GERMANY IN TRANSIT

WEIMAR AND NOW: GERMAN CULTURAL CRITICISM

EDWARD DIMENDBERG, MARTIN JAY, AND ANTON KAES, GENERAL EDITORS

GERMANY IN TRANSIT

NATION AND MIGRATION | 1955–2005

EDITED BY

DENIZ GÖKTÜRK

DAVID GRAMLING

ANTON KAES

University of California Press   Berkeley Los Angeles London

University of California Press, one of the most distinguished university presses in the United States, enriches lives around the world by advancing scholarship in the humanities, social sciences, and natural sciences. Its activities are supported by the UC Press Foundation and by philanthropic contributions from individuals and institutions. For more information, visit www.ucpress.edu.

University of California Press
Berkeley and Los Angeles, California

University of California Press, Ltd.
London, England

Library of Congress Cataloging-in-Publication Data

Germany in transit : nation and migration, 1955–2005 / edited by Deniz Göktürk, David Gramling, Anton Kaes.
   p.   cm. — (Weimar and now ; 40)
Documents translated from German.
Includes bibliographical references and index.
ISBN-13: 978-0-520-24893-9 (cloth : alk. paper),
ISBN-10: 0-520-24893-7 (cloth : alk. paper);
ISBN-13: 978-0-520-24894-6 (pbk. : alk. paper),
ISBN-10: 0-520-24894-5 (pbk. : alk. paper).
   1. Germany—Ethnic relations—History—20th century—Sources.
2. Germany—Ethnic relations—History—21st century—Sources.
3. Germany—Race relations—History—20th century—Sources.
4. Germany—Race relations—History—21st century—Sources.
5. Pluralism (Social sciences)—Germany—History—20th century—Sources.   6. Pluralism (Social sciences)—Germany—History—21st century—Sources.   7. Xenophobia—Germany—Sources.   8. Immigrants—Germany—Social conditions—Sources.   9. Germany—Emigration and immigration—Sources.   I. Göktürk, Deniz, 1963–.
II. Gramling, David, 1976–.   III. Kaes, Anton.   IV. Series.
DD74.G47   2007
304.8'43009045—dc22   2006011622

Manufactured in the United States of America

15   14   13   12   11   10   09   08   07
10   9   8   7   6   5   4   3   2   1

The paper used in this publication meets the minimum requirements of ANSI/NISO Z39.48-1992 (R1997) (*Permanence of Paper*).

CONTENTS

DOCUMENTS

4 WHAT IS A GERMAN? LEGISLATING NATIONAL IDENTITY 149

5 RELIGION AND DIASPORA: MUSLIMS, JEWS, AND CHRISTIANS 193

ILLUSTRATIONS

PREFACE

HOW DOES MIGRATION change a nation? At the beginning of the twenty-first century, nearly 200 million people reside outside their countries of birth. Their personal histories vary as greatly as the routes that have led them across borders and continents to new homelands. Their presence is often contested, especially in times of war, and the transnational ties they maintain challenge the very idea of a territorially bound nation-state. In Germany, the economic, legal, and cultural transformations associated with global migration have generated fervent public debates over the past fifty years—debates that provide a particularly instructive case study for understanding the dynamics of nation and migration.

Germany's increasingly diverse immigrant population routinely surpasses efforts to document and represent it. A rough sketch at present would include former guest workers, primarily from Turkey, repatriated ethnic Germans, Jews from the former Soviet Union, asylum seekers and political refugees from Asia and Africa, high-tech industry recruits from India, citizens of other European countries, and an estimated 1.4 million undocumented migrants. According to the 2005 German microcensus, no fewer than 15 million of the country's current population of 82 million have a "migration background." This means that every fifth German is an immigrant or has parents or grandparents who came to Germany from elsewhere. Today every third German child is born to non-German parents, and schools in urban centers enroll students of more than 100 nationalities. Large-scale immigration has arguably changed the face of contemporary Germany in more lasting ways than reunification.

This book presents 200 texts and documents that chart Germany's irreversible transformation into a multiethnic society against the backdrop of the Cold War and European integration. The documentation spans half a century, beginning with the first labor recruitment contract in 1955 and ending with the country's long-awaited comprehensive immigration legislation in 2005. The collection is divided into eleven thematic clusters that serve as an analytical grid for identifying the divergent yet overlapping aspects of migration history. Using the principle of montage to juxtapose multiple perspectives, we seek to do justice to the complexity of such issues as citizenship, religion, and globalization. Included are a variety of genres, from newspaper editorials, political manifestoes, and legal statutes to interviews, song lyrics, and autobiographical essays. By adhering to a chronological order within each chapter we have tried to capture the immediacy and vigor of past debates. Although these debates are inevitably bound to their historical moment, they set forth arguments that have not lost their poignancy and critical acumen for the present.

As the U.S. Congress weighs the possibility of a German-style guest worker program, parallels between the two countries become all the more striking: a recurring need for foreign labor in both low-wage and professional sectors, multilingual neighborhoods and classrooms, and a perennial stalemate regarding the question of illegal immigration. What renders mass migration to Germany unique, however, is the constant interplay between labor-market forces and the ethical imperatives of the nation's history. In a deliberate attempt to make amends for the genocidal crimes of the Third Reich, Germany accepted more political refugees and Jewish immigrants throughout the 1980s and early 1990s than any other European country.

Germany in Transit is a cultural history of postwar Germany through the lens of migration. The texts articulate bold visions, tragic setbacks, and unintended consequences. They exemplify the rhetoric of integration and intercultural exchange and of racial prejudice and discursive violence. Above all, the book offers a rich archive for readers who wish to situate Germany's cultural production over the past half-century in its historical context. For instance, R. W. Fassbinder's 1974 film *Angst essen Seele auf* (Ali: Fear Eats the Soul) resonates more fully when viewed alongside documents about the status of guest workers at that time. Even films and novels that do not explicitly address immigration tend to reveal a Germany in a state of transition.

This volume grows out of the Multicultural Germany Project, an interdisciplinary research initiative started in 2001 in the German Department at the University of California, Berkeley. A companion Web site, which includes periodic updates and additional materials, may be found at www.german.berkeley/mg. The venture has been generously funded by the Institute for European Studies at the University of California, Berkeley, and we would like to thank Gerald Feldman and Beverly Crawford for their steadfast support. Our special thanks go to Tes Howell, who was principal research assistant and translator from 2001 to 2003. This book would not have been possible were it not for a devoted research team of undergraduate and graduate students: Şener Aktürk, Joseph Baumgarten, Cristelle Blackford, Christian Buss, Erin Cooper, Paul Dobryden, David Eaton, Jeffrey Ezell, Nicola Gladitz, Priscilla Layne, Gabrielle Owen, Lore Phillips, Sabrina Karim Rahman, Alexander Randolph, Rob Schechtman, Leilah Vevaina, Yasemin Dayıoğlu Yücel, and Jennifer L. Zahrt. We also thank Hilary Menges for her superb editorial skills and Efthymia Stathis Drolapas and Mettabel Law for their expert help in proofreading.

Leslie A. Adelson, a pioneer in German-Turkish studies in the United States, gave us invaluable feedback, and her enthusiasm for the project kept us going when its sheer scope threatened to overwhelm us. We would also like to thank Pipo Bui, Pheng Cheah, Tom Cheesman, Edward Dimendberg, Aytaç Eryılmaz, Fatima El-Tayeb, Ulrich Everding, Angela Göktürk, Roger Hillman, David Hollinger, Peter Kaes, Claire Kramsch, Claus Leggewie, Oliver Lubrich, Rolf Mehldau, Barbara Mennel, Minoo Moallem, Damani Partridge, Peggy Piesche, Patrice G. Poutrus, Martin Rapp, Eric Rentschler, Regina Römhild, Tim Rosenkranz, Werner Schiffauer, Hinrich C. Seeba, Zafer Şenocak, Werner Sollors, and Barbara Wolbert for their input, critical commentary, and suggestions of texts for inclusion. We are indebted to the anonymous reviewers of the manuscript for their helpful comments. We appreciate the interest of our editor, Niels Hooper, the dedicated collaborative work of Suzanne Knott and Adrienne Harris, and the elegant design by Nola Burger of the University of California Press.

Berkeley, September 4, 2006

ABBREVIATIONS

ADN	Allgemeiner Deutscher Nachrichtendienst / General German News Service
ARD	Arbeitsgemeinschaft der Rundfunkanstalten Deutschlands (First German Television station)
AL	Alternative Liste / Alternative List
APO	Ausserparlamentarische Opposition / Extra-Parliamentary Opposition
BRD	Bundesrepublik Deutschland / Federal Republic of Germany
CDU	Christlich-Demokratische Union / Christian Democratic Union
CSU	Christlich-Soziale Union / Christian Social Union
DAAD	Deutscher Akademischer Austauschdienst / German Academic Exchange Service
DDR	Deutsche Demokratische Republik / German Democratic Republic
DGB	Deutscher Gewerkschaftsbund / German Trade Union Federation
DW	Deutsche Welle (radio and television station equivalent to BBC World Service)
EC	European Community (1958–)
ECSC	European Coal and Steel Community (1951–2002)
EEC	European Economic Community (1957–92)
EU	European Union (1993–)
FAZ	*Frankfurter Allgemeine Zeitung* (newspaper)
FDP	Freie Demokratische Partei / Free Democratic Party
FRG	Federal Republic of Germany / Bundesrepublik Deutschland
GATT	General Agreement on Tariffs and Trade
GDR	German Democratic Republic / Deutsche Demokratische Republik
IAB	Institut für Arbeitsmarkt- und Berufsforschung / Institute for Labor Market and Occupational Research
IBA	International Building Exhibition
KPD	Kommunistische Partei Deutschlands / Communist Party of Germany
NATO	North Atlantic Treaty Organization

NPD	Nationaldemokratische Partei Deutschlands / National Democratic Party of Germany
PDS	Partei des Demokratischen Sozialismus / Party of Democratic Socialism
PISA	Program for International Student Assessment
PKK	Partiya Karkeren Kurdistan / Kurdistan Workers' Party
RAF	Rote Armee Fraktion / Red Army Faction
RTL	Radio Télévision Luxembourg (first private German television station)
SED	Sozialistische Einheitspartei Deutschlands / Socialist Unity Party of Germany
SFB	Sender Freies Berlin / Radio Free Berlin
SPD	Sozialdemokratische Partei Deutschlands / Social Democratic Party of Germany ("Red")
SRV	Socialist Republic of Vietnam
taz	*die tageszeitung* (newspaper)
TBB	Türkischer Bund Berlin / Turkish Federation of Berlin
TRT	Turkish Radio and Television
UNHCR	United Nations High Commissioner for Refugees
UNESCO	United Nations Educational, Scientific and Cultural Organization
WDR	Westdeutscher Rundfunk / West German Radio
WTO	World Trade Organization
ZDF	Zweites Deutsches Fernsehen / Second German Television

A GERMAN DREAM?

PORTABLE PLENITUDE, 1962. Sporting four new battery-powered radios, Italian guest workers at the VW plant in Wolfsburg delight in their ability to listen to music while on the move. As early as 1961, West German radio stations began airing weekly half-hour programs for the country's 120,000 Italian migrants. The image depicts Germany's guest workers as members of a dynamic consumer society in an age of border-crossing technologies.

By now,
all the survivors, all who avoided headlong death
were safe at home, escaped the wars and waves.
— HOMER, *THE ODYSSEY*

"Well, what's your name?" you ask him.
"Odradek," he says. "And where do you live?"
"Residence unspecified," he says and laughs.
— FRANZ KAFKA, *THE CARES OF A*
FAMILY MAN

"We Are Not an Immigration Country"

Picture the following scene: Several hundred immigrants wearing native garb from their homeland line up on a stage. They march through a huge "melting pot" and, after a quick change of clothes, emerge as Americans in workers' uniforms. This spectacle was Henry Ford's way of celebrating the mandatory Americanization of his immigrant workforce in 1908. Since then, the mythic ideal of an American melting pot has undergone a century of revision and critique, but the collective swearing-in ceremony that transforms immigrants into American citizens continues to this day. Drawn by the promise of the American Dream, more than 100 million immigrants, including 6 million Germans, have come to America in the past 150 years, making the United States the world's preeminent immigration country.

Germany, in contrast, has never been known as a country of immigrants, and a German Dream is difficult to imagine. Indeed, former Chancellor Helmut Kohl's insistence that Germany is *not* an immigration country accurately represented the legal realities throughout the 1980s and 1990s. Unlike France, which was eager to grant citizenship to new immigrants, Germany held fast to its notorious Empire- and State-Citizenship Law of 1913, which invoked an ethnic, descent-based principle of national belonging. Under this law, a person could be born, work, and die on German soil without ever becoming a German citizen.

For decades, German governments (regardless of party or political orientation) responded to the presence of immigrants with ad hoc regulations, ambiguous policies, cultural initiatives, and social programs, but the basic legal definition of Germanness remained unchanged. Though residency laws for foreign nationals were relaxed as early as 1965, the federal government did not establish a coherent system to naturalize migrants who wished to reside permanently in Germany. Guest workers on temporary visas were expected to go back home eventually; refugees and asylum seekers were informally "tolerated" year after year; and "ethnic German" migrants from the former Soviet Union were already considered *de facto* citizens according to the 1913 citizenship law. A confusing array of residency categories substituted for a clear path to citizenship. As a consequence, native Germans tended to refer to all migrants, regardless of their residency status, as *Ausländer*, or foreigners—a pejorative shorthand for any person not born into the national community.

Although several attempts were made in 1977 and again in 1990 to reform the exclusionary citizenship policy, naturalization was rare because no unified principles existed to promote it. Each state of the Federal Republic could apply its own rules as to the desirability of an applicant. This strong federalist structure delayed legislative progress on immigration policy throughout the 1980s and 1990s. As late as 2004, the Bavarian CSU party declared: "Germany is not a classic country of immigration, and because of its history, geography, and economic conditions, it cannot be one."

Naturalization in the 1970s and 1980s was restricted to immigrants who had lived in Germany at least 10 years and could prove a "lasting commitment to Germany." Dual citizenship was only granted under exceptional circumstances. For their part, most migrants found the benefits of pursuing a German passport dubious at best. Giving up their previous citizenship often meant forsaking ancestral property, as well as the unrestricted right to seek employment and visit relatives in the home country. It is thus not surprising that no more than 1 percent of the non-German population opted for citizenship.

A sea-change occurred in 1999, when the newly elected government of Gerhard Schröder complemented the blood-concept of German citizenship with a territorial principle akin to that in France and the United States. As of January 1, 2000, a child of non-German parents with eight years of residency is automatically entitled to German citizenship at birth. Because children of immigrant parents are now counted as Germans, the percentage of "foreigners" is slowly declining.

After a five-year struggle with the opposition CDU/CSU parties, Schröder's coalition government passed the country's first-ever comprehensive immigration law in June 2004, bringing Germany's immigration statutes into accord with those of other European states. The Immigration Act took effect in 2005 and was widely hailed as the end of one chapter in German history and the beginning of a new one. However, naturalization remains a cumbersome and mundane bureaucratic procedure, and no collective, American-style ritual marks the conferral of German citizenship.

Nonetheless, the demographic shifts of the past 50 years are indisputable.

The 2005 German microcensus revealed that some 15 million of Germany's 82 million inhabitants are of immigrant descent, including 6.76 million noncitizens. Between 1955 and 1973, approximately 11 million guest workers came to Germany; many of them brought their families and stayed. Between 1991 and 2004, 2 million ethnic Germans from the former Soviet Union moved to Germany and became repatriated; in the same period, 2 million asylum seekers from eastern Europe, Asia, and Africa applied for residency. In 2004, 1 million political refugees and asylum seekers were living in Germany. At some schools in Berlin-Kreuzberg today, more than 90 percent of the student body is of Turkish or Arabic descent. Berlin boasts 100 mosques for its 200,000 Muslims, out of a total 3.5 million Muslim residents throughout Germany. Though ethnic distribution differs widely by region and within major cities even by district, the statistics show that Germany's multiethnic population resembles that of other Western European countries.

Migration to Germany would not have been possible without the larger framework of the European Union and its predecessor organizations, which emerged in the wake of the Marshall Plan in the 1950s. West Germany's postwar economic dynamism necessitated the recruitment of migrant laborers from its European neighbors; labor migration in turn helped bring down Europe's internal borders. During the 1960s, European Community members saw the need for collaboration in matters of law, defense, agriculture, environment, energy, and transportation, as well as immigration. In 1985, the Treaty of Schengen abolished passport and customs controls at most borders between European Community states, allowing workers to move freely among 15 member countries. Since the treaty took full effect in 1995, Germany has become one of the "Schengen countries" that does not share a border with any non-EU member state, thereby making coordination with neighboring European countries a necessity. In 2002, Germans gave up their beloved German mark and adopted the euro as the common currency among 15 states. Like migration, European integration has become fundamental to German everyday life. Mobility within Europe is now considered as much of a basic right as citizenship, and civic affiliation is no longer purely a national matter.

A Brief Prehistory

Germany has always been more ethnically diverse than the Nazi assertions about the purity of the "Aryan race" claimed. Located in the middle of Europe, it was at the crossing point for ethnic groups from the West and East, North and South. In 1685, Brandenburg-Prussia provided refuge for 20,000 Huguenots fleeing France because of their Protestant faith. Throughout the eighteenth and nineteenth centuries, nobility was transnational, from Prussia's French-speaking Frederic the Great to the German-born Russian em-press Catherine the Great. For centuries a conglomerate of territorial states comprising the Holy Roman Empire of the German Nation, Germany did not become a modern nation-state with defined borders and a unified national government until 1871, when it vanquished France in the Franco-Prussian War. Kaiser Wilhelm II, who ruled Germany from 1888 to 1918, boisterously vowed to make the belated nation powerful and give it a "place in the sun." As Germany's economy boomed, its universities attracted top scholars and scientists, especially in the new electrical engineering and chemical industries.

When German agriculture and heavy industry suffered a serious labor shortage in the 1870s and 1880s, German businesses recruited close to half a million unskilled laborers from the eastern provinces (now Poland) to work in the coal mines and steel factories of the Ruhr region. Industry leaders saw only advantages in this program: the foreign workers did the hard work that German workers were unwilling to perform, they kept the wages down, and they could be sent back when German industry no longer needed them. But many of the so-called Ruhr Poles (derided as *Pollacken*) married Germans, settled, and created a distinct subculture proud of its Polish-Catholic origins. In reaction to discrimination and harassment, they organized themselves and founded a combative Polish workers' union that staged well-publicized strikes in 1899, 1905, and 1912. Under pressure from nationalist circles interested in preserving "Germany for the Germans," the government felt compelled to pass a law in 1908 that regulated and curbed the influx of foreign labor. At that point, the number of non-German workers had already reached 1 million, and Germany's reputation as a destination for migrant laborers was second only to that of the United States.

The outbreak of World War I in 1914 changed the status of seasonal workers. The German government forbade them to return home because the country needed them (along with its prisoners of war) to fill in for millions of young men who had been drafted. In 1918, when German soldiers returned from the front, the foreign workforce of some 2 million was ordered to leave, although not everyone heeded this command. World War I also uprooted millions of German military recruits, who found themselves fighting in faraway countries they would otherwise not have known.

Escaping the upheaval of the Russian Revolution, about 200,000 Russians emigrated to the West throughout the 1920s. Most of them ended up in Berlin, which soon became the most Russian city in Western Europe. Vladimir Nabokov, for instance, lived in Berlin from 1923 to 1930, before moving on to Paris and the United States. The German capital, boasting 4 million inhabitants in 1920, was also the destination for 70,000 Orthodox Jews from Eastern Europe. These immigrants formed a Yiddish-speaking community in the Scheunenviertel, a shtetl-like district of Berlin. As their numbers increased during the Weimar Republic, nationalist critics engaged in increasingly aggressive polemics that blended anti-Semitism with xenophobia. In 1933, many Jews emigrated to the United States; those who remained faced imprisonment and deportation. Even assimilated Jews with German passports were not safe after a change of the citizenship law on September 15, 1935 (the so-called Nuremberg law), which deprived all Jews of their German citizenship. The industrial genocide of the 1940s killed 6 million Orthodox, secular, and assimilated European Jews, regardless of their nationality.

One of the sources of Germany's geographical and political instability since the Middle Ages has been its lack of a natural frontier in the East, leading to repeated encroachments on Slavic territory. Vulnerable to German conquest and colonization, the border regions were often traded back and forth in treaties. In their century-long push to the East, migrant Germans settled and stayed, even if the territories were reclaimed, thus forming German enclaves throughout Eastern Europe and Russia. At the end of World War I, 8.5 million ethnic Germans lived outside the borders of Germany: 3.5 million in Czechoslovakia, 1.8 million in the Soviet Union, 1.2 million in Poland, 800,000 in Romania, 700,000 in Yugoslavia, 550,000 in Hungary, and 50,000 in the Baltic States.

Hitler's pan-German ideology sought to unite the various ethnic Germans into one Reich with a newly expanded eastern border. The annexation of Austria and the Sudetenland (now part of the Czech Republic) and the occupation of Poland in the fall of 1939 were supposed to create sufficient *Lebensraum,* or living space, for all Germans from farther east. Native Poles were brutally driven from their farms to make room for resettled Germans. The Nazis brokered treaties with most of the affected countries for a transfer (or more precisely, forced emigration) of all ethnic Germans who lived there. A total of almost 1 million (a third of them Germans from Russia) were thus "brought home" into the Reich.

When the Red Army advanced toward the Reich's borders in 1944, millions of Germans were forced to flee to the West under chaotic conditions. Rightly blamed for the ruthless expulsion of native Slavs, Germans were now themselves mercilessly expelled from Eastern Europe. Joseph Stalin ordered the newly installed Polish government to incorporate large parts of Pomerania, Silesia, and East Prussia, where approximately 5 million Germans resided. Over a million from the Sudetenland and former German territory east of the rivers Oder and Neisse were driven out. Of 16.5 million Germans living in the eastern provinces in 1945, close to 12 million survived the trek to the West, 2 million perished, and the rest, some 2.5 million, did not leave. They formed the bulk of the Russian and Eastern European population that could later, after the collapse of the Soviet Union in the early 1990s, claim

German ancestry and move to Germany as *Aussiedler,* or ethnic German resettlers.

The National Socialists had relied on forced laborers, euphemistically called *Fremdarbeiter,* or foreign workers, to build highways, toil in agriculture and the armament industry, and supply the country's workforce when 10 million Germans were called to arms. Estimates indicate that as many as 13.5 million foreign laborers worked involuntarily in Germany, including prisoners of war, Sinti and Roma, political prisoners, Jews, as well as foreign-born civilians and *Ostarbeiter,* or workers from the East—half of whom were women and children. Because of Nazi paranoia about miscegenation, the Slavic laborers were strictly separated from the German population and housed in barracks, which incidentally were reused in the postwar period to accommodate the first guest workers.

In 1945, most of these foreign laborers left Germany to return to their home countries. At the same time, about 8 million to 10 million displaced persons—liberated prisoners of war, political detainees, deserters, refugees, and survivors from the concentration camps—were stranded in the four occupied zones. Some 4.6 million were repatriated in massive transports by the end of 1945, but many refused to go back, especially to the Stalinist eastern zone. After the fall of the Third Reich, 11 million Germans were prisoners of war: 7.7 million on the western front, 3.3 million on the eastern front. Although most of the POWs from the West returned to Germany between 1945 and 1950, the last POWs in Soviet hands were not released until 1955; the fate of about a million of them remains unknown. Many returning veterans found themselves in competition with refugees, expellees, and evacuees for housing and food. At the close of the war, no fewer than 12 million people, among them 2.5 million children, wandered across a scarred landscape of ruins and rubble.

This mass migration within Germany and across Europe had enormous consequences for the future of both Germanys. The influx of Germans from the East who had lost their homes and were compelled to make their way in the new environment gave the Federal Republic the labor and energy necessary to rebuild the country in a relatively short time. Their number soon exceeded the 5 million Germans who were killed in the war. Because of the destruction of urban areas, the refugees often ended up in places like rural Bavaria or Holstein, thereby changing the villages' demographics for the first time since the seventeenth century. Although the refugees spoke their own dialects and organized themselves politically around their status as expelled persons, the domestic population did not call them "foreigners." Over time, they integrated into the community and exemplified upward mobility.

In its economic dynamism, West Germany of the 1950s and 1960s resembled an immigrant society, but it was also radically different: the majority of migrants were German refugees who had escaped to their "native land," which welcomed them. West German society for all its large-scale displacement and dislocation remained fundamentally homogeneous. In 1955 the number of those living in Germany without German citizenship hovered around 1 percent.

Coming to Germany

In the early 1950s, the United States, Britain, and France had a vested interest in reconstructing West Germany as an anti-Soviet, market-oriented society. After initial assistance of the Marshall Plan, domestic corporations boosted productivity and revenues. To maintain the "Economic Miracle," the private sector needed a highly mobile workforce that it could deploy to specific sites throughout the country. Most of West Germany's 1 million unemployed workers were unable or unwilling to relocate with their families to these new industrial sites, and the labor shortage was becoming acute. In December 1955, the Labor Ministry devised a plan to recruit Italian workers to operate machines, work assembly lines, haul trash, and perform other hard labor that did not require more than a rudimentary knowledge of the German language. Unlike the forced "foreign laborers" of the Nazi period, these foreigners were "guest workers"—welcome to stay for a restricted period and expected to return home with the host's gratitude. In the midst of a roaring economy, this stopgap measure appeared to be a winning solution for all parties. From the outset, the language of the bilateral guest-worker agreements presaged the Europeanization of the West German labor market, promoting a "spirit" of labor mobility among postwar European states. This initially European rationale for labor recruitment signaled the beginning of a common economic policy that culminated 40 years later in the dismantling of border controls in the European interior.

The postwar German labor shortage worsened drastically in August 1961, when the newly constructed Berlin Wall abruptly cut off the steady flow of workers from East Germany. A total of 3.8 million East Germans had left the Communist-ruled country for the West between 1949 and 1961. Less than half a million moved in the other direction. Each year during that 12-year period, hundreds of thousands of *Übersiedler*, or settlers from "the other side," had relocated to the Federal Republic for political, economic, or personal reasons. The moment this influx stopped, the call for more guest workers became inevitable.

In the sphere of international relations, the expansion of the temporary-worker program appealed to the diplomatic objective of economic collaboration with anticommunist allies such as NATO member Turkey. The West German Labor Ministry also saw the program as the perfect supplement to the curtailed "internal" migration from the communist East to the capitalist

West. After initiating labor recruitment contracts with Italy, Spain, and Greece, the federal government signed agreements with Turkey in 1961, Portugal in 1964, and Yugoslavia in 1968.

The guest workers rapidly altered labor relations throughout the country. Between 1960 and 1970, approximately 2.3 million West Germans left industrial and agricultural jobs to become managers and clerks, while foreign "temporary" laborers took up the vacated positions. The West German Ministry of Labor also reported in 1976 that guest workers had paved the way for a shorter workweek and longer vacations for Germans. In September 1964, a representative of the Employers' Association opened the welcome ceremony for West Germany's millionth guest worker by acknowledging the cooperation of guest workers, who made the country's economic development possible. The strictly rotational design of the program proved too expensive for industry, and it was quietly abandoned in 1964, when Germany renewed its contract with Turkey.

Although immigrants had become an integral feature of West German workplaces, the government had passed no new legislation on foreign residents since the Nazi period. Germans hailed the 1965 *Ausländergesetz*, or Foreigner Law, as a progressive measure at the time, but it had a destabilizing effect on migrant workers and families. According to this law, foreigners could reside in Germany as long as they had a valid visa and continued to serve "the needs of the Federal Republic." Interpretation of this notoriously vague concept was left up to thousands of semiautonomous agencies and their myriad employees throughout the country. Noncitizens had few options for challenging visa decisions made at their local *Ausländeramt*, or foreigner bureau. Ultimately, the 1965 law created general confusion about the legal status of labor immigrants, and ambiguity in bureaucratic procedures led to greater disparities in housing and workplace rights.

The plight of guest workers and their status as outsiders attracted the attention of the New German Cinema, which perceived itself at the margin of the commercial film industry. Rainer Werner Fassbinder's film *Katzelmacher* (1969) focuses on a Greek guest worker whose very presence disrupts the close-knit community of a Munich neighborhood. "Katzelmacher" is a derogatory Bavarian slang term for migrants from the South who breed "like cats." The film shows German society through the eyes of the outsider as bankrupt, dim-witted, and xenophobic. Fassbinder uses Brechtian techniques to lay bare the social and sexual forces unleashed by the arrival of the guest worker, and he ups the ante in his highly stylized parable by playing the "Greek from Greece" himself. In his later film *Angst essen Seele auf* (*Ali: Fear Eats the Soul*, 1974), Fassbinder casts his Moroccan partner, El Hedi ben Salem, in the leading role of Ali. In the tradition of Sirkian melodrama, the camera comments on the doomed relationship between Ali and Emmi, an older German woman. As in *Katzelmacher*, a courageous female reaches out to the foreigner, but the social reality of Germany in 1974—unemployment, racism, discrimination—takes its toll. Fassbinder's film, which won him international recognition at the Cannes Film Festival, was an early response to a shift in the economic climate.

By 1973, a global oil crisis and recession had stunted the burgeoning West German economy. In November of that year, the federal government ordered a moratorium on guest-worker recruitment. By that point, the guest-worker population had reached 2.6 million, with 605,000 Turks forming the largest group. In the period between 1973 and 1979, immigration emerged as a major national topic. Politicians and employers strategized to limit West Germany's reliance on the foreign labor force. The government made only rare exceptions to the 1973 moratorium until the end of the Cold War, when it reimplemented smaller-scale recruitment programs with Yugoslavia (1988), Hungary (1989), and Poland (1990).

At the time of the moratorium, Turks formed 23 percent of the noncitizen population, followed by Yugoslavs (17 percent), Italians (16 percent), Greeks (10 percent), and Spaniards (7 percent). When the Labor Ministry announced the ban, non-EC immigrant workers realized that they could no longer leave Germany if they intended to return safely. In 1974, the German government passed a law that enabled their families to join them. This law resulted in a population boom diametrically opposed to the state's intentions. By 1980, the noncitizen population climbed to 4.4 million, as workers' spouses, children, and parents entered Germany from non-EC countries under "family unification" statutes.

The circumstances for migrants and refugees in the communist German Democratic Republic were a different story. Whereas the West German guest-worker program embodied the idea of an economic symbiosis between developed and developing capitalist countries, East German initiatives appealed to an internationalist doctrine of solidarity and struggle against the capitalist West, particularly during the period of the Vietnam War. Addressing its comparatively small number of guest workers as "our socialist friends," the East German government maintained networks with Mozambique, China, North Korea, North Vietnam, Cuba, and other emerging socialist states. As a result, the GDR could promote its forays into international labor recruitment as a visionary measure, strengthening a global movement of like-minded socialist citizens. East German critiques of the West's "exploitative and racist" guest-worker program grew fiercer as the 1970s drew to a close.

In 1982, Helmut Kohl's call for a "change in our *Ausländerpolitik,*" or foreigner politics, and his promise of a 50 percent reduction of the guest-worker population aided his successful run for West German chancellor, a position he held for the next 16 years. In the early years of the Kohl administration, the right of Turkish citizens to travel back and forth between Turkey and Germany remained a sore diplomatic subject, particularly after Kohl paid a state visit to Ankara in 1983, during which the "mobility question" was left unresolved. During this period, metropolitan areas with high percentages of noncitizen residents, like Frankfurt am Main, considered ordinances that would essentially close the city to new immigrants. As members of the EC, Greek and Italian citizens enjoyed a mobility unavailable to Spanish and Portuguese citizens, whose countries would not join the EC until 1986.

The early 1980s also ushered in new statutes on the minimum amount of domestic space required for each noncitizen family member. The 1971 minimum standard of 12 square meters per resident increased steadily throughout the 1980s, introducing a requirement for immigrant families that even 1.2 million German-born wage earners could not meet. The debate about domestic space found its way into a range of stories and films, such as Tevfik Başer's drama about the entrapment of a migrant woman from rural Turkey in a Hamburg apartment, *40 Quadratmeter Deutschland* (*40 Square Meters of Germany*, 1986). An ironic reversal of this scenario of spatial confinement occurs in Sinan Çetin's film *Berlin in Berlin* (1993), which was produced in Turkey. In this comedy, a German man on the run must seek "asylum" in a Turkish family's home in Berlin's Kreuzberg district, eventually adopting their customs and integrating into the microcosm of their apartment.

In the 1980s, bureaus of foreigner affairs began to emerge in West Germany, popularizing the concept of an open, multicultural society. Commissioner of Foreigner Affairs Barbara John mounted a large-scale poster campaign with the motto "Living Together in Berlin," which depicted German and immigrant workers harmoniously coexisting in various workplace settings. Immigrants often understood the bureaus as one more mediating buffer between them and the federal legal apparatus; activists, academics, and immigrant community leaders criticized the paternalistic attitude of these agencies' employees. Nonetheless, throughout the 1980s, foreigner bureaus and church organizations played a major role in defending immigrants' rights to social and legal equality amid rising anti-immigrant sentiments in the German Parliament.

After the Wall

Debates on asylum took the national stage during German reunification in 1990. The liberal asylum policies in the West German constitution contributed to a xenophobic backlash, fueled by the notion that foreign "freeloaders" were abusing the Federal Republic's magnanimity. This alarm about alleged abuses of asylum rights was not new in West Germany; as early as 1949, refugees fleeing the Soviet Occupied Zone were often met with ambivalence and rancor for invoking article 16 of the West German constitution, which clearly stated, "The politically persecuted enjoy the right to asylum."

In the early 1990s, resentment toward foreigners led to physical assaults and arson attacks on asylum residences in Rostock-Lichtenhagen, Hoyers-werda, Frankfurt an der Oder, and Magdeburg in the former German Democratic Republic. Arson attacks occured in the West as well—in Mölln and in Solingen, where five Turkish women and girls burned to death in their home. Such crimes, which reminded Germans of the Nazi persecutions, triggered nationwide protests. In December 1992, close to half a million Germans gathered in Munich for nighttime *Lichterketten,* or candlelight vigils, to take a public stance against neo-Nazism and racist violence. All other major cities followed, and by the end of the year, about 3 million Germans had come out to declare their solidarity with the foreigners in their midst. The government initiated publicity campaigns for tolerance.

Simultaneously, however, the major political parties were calling for a constitutional amendment to implement strict limits on claims to asylum. The so-called asylum compromise of 1993 resolved that no one could seek asylum in Germany if he or she had set foot in a "secure" country before entering German territory. Asylum policy and deportation strategies subsequently focused on airports rather than traditional checkpoints. As a consequence of the open borders, illegal immigration increased at an unprecedented rate in the mid-1990s. Like other immigration countries, such as France and the United States, Germany has yet to develop policies to deal with its undocumented migrants. The categories "asylum seeker" and "refugee" became all the more complex in 1994, when the government granted temporary residence to 200,000 war refugees from Bosnia-Herzegovina.

Osman Engin's novel *Kanaken-Gandhi* (1998) gives a comic edge to this shift from guest-worker to asylum politics. The main character, a guest worker without any desire or need for asylum, suddenly receives notification that his asylum request has been rejected and that he is scheduled for deportation. The narrator, Osman, alarmed by his unclear legal standing in Germany, spends the remainder of the novel attempting to clear up this bureaucratic fiasco, but to no avail. The novel also satirically stages the competition for resources between former East Germans and former immigrants—all residents of the new Germany.

Historical events in 1989 and 1990—the fall of the Berlin Wall, the collapse of the German Democratic Republic, and the opening of the entire East Bloc—once more triggered mass migration that changed the demographics of the Federal Republic. No fewer than 1.4 million people emigrated from the former East Germany to West Germany between 1989 and 1993, whereas only 350,000 moved to the East. The drain from the East to the West has since slowed, and economic incentives (new factories, universities, and improvement of infrastructure) have tried to reverse the trend.

In the glow of reunification, the West German government handed all East Germans who came west a small gift of a 100-mark bill, the so-called *Begrüs-*

sungsgeld, or greeting money; it also levied against its own citizens a special *Solidaritätsbeitrag,* or solidarity tax, to help defray the enormous costs of rebuilding the East. The hurried absorption of the communist German Democratic Republic (a population of 23 million) by the capitalist Federal Republic has left many wounds and mutual suspicion. Terms like *Ossi* and *Wessi* (diminutive shorthand for East and West Germans, respectively) highlight the lingering divisions to this day. Wolfgang Becker's international film hit, *Good Bye Lenin!* (2002), put a satirical spin on the sudden disappearance of East Germany as an independent state. With a light touch, the film emphasizes displacement and disorientation in the newly unified Germany.

The end of the Cold War and fall of the communist regimes in Central and Eastern Europe in 1989 and 1990 brought new waves of immigrants to the Federal Republic. Ethnic Germans (*Volksdeutsche,* also known as *Aussiedler,* or resettlers) from Eastern Europe and the Soviet Union saw economic opportunity and a generous social-welfare system in the West and migrated in the hundreds of thousands to Germany. These so-called resettlers had an easy time crossing the border because the Kohl administration extended citizenship to anyone who could prove German ancestry. In 1989, amid reports of rising anti-Semitism in the Soviet Union, the German government also offered unrestricted residence and eventual citizenship to Soviet Jews.

Both of these groups, German-heritage resettlers and Jews from the former Soviet Union, were entitled to German citizenship, whether or not they had any practical, linguistic, or emotional ties to Germany. Many liberal critics in the 1990s charged the Christian Democratic Kohl government with courting the socially conservative votes of resettlers. A prominent Christian Democrat even referred to resettler children as "our gold treasure." At the same time, many German Jewish community leaders discovered that the mostly secular Soviet Jews entering the country had little interest in worship services or religious community.

Religion became one of the rallying points for post-Wall immigration politics. In 2003, the Federal Constitutional Court reached a key decision defending the right of an Afghan-born schoolteacher to wear a head scarf in her southern German classroom. The plaintiff, Fereshta Ludin, a German citizen, insisted that her wearing a head scarf had no effect on her teaching of German history. Nonetheless, her home state of Baden-Württemberg interpreted head scarves as religious symbols and banned them among teachers in 2004. Currently seven of sixteen German states have enacted such a ban.

Right-wing violence against non-Germans flared up again in the summer of 2000. In July, a bomb in Düsseldorf injured nine immigrants from the former Soviet Union. In August, three German skinheads in Dessau (a city with an unemployment rate of 21 percent) were charged with the brutal murder of a Mozambican asylum seeker. The German chancellor himself went on a trip through East Germany, pleading for "civic courage against right-wing extremism." The government attempted to ban the openly racist NPD, or National Party of Germany. Foreign minister Joschka Fischer declared that anti-immigrant violence was doing "devastating damage to the image of Germany abroad." Another antiracist campaign began. The most famous German soccer team, Bayern München, took out an ad boasting players from 13 nations. The automobile company Opel heralded the fact that workers from over 40 countries built cars in its German plants.

These efforts to fight right-wing violence came at a time when German industry was desperate to attract computer programmers from abroad. The shortage was so acute that the state lifted the moratorium on foreign labor recruitment by way of a so-called Green Card program. Whereas the American Green Card is equivalent to permanent residency and a first step toward citizenship, the German Green Card was limited to five years. The program placed approximately 17,000 workers in German firms, with Indian nationals forming the largest contingent. Despite the Green Card's relative success, German businesses still reported a continued need for information-technology workers. The 2005 Immigration Act renders the Green Card obsolete, but it incorporates controlled recruiting of high-tech professionals and financially independent entrepreneurs. Although in this era of automation and outsourcing, German industry no longer needs a massive influx of blue-collar workers, the informal labor economy of the service sector—from domestic help to restaurant workers and cleaning crews—depends on migrants more than ever.

A Multicultural Germany?

In February 2004, Fatih Akın won the top prize at the International Berlin Film Festival for his feature *Gegen die Wand (Head-On)*. It was the first time in 18 years that a German film received this prestigious award. The film, set in Hamburg and Istanbul, depicts the relationship between Cahit, a suicidal widower, and Sibel, a headstrong woman in her twenties who is at odds with her family's expectations. Both protagonists are Germans of Turkish background—like Akın himself, who was born in Hamburg in 1973. Though not a story of conflicts between Germans and Turks, the film nevertheless persistently alludes to issues of citizenship, plural cultural identities, languages, and loyalties. This film epitomizes genre cinema in the era of transnational networks, drawing on Turkish, German, and American traditions of melodrama. The characters show little concern for assimilation to either Germany or Turkey; instead, they challenge binary oppositions between native and foreign, here and there, them and us.

Second-generation immigrants like Akın have established affiliations across ethnicities that have transformed the image of what and who is German. Just as Latin-, African-, and Asian-American literature, music, and film have played a crucial role in circulating new hybrid forms of identity, binational and multilingual artists in Germany are "writing back." Authors, essayists, and filmmakers of migrant backgrounds have begun to take influential positions on the national stage—speaking out not only on domestic migration politics but also on language policy, education, and the global labor economy. The pejorative slur "Kanake" took on unexpected subversive power in the 1990s, as transethnic activist groups consciously appropriated the label.

Akın's film *Head-On* draws on this countercultural aesthetics through its explosive energy but also in its wistful musical interludes that feature gypsy songs from Thrace. Although the film enjoyed critical acclaim and even a brief run in American art cinemas, it did not draw a mass audience. It was soon pushed off the screen by dubbed Hollywood hits like *Shrek II* and a German science-fiction parody, *(T)raumschiff Surprise.* This spoof on both the American sci-fi series *Star Trek* and the corny German television serial *Traumschiff (Dream Ship),* itself an adaptation of the American television series *The Love Boat,* illustrates the fusion of American and German pop culture.

Since the 1950s, television has inundated German viewers with Hollywood blockbusters and American television shows, all dubbed into German. *Sesamstrasse* and *Die Simpsons* have become programming staples. In the 1950s and 1960s, Elvis Presley and rock and roll dominated American and British Forces network radio and helped "Americanize" West Germay's postwar generation. East German youth craved Western rock bands, as Leander Haussmann's film comedy *Sonnenallee* (1999) demonstrates. There is no escaping the global culture industry today; even German-Turkish hip-hop groups adopt rap styles from American record labels. Quests for a purely German *Kultur* and its guiding value for new immigrants rest on shaky ground.

As one of the leading eight industrial nations in the world, Germany cannot disengage from recent developments in information technology, outsourcing practices, and global markets that ignore the borders of the nation-state. Germany's status as a flourishing export nation has depended on immigration since the 1950s, and the country's low birthrate of 1.37 children per woman makes immigrants indispensable—as workers, taxpayers, and guarantors of the older generation's retirement. According to recent estimates, Germany would need as many as 200,000 immigrants annually to sustain its labor ranks and uphold its social welfare system. Not unlike other Western nations, Germany is busy asserting itself within the new global economy, torn between an insistence on national autonomy and the recognition of political, social, and cultural forces that continuously question this autonomy. In this light, German discussions about migration are part and parcel of a broader debate about the future of national sovereignty and the global distribution of labor.

Today, Germany offers two divergent perspectives on its status as an immigration country. One view is that multiculturalism has utterly failed, not just in Germany but on an international scale. The 2001 World Trade Center attacks, the 2004 murder of Dutch filmmaker Theo van Gogh by a Moroccan Islamist (and Dutch citizen), the 2005 London suicide bombings perpetrated by four al-Qaeda members (all British citizens), and riots by disenfranchised youth in French cities in November 2005—each instance has been fodder for the media to decry migration as dangerous and multiculturalism as naïve. Further ammunition for this position is the high unemployment rate among immigrants in Germany, now approaching 30 percent. Racist assaults are reported to be on the rise, and in some former East German cities, skinheads and neo-Nazi vigilantes have declared certain areas "no-go zones" for foreigners. In addition, an undifferentiated fear of Islam is gaining legitimacy in the public debate.

Yet in spite of the media's often apocalyptic visions about unbridled migration and the unraveling of the social fabric, another, much less dramatic view pertains. Over the past fifty years, millions of immigrants, their children, and grandchildren have made a life for themselves in Germany, selectively incorporating "German ways," while maintaining their customs and communities. The Internet and other media connect global diasporas across national borders, and the German story of migration is not confined to Germany alone. It is also being written in Istanbul, Maputo, and Mumbai. When Shermine Sharivar, an Iranian-German student, was crowned Miss Deutschland in 2004 (and Miss Europe in 2005), Iranian satellite television from Los Angeles broadcast her triumph with great pride. Such networks of communication transcend the idea of belonging to one single country. Migration today can no longer be framed as a one-way narrative of leaving home and settling in a new land.

In the unspectacular realm of daily existence, even the German authorities are beginning to adapt to their new arrivals. On weekends in Berlin-Wilmersdorf's Preußen Park, now commonly known as the Thai Park, Thai-German families and their friends gather to picnic and socialize in the mild afternoon sun, enjoying the freedom of assembly that the German Basic Law guarantees them. Old and new Berliners relax together, while their kids play soccer—all far removed from the official debates about integration and identity. To keep order, the city has posted rules for the use of the park in German, in English, *and* in Thai—a tacit, yet permanent acknowledgement that everyday life in Germany has become a transnational project.

DOCUMENTS

WORKING GUESTS

GASTARBEITER AND GREEN CARD HOLDERS

THE MILLIONTH GUEST WORKER, 1964. Amid banners, dignitaries, and flashing cameras, Armando Rodrigues de Sá balances awkwardly on his welcome gift after a two-day train trip from Portugal to Cologne-Deutz. West Germany's financial newsweekly greets him with the following words: "Señor Rodrigues, welcome to the Federal Republic. . . . You shall be made as comfortable here as possible, as any guest should expect. . . . Now off to the fight, Torero!"

WE BEGIN THIS VOLUME with documents tracing the turbulent itinerary of foreign labor recruitment in West Germany from the postwar era to the present. Though Italian seasonal workers had been employed in the southwestern province of Baden-Württemberg since 1952, recruitment on the federal level began in January 1956. Our first text is a 1955 contract between Italy and West Germany "in the spirit of European solidarity" that would place Italian laborers for a maximum term of nine months. Members of the center-left Social Democratic Party objected to the program, claiming that the government should reduce domestic unemployment before hiring foreign labor power. Many questioned whether the postwar German infrastructure was prepared to house, transport, and provide basic services for the 100,000 new recruits expected in 1956.

Despite the plan's detractors, the "guest-worker initiative" evoked a progressive vision of pan-European mobility, foreshadowing many of the transnational features of 1990s labor policy. The contract idealized a flexible, multifunctional laborer who, in contrast to unionized domestic wage earners, could be transplanted to new sites and milieus with ease. This mobile Italian worker would benefit from a symbiotic relationship with the capital-rich, labor-poor West German economy, while continuing to support family members in Italy. The logic of the contract precludes classical immigration by assuming the recruits would neither desire nor need permanent civic membership in the host country. This pro-European, transnational outlook among the contract's negotiators led them to ignore the concrete manifestations of the nation-state: borders, passport controls, xenophobia, and restricted visas.

In the late 1950s, as industry leaders dubbed Italian recruitment a success, the Labor Ministry began to explore similar possibilities beyond the European Economic Community, which then had only six member states. Texts such as "The Verona Bottleneck" (1960) and "The Turks Are Coming" (1961) announce the recruitment of Spanish, Portuguese, and Turkish workers. In these articles, government spokespersons and journalists question the prudence of expanding the guest-worker program beyond the European Economic Community. A 1961 press release from the Confederation of German Employers' Associations suggests that West Germany should consider expanding its economic aid to Turkey instead of expropriating that country's labor power.

Like the recruitment contract with Italy, several of the documents in this chapter exemplify the more "performative" artifacts of early labor migration—informational pamphlets, sociological and demographic research studies, and invitations for labor placement. For example, "How the Turkish Worker Should Behave and Defend His Character in a Foreign Country," a Turkish-language pamphlet distributed by the Istanbul-based Turkish Labor Placement Office in 1963, advertises West Germany as an anticommunist, nationalist country that values hard work above all. Recruits, it suggests, should honor and reflect the virtues of the Turkish Republic and its Ottoman predecessors at all costs. Another text, from 1973, "Invitation for Labor Placement," notifies the addressee of his pending placement in Western Europe and instructs him to present himself for transport at a specific date and time.

Other texts document the public image of immigrants in these early years—whether as caricatures, homesick displaced persons, or future citizens. Giacomo Maturi's 1961 lecture at a nationwide meeting of employers advanced a culturalist theory of guest-worker productivity, suggesting that mental and emotional differences between German and Italian workers required two distinctly different managerial approaches in the workplace. Conny Froboess's popular 1962 song, "Two Little Italians," illustrates this exoticized nostalgia, picking up on the romantic image of the homesick Italian worker.

Though the nine-month "rotation principle" was supposed to be one of the structural mainstays of labor migration in West Germany, it had been all but abandoned in practice by the mid-1960s. A 1965 text, distributed by the Nuremberg-based Federal Labor Placement Office and entitled "Support for the Foreign Employee," took initial steps to acknowledge the permanent nature of immigrant cultures in West Germany. This text asks politicians and citizens to support "coexistence" initiatives, occupational advancement, and cultural programs for guest workers.

A further group of texts index a corpus of political journalism in West Germany that critiqued the inequities and political foibles arising from the guest-worker program. These texts reveal the persistence of a fundamental ambivalence in the mainstream press about the sustainability of temporary, rotation-based labor. "Big Welcome for Armando sa Rodriguez" (1964) reports on an official reception ceremony for the country's 1 millionth guest worker. Later articles, including "Come, Come, Come!—Go, Go, Go!" (1970) and "Recruitment of Guest Workers Stopped" (1973), speak to the living conditions that had arisen from temporary recruitment, including workplace xenophobia and housing inequity. "The Turks Rehearsed the Uprising" (1973) documents a "wildcat strike" at the Ford factory in Cologne, where Turkish autoworkers led a sustained campaign against unfair labor practices and inadequate union representation. Two other texts from the postrecruitment era—Chancellor Helmut Kohl's "Coalition of the Center"

(1984) and Irina Ludat's "A Question of the Greater Fear" (1985)—address the exclusionary after-effects of the 1973 moratorium. Ludat's exposé critiques Chancellor Kohl's "remigrant incentive" program, which sought to pay immigrants a one-time sum to leave Germany for good.

"The Card Trick" (2000) comments on the federal government's sudden announcement of a Green Card initiative to attract high-tech workers and suggests that parliamentarians across the political spectrum have bowed to corporate interests, instead of acknowledging immigrant communities' pleas for equal rights in employment. "The Campus That Never Sleeps" (2000) and "Carte Blanche in Green" (2002) comment on the itineraries of high-tech migrants from India and Eastern Europe and on Germany's struggle to counter its own IT brain drain to the United States. We conclude this chapter with Fotini Mavromati's 2005 article "Odyssey into the Promised Land," which surveys illegal immigration in a Europe that no longer has internal border controls.

The guest-worker program of the 1960s and 1970s brought about the transcontinental shift of millions of families, along with their assets, ideals, institutions, languages, music, and food. No one at the Ministry of Labor in 1955 could have imagined the transnational cultures that would soon emerge from this experiment. A comparative look at the guest-worker program and the Green Card initiative reveals that, in both cases, the federal government relied on similar conceptions for securing flexible, temporary "labor power" to boost German competitiveness in world markets. In surveying Germany's two major international labor-recruitment programs of the past 50 years, we encounter a number of questions. Can temporary labor programs succeed without systematically exploiting those who participate in them? Could Germany have avoided the xenophobic developments of the 1980s if it had afforded migrant laborers permanent resident status or citizenship? What role did the ideal of a mobile, borderless Europe play in the guest-worker program, even in its early years? As the U.S. government considers implementing bilateral "guest-worker" programs with Latin American countries, what lessons can be learned from the German case?

1

A HUNDRED THOUSAND ITALIAN WORKERS ARE COMING

First published as "Hunderttausend italienische Arbeiter kommen" in *Frankfurter Allgemeine Zeitung* (December 21, 1955). Translated by David Gramling. The term *zone border* in this text refers to the border between the Federal Republic of Germany and the German Democratic Republic, established in 1949.

Rome: Storch and Martino Have Signed the Contract

With a certain celebratory air, Foreign Minister Martino and Federal Labor Minister Storch signed an agreement on the employment of Italian laborers at the Palazzo Chigi on Tuesday. Martino commented, "A new period of fruitful cooperation between the two countries has begun."

The preamble makes a pledge to the spirit of European solidarity. Italian workers will enjoy the same working conditions as are stipulated for German workers. The agreement was sketched out on July 18, though some details were resolved later by Director Dr. Rudolf Pertz and an advisory panel at the Federal Ministry of Labor. These details were primarily concerned with questions of social services and provisions for workers' family members. The Italian negotiators did not conceal their contentment with one particular aspect: in contrast to Italy's labor agreements with other countries, Germany will pay family allowances even when family members remain in Italy. The Federal Ministry of Labor was concerned that Italian workers in Germany could not be housed in as "homelike" a way as would be necessary in today's times. This problem could, the officials contend, be overcome. But the flow of Italian workers into Germany can only be promoted to the extent that housing is available for them.

In the coming years, a hundred thousand Italian workers are expected, although the German economy could accept many more. Recruitment will begin in January [1956]. All economic sectors will be involved, but primarily the agricultural and building trades, as well as the mechanical industries. Later, when Italian workers have acquired the necessary German-language skills for occupational safety standards, mining positions will be added. A joint German-Italian advisory board will assess and regulate all issues that pertain to the agreement.

The Social Democrats' Concerns

BONN—DECEMBER 20. On Tuesday, the Social Democratic faction objected to the plan, claiming that organized recruitment of foreign workers should commence only when the domestic economic market has no more labor power. Such is their position on the German-Italian agreement. Here, the faction is referring to the high level of permanent unemployment in the zone-border regions and is calling on the government of the Federal Republic to undertake all possible efforts to bring these unemployed people to the industrial centers.

Federal Labor Minister Anton Storch responded by pointing out that the Federal Institute for Labor Placement and Unemployment Insurance in Nuremberg will only distribute work permits for foreign workers if the foreigners have the same working conditions and the same employment protections as German workers.

State Secretary Sauerborn from the Federal Ministry of Labor spoke to the concern that recruiting Italians could lead to a destabilization of German salary standards, alleging that the German-Italian agreement mitigates such concerns. The costs of recruitment, he continued, would be covered by the Italian government and by German employers, who would have to pay a uniform flat rate to cover travel costs from the Italian border to the German labor site.

2

DECLARATION OF ACCORD BETWEEN THE GOVERNMENT OF THE FEDERAL REPUBLIC OF GERMANY AND THE GOVERNMENT OF THE ITALIAN REPUBLIC CONCERNING THE RECRUITMENT AND PLACEMENT OF ITALIAN WORKERS IN THE FEDERAL REPUBLIC OF GERMANY

Published as "Bekanntmachung vom 11. Januar 1956" in *Heimat: Vom Gastarbeiter zum Bürger* (Bonn: Die Beauftragte der Bundesregierung für die Belange der Ausländer and Haus der Geschichte der Bundesrepublik Deutschland, 1995), 79. Translated by Tes Howell. This document, signed on December 20, 1955, in Rome, represents the first in a series of bilateral agreements on labor recruitment in West Germany. Subsequently, similar agreements were signed with Spain and Greece (1960), Turkey (1961), Portugal (1964), Tunisia and Morocco (1965), and Yugoslavia (1968).

The government of the Federal Republic of Germany and the government of the Italian Republic,

Guided by the desire to promote and deepen relations between their peoples in the spirit of European solidarity, to benefit both countries, and to strengthen the existing ties of friendship between them; in the endeavor to achieve a high employment rate and to utilize productive potential to the fullest; and with the conviction that these efforts serve the common interests of their peoples and promote their economic and social progress, have reached the following Accord concerning the recruitment and placement of Italian workers in the Federal Republic of Germany.

Section I: General Provisions

Article 1: (1) When the government of the Federal Republic of Germany (herewith referred to as Federal Republic) determines a demand for workers, which it wishes to fulfill through an in-sourcing of workers with Italian citizenship, it will notify the Italian government as to which occupations or occupational groups and to what approximate extent there is a need for workers. (2) The Italian government will notify the Federal Republic whether there is a possibility of accommodating this demand. (3) On the basis of these communications, both countries will agree to what extent, in which occupations or occupational groups, and at what point the recruitment and placement of workers of Italian citizenship in the Federal Republic shall be undertaken. [. . .]

Section II: Recruitment and Placement

Article 6: The Italian applicants must provide the following identifying documents to the German Commission:

- a certificate providing the results of an examination of their occupational and health qualifications;
- a personal identification card with photo;
- a certificate issued by the respective mayor, stating that the holder has no criminal record;
- an official certificate of their marital status. [. . .]

Section IV: Support, Wage Transfer, and Workers' Families

[. . .] Article 15: In accordance with the relevant German foreign exchange regulations, Italian workers can transfer their entire earned income back to Italy.

Article 16: (1) Italian workers who wish to arrange for their family members to join them can apply for a promissory note for a residence permit for these family members from the Foreigner Police by providing official documentation that there is sufficient living space for the family members. The authorities will prudently consider the applications and render a decision as soon as possible. [. . .]

Section VII: Final Provisions

[. . .] Article 22: The terms of this Accord do not countervene more favorable international regulations governing free movement of workers between European countries, but are nonetheless binding for the Federal Republic of Germany and the Italian Republic.

Article 23: This Accord will come into effect on the day of its signing. It is binding for one year and will be automatically extended each year if it is not discontinued by either government at least three months before its expiration date.

Signed in Rome on December 20, 1955, in two copies, German and Italian, whereby the provisions are binding in both languages. [Signatories were Anton Storch, Federal Minister for Labor for Germany; Gaetano Martino, Minister for Foreign Affairs for Italy; and Clemens von Brentano, Ambassador for the Federal Republic of Germany in Rome.]

3

THE VERONA BOTTLENECK

First published as "Engpass Verona" in *Der Spiegel* (April 27, 1960). Translated by David Gramling.

In recent days, that perennially restless search through Europe's economic hinterlands, aiming to drum up fresh reserves for West Germany's rural-flight-stricken labor market, came to a successful conclusion at the Bonn Foreign Ministry. The Foreign Bureau's State Secretary, Dr. Albert Hilger van Scherpenberg, signed a document in Bonn that will open up employment opportunities for Spanish workers in the Federal Republic; the director of his department, Ministerial Director Dr. Friedrich Janz, signed a second agreement that provides for the recruitment of Greece's unemployed for West Germany.

Bonn has been engaged in a labor-power search since 1955, when West Germany's labor market began to strain against its mere 500,000 unemployed (2.7 percent of those able to work). Since then, the number of unemployed has sunk to 255,000, or 1.3 percent.

West Germany thus boasts the world's lowest unemployment rate. Even the United States, the classic land of affluence, cannot produce a rate under 3 percent, even in boom times. Theo Blank's labor-market specialist, Dr. Rudolf Petz, explained, "The German labor-power deficit will become chronic in the next half decade."

It was also Petz who paved the way for the first agreement with Italy in December 1955, which sought to fill vacant positions with imports. In 1956, 15,608 Italians came over the Alps; in 1958, it was 24,047, and last year [1959] 45,000 Italians signed a German work contract. The majority of these import workers stay for a season, mostly in well-paid building trades.

In accordance with Petz's ordinance, the Federal Institute for Labor Placement and Unemployment Insurance (in Nuremberg) established two German recruitment centers—in Verona and Naples. Neither recruitment office can complain that business is slow. This year already, 15,184 Italians have committed to the Federal Republic. The German labor offices have also reported an additional cohort of 29,200 from Naples and Verona.

At the recruitment centers, the unemployed are examined by a doctor for their health status, and then presented to a commission, which instructs the potential recruit to demonstrate a few moves on the lathe or scaffolding—if they have indicated that they hold a trade qualification—in order to deter frauds and cons from making their way into West Germany. Upon approval by the commission, the seasonal emigrants receive a signed contract from their future employer and are brought to a mass residence hall to be freighted north the next day in a special transport train.

Before the new employee even sees his new West German employer, he must hand over 60 marks to the Federal Institute for transport costs at the border. This process does not always benefit the employers; driven by home-sickness, every fifth Italian aborts seasonal labor in the initial period. Today, seven of eight hired laborers honor their work contracts in West Germany until they expire.

Though this labor traffic was promising at the outset, the capacities of the Italian recruitment office were quickly exhausted. Verona sends 300 to 350 Italians daily; Naples sends 150. It will take the 29,200 requested laborers a good 10 weeks to reach their assigned site.

It was not for this reason alone that Petz and his colleagues began to look around at other European labor markets. Against Bonn's will, the Italian labor bureaus are attempting to send their labor power as more than mere place fillers for the highly industrialized Federal Republic; they are also seeking to strengthen the legal standing of these seasonal emigrants as well.

For example, the director of the department of "social issues" at the Brussels-based EEC Commission, the Italian Giuseppe Petrilli, prepared a draft for a European regulation that would ensure unrestricted freedom of mobility for laborers during the 12-year EEC transition period. The draft would stipulate that foreign laborers from any of the six member countries within the EEC would have to be granted a labor permit within three weeks' time, if the position vacated cannot be filled by a domestic applicant within this period.

4

CONFEDERATION OF GERMAN EMPLOYERS' ASSOCIATIONS

THE TURKS ARE COMING

First published as "Die Türken kommen" (1961). Reprinted in Christoph Kleßmann and Georg Wagner, eds., *Das gespaltene Land: Leben in Deutschland, 1945–1990: Texte und Dokumente zur Sozialgeschichte* (Munich: Verlag C. H. Beck, 1993), 191–93. Translated by Jeremiah Riemer.

Alongside the recruitment of workers from Italy, Spain, and Greece, the hiring of Turkish workers will soon begin, according to the Federal Employment Agency's recent announcement. On the basis of a provisional arrangement with Turkish government authorities, in cooperation with the Federal Employment Agency and the Turkish Labor Administration, workers will be recruited in Turkey and transported to the Federal Republic. Recent news reports may have already suggested that German authorities had this intention; nevertheless, the announcement of the realization of these plans is somewhat surprising. For one thing, the reservoir of manpower from previous countries of recruitment has hardly been exhausted; moreover, countries belonging to the EEC should have a certain priority over countries not yet included in the recruitment of workers. In addition, Turkey numbers among those countries in need of development aid, and in this respect, it is not entirely unfair to ask if it is sensible to deprive a country like Turkey, which is dependent on its manpower for the continued expansion of its economy, of those very workers. Certainly, one has to make sure that these workers are not needed back home at the same time. For the practical implementation of a collaboration between the Federal Employment Agency and the Turkish Labor Administration, a provisional agreement was signed. It provides for the following: effective as of July 15, 1961, a German liaison office in Istanbul will handle the placement of Turkish workers suitable for the Federal Republic.

For the time being, placement will be restricted to the regional labor bureau districts of Baden-Württemberg, North Rhine–Westphalia, and Hamburg, which already employ a considerable number of Turkish workers, and where there is already experience with hiring Turkish workers. Because the German Federal Railway is interested in hiring a large contingent of track and loading workers, this restriction does not apply to contracts with the German Federal Railway. For the time being, however, companies can make hiring requests for Turks at the employment offices only if they are orders for male workers not specified by name. For unskilled and semiskilled male workers, who are available in as large a number as anyone might want, only orders for larger groups (at least 25 workers) will be accepted. Beyond that, presumably, it should be possible to place qualified workers in the textile industry; metalworking industry; food, drink, and tobacco industries; shipbuilding; building trades; mining; as well as quarrying and brick making. Here, though, it should be noted that though qualified Turkish workers have a certain amount of professional knowledge and experience, their practical training is not as systematic as that which is customary in the Federal Republic. For every Turkish worker requested—subject to final approval by the governing board of the Federal Employment Agency—companies must pay a lump sum for expenses in the amount of 120 German marks—corresponding to the amount for recruitment in Greece—and a travel supplement of 30 German marks, coming to a total of 150 German marks. The German liaison office in Istanbul will routinely inform the employment offices about placement prospects as soon as it receives a comprehensive overview of the manpower supply. It is recommended that interested employers turn to the employment office in their area for further information.

5

GIACOMO MATURI

THE INTEGRATION OF THE SOUTHERN LABOR FORCE AND ITS SPECIFIC ADAPTATION PROBLEMS

First published as "Die Eingliederung der südländischen Arbeitskräfte und ihre besonderen Anpassungsschwierigkeiten" in *Ausländische Arbeitskräfte in Deutschland* (Düsseldorf: Econ, 1961), 121–27.

Translated by David Gramling. Maturi, a psychologist from Freiburg, presented this paper at a 1960 convention of German employers on the topic "Integrating the Foreign Worker."

Many of the difficulties in the integration of foreign labor power in the German economy originate in the *differentness* of these southern people. These are psychological difficulties, which cannot always be resolved by adapting these people to the German mentality and German forms. These difficulties can only be mastered by getting to know the eccentricities of these foreigners. They arise primarily when one tries to handle these people like Germans. It is only when one knows foreignness that a right-minded negotiation with them is possible, in which case the difficulties cease to exist, or are not that bad after all. They are only new manifestations that one must take into account; they can even be useful for the business milieu. [. . .]

The roots of these differences lie in the climate, in the landscape, in the historical development, in the culture and education, and in the societal structure of these peoples. The depth and momentousness of these factors show that it is impossible and irrational to demand a quick and total adaptation.

The Influence of the Climate on Life Rhythms

The southern climate demands and enables a different life rhythm than here in the north. Life is livelier; it is less strict and regulated. Without affecting actual productive potential, the climate has an effect on people and demands a different daily schedule, conditioning the distinct habits of these people, in private as well as in business life. Labor takes place in a different way than in the northern countries; it does not have the haste and the tempo that is common here. These people are no less willing to work or capable of work. This fact needs no further proof, because everyone praises the industriousness and the joy in working evident among the Italians. The legend of lazy Italians is, after all, a thing of the past. The overtly negative aspects can also be attributed to the climatic influences; it is also true, nonetheless, that southerners have another understanding of work.

The Southerner's Idea of Labor

Southerners are more conscious than others that they do not live to work but work to live. They are, after all, the heirs to the ancient Roman and Greek societies that regarded handiwork as slave labor and saw life's ideal as an *otium*—meaning liberation from material handiwork—in order to devote oneself to the greater values of life. They carry themselves with a distinct sense for the truly human aspects of life, because they do not really need to give themselves over to a hasty industriousness in order to drive away boredom. They value many things much more than financial affluence and the comfort of technology. Moreover, their deeply religious, sometimes fatalistic sense for life leads them to undervalue many external things.

The beauty of the landscape, the mild climate, the clear blue sky and sea on the heavenly coasts are not inconsequential for them, in that they encourage a more contemplative and nature-bound way of living.

The pressure of work and income has, however, become great among these people of late. This fact is evident in their desire for overtime and their thrifty intentions to send as much money back home as possible. But one may not forget the conventional attitude of these people toward material labor if one wants to understand this or that particular manifestation. Their lack of hardiness and reliability, which is cause for complaint here and there, can certainly be understood from this point of view. [. . .]

The Psychological Differences between Germans and Southerners

The southerner wants to be dealt with in a very personal manner; he does not want to be a number. He needs warmth, sympathy, open and affectionate friendship, as well as recognition for work performed. Equality of rights and compensation is not sufficient for him; he is receptive and looks for a smile from his boss or employer.

The German, in contrast, is cold and objective; he is usually honest, just, and shies away from playing favorites, but he smiles too infrequently. For the southerner, he is not human enough. The tone one finds in the businesses here, particularly in construction work, is too tough and raw for southerners and sometimes appears almost brutal to them. These people are not exactly sensitive but they do tend to react more quickly. Even their voices sound different, particularly when they are fighting. They are impulsive and sometimes violent, but this behavior is only their passions coming to the surface. [. . .]

Most German employers are happy with the performance of these newly recruited foreigners, but the latter are too often conceived of only as labor power, as an economic factor, not as people. This perception does not mean that too little is being done for them; many firms even provide housing and supplies for them. But the human contact is missing. Coworkers also do not do much to foster intimacy with these people, to understand them. Foreign labor power is certainly not merely "foreign workers" anymore, but these people are still not perceived as full humans; they are isolated. Families living in the area also tend to avoid contact with these people as much as possible. There are no free rooms to rent for them; they are not wanted.

One should greet them, invite them in, receive them warmly, in order to introduce them into the new society. The economic problems of immigration should not overshadow the purely human problems. Inclusion in the economy demands inclusion in society. [. . .]

6

CONNY FROBOESS
TWO LITTLE ITALIANS

First released as "Zwei kleine Italiener" on *Conny's Party* (Electrola: EMI, 1962). Translated by Tes Howell. Born in Berlin-Wedding in 1943, Froboess became a teenage idol by 1958, with halcyon tunes like "Pack Your Bathing Suit" and "Oh, It's a Snowball Fight!" (1951). "Two Little Italians," a German chart topper, was the high point of her singing career. It was also Germany's entry for the 1962 Eurovision Song Contest.

A journey to the South
is for others chic and good,
but the two little Italians
would rather be at home.

Two little Italians,
dreaming of Napoli,
of Tina and Marina,
who've long been waiting for them.
. . . .
Two little Italians
never forget their home,
the palms and the girls
on the beaches of Napoli.
. . . .
Two little Italians,
a familiar sight at the station;
they leave every night
on the train to Napoli.
. . . .

7

TURKISH LABOR PLACEMENT OFFICE
HOW THE TURKISH WORKER SHOULD BEHAVE AND DEFEND HIS CHARACTER IN A FOREIGN COUNTRY

First published as "Türk İşçisi Yabancı Ülkede Nasıl Davranmalı, Nasıl Benliğini Korumalı" by the Turkish Institute for Labor and Labor Placement (1963). Reprinted in *Fremde Heimat: Eine Geschichte der Einwanderung aus der Türkei*, Aytaç Eryılmaz and Matilde Jamin, eds. (Essen: Klartext, 1998), 64. Translated by David Gramling. Each worker recruited from the Turkish Republic between 1961 and 1963 received the following Turkish-language pamphlet introducing the German culture and economy.

The Federal Republic of Germany is a nationalistic state. The Germans living there are nationalist and anticommunist, just like us. But even there, some harmful people will slip in among our workers and spread all sorts of propaganda to isolate them from their nationality and religion, luring them into the merciless, scarlet trap of communism, seeking to infect them with poisonous ideas. They will attempt to alienate our workers from the work they are doing with promises of money and women, and try to deceive them by saying that they will find them better jobs. But more importantly, if encouraged, they will defame our homeland, our government, our state, our regime, and our glorious army and will attempt to lure you away from your straight path. To this end, they will take advantage of your drunken, tired, and weary moments to insinuate themselves among you. When you sense that someone like this is present, remove him from your social circle immediately. There are some among our colleagues whose will is weak. Do not leave them to their devices. Notify our consular officials.

Should you have friends who may be ensnared by the lies of communist radio programming, remind them of the realities of the situation.

So you are able to receive news from your homeland in a timely way and hear the *türkü* folk songs that you miss, our Ministry for Press, Publishing and Radio is currently making Turkish programming available via radio and shortwave frequencies.

Do not cause trouble or fight with our allies and friends among the Germans, with your own countrymen in Germany, or with other foreigners who have likewise come to make their livelihood. Each time such occurrences appear in the newspapers, the reputation and fame of Turkishness are denigrated. Because German women love the heroism of the Turk, they will behave cheerfully and politely toward you. Do not misunderstand this friendliness. You must regard the honor of these people with whom you are now living just as you regard your own honor. One thing that will elicit the most negative of reactions and is not kindly looked upon in Western countries is to aggravate a woman in any way or to attempt to establish intimacy with her in a way she does not want.

Family bonds in Germany are held sacred, just as they are in Turkey. Looking improperly at a married woman will not be forgiven. If you are married yourself, do not do anything that would cause you to forget your loyal spouse patiently awaiting you at home.

Every Turkish worker living in a foreign country must also not forget that our heroic ancestors, who went as far as Vienna and the shores of the Danube, never infringed upon the honor of others. When they took a bunch of grapes from a deserted vineyard, they left behind appropriate payment at the base of the vine, and if they took a fig from a tree, they tied a small purse of money to the branch. To this day, no Turk is considered as thieving, honorless, unjust, or mischievous. You will also not bring such labels upon yourself.

Germans are known throughout the world as a hardworking nation. They do not play around once work has begun and do not disobey the words of their superiors. German employers request workers from us because they have heard and know from experience that Turks are hardworking and discipline loving. Do not soil the Turks' reputation. Work like bees, be cautious, be quick to learn what you do not know. Do not deviate from the order of the workplace. Begin work on time; end on time. Do not seek medical leave unless it is especially necessary. Do not resist your supervisors or employers. Choose a trusted colleague from among you to be a spokesperson so that your rights will be represented and so that your wishes and complaints will be appropriately heard by the employer. Seek mediation from the agents at what is called the workers' council at German workplaces and become a member of the unions. If you have tried all of these venues and you continue to believe that you are in the right with regard to a complaint or request that has not been resolved or responded to, appeal to the nearest German Labor Placement Office or notify our labor attaché in Bonn in person or by letter. More labor attaché positions will be established soon. For now, you can explain your situation to the consulate in your region. Our consulates will try to do everything in their power to be of assistance to you. But they also will have some expectations of you.

8

BIG WELCOME FOR ARMANDO SA RODRIGUES

First published as "Grosser Bahnhof für Armando sa Rodrigues" in *Frankfurter Allgemeine Zeitung* (September 11, 1964). Translated by David Gramling. In September 2004, a conference took place at the Cologne-Deutz train station in commemoration of Rodrigues and the 500,000 workers from Portugal and Spain who had come there by train.

The Federal Republic Receives Its Millionth Guest Worker

COLOGNE. The millionth guest worker to arrive in the Federal Republic was ushered in with a "big welcome" on Thursday upon his arrival in Cologne-Deutz—not without betraying a little embarrassment and perplexity toward the honors bestowed upon him. After a 48-hour train ride, the 38-year-old carpenter, Armando sa Rodrigues, from the Portuguese village Vale de Madeiros, was suddenly surrounded by a flock of reporters and television cameras, boisterous marching music, and the reception committee of the Federal Republic's Association of Employers, which hailed him as its "millionth."

Rodrigues arrived in the second of two special trains delivering 173 guest workers from Portugal and 933 from Spain. Rigidly and with an almost affectless facial expression, he stood under a banner with the words "The German Association of Employers Greets the 1,000,000th Guest Worker" amid the flash of cameras and spotlights. Even the news that the two-seated moped standing next to him was his welcoming gift could not conjure a smile from his face. After some hesitation, the gaunt man in blue worker's pants gave some information about himself. He did not know how long he intended to stay in the Federal Republic. Nonetheless, he plans to have his wife, his 15-year-old son, and his 11-year-old daughter come join him.

During the short celebration—the greeting podium was flanked with the flags of Portugal, Spain, and the Federal Republic—a representative of the Employers' Association welcomed the millionth foreign employee and his newly arrived colleagues. "Without the additional work of foreigners, our economic development in recent years would be unthinkable," he stressed. Their efforts were, he continued, all the more formidable, considering the difficulties of adapting and reorienting to a foreign, highly industrialized world, despite differences in mentality, the change in climatic conditions, and the linguistic difficulties. It was, he said, the task of the German businesses and their workers to help them overcome these integration difficulties.

This "millionaire" is not uncontroversial; there are conflicting statistics about the number of guest workers in the Federal Republic. As recently as Wednesday, the president of the Federal Institute for Labor Placement and Unemployment Insurance, Anton Sabel, expressed doubts as to whether a million foreign guest workers were indeed working in the Federal Republic. According to his statistics, only 970,000 foreigners were accounted for on September 30. Most of the foreigners working in the Federal Republic, about 31 percent, come from Italy. Spain and Portugal come in second, with 15 percent each. Recruitment from Portugal has only recently begun. Thus far, 3,500 Portuguese are working in the Federal Republic. About 20 percent of all foreign guest workers in the federal territory are women.

9

FEDERAL LABOR PLACEMENT OFFICE

SUPPORT FOR THE FOREIGN EMPLOYEES

First published as "Betreuung der ausländischen Arbeitnehmer" in *Amtliche Nachrichten der Bundesanstalt für Arbeitsvermittlung und Arbeitslosenversicherung* (1965). Translated by David Gramling.

All sides seem to be in agreement that the economic growth of the Federal Republic of Germany will continue in the foreseeable future. However, according to the statistics of various federal bureaus, the number of Germans capable of working, a group whose growth rate has begun to slow in recent years, will decrease by several hundred thousand by the year 1970 due to natural population developments and the lengthening of school-attendance requirements. In order to acquire the necessary supplemental labor power and to replace the foreign employees who are returning to their homelands, recruitment countries will remain the main source of this labor power.

In the Federal Republic of Germany, a large number of foreign employees will work here for an extended duration. It is thus necessary to provide assistance to these foreign employees on as broad a basis as possible, in order to facilitate and accelerate the adaptation process. [. . .]

Given the lack of qualified personnel, businesses are increasingly directing their efforts to training those foreign colleagues who are capable of an apprenticeship or continuing education. Foreign employees are already foremen and hold other advanced positions at many work sites. Professional-development opportunities sponsored by the unions are also open to foreign employees. However, they do not tend to take advantage of this opportunity. It should be observed that most foreign employees are not strongly interested in professional training outside the factory milieu. They shy away from the financial costs and effort that are necessary for an apprenticeship. The acquisition of the German language is the intractable root cause for this reluctance. [. . .]

Efforts toward a greater mutual understanding between foreign employees and the German population have been supported through press, radio, and television programming. The media have been given the task of bringing mutual clarity to both sides through objective reporting. Newspapers and magazines from the homelands are available to foreign employees. There are also special newspapers and magazines in their mother languages. The distribution of these kinds of newspapers is partially supported by the federal government, as is the case with the Italian workers' newspaper *Corriere d'Italia,* the Greek *I Eliniki,* and the Turkish *Anadolu.*

Unfortunately, efforts toward a greater mutual understanding have been destroyed by sensational reports in some papers and magazines that represent foreign labor in the public sphere. The faults of a handful of foreign employees are grandly touted, reports of ostensible discrepancies in the provision of social services are published without being closely investigated, and the emphasis is placed on those aspects that ensure a negative overall impression. [. . .]

Given the current economic developments, the German population will need to come to terms with the idea of living together with a greater number of foreign workers. Efforts toward a greater mutual understanding should be maintained and fostered for this reason. In particular, developing tactics for clearing up misunderstandings and dismantling prejudices is an integral aspect. Assistance programs should be streamlined and their base broadened. In order to accomplish this task, it is necessary that all private and bureaucratic institutions of the federal government, the federal states, and municipalities work together. Our support work must proceed on the knowledge that foreign employees are cooperating to uphold the economic growth of the federal government and its tax base and that these workers should be supported in the development of their personal sphere by all means necessary.

10

COME, COME, COME!—GO, GO, GO!

First published as "Komm, Komm, Komm—Geh, Geh, Geh" in *Der Spiegel* (October 19, 1970). Translated by David Gramling. The national weekly news magazine *Der Spiegel* published this report as part of a series on underprivileged minorities in West Germany.

On the village green in the community of Gülnow in the Duchy of Lauenburg in Schlesswig-Holstein, Red Cross workers are heating up 10,000 knackwursts. Next to the goulash pot, a lamb side is sizzling on a spit. Some 120 Greeks are supposed to feel at home here. Social worker Gerda Fink from Stormarn is laying out sacks for a potato-sack race, saying in an admonishing tone, "We have to do something for these people."

At the main train station in Stuttgart on track 11, government functionaries in black are waiting for Zvonimir Kanijr, 32, from Voca Donja in Yugoslavian Croatia. President Dr. Karl-Otto Fritze from the Provincial Labor Office of Baden-Württemberg presents the man with a pocket radio upon his arrival and commands, "We must not think of these people as a disturbing element."

At the foreigner counter of the Stuttgart Provincial Bank headquarters, Adriano Piccolini works every day from 8:30 to 6:00. As a bank clerk, he is supposed to teach his countrymen and women how to maintain a savings account. Department Director Rudolf Köhler from the Württemberg Provincial Bank says, "We cannot just allow these people to carry thousands of marks around in their jacket pockets."

At the information kiosks of West German department stores, hostesses hand out nutrition pamphlets in four languages (Italian, Spanish, Greek, and Turkish) with tips on men's socks and laxatives, bottled capers, and blood sausage (Spanish: *salchichón de sangre y gelatina salada*). Business Director Albert Oink from the Karstadt department store in Hamburg demands, "We must help these people to shop."

"These people"—fed in Gülnow by the Inner Mission and encouraged to participate in potato-sack races, given gifts by the state in Stuttgart, and shepherded around Hamburg department stores—are guest workers. Zvonimir Kanijr from Yugoslavia was the 500,000th—in Baden-Württemberg alone. There are currently 1.95 million of them in the Federal Republic.

There are 1.5 million men and 500,000 women; among them are 424,500 Yugoslavians, 381,800 Italians, 353,900 Turks, 342,200 Greeks, 171,000 Spaniards, and 44,800 Portuguese. According to the German Industry Institute in Cologne, the number will be 2 million by the end of the year: 1 out of 10 workers in West Germany.

For a long time, these workers have belonged to the "typical imagery of a modern industrial state," as Assessor Rolf Weber from the Federal Union of German Employer Associations says. In Cologne-Weidenpesch, the Ford

Company built barracks for its laboring guests. Volkswagen built a whole village for them across from the factory gate called "Castel Lupo" (Wolfsburg). The Nuremberg Federal Institute for Labor has been administering the affairs of these 8.3 million people since 1959, building "makeshift spaces, cooking stations, photo labs, and hobby centers."

Public institutions have been offering services to guest workers for a long time now: radio stations with programs in the home language, the Bundesbahn railway company with special trains. No fewer than 180 institutions have begun to work with guest workers: 6 federal ministries, as well as the Salvation Army, 11 provincial labor ministries, the Union of Women Friends of Young Girls, the German Alliance of Unions, and the Frankfurt-based Foreigners' Brotherly Service.

FAZ coeditor Karl Korn dubs guest workers "potential conduits of understanding and communication," who are now a constitutive part of the West German milieu: the gesticulating, parlaying Italians who bring a breath of Calabria into the Hansiatic train station halls, the dandified Turks who have changed out of their Anatolian footwear into fancy duds with white leather ornaments; all the foreigners, called "salami breeders," "macaroni munchers," "Spagnols," "camel drivers," "mutton munchers," and "spaghettis" in the colloquial language of the people. [. . .]

Guest workers in Germany are not guests at all. They are not given any gifts; they do not enjoy any special status; they are only invited to join in the production process. They are allowed to work—and protecting this privilege is indeed a German tradition.

"Foreign workers" was what they called the more than 1 million foreigners who sold their labor power in the time of the kaisers: on the lands of Pommeranian farm estates and in the mines of Rheinish heavy-industry sectors. The "Yearly Report of the Prussian Industry's Oversight Officers" from 1908 registered a "larger reserve of domestic labor power than usual, because the jobs are, for familiar reasons, filled by foreigners—Italians, Poles, and Bohemians." The familiar reason: the foreigners' willingness to sacrifice themselves to the most difficult work for the lowest wages.

Such social disparities are not to be forgotten when considering the development of civilization and progress within Western industrial nations, as the French philosopher Claude Lévi-Strauss believed. To the Lévi-Straussian formula of historical exploitation—"first slavery, then bondage, proletariat, colonialism"—a group of Cologne-based analysts added two contemporary posts: "forced laborers and today's guest workers."

Within six years, the Nazis brought back at least 5.3 million civilians and 1.5 million prisoners of war to Germany. Armed with the spoils *rapoti* and *dawai,* they forced tens of thousands of Soviet citizens into the German war industry. Deportees from Poland, Belgium, and France worked on German fields. They were, according to the publisher Wolf-J. von Kleist, "people of stigma . . . valued as labor hands, yet meanwhile the object of astonished disbelief when they recognized what a bicycle was or knew how to turn the right knobs on the transistor radio."

The fact that the "camel drivers" and "mutton eaters" of today are often categorized as uncivilized or dumb signifies a continuity in this minority discrimination. But today these pigeon-holed, devalued people come of their own free will and are called "guest workers." This "switch of concepts," writes the Cologne-based psychology professor Edeltraud Meistermanns-Seeger, "which led to the discontinuation of 'foreign,' to the euphemism 'guest,' and ultimately to the neutral label 'foreign employee,' is a sign of uncertainty and ambivalence, best understood in the context of the repression of problems associated with the previous period of forced labor." [. . .]

11

TURKISH LABOR PLACEMENT OFFICE

INVITATION FOR LABOR PLACEMENT

First published as "Einladung zur Arbeitsvermittlung" by the Istanbul Branch Office of the Turkish Labor Placement Office, 1973. Reprinted on www.domit.de. Translated by David Gramling. This form letter represents the administrative portal through which workers were screened and scheduled for labor migration to Germany. This invitation would have been one of the last sent, given that Willy Brandt announced the recruitment moratorium on November 22 of the same year.

Istanbul Branch Office

July 2, 1973

First and Last Name of the Invited Party: Ismail N_____ :

1. According to our branch office records, it appears that it is your turn to be placed abroad.
2. Please present yourself without fail on the day and at the hour indicated below; doing so will result in the preselection of your application.
3. If you are unable to appear at this appointment, please note the instructions on the reply form attached in this communication (Form no. 49/A). Please check one or more of the reasons that would prohibit you from appearing at the indicated appointment time. Mail this reply form in time for it to reach our branch office by July 5, 1973, at the latest. (Mail delays will not be considered as valid grounds for exception.)
4. Enter your signature on the reply form and include this as a separate attachment. Mail it in an envelope with 200 kurus postage.

For men: If you are younger than _____ years of age, you need not appear. If you have more than four children under 18 years of age, you also need not appear.

For women: If you have more than four children under the age of 18, you need not appear. If you have a child younger than 12 months old or are pregnant, you need not appear.

If you are unable to read and write, you need not appear.

Branch Office, Department of Applications for Foreign Employment

Please appear on:	July 9, 1973
at:	8:30 A.M.
at:	1st Floor, Room 8
Recruiting country:	Germany
Type of work:	Carpenter

12

FRIEDRICH K. KURYLO

THE TURKS REHEARSED THE UPRISING

First published as "Die Türken probten den Aufstand" in *Die Zeit* (September 7, 1973). Translated by David Gramling. From August 24 to August 30, 1973, Turkish autoworkers at the Ford plant in Cologne staged a strike and sit-in against the wishes of the German Alliance of Unions as well as their own umbrella union, IG-Metall.

Some Background to the Wildcat Strike at Ford

"We sat in the foreman's office and hid under the desks as the Turks made their way through the warehouse." Even now, fear seems to linger in this worker's body. He was a witness to the most consequential strike among guest workers in the Federal Republic to date. For seven days, around 2,000 Turks took to the barricades at the Ford factory in Cologne. They stopped their work on the auto manufacturer's conveyor belts.

The Turks' wildcat strike began after the management fired 300 of their countrymen and women for returning late from vacation.

This layoff was, however, just the straw that broke the camel's back. The angry men who blocked production day after day felt provoked by other unfair labor practices as well. They decried the work conditions, demanded higher compensation, and complained of discrimination by their German colleagues.

At Ford, what has been simmering just below the surface at many factories appears to have forced its way into the public eye for the first time. The guest workers, this new German proletariat, wanted something better. The fact that it happened here in Cologne is no coincidence. In this metropolis on the Rhine, the problems of guest workers have become evident in an intense way, in residential conditions as well as in the workplace.

Foreigners, primarily Turks, tend to live in prewar buildings from the 1870s between Ring Street and the railway tracks near the city center. Most

Germans moved out of these buildings long ago; the noise of traffic comes in day and night. The sanitary facilities of these tenements are generally inadequate, and sun hardly makes its way into the backyards.

The Turks' workplace appears much more inviting at first glance, but even there, one can sense their second-class social status. Nonetheless, the union representatives at Ford allege that "they are working at the same rate as us; they are receiving the same wage for the same work." But in reality, the 12,000 Turks are a large, disadvantaged minority among the staff of 32,000 workers. The language barrier bars them from accessing better wages. As a rule, Turks do monotonous, dirty, and uncomfortable work—like removing screws in very hard-to-reach spaces—work that does not require a common language and understanding with one's neighbor. With a little teamwork, the Germans and the few German-speaking Turks can make up to 2 marks more per hour.

A number of internal production-rate differences cement this inequity. There are many difficult jobs that are simply not done by Germans anymore, jobs that have been entirely given over to foreigners. The productivity standards for those jobs are, without a doubt, guest-worker standards.

Unions and workers' councils, which are supposed to represent the interests of all employees, are hardly able to provide assistance. In many ways, language difficulties stand in the way of trust and cooperation. The union functionaries cannot speak Turkish. The management's interpreters are often considered extensions of the power of the management, and justifiably so.

Last year, it appeared as though no Turk would be able to remedy this lack of representation. Their countryman Mehmed Ozbăgcı was elected to the workers' council staff. But what was the reaction of the workers' council, which was run by an absolute IG-Metall majority? It refused to accept Ozbăgcı into the tight circle of at-large members. Ernst Lück, the chair of the workers' council, complained that "this man did not know German and did not even have a workplace constitution on hand."

Since then, Ozbăgcı has had to do the work of a workers' council member as well as his work on the assembly line. Turkish colleagues support him financially so that he can sustain this double duty. Along with Özbağcı, four other Turks and an Italian, all IG-Metall members, have become workers' council members. The percentage of guest workers on the workers' council is now 12.7 percent, whereas their share of the overall company workforce is 53.1 percent. These numbers disprove the claim that guest workers have equal representation in the Cologne Ford factory.

The layoff of 300 Turks then turned simmering unrest into open rebellion. Most are allowed no vacation, unlike their German colleagues. They often have to travel days to reach their home villages to settle rent claims and debts, and once there, they frequently encounter tumultuous family issues such as inheritance disputes. But neither the workers' council nor their German colleagues have much interest in or understanding of such situations.

One German worker says, "There are lots of them who take so much extra vacation that they run out of money and don't have anything left to eat."

Meanwhile, Turks feel that they are being unjustly treated. They fear having to overcompensate for the absence of those who have been fired from the assembly line, where they claim the pace is too fast and allows for too few breaks. The strike could be avoided no longer.

Then, who else took over the coordination of the strike but leftist extremists. It remains unclear whether they intentionally weaseled their way in, as in the case of the Brechnjew unrest in Bonn. The university student Dieter Heinert maintains that he had learned some Turkish before taking the job at Ford. Moreover, the charismatic Turkish agitator Sulaiman Baba Targün (30) began work at the factory only four days before the strike broke out.

The strikers' demands—a cost-of-living bonus and a 13 percent wage increase, long-time goals of the workers' council—generated solidarity among many German workers with their Turkish colleagues. But the solidarity was soon overshadowed by misunderstanding and fear—and was finally crowded out by enmity and hate.

This strike was not a German strike. It fostered resentment about the foreigners' rabble-rousing. "You should just send all of them away," said many; such were the most harmless commentaries on this Turkish impertinence. In a mass counterdemonstration condemning the event, the German employees defeated the foreigners' strike. When police commandos arrested the agitators, vigilantes moved in, saying "One should just give them a good beating; then it will be all over with."

The ultimate gain of the strike—a cost-of-living bonus—benefited the Germans as well. As for the Turks, only a repeal of some layoffs was promised. The management and IG-Metall in Cologne declared they have learned a lesson from the strike and are going to take a close look at their guest-worker policies. It is high time for it.

13

RECRUITMENT OF GUEST WORKERS STOPPED

First published as "Anwerbung von Gastarbeitern gestoppt" in *Süddeutsche Zeitung* (November 24–25, 1973). Translated by David Gramling.

No more guest workers will be recruited from countries outside the European Community from now on. At this time, about 2.6 million foreigners are working in the Federal Republic. Of those, 23 percent are Turks, 20 percent are Yugoslavians, 18 percent are Italians, 11 percent are Greeks, 8 percent are Spanish, and 20 percent are from other countries.

BONN, NOVEMBER 23. The Federal Institute for Labor in Nuremberg can no longer accept any foreigners into the Federal Republic and West Berlin for the time being. A declaration to this effect came from Federal Labor Minister Walter Arendt on Friday, with the consent of the Federal Cabinet at the Institute. The Labor Promotion Act entitles the federal labor minister to take such measures. Arendt made it known in his declaration that the intention was to stem the employment of foreigners as a precautionary measure. For those who are already working in our country, there is, he reports, "no reason for serious concern. However," added the federal labor minister, "we cannot rule out the possibility that the energy shortage might lead to some employment risks."

European Community countries, particularly Italy, are not affected by this measure.

According to paragraph 19 of the Labor Promotion Act, those foreigners who are not German in the sense of article 116 of the Basic Law must acquire a permit from the Federal Institute for Labor in order to enter into employment, "as long as no diplomatic agreements stipulate otherwise." These permits will be distributed in individual cases according to developments in the labor market. Because the work permit is limited to two years and may also be restricted to certain vocational sectors, businesses, and economic branches, or districts, the Federal Institute for Labor reserves the right to intervene in and manage the employment of foreigners.

These options have been invoked sporadically in the past to the benefit of certain economic branches or districts, but it has not generally been perceived as restricting the employment of foreigners. In the past few months, however, there have been more and more attempts to counteract the "concentration" of foreigners in certain cities and the consequently excessive demands on the infrastructure. The Federal Ministry of Labor stresses that, in the future, the control measures included in paragraph 19 of the Labor Promotion Act will be enacted throughout the labor market. Considerable effort has been made to not appear dramatic when referencing foreigners in these control measures, because, according to the undersecretary responsible, "it is the natural implementation of legal measures in light of labor market conditions."

The discontinuation of foreign labor placement affects 60,000 current placements that were distributed after September 1, 1973, under the new 1,000-mark placement surcharge. (The placement surcharge for EC citizens is 60 marks.) [. . .]

14

HELMUT KOHL

COALITION OF THE CENTER: "FOR A POLITICS OF RENEWAL"

Published as "Koalition der Mitte: Für eine Politik der Erneuerung" in *Bundeskanzler Helmut Kohl: Reden 1982–84* (Cologne: Presse- und Informationsamt der Bundesregierung, 1984), 143–44. Translated by

David Gramling. Kohl delivered this speech before the Bundestag on October 13, 1982. His first campaign for West German chancellor was bolstered by his protectionist position on "foreigner politics." The following excerpt marks a rhetorical turn in the federal government's policy on future immigration.

[. . .] The third focal point of our urgent program for the upcoming elections is foreigner politics.

The coexistence of a great number of people of a different mentality, culture, and religion alongside Germans demands effort from all sides—state and society, foreigners and Germans. This task requires patience and tolerance, realism and humanity.

The federal government's policies for foreigners will be guided by three basic principles.

First: Integrating the foreigners living with us is an important goal of our foreigner politics. Integration means not the loss of one's own identity but rather the most frictionless coexistence possible between foreigners and Germans. Integration will be possible only if the number of foreigners living with us does not continue to increase. It is crucial to avoid an unbridled and uncontrolled immigration.

Second: The federal government will continue the recruitment moratorium and restrict the number of new family members coming to West Germany, and it will do so precisely in the interest of the children, who have a right to their own family. The government will work within the Association Agreement [with the Turkish Republic] to avoid another immigration wave.

Third: The foreigners who would like to go back to their homeland must be assisted in doing so. Every person has the right to live in his homeland. Foreigners in Germany should be able to decide freely, but they must decide if they want to return to their country or stay here and integrate.

The federal government will establish a working commission focused on the realization of this program, including representatives of the federation, states, and municipalities, who will present their suggestions and recommendations at the beginning of the coming year.

We will do everything to prevent abuse of the right to asylum. [. . .]

15

IRINA LUDAT

A QUESTION OF THE GREATER FEAR

First published as "Eine Frage der grösseren Angst" in *Die Zeit* (October 18, 1985). Translated by Tes Howell. After a no-confidence vote ousted Helmut Schmidt as West German chancellor on October 1, 1982, Helmut Kohl succeeded him, promising to reduce the "flow" of foreigners. The "border-crossing certificates" mentioned in this text are one-way exit permits tantamount to voluntary self-deportations.

*The End Result of Encouraging Immigrant Workers to Return
to Their Native Country*

It almost looked like a state visit on September 10, 1964, at the Cologne-Deutz train station: the train arrived from Portugal; the country's national hymn was playing; city officials were waiting on the platform. The red carpet treatment for Armando Sa Rodrigues, the 1 millionth "guest worker" in the Federal Republic. He received a moped, flowers, and a certificate.

Twenty years later at the Frankfurt Airport: suitcases, boxes, bags, and a stifling crowd at the Turkish travel-agency counters, lines in front of the Federal Border Guard's office. Stressed officials stamp border-crossing certificates and invalidate the residence permits in Turkish passports. For charter-flight passengers, this stamp means bidding a definite and irrevocable farewell to Germany.

This time, officials stay far away from the event, and the politicians in distant Bonn celebrate the law encouraging immigrant workers to return to their native countries as a demonstration of "our successful policy."

Upon taking office, Chancellor Helmut Kohl promised to halve the number of foreigners living here. A joint federal/state commission, under the direction of Friedrich Zimmermann, was to submit proposals on the topic, but a coalition dispute has prevented the federal interior minister from getting started.

Then the administration reached into the drawers of its predecessors and found the draft for a law encouraging immigrant workers to return to their native countries, which—slightly modified—was adopted on November 29, 1983. "Our assistance accompanies those returning home," declared Federal Labor Secretary Norbert Blüm at the time.

With the window of opportunity restricted to just eight months, the law provided "remigrant incentives" of 10,500 German marks for unemployed or partially employed foreigners. Most importantly, the law offered Turks and Portuguese the opportunity to immediately access the contributions they had made to their pension funds.

Shortly before the law's adoption, headlines declared in the press, "Half want to go home" and "A third want to leave today." Then in July, after the eight-month mark had passed, officials announced: "Three hundred thousand foreigners left the Federal Republic through the remigrant incentives program."

Today, one year later, it is still unclear how many foreigners have actually taken advantage of the law's provisions and how many were thus induced to leave. This same conclusion was reached at a recent Friedrich Ebert Foundation conference entitled "The New Immigrant Policy in West Europe." Unofficially, those in Bonn speak more moderately on the topic.

Two questions arise: Have the expectations associated with the law been fulfilled? And do targeted repatriation measures offer an adequate "solution to the foreigner problem"?

First, a definition: "remigrant incentives" are one among various measures stipulated in the law to encourage immigrant workers to return to their home countries and constitute a one-time payment of 10,500 marks (plus 1,500 marks for every child).

Last year's report that 300,000 foreigners have left this country through "remigrant incentives" was erroneous. Rather, exactly 13,716 foreigners have left, of whom 94.2 percent possessed a special work permit. With this permit, they would have been entitled to extended unemployment benefits if they had chosen to remain in Germany. As a result of their departure, the German Federal Labor Office will save approximately 330 million marks.

Bonn also dressed up the balance by including those who left after requesting restitution of their pension funds. Previously, remigrants could always reclaim their pension contributions (instead of drawing a pension in Germany), though only after a two-year waiting period, which was and is still an important buffer. But because Bonn's success statistics include all repayment claims since the inception of the remigrant law, the recently approved claims of some 30,000 Turks already living in Turkey have also been paid.

In contrast to the situation with "remigrant incentives," far more than Bonn's early estimate of 55,000 foreigners have filed claims for premature restitution. However, no one knows the exact number, explained Elmar Hönekopp from the Institute for Labor Market and Occupational Research at the Ebert Foundation conference. According to Hönekopp, the institute counted approximately 100,000 applications, some 40,000 fewer than the government alleged a year ago. Because only the employee contributions were reimbursed without interest, the government saved 4 billion marks of otherwise future pension payouts abroad, a sum that is now helping to safeguard German pensions.

For Elmar Hönekopp and Ursula Mehrländer, who works in the Research Institute of the Ebert Foundation, these statistical confusions are mere embellishments that raise fundamental concerns about the law's effectiveness. Encouraging foreign workers to return home may indeed have influenced their date of return, but it hardly affected the total number of remigrants. Since 1966, an average of 300,000 foreigners have returned to their home countries every year; last year [1983], when the law went into effect, only 55,000 more returned. The reason for the decrease of the foreign population is not this law but rather the drastic drop in the number of foreigners coming to Germany.

Due to the various restrictions in the law's original language, the most crucial of which are its time restrictions and narrowly conceived population groupings, the law was not suited to promote the return of a greater number of foreigners. It is logical that a foreign worker who has lived in Germany for 20 years would need some time to consider the government's proposition. The federal government, however, demanded they decide and leave within four weeks—otherwise there would be "aid" deductions of 1,500 marks for every additional month.

The unspoken desire to use this foreigner policy to free up jobs for unemployed Germans was not fulfilled. Anyone leaving the country with "remigrant incentives" following bankruptcy or a company closure—and this situation constituted the majority of cases—does not free up a job. And the positions of those who quit and went home on their own were difficult to fill. Whether hired in fish processing or in the slaughterhouse, the Germans sent by the Employment Office usually threw in the towel shortly after taking the job.

To cite another case, German replacement workers were not sufficiently qualified for the positions at the Howaldtwerke-German Dockyards. The Foreigner Office in Kiel reports that HDW was seeking Turkish welders who, because of their specialization in welding techniques for submarine construction, could not be replaced at such short notice.

At the Ruhrkohle AG in Duisburg, the largest employer of Turks, there were shortages as well. When 2,700 Turkish miners left the company, this disadvantaged the German personnel: overtime and lower chances for early retirement.

Incidentally, the area between the Rhine and Ruhr basin was the regional center of the remigrant carousel. According to the Institute for Labor's calculations, most applications for "remigrant incentives" came from the iron, steel, mining, and energy industries. This fact is hardly surprising, because firms such as Hoesch, Thyssen, Mannesmann, and others used the Bonn model for their operational personnel policies. They supported legal regulations promoting "melting pots" and "assimilation," which consequently led to staff reduction.

IAB calculations prove the connection. In 68.7 percent of all applications, the remigrant award was paid subsequent to company closures; this case held in 98.5 percent of mining applicants and in 96.5 percent of iron and steel applicants.

Take Hüttenheim, for example: reporters descended upon the area in droves after 900 Turks were "encouraged to move on" and "sent home with incentives" in one concentrated action by Mannesmann's executives, the workers' council, and the Labor Office. It was a serendipitous convergence of the remigrant law and business strategy; the firm could list the "incentives" and the restitution of pension funds next to the operational severance payments on their corporate reports. The Turkish fathers "became docile by the dozens," argued workers' council member Mahler, though he did not mention that the employee advocate and German personnel had intervened.

When the Mannesmann management excluded only Turks from the early-retirement program, consequently blocking the path to retirement for a number of Turks over 55, the employee advocate put up minimal resistance. Faced with the alternative of leaving the firm with or without compensation, the Turks finally signed this "offer to foreign fellow citizens" from Mannesmann and the federal labor minister, consequently ensuring their own untimely departure.

Even the Labor Ministry's secretary of state Vogt had to conclude recently that the return of foreign workers has opened up few jobs for Germans. Most jobs vacated by foreigners—according to Vogt at a press conference—have fallen victim to downsizing.

One must ask why Chancellor Helmut Kohl, speaking to the CDU's employment committees in Saarbrücken, kept attributing the high unemployment rate to the fact that there are "still too many jobs taken by guest workers"—a statement largely unnoticed by the press.

An investigation into the political effects of this remigrant law yields four important discoveries:

First: The premise of "remigrant incentives" was a structural constraint—namely, the real or imminent loss of one's job.

Second: The law's temporal restriction was meant to force a decision by foreign employees.

Third: The "remigrant incentives" forced the foreign employee and his/her family to leave the Federal Republic permanently, even if resettlement in the home country later proved to be impossible.

Fourth: The good publicity the government received for these "incentives" did not acknowledge the premise that restitution claims were based on employees' own contributions and labor over the years. Instead, the notion prevailed that these payouts were "rewards," gifts to unemployed foreigners. Consequently, the law also fueled prejudices and violence against foreigners and intensified the social constraints for foreign families.

Felix Rodriguez, a Spanish pastor, paraphrased this dynamic: "When a foreigner's fear of staying here outweighs his fear of returning home, then he will 'voluntarily' go home."

Immigrants' fear of a future in their home countries is still greater. More than 4 million foreigners continue to live in Germany, and politicians know that targeted remigrant measures, in the best-case scenario, increase the number of those returning home only slightly.

As the Ebert Foundation conference tried to demonstrate, programs that encourage foreign employees to return home have primarily symbolic meaning because they lead proponents of tough policies on foreigners to believe in active negotiation. At some point, however, this line of reasoning will exhaust itself and its stopgap character will become evident. Then, three possibilities will remain:

The first would be the intensification of the returnee program through large-scale, forced repatriation. Despite current debates about a stricter stance on the foreigner law, this outcome is improbable. International considerations, interstate treaties, and economic factors hardly provide options in this regard. Already, the damage done by the remigrant law is a perennial burden on relations between southern European countries and the Federal Republic. These countries were not consulted prior to the law's implementation.

The second possibility would be to recognize that the indisputable contemporary problems among foreigners will not be resolved by sending some away but must be dealt with here instead. According to Ursula Mehrländer of the Ebert Foundation, recognition of foreigners as "permanent immigrants" or "migrants" must occur. The Hessian government is formulating it more cautiously; Interior Minister Horst Winterstein declared in Parliament, at the request of the CDU/CSU, that "fundamental considerations" precluded the "remigrant incentives" from becoming the cornerstone of their foreigner policy. According to Winterstein, "The children born and brought here will stay here, as they have little or no connection to their parents' country of origin."

The third possibility is the most probable at present: we continue talking about remigration. We can do so by looking at the "Draft of a Law on Reintegration Aid for Residential Construction for Returning Foreigners," which the Parliament is still discussing but which is supposed to become law on January 1, 1986. According to the draft, remigrants can create a savings account with a building and loan association in their home country without penalty if they simultaneously commit to going home within four years after the loan disbursement.

The haggling over numbers has begun: the law, according to the government, could be used by 185,000 foreign building-and-loan clients (among them 130,000 Turks). The parliamentary speeches are already being written. On the topics of home construction and German-Turkish friendship, Norbert Blüm claimed, "This will last forever and remind all generations that their fathers and grandfathers once worked in Germany. Could this not be a contribution to the friendship between our two countries?"

If this policy continues to be promoted, the conflicts will continue to intensify. And there is no sign that the trend will be reversing any time soon.

16

FLORIAN SCHNEIDER

THE CARD TRICK

First published as "Der Kartentrick" in *Süddeutsche Zeitung* (February 27, 2000). Translated by Tes Howell.

In with the Foreigners: Why the Boat Is Suddenly Not So Full Anymore
How quickly times change. For over 10 years in this country, everyone from the neo-Nazi to the parents' group spokeswoman, from Schönhuber to Schily, has been singing the same tune in this country: Germany could not, despite its best intentions, take in any additional immigrants. The boat is full, the pain threshold finally reached. Those who contradicted this maxim were seen as so-called do-gooders or, worse, as hopelessly delusional.

Then the report blew in on Tuesday afternoon that the computer industry's leading representatives are warning of imminent ruin: if they do not recruit at least 250,000 employees from abroad, their chances in future markets will be dim. Reactions from the unions and the Ministry of Labor ranged from indignation to dismissal, and the chancellor, who clearly seeks yet again to say what everyone wants to hear, pulls the Green Card out of the hat for the "best of the best."

The employers' goal is to compensate for highly trained workers, who are leaving narrow, globally withdrawn Germany for California, by offering young Eastern European and Middle Eastern specialists comparably favorable conditions and thus the chance of a lifetime.

Union functionaries are already scared; they fear that a majority of their members could soon become openly hostile to foreigners. And the federal government is still dodging what has long been overdue: fundamentally questioning the work-permit requirement, in all its forms that contradict national and international law.

Herein lies the actual explosive force of the debate on high-tech guest workers: non-German employees, provided that they are not EU citizens or do not have an unrestricted residence permit, need a work authorization or a work permit. The Bureau of Labor grants only temporary permits—if at all—and limits this practice to certain industries, mostly involving what is justifiably labeled dirty work.

Worse yet, the "work-permit requirement" presumes a job-placement agreement with the Bureau of Labor, which means that the potential employer and his non-German employee commit to supporting the bureau by finding an employment-seeking German within at least four weeks. Since the oil crisis in the 1970s, there has been a freeze on recruitment of foreign workers. The so-called Exception Guidelines for the Freeze on Recruitment are implemented so restrictively that they allow for few exceptions and in specific industries only—for example, agriculture or construction—ultimately leading to the familiar side effects of extremely low wages and inhuman working conditions.

While the German political party representatives are demonstratively displaying their disgust for right-wing party demagogy and pointing the finger at Austria on election days, politicians and lawmakers from Schily to Stoiber have created a situation in which almost only Germans may work in Germany.

Employers in all branches of industry have bemoaned the consequences of this policy behind closed doors for years, especially because the specialized knowledge of many government officials is not nearly as strong as their ideological stubbornness when it appears necessary to protect the fatherland from the tide of foreigners. Personnel managers of large international firms are often told that German sinology students could in principle be just as successful in conquering the Far Eastern market for mobile-radio networks, for all one really needs is the right linguistic knowledge. Or a video technician who, due to his dark skin and lack of a work permit, must work as a bartender because the authorities, cashing in on popular clichés, clearly do not want to cause trouble.

The outcry of the information industry belies a policy that in the past few decades has not only declared the walling off of the German labor market beyond all party lines but has also flagrantly pursued it, despite all enthusiastic insights into the "inevitability of globalization." Years ago, the French government had to recognize that the biological working hypothesis, according to which the body politic repels everything foreign, led only to its own lasting detriment: young African elites made a grand detour around the colonial motherland.

One perhaps more comparable process of recognition appears to be starting in Germany, aside from the notorious attacks. There is an interesting question here: will the result be an ideological dispute among factions, in which hopeful candidates for the German version of Haider may prove their demagogical suitability? Or is this the beginning of a serious discussion about the social and political implications of a new market that ignores nation-state borders?

The alignment of employee rights with the market's unrestricted freedom is at the top of the agenda. After all, the "red-green card" issue could serve as an introduction to Asian conditions in which, for working migrants in high- and low-tech sweatshops, the privilege of being shamelessly exploited is coupled with the subsequent pressure to leave the country as quickly as possible after the work is done.

The unions have a choice: either they move decisively into the right-wing camp with their fixation on German jobs for Germans, or they join their Italian and French colleagues, for whom even the representation of illegal workers has long been a given, in seeking a critical analysis of non-German workers and the German workforce and developing from that a contemporary conception of internationalism. [. . .]

17

KARIN STEINBERGER

THE CAMPUS THAT NEVER SLEEPS

First published as "Der Campus, der niemals schläft" in *Süddeutsche Zeitung* (August 1, 2000). Translated by David Gramling. In spring 2000, the North Rhine–Westphalian Bundestag candidate Jürgen Rüttgers campaigned on the slogan "Kinder statt Inder" ("Children, Not Indians") to counter the German government's Green Card program. Steinberger's article reports on the effect of this slogan in Bombay, India.

How enthusiastically young people in Bombay work on the computer—and why the Berlin Green Card government leaves them so indifferent

BOMBAY, THE END OF JULY [2000]. By the time Ramashish was 18 years old, everything had happened for him already. He had been accepted at the Indian Institute of Technology, and since then, nothing has or will come between him and moving up. Now he is 21, and the world is his oyster. Well, not exactly—yet. Actually, he and several other colleagues possess not much more than an idea. But it might catapult him directly into the Olympus of the computer industry.

The room from which the seven young men intend to launch their conquest of the world has scummy walls, wobbly cubicle dividers, and the temperature is more than thirty degrees Celsius. The only things that look in good shape here are the computers. But Ramashish is extremely confident. In one year at most, he says, his Internet firm will be a success, even if he cannot exactly divulge what the firm is going to offer. The idea is priceless, however: the young men have to wait until it is ready before they can tell the press exactly what it is.

Would he go to Germany if he were offered a good job? A short silence, then laughter. Ramashish looks as if someone had just made him an indecent proposal. Europe? People might go there for vacation but definitely not to work. The best of the best of the computer sector are found in America, definitely not in Germany. And now this whole discussion about the Green Cards. He does not understand what it is about exactly, but the feeling of not really being wanted in Germany is omnipresent here. But this hostility is not the only concern: how would he fare with the language, with the food? "We just know too little about Germany, industrially and culturally." Ramashish leans back, "No, if I had to go anywhere, I'd go to the USA." And then, in a tone that allows for no further questions, he says, "But man, we're in the hot spot right here."

200,000 Applicants

Whoever makes it to this hot spot first has to go through the "minefield," as they call this boulevard blanketed with bird droppings. Thousands of crows inhabit the trees just behind the main door to the Indian Institute of Technology in Bombay. Here they make the race to the world of elites into a dirty business. But what is a little bit of bird droppings compared to what applicants must go through to get into this campus? The acceptance exam at the six IITs—in Delhi, Kharagpur, Chennai, Kampur, or Guwahati, along with Bombay—is one of the most difficult in Asia. Even to participate in test preparation, one must already have passed one exam. For up to three years, the applicants ready themselves for the test, and each year only 2,500 out of 200,000 are accepted. "The Chosen," they call themselves, who have succeeded. The Selected.

The IIT perceives itself as a "production center for the brightest minds in the land," as a producer of "leadership material." So says IIT Director Ashok Misra, and this is exactly what everyone here has internalized. On the 220-hectare campus 30 miles outside of Bombay, an "atmosphere of intellectual agitation" prevails, as the magazine *Outlook* described it. What counts here is intelligence, talent, and leadership qualities. Learning from the heart is frowned upon. And one's best friend is one's worst competitor. [. . .]

"Whatever the IIT graduates in Silicon Valley can do, the students here can do as well," says [Deppak] Phatak. For him, it's an issue of giving students the confidence to feel that they don't need to go to America in order to achieve something. Too many, he says, have gone, stayed, and never come back. That is the good thing about the "Children, Not Indians" ["Kinder statt Inder"] slogans in Germany: "with Germany, we don't have to worry that our elite is going to disappear there." [. . .]

Two floors below Director Phatak's office, there is a crowd in front of the job-placement office. The firms Veritas, Tata Consulting Service, and Cisco Systems have their application tests there. In the office itself, firms have hung up posters with prophecies from the beautiful new dot-com world, messages like "Step into the cyber era," "The world is smaller, the market is bigger," "You too can be a part of an unbelievable success story," or "We offer a career, not just a job." Texas Instruments, Amazon.com, Sun Microsystems, Cisco, McKinsey—large employers are fighting over the next generation here. "These firms buy the brains of the IIT students; they know that these people are the ones who can learn anything," says Ashok Misra. But he cannot remember a German firm ever having done on-campus recruiting. It is astounding: didn't Germany want to drum up some Indians with its August 1 initiative? "It seems that Germany should put more effort into presenting itself in a positive way," says Misra. IIT students are used to people fighting over them: "Our students know what they are worth. World-class firms pay to become the first to come and recruit them." Almost all have a job even before they have finished their studies. Or they have their own firm.

In the IIT, time flows only in one direction: what counts is the future. And in that sense, everything is possible for these students and for this country. [. . .] "Everyone here in IIT knows that he will have a great career, why should we not be optimistic?" says Ramashish. "But we want to use our knowledge in our own society. Why go to Germany?"

"We are far too motivated to work less," say Ramashish and his friend in the computer room.

18
BERND HOF

SCENARIOS FOR THE DEVELOPMENT OF LABOR-FORCE POTENTIAL IN GERMANY

First published as "Szenarien zur Entwicklung des Arbeitskräftepotenzials in Deutschland" in *Politik und Zeitgeschichte* (August 2001). Translated by Tes Howell. Since 1973, Hof has been project manager at the Institute for German Economics in Cologne, researching structural change in the German and European labor markets. In 2001, he was appointed professor of empirical economic research at the International School of Management in Dortmund.

I. Preliminary Remarks

There is an established tradition in Germany of predicting the future development of employment potential. The first wave of potential scenarios came in the second half of the 1970s, when all the notable economic-research institutes were addressing the challenge of several high-birthrate years, which drastically increased the labor force in the years between 1977 and 1987. At the time, they predicted that weak economic growth would lead to intolerably high unemployment rates and that the number of unemployed would climb to 2 million or 3 million in the 1980s. The media broadcast horror stories, and most did not want to believe that something like this could really happen. We have known for some time that high unemployment did occur in the course of the 1980s and that in the former West German states, unemployment numbers actually exceeded 3 million, even though this did not take place until 1997. [. . .]

V. Migration: From the Guest Worker to the New Citizen

Foreign migration has shaped the population as well as the job market since the early 1960s. One thing is clear: without immigration, the population figures in the Federal Republic would already have been declining by 1972. Had there been no immigration in the past 30 years, only 54.7 million people would now be living in the former West German states—fewer than in 1960. Germany would not only be economically poorer but culturally [poorer] as well.

The updated result of a previously published retroactive projection shows that, regardless of how the immigration history in the Federal Republic of Germany is configured, the gap (which until 1999 had grown to 12.2 million people) between both population curves with and without migration reveals the deep divide between the population's actual experiences and political declarations to the effect that Germany is not an official immigration country.

The Federal Republic is undoubtedly experienced in immigration. But it must abandon the old guest-worker concept based on the principle of rotation and clearly and decisively adopt the concept of the "new citizen" with concrete opportunities for permanent residency. This change in orientation is urgently needed, for the migration numbers of the past will eventually overstrain every institutionalized integration plan promoting linguistic, academic, educational, and technical development. If Germany wants to elevate integration to an actual agenda, and at this point there really is no alternative, the turnstile at the borders must be replaced by transparently monitored entrance doors. Here one can learn from classic immigration countries. Comparing the migration totals in Germany to those of the United States or Canada clearly demonstrates this necessity. In the 1970s and 1980s, for every 80 people leaving Germany, there were only 100 immigrants arriving. In this sense, Germany was a pit stop on the way to other countries. The circumstances marginally improved in the 1990s. The situation in the United States was different: for every 100 immigrants entering the country annually, only between 22 and 26 left. These ratios apply to Canada as well.

The application of ratios to the migration totals in Germany is possible with the statistical measure of so-called migration efficiency, which correlates the migration balance with the migration volumes. For Germany in the 1990s, this approach would have meant that in order to reach an actual migration balance totaling 1.9 million people, only 2.4 million immigrants would have been necessary, not 7.3 million. This former figure is based on the situation of immigration countries that provide concrete opportunities for permanent residency. Such would also be a model for Germany.

For when one inserts an annual long-term migration balance of 300,000 people into the computation scenarios for Germany, a net increase of 385,000 migrants results based on the North American migration efficiency, as opposed to 1.2 million according to previous trends in Germany. Every integration plan would necessarily fail in the latter case, due to high costs as well as social-acceptance problems.

The Canadian experience after the introduction of an immigration law in the late 1970s proves that migration movements are alterable in this sense. The ratio of emigrants to immigrants has also noticeably improved, from 56 out of 100 to 22 out of 100.

Potential Effects of Immigration and a High Birthrate

If future computations are meant to be more than just numbers, then an increase in the resident population is necessary; the following four insights support this claim:

- In a society with a steadily declining and subsequently aging population, the structure of relations changes. This pattern affects the solidarity between young and old as well as social-support systems.
- The assimilating society accentuates the rules of social coexistence and expects them to be externally transparent. This action provides clarity for immigrants.
- The assimilating society is aware that immigration can trigger anxieties within its native population.
- Continuous immigration places greater demands on the capacity of the individual to allow for difference. This situation requires tolerance.

Consequent to these insights, the prediction focuses on institutionalized integration, primarily in the educational system. Migrants will eventually become new citizens.

Looking toward the job market, the computation is based on the elements of active guidance in consideration of the labor market. Immigration of exclusively unqualified workers remains a risky strategy for Germany. Underlying this claim is the presupposition that global controls—in tandem with an immigration policy commensurate with middle-term job-market demands and a long-term perspective—will lead to a successful immigration program. Starting from the higher migration efficiencies, an annual increase of 192,000 people until 2010 yields the previously mentioned totals, an increase of 256,000 until 2020, and after that, 385,000 people per year, based on the expected labor shortage. [. . .] In combination with an increasing employment capacity, the following results can be deduced from the aforementioned phases:

- In phase 1, the labor pool will rise to 41.6 million people until 2010 as a result of migration and increasing employment capacity. This number is 1 million more than in the year 2000. Without migration, the level of this employment variant would have been 40.4 million in 2010. This estimate makes clear that the labor pool is less likely to relieve the job market in the coming decade. Under these conditions, a job-market improvement would have to come from the demand side via a continuously dynamic employment trend.
- After 2010, the decline of the labor pool can no longer be intercepted by means of migration; therefore, the job-market result will benefit in phase 2. In these 20 years, migration will slow the process of national negative growth by 4.8 million people. This development will provide a baseline of 35.8 million workers in 2030—only 5.3 million fewer than in 2010.
- In phase 3, the labor pool will shrink to 32.5 million people despite migration. If a boost in the birthrate were to prevail, stabilization at 35.4 million workers would be possible in phase 3.

This perspective would mean a decisive advantage for Germany. Compared with the status quo, the path to the knowledge society would be eased by a young labor force, as the comparison of current age structures with those of the year 2050 demonstrate. Migration and an increase in the birthrate considerably strengthen the secondary growth and midlevel positions for the available personnel resources. Increasing labor participation, in contrast, intensifies the aging trend.

Conclusion

The double dimension of this demographic change—a noticeable decline and progressive aging of the labor force—jeopardizes conditions in Germany. Migration directly counteracts both of these unpreventable tendencies. The potential effects of a rise in the birthrate will bear out only in time. [. . .] The notion that migrants should continue to come to Germany may appear misguided in light of increasing social burdens. In the long term, Germany must address this problem conceptually. Otherwise, new disappointment could soon set in—similar to the one that followed Adenauer's attempt to console the forward-thinking social-policy makers in the late 1950s: "People always have children."

19

MARC BROST

CARTE BLANCHE IN GREEN

First published as "Freikarte in Grün" in *Die Zeit* (March 30, 2002). Translated by David Gramling.

The Green Card is a success. It attracts labor power that cannot be found among the domestic unemployed.

It is 467 kilometers from Bratislava to Munich—or 51,000 euros. This amount is how much Ondrej Kelle earns as a programmer in the Bavarian capital; the 31-year-old Slovakian came to Germany for the job in August 2000. Ondrej came with a Green Card, just as 2,138 other foreign immigrants in Munich have done. He was the first.

For about two years previously, his employer had been looking for an IT specialist who was as proficient with Microsoft Windows programming as with the Internet and who could develop interfaces between the two worlds for the firm-specific editing system. "About 50 or 100 people worldwide can do what he does," says Armin Hopp, a director of digital publishing and Ondrej's boss. They found him over the Internet, where a colleague from Munich had become acquainted with the Slovakian. Just at that moment, the federal government closed the deal on the new Green Card, the special work and residence permit for computer specialists from outside the EU. Then everything went quite fast. "Within 24 hours, I had my visa," says Ondrej Kelle. "I was able to begin working the next day." His employer produces software for people who want to learn foreign languages at home, and since Kelle has been there, the programmers have been improving their language skills as well. English is spoken at work.

German Job Seekers in the Lurch

More than 11,000 foreign immigrants have moved to Germany with a Green Card since August 2000—more than expected. Most come from Eastern Europe. Lately, however, few Green Cards are being distributed. The demand for foreign specialists among employers has decidedly "cooled off," says Jürgen Rohrmeier, a member of the administration at the personnel consulting firm Kienbaum Executive Consultants. The crisis of the New Economy has fully gripped the labor market: there are only a few new jobs; in fact, positions are now being cut. High-tech firms that were looking hopefully into the future only a year ago have long since pulled in the reins. Even immigrants with Green Cards have not been shielded from the crisis. In Munich, for example, every tenth foreign computer specialist has changed jobs. Now newspapers are reporting that more and more Green Card holders are unemployed.

This kind of reporting galvanizes those who are critical of immigration for foreign IT experts. Why, they ask, do we continue to recruit immigrants if they are just going to be unemployed? And why don't we just take domestic workers who are looking for jobs anyway?

Erich Blume hears such questions often. When he gives answers, he quickly talks himself into a rage. "There is no such thing as high unemployment among Green Card holders," says the chief of the Labor Bureau in disgust. "Whoever makes these claims is intentionally making false claims." Throughout the country, about 1 percent of the immigrant IT specialists are out of work. "After two to four weeks, most have found a new position," says Blume. If anyone is being hired during the crises, it is the highly trained specialists who are getting a free job—Green Card computer specialists, for example. They are always ready to start anew in another part of the republic; they are working far away from home no matter what.

Computer specialists are modern nomads: they offer their knowledge where they are needed, and they move on when there is a better job somewhere else—or a better-paid one. "I came because of the job, not because of Germany," says Ondrej Kelle. That statement sounds egotistical, but others also profit from this fact nonetheless. Across the country, every Green Card holder has created 2.5 new jobs at his workplace, says Labor Bureau Chief Blume, because employers can then expand.

The question remains, why could this strategy not work with domestic labor? Some 20,000 German computer experts are still looking for a job, says the Federal Union of Employer's Associations. Yet these experts are not the ones who are currently needed. Behind the concept "IT specialist," as it is understood in the Labor Bureau and as it is used in official statistics, any number of factors linked to the market in the broadest sense are obscured. There are experts for complex calculation devices and cellular-telephone programmers, specialists for machines, and specialists for the software. Only the last are needed, however. And there is also the age of the unemployed to be considered. Seventy percent of computer experts in the proper sense who were seeking a job in Munich in March 2000 were older than 55. The numbers are similar throughout the country.

The problem for the older people is not their age but the qualifications that relate to it. The unemployed over 55 are often programmers of the older type: "highly qualified people who do not, however, have the qualifications that employers currently are seeking," says Blume. The software market is, after all, growing at a raging pace.

Many More Hurdles for Foreigners

[. . .] Ondrej Kelle has been a professional programmer for 10 years now and threw away his university study to do so. The Slovakian knows that there is not much time for him to earn a lot of money. Soon his abilities will be obsolete as well.

"Of course, here and there, a Green Card holder returns frustrated to his homeland," says consultant Rohrmeier. The language barriers might have been too great; the conceptions among employers and computer experts were too different. Of every 10 immigrant specialists, 6 work in businesses with fewer than 100 workers.

"The Green Card is good but not good enough," says Jürgen Rohrmeier. Because spouses of immigrants must wait a year before they are allowed to work, integration is difficult for them. Because the various bureaucracies often do not work well together, it takes "days and weeks before the necessary documents are correct," says Rohrmeier, which was not the case with Kelle and the Munich Labor Bureau. And therein lies the arbitrary issue in the eyes of many employers: because Kelle has no university diploma, he must earn at least 51,000 euros, according to the Green Card statute. If he had a diploma, the employer could pay him less. The federal government wants to avoid such "dumping salaries" and the recruitment of underqualified immigrants. But if Kelle had had more university knowledge and less practical programming experience, digital publishing would never have been attractive to the Slovakian. "The regulations make the workers whom we urgently need more expensive," says Director Hopp. "That is a joke."

20

FOTINI MAVROMATI

ODYSSEY INTO THE PROMISED LAND

First published as "Odyssee ins gelobte Land" in *Freitag* (March 4, 2005). Translated by David Gramling.

In a factory in Tangier, women are shelling East Friesian prawns that will then be packed into a cattle trailer and driven back to Europe—for extremely low wages. Many of the young men hanging around the cafés and plazas of the old city are planning their departure to Europe. The black Africans among them already have a long journey behind them. In buses, hitchhiking, and on foot, they crossed the Sahara, fighting their way through to Tangier, the marketplace of refugees. Here, bands of smugglers, called "brokers," await them, offering passage from Gibraltar to Spain over the strait. This heavily trafficked sea route is about 14 kilometers at its most narrow spot; it divides the first from the third world.

The risky crossing in a dinghy can cost up to $1,500 (U.S.). Those who can afford it also pay 250 dollars for a life vest. Those who choose to undertake the illegal journey to Europe must have succeeded in an already grim and prospectless struggle—with the goal of securing a piece of the middle-class cake. Europe is tempting. Those who want into the promised land must try to enter without a visa or a work permit. These unwelcome foreigners must first set foot in a Schengen country like Italy. Then the rich Central European countries are within attainable reach. The Schengen agreement guarantees that the citizens of its member states may cross its internal borders without passport checks. And Schengen Europe reaches from Helsinki down to the Algarve. Still, this Europe of free mobility has armed itself with highly fortified borders and rigid laws against unauthorized entry. Patrol boats and infrared monitors are prepared to spot illicit border crossers, and biometrical data is collected from all new citizens outside the EU, in accordance with the new Italian immigration law. No revenue is spared for developing an ever more perfect border control or a new technical monitoring device.

In the meantime, the negative headlines about rusted-out boats with more than 800 refugees on board that land somewhere on the Mediterranean have receded from view. This trend has to do partially with the winter weather. Illegal migration has come back into the debate because of the new dispute about visas. As has always been the case, most immigrants come by land routes. A great portion of "illegals" even come over the borders with legal papers and stay long beyond their prescribed residence allowance.

The visa debate overshadows the more important question: whether we need immigration. Demographers, businesses, and the Red-Green federal government are answering this question with a tentative yes, in view of the declining birthrate in Germany. The CDU, however, sees the integration of the foreigners living here as the priority and laments the looming specter of parallel societies and shadow economies in which criminals and terrorists can thrive. The German Immigration Act does not address those who are already living here illegally. Experts calculate that there are approximately a million people living in Germany without residence permits. They are not welcome but are necessary. They work without social security and health insurance for rock-bottom wages on construction sites, in the restaurant industry, or in the domestic sphere.

In the current debates about travel visas, the prejudicial notion is being advanced that illegal immigrants would take away jobs from federal citizens. A study by the Research Center of Berlin [Wissenschaftszentrum Berlin], however, considers this generalizing assumption of a "danger to domestic wages and employment arising through illegal migration." The European need for (often seasonal) labor power in the minimum-wage sphere is extensive, and EU states count on illegals to deliver on the economic market. Whoever buys Spanish tomatoes at a decent price is profiting from the shadow economy.

Yet illegal laborers are beyond public control. No state can tolerate this situation in the long run. In countries like Spain, Greece, and Italy, there are consequently ever-new offers for legalization. A pan-European immigration law with a humane set of regulations is nowhere in sight. When the weather warms up again soon, many people will once again undertake the life-threatening Mediterranean crossing.

2

OUR SOCIALIST FRIENDS
FOREIGNERS IN EAST GERMANY

SOLIDARITY AND PROGRESS, 1980. East German general secretary Erich Honecker and Mozambican president Samora Machel sign a labor recruitment treaty beneath the watchful eyes of Lenin, who wrote in 1913: "Dire poverty alone compels people to abandon their native land, and the capitalists exploit immigrant workers in the most shameless manner. But only reactionaries can close their eyes to the *progressive* significance of this modern migration of nations."

T HE DIVISION OF GERMANY into two states in 1949 was a major catalyst for the guest-worker programs of the 1950s, both in the Federal Republic of Germany and the German Democratic Republic. In West Germany during the "Economic Miracle" years, the labor shortage was most acute in the regions bordering on the East, where militarization and political uncertainty had scattered thousands of families into the interior of the Allied zones. Meanwhile, East Germany was losing millions of its citizens to the West, and it continued to suffer crippling labor droughts even 10 years after the Berlin Wall was erected in 1961. This second chapter tracks the recruitment and representation of foreigners in the German Democratic Republic, from the Korean War to the postreunification period of the 1990s. The documents included here illustrate the mutual influence that the two estranged German states exerted on each other's immigration policies and intercultural imagination over four decades.

The GDR's first contract workers arrived from Poland in 1963. Each month, East Germany had been losing between 10,000 and 20,000 of its most able-bodied residents to the West's open-door policy, until the "antifascist border wall" was constructed on August 13, 1961. Sluggish birthrates and the long-term effects of mass exodus over the zone borders left East Germany with a dearth of unskilled workers. In 1967, Hungary agreed to send 13,000 workers, and additional contingents followed from Algeria (1974), Cuba (1975 and 1978), and Mozambique (1980). Once these laborers had settled in collective housing in the GDR, their primary contact with the domestic population occurred through conversations with their overseers, also known as "cultural liaisons," and with the few Germans who would speak with them in the workplace.

The immigration policies of the Socialist Unity Party (SED), East Germany's sole political party from 1946 to 1989, is important to European migration history for two reasons. First, the SED's platform on internationalist solidarity sought to distinguish the East's "socialist friends" from capitalist West Germany's guest workers. Since the GDR's first ceremonial embrace of North Korean orphan children in 1954, the party had framed its immigration policy in terms of a visionary struggle against the "American aggressor" and its West German accomplices. Even GDR citizens critical of their government's policies perceived the Turkish or Greek laborer in West Germany as a spectral icon of capitalist exploitation. The SED's widely heralded magnanimity toward war refugees served as a potent—though unverifiable—symbol of East Germany's commitment to human rights and the Geneva Convention. Quite a few Western journalists in the 1970s who were critical of West Germany's treatment of its foreign recruits decried the ostensible disparity between nationalist expropriation in the West and internationalist cooperation in the East. See, for example, the first West German piece in this chapter, "In the GDR, They're Called Friends," from 1973.

The first prominent image of the guest worker in the West was that of a midtwenties, single, able-bodied man or woman. Only in the 1970s would the West German public face the uncertain fate of the "guest-worker child" in the host country. In contrast, the first public images of non-Soviet foreigners in the East were of war-ravaged children and adolescents. The press hailed the residence halls that housed refugees, children, and contract workers—at a functional distance from any GDR citizens—as state-of-the-art "colonies" with all the amenities necessary for a thriving collective. Even the most skeptical East German reader was likely to picture the foreign guests as a privileged delegation rather than as an isolated and malleable labor force.

East Germany's first publicized reports on its foreigner residents exalted the newly arrived guests for their patriotic bond to their homeland, their courageous gesture of faith in the new socialist German state, and their confidence in the GDR's unique capacity to provide less-developed socialist societies with expert medical care, technical training, and financial subsidy. By documenting the encounters between East Germans and their North Korean, North Vietnamese, Mozambican, and Cuban visitors, the GDR press could showcase its role as an industrial leader and global "outpost of peace" for the future of socialism. Most of these early reports were written and distributed by the General German News Service (ADN), a state bureau founded in 1946, which distributed around 90,000 stories annually to local and regional newspapers throughout the German Democratic Republic.

In the early 1970s, the GDR press began to report on the thousands of Vietnamese "apprentices" who were granted three-year rotations in East German technical-training institutes. The laborers, though seldom visible in public life, were depicted in print as ambassadors. Some reports even indicated that newly arrived workers could sing the GDR anthem in German, as a gesture of spontaneous praise for their hosts. Native GDR residents were encouraged to take an active role in the international solidarity movement. Free German Federation of Trade Unions members paid a compulsory donation each month to the GDR Solidarity Fund, which then financed development projects around the socialist world. This prescribed national devotion to solidarity enabled the SED to issue regular disavowals of racism and xenophobia in its social policies, and East German dictionaries defined ethnic discrimination as an epiphenomenon of the capitalist distribution of labor. Yet hostility toward Poles and Hungarians grew throughout the 1970s, after some Warsaw Pact countries began to relax their rules for tourist transit. Suddenly, East Germans in cities and border regions found themselves in the constant company of Polish consumers, who bought high-profile East German products and took these purchases back to Poland.

In 1980s West Germany, many public intellectuals like Hans Schueler faulted the East German government for increasing hostility toward asylum seekers and other migrants in the West. Schueler, in his 1986 piece "Panic Is the Wrong Answer," charged the GDR airline Interflug with running a trafficking operation that flew political refugees from Iran, Nigeria, Libya, and other states to East Berlin for a fee and then released them into the West by way of Berlin's Schönefeld sluice. The daily spectacle of these GDR-recruited refugees' arrival in West Berlin cast widespread doubt on the West German constitution's magnanimous asylum provisions. East Germany's traffic in foreigners thus helped assure the passage of the restrictive 1993 amendment to West Germany's article 16, which had previously guaranteed asylum to all politically persecuted persons since 1949.

Since the collapse of the GDR state in 1990, the SED's 40 years of immigration policy have continued to cast a long shadow on the postunification period. Sixty thousand Vietnamese, 52,000 Polish, 15,000 Mozambican, and 8,000 Cuban "socialist friends" were living in the GDR at Reunification. After 1990, they faced deportation, premature discontinuation of their residence permits, bureaucratic chaos, and more openly sanctioned and violent xenophobia than they had seen in the GDR. By 1989, approximately 100,000 non-Soviet contract workers were living in the GDR: Angolans, Mozambicans, Cubans, North Vietnamese, and Chinese. Many were on their second or third "tours" of employment, had established themselves in the GDR, and had no plans to return voluntarily to their countries of origin.

By 1992, however, four-fifths of these workers had left Germany because of severe unemployment, discrimination in the workplace, and xenophobic violence. The East's remaining Vietnamese were often eager to take low-paying or illegal jobs as bricklayers, seamstresses, factory workers, and cigarette vendors. Nonetheless, with national unemployment at a 60-year high, foreigners were promptly vilified for taking jobs away from both eastern locals and western settlers. By 1993, many native eastern Germans realized that reunification would not bring them the burgeoning economic landscape they expected, and they began to view foreigners as provocateurs from renegade socialist states.

The last three articles in this chapter—Robert von Lucius's 1994 "Nostalgia Despite Unfulfilled Promises," Mark Siemons's 1995 "Smuggling Discerned—Fingers Burned," and Dennis Kuck's 2001 "Those Foreign Socialist Brothers"—describe the hurdles and dangers that foreign workers faced in the East after 1989.

1

WARM WELCOME FOR 200 KOREAN CHILDREN

First published as "Herzliches Willkommen für 200 koreanische Kinder" by the *Allgemeiner Deutscher Nachrichtendienst* (March 2, 1955). Translated by David Gramling.

This Sunday, in the small community of Moritzburg, 200 Korean children were welcomed into their new home at the Käthe Kollwitz Residence Hall, just outside the city of Dresden on the Elbe River, after making a three-week journey through the People's Republic of China and the Soviet Union. The guests made their way into the residence through a long column of local youth holding torches. They were surrounded on all sides by the sounds and sights of a heartfelt welcome. By the bright light of a peace fire and hundreds of torches, the population of Moritzburg made a commitment to support the Korean people now more than ever in their heroic fight for freedom and independence, and to not relent in the struggle against American imperialism.

A delegation of boys and girls from the Greek colony in Dresden-Radebeul, youth who have been living and learning in the German Democratic Republic for two years now, offered the Korean pioneers a sincere welcome. The Korean children conquered the hearts of the Moritzburg inhabitants when, at the end of the ceremony, they sang the first stanza of the national hymn of the German Democratic Republic in German.

Then, with happy eyes, the children, now thousands of kilometers from their homeland, which has been laid to waste by American interference, moved into the Käthe Kollwitz Residence. Its complex of twelve buildings right next to the well-known Moritzburg surge tank forms a living colony in its own right. The four residence buildings for the Korean children bear the names of Ernst Thälmann, Georgi Dimitroff, Rosa Luxemburg, and Karl Liebknecht. The complex also boasts a school building with eight classrooms, including music rooms, pedagogical materials, and teachers' rooms, as well as a library and a gymnasium. An infirmary, conference rooms, and showers have been installed in the administration building.

Kurt Geister will look after the nutritional well-being of the guests, whose ages range from 12 to 16 years. Geister has been a sailor for fifteen years and has visited Korea. Successful taste tests among Korean students who are studying at the University of Leipzig have proven that he understands his craft and knows the "secrets" to preparing Korea's traditional rice dishes. [. . .]

2

VIETNAMESE CHILDREN ACCEPTED INTO THE GDR

First published as "Vietnamesische Kinder in der DDR eingetroffen" by the *Allgemeiner Deutscher Nachrichtendienst* (September 22, 1955). Translated by David Gramling.

FRANKFURT (ODER). On Thursday, the minister of people's education for the GDR, Fritz Lange, greeted 149 Vietnamese girls and boys aged 9 to 14, who will attend school in Moritzburg near Dresden and learn a trade. Cries and cheers of friendship accompanied the arrival of the special German Imperial Railway train that had picked up the Vietnamese children in Brest. Since August 25, the children have been on a long journey through Vietnam, the People's Republic of China, the Soviet Union, and People's Poland. At the festively decorated train platform, the state flags of Vietnam and the GDR encountered one another, as did banners in German and Vietnamese and pictures of Ho Chi Minh, Woroschilov, and Wilhelm Piecks.

With loud jubilation, Frankfurt's Thälmann Pioneers [youth group] received the little black-haired girls and boys in their blue dresses and suits. Waving gaily, the visitors disembarked the train and ran toward their German friends. The pioneers offered them dolls and bouquets of flowers as a sign of solidarity between peoples. Clutching the small gifts, the Vietnamese boys and girls sang a song from their homeland in honor of their German friends.

Then the Minister for People's Education of the GDR, Fritz Lange, spoke and greeted his little guests in the warmest manner possible. "The long journey has shown you how large the world's Outpost of Peace is. As you enter the German Democratic Republic, you will find many friends of your people. We know that many of you have lost fathers and mothers. We promise to care for you like mothers and fathers." He expressed certainty that the Vietnamese children will learn just as successfully as the young Greeks and Koreans, who have been in the GDR for a long time already.

The leader of the Vietnamese Youth Pioneers offered friendly greetings on behalf of his fatherland to the president of the GDR, Wilhelm Pieck. "During the construction of our homeland, we have received much support from the German people. Our children will learn here and then after a few years return to Vietnam. This will be a great help to us."

3

VIETNAM'S CHILDREN GAVE THANKS FOR THE PRESENTS FROM THEIR GERMAN FRIENDS

First published as "Vietnams Kinder dankten für Geschenke ihrer deutschen Freunde" by the *Allgemeiner Deutscher Nachrichtendienst* (January 24, 1958). Translated by David Gramling.

A delegation from children's Radio GDR has returned from Hanoi.
BERLIN. The staff of Radio GDR brought back warm greetings from tens of thousands of children from the Democratic Republic of Vietnam to the boys and girls of the German Democratic Republic. The Children's Radio staff returned from Vietnam in a special German Lufthansa airplane to Berlin's Schönefeld Airport. [. . .] In the presence of the Vietnamese consuls and businesspeople in the GDR, Nguyen Song Tung told the radio staff about the warm and friendly reception they received in Vietnam. Some 1,500 children had gathered to greet them at Hanoi's airfield. The radio staffers met with Vietnamese children in all parts of the country and learned that the boys and girls of this faraway country are highly interested in and curious about the lives of the GDR's youth. The high point of their visit was a reception with President Ho Chi Minh.

4

SEVENTEEN WOUNDED CUBANS RECEIVED
FOR REHABILITATION IN THE GDR

First published as "17 kubanische Verwundete zur Genesung in der DDR eingetroffen" by the *Allgemeiner Deutscher Nachrichtendienst* (March 15, 1963). Translated by David Gramling.

BERLIN. Seventeen young Cubans who took part in the battle at Playa Giron were received at the GDR's tarmacs on Thursday for a period of rehabilitation and rest. After a short stay in the airport hotel in Berlin-Schnabel, eleven made the journey to the Kirchmoeser Hospital on Friday, while the other six will be treated at the Berlin Charité hospital. The group is here at the invitation of the Committee for Solidarity with the Cuban People of the GDR's National Front Council. This group is already the third group to enter the GDR at the invitation of the Committee for Rehabilitation. The eleven patients in Kirchmoeser have lost arms and legs in battle and will learn, under expert tutelage, how they can assist in the reconstruction of their socialist homeland, equipped with prosthetics and the best technologies available. The six Cubans at the Charité Hospital will be cured of the wounds they received during heavy assaults.

All members of the group are full of confidence, despite the serious wounds they sustained as young people, and want to spend their rehabilitation time learning as much as possible. With the excited corroboration of his comrades, Captain Victor M. Sotomayor said, "We are so happy and grateful to be in the GDR. We will regain our health here in this socialist brother country. In the GDR, socialist development is already so advanced. We are only at the beginning, and there is so much for us to learn." Captain Juan Rodriguez Infante added, "The most important thing, the thing that we are all fighting for, is peace. Peace for the GDR, peace for Cuba, peace for the whole world." One of the first questions the Cuban friends asked after their arrival was: what are the best opportunities for learning German? All seventeen are abroad for the first time in their lives; they were most impressed by the snow covering the Berlin airfield upon their arrival.

5

LY THUONG KIET

REPORT ON THE SOLIDARITY MOVEMENT IN THE GERMAN DEMOCRATIC REPUBLIC IN SUPPORT OF THE STRUGGLE OF THE VIETNAMESE PEOPLE

First published as "Bericht über die Solidaritätsbewegung in der Deutschen Demokratischen Republik zur Unterstüzung des kämpfenden vietnamesischen Volkes" by the Vietnam Committee for the Solidarity of Afro-Asian Peoples (April 1966). Translated by David Gramling.

Every adult citizen of the German Democratic Republic is personally committed to active solidarity with Vietnam. The members of the socialist Pioneer Association "Ernst Thälmann"—comprised of children from 6 to 14 years old—and other boys and girls in elementary and secondary schools have done innumerable good deeds in the solidarity movement with Vietnam.

Ten thousand protest resolutions against the dirty American war and against the West German government's participation in the United States' crimes in Vietnam, as well as solidarity declarations in support of the righteous struggle of the Vietnamese people, carry the signatures of some 8 million citizens. Workers' collectives, youth brigades, research associations, students and professors, residence communes, and members of all classes have sent protest letters to U.S. President Johnson. Every day, print media, radio, and television bring forth new expressions and opinions from the population as well as examples of active solidarity.

In thousands of assemblies, demonstrations, matinees, and speak-outs large and small, the entire population of the GDR has expressed its steadfast and true solidarity with Vietnam's struggles. [. . .]

Factory employees, workers in agricultural production cooperatives, and artisans in various labor sectors have committed to high production levels and excellent quality in order to create more economic and political opportunities for the German Democratic Republic by way of an exemplary fulfillment of the people's economic plan, with the goal of strengthening their solidarity with Vietnam and galvanizing its own position in the anti-imperialist struggle. [. . .]

The backbone of the solidarity movement in the GDR is the working class. This fact becomes clear when one considers that every month, 80 percent of all union members pay a special solidarity fee along with their membership contributions in an expression of loyalty to proletarian internationalism and to the principles of anti-imperialistic peoples' solidarity. Since the founding of the Vietnam Committee and the beginning of its active propaganda efforts for solidarity with Vietnam, these contributions have increased steadily. In recent months, many millions of marks from the unions have gone into increasing material assistance for the struggling country.

6

PETER BETHGE

WHAT STATUS DO FOREIGN WORKERS HAVE HERE?

First published as "Welchen Stand haben ausländische Arbeiter bei uns?" in *Junge Welt* (September 28, 1972). Reprinted in *Anderssein gab es nicht: Ausländer und Minderheiten in der DDR*, Marianne Krüger-Portratz, ed. (Münster: Waxmann, 1991), 206. Translated by Tes Howell.

Question: "In order to successfully realize our people's economic goals, we are currently relying on young workers from the People's Republic of Poland. Is their role comparable to the guest workers in Western European countries?" asks Dieter Uhlig from Eisenhüttenstadt.

Answer: There are certain concepts, dear Dieter, that are inextricably linked to capitalism. Among them are exploitation, profit, and, yes, the guest worker. This deceptive concept denotes those countless Moroccans, Italians, Greeks, and Turks who resort to working and living in the Western European industrial strongholds because there is no work for them in their homelands.

They play an outsider's role in capitalist society. They are forced to sell their labor power wherever the monopolies hope to gain the highest profit margins. The guest workers in Western European countries have little governmental or trade-union protection. They are forced to sell their labor power on the cheap, and their earnings lie far below those of other workers. They are thus all the more dependent. If they resist the directives of their capitalist employers, they are often fired without notice and deported to their homelands. Their positions can be filled immediately by other "guest workers."

In addition to the exploitation of their labor power, foreigners in many places face deeply entrenched mistrust, nationalism, and chauvinism. Italians, for example, must endure daily insults such as "dago" or "macaroni muncher." They are not served in many restaurants and often must use separate bathrooms. Even in churches, the biblical phrase "all are equal under God" has no meaning. Separate refrains are reserved for foreigners. The monopoly press discriminates against them. They are the slaves of the twentieth century.

Meanwhile, when I think about the role of our Polish and Hungarian friends, I am reminded of a conversation I had with a Polish brigade leader in a Frankfurt (Oder) semiconductor factory. She characterized the work of her collective as "socialist teamwork for a common goal." Indeed, our friends help us carry out our economic tasks, while simultaneously increasing the overall strength of socialism. Many of them enjoy careers as highly qualified skilled laborers in our factories. In every respect, they are true partners from a socialist neighboring country—for example, Poland, where the population has grown more quickly than industry in the past few decades.

Our Polish and Hungarian friends are respected citizens within our socialist society. More than a few of them proudly display the activist badge. Brigades of our Polish friends are distinguished with the honorary title "Collective for Socialist Labor."

At the same time, many have used their temporary work here as technical preparation for an eventual return to their homeland, where they will work in factories that specialists from Poland and the GDR have established for common production and common use. [. . .]

7

APPRENTICE TRAINING WORKSHOPS FOR THE DEMOCRATIC REPUBLIC OF VIETNAM: MORE VIETNAMESE INTERNS COME TO THE GDR

First published as "Lehrlingsausbildungsstätte für die DRV—weitere vietnamesische Praktikanten in der DDR" by the *Allgemeiner Deutscher Nachrichtendienst* (February 28, 1973). Translated by David Gramling.

An apprentice workshop for skilled metalworkers, financed through the GDR population's solidarity donations, will begin instruction near the Vietnamese capital this year. This project was a stipulation of the 1973 GDR-Vietnam agreement, and was supported by 4 million marks from the Vietnam Committee. It is the first apprenticeship workshop of its kind to train skilled workers for the construction of their socialist brother country. Soon 540 students will be enrolled in three-year cycles to learn the ropes as locksmiths, lathe operators, molding cutters, blacksmiths, toolmakers, mechanics, and foundry workers. If there is enough room on the premises for more students, the number of apprenticeships will be increased.

Currently, Vietnamese laborers are preparing for this new task. Many of them have been trained in the GDR as engineering pedagogues. Eight GDR specialists, master teachers, engineering pedagogues, and qualified engineers will assist and advise their Vietnamese colleagues on-site regarding the administration, planning, and implementation of the training course.

Training assistance for the brother people will also continue in the factories of the republic. In the past year, 2,700 Vietnamese interns in more than 60 GDR factories became technicians, specialized engineers, and skilled workers in a variety of fields. [. . .]

8

MARLIES MENGE

IN THE GDR, THEY'RE CALLED FRIENDS

First published as "In der DDR heissen sie Freunde" in *Die Zeit* (August 18, 1973). Translated by David Gramling.

The guest-worker problem is not only an issue for the Federal Republic but for other countries as well

They are named Marika, Ilona, and Mariena, and they are from Györ, Szombathely, and Budapest. They are 3 of the 140 Hungarian women and 40 Hungarian men who, for the past year or so, have been assembling transistors in the GDR city of Neuhaus at the collectively owned metal factory. Guest workers in the "Economic Miracle country" of the GDR. One must, however, not label them that way. According to East German newspapers, they are "foreign friends."

Last year, in the GDR magazine *Wirtschaft*, Jozsef Rozsa, a high-ranking administrator of the Labor Ministry of the People's Republic of Hungary, asked, "What is the fundamental difference between the guest-worker system in capitalist countries and organized labor-power cooperation in socialist countries?" He got a quick and ready answer: "The difference is essentially that in capitalism the underdevelopment of various countries necessitates labor migration. In socialist countries, there is no such pressure. These countries—Hungary, for example—can guarantee employment for all citizens of working age. Socialist governments seek out opportunities for international cooperation so that certain workers may acquire further training in their field and supplementary experience in dealing with modern technology. Furthermore, coming to a new country lets workers learn a new language and learn about life in another socialist partner country."

The actual number of foreign workers in the GDR is unknown. Hungary and the GDR signed an agreement in 1967 in which the Hungarian government declared its willingness to send 13,000 workers to the GDR—the first large contingent of foreign assistance. In an interview with the *New York Times* at the end of last year, Erich Honecker said that 13,000 Hungarians and 12,000 Poles are working in the GDR. Some experts believe that there are far more. Smaller groups have come from Czechoslovakia, Bulgaria, and Romania. These people are not merely supposed to acquire greater knowledge of their profession, the German language, the country, and its people; they are expected to put their labor power at the disposal of the GDR. The population of the GDR is, after all, aging faster than its birthrate is growing. Furthermore, the country is not growing as quickly as an aspiring industrial nation ought to. Another problem is that the GDR's workers are very competent and are constantly improving their qualifications; thus, few are willing to perform unskilled labor. It is thus no coincidence that many of the working guests are employed in service industries as cooks and waiters, maids and sales clerks. Most, however, work in factories and obtain continuous training there.

Of course, these guest workers are not coming to their socialist brother country only for professional development and the beautiful German language. When GDR television recently asked young Hungarian workers what their motivation was for working in the GDR, many mentioned the opportunity to learn German; yet the German money they are earning seemed to be the greater priority. Seventy-five percent of them earn a gross monthly salary of 500 marks, and 23.7 percent of the Hungarians are earning more than 700 marks. One young Hungarian proudly announced, "With my first words of German and my second pay raise, I bought a motorcycle."

Foreigners working in the GDR are between 18 and 25 years old, and their contracts last two to three years. They enjoy parity with their German counterparts in salary and social benefits. To the extent that they can take part in professional development, they can learn a new career in the GDR. Skilled specialists can supplement their knowledge. They may work in the Socialist Brigades (Work Competition Groups) and earn the title of a Young Activist. [. . .]

Poles on the Prowl for Girls

When Poland's Party Chief Gierek visited Honecker in June, he also met with Polish workers from East Berlin factories. His expectations were confirmed: "We feel at home here. The work makes us happy, and we get along well with our colleagues from the GDR." The declaration that he and Honecker wrote together stated, "We attach particular meaning to the contracts between the youth of both countries, who embody the future of socialism in the German Democratic Republic and the People's Republic of Poland. They will devote great attention to the education of youth in the spirit of proletarian internationalism and the brotherly relations of the socialist community."

In private, GDR citizens often complain about their Polish friends. The mean-spirited call them "Polacks:" "they're always showing up in big groups, taking away our girls, and then beating us up!" After dance parties, street fights often break out between Germans and Poles. "And then our police prefer to help the Poles, not us," reports one young East German man bitterly.

If GDR journalists ever admit to tensions between Poles and Germans, they blame them on the Germans; they, and only they, have made a vow to socialist brotherhood. For example, a reporter from the student magazine *Forum* drove to the VEB Factory Black Pump, where some 500 Poles work. He reported on collective sports events, archery tournaments, youth dance parties, and activity days, but these common engagements have their limits. "Although the friends spend most of their free time together, none of the Poles were allowed to ride the motorcycles that belong to the Society for Sport and

Technology. They might drink their beer together, but at home there is still a German and a Polish entrance."

Since January 1 of last year, the animosity between Germans and Poles has intensified. On that day, visa-free transit between the GDR and its neighboring socialist states was introduced. Polish workers in the GDR suddenly had to answer for something that was entirely out of their hands: In 1972 alone, 12 million of their countrymen visited the GDR and bought out the department stores. East Berliners read in the *Berliner Zeitung* that the department-store manager of the Polish border city Zary complained "Every month, GDR tourists alone buy 50 carpets, not to mention the many parkas and leather jackets." This complaint must have sounded to them like derisive mockery, just as when another Pole in the *Berliner Zeitung* complained that a GDR tourist snatched up the last batch of asparagus and the last jar of chanterelles from under his nose. Polish women have been coming by the busload to the Centrum Department Store at East Berlin's Alexanderplatz to buy anything they can get their hands on, and it was reported that the Polish women who did not get what they were looking for yelled "Nazi pigs" at the clerks.

Despite this hostility, there are nonetheless examples of amicable relations between Germans and Poles. GDR girls appear to hold Polish men in rather high esteem, much to the consternation of their male countrymen. Three Polish commuters, Marian, Attek, and Johann, who travel daily to work in the GDR town of Weisswasser, learned five German words right off the bat: first, "work," "assembly," "food"; then "classy" and "immaculate," which referred to their new GDR friends Inge, Andrea, and Jacqueline. [. . .]

In Frankfurt (Oder) last year, 23 GDR citizens got engaged to 23 Polish women. The *(Ost-)Berliner Zeitung* admits, "Of course not every flirt leads to marriage. Old prejudices born out of centuries of cultivated enmity between Germans and Poles cannot be so quickly pushed aside."

Time and again, one is reminded of the past. When a young Pole makes his GDR girlfriend into a mother without marrying her, the GDR population calls it "the revenge for Warsaw." "Why must we always atone for the crimes of our fathers and grandfathers?" asks one young man from East Berlin, whose family was ruined in this way. "It is fine that people always remind us we and the Poles are socialist brothers. That's just fine, but if everyone is going to continue talking about brotherhood, then we would ask them to kindly deal with us like brothers someday as well."

9

SERVICE PROTOCOL ON THE RESIDENCE OF NONCITIZENS IN THE GERMAN DEMOCRATIC REPUBLIC

First published in German as "Protokoll No. 041/77" by the Minister of the Interior and Chief of the German People's Police on December 20, 1976. Translated by David Gramling.

Permanent residence may be withheld from persons who:

1. Let it be known that they oppose the socialist societal order of the GDR or can be expected not to integrate into the socialistic life of the GDR;
2. Are considered as having a criminal record according to the laws of the GDR or who have been prosecuted abroad for a crime that would be considered an indictable offense in the GDR, or those for whom the character of their felony demonstrates they cannot be integrated into the societal life of the GDR;
3. Do not carry identifying documents on their person, or are in possession of invalid or falsified documents and the identity of the person cannot be determined in short order;
4. Are mentally disturbed, incurably ill, or are so ill that the convalescence process requires a longer period of time than can reasonably be accepted, or are drug addicted;
5. Knowingly make false statements in order to obtain residence in the GDR;
6. Live in ambiguous familial relations;
7. Are, on account of their age or other reasons, incapable of working or are in need of supervision and have no close relatives in the GDR, or whose family members in the GDR have denied them assistance and supervision;
8. Are clearly to be seen as asocial elements, and integration into societal relations is not to be expected;
9. Have left behind large financial responsibilities and personal debts and are hoping to evade these by taking up residence in the GDR, or are suspected of seeking residence for personal gain;
10. Are not in possession of work papers or have had no orderly employment in the past due to their own actions, and will most likely not change their attitude toward work once in the GDR;
11. For whom a permanent residence does not appear to be in the interest of state and society;
12. When considerations of foreign affairs appear to compel such action.

10

UNION MEMBERS FROM THE SOCIALIST REPUBLIC OF VIETNAM RECOVER IN THE GDR

First published as "SRV-Gewerkschafter erholen sich in der DDR" by the *Allgemeiner Deutscher Nachrichtendienst* (August 11, 1977). Translated by David Gramling.

A Proof of Solidarity: Donations from the Free German Association of Unions
BERLIN. On Thursday, 30 more unionists from the Socialist Republic of Vietnam were received in the GDR. At the invitation of the Free German Associ-

ation of Unions, they will rest and recover for several weeks at the rehabilitation center at Graal-Moritz. Thereafter, they will become acquainted with the union operations of the host country during a period of study at Magdeburg.

This group of Vietnamese guests, which includes guest workers from factories and agricultural institutions in the north and south of Vietnam, are a subset of the 190 unionists who have been able to spend a rehabilitation period and vacation in the republic during 1977. The first such group of 20 unionists was greeted in the GDR in 1968. By the end of 1976, the number had grown to 500.

Many of the guests still suffer from war wounds so severe that a hospital stay is often necessary. Others who have been wounded in war receive arm or leg prostheses, therapeutic massages and baths, and are seen by ophthalmologists or other medical specialists. Doctors, nurses, and countless other staff in the rehabilitation centers are constantly making an effort to improve the health of the Vietnamese unionists, so they can dedicate their energies to peaceful development in their country.

Nguyen Minh, the leader of a group that recently returned to its home country, represented the sentiments of the many recovering 18- to 20-year-olds in the following words: "Everywhere we stayed—whether in factories, schools, or during rehabilitation—we felt the steadfast and honest friendship of the people of the GDR with the working class and the entire people of Vietnam. We would like to express our thanks for the heartfelt solidarity that the citizens of the socialist state offered us, not only in the struggle against U.S. aggression but also in the socialist construction of our fatherland."

11

KURT SEIBT

SOLIDARITY: AN IMPORTANT FORCE IN THE FREEDOM STRUGGLE

First published as "Solidarität—wichtige Kraft im Befreiungskampf" in the East German *Neue Deutsche Presse* (August 19, 1979). Translated by David Gramling. Seibt (b. 1908, Berlin) served as the president of the Solidarity Committee of the German Democratic Republic during the late 1970s. For his international solidarity efforts, he received the Star of Friendship between Peoples (Stern der Völkerfreundschaft) from the East German government in 1978.

In a few weeks, our people will celebrate the thirtieth anniversary of the founding of the republic. Thirty years of the GDR also means 30 years of active anti-imperialist solidarity—solidarity with all peoples fighting for freedom and justice, human rights, and human dignity.

The journalists of our republic have made a meaningful contribution to the solidarity concerns and negotiations in the GDR, including journalists who are active in the mass media. Their activities in the print media, radio, and television bring the freedom struggles of various peoples into living rooms everywhere and arouse pride in the triumphs of our class brothers, as well as pain and anger about tyranny, repression, and imperialistic barbarism. Out of their engagement grows empathy, willingness, and deeds of assistance and solidarity.

At its March convention, the Presidium of the Solidarity Committee of the GDR expressed its special thanks to our country's journalists for their indefatigable efforts on issues of solidarity. We are grateful for more than just the half million marks that the Alliance of GDR Journalists has contributed to the Solidarity Fund. Our thanks go out most of all to the thousands of journalists in newspapers, radio, and television who facilitate the power of party expression that flows into the hearts and minds of readers, listeners, and spectators. Some examples are the programs *Voices of the GDR* and *Freedom to Peace,* or the decade-long work of the *NBI* [*New Berlin Illustrated* newspaper] under the motto "Peace to the Children," or the annual solidarity action on Berlin's Alexanderplatz for the People's Republic of Vietnam, an event in which all of the capital's editorial staffs took part.

In the 30 years of our republic's existence, the working class and the people of our country have benefited from active international solidarity. When the imperialistic states, mobilized by reactionary circles and the Bonn State's reinvigorated imperialism, sought to isolate us and undermine the socialist state's equal-opportunity participation in international life, they failed to defeat this active international solidarity and the conscious position of the citizens of the GDR. Our people exercised and continue to exercise solidarity, as long as there are politically, socially, colonially, or racially oppressed people, as long as there is hunger and need in our world.

Such is the declared policy of our party and our state, anchored in the party program and in the constitution. It is a profound necessity among the entire population of the GDR, beginning with the Young Pioneers with their regular secondhand goods drives and solidarity bazaars, all the way to the retirees, who do not hesitate to contribute their energies to broader solidarity work. About 20 million marks were donated to the Solidarity Fund last year. Without exception, all levels within our society took part in this donation campaign. [. . .]

Thanks to the internationalist position of the employable worker, the Solidarity Committee of the GDR was able to deliver urgently needed humanitarian aid to the severely afflicted Vietnamese brother people. The campaign "Hands Off Vietnam," which was born literally hours after the criminal invasion of the high-powered Chinese chauvinists, mobilized various efforts and special solidarity alliances with Vietnamese class comrades. The Free German Association of Unions gave an additional 50 million marks, and all broad-base mass organizations offered additional solidarity donations in the millions. Tens of thousands of citizens donated blood, and tens of thousands of youth declared their willingness to stand by their Vietnamese brothers as volunteers in the struggle against aggression. Our government also made an additional 172 million–mark donation so that the first deliveries of medications, plasma, blankets, and foodstuffs could reach those most severely affected.

It is obvious that our attention must be focused on those among our brother peoples who are under the most duress: Vietnam, Laos, and the people of Kampuchea, who have just recently been liberated at long last. But we are in no way neglecting our inherent responsibility for the struggling people of the African continent. Our solidarity support is also geared toward the people of Angola, Ethiopia, and Mozambique, as well as the People's Republic of Yemen, whose independence from imperialist intrigues is constantly threatened. Neither do we want to forget the struggling peoples of South Africa, Zimbabwe, and Namibia, to whom we have committed considerable support in the form of medical supplies, vitamins and other nourishment, primarily for the many refugee camps. [. . .] Our solidarity assistance also reaches the Palestinian Liberation Organization and other patriotic forces in the Near East, with whom we join in condemning the Camp David Separation Agreement. [. . .]

12

SIEGFRIED MANN

HOW DO FOREIGN WORKERS LIVE IN THE GDR?

First published as "Wie leben ausländische Arbeiter in der DDR?" in the East German newspaper *Die Wahrheit* (April 22, 1985). Reprinted in *Anderssein gab es nicht: Ausländer und Minderheiten in der DDR*, Marianne Krüger-Portratz, ed. (Münster: Waxmann, 1991), 207. Translated by Tes Howell.

Welcome Guests — Not Low-Paid Guest Workers

She is pretty, friendly, and smart, the delicate Diep from Vietnam, who has worked for three years with 100 Vietnamese compatriots in the Berlin lightbulb factory, the main branch of the state-owned conglomerate NARVA [a subsidiary of the lightbulb company Osram]. A further 180 Vietnamese youth study and work in other branches of the conglomerate, in Tambach-Dietharz, Brand-Erbisdorf, and Oberweissbach.

Diep works in Berlin as a translator; she studied *Germanistik,* or German philology, in Hanoi and learned English during a previous stay at a GDR university. She is proud of her good grade on the final examination. Accompanying her in this conversation were 28-year-old Duong, 27-year-old Nhuan, and 24-year-old Tram.

They are all guests in the GDR, but are they "guest workers" like in the West? Why are they here? What are their work and living conditions? These questions are important, and the answers revealed serious differences.

First, some introductory information: The young Vietnamese will be at the conglomerate NARVA for four years under the December 4, 1977, government accord between the GDR and the Democratic Republic of Vietnam. They must first complete a German language course, then a semiskilled-labor apprenticeship. The third step is a skilled-labor apprenticeship, which occurs on a voluntary basis and was undertaken by more than 50 percent of the Vietnamese girls, women, and men here in the lightbulb factory. The specific job titles are electric installer and metallurgist for rolling-mill technologies (skilled labor) and installer for illuminants and cable (semiskilled labor).

Duong, who qualified to be a metallurgist for rolling-mill technologies, explains the purpose of his stay in the GDR: "We are here to acquire as much modern, scientific knowledge as possible so that we can apply it later in the development of our homeland." He describes the management's heartfelt reception at the airport three years ago and how all his compatriots received help in overcoming the first pangs of homesickness.

The petite Tram, who will become an electric installer, continues, "In the beginning, we had difficulties with the food, the climate, and the German language. But everyone made such an effort to help us. They provided meals with rice in the cafeteria because we could not get used to potatoes, and we cook in the residence hall where we live comfortably in double-occupancy rooms. The rent is 30 marks a month, including heat, hot water, and electricity."

Nhuan, on his way to becoming a skilled laborer in rolling-mill technology like his friend Duong, reports that all his compatriots work together in brigades with German colleagues. "We participate in meetings and are informed on all questions important to us. Representatives from our group are also included in the monthly meeting with the conglomerate's general manager."

The Vietnamese colleagues have a labor-union official who is an equal member of the factory's union board. Nhuan reasons, "We are informed on all measures. Whoever is not in the know has only himself to blame. There are no differences between our German colleagues and us. This also applies to health care. Sometimes we even have priority at the clinic."

And what is the pay like? Their pay is comparable to the salary rate and performance quotas of their German colleagues. This parity also applies to the year-end bonus. The shop committee recognizes the industriousness and considerable dexterity of the Vietnamese workers. For this reason, the Vietnamese sometimes earn more than their German colleagues, based on performance.

Tram, Diep, Duong, and Nhuan: "We are always trying to save money and help our families as much as possible. This is part of our mentality."

So much for the work. What does their free time look like? Our interviewees report that they also receive support in this area and have many diverse opportunities at hand. For example, they can go on outings together with their German work colleagues. Diep says, "We will soon know the entire GDR!" They have a soccer team and have even won first place in a competition with other factory teams. They have a choral group, which is very popular. They enjoy talking with the young Vietnamese in the schools, where they discuss the struggles and lives of their people.

When asked how they see their future, Nhuan speaks for all: "We are building socialism in our homeland. And for this we need a workforce. Industrial firms are being established throughout our country, but Vietnam is still known to be antiquated and agricultural. When we return to our homeland, we will be placed where the industry needs us. And we believe that this assignment will correspond to our wishes."

It is clear, even from this one discussion, that there can be no comparison between guest workers' living conditions in West Berlin and those of foreign workers in the GDR. The primary goal here is a concrete form of solidarity and a well-paid workforce that will increase profits. It is not mere lip service when Duong says: "We are working here in a brother country. We feel at home, working and learning here for our homeland."

What moves these young people today? What do they feel? The happiness drains from Diep's pretty face as she explains: "We have all experienced war. Especially in the north, where we lived. The battles were horrendous. Almost all the cities and bridges were destroyed. We saw with our own eyes as the American bombs fell. Being children, we only wanted to live with our parents. But this desire was not fulfilled. From age four to six, I had to live away from my parents out in the country. Sometimes they could only visit me once a month. I want to say that whoever has experienced war yearns for freedom. War is the worst for the children."

13
HANS SCHUELER
PANIC IS THE WRONG ANSWER

First published as "Panik ist die falsche Antwort" in *Die Zeit* (July 25, 1986). Translated by David Gramling.

The asylum flood does not mean that a basic right must be sacrificed

GERMANY, SUMMER 1986. A divided country gets ugly. And it's difficult to say if the Communist dictatorship in the East or the free democracy in the West contributes more to the darkening of Germany's image.

At East Berlin's Schönefeld Airport, the GDR airline Interflug lands with masses of human cargo from the Third World's lands of misery—now mostly young Iranians seeking to escape recruitment for the ayatollah's war against Iraq, Ghanaians and Nigerians hoping for a better future in the golden West, and Indians.

The GDR surely has nothing more in mind for its numerous passengers than to deport them to West Berlin. They'll be carted off to the Friedrich-strasse train station in buses and loaded onto the streetcars, which will bring them nonstop and beyond their control over the sector border into the west of the city.

Over here, however, the foreigner bureaus in Berlin and Helmstedt do not know what to do with the hundreds of new arrivals. In West Berlin, radical-right skinheads have been fighting with the police, who were ordered to provide protection for the foreigners. Sending them back to the GDR is not a possibility. Everywhere, respectable citizens are astir; fear of foreign infiltration is growing, and our political spectrum's middle-right is once again making a formidable racket about the Asylum Article of the Basic Law.

Enterprise of the Persecuted

The Workers and Farmers State is systematically managing an enterprise for refugees fleeing poverty and persecution at the expense of the Federal Republic. In 1980—the year with the strongest stream of refugees in recent memory—10,000 out of 108,000 asylum seekers came over the West Berlin border. Five years later, more than half of the 74,000 applicants entered in this way. In the first half of 1986, 42,268 refugees have traveled into our country. Of those, 53.9 percent used the Schönefeld sluice. In Ghana and Nigeria, Interflug is recruiting with brochures for "fast and smooth transit" to West Berlin.

A cynicism more wicked is hardly imaginable. A regime that locks up its own population until retirement age and does not think twice about it is now pretending to provide the persecuted of other dictatorships (not to mention *renommée* communists) asylum in their own country but then pumps suffering people by the thousands into the "capitalist" neighboring country, while simultaneously barricading its exits with walls, mines, and barbed wire.

The federal government must bring about a change in the current practice. Because Bonn does not exercise sovereignty in West Berlin, this issue must be put to the Americans, British, and French. The federal government can underscore their decisiveness by denying the GDR any economic relief and preferential treatment that is not based on contractual stipulation.

How are the powers that be reacting in our country? They respond with bureaucratic panic and thinly dissembled propaganda against a new "asylum flash flood," which—as was said six years ago—could burst all the dams. We should, however, be wary—not just of the exploitation of the Basic Law but also of assaults upon it.

First, the facts: about 600,000 refugees are currently living with us, according to the federal minister of the interior. However, this number is questionable. Nevertheless, 200,000 have come from the East Bloc, and they cannot be deported. About 100,000 are asylum seekers whose admission proceedings have not yet concluded. Approximately 60,000 are people whose asylum applications were declined but who are still permitted to live in the country, partially for humanitarian reasons. This number constitutes 70 percent of those declined. Asylum has been granted to only 63,000. Are we unable to cope with this amount?

Given these circumstances, the reaction of the coalition politicians is more than astounding. They do not concern themselves with arresting the human smugglers from the GDR or with enforcing legal regulations. They settle for restriction itself: headlines are calling for the abolition of the basic right to asylum.

Even just a few weeks ago in top-level talks chaired by the chancellor, the Bonn Coalition parties agreed to not undertake "any change in the basic right to asylum but rather to strengthen the practical measures for the abridgement of the asylum procedure." New disincentives will be provided: a prohibition on gainful employment for all asylum seekers during the entire duration of the recognition procedure, streamlining the legal pathways for rejecting applications that were developed to ensure equal dispensation of justice, and immediate rejection of asylum seekers who have previously resided in an EC state (or Switzerland, Austria, or Norway) for more than three months.

One would think that seeking recourse to disincentives already provided in the existing law would suffice. The Law of Asylum Procedure grants the Federal Bureau for the Recognition of Foreign Refugees and its deputies the opportunity to hear the cases of asylum seekers immediately upon their arrival, if they so desire. A person who says he suffered from hunger at home or that civil war overtook his land or that he did not want to be forced into military service against Iraq might be immediately rejected and deported. In such a case, there remains a legal defense only against the immediate execution of the deportation notification. In contrast to other asylum procedures, the courts may rule on these cases within a few days.

For a long time, applicants have availed themselves of this approach taken in fewer than 10 percent of the cases in West Berlin. Asylum seekers with clearly groundless applications could certainly not be sent back into East Berlin, but they could be flown back to Istanbul, Tehran, or Delhi—whether by way of Tegel or an airport in the Federal Republic—if necessary at the expense of the GDR, which brought them to us.

Instead, the chancellor's ministers and the minister presidents from federal states governed by the CDU and CSU are almost unanimous in demanding the repeal of article 16 of the German federal constitution, which states, "The politically persecuted enjoy the right to asylum."

Dangerous Legal Plans

At the beginning of the week, these appeals from the right were still unclear. They seemed to be suggesting that a clarifying sentence be added to article 16, which would read "The full particulars regulate the law." Then Franz Josef Strauss finally stated openly what would be in this law:

- In the future, the guarantee of a lawful claim to asylum for all people who are politically persecuted in their homeland will apply only to those persecuted people from the East Bloc countries and Afghanistan—since they are occupied by the Soviet Union.
- The federal government will be empowered to establish quotas for refugees according to their country of origin.
- The guarantee of due process will fall away, as it will not apply to measures concerning foreigners seeking asylum.
- Controls will be bolstered at the Berlin sector borders (Strauss does not see Berlin's status as sovereign enough to forgo this measure).

The momentousness of these plans must be understood. According to Strauss's theses, only people from leftist dictatorships would have the right to asylum. White opponents of apartheid or even blacks from South Africa, who will certainly come to Europe in the next few years fleeing the Buren regime, would find no mercy under the new regulations.

There are already "quota refugees" here in the Federal Republic. They are the boat people, some 30,000 Vietnamese rescued from the Chinese Sea, whose accommodation the minister presidents of the federal states already battled over back at the beginning of the 1980s. They are often economic refugees; they have no real asylum status and need it as little as the Poles, Czechs, and other refugees from the East Bloc. Yet Federal Minister of the Interior Friedrich Zimmermann industriously counts them into his statistics, as well as the surviving 40,000 forced laborers recruited by the Nazis during the Second World War.

The refugee contingents of the future shall be held separate from the truly politically persecuted, who come to us from the "wrong" region and with the "wrong" skin color. For them, the consequences will be like those of the German Jews who, until the beginning of the Second World War, knocked on Switzerland's door and were turned away with a cool gesture and a declaration that, unfortunately, the contingent for immigrants of Jewish belief or Jewish race had already been exhausted.

The claim that the Federal Republic is overflowing with asylum seekers runs contrary to the facts. Among the 4.7 million foreigners who live in our midst, political refugees are still a small minority. They will also stay a minority if agencies and courts make consistent use of the Law of Asylum Procedure. Efforts toward improvement must be focused there, rather than on the guarantee within the Basic Law, which promises a home in the Federal Republic to truly politically persecuted people.

14

AGREEMENT ON THE PROCEDURES CONCERNING PREGNANCY AMONG VIETNAMESE WOMEN LABORERS IN THE GDR

Reprinted as "Vereinbarung" in *Anderssein gab es nicht: Ausländer und Minderheiten in der DDR*, Marianne Krüger-Portratz, ed. (Münster: Waxmann, 1991), 204–205. Translated by Tes Howell. This memorandum of understanding was drafted to reaffirm and clarify aspects of a bilateral 1980 state treaty, particularly issues surrounding pregnancy among Vietnamese contract workers in the GDR. It was signed on January 26, 1987, by the two states' ministers of labor.

The common goal of the Labor Cooperation documented in these pages is as follows: Vietnamese workers are employed and trained in GDR firms for a specific time frame. The concomitant obligations place heavy demands on both sides as well as on the Vietnamese workers themselves. Pregnancy and motherhood change the personal situation of the affected female workers so profoundly that they are subsequently no longer able to realize the demands of temporary employment and training.

The representatives of the operational firms as well as the work group leaders are responsible for discussing the use of prophylactics with Vietnamese workers and informing them that pregnancy and motherhood are incompatible with the terms of their contract. Vietnamese women—like women in the GDR—have the right (in accordance with the agreement between the ministers of health in both countries) to terminate their pregnancies cost-free.

Vietnamese women who do not avail themselves of contraception or abortion must report at a predetermined time for their premature return to Vietnam, upon being cleared by a doctor to travel. In the case of a refusal to leave the country, the embassy of the Socialist Republic of Vietnam in the GDR will take immediate, necessary steps toward the execution of the deportation order and will be responsible for all costs incurred in the process.

In special circumstances, when the personal, social situation of the Vietnamese woman in question justifies a delivery in the GDR, the permanent secretary for labor and wages of the GDR, in consultation with the embassy of the SRV in the GDR, can approve the prolonged residence of mother and child until both are able to travel.

The Vietnamese government will inform new delegations of the provisions of this agreement and will notify the women in these delegations of the prerequisites to their employment.

15

JUST GO TO ISRAEL

First printed as "Geht doch nach Israel" in *Der Spiegel* (October 1, 1990). Translated by David Gramling.

Forty-five years after the end of the Holocaust, thousands of Soviet Jews are pushing their way into exile in Germany—but the federal government and states do not want to take them in. The Central Council of Jews considers this ban on entry "uncompassionate," yet individual spokespersons from Jewish congregations express "understanding" for Bonn's position.

The setting is macabre. In the former Nazi Propaganda Ministry, of all places, some 60 Russian Jews have gathered, excited and afraid, in front of a small office: the East Berlin Advice Office for Jewish Immigrants from the Soviet Union. It's time for office hours.

Karina, 36, is among them—a German teacher from Moscow. She is in luck. After waiting an hour, she finally catches the director of the help desk as he is slipping out the back door. Now she can tell him her story.

At the beginning of July, she read in the Moscow newspapers that the GDR government would offer refuge to all Soviet Jews "on humanitarian grounds." Two weeks later, with her computer-engineer husband and two sons, she arrived in Berlin. Now, she says in an excited voice, "I am so grateful to the Germans."

The past few years in Moscow have been "horrible." Their 14-year-old son, Nikolai, would return from school in tears daily because his schoolmates would constantly write "Jew" in chalk on his back. All at once, the family gave up its livelihood and property.

The GDR, Karina reports, had accepted them openly, but now "we need help again," she says to the director of the Berlin help desk. Their parents also want to come, but they do not know how, when, and if they still can. "October 3rd," she explains with a worried expression, "is the German reunification."

Matthias Jahr, 39, the director of the help desk, can hardly help her. The provisions for Soviet Jews will be guaranteed only as long as the GDR exists.

Jahr does not even know if his help desk will still exist on the day after the German Reunification. The Bonn federal government is responsible for this uncertainty. At the beginning of September, it advised all West and East German consular officials in the Soviet Union that the "acceptance applications" for Jewish citizens "will no longer be processed."

The reason for the ban on entry is that the Foreign Ministry recently experienced an "explosive increase in emigration inquiries" among Soviet Jews. The German General Consulate in Kiev alone had been processing "almost 10,000 applications." Only after "the establishment of an acceptance quota" by the federation and the states will the entry applications be approved, declares Interior Minister Wolfgang Schäuble.

This reaction is almost as inconceivable as its cause; 45 years after the end of the Holocaust, a large number of Jews want to settle in Germany—and Bonn is putting up barriers.

The GDR commissioner of foreigner affairs, Almuth Berger, has protested in vain against the "scandalous ban on entry." Heinz Galinski, the chair of the Central Council of Jews in Germany, calls the decision "uncompassionate."

Bonn's behavior has very little to do with a lack of compassion, maintains the Christian Democrat Schäuble. "The pent-up desires among Jewish people," who have long sought to emigrate from the Soviet Union, are now finding "new options."

It is not just the liberal emigration praxis of the Gorbachev era that is driving Jews out of the country but a pernicious anti-Semitism as well. Insults and violence in broad daylight—not to mention unabashed anti-Jewish elements in the media—are among the darker aspects of perestroika.

The fascist Pamjat movement is at the political forefront of this anti-Semitic campaign. It calls forth a hatred of Jews that is deeply rooted in Russian history. Nonetheless, the ruling Soviet bureaucracy is tolerating the activities of the Pamjat agitators; once again, Judaism has become the scapegoat. This new anti-Semitism, says the Moscow author Jurij Ginsburg, blames Jews for "Bolshevism and its consequences, for mass hunger and for the contamination of nature." The fall of the "state of many peoples" has also contributed to an increase in anti-Semitism. "In order to protect the Soviet empire," explains the author Andrej Sinjawski, a "powerful militant Russian nationalism is developing and is turning against Jews."

Of the 2 million Jews living in the Soviet Union at the beginning of this year, more than 100,000 had emigrated to Israel by August. The small state has been overburdened by this mass influx. Impoverished Israelis are already calling on Gorbachev: "Don't let the Jews move."

Israel is apparently "taking more people in than is actually possible," says Mikhail Boguslawski, 35, who left Czernowitz for East Berlin two months ago. This situation is one of the reasons he emigrated to Germany—a country that, for him, is just like any other. "Our generation," Boguslawski says in justification of his decision, "has confidence in Germany again." [. . .]

16
ROBERT VON LUCIUS
NOSTALGIA DESPITE UNFULFILLED PROMISES

First published as "Nostalgie trotz unerfüllter Versprechen" in *Frankfurter Allgemeine Zeitung* (August 30, 1994). Translated by Tes Howell.

Bonn is No Longer Interested in German-Speaking Mozambicans

MAPUTO, MOZAMBIQUE. He has the GDR to thank for what he is today. Germany is his second home, reports Samuel da Graça Chioco. But, as with many tens of thousands of other German-speaking Mozambicans, Bonn no longer wants to hear anything of him and ignores the potential that nostalgia and language skills would give him. Though difficult and expensive German language courses are offered in other countries, there are no opportunities for contact and cohesion among the Mozambicans returning from the GDR; they represent a high percentage of the elite. They do not even have access to German-language films, although they have repeatedly reported that they would be interested in obtaining some. Why not? "We don't have a projector," explains the German embassy, and there is also no room for showing the films.

There would also be economic benefits to such outreach. Samuel, for example, who trained in Chemnitz as a textile engineer, now works for a printing firm. Because of his language skills and connections, he imports printers exclusively from Heidelberg for a new print shop in Beira, to the benefit of German exporters.

Anyone who meets the young entrepreneurs of today, those who are driving the reconstruction of an economy that was destroyed by a long civil war, frequently encounters German speakers. Those who were allowed to leave Mozambique were lucky, says Samuel. They received training and a stable life in the eastern part of Germany; moreover, they escaped being drafted into the army. Nearly every fifth or sixth person in this small elite community has the GDR to thank for his training. The Germans had "a good culture: work," Sam smirks. Mozambicans who had worked in the GDR were "different."

The son of an attorney, Samuel came to Magdeburg for the first time at age 17, but he spoke only Portuguese and a little English. He learned German quickly because, at that time, Germans, Mozambicans, and Namibians shared rooms at the School of Friendship. In the six years of his training he never traveled home and learned little about the West. When he made a West German friend in Berlin and applied for a visitor's pass to the FRG, he encountered difficulties. The GDR ultimately sent him home. Samuel likes Germany and was sad not to have been there for the reunification, an event that brought him great joy nonetheless. In Maputo, he has little access to a German-speaking community, although he would gladly participate if he did.

There were two distinct groups among the approximately 50,000 young Mozambicans who worked in the GDR between 1979 and 1991: one group earned money; the other completed job training. Anyone who came before 1988 belonged to the lucky cohort that obtained solid vocational training. Then, amid vague promises, these trained workers were sent to places that were short-staffed—in the auto industry in Eisenach and Nordhausen, for instance. Their experiences after returning were a lesson in the importance of training. Those in the group of *regresados,* the returnees, who came home with consumer goods that were often stolen on the way or were useless in Mozambique, were seen as show-offs and quickly became outcasts; the others came without money but found jobs and social prestige.

Roberto Julião was among this latter group. He became a radiator technician in the GDR. Why, he does not know, for radiators are not particularly necessary in warm Mozambique, but he did not have a say in his training. Now he is working at the concierge desk for a large hotel in Maputo because of his language skills and experience abroad. Roberto's brother is married in Magdeburg. Roberto, who had enough money for a return ticket, wanted to visit him there, but the embassy refused to grant him a tourist visa, without grounds. Acasio Castro, whose brother is married to a German, reports similar experiences. He was also refused a tourist visa to visit his brother and his sister-in-law, again without grounds, although he leads a prosperous and stable life in Mozambique. He was sad about that, he says. Samuel thinks about his son in Chemnitz often, despite not having seen him since his return in 1989. They both speak of pleasant, good memories.

At any rate, Bonn responds with unvarnished and sedate disinterest in keeping with its tradition. The past five years have seen an uninterrupted sequence of broken promises by the former GDR, the Federal Republic, Eastern German businesses, and the Mozambican government. Shortly before unification, the two German states did not know what they should do with the foreign guest workers in the GDR. Mozambicans, who still numbered around 15,000 at the time of the GDR's collapse, represented the largest group of foreigners after the Vietnamese. By then, at least those who had done their training there, instead of just working and earning money, had integrated themselves sufficiently: they spoke German well, unlike the guest workers.

The authorities sought a quick return of all foreign workers. They offered three options: an immediate return home, a continuance of employment until the termination of the standing labor agreements (most ending in 1994, at the latest), or an individual work permit, valid as long as the workers could prove they had a job and a residence. After months of silence, the state mentioned that no one would be expelled against his will. In the meantime, this silence had created great uncertainty among foreign workers. "Gentle" pressure, cost-of-living and rent increases after the currency reform, employers' bankruptcies, xenophobic violence, and a lack of information led approximately 3,000 Mozambicans to choose premature return.

The strategies to entice workers to choose this option were tempting: 3,000 marks, a full two months' salary, help with transporting possessions, and a free flight. But the businesses broke their promises, paid either none or only some of the money, and contrary to the agreement, paid only transport to Maputo, not to the workers' homes. Many of the containers were looted upon arriving in Maputo; former employers did not insure the wares or underinsured them. When the Mozambicans arrived at their home villages with refrigerators and stereos after weeks in encampments, they could not use the appliances because there was no electricity. In Maputo, they were eligible for claims on the government for a part of their salary. Only 40 percent of these wages had been paid to them in the GDR, and Maputo was supposed to pay the rest in local currency. The GDR government reduced this remaining sum according to the foreign debts of the Mozambican government. This disbursement took place only irregularly, based on a surreal exchange rate, or not at all. And the money entitled to them was again taxed according to the customs claims on their goods from Germany.

Several German aid organizations, including the German Society for Technical Collaboration and the Friedrich Ebert Foundation, at least recognized these difficulties and made an effort at assistance. They suggested programs for establishing new businesses and assisting returnees. Government representatives in Bonn said at the time that Mozambique must become a priority for German foreign aid and that the GDR programs should be continued. This plan also failed miserably. There was too little money and interest in Bonn.

17
MARK SIEMONS
SMUGGLING DISCERNED—FINGERS BURNED

First published as "Schmuggel erkannt—Finger verbrannt" in *Frankfurter Allgemeine Zeitung* (February 25, 1995). Translated by Tes Howell. Subsequent to this article, negotiations between Bonn and Hanoi recommenced, eventually leading to an agreement on August 25, 1995, on the repatriation of Vietnamese contract laborers from the former GDR. The parties agreed that 40,000 Vietnamese nationals, particularly those with criminal records, would be repatriated to Vietnam in yearly quotas, in exchange for an extensive German aid package to Hanoi.

Between the Mafia, the Police, and Deportation: What Will Become of the Vietnamese Contract Laborers from the GDR?

The illegal cigarette trade in Berlin lost its innocence long ago, if indeed it ever had any. When Vietnamese gangs from North Vietnam and the Czech Republic forced their way into the market and backed up their demand for protection money with strategic murders, naiveté became a thing of the past. Others from Central Vietnam avenged these deaths by murdering mafia leaders and taking over their organizations. Today, city officials suspect that protection money covers every area in Berlin where untaxed cigarettes are sold and where Vietnamese participants are connected to a larger organization. Escape is hardly an option.

The police are somewhat perplexed. By raiding stores or the apartments of suspects known to be selling cigarettes illegally, they can usually catch the little fish but not their bosses, who pull the strings. Few Vietnamese are willing to give statements, for the police cannot protect their informants from henchmen seeking revenge. Murders among the Vietnamese mafia have been on the rise since 1992. The scenario is now all too familiar: a few Vietnamese are sitting in their living room playing cards or watching videos; the door opens, and masked men open fire on one of them, then leave again without a trace. Some victims have even faced execution by samurai sword.

Negotiations in Bonn and Hanoi

Illegal cigarette sales are like a permanent, open wound in the constitutional state's sense of security. The Vietnamese stand on every corner, square, and subway platform in East Berlin. Sometimes young men drive up in sporty, expensive sedans and buy several cartons from them after a brief negotiation. Sometimes the police come, but by then the Vietnamese, warned by lookouts, have already disappeared. The aspect that irritates officials most is that there is nothing they can do about it, even though they have already confiscated 85 million untaxed cigarettes and initiated more than 8,000 criminal proceedings. Trade continues to flourish. Posters with a large cigarette broken in two hang all over the city. They are advertisements sponsored by the federal minister of finance promoting legal behavior, a powerless entreaty in the futile battle against organized crime: "Smuggling Discerned—Fingers Burned" reads the caption, or "Better taxed than locked up." Obeying the law seems like just one option among many for making one's way through the city.

Hanoi broke off high-level talks with Bonn this week over the repatriation of the Vietnamese. The German government is offering Vietnam massive economic assistance so that it might take in as many Vietnamese as possible: up to 40,000. The Federal Chancellery is calling this step an "integral starting point." Until now, Vietnam had refused entry to deported Vietnamese who had not signed a voluntary statement. Last year, the Federal Republic responded by suspending all foreign aid, blocking a collaborative program of the European Community, and freezing the Hermes low-interest loan guarantees. The Vietnamese in Germany set in motion a highly complex interplay among various ministries: in order to solve the problem of the interior minister while simultaneously mitigating its effects on the finance minister (the illegal sale of cigarettes causes losses of a billion German marks in taxes every year), the Foreign Ministry calls on the services of the Ministry of Economics as well as the Ministry of Development. Also participating in the negotiations is Minister of State Bernd Schmidbauer from the Chancellery. The cabinet approved the negotiation strategy in January.

When the Vietnam demonstrations took place in Berlin in the late 1960s, no one could have dreamed of how close the Vietnamese would actually come to the Germans. At the time, people wanted to fight not only against

"U.S. imperialism" but also "for a red Vietnam—for the victory of revolution" as part of a worldwide youth movement. Now that today, at the end of their revolution, Vietnamese are in Berlin by the thousands, no one wants to take to the streets for them. The problem is not that members of a certain population group have become delinquent, as could happen with Italians, Poles, or Germans. Rather, the problems of the Vietnamese are intimately related to the reunification of the German state.

After the victory of communist North Vietnam in the 1970s, the Federal Republic agreed to take in a contingent of 12,000 "boat people" [original in English] fleeing from the South; they received permanent, unconditional right of residence. The GDR contracted with North Vietnam for workers and apprentices, as well as with the other socialist brother nations of Mozambique, Angola, and Cuba. Whereas a portion of the country's elite could be found among the South Vietnamese, many of the contract laborers sent from North Vietnam were underqualified. By the time the Berlin Wall fell, 60,000 Vietnamese lived in the GDR.

After reunification, contract laborers received a severance settlement and were offered a return plane ticket. Most accepted the offer. The remaining 15,000 Vietnamese received a restricted residence permit for the duration of their original contract, even if in reality they had been laid off long ago. In 1993, a conference among the interior ministers converted the status into a two-year temporary permit, on the condition that workers provide proof of current employment. They did not receive credit for their labor time in the GDR and must wait until 2001 for a permanent residence permit. Some of them who had worked in the GDR since 1985 will have lived 16 years in Germany before being able to receive a residence permit, although the Foreigner Act states that they can obtain the right of residence after just five years.

The situation of the approximately 45,000 Vietnamese asylum seekers who came to a reunified Germany is even more complicated. The designation *asylum seeker* kicks off a routine and rather predetermined course of events. Fewer than 1 percent of asylum applications are recognized; people whose applications are rejected receive a deportation notice but cannot be deported because Vietnam has not accepted them yet. They are in a state of flux: they cannot live anywhere except in Germany but are not allowed to work here legally. The value of a residence permit is growing quickly; a permit on the black market is supposedly worth 30,000 marks.

Asylum seekers came to Germany in different phases and for different reasons. First, family members and contract laborers from other East Bloc countries entered after the Wall fell. Later, boastful fellow countrymen and -women charmed increasingly more Vietnamese with their siren calls, describing a fantasy land of unlimited possibilities. Many contract laborers in the GDR worked in the textile industry—for example, in the Berlin's Men's

Clothing Progress, which is called Beacon Classic today. They lived in separate contract-laborer residences, crowded into rooms separated by gender. An advisor paid by the state watched over the women in the case of pregnancy. Whoever wanted to keep her child had to return to Vietnam; if staying here was more important, the woman was forced to have an abortion. The GDR made no provision for a private life. With considerable talent for improvisation, residents would rearrange the cabinets in the bedrooms so as to effect a modicum of intimacy for couples; but when the inspector came around, they quickly returned the cabinets to their original positions.

Contract laborers were the first to lose their jobs after the Wall fell, even in the firms that survived the transition to a market economy. The Vietnamese tried to maintain their hold on the traveling vendors, but the Turks and Poles were well established in that profession. Then they established the black market for cigarettes. The necessary infrastructure had already developed in the GDR. The Vietnamese had earned extra money by making those famous GDR stonewashed jeans. GDR citizens who wore hard-to-find sizes especially appreciated this service: the Vietnamese would tailor pants and jackets for them. At the time, this part-time work established a functioning system of labor division, from the acquisition of material to the fastening of rivets.

The Vietnamese also had come into contact with the Poles in the GDR. Because packages shipped from the GDR to the homeland were always thoroughly inspected, the Vietnamese found an alternate route: they sent their often-bulky postal parcels filled with bicycles and mopeds through the Danzig port. And now Polish gangs smuggle the cigarettes over the border or bribe customs agents to get the necessary stamps. The profit margin is considerable: a pack bought for 60 pfennig is sold for 2.40 marks. Meanwhile, the trade has grown into a billion-mark industry. The police in Berlin have formed a Tobacco Task Force. In other federal states, it is called Special Commission Samurai or SoKo Blue Smoke.

Trials against Police Officers

Life for the Vietnamese is not particularly enjoyable. The contract laborers' residences, in which most still live together in close quarters, are located in the most forlorn areas of Berlin-Lichtenberg and Marzahn. The Vietnamese were already culturally isolated in the GDR, attracting less attention than even the Mozambicans. They also encountered less resentment. Still, after the Wall fell, they became the object of skinhead aggression. Taking cigarette cartons from the *"Fitschis"* became a favored sport, but the well-organized Vietnamese knew how to protect themselves as a group. Interest in attacking them soon dwindled. However, they still avoid going out after dark if possible. In the evenings, they sit together at home. They spend little money on themselves in order to send as much as possible back home. On the weekends, they drive to relatives, eat Vietnamese food, and watch the Vietnamese videos that are available in Germany.

Tamara Hentschel was an advisor to the Vietnamese in the GDR. When her charges had problems with the bureaucracy after the Wall fell, she helped establish the German-Vietnamese Friendship Association, "Rice Drum." She helps them communicate with the authorities and come to terms with living in Germany. Many still do not speak German proficiently. The long-term goal is to facilitate residence in Germany for contract laborers and secure a realistic chance at job training for all others. It would be ideal if the Vietnamese could find jobs with German firms that invest in Vietnam, but the laws must be changed before that can happen.

Tamara Hentschel has a position of trust that became important when complaints about police abuse increased. The Rice Drum collected records about what allegedly happened in the police posts in Bernau and several Berlin districts. Police reportedly kicked and beat Vietnamese suspects and forced them to undress and "make a Chinese face." More than 50 officials have faced indictment. However, it is still unclear how many will go to trial. Today, the U.N. Committee on Human Rights is organizing lectures at police stations about Vietnamese history and culture.

Berlin is still divided for the Vietnamese. They sell their cigarettes and, more recently, pirated videos almost exclusively in the East—familiar terrain for them. In the West, there is a Vietnam House, but it is dominated by South Vietnamese boat people, who believe their northern compatriots living in the East are Communists and spies for the government. For many East Berliners, however, the black market is a demonstration of solidarity: they still call the cheap goods "Soli cigarettes." They recognize in the Vietnamese, despite whatever foreignness, their poorer companions in misfortune after the collapse of communism—and secretly they are happy that the Vietnamese, too, have found a crack in the supposedly perfect new system.

18

DENNIS KUCK

THOSE FOREIGN SOCIALIST BROTHERS

First published as "Die fremden sozialistischen Brüder" in *Frankfurter Allgemeine Zeitung* (October 11, 2001). Translated by Tes Howell.

The "Friendship of Peoples" Has Become an Issue for Secret Service Organizations: On the Fate of the Guest Worker in the GDR

When Nguyen, barely 20 years old, came to the GDR in 1980, he was lucky. According to aptitude tests, he belonged to the 5 percent of Vietnamese who would receive proper training. For three years, he was trained as a bracing technician, after which he worked for two more years. Actually, Nguyen should have already returned to his homeland, but the GDR and Vietnam had agreed to allow "highly qualified workers" to remain on the job for seven years. Nguyen stayed in the factory for two years and was even admitted to university to study engineering because of his accomplishments. The ambitious Vietnamese man also gained ground on a personal level. He had a German girlfriend and two children with her. But his problems began there. The authorities demanded that Nguyen leave the country, and the Stasi [State Security Police] put more and more pressure on him to do so. Finally, he went underground for months—until the Wall fell—living in various worker apartments for Vietnamese, whose inhabitants often all looked the same to the monitors and Stasi agents. Nguyen does not know how long he might have continued on in this way. For him, reunification was a godsend, for now he could resurface. He even found work as an engineer in Brandenburg. Nguyen's history is atypical for the majority of contract workers in the GDR; however, it clearly demonstrates the fundamental problem of foreigners' employment in the GDR. The SED needed the foreign workforce, but it soon encountered the consequences of this exchange, especially those arising from interaction between foreigners and the native population, and responded with deep-seated distrust. Integration was not a desired outcome.

Foreign workers and students had been coming to the GDR since the 1960s, where there was always a labor shortage despite the building of the Berlin Wall. The state signed a short term Qualification Agreement with its Polish neighbor in 1963 and a commuter agreement in 1966, on the basis of which 3,000 to 4,000 Polish men and women worked in the border region every year. Agreements followed with Hungary (1967), Algeria (1974), Cuba (1975 and 1978), and Mozambique (1979). Official propaganda represented the presence of "foreign workers" in "the Worker and Farmer State" as "workforce cooperation" within the framework of "socialist economic integration." As long as the GDR was economically superior to the other socialist states, workers would come from those states to "build socialism in their homeland" after their residence in the GDR. The GDR promoted this cooperation as a kind of "solidarity through training," meant to aid other countries' liberation movements as well as younger nation-states.

With these buzz words, the GDR deliberately set itself apart from the Federal Republic, denouncing the latter's guest-worker policies as the continuation of the National Socialist policy on foreign workers. Meanwhile, the notion of solidarity became increasingly suspect among SED leaders in the 1970s. Because there were not enough workers from the European brother states in the Eastern Trade Association, the socialist developing countries presented an attractive alternative. Political policies now competed with economic considerations. The advent of the agreement with Mozambique is particularly interesting.

Socialist Discipline

In November 1977, the government office responsible for employment and wages in the GDR rejected the placement of untrained Mozambican workers as politically intolerable. In early 1979, this policy expired, and 2,000 Mozambicans could soon accept "paid employment in socialist factories." Mozambique's fiscal debt to the GDR must have played a role in this policy change. According to the agreement, the debt was supposed to be amortized through the partial remuneration of the contract workers.

Twenty years ago, the SED finally began to use foreign workers out of economic interests. On April 11, 1980, the GDR signed a new agreement with Vietnam, which had been sending apprentices to the GDR since the (1967) Vietnam Solidarity Action "for the temporary employment and training of Vietnamese workers in factories" in the GDR. In terms of training, the agreement refers tersely to the "acquisition and enhancement of practical job experience in the process of productive operation" and advanced training in adult education. The agreement offered employment for technical workers from 18 to 35 years old, for university cadres up to 40 years old, as well as for Vietnamese who had previously completed their training in the GDR. If the agreement placed a great deal of focus on training and professionalization, it had little relevance in the individual company. The contract workers sought material advantages from their stay in the GDR in order to support their families at home. The Vietnamese saw the advanced training, which often took place in addition to their regular work schedules, as an unnecessary additional burden.

The agreement between the GDR and Vietnam provided a model for further contract agreements. On July 1, 1980, the corresponding framework directive "on the temporary employment of foreign workers in GDR factories" took effect. The directive clarified where the GDR would recruit workers from, explicitly excluding "workers from European socialist countries." Agreements on a smaller scale followed with Mongolia (1982), Angola (1985), and China (1986). Only in 1987 did the last phase of the GDR's foreign-worker plan begin with the massive introduction of Vietnamese contract workers. In an addendum to the bilateral agreement, the GDR clearly stipulated that labor was of higher priority than professional training. With Vietnamese help, the SED hoped, for example, to remedy shortages in the clothing industry. Within two years, 50,000 Vietnamese came to the GDR; the number of contract workers reached a high point in 1989 with approximately 91,000. The largest groups among them were the 60,000 Vietnamese, 15,000 Mozambicans, 13,000 Hungarians, and 8,000 Cubans. Statistics according to gender and age exist only for the foreign-resident population in the GDR: in 1989, 76 percent of the contract workers were between 18 and 39 years of age, 54 percent were men and 22 percent were women.

Few GDR citizens knew anything about the foreign workers. Contrary to the government's propaganda, foreigners' employment and residence were politically sensitive topics, which few newspaper articles addressed during the entire 1980s. In everyday life, the contract workers felt the effects of this political insensitivity on two levels: they lived isolated from the GDR population, and they were subject to strict behavioral norms that led to conflicts. From the perspective of the SED and their homelands, they were national delegates who were there to fulfill their training and employment contract with "socialist discipline." Their individual interests and needs were subordinate. [. . .]

Sometimes One Just Had to Fight Back

[. . .] To a great extent, the relationship between native workers and contract workers was shaped by the factory's internal hierarchy. It was not difficult to discover that foreigners were at a disadvantage in conflicts. [. . .] There were often disputes about everyday affairs, such as wages. The contract workers could lose wages if they did not attend training events. Because the German foremen determined the contract workers' wage brackets, their fulfillment of production quotas, and whether or not they were performing satisfactorily at work, racist motives were always afoot. Discrimination took on complex quotidian forms: German colleagues took longer on their breaks or left work earlier—liberties their foreign colleagues were not allowed to take. Sometimes they had to work demeaning jobs in the factories. Mozambicans were sent to particularly grimy large machines with the comment that "they were black anyway." Offensive names such as "coal" for persons of color and "Fijis" for Vietnamese became part of the everyday cultural landscape. When contract workers refused to carry out directives that they felt were unfair or exploitative, many a German boss reacted with threats to call the police or to begin processing their return to the homeland. A Mozambican named David from Hoyerswerda reports that his employer occasionally hit them in such situations: "then there was a discussion about it, or the guy just hit back. The factory management discussed it and determined that the Mozambican should be sent home." When in one case the Mozambican group leader insisted on noting the racist assault in the employee's record, management decided to move the worker to another area. In this way, officials avoided trouble with their superiors, trouble that such a breach of taboo would certainly have provoked in the officially antifascist and antiracist GDR.

This ideological framework influenced not only contract workers' work in the factories but also their private lives. Most were housed collectively in factory-owned residence halls. The halls were often remote or located on the factory lot and were always monitored. A young contract worker complains, "We felt a little like prisoners, since it was difficult for others to visit us. From Monday to Friday we could only stay out until 10:00 P.M., couldn't have female visitors in our rooms, and if a fellow worker or a German colleague came to visit us, he had to produce personal identification and answer questions for the guard. I didn't think that was right; it made people uncomfortable, the few who trusted us." Because the contract workers came to the GDR primarily without family and were separated by gender in their living quarters, there was a de facto demand on the part of the government that they relinquish any thought of a family life during their years in the GDR. In practice, the factories could enforce this segregation only on a limited basis. Some guards were understanding, and many were overwhelmed when their residents rebelled against the visitor regulations.

Thus, the "foreign workers'" private contacts remained a sticking point for authorities. The intensity of oversight also depended on the home countries' stance. Representatives of the Vietnamese embassy were particularly harsh. With the help of the German residence-hall directors, they organized nightly raids to root out "illegal overnight stays" in the halls. The embassy was also suspicious of Vietnamese-born interpreters in the factory, as well as former students who had come to the GDR in the 1960s and were now GDR citizens. Vietnam apparently wanted to remove every temptation for the newly sent "workers." In 1987, when the largest Vietnamese contingents came to the GDR, the Vietnamese Interior Ministry began working with the Stasi [State Security Police] on the general "political-operative security" of its contract workers.

Some Worked, the Others Cashed In

It was particularly precarious for contract workers when, despite the restrictions, they cultivated private relationships—especially when they did so with GDR citizens or when female workers became pregnant. Seeing the reality of the situation, some factory officials did distribute birth-control pills, but the women sometimes had problems with them, and pregnancies still occurred. Only Polish women could deliver their babies in the GDR. Until 1988, most contract workers were forced to abort or were sent home. Mozambicans were sent home automatically in all cases of pregnancy. When a German woman became impregnated by a contract worker, she frequently concealed his identity in order to prevent disciplinary action by the homeland. In the late 1980s, an increasing number of Vietnamese sought to avoid being sent home. Several were spending a second employment period in the GDR and were estranged from their homeland. Some went underground like Nguyen; others paid an exoneration fee based on their level of training.

The Stasi feared for the GDR's reputation because of this "buying one's freedom" policy. According to their information, the unskilled had to pay the Vietnamese state 5,000 marks; technical workers, 10,000; and college graduates, 24,000 to the Vietnamese state. From the Vietnamese perspective, the workers' residence in the GDR was a privilege that came with monetary value. Foreign workers contributed to the economy in the most varied ways: during the contingents' official selection according to achievement and social criteria, such as relationship to war victims, there was widespread corruption. Whole families went into debt while bribing officials in the Vietnamese Labor Ministry to send one of their own into the GDR. The Vietnamese state officially collected 12 percent of the contract worker's wages as a contribution "to the reconstruction and defense of the fatherland," and child support and social security contributions flowed into the country from the GDR. However, the children did not receive a part of the Vietnamese state's take. Nor did the former contract workers, who suffered from the consequences of their health-damaging work in GDR factories, receive the social security money they paid into the system.

Though the original source of conflict and difficulty in the contract workers' lives was the arbitrariness of the authorities, increasingly uneasy relations with the GDR population added to the tension between the workers and their surroundings. After 1981, David also began feeling the daily effects of some GDR citizens' latent racism. His complaints to the police fell on deaf ears. But there were also conflicts about supply shortages that were unique to socialism. Whoever had come to terms with the GDR's employment opportunities and culture of scarcity—no great expectations but a modest prosperity—were vexed by the ambition of some contract workers. These workers tried to yield maximum results from their stay, and their efforts often collided with the interests of German colleagues or German customers in the "purchasing chain." By the early 1980s, youths had already attacked a Vietnamese residence hall in Thuringia.

[. . .] According to a Free German Federation of Trade Unions report, this assault was supposed to keep the contract workers from overfulfilling production norms, which eventually would have placed the factory's German workers under additional pressure to perform. Despite widespread consciousness of "Germans' high-caliber workmanship," workers constantly asked themselves how much effort they wanted to make in the factory considering the limited consumer product lines that were available for their purchase.

The contract workers, whose standard of comparison was their impoverished homeland, worked for hard cash. In one report, the Stasi found fault with the Vietnamese workers' "ostensible material interests and ideological disinterest," but the organized "purchasing" of scarce products raised particular distrust among the population and attracted the secret police's attention. Many contract workers chose one among them to go into stores when desired products arrived.

Outside of work, the Vietnamese sewed and sold jeans and traded electrical appliances. Many of the desired products were also meant to be sent home: the sale of two motorcycles could be enough to buy a house in Vietnam. Broad sections of the population viewed these aggressive consumer practices as illegal "speculation." [. . .] The GDR government made use of such prejudices as well. In 1981, it launched a campaign against the "all-consuming" Poles, which ultimately served to discredit *Solidarnosc* and Polish reforms. In 1989, this development reached its high point: the SED limited the quantities of consumer products that foreigners were allowed to purchase. This included restrictions on contract workers' product shipments back home. The GDR media reported widely about the "buying up of consumer products" and the government's countermeasures, which were largely supported by a majority of the population. The GDR's final crisis brought more than reunification and the end of the SED regime. Many citizens also saw the situation as a crisis and used the new freedom of speech to air their sentiments; these expressions often were directed at foreigners. [. . .]

Most contract workers returned to their homelands after their contracts expired. In 1995, the number of former contract workers in united Germany was reduced to 10,000. In 1991, just a few weeks after the riots in Hoyerswerda, David boarded a plane back to his homeland. A positive assessment of the situation was difficult for him. Whether or not contract workers remain in Germany today depends on whether they retained their jobs, found new ones, or achieved independence. In 1997, these criteria became the foundation for permanent legal residence in Germany. Originally, most had come to find work; only a few could do so once the GDR disappeared.

3

IS THE BOAT FULL?

XENOPHOBIA, RACISM, AND VIOLENCE

SOLINGEN, 1993. The aftermath of a fatal arson attack by four local youth that killed five members of the Turkish Genç family. The charred ruins of their house, set off against a bucolic landscape, came to epitomize the brutality of racist attacks in the newly unified Germany. The banner hanging outside the second floor reads, "We demand a general strike now! Germans and foreigners together against racism."

ALTHOUGH THE YEARS directly following reunification gripped Germany in a cycle of high-profile racist attacks—followed by investigations, candlelight vigils, human chains, trials, mourning, coalition building, and fear—the German debate on anti-immigrant violence had begun at least 20 years before. This chapter presents a historical account of the interplay between immigration policy and racist violence.

We begin with a cover story from the mainstream magazine *Der Spiegel*, published four months before West Germany's November 1973 moratorium on foreign-labor recruitment. The article sets an alarmist tone that would characterize public sentiment on immigration throughout the decade—giving voice to the fear that "a new Harlem" was growing beyond control in Germany's metropolitan areas. Catalyzed by a mounting concern about domestic and pro-Palestinian terrorism, the xenophobic discourse of the mid-1970s called forth a threatening metaphorical vocabulary of floods and waves, shrinking islands and beleaguered boats. This rhetoric in refugee policy hearkened back to 1942, when Swiss Federal Council member Eduard von Steiger explained Switzerland's selective refugee policy as follows: "He who must captain a small, heavily occupied lifeboat, while thousands of victims of a shipwreck are screaming to be saved, will inevitably appear insensitive when he cannot accept all of them. And yet he is still humane when he warns against false hopes and tries at least to save those he has already accepted in."

The new period of recession and financial sobriety after 1973 recast the children and relatives of guest workers as a collective oceanic force overwhelming the German populace, its neighborhoods, and its magnanimous social-welfare apparatus. A new narrative emerged in the immigration discourse of the early 1990s, according to which Turkish and Italian businesses and religious institutions were uprooting traditional German merchants and neighborhood norms. This anxiety finds its extreme expression in the parodic fairy tale "The Last Germans" and the 1982 "Heidelberg Manifesto," included in this chapter. The manifesto arose from a movement among Germany's university elites to contest the "tide" of immigration, for the good of natives and foreigners alike. Its academic signatories were quick to deny any sympathy with National Socialist racial ideology and openly lamented the conflation of anti-immigrant sentiment with proto-fascist ideas. In demanding a new public debate on migration, the Heidelberg platform exemplified a gradualist and cautionary stance that appealed to many liberal intellectu-als and politicians, who sought to counter xenophobia by reducing immi-gration. The manifesto also evinces a preoccupation with West Germany's low birthrate, juxtaposing the ubiquitous icon of the "guest-worker child" with that of the stagnating German nuclear family. The professors' urgent appeal for the regeneration of the German family would reemerge later in the "Children, Not Indians" *(Kinder statt Inder)* anti-immigration demonstra-tions of May 2000.

In August 1983, a 23-year-old asylum seeker, Kemal Altun, committed sui-cide by jumping from a window of West Berlin's Administrative Court build-ing. Altun's choice of death over deportation refocused the national debate about asylum. Still, in an editorial entitled "Victims of Freeloaders" (1985), the former mayor of Berlin, Heinrich Lummer, employed the "flood" metaphor to galvanize his call to restrict asylum. According to Lummer, West Germany had a worldwide reputation as the most accommodating of asylum destinations, attracting a large number of "inauthentic"—that is, economic—refugees.

A year after Lummer's 1985 editorial, Theo Sommer, editor in chief of the left-center weekly *Die Zeit,* attempted to address the conflation of asylum and immigration in public debate. For Sommer, the mid-1980s' alarmism about an impending asylum disaster was a result of German politicians' unwilling-ness to take responsibility for the labor-recruitment strategies of their pre-decessors. Sommer emphasized that among the 270,000 rejected yet "toler-ated" asylum seekers living in Germany in 1986, two-thirds were from Soviet Bloc countries, not from the usually suspected labor-recruitment countries.

The 1993 *Spiegel* feature "A Riot in the Eyesore" considers the political af-termath of the Solingen murders in the context of the three high-profile at-tacks in Hoyerswerda, Mölln, and Rostock that preceded it. Another feature piece, "A Protector Who Yearns for Protection" (1993), tracks the career of the first black police officer in the former GDR, Sam Meffire, and his expe-rience growing up as an Afro-German and Dresden resident, before and after reunification. In the wake of the high-profile hate crimes of the early 1990s, many public intellectuals began to question the fundamental terms of the asylum and immigration debates. Essayist Lothar Baier scrutinizes main-stream concepts like xenophobia, racism, and antiracism in his 1993 essay "The Grace of the Right Birth" by contrasting American and German con-ceptions of race and critiquing the principles of the German antiracist movement. May Ayim's 1993 essay on race and German reunification elabo-rates on Baier's critique of leftist antiracism from a feminist point of view. For Ayim, the left's preoccupation with the psychological profile of right-wing youth overlooks the global causes of refugee movements: war, poverty, and environmental destruction.

Two further texts, by Alexander Böker and Uta Andresen, analyze right-wing youth identity and affiliation from two nearly opposing angles. Focusing on music, fashion, and subcultural forms, Böker considers the social benefits of group-level identity in apolitical skinhead youth communities. Andresen's article attributes right-wing ideology among youth to the authoritarian educational system and conformist socialization in East Germany. Our documentation would be incomplete without the platforms of Germany's right-wing political parties. This chapter includes the Republican Party of Germany's 2002 anti-immigration platform and a speech by Bundestag member Martin Hohmann, formerly of the Christian Democratic Union.

Racism and violence in the early 1990s profoundly influenced German music and literature. In 1992, the transethnic hip-hop group Advanced Chemistry produced "Foreign in My Own Country," a song about Europeanization, racism, and political profiteering in the face of xenophobic attacks. When the Mozambican Alberto Adriano was murdered in June 2000, another hip-hop group, Brother's Keepers, produced a tribute to him, in which the singers lamented "throwing away their airtime" on less urgent topics in the 1980s. Daniel Bax's 2000 article examines the self-fashioned notoriety of the right-wing hard-core band Die Böhsen Onkelz (The Evil Uncles), who describe themselves as the "burr in the ass of the nation." After publicly disavowing their more anti-Turkish lyrics from the 1980s, the Onkelz have recently experienced a revival among their skinhead youth base. The chapter concludes with an appeal for vigilance from Berlin's *Islamische Zeitung*, more than a decade after the Mölln and Solingen attacks.

1

THE TURKS ARE COMING! SAVE YOURSELF IF YOU CAN!

First published as "Die Türken kommen: Rette sich wer kann" in *Der Spiegel* (July 30, 1973). Translated by David Gramling.

Almost a million Turks are now living in the Federal Republic. Some 1.2 million more are waiting their turn back home. The pressure from the Bosporus is exacerbating a crisis that has been smoldering in metropolitan areas already overrun with foreigners. Cities like Berlin, Munich, and Frankfurt can barely withstand the invasion any longer. Ghettos are developing, and sociologists are prophesying the downfall of the cities, increased criminality, and social misery like that found in Harlem.

The pub at Kottbusser Gate was once the stuff of authentic Kreuzberg: a corner storefront, Berliner Kindl beer, beef sandwiches, a banking club in the back room. These days, there is a lamb spit rotating on a vertical axis at the counter, the coffee is sweet and translucent, and Oriental sing-song is coming from the music box.

Hisar is the name of this corner joint now; it means "fortress"—and the name does not seem inappropriate. Under the bullet holes in the ceiling, another new proprietor is keeping watch. Way in the back, Zeki, Ahmet, and a few others are crouching around, playing a game called Jokey. The dealer, Hasan, is cashing in tenners at the table.

The Berlin dialect of German that the Turkish residents speak is only a ruse for business purposes. And around the corner, on the next street, and on the next street after that, an inexhaustible clientele from the "land of the morning" is alive and well.

At the entrance to 50 Lausitzer Street hang the mailboxes of 30 renters, all of whose names end with "-oglu," "-ek," or "-can." On Oranien Street, where Paul Lincke once lived at 64 and where one can almost hear the melody from "Berlin Air," men in pedal pants are strolling like flaneurs. The vegetable stands are colorful and opulent. In front of the butcher shops hang gutted mutton chops, and everywhere Turkish flags with stars and half-moons indicate that Kreuzberg is indeed "Little Smyrna"—pronounced in good Berlinish, of course. [. . .]

Some 1.2 million have signed up on the waiting list in Turkey. This reserve "could make its way to Germany if new regulations are implemented for 1976," reports Josh Stingl, president of the Institute for Labor, who sees insurmountable problems ahead. Still, today's problems are difficult enough. The fact that the officials now call them "foreign employees" does not mean that the Legacy of the Guest Worker has disappeared. An official fiction persists in which foreigners are only welcome in the Federal Republic as exotic and cheap helpers for the affluent classes who will soon go back to where they came from. [. . .]

How naturally the phrase *Turkish ghetto* rolls off the tongues of city-council members and politicians alike. Back when he was mayor of Munich, Hans-Jochen Vogel, now federal housing minister, observed that "a small Harlem has developed here." Indeed, this nightmare is still upon us: a city of marginal groups, condemned to the chronic malaise of apathy amid racial conflict, criminality, and dilapidated buildings. The first Harlem symptoms are already visible. In the eroding sectors of German cities, "a new subproletariat is growing in which the seed of social diseases is sown," says Richter Franz. [. . .]

"If someone gets stabbed," says a northern German police commissioner, "a Turk is usually involved." Even with such ethnically specific forms of criminality, the statistics are lower than one might expect. In Bremen, for example, the number of dangerous or serious physical assaults perpetrated by members of the foreigner population has doubled, whereas it has quadrupled among the entire population. [. . .]

Segregation and the displacement of minorities into underprivileged subcultures are widespread. The authors of the Stuttgart Foreigner Study sought insights from the American experience; in the famous "melting-pot country," the immigrant ghettos from the era 1910 to 1960 still remain, "even in the generation of the children and grandchildren," says the American sociologist [Barbara] Kantrowitz. The Stuttgart study claims that this phenomenon is "one more reason to sound the alarm against segregation in residential areas."

Perhaps the warnings are coming too late. Heeding the Kreuzberg slogan "Save yourself if you can," a few thousand residents are now setting their sights on new districts. The cities themselves, however, cannot escape.

2

HEIDELBERG MANIFESTO

First published as "Heidelberger Manifest" in the *Frankfurter Rundschau* (March 4, 1982). Translated by Tes Howell. The signatories of this document were Prof. Dr. Bambeck (Frankfurt), Prof. Dr. R. Fricke (Karlsruhe), Prof. Dr. W. Haverbeck (Vlotho), Prof. Dr. J. Illies (Schlitz), Prof. Dr. P. Manns (Mainz), Prof. Dr. H. Rasch (Bad Soden), Prof. Dr. W. Rutz (Bochum), Prof. Dr. Th. Schm.-K. (Bochum), Prof. Dr. K. Schürmann (Mainz), Prof. Dr. F. Siebert (Mainz), Prof. Dr. G. Stadtmüller (Munich).

We are observing a development with great concern, a development initiated by a euphorically optimistic economic policy that has resulted in a state of affairs in which approximately 5 million guest workers and their families are now living and working in our country. Obviously, it has not been possible to halt the influx, despite a moratorium on recruitment. In 1989 alone, the number of registered foreigners rose by 309,000; 194,000 of those were Turks.

The situation has been exacerbated by the fact that little more than half of the necessary amount of children are being born in order to maintain zero growth of the German population in West Germany. A renewal of the procreative function of the German family is urgently needed.

Many Germans already feel foreign in their own neighborhoods, workplaces, and homeland in general—just as foreign as the guest workers are in their new surroundings.

The government's decision to promote the influx of foreigners in an era of unbridled economic growth is now widely recognized as questionable. Up to this point, the German population has not been informed of the significance and consequences of this process. We believe that the establishment of a politically independent consortium is necessary, one that will work in dialogue with politicians toward a (preferably) universal solution. This problem must be resolved if it is not to become a fateful impasse for guest workers as well as the host country.

One complication in the search for a solution to this problem is the fact that one can no longer pose the necessary questions in public debate without incurring accusations of Nazism. For this reason, we must stress that we stand firmly on the foundation of the Basic Law in all our efforts toward a solution. We emphatically oppose ideological nationalism, racism, right- and left-wing extremism.

The integration of large masses of non-German foreigners is not possible without threatening the German people, language, culture, and religion. Every people, including the Germans, has a natural right to preserve its identity and character in its residential areas. Respect for other peoples necessitates their preservation as well, not their assimilation ("Germanization"). We perceive Europe as an industrious community of peoples and nations that gives rise to a coherent higher order through culture and history. As Solzhenitsyn suggests, "Every nation is a one-time facet of a divine plan." On April 5, 1981, the voters of a multiracial nation, Switzerland, approved a model.

Although we know about the abuse of the word *Volk,* we must remind the reader that the Basic Law emanates from the term *Volk,* indeed from the German *Volk,* and that the federal president and the members of the government take this oath: "I swear that I will dedicate my energies to the good of the German *Volk,* further its interests, and prevent injury to it." Whoever understands this oath cannot deny that it is the German people whose "preservation" is at stake. And those who decide that there are no peoples worth preserving disregard the rules of scientific hermeneutics and grossly misinterpret our concerns.

We do not hesitate to remind you that the goal of reunification—an obligation established in the preamble of the Basic Law—could be most grievously endangered through the current foreigner policy.

How is reunification to remain a possibility when many regions of Germany are becoming ethnically foreign? What hope for the future do the hundreds of thousands of guest-worker children have if they are illiterate in both their native language and German? What hope do our own children have when they are being educated predominantly in classes with foreigners? Only active and viable German families can preserve our people for the future.

Technological advancement continues to offer various possibilities to make the employment of guest workers superfluous. The highest priority of economic management must be to bring machines to people, not people to machines. Solving this problem means improving the living conditions of the guest workers in their own countries through targeted development assistance—not here with us. Reuniting guest workers with their families in the ancestral homeland—on a voluntary basis, of course—will relieve the burden on our overindustrialized country, a country suffering from environmental destruction.

Almost none of the responsible persons or the functionaries from prominent social institutions have dared to face facts, let alone to propose a realistic concept for a long-term policy. To this end, we believe the formation of a politically independent consortium is necessary, one that will encourage organizations, associations, and individuals to collaboratively dedicate themselves to the preservation of our people—its language, culture, religion, and way of life.

We as university instructors, a profession with lofty tasks and responsibilities that compel us to ensure an appropriate and reasonable education for foreigners in our country (especially those from the so-called third world), must, on the grounds of our professional legitimacy, point out the seriousness of the current situation and the menacing consequences of a trend already under way.

3
HEINRICH LUMMER
VICTIMS OF FREELOADERS

First published as "Opfer von Schmarotzern" in *Die Zeit* (April 26, 1985). Translated by Tes Howell. Lummer (b. 1932, Berlin) was a Christian Democratic Union member of the Bundestag from 1987 to 1998. He published this editorial during his term as mayor of West Berlin.

A Constitutional Right Is Being Abused

A twofold problem is confronting our asylum policy. How can abuse of the asylum system be effectively countered, and what steps must federal law enforcement take upon realizing that the Federal Republic of Germany is *not* in a position to accommodate even a fraction of the potentially qualified asylum seekers?

Everyone familiar with the issues understands that a large percentage of asylum seekers are coming to our country not because of "political persecution" (article 16 of the Basic Law) but for economic reasons and because the drawn-out legal process allows them to receive social-welfare assistance for many years, thanks to German taxpayers. Meanwhile, the message has spread through the global grapevine that any foreigner who comes to the Federal Republic seeking asylum can live here indefinitely at our expense. An alarmingly large contingent of asylum seekers is making its presence felt through violent crime and drug offenses, as well as through prostitution and illegal employment. Law enforcement has investigated one in two Lebanese men living in Berlin for such offenses; foreigners are responsible for 90 percent of the city's large-scale heroin dealing.

A policy that turns a blind eye to these occurrences and that rejects—allegedly for humanitarian reasons—the precautionary measures necessary for protecting the state and its citizens does not fulfill its obligation toward the native population. More importantly, such a policy discredits the asylum law, disadvantages those who really are in need, and causes consternation among those citizens who agree with the asylum law as such but do not wish to see their state fall victim to freeloaders. Such a policy is incapacitated and estranged from reality. It fails to follow the example of other, no less liberal and constitutional countries, which have, in their sober estimation of the situation, long since instituted provisions to prevent an excessive stream of asylum seekers and asylum abuse. The designation "asylum seeker" must not become derogatory. [. . .]

It would be presumptuous to believe that the spatially restricted Federal Republic, which has accepted the largest portion of displaced persons from Germany's eastern areas, several million refugees from the GDR, and nearly 4 million foreigners, could be Noah's Ark for the entire, unsettled world.

I can suggest one possible solution to this problem: a supplement to article 16 [of the Basic Law] that would include a legal caveat, international harmonization of asylum law, regionalization of asylum (i.e., granting asylum only in the region of origin), elimination of the necessity for asylum through diplomatic pressure and foreign aid to applicants' countries of origin, and equalization of the financial burden between heavily and minimally burdened host countries. [. . .]

There should and must be a rigorous and controversial discussion on the subject. But empty pseudoliberal phrases and ideology, in place of substance, are not beneficial to the debate.

4

THEO SOMMER

CLOSED DUE TO OVERFLOW?

First published as "Wegen Überfüllung geschlossen?" in *Die Zeit* (August 29, 1986). Translated by David Gramling. Sommer (b. 1930) was editor in chief of *Die Zeit* from 1973 to 1992.

Hysteria and Folkish Small-Mindedness in the Asylum Debate

"Will it be mere coincidence or a dearth of means of transportation that will prevent us from soon becoming a country with a majority African-Asian population, rocked by the social, national, and religious conflicts brought about by overcongestion?" This sentence comes from a *Frankfurter Allgemeine Zeitung* lead article. It cannot be mere coincidence that the same sentence was then touted in the *National-Zeitung*, a newspaper that has been keeping steadfast watch over the increasing threat of an "asylum-seeker state-of-emergency" and demanding "tough crack-down measures . . . to preserve the German character of Germany." The *FAZ* lead reporter sees the issue no differently. The unbridled guarantee of asylum, he suggests, could force our state "to surrender the German Nation in the western part of Germany."

Let's get real. The numbers cannot justify the doomsayers' dam-breach metaphors: refugee flash floods, fountains of asylum seekers, streams of foreigners, waves of immigrants. A hundred thousand asylum seekers per year— 20 percent of whom are officially recognized and a further 30 percent of whom stay in the country despite being turned down—does not throw us off kilter, economically or socially speaking. Neither does a population with 7.2 percent foreigners throw us off balance in terms of blood. Some 4.5 million out of 61 million: is that really too much to contend with? The number of naturalizations does not present any cause for anxiety either; all of 38,000 in 1984. Among those, if one does not count the "naturalizations by entitlement" of ancestral Germans, were 15,000 "discretionary naturalizations." There is just as little justifiable cause for excitement about asylum figures; the Federal Republic has distributed 67,000 allowances since its founding; 270,000 rejected applicants still live among us, and of those, two-thirds are from East Bloc countries. [. . .]

On one point we may not deceive ourselves. The topic under discussion these days in this country is not merely how to defend against the abuse of the constitutional right of asylum. Truthfully, the debate is about how we encounter the foreigners in our midst. Behind this debate, though, is the question of our self-understanding as a people. Do we want to stay only among our own kind—together, like they said in the Thousand Year Reich? Or do we open ourselves, within the parameters of reason, to the influx of the foreign, to the burden as well as the enrichment that immigration brings? [. . .]

It should give us pause when 150 Tamils put everything on the line to escape to the Federal Republic on a rusted-out boat. What is wrong with us? Do Germans—of whom 800,000 were refugees during the Nazi period—have no heart left for suffering people? And no vision for the future other than folkish small-mindedness?

5

ADVANCED CHEMISTRY

FOREIGN IN MY OWN COUNTRY

First released as "Fremd im eigenen Land" on the album *Fremd im eigenen Land* (MZEE) in 1992. Translated by Tes Howell. Advanced Chemistry, founded in 1987, is considered Germany's first political hip-hop band. Members are Toni L, Linguist, Gee-One, DJ Mike MD, and Torch. AC is one of the few German-language groups to become a member of the Universal Zulu Nation, an international hip-hop awareness group founded in New York in the 1970s by Afrika Bambaataa. A radio news clip that precedes the recording of "Foreign in My Own Country" frames the song as a response to the arson attack of Rostock-Lichtenhagen in August 1992.

I have a green passport with a golden eagle on it
that shows that I pull my hair out all the time.
But seriously: I get so much grief,
even though I drive slowly and never get drunk.
All that talk of a European federation—
When I go to the border by train or bus,
I ask myself why I'm the only one who has to show identification,
who has to prove his identity!
Is it so unusual that an Afro-German speaks German but
doesn't have pale skin?
The problem is the ideas in the system:
a real German must also look German—
blue eyes, blond hair, then you're okay.
Was there ever a time when it wasn't like that?!
"Are you going back to your homeland someday?"
"Where? To Heidelberg? Where I live?"
"No, you know what I mean. . . . "
Come on, I've heard these questions since I was young.
I was born in this country twenty years ago,
but I still ask myself sometimes:
what am I doing here?
Ignorant babble with no end;
dumb comments, I already know them all:
"Um, are you an American or are you from Africa?"
Another comment about my hair—what's so strange about it?
"Oh, you're German? Come on, don't try to fool me":
You want proof? Here is my proof:
If you please, my name is Frederick Hahn.
I was born here, but I probably don't look like it,
I'm not a foreigner nor a resettler, tourist, or immigrant,
but a German citizen, from this country.
Where's the problem? Everyone should go wherever they want:
to ski in Switzerland, to be a tourist to Prague,

to study in Vienna, to be an au pair in Paris.
Others don't even want to leave their country, but they have to flee
xenophobia, inferiority complexes.
I want to shock and provoke,
to motivate my brothers and sisters again.
I already have a plan,
and when I'm ready, it'll be an eye for an eye, tooth for tooth.
I hope the radio stations will play this song,
for I'm not an exception but one of many.
Not recognized, foreign in my own country,
Not a foreigner yet still a stranger.

I have a green passport with a golden eagle on it,
but I grew up here with an Italian heritage.
Because of this, I've been taunted.
Politicians and the media report that, sooner or later, the
"capacity for assimilation" will be "reached."
The public is given explanations, its collective head is turned,
prompted to believe that its existence will be threatened by foreigners.
So the citizen cultivates prejudices and thinks
that there is a grave possibility of losing his all-important
German standard of living.
Unfortunately, no one comes along asking who would do
the low-paying, undesirable work.
Hardly anyone considers or values the knowledge of
why this country is doing so well—
how the guest worker has contributed significantly
to the raging economic development since the 1950s
but lives with a weak foothold in society,
plays the role of scapegoat in times of crisis,
and the actual problem being ignored is simply
swept under the rug inconspicuously.
Not recognized, a foreigner in my own country.
Not a foreigner yet still a stranger.

I have a green passport with a golden eagle on it,
but no one asks about it when I end up in the wrong neighborhood.
"Hey, let's get him!"
Good thing I was always fast in the hundred-meter dash.
Violence in the form of a clenched fist,
or a glistening knife or a striking weapon.
Many will say we are exaggerating,
but we've lived here for twenty years and are
tired of being silent.

Pogroms happen, the police stand by,
a German citizen fears for his life.
The reunification on television:
in the beginning I was excited, but I regretted
that quickly,
for it's never been so bad as it is now!
Politician types talk a lot but remain cold and calculating—
all this plays right into their plans;
they look concerned and travel to the scene,
hold a child in their lap, and show off for the press,
a new seat in the Bundestag with every flash of the camera;
there they pass a new law.
Of course, asylum seekers must leave,
and no one messes with the fascists!
This is not my world if only skin color and heritage count;
the illusion of foreign infiltration accrues political value.
Every Hans or Franz passes judgment in ignorance, complains
and bellows, considers himself an expert.
I have been raised to see things differently:
to look behind façades, understand contexts,
to face every human being *en direct* with respect,
ethical values that transcend national borders.
I have a green passport with a golden eagle on it,
but I'm still foreign here.

6

A RIOT IN THE EYESORE

First published as "Mal Randale im Schandfleck" in *Der Spiegel* (June 7, 1993). Translated by David Gramling. This article is a follow-up analysis of the arson attack that took place in Solingen on May 29, 1993.

Everyday Discrimination in the City of Solingen

A dark hole cleaves the charred-out ruins of the house at 81 Lower Werner Street. Where the low side door used to be, three pairs of children's sneakers are still sitting neatly ordered on the doormat, just as they were on the evening of the arson attack.

The neighbors have always valued such things; order must reign in this district of tidy, quiet people who know very little of the charged atmosphere of metropolitan neighborhoods like Berlin's Kreuzberg or Hamburg's St. Georg. The Turkish Genç family was thought of as assimilated on this narrow street, where the people and the houses are of equally solid build.

"They were nice, orderly people," says an assembly-line foreman named Klaus Stamm from the neighborhood. "They were always friendly and said hello," said one local fitter, Klaus Schulze, "and the women didn't even wear head scarves."

But the 19 people living at house number 81 didn't really belong, no matter how well they ascribed to German secondary virtues. Even after 13 years, there was still very little contact with the outside, except with the Keinerts next door.

"We had parties together and helped each other with tasks around the house," recounts Hubertus Keinert. Eighteen-year-old Hatice, who died in the fire, was "like a daughter" to his wife, Käthe. The close friendship emerged out of a common fate. "We have no contact with anyone else here. We are also foreigners, so to speak." The Keinerts moved here from Saxony about ten years ago.

This mix of stubborn indifference and invisible apartheid is characteristic of the climate in Solingen and other places. It has a way of outlasting all the candlelight vigils, the moments of silence, and the declarations of political intention.

After the arson in Mölln, Solingen staged its own human chain of solidarity. For a while now, the Solingen Coalition against Racism and Fascism has been attempting to integrate Solingen's 7,000 Turks and has been struggling against extreme-right activities. After the arson [in Solingen], the Christian Democratic mayor, Bernd Krebs, went on camera before the world yet again and reported that there are absolutely no right-wing radicals in his city. The provincial legislator Erika Rothstein, majority leader of the SPD, had considered herself to be living on an "island of peace" until the attack. Now she must admit "we were dozing like Sleeping Beauty."

The facts belie the mayor's claims. According to his colleague Ms. Rothstein, there were plenty of reasons for the officials to wake from their slumber. Last year, the coalition counted two dozen xenophobic events, and the police came up with similar numbers.

About a year before the murderous arson, on May 16, 1992, two drunken young men from the Solingen skinhead scene stormed an asylum residence and beat three Tamils to the point that they required hospitalization.

In court, the attackers claimed that they had decided, quite spontaneously, to "go on a riot in that eyesore" of a building. A court sentenced the 25- and 20-year-old perpetrators to two years of probation. The presiding judge did not deem their action a "classical case of xenophobia," because the attack was not planned.

On the day after [the attack on the Genç family], a steady stream of ministers flocked in with words of sorrow, repulsion, and outrage, making the German audience all the more perplexed and the Turks all the more enraged. The tension was released on the following nights. With every windowpane broken by raging young Turks and with every burning car, the locals' sense of guilt for the five deaths decreased. With bleeding police officers and screaming crowds, the situation had gotten out of hand.

As the Turks came in from around the country, the opposing camps let loose on one another; vigilantes demanded blood and arms, and many local Solingen residents were racking their brains, thinking, "Now they want to carry out their war in our town! Wasn't there something going on in Mölln with drug dealers and pimps as well?"

But this time the Turks have no intention of scurrying away. After every death until now, they have called for prudence and caution. "Thus far it has just been the same old lip service," says Taner Aday, a spokesperson for the Turkish Association. "It appears that every city will have to go through the experiences that Hünxe, Mölln, and Solingen have gone through." But apparently the Turkish minority will not wait for this to happen.

7

ARTICLE 16 OF THE BASIC LAW OF THE FEDERAL REPUBLIC OF GERMANY

Translated by David Gramling. Three days before the Solingen arson attack, on May 26, 1993, the Bundestag amended the German constitution, or Basic Law, to restrict the provisions for political asylum in article 16. The amendment became law on July 1, 1993. Both versions are reprinted here.

Before July 1, 1993:

1. German citizenship may not be revoked. The loss of citizenship may only occur by mandate of a law and against the will of an individual if the individual will not consequently become stateless.

2. No German may be deported to foreign soil. Politically persecuted persons enjoy the right to asylum. [. . .]

[The following amendments went into effect after July 1, 1993:]

Article 16a:

1. Persons persecuted on political grounds shall have the right of asylum.

2. Paragraph 1 of this article may not be invoked by a person who enters the federal territory from a member state of the European Community or from another third state in which the standards of the Convention Relating to the Status of Refugees and of the Convention for the Protection of Human Rights and Fundamental Freedoms are assured. States outside the European Communities to which the criteria of the first sentence of this paragraph apply shall be accordingly specified by a law requiring the consent of the Bundesrat. In the cases specified in the first sentence of this paragraph, measures to terminate an applicant's stay may be set in motion without regard to any legal challenge that may have been raised against said measures.

3. By a law requiring the consent of the Bundesrat, states may be specified in which, on the basis of their laws, enforcement practices, and general political conditions, it can be safely concluded that neither political persecution nor inhumane or degrading punishment or treatment exists. It shall be presumed that a foreigner from such a state is not persecuted, unless he presents evidence justifying the conclusion that, contrary to this presumption, he is indeed persecuted on political grounds.

4. In the cases specified by paragraph 3 of this article and in other cases that are plainly unfounded or considered to be plainly unfounded, measures to terminate an applicant's stay may be suspended by a court only if serious doubts exist as to their legality; the scope of review may be limited, and tardy objections may be disregarded. Details shall be determined by further legislation. [. . .]

8

GIOVANNI DI LORENZO

A PROTECTOR WHO YEARNS FOR PROTECTION

First published as "Ein Beschützer voller Sehnsucht nach Schutz" in *Süddeutsche Zeitung* (April 1, 1993). Translated by Tes Howell. In 1996, 3 years after the publication of this article, Sam Meffire (b. 1970) was convicted of armed robbery and blackmail and sentenced to 10 years in prison. A 2000 film, *Dirt for Dinner* (*Dreckfresser*), directed by Branwen Okpako, narrates Meffire's story.

The tests a black Saxon must face and how he is determined to become a good police officer in Germany: A crazy mission

Sam is a Saxon. He has spent his life in Leipzig and Dresden. He came into the world on July 11, 1970, at 12:45 A.M. a few hours after his father, Samuel Njankouo Meffire of Cameroon, died. Sam grew up with his German mother and German grandparents. He likes Dresden, especially when the squares and streets in the old part of town are empty or when the Elbe reflects the colors of the dawning day. When he speaks of his city, the words "at home" flow naturally from his lips. The fact that Sam, a person who neither knew his father nor the land of his ancestors, identifies himself as an "Afro" and not as a German, which he actually is, has more to do with the people in this area than with any experience of a better life in another country. And still, he undertook the crazy mission of becoming the first black police officer in the new federal states—the part of Germany where the past three years of headlines have reported that it's open season on people like Sam.

Federal Interior Minister Seiters has announced he will make the police force more accessible to foreigners. Even Bavaria's Interior Minister Stoiber has embraced this project. Sam read about it: "A Turk or a Greek," he says, "has a much easier time of it. He looks different." As long as he is quiet, Sam looks like a combination of Roland Gift, the lead singer of the Fine Young

Cannibals, and Charly Muhamed Huber, who plays Commissar Kress's dark-skinned assistant on the detective series *The Old Man [Der Alte]*. But when he speaks, he attracts attention with his slight Saxon accent and a missing front tooth; Sam knocked it out himself while handling Asian nunchakus. He is wearing a T-shirt proclaiming "The Rebel" and shows an upper body sculpted by years of training. It is difficult to say whether Sam will really make it, whether he will lead a life as a civil servant in law enforcement, but he can at least explain his decision to become a cop in Saxony.

When the Wall fell, Sam had just completed an apprenticeship as a mason. He had become a father six months earlier; he and his former girl-friend named the child after his grandfather Samuel. The boy is now four years old, and Sam says that little Samuel can already sense whether someone really likes him or simply sees him as a "strange animal."

The new freedom [after the Wall fell] was also the freedom to think dif-ferently. Sam was suddenly treated with hostility. Sometimes young men in blue overalls deliberately crashed shopping carts into his legs at the super-market. Other times passersby would hiss "nigger" behind his back. Sam was afraid, and he had been afraid ever since young Nazis shot at him with tracer bullets and tried to storm his apartment in Dresden. Sometimes he did not leave the house for days. A girlfriend, also black, wanted to get him to safety. In Radebeul, near Dresden, she arranged a room for him in a women's flat-sharing collective immediately following reunification. "They did not see me as a man," Sam says, as though he were quoting a satire on the feminist mi-lieu, "but rather as an Afro."

Sam proposed to the Social Welfare Office in Radebeul that they establish a youth meeting place. The office set up rooms in a small, rundown castle on the outskirts of town. On a daily basis, he met young neo-Nazis here who re-spected him and probably even liked him, but Sam remarks that this fact did not stop them from attacking Vietnamese or nearly beating Afros to death on other occasions. [. . .]

Last October, Sam posed for a prominent Western advertising campaign on behalf of *Sächsische Zeitung* (newspaper). The photo's caption read, "A Saxon." Sam recalls that the agency originally hesitated to use his portrait; the black, shaved head seemed "too tough" to the advertising executives, but the cam-paign became a huge success for the agency: it was selected as the advertisement of 1992. To the frustration of many of his colleagues at the police department, Sam was suddenly a darling of the press. According to him, "They explained to me that I, as an Afro, am a real sympathetic character for the people." [. . .]

In the early 1960s—Sam does not know when for sure—a young man from Cameroon came to Leipzig to study; Samuel Njankouo Meffire's head was full of plans; he was ambitious. Soon he married a German woman, and in 1963, Sam's older brother, Moise, was born. Their German relatives tortured his mother, Christine. Sam still has his uncle's letter to her, in which he begs her to leave her black husband and claims she is in danger of gambling away the Western cultural heritage of two thousand years in her genes; Meffire meanwhile only cares about bragging to his tribe that he has a blonde, white wife.

For seven years, Christine could only make secret visits to her mother in Leipzig; her father no longer wanted to see her. When he [her father] came home early one day unannounced, Christine's mother hid her in a closet. Later, the grandparents tried to reconcile relations by taking in the five-year-old Sam for a while. For the young boy, this was the best time in his life. [. . .]

Deceptive Kindness

We met Adolf Hitler in front of the youth hangout Contact in Radebeul. Side part, moustache, brown belt, black boots—the leader of the local Nazi scene apparently felt safe in this city despite his appearance. Inside the club, almost all the youths are right-wing extremists. Sam is not afraid of them. His self-confidence is evident; he is physically well conditioned and feels a rush of adrenaline in this situation. As he enters the locale, the neo-Nazis remain calm; one of them even greets him amicably. Sam is still known around here from the time when he managed the hangout. Still, he says, one must not be deceived by the peacefulness; if they were drunk or one of them was being really nasty, these same, seemingly harmless youths could be murderers. He believes that nothing curbed the Dresden Nazi scene as well as the powerful special police unit Soko Rex [Special Command Right], established in July 1991, by Interior Minister Eggert. "Upon encountering these officers," says Sam, "most Nazis realized that there is resistance to them."

Sam is certainly a dedicated officer, and yet he still remains an outsider in his own country. "They'll never accept you," said the owner of a business across from Sam's old apartment in the women's collective, "the way you look." He meant German citizens, a designation he himself does not have, not neo-Nazis. Sam did not react to it, although his facial expression froze: "I'm afraid of what will happen if I let all my aggression out." In order not to lose self-control, he does not drink, not even liqueur-filled candy.

Someone at work suggested that he become an undercover agent someday. Sam politely declined, not so much because he fears for his safety but rather because he has recognized the trap in time. He says he wants to live in Germany, not just survive there.

9

LOTHAR BAIER

THE GRACE OF THE RIGHT BIRTH

First published as "Die Gnade der richtigen Geburt" in Lothar Baier, *Die verleugnete Utopie* (Berlin: Aufbau Taschenbuch Verlag, 1993). Translated by Tes Howell. Baier (1942–2004) was a prominent essayist, translator, author, and activist closely associated with the 1968 student revolts.

The New Racism and Raging Antiracism

There are countries in which the expression *racism* is not merely a vague ideological accusation. It possesses a precisely circumscribed meaning, for "race" in such contexts signifies something quite specific. In the United States, for example, "race" is an administrative category like religious affiliation. Under this rubric, the individual indicates that he is black or American Indian. This indication potentially enables him to participate in quota systems and promotional measures designated for these "races." To use a person's affiliation with one of these "races" against them is "racist" behavior—for instance, rejecting one's claim to promotional subsidy or social support. Racism is understood as something practical; the convictions behind it are not in question, nor is the biological implication that racism, understood as a derivation of earlier race theories, might entail.

This concept of racism cannot be transferred to German circumstances, because the social premises it relies upon do not exist here. But considering the crimes of National Socialism, one might doubt the logic of categorizing the crimes in Rostock, Hünxe, Mölln, or Solingen as racist. Attributing the monstrous National Socialist crimes to racism seemed increasingly questionable to me the more I studied National Socialism.

In his 1939 Reichstag speeches, Hitler spoke of the annihilation of the "Polish race," but I do not believe that Hitler's proclamation of genocide had anything to do with racial-biological concepts. Instead, the Poles simply had settled in the geographic area that Hitler's geopolitical nightmare had reserved for the Germans and had to disappear as a result—whether as a "race" or simply a "population." The mass murderers in doctors' coats at Auschwitz were clearly no strict observers of the racial biology their colleagues taught at the university, for when it came down to it, before putting the Jews to death, they kept their allegedly contaminating blood in order to produce a serum for the pure German armed forces. The lessons to be drawn from the civilizational catastrophe perpetrated by Germany are as complex as the network of factors from which the annihilation process emerged. The concept of racism does not sufficiently describe this complexity.

In my opinion, there are many good reasons for placing a question mark behind the contemporary agitation against "racism." But "antiracism," motivated by immediate human indignation over heinous acts of violence, is just as intellectually unsatisfying and in the long run politically ineffective. It is certainly a well-intentioned answer to the inflammatory violence in Germany. Can someone committing these acts be calmed? In *Minima Moralia,* written in 1944–45 in American exile, Theodor W. Adorno raised objections to the equality postulate contained in the call for tolerance: "Mélange. The familiar argument of tolerance, all men and all races are equal, is a boomerang. It is vulnerable to simple refutation by the senses. The most compelling anthropological proof that the Jews are not a race will, in the event of a pogrom, scarcely alter the fact that the totalitarians know full well whom they do and whom they do not intend to murder." There seems to be a clue hidden here that is crucial to the current situation. Today's totalitarians also know precisely whom they do and whom they do not intend to murder. How do they know this, [and] what denotes a victim for them? [. . .]

"No, we are not xenophobic. We are not afraid of your skin color or religion, and we respect your foreign culture and are interested in it. But we hate poverty." With this thesis, Christoph Hein has incurred much negative critique. [. . .] In my opinion, Hein is entirely correct; *xenophobia* is an idiotic word, a creation of shallow-thinking bureaucrats and journalists. It signifies nothing socially concrete and illustrates even less.

Horror in the face of impoverishment is a much more convincing motive for the bureaucratic rejection of refugees and violence against asylum seekers, who have long been depicted in the media as greedy impoverished swindlers. It is thus easier to understand why, in a December 1992 candlelight vigil, people talked of a cost-free "tolerance," yet no one mentioned the recent movement to strengthen asylum laws, which led to the increased rejection of refugees. Tolerance yes, but please leave the poor outside. [. . .]

In Hannah Arendt's 1951 *The Origins of Totalitarianism*—a book often quoted and readily exploited for ideological purposes yet very poorly read— I once came across a line of thinking that has gradually clarified the phenomenon of civilized aggression to me. Toward the end of "The Perplexities of the Rights of Man," in the conclusion of the section on imperialism, Arendt contradicts the optimistic expectation, propagated after the end of World War II, that the future progress of civilization would cause atavisms like hatred of foreigners to disappear. She recognizes a connection between the development of civilization and an increase in aggression. "The more highly developed a civilization, the more accomplished the world it has produced, the more at home men feel within the human 'artifice,' the more they will resent everything they have not produced, everything that is merely and mysteriously given them." This "highly developed political life breeds a deep-rooted suspicion of the private sphere, a deep resentment toward the disturbing miracle contained in the fact that each of us is made as he is— single, unique, unchangeable."

What can be the target of this resentment in our civilization? "Nature," which unsettles us with ailments and death? No: according to Hannah Arendt, resentment has rather made the alien a symbol of everything that damages the pride in our civilization's omnipotence. It has selected him "because [he] indicate[s] all too clearly those spheres where men cannot act and cannot change at will, i.e., the limitations of the human artifice." The alien, she continues, "in its all too obvious difference, reminds us of the limitations of human activity—which are identical with the limitations of human equality." We can barely tolerate this fact and ultimately exploit those who remind us of it. [. . .]

The foreigner, whether handicapped, a vagabond, or a refugee from Afghanistan, encounters rejection, not because he costs money, but because he calls to mind the hidden proximity and power of the nongoverned and nondomesticated in the midst of our artifice. Why is a poor country like Pakistan in the position to take in 20 times as many refugees as the rich Federal Republic, never needing to mention the famous "tolerance threshold"? I believe it is because their civilization is much less sensitive to the presence of "givenness" so visible and mysterious in the refugee—the sight of whom, even in small doses, threatens to throw off our civilization's balance. [. . .]

10

MAY AYIM

THE YEAR 1990: HOMELAND AND UNITY FROM AN AFRO-GERMAN PERSPECTIVE

First published as "Das Jahr 1990: Heimat und Einheit aus afro-deutscher Perspektive" in the 1993 collection *Entfernte Verbindungen*. Reprinted in May Ayim, *Grenzenlos und unverschämt* (Berlin: Orlanda Frauenverlag, 1997). Translated by Tes Howell. Ayim was born in Hamburg in 1960 and lived in Berlin from 1984 until she committed suicide in 1996. Under the name May Opitz, she was a coeditor of the groundbreaking 1986 essay collection *Showing Our Colors: Afro-German Women on the Trail of Their History*. Her collection of poetry, *Blues in Black and White*, was published in 1995.

[. . .] I scroll back to my thoughts at the end of 1989 and into 1990, to the confusion and contradictions, the departures and disruptions, the memories of repressed experiences, the new discoveries. At the time, I felt as though I were on a boat in choppy waters. I was so preoccupied with not getting shipwrecked in the whirl of events that I could barely differentiate and process the events happening around me. In hindsight, I see only the shadows of some things; others I can make out much more clearly from a distance. [. . .]

Talk in the media was of German-German brothers and sisters, of unified and reunified, of solidarity and togetherness. Yes, even concepts such as homeland, people, and fatherland were suddenly—again—on many tongues. Words came back into official circulation that had not been used without hesitation in either German state since the Holocaust, words that were frowned upon generally but enjoyed uninterrupted popularity in right-wing circles. Times change, people too. Perhaps the contemporary questions change only slightly, and humanity's answers to them almost not at all. [. . .]

In the first days after November 9, 1989, I noticed that there were hardly any immigrants and Black Germans visible in the cityscape, at least those with dark skin. I asked myself how many Jews were (not) in the streets. A few Afro-Germans, whom I had met the year before in East Berlin, crossed my path by chance, and we looked forward to new opportunities to get together. I was walking alone, wanted to experience a bit of the general enthusiasm, feel the historical moment, and share my cautious happiness. Cautious because I had heard of the impending legislative restrictions on immigrants and asylum seekers. Like other Black Germans and immigrants, I knew that even a German passport did not constitute an invitation to the East-West festivities. We sensed that an increasing dissociation from the outside would accompany the imminent German-German unification—an outside that would include us. Our participation at the party was not requested.

The new "we" in "this country of ours"—as Chancellor Kohl loved to say— did not and does not have room for everyone.

"Get lost, nigger, don't you have a home?"

For the first time since I moved to Berlin, I have had to defend myself on an almost daily basis against blatant insults, hostile looks, and/or openly racist defamations. I began again—as I had in the past—to look for the faces of Black people while shopping and on public transportation. A friend was holding her Afro-German daughter on her lap in the subway when she heard, "We don't need people like you anymore; we've got more than enough now!" A 10-year-old African boy was thrown out of a full subway car onto the platform to make room for a white German. . . .

These incidents took place in West Berlin in November 1989, and since then, reports of racially motivated assaults, primarily against Black people, have increased—mostly in the eastern part of Germany. Officials took little notice of these reports of violent riots, which were first acknowledged only in immigrant circles and among Black Germans. [. . .]

I began to get irritated with the East-West festivities and events that did not include the North-South dialogue. German-German was discussed and celebrated even in the women's movement as though Germany were exclusively white and the center of the world. Congresses and seminars were organized, complete with travel vouchers for women from the GDR, without simultaneously thinking about asylum-seeking women, who—regardless of whether they were in East or West Germany—had to live on the edge of subsistence. Such treatment was consistent with the inadequate and half-hearted solidarity activities staged on an administrative level by the "know-it-all West Germans" for the "poor East Germans."

Looking back, I remember a movie advertisement promoted by the Berlin Senate: East German workers at a construction site in West Germany. A voice offstage explains that these women are citizens of the GDR who are taking underpaying jobs that are unappealing for West Germans. The commentator implores the audience, urgently yet pleasantly, to graciously accept "the people" who have come to "us" in the last weeks and months. Why are only white German men featured when the topic is respect between men and women from both parts of Germany? I wholeheartedly support a call for solidarity but not one that leaves unmentioned the fact that the least attractive and lowest-paying jobs are taken by migrant laborers from European and non-European countries. Where is the call for solidarity with those people who, in the face of the German-German appropriation and competition, are the first in jeopardy of losing employment opportunities or housing, positions and apprenticeships?

There are no widespread solidarity events for asylum seekers with catchy slogans and reduced admission prices. On the contrary, new legal measures have drastically reduced the right of residence, particularly for people from mostly impoverished non-European countries. Moreover, until the end of 1990, white citizens and politicians—East and West German—watched the increasing racist violence on the streets with the greatest degree of passivity. I found the "receptiveness" and "hospitality" toward white GDR citizens duplicitous considering the constant warnings to our so-called foreign fellow citizens that the "boat" is full. [. . .]

In 1990, I found this silence and resistance surrounding racism, even among "progressive" leftists and feminist women, frightening and shocking, and yet I was hardly surprised. To be sure, discussions on the topic of a "multicultural Federal Republic" have occurred more frequently since the mid-1980s. Only in exceptional cases, however, have these discussions changed lives and political connections in such a way that an uninterrupted, equitable collaboration with immigrants and Black Germans would become an indisputable given and the analysis of racism a permanent undertaking. The Second Women's Refuge in Berlin and the Orlanda Women's Publishing House belong to the few autonomous women's projects fighting for a quota of posts reserved for immigrants and Black women. [. . .]

The voices of immigrants, Black Germans, and Jews finally gained an audience in the election campaigns in late 1990. At the time, conferences and events concerning racism multiplied but were mostly and almost exclusively organized by white Germans. Such was the case, for example, at the conference "Exclusion and Tolerance" that took place in Eindhoven in November 1990. Of course, Black as well as white scholars from the Netherlands and the Federal Republic gave lectures and seminars on the topic. However, Black women did not take part in the conception and realization of the conference. Fortunately, at several other events, such painful offenses did not occur, and fruitful impulses materialized toward a real collaboration between Black and white women. [. . .]

Discussion has intensified in recent weeks about the situation of marginalized youth, who are currently the main perpetrators of neo-Nazi attacks. Discussions about the causes behind refugee movements have not taken place, nor about measures that could put an end to hunger, war, and environmental destruction in impoverished countries ultimately kept dependent on Europe. A hasty and strident encroachment on the asylum law is dauntingly imminent; and for the foreseeable future, asylum seekers will not be lightheartedly referring to the Federal Republic as their "homeland." Immigrants, Black Germans, and Jewish people, who have lived here for a long time or their whole lives, will be just as reluctant to do so.

The blatant violence on the streets is in step with the words of leading politicians and is part of their practical implementation. But I am convinced that we—and by that I mean all the people in this country who will not tolerate racism and anti-Semitism—have the will and the capacity to form alliances. There are examples that we can follow and with which we can connect. One such example is the Black Germans Initiative, which arose out of a small group of Afro-Germans in the mid-1980s and currently has working groups in numerous cities throughout the Federal Republic. Organizations of immigrants, Black Europeans, and Jews network their groups and activities beyond national borders. [. . .]

11

ALICE SCHWARZER

HATE IN SOLINGEN

First published as "Hass in Solingen: Zum zwiefachen Herren- und Untermenschentum" in *So sehe ich das!: Über die Auswirkung von Macht und Gewalt auf Frauen und andere Menschen* (Cologne: Kiepenheuer & Witsch, 1997). Translated by Tes Howell. Schwarzer (b. 1942), editor of the women's magazine *EMMA* since 1977, is one of Germany's best-known mainstream feminist journalists.

No, these are not "lunatics"—as Foreign Minister Kinkel consolingly declared. This is also not "antisocial violence," as citizen Kohl alleges. They are not "loners," as some of the press are quick to believe. Nor is it "the racist beast," as Ralph Giordano maintains. And they are not always "Nazis," as the *tageszeitung* chants ("Nazis out!"). They are our own children.

More precisely, our own sons. They are the ones who are rampaging in Solingen and everywhere else, setting fires and "bashing foreigners." There is Christian R.: age 16, fatherless, a special-needs student, occasional foster child, his first arson attack at the age of 9, known for his xenophobia, Schalke-04 fan. There is Christian B.: age 20, son from a middle-class home, his father a certified plumber, Christian himself almost a paratrooper, held back because of mental unsuitability. There is Markus G.: 23, unemployed insurance agent, drinker, member of the heavy-metal band Determent and the right-wing radical German National Union. And there is Felix K.: age 16, a doctor's son (father involved with the Doctors against Nuclear Death and mother an active environmentalist). Felix is a fan of karate, baseball, and the right-wing radical band Störkraft.

Sixteen-year-old Felix looks like every mother's dream: he has a sweet youthful face with a long, blond mop of hair, big, blue eyes. He is neither Kinkel's "lunatic" nor Kohl's "antisocial element," and not even Giordano's "beast." Who is he then? "What did the parents do wrong?" asked the *Bild* newspaper (for apparently only the parents are capable of doing something wrong) and promptly responded with a centimeter-high headline: "The mother was often away from home."

And, feeling guilty as well, the single mother of Christian R. confessed: "I chose to concentrate on my career—that was a mistake." As though this mess was the mothers' fault and not the fathers', who are making loads of money from porno and thug productions!

The Federal Office for the Protection of the Constitution [Bundesverfassungsschutz] currently counts 6,500 right-wing skinheads in Germany. The number of sympathizers runs in the five and six digits. These young people come from the most varied social milieus, are either students (sometimes with special needs), unemployed, or career men. Most are between 15 and 25 years old, and all have one thing in common: they are men! At most, every twentieth skinhead is a female (including wives), and the proportion is similar in right-wing political groups. With so many active male organizations—motorcycle clubs, concerts, soccer teams, or groups of "foreigner bashers"—the gentlemen go unaccompanied.

These new members of the master race are the first completely brutally dehumanized and "pornographied" generation, and not only via the media. These new members of the master race, who usually look so pitiful, practice their triumph on a daily basis: beating people down, beating them up, violating them, committing murder. They play computer games under school desks and in their rooms, they see violence in the living room on videos and television, they rehearse it at concerts and in stadiums. And finally, they want to get serious about it. Raping women—yeah, sure. Bashing foreigners—now that's a turn-on.

Yes, these young men are not only members of the master race but also generally poor wretches. Still, what use is it to the victims that the perpetrators are helpless, lonely, and insecure? And: women are helpless, lonely, or insecure too—often more so. And the many female incest victims? Why don't frustrated women react like that? Why do twice as many women vote for the Green Party, whereas twice as many men support right-wing parties?

The answer must not only be sought in social conditions, for then we would have just as many rampaging and pillaging girls on the streets as boys. But we see only young men, incidentally, on both sides—the rampaging young members of the master race and the Turks who rage back at them. While their fathers and husbands work, interact with the Germans, or debate in the mosque, the women sit confined by their four walls: an ideal target.

That the kind of attacks—sneaky, cowardly tricks with fire—do not actually correspond to this new master race's "code of honor" do not seem to bother these perpetrators. They do not take their victims seriously enough to feel in any way bound to their "manly honor" after having killed them.

The "Rambo cult" has seized even young German men (not all but too many).

In their fantasy, these men see themselves as radiant, tough, brutal victors and others as subcreatures: women who mean yes when they say no, foreigners who have no reason to be here and who steal their girlfriends. And we expect humanity and even empathy from these young men? Where is this supposed to come from?! They are completely filled with contempt for humankind.

However, the situation is similar for young men on the other side of the tracks. It was no coincidence that fundamentalist Turkish groups were responsible for the brutal rioting. The Turkish Khomeini, Cemalettin Kaplan, who resides unchallenged in Cologne, "sentences" writers to death who do not produce devout literature and incites Islamic holy warriors against (un-) Christian believers of other faiths. Cologne is the stronghold of Islamic fundamentalism in Germany. At the funeral in Cologne for the women murdered in Solingen, the mosque's imam, in his official address, used the opportunity to call on all Turkish women to don the head scarf and all Turkish men among the mourners to separate themselves from the women!

Fundamentalism is the Middle Eastern variant of Western fascism. Both are lodged in the male realm. Against this background, whenever one appeals to the Turkish men's manliness and capacity for self-defense, one contributes to the escalation of the "men's war." Meanwhile, the women continue to die in their apartments on the home front.

No, the answer can no longer be "self-defense capabilities" for the Rambos of all nations. The answer must be "truthfulness" ([Federal President Richard von] Weizsäcker): everyone, even the men, who would prefer not to, must trace the causes of this newly ignited virility craze and fight them. As long as we women expect every woman and every man to stand up for all those threatened by sexism, which we have done until now in vain, then it must be a given that every woman will intervene anytime and anywhere against racism: stop the perpetrators and help the victims!

12

ALEXANDER BÖKER

HE IS NOT AS SWEET AS HE SEEMS

First published as "Lieb ist er wirklich nicht" in *Süddeutsche Zeitung* (July 20, 1998). Translated by Priscilla Layne.

Marc has polished his boots for such a long time that you can see your reflection in them. Actually, Marc always cleans his shoes, but today he has taken even more trouble than usual. Marc is taking the train from Berlin to Potsdam; he's happy because today is an important day. He is meeting with friends who will be coming from all over Germany. Most of them look just like Marc. They shave their heads once a week, wear polished Doc Marten boots, rolled-up jeans, Fred Perry polo shirts, and bomber jackets. Sometimes they wear suits; it all depends on the occasion. Marc is 26 years old, and he's a skinhead. A "smartly dressed" skinhead, he says: "Always well-groomed." Marc is good-looking. He has a dark complexion and dark eyes, because his mother is Peruvian. When he talks about himself, the words gush right out of him: he thinks dirty shoes are "disgusting"—people with long hair, too. Nonetheless, he is on his way to Potsdam to see a few long-haired musicians, like Prince Buster, a Jamaican reggae and ska legend who has come to Germany for the two-day ska festival at Linden Park. Skinheads love ska, and a few hundred of them have come to Potsdam this weekend to have a good time. This gathering is why there are policemen scattered all around the festival grounds. They casually lean against their police vans and wait. But nothing happens. [. . .]

Some people who call themselves skinheads shout out German songs, march through the streets, and kill foreigners, in the East as in the West. They wear the wrong shoes—military boots—and shave their heads completely, not leaving even a millimeter of hair. Real skinheads laugh at those kinds of neo-Nazis. "They have no idea what it's all about," says Fabian from Gelsenkirchen. Fascist skinheads don't dare come to the ska festival anymore, because they know they would get beaten up and thrown out. That's what happened two years ago, when a group of neo-Nazis showed up giving the Hitler salute. Still, while many of those attending the festival do not consider themselves right wing, they still don't make a secret of not especially liking foreigners. One of them says that he has "Turkphobia," but no one is interested in that this weekend. Only ultra-left-wing skinheads talk about politics and society's view of skinheads. This political talk annoys Fabian, even though he seems to consider himself left wing, just like Marc. Like many left-wing skinheads, he no longer cares that he's always being misjudged. Most left-wing skinheads have put away their SHARP patches. SHARP stands for Skinheads Against Racial Prejudice, but Fabian asks, "Why do we have to justify ourselves, just because a few East German Nazis have ruined our reputation?" He'd rather spend the weekend with right-wing skins. "They at least know how to party."

13

UTA ANDRESEN

GENERATION HATE

First published as "Generation Hass" in *die tageszeitung* (March 27–28, 1999). Translated by Tes Howell. On February 13, 1999, the Algerian-born Farid Guendoul died when a group of right-wing youth attacked him and two of his friends in the city of Guben.

The number of right-wing radicals is on the rise, not only in Saxony but also elsewhere in the former GDR. Violence against foreigners is apparently an

East German problem. Researchers are diligently looking for the causes of this phenomenon. It is said that the socialist upbringing in the GDR, the compulsion toward the collective, is at fault. However, neo-Nazism exists in the West as well—despite efforts at rehabilitation. Youth respond by lashing out against the foreign. Have both systems failed?

She would like a fully equipped kitchen; he is suffering from *Teewurst* syndrome, the desperate wish for a completely normal dinner. Anna and David dream of living an average life. They would like life to be bourgeois, manageable. This is the dream of former *Kinderladen* children, for whose parents *Teewurst* and a fully equipped kitchen were undesirable—too bourgeois. With this teetotaler pedagogy, their leftist parents hoped to raise nonconformist and individual offspring. [. . .]

Right-wing extremism in eastern Germany is, according to criminologist Christian Pfeiffer, a consequence of the repressive state-run upbringing in the GDR. Pfeiffer is trying to explain, for example, events in the Brandenburg town of Guben, where a gang of adolescents chased an Algerian man through the small town and then left him to bleed to death.

According to Pfeiffer, the Socialist Unity Party state reared its citizens to become conformist, dependent subjects who long for strong leadership and vent their aggressions on foreigners. The effects of this upbringing still linger. After all, it is the same caretakers, the same parents and teachers the youths of today turn to. In Thuringia, for example, colleagues mobbed a fellow teacher who had rejected their "just-act-like-nothing-happened" attitude.

Youth crime in Germany has particular characteristics. There are more murders and rapes in the West than in the East, but the danger of a foreigner becoming a victim of a right-wing extremist attack is considerably higher in the East. In 1997, there were 4.7 times as many attacks in the new federal states than in western Germany. The number of suspects is five to six times as high.

Investigations have shown almost without exception that young East German perpetrators attack in groups; only about half of young West right-wing extremists show this tendency. The foreigner population in the new federal states is low, only about 1.8 percent, compared to 10.2 percent in the West. The chances of becoming the victim of a xenophobic attack between Rostock and Cottbus are high—27 times higher than in the West. So it is no wonder that many asylum seekers now fear nothing more than being shipped off to asylum residential centers in the East. Given the comparatively greater violence against foreigners, predominantly in the form of group attacks, there is also the question of motivation. Something must be provoking the East German right-wing extremist to engage in such aggressive behavior. And this tendency, says Pfeiffer, could only arise from the collectivist and conformist values transferred from the GDR. Orders from above are not questioned. Why develop a guilty conscience when all are joining in the attack? The group is everything, the individual nothing. [. . .]

The goal of the educational system in the GDR was to foster the "socialist personality." In this schema, upbringing was supposed to foster "collective life organization," beginning as a baby. Day care until three, kindergarten until six. After-school daycare until grade four. Young Pioneers until nine. Thälmann Pioneers ("the Combat Reserve of the Working Class") until fourteen. Then the Free German Youth, Free German Federation of Trade Unions, and finally national solidarity. From the cradle to the grave in the clutches of the socialist state. [. . .]

The fact that the East Germans are now reacting with such intense indignation to Pfeiffer's thesis and that bags of letters are appearing at newspapers such as *The Magdeburg People's Voice* means that "the people have obviously forgotten what the GDR was like in those 40 years," says civil-rights activist Hans-Jochen Tschiche. He explains this outrage: "those who lived here for 40 years simply developed their own conformity rituals." The GDR's proletarian petty bourgeoisie did not cultivate a culture of discussion, according to Anetta Kahane [an East Berlin social scientist and executive director of the Regional Centers for Intercultural Understanding in Berlin]. That which is outlawed does not exist. There was no talk of unpleasant things and no debate on the past. Citizens who criticized the GDR were portrayed as soiling the nest. Whoever is not for us is against us. Whoever is not us is them. [. . .]

Generally speaking, right-wing radicals in the East and West come from families that did not place great importance on their upbringing. Sweets instead of comfort, shouting instead of help with homework, beatings instead of discussion. Still, while the right-wing biography in the East is a social one, shaped by the group and previously by the state, the one in the West is personal. The abused son, feeling inferior, failing in school. Then the neo-Nazi gang swoops in at the right time for quick validation. To feel big and strong for once and demonstrate this strength to the weaker! "Militancy provides a quick narcissistic victory," says psychoanalyst Streeck-Fischer. [. . .]

When assaults by right-wing radicals come to light, politicians, social workers, and citizens begin to squirm. After the attack in Guben, Manfred Stolpe, the minister president of Brandenburg, spoke of it as an "out of the ordinary" event. When the Brandenburg community of Gollwitz refused to accept 60 Jewish immigrants from Russia, Stolpe defended "the ordinary citizens" of the village who had apparently made some "mistakes in planning." The right-wing scene practically took over control of the Leipzig youth center Kirschberghaus; the tolerant social workers there had allowed the right-wingers more and more freedom. [. . .]

When 12.9 percent voted for the German People's Union in Saxony-Anhalt, the Brandenburg SPD leader, Wolfgang Birthler, expressed his sense of "crisis, protest and disappointment concerning the path of German unity." About 1,000 skinheads gathered for the National Party of Germany's demonstration in Magdeburg against dual citizenship; a mere 400 people came for the counterdemonstration. Antifascist organizers then brought 600 together. Right-wing radicalism catalyzes little resistance anymore; it is trivialized and hushed up. Some suggest that the perpetrators are actually the victims.

Given such responses, it is not surprising that good youths continue to "beat up foreigners." The perpetual excuses from politicians—and from researchers who argue that violence against foreigners is a consequence of poverty and lack of prospects—are counterproductive. According to criminologist Christian Pfeiffer, "they are just simplifying the problem"—especially since the majority of xenophobic perpetrators, in the East as well as the West, are neither unemployed nor poor. They are usually workers, apprentices, and lower-level employees with little education. [. . .]

What is happening in these "nationally liberated zones," which the Bielefeld youth researcher Heitmeyer prefers to call "spaces of fear"? To what extent do the community leaders support extremism? How is violence transformed into power? How does this social-control mechanism function? [. . .]

14
RÜDIGER ROSSIG AND ERICH RATHFELDER
WELCOME! BON VOYAGE!

First published as "Willkommen! Gute Reise!" in *die tageszeitung* (March 6, 1999). Translated by David Gramling.

Some 345,000 refugees from Bosnia used to live among us. Barely 100,000 are still here. The others went back—into a land destroyed and torn asunder. Many find themselves standing before the abyss. Some see no other option than to make their way back to Germany secretly, where they must fear forced deportation just like those who stayed here.

Sabaheta Barjaktarevic can hardly sleep anymore. "She is always thinking about how my brothers and sisters are all alone down there," explains her daughter Aida. The stress of the past few days is written on the face of this 26-year-old as well: "On the 22nd of February at six in the morning, someone pounded on our door and shouted 'Police! Open up!' " Four officials from the Federal Border Patrol were standing at the door in full uniform and demanded to speak with Aida's mother.

Sabaheta Barjaktarevic was, however, not at home in her Berlin apartment—which is common since the 45-year-old Bosnian received her Certificate for Border Crossing. This document instills fear in the approximately 99,000 Bosnian refugees who still live in the Federal Republic. The Certificate for Border Crossing is a one-way ticket without an option to return—the discontinuation of the "exceptional permission to remain" for war refugees and thus an ultimatum to leave Germany. Again and again, this certificate results in deportation, such as in Barjaktarevic's case. The UN refugee organization, UNHCR, in Germany had stepped in on behalf of the family several times last year at the State Residents' Office, but to no avail.

"When the police realized that Mother actually was not there, they got angry," Aida recounts. The officials demanded that Aida, whose "exceptional permission to remain" is valid until the end of June, wake her younger sister, Vahida (24), and the younger sibling Adnan (12). "They said, 'If we don't get your mother, then we'll take these two. That way we didn't come for nothing.' " The family was not permitted to notify its lawyer nor its host, the Berlin Rollbergen Church Congregation. Six hours later, the brother and sister called from the Sarajevo airport, where workers from the local UNHCR High Commission had arrived to meet them.

The family had come to Berlin in August 1992 from their home village, Bratunac, after it was easily overtaken by the Serbian military and then finally "ethnically cleansed." The family fled into neighboring Tuzla. There, the city was already filled beyond capacity and was under constant fire from Serbian artillery. The Barjaktarevics had to keep going. They went to Germany.

Upon their arrival in Berlin, a neurologist diagnosed the mother as having "depression with psychic decompensation." She appeared to be suffering from "insomnia, fear, nightmares, *pavor nocturnus,* and sweats"—typical symptoms of war trauma. The physician reconfirmed this diagnosis as late as December 1998. A Berlin police physician, however, saw the situation quite differently; he deemed the woman "capable of air travel" and determined that a "permanent, severely compromising traumatization of personality structure and everyday functioning" was not evident.

Sabaheta Barjaktarevic is still in Germany. Underground, out of sight. Fatima Sombecki is also here again. Illegally. Her fate is emblematic for many. She was deported in September—along with her 9- and 13-year-old sons. "At the Sarajevo airport, two workers from the Bosnian Refugee Ministry were waiting for us," she explains. "They only said 'Welcome home! Enjoy your further travels!' " The 32-year-old Muslim from Breko, in today's Serbian sector of Bosnia, did not know where these "further travels" would take them. "When after 12 days in the Sarajevo reception camp near Tuzla we were told we had to go to make room for new refugees, I tried to do just that," she says.

The three actually did make it as far as Breko. Contrary to their expectations, the Muslims even found a room to live in. Two days later, Serbian youth beat the older son until he bled. "That evening, Serbian police officers came to us and told us they could not guarantee our safety." The Sombeckis fled once again, this time over the nearby border into Croatia, and from there to Germany—illegally, for 500 marks.

On the streets of Sarajevo, it is easy to ascertain who stayed here during the war and who fled and has now returned. The difference can be noticed in people's facial expressions, in their movements, in the way they behave.

Those who stayed behind are usually poorly clothed but are more self-possessed. Those who returned compensate for their sense of insecurity with an exaggerated, raucous manner.

This behavior is understandable. The world they once knew no longer exists. Their friends have scattered; many families are torn apart. Only those who came from the respective majority regions can return home to the place they were driven out of. Any Muslim who wants to go to Sarajevo can do so relatively easily—just as Croats can go back to Croatian-dominated Lasva-Tal and Serbs can go to Serbian-dominated regions. However, most of these refugees find their houses or apartments destroyed or looted. Or refugee families from other parts of the country are living there, people who were made to suffer an even more difficult fate. Encounters between the "home-comers" and the "squatters" lead to conflicts.

At the same time, the new arrivals are usually coming from other ethnic groups' majority regions. Muslims from Serbian-occupied East Bosnia have hardly had a chance to return to their homes. In other parts of the Republika Srpska, few dare to; out of 1,921 refugees returning from Germany this February, only 132 registered in the Serbian-controlled part of the country. Of course, the bureaucracies in the Muslim regions also try to prevent the return of Serbs and Croats with all kinds of tricks. The Croatian radicals leave no doubt that they intend to hinder the Serbs' and Muslims' return to their regions.

No more shots are being fired. Threats are enough to instill fear. So most returnees are forced to slip in among their own ethnic group in order to find work and an apartment. And then they wait. But there are hardly any empty apartments anymore, and these are available only at horrendous prices. How is one supposed to find a decent job when 60 percent of the population is unemployed? If one finds an illegal job, the paycheck is so small that it hardly even covers the rent.

At most, the German state has paid 1,300 marks per family in return assistance. Those who did amass savings in Germany lost most of it in fees for various documents from the bureaucracies back home. Those with a little luck can stay with family members when they arrive. The others have to go back to the places they never want to see again: one of the numerous refugee camps.

Of course, there are assistance organizations and programs to facilitate return. Funds have been raised for this purpose, but neither the Refugee Assistance Bureau at the UNHCR nor the International Organization for Migration has statistics about the living conditions of returnees. If the city of Tuzla, which had 110,000 inhabitants before the war, has to take in 40,000 refugees, and 31,000 of them last year as returnees, one can imagine the hardships.

International efforts help only a few. Even the projects of the federal commissioner for returnee assistance have petered out. New apartments are indeed being built, and Hans Koschmick is trying, just as his predecessor Dietmar Schlee did, to prevail upon the Serbian agencies to accept returnees. In the state of Kozarac, more than 1,000 houses are being refurbished with German help. But in the end, this is only a drop in the bucket.

15

CAROLINE FETSCHER

THE NEW WALL

First published as "Die neue Mauer" in *Der Tagesspiegel* (July 30, 2000). Translated by Tes Howell.

A scandal as taboo: Citizens with dark skin live in fear here. Racism is rampant. In the East—and the West. The entire country needs a campaign against right-wing extremists.

Now they are waking up. Even the chancellor admitted on Wednesday, "I am tired of having to read almost daily accounts of right-wing-extremist beating frenzies against foreigners." Before his departure for the summer, Gerhard Schröder spoke out last week against the delay in reforms, and he was moved to speak on the topic of racism as well. "There is no excuse for murder," he said, adding, "for bodily harm, or for desecrating graves and memorials." After the allegedly racially motivated bombing in Düsseldorf, Otto Schily also adopted a sharper tone against right-wing radicalism.

Racists do not take a summer break. We saw proof of this fact in places other than Düsseldorf. Every day, we read those ugly reports the chancellor has grown to expect—from Mecklenburg-West Pomerania, Brandenburg, Saxony-Anhalt. As the Berlin Republic grows, we hear constant talk of its darker side. Embassies are opening in the center of this republic, in the new Berlin. Construction sites are evolving into magnificent buildings, attracting artists into the capital. How cosmopolitan it is becoming here, they gush. How exciting the cultural scene is—in Berlin-Mitte and in Prenzlauer Berg. And so it is.

Reports about right-wing violence, though, are not only showing up in the brief reports about right-wing thugs and the Düsseldorf bombing. Violence is a latent and perpetual threat for all nonwhites and Jewish communities. Nonwhite employees of Berlin firms do not travel on business trips to the surrounding countryside, and a chef named M. from Sri Lanka, who lives in Neukölln, only takes her daughter out with her in the west side of town. Potsdam? Sanssouci? Even those are not destinations for a family of color, she says with a shrug of her shoulders. That's just the way it is. We go to the Charlottenburg castle; it is nice there.

A Political State of Emergency

[. . .] As long as large parts of the country, particularly in the East, are "no-go" areas for nonwhites, the country and its capital carry an unbearable stigma. As long as we tolerate, approve, or ignore this infraction of the constitutional agreement, we accept both latent and open racism—harmlessly labeled "hostility to foreigners." The fact that nonwhites live with fear and restricted freedom of movement is politically, socially, legally, and culturally intolerable. There is a new wall; it is not only in Berlin. And it must fall.

When the German capital moved from Bonn to Berlin, it moved east politically and geographically: to the new federal states of the republic and the neighboring countries in Eastern Europe. From its new position, the current capital communicates with the surrounding countryside and with foreign countries, and the East communicates with the West in a way that was not possible for many years. But if, alongside all the new texts and images, faces and stores, buildings and landscapes, primarily the latent or open racist text is powerfully intervening in this exchange, then an acute political state of emergency is at large. We must ask why the Federal Republic's citizens have become accustomed to this situation and why they do not want to see it as a crisis.

The "wall-in-the-mind" metaphor, popular after the Berlin Wall fell, referred to prejudices between "brothers and sisters" in East and West. Emotional statesmen emphasized that we are all German, that we should come together. As we attempted to do this, and the Black-Red-Gold coalition receded into the fallow land of the "Eastern zone" (and the Allies, under whose eyes we had become democratic, cleaned out their barracks), the other New Wall of racism and exclusion grew.

This new wall is at its thickest where the real wall once stood. An invisible force, it encloses western Berlin just as it did in the transition period: nonwhite foreigners do travel to West Germany, but they prefer not to stop along the way. Many say they "just fill up beforehand." And they completely avoid "the zone" if possible. In early June at a Berlin "Forum on Foreign Cultural Policy," Foreign Minister Fischer complained that foreign intellectuals can only seldom be placed at universities in the East because of rampant racism.

Nonwhite train conductors and Mitropa dining-car waiters now have protection in the East. Foreigners live there with a self-imposed evening curfew, especially in villages and small towns. If possible, they avoid walking on the streets alone. Some asylum-seeker residences, such as the one in Brandenburg Kunersdorf, must be secured with NATO barbed wire and video surveillance, like Serbian enclaves in Kosovo. The only things missing are the tanks.

Another type of resentment is generally accepted as well, namely an antiurban trend, a hatred-of-Berlin attitude. Berliners are seen as privileged, arrogant, rich, "different." They are "enemies." Berlin teachers do not like to travel in the East with their classes, because students there frequently suffer attacks at the hands of the local youth. Berlin is not yet the capital of the new federal states, not truly a city that represents the East. [. . .]

In other countries, the new German racism is not a taboo topic. The fact that Berlin correspondents dependably report on the conditions and search desperately for "any other topic" does not improve the country's reputation. Their reporting will not attract urgently needed computer experts from abroad. [. . .] According to Foreign Minister Fischer, this situation will be devastating and expensive.

At the moment, however, almost nothing is in the works, neither on the federal nor the state level. There is no committee or subcommittee on the problem of racism and xenophobia. There is no comprehensive institutional and financial framework for the topic. This absence can very easily look like tolerance or approval of the status quo. There is also no broad citizen movement. At least Vienna has its Thursday street demonstrations: it seems to be enough for Berliners that the Red-Green coalition is in power. And those eastern Germans who are indeed aware appear not to see their own responsibility in this. [. . .]

The primary issue is how to control this criminality—no less a crisis than the RAF, against which the state fought with hundreds of millions of marks. The deaths and terrorist acts, the "national liberated zones" proclaimed by social marauders, are no less threatening than the criminal acts of the Red Army Faction. Henryk Broder proposes dispatching an EU commission to Brandenburg instead of Austria. "Democracy Watch" in Germany? At second glance, the proposal seems less polemical than inevitable. [. . .]

16

DANIEL BAX

IN PRAISE OF PROVOCATION

First published as "Gelobt sei, was provoziert" in *die tageszeitung* (June 3–4, 2000). Translated by David Gramling. This article surveys the career of the Böhsen Onkelz (The Evil Uncles), a right-wing band from the 1980s whose members renounced their racist lyrics in the postunification era.

The Böhsen Onkelz have plenty of practice in the art of spiteful self-assertion. *A Wicked Fairy Tale* is the name of their new album, which shot to the top of the charts as soon as it came out at the end of April. Despite—or perhaps because of—the fact that these brute rockers are ignored by a broad sector of the music press—because of their radical-right early years in the 1980s and because many record stores, including the record chain WOM, refuse to stock their albums—

the Onkelz have no intention of disappearing into obscurity. On the contrary, it could not have hurt their career when, in the middle of the 1990s, they publicly disavowed the right-wing scene and offhandedly characterized a few of their one-time partners in crime as "brown shit" in one of their songs. The conflict about their past was the first thing to make them truly well known, causing their following to grow steadily through the years. That they kept their name is a sufficient symbol of the continuity: the wicked remain wicked *[Böhse bleibt böse]*. With the countenance of a martyr, they enjoy the sympathy of all those unfortunates who seek to imagine their idols as the last of the righteous in a world that demands false, questionable concessions. [. . .]

The Böhsen Onkelz no longer offer much in the way of a platform for assault. Their aggressive self-pity is diffuse and can be interpreted in any of a number of ways, and their music is commercial punk rock of the same sort that the Toten Hosen have mastered. It has long remained an uncertainty whether the Onkelz's commercial success would be any different if they were still shouting "Turks Get Out." Only after renouncing extremist rhetoric did they achieve their current popularity. [. . .]

But what's behind all this? Is this rampant Teutonism the consequence of pop-cultural regression? Is it an indication of a general shift to the right? Or is it simply a subtle form of the German disposition? [. . .] Either it is the return of the repressed in the form of travesty or perhaps a knee-jerk reaction against Hollywood's banalization of evil. A touch of self-ethnicization is also certainly in play here: look at us, we're the ones you were always warned about. [. . .]

17
BROTHER'S KEEPERS
ADRIANO (LAST WARNING)

First released as the single "Adriano (letzte warnung)" on the album *Am I My Brother's Keeper?* in 2001. Translated by David Gramling. Brother's Keepers dedicated this song to the 39-year-old Mozambican-German Alberto Adriano, who was murdered by right-wing extremists on June 10, 2000, in his hometown of Dessau. This song references poems by the Jewish German lyricist Heinrich Heine (1797–1856). The final stanza is in English in the original.

Torchman:
Now is the time, here is the place,
this is the night, Torchman has the word.
When I think of Germany at night, it robs me of sleep.
My brother Adriano was taken down,
skin color black, blood-red, silence is gold
thoughts are deep blue, a citizen is afraid of his people,
a winter fairytale from Germany. Blue velvet.

Recognized already as a child—here I am foreign in my own land.
Operation article 3—you laughed at that!
Boys, this is my life, we didn't think it through
in all those years when we tossed away our airplay.
You might think that we rappers have nothing to say,
but it will come back at you, you will see, it is catching up to us—
unity makes us strong—Adriano died alone.

G.E.R.M.:
all at once your life hangs on a silken thread, then the warning signals
    blink under the heaving stoplights.
The time is ripe, now heads have no more prices,
we have to stop babbling and proceed strategically,
watch the enemy and then slowly make ourselves known.
Words are like the wind, and deeds speak loudly.
We won't wait, dig holes with spades.
You should know: karma will tell you what's what.

Xavier Naidoo:
this is a kind of last warning,
our fight back has been in the planning,
we will come get you where you are at, we'll arrest your brown shit in
    the end,
for you seek your own demise, and what we're putting out
is clenched fists, not hands to shake—
your defeat forever, and what we will hear is
your crying and whimpering.
. . . .
Sekou:
how many more men must die, pass by the public eye,
on both sides of the Atlantic watch the panic multiply,
walk on by, we divided supposed to coincide,
side-line observers disturbs trying to stay alive.
I realized at a young age life's design maze like,
but it's amazing the way hate spreads when it's been raised right,
without daylight, the truths often hard to swallow,
why we're sending out our love to Amadou and Adriano.

18

REPUBLICAN PARTY OF GERMANY

EXCERPTS FROM THE 2002 PARTY PROGRAM

Published online at www.rep.de. Translated by Hilary Menges. The Republican Party of Germany (Republikanische Partei Deutschland) splintered off from the Christian Social Union in the 1980s. Its first party chair in 1983, Franz Schönhuber, had been a member of the Waffen-SS during National Socialism.

German Identity Instead of Multiculturalism

Everyone has an inalienable human right to a homeland. It grants security and support in a trusted environment through the feeling of not being alone, of belonging to a group that has grown together through history, language, and culture; a group that assumes responsibility for its members.

One can be expelled from one's homeland without changing locations: through cultural infiltration and mass immigration of foreigners. Those who support the now-arising "multicultural society" because they do not value homeland are not authorized to dismiss another's right to homeland. Furthermore, as experience shows, every multicultural society is a society of conflict.

Therefore, the most important demand of the Republican Party is protection of the German homeland, no multicultural society, no multiracial state!

Culture

Germany is one of the world's greatest cultural nations. Representing this culture with self-confidence is valid and legitimate; there is no reason for inferiority complexes.

Priority of the Christian-Western culture—especially the German interest—in pedagogical education.

Care for German customs and resuscitation of the treasury of German songs, including those of the expelled regions.

Protection of the German language from excessive foreign-language influence, particularly in the media.

At least 50 percent of German-language music titles in radio programs.

No fostering of so-called multicultural or intercultural projects.

Foreigners

In Germany, maximum capacity has been exceeded. The high number of foreigners in many cities and districts has helped make Germans a minority. Schools are composed mostly of foreigners, and parallel societies are emerging—especially in the case of the Turks. The ability to receive foreigners from other cultural spheres is exhausted—partly already exceeded—and integration is barely taking place.

Moreover, foreigners are not needed to balance out the German population decrease or save the social security system. In one of the most thickly populated world states and in light of large environmental problems, a certain drop in population density would be a blessing. In addition, the elderly must be protected, especially through the promotion of the German family.

Appropriate measures become even more necessary as the foreigners no longer relieve but burden the social system.

Therefore, we must seek all opportunities to limit the immigration of foreigners and send certain foreigner groups back to their homeland. [. . .]

Asylum

The practice of political asylum rights is characterized by abuse on a massive scale. It must be restricted to address the real victims of political persecution. We therefore call for:

Cancellation of the basic right of asylum, replaced by regulation through law.

No extension of the right of asylum to non-state-persecuted and so-called poverty refugees. [. . .]

Acceleration of court hearings determining rights to asylum, restriction of the process to two legal proceedings and denial of any reapplications.

Consistent deportation of all rejected asylum seekers.

Coercive detention of all rejected asylum seekers who delay their deportation through the destruction of identity papers.

Deportation of criminal asylum seekers even prior to the conclusion of legal proceedings.

Use of police enforcement and possible criminal prosecution to end the so-called church asylums. [. . .]

19

REPUBLICAN PARTY OF GERMANY

THE LAST GERMANS

Published as "Die letzten Deutschen" (2002) on the web page of the Republican Party of Germany in Saarbrücken: www.rep-saar.de. Translated by David Gramling.

I awoke to the muezzin calling into my ear on the loudspeaker from the mosque next door. I had gotten used to it a long time ago. The building used to be a church, but it was converted into a mosque when the Islamic congregation in our district outgrew its old mosque.

The few Christians who were left did not raise any objections. Our Turkish mayor, Mehmet Özal, suggested that the time had come to grant the one true religion, Islam, more space. The few Germans who live in our district send their children to Koran school so that they can integrate with more ease later. In schools, lessons are conducted mainly in Turkish, sometimes in Russian or Arabic depending on the majority. The classes are assorted accordingly. The German children must adjust to this arrangement, but children have little difficulty acquiring foreign languages. Alex, our 10-year-old, speaks broken German at home, but sometimes he falls back into Turkish.

We have to remind ourselves that we do not know how to speak Turkish, and we are often ashamed. Alex is the only pupil in his class with German parents, and he tries to adapt as well as he can.

I try to listen to the news on the radio, but it takes me a long time to find the German-language station. [. . .] The announcer says that because of the pressure of the Party of the One True Way in the Bundestag, a head-scarf mandate will be implemented for all women. My wife has worn one for a long time now, in order to not attract attention in our district. She is now less frequently recognized as a German and is thus much more kindly received. Meanwhile, after a unanimous decision, a "Day of German Shame" will be introduced, on which the evil deeds of the Germans will be pondered, particularly our xenophobia. [. . .]

My wife has found work again, this time at a Turkish restaurant. Because foreigners are now privileged in the distribution of jobs (a consequence of the new antidiscrimination law), her job was quite a stroke of luck for us. I am not supposed to go to the Labor Bureau anymore. The case manager, Mr. Hassan Muftlu, says I am no longer fit for labor placement because I lack knowledge of Turkish. He offered me a language course, which I accepted because one does not get a chance like that every day. Our landlord, Mr. Ali Yüksel, mentioned yesterday in passing that he had promised our apartment to his brother's family and that we should probably look around for something else. When I timidly objected, he said only that he had good connections with the local authorities.

So we have to go, but it is not all that difficult to say goodbye to our old neighborhood. Like many of our acquaintances, we will probably emigrate to the Anatolian steppe. The Turkish government there has generously offered the Germans a piece of land, a kind of reservation for us. We would be among our own people and could maintain our own language and culture. We have been considering this option for a long time.

20

MARTIN HOHMANN

SPEECH ON THE DAY OF GERMAN UNITY

First published as "Ansprache von MdB Martin Hohmann zum Nationalfeiertag, 30 Oktober 2003" on the CDU-Neuhof website on October 30, 2003, and then promptly retracted due to public outcry. Translated by David Gramling.

Today we will be directing our thoughts toward the theme "fairness for Germany," toward our people and its somewhat difficult relationship to itself. We will not dwell very long on outward appearances. But it is certainly strange, and many Germans take issue with the fact that a sentenced Turkish murder accomplice, after serving his sentence, may not be deported to his Turkish homeland. A German court construes German laws such that the so-called

Caliph of Cologne does not see himself compelled to return to Turkey and continues to receive German social-welfare assistance. Many of you know similar examples in which the abiding German social-welfare state or the legal state is mercilessly abused. Thus, the individual, whom one used to call a freeloader, generally has no bad conscience. Well-meaning socialist politicians of all colors have significantly strengthened these individuals' sense of entitlement; one can even say they have made it a matter of course. [. . .]

It is the community bond of the "we" that must be strengthened. It is bitter for us that we must undertake such a taxing strategy, especially at the current moment of economic stagnation. The number of cutbacks is significant, and the number of cutbacks to come will be even greater; one need not be a prophet to predict this eventuality. [. . .] Many Germans sense a lack of fairness on the part of their own state. They have the feeling that normal Germans are handled more poorly than others. Those who fulfill their civil responsibilities, work hard, and raise children may expect no praise in Germany. On the contrary, they feel like the dumb ones, for the chronically stingy state can fill its empty coffers at their expense. Unfortunately, ladies and gentlemen, I cannot repudiate this suspicion that Germans do not enjoy advantageous treatment in Germany. On the contrary. I have posed three questions to the federal government:

1. Is the federal government prepared, in view of the economic developments and the decrease in state revenues, to reduce its payments to the European Union? The answer: The German responsibility to the European Union will be maintained without any reductions.
2. Is the federal government prepared to advocate for German forced laborers now that 10 million German marks have been made available to foreign and Jewish forced laborers? The answer: One may not compare the cases. The federal government will not even advocate for symbolic reparation or an apology from Russia, Poland, and the Czech Republic.
3. Is the federal government prepared, in view of the economic developments and the decrease in state revenues, to calibrate its reparations payments as directed by the Federal Reparations Law (i.e., to the primarily Jewish victims of National Socialism) according to the decreased performance output of the German state? The answer was: No, respect for the previous sufferings of these people dictates that the level of reparations be maintained without cutbacks. [. . .]

With these answers in mind, I will ask the provocative question: in modern history, is there not also a dark side to the Jewish people, whom we exclusively perceive in the victim role, or were Jews exclusively the victims, the ones who suffered? [. . .]

We must take a more precise look. The Jews who subscribed to Bolshevism and the revolution had already severed their religious connections. They were Jews by ancestry and education, but their worldviews demonstrated that they were ardent haters of every religion. Such was also the case among the National Socialists. Most of them grew up in a Christian home, but they had set their religion aside and became enemies of the Christian and Jewish religions. The element linking Bolshevism and National Socialism was thus the antireligious trajectory and godlessness. Thus, neither "the Germans" nor "the Jews" were a perpetrator people. One may, however, quite justifiably maintain that the godless with their godless ideologies were the perpetrator people of this past, bloody century. These godless ideologies gave the "executors of evil" the justification, and even a good conscience, for their crimes. In this way, they could defy the divine commandment "Thou shalt not kill." The result was a historically unprecedented killing of millions. Thus, ladies and gentlemen, I decisively plead for renewed reflection upon our religious roots and bonds. Only they will prevent these kinds of catastrophes, which the godless have created for us. The Christian religion is a religion of life. Christ said, "It is my will that you have life and that you have it in its fullness" (John, 10:10). This directive applies not only to the world beyond but very concretely to our real life and survival today. For this reason, we are advocating for a reference to God in the European Constitution.

My dear ladies and gentlemen, we have seen that the allegation that Germans are through and through a perpetrator people misses the point and is unjustified. We should defend ourselves against this claim in the future. Our maxim shall be "Justice for Germany, Justice for Germans."

I shall conclude by saying, May God grant a good future for Europe! May God grant a particularly good future for our German fatherland!

21
AGAINST FORGETTING

First published as "Gegen das Vergessen" in *Die Islamische Zeitung* (June 2004). Translated by David Gramling.

The Muslim death prayer is not easily forgotten. It is now exactly 11 years since the right-radical Solingen arson attack burned five Turkish women and girls to death on May 29, 1993. Four youths lit the Genç family's house ablaze, annihilating the family in one strike. The attack catalyzed not only worldwide horror but a domestic political discussion as well. In addition, the act demonstrated the incommensurability of rightist and racist theses with Islam and the lives of Muslims.

These days in Germany, the event and the debate around it have fallen out of the headlines. Despite constant appeals for remembrance—11 years after the xenophobia-motivated Solingen attack—there is hardly anything to read or learn about it. Surely, forgetting is not the solution, but neither is a profane memory tourism. The Central Council of Muslims in Germany demands that "memory must be kept alive, so that nothing like this may ever happen again, particularly in these hectic times when the call for increased security and tougher laws predominate."

Many Muslims fear that the public rhetoric about Islam could soon lead to increased attacks against Muslims, particularly against Muslim women. Many Muslims in Germany believe that the struggle against Islam has become a politically correct form of xenophobia. [. . .] Recently, the dividing line between Turks and Germans has again grown more acute. Many understand European conservatives' rejection of Turkey's desire to enter the EU as a message that Turks are unwelcome in Europe. And Germany is most certainly in Europe.

4

WHAT IS A GERMAN?
LEGISLATING NATIONAL IDENTITY

DEMONSTRATING FOR VISA REFORM, 1977. This woman's hand-written sign, demanding an "unlimited residency permit," was part of a Protestant Church convention in Berlin that openly criticized the government's anti-immigration policies. Her protest challenges the rationale of a rotating foreign workforce and the restrictions on permanent residency. Comprehensive laws on naturalization for recruited laborers and their families would not be passed until some twenty years later.

WHEN MAHMUT ERDEM, the protagonist of Christian Wernicke's article "The Long Road to the German Passport," obtained West German citizenship in 1989, he had fulfilled all of the criteria that nineteenth-century applicants had to demonstrate: unequivocal moral character, solvency and fastidious financial planning, exemption from foreign military service, and release from previous citizenship. Like the new Prussian citizens of the early nineteenth century, Erdem received his confirmation of citizenship not from a centralized federal office but from a local agent of the province of Braunschweig. Even for a highly educated applicant like Erdem, the naturalization process was ambiguous, arbitrary, and prohibitive.

The German word for citizen, *Staatsbürger,* is derived from the medieval status denoting those who were permitted to live within the castle walls of a given city, or *Burg.* The late twentieth-century term *ausländischer Mitbürger,* or *foreign fellow citizen,* sought to broaden this ideal of civic community while withholding the more technical status of "citizen." Thus, the discourse on foreign fellow citizens prized a romantic ideal of civic participation over the pragmatic legal status of "citizen." Most of the texts in this chapter, however, illustrate the everyday dilemmas of citizenship rather than the ideal of civic subjectivity.

The feud about the prospect of "double-passport holders" is the subject of five texts in this chapter. Four of the five adopt clear pro and con stances, whereas the fifth, "Ethnicism in the Cloak of Multiculturalism," by Sonja Margolina, abstains, viewing dual citizenship as an overladen ruse in the debate about Germany as an immigration country. Other texts, like Irina Wießner's "Conservative and Manipulated," propose that the Turkish state and media have exerted such relentless ideological pressure on German residents of Turkish descent that they are caught in an aporia of loyalty between their ancestral, imaginary homeland and their estranged, immediate surroundings. For Margolina, dual citizenship serves only to uphold the logic of German blood lineage, instead of forging a new definition of the citizen that is not ethnically defined. Margolina further cautions the German left that affording immigrants dual citizenship will neither ensure integration nor mitigate ethnic nationalism.

In October 1998, the governing Social Democrat/Green coalition under

Gerhard Schröder took the epoch-making step of reformatting the law of blood citizenship *(ius sanguinis)*. The idea that the *normal* citizen was of German ethnicity or blood lineage had persisted through two empires and two republics, since its most recent and binding articulation in 1913. The new legislation, the 2000 Citizenship Law, immediately availed 900,000 Turks of a significantly more streamlined naturalization process. Turkish daily newspapers hailed the action as the end of Germany's "guest-worker ideology." The law provided for optional dual citizenship until one's twenty-third birthday, except in some special circumstances.

Jeannette Goddar, in her essay "Naturalization Impediments for Women," focuses on immigrant women's often-ambiguous legal status as wives, fiancées, and daughters—long-term residents in Germany who have had neither the opportunity nor the legal standing to file independent residence applications. Furthermore, Goddar contends, many aging Turkish women who have worked in Germany for decades are hesitant to apply for naturalization because they would then be barred from inheriting ancestral land in Turkey—often their only potential source of income or collateral for retirement. Thus, even though the 2000 Citizenship Law conferred citizenship upon any child born on German soil whose parents had lived there legally for eight years, Goddar points out that much conjecture remains about whether the new law would assist migrant women in overcoming familial pressures, sexual servitude, and economic privation.

Michael Brenner's 1999 article "Rewarded for Good Behavior" contrasts the historical development of French and German citizenship law and then compares the citizenship options for nineteenth-century German Jews with those available to twentieth-century German Turks. Dieter Grimm, a former justice of the Federal Constitutional Court, then discusses the historical disjunction between multicultural concepts such as "cultural tolerance" and the Basic Law, Germany's constitution. For Grimm, the German constitution emphasizes freedom and liberty in the intracultural, not the intercultural, sphere. Consequently, it does not offer an adequate basis for a jurisprudence of immigration. Nonetheless, coercive assimilation, claims Grimm, is incommensurable with the Basic Law. He further points out that exception from military service, religious taxes, and other duties is ubiquitous among the domestic population. Thus, one ought not consider special provisions for Muslim employees at prayer time to be a volatile new development in German everyday life.

A 2000 working paper by the Christian Democratic Union, the center-right party of Helmut Kohl and Angela Merkel, foreshadows the 2005 Immigration Act. According to the CDU's "working principles," Christian values require justice and solidarity with all peoples of the world, but Germany must focus on attracting entrepreneurs and elite immigrants, rather than the unskilled laborers it recruited throughout the 1960s. A pivotal moment in citizenship and immigration law came with the establishment of the Independent Commission on Immigration, chaired by former Bundestag president Dr. Rita Süssmuth. The commission's report effectively closed the tumultuous 20-year-old debate on Germany's status as an immigration country, unequivocally stating that immigration must be recognized as a structural feature of Germany's society and economy. This declaration notwithstanding, the Süssmuth report espouses many of the same goals and recruiting principles as the CDU working paper: theoretical solidarity with the world's poor, the full cultural and linguistic integration of the current immigrant population, and strategic recruitment of highly qualified transnationals in order to counteract Germany's low birthrate and balance out its aging population. Despite its restrictive scope, the 2005 Immigration Act was the first in the Federal Republic to extend the option of naturalization to legal residents with work permits.

The chapter concludes with three critiques of the predominant immigration principles shaping legislative affairs between 2000 and 2005. According to the Central Council of Muslims in Germany, the Süssmuth Commission devoted insufficient attention to religious freedom and to compliance with the European Parliament's antidiscrimination statutes. The refugee-advocacy network PRO ASYL critiques the 2005 Immigration Act for overlooking long-term undocumented residents on German soil. PRO ASYL demands that any immigration law provide the undocumented with an opportunity to enter into legalization proceedings. For migration researcher Rainer Münz, Germany's first-ever immigration law does not deserve that precedent-setting distinction; its directives are far too tentative to address Germany's urgent need for new immigrants. The 2005 Immigration Act will provide only a temporary reprieve, as new industry needs and national security concerns arise within the European Union.

1

EMPIRE- AND STATE-CITIZENSHIP LAW (1913)

Published as "Reichs- und Staatsangehörigkeitsgesetz" in *Reichsgesetzblatt* (1913), 583–93. Translated by Tes Howell. This law refers to "refuge areas," which are the colonies that Germany acquired between 1884 and 1885: German Southwest Africa, Cameroon, the South Sea colonies, and German East Africa. Tsingtau, acquired in 1897–98, had a distinct legal designation.

Section 1. A German is someone who possesses state citizenship in a federal state or direct imperial citizenship.

Section 2. Alsace-Lorraine is a federal state in this sense of the law.

Section 3. Citizenship in a federal state is acquired
1. By birth,
2. By legitimation,
3. By marriage,
4. For a German by acceptance,
5. For a foreigner by naturalization.

Section 4. Legitimate children of a German man acquire the citizenship of the father at birth; illegitimate children of a German woman acquire the citizenship of the mother. [. . .]

Section 8. A foreigner who has settled in a federal state can be naturalized by the federal state per application when he
1. Is legally competent according to the laws of his previous homeland or would be according to German laws, [. . .]
2. Has lived a morally upright life,
3. Has found his own dwelling or residence in the area of his settlement, and
4. Is able to care for himself and his family according to the circumstances prevalent in his chosen area.

Prior to naturalization, requirements 2 to 4 must be discussed by the community of the area of settlement and, insofar as they do not also act as independent charity organizations, by the respective charity organizations.

Section 9. Naturalization into a federal state may occur only when the imperial chancellor has determined that none of the other federal states have objected to it; should a federal state object, then the Federal Council will decide. Objections can be based only on facts that justify concern that the candidate's naturalization would endanger the welfare of the Reich or a federal state. [. . .]

Section 33. Direct imperial citizenship may be granted
1. To a foreigner who has settled in a refuge area or to a native in a refuge area;
2. To a former German who had not settled in a federal state; this applies to his children or to those who are considered to be his dependents. [. . .]

2

ARTICLE 110 OF THE WEIMAR CONSTITUTION (1919)

Passed in 1919 as Die Verfassung des Deutschen Reichs. Translated by Tes Howell.

Citizenship in the Reich and the states is acquired and lost according to the determinations of the Imperial Law. Every citizen of a state is simultaneously an imperial citizen.

Every German has the same rights and duties in every state of the Reich.

3

LAW ON THE REVOCATION OF NATURALIZATIONS AND DENIAL OF GERMAN CITIZENSHIP (1933)

Published as "Gesetz über den Widerruf von Einbürgerungen und die Aberkennung der deutschen Staatsangehörigkeit" in *Reichsgesetzblatt* 1 (1933), 480. Translated by Tes Howell.

Section 1. Naturalizations completed between November 9, 1918, and January 30, 1933, can be revoked if the naturalization is considered undesirable.

Upon this revocation, the naturalized individual loses not only his naturalized status but also German citizenship, which he would not have acquired without naturalization.

The revocation will take effect upon delivery of the revocation decree or at the time of its publication in the Imperial Index. [. . .]

Implementation provisions for section 1:

1. Whether or not a particular naturalization is considered desirable will be adjudicated according to national principles. In the foreground are those racial, civic, and cultural factors that promote an augmentation of the German population through naturalization, conducive to the interests of Reich and *Volk*. In addition to considering the facts from the period prior to naturalization, a decision must also take into account the circumstances that developed after naturalization.

Hereafter, the following are to be considered for revocation of naturalization:

a. Eastern Jews, unless they fought on the German front during the world war or have made themselves particularly useful to German interests,

b. Persons who are guilty of a serious misdeed or a crime or have otherwise behaved in a manner harmful to State and *Volk*. [. . .]

4

BASIC LAW OF THE FEDERAL REPUBLIC OF GERMANY (MAY 1949)

Passed as Grundgesetz der Bundesrepublik Deutschland. Translated by Tes Howell. For an excerpt from article 16 on the right to asylum, see reading 7 in chapter 3.

Conscious of their responsibility before God and man,

Inspired by the determination to promote world peace as an equal partner in a united Europe, the German people, in the exercise of their constituent power, have adopted this Basic Law. [. . .]

Article 3 [Equality before the Law]

All persons shall be equal before the law.

Men and women shall have equal rights. The state shall promote the actual implementation of equal rights for women and men and take steps to eliminate those disadvantages that now exist.

No person shall be favored or disadvantaged on the basis of sex, parentage, race, language, homeland and origin, faith, or religious or political opinions. No person shall be disadvantaged because of disability. [. . .]

Article 12 [Occupational Freedom; Prohibition of Forced Labor]

All Germans shall have the right to freely choose their occupation or profession, their place of work, and their place of training. The practice of an occupation or profession may be regulated by or pursuant to law.

No person may be required to perform work of a particular kind except within the framework of a traditional duty of community service that applies generally and equally to all.

Forced labor may be imposed only on persons deprived of their liberty by the judgment of a court. [. . .]

Article 116

According to the Basic Law and subject to further legal regulations, a German is whoever possesses German citizenship or was accepted as a refugee or displaced person of German origin or as said person's spouse or descendant in the territory of the German Reich as it stood on December 31, 1937.

Former German citizens, whose citizenship was revoked on political, racial, or religious grounds between January 30, 1933, and May 8, 1945, and their descendants can be naturalized again per application. They are not considered expatriated provided they took up residence in Germany after May 8, 1945, and did not express a contrary will.

5

CHRISTIAN WERNICKE

THE LONG ROAD TO THE GERMAN PASSPORT

First published as "Langer Weg zum deutschen Pass" in *Die Zeit* (March 24, 1989). Translated by David Gramling.

The Pressure to Decide on One State Makes Changing Allegiances Difficult
Mahmut Erdem stays calm and acknowledges the CDU representative's assertions with a gracious smile and the five words "That is just plain dumb." The speaker on the stage fidgets nervously with his tie and papers. His doctrine, that human-rights offenses in Turkey are "rooted in the Oriental mentality," aggravates the audience of students who have come to this evening's Amnesty International event at the trendy Göttingen theater The Lumiere. Excited interjections, demands for an "apology to the Turkish guests in the room," even a threat of "criminal charges for sedition" do not persuade the young CDU politician to retract his declarations about torture and repression in Anatolia. Mahmut is enjoying himself. "I am indeed a Turk, but since February 28, I cannot accept his apology."

Since then he has held German citizenship, as documented by Form 10 001: dull green with a watermark of the federal eagle. The naturalization certificate confirms that Mahmut Erdem, born January 1, 1963, in Gemerek, Turkey, with file number 301.11020/1-Er from the Bureau of Public Order of the City of Göttingen is hereby declared a German in the sense of the Basic Law. The 26-year-old law student, who has lived in Lower Saxony since age eight, has taken a step that only a few of his (former) countrymen dare. Mahmut knows from experience, and the statistics prove it. Of the barely 900,000 Turks who are entitled to apply for "discretionary naturalization" after a residence period of at least 10 years, fewer than 1 percent sought a German passport between 1973 and 1986—8,166 to be exact. Whereas the number of eligible foreigners and their prospect of success increase each year, the number of naturalizations has stagnated at a steady 14,000 per annum. [. . .]

At an SPD press conference last year, Federal Interior Minister Friedrich Zimmermann speculated about the reasons for immigrants' hesitation. "Strong national, cultural and religious ties to their homeland," "social pressures," "overall parity between the legal status of foreigners and Germans," the government's "demand for the forfeit of one's previous citizenship," and "the fear of problems when visiting the homeland," especially among children and grandchildren of recruited workers, are said to stand in the way of naturalization. Results from a Friedrich Ebert Foundation survey corroborate this reluctance to switch allegiance. 38.7 percent preferred to remain citizens of their homeland, 23.6 percent wanted to return there sometime, and 13.8 percent disapproved of the pressure in Germany to give up their previous citizenship.

Conflict with the Family
[. . . Though Erdem is] the typical son of a working migrant woman, he recalls early experiences that would later make him an exception and a candidate for naturalization. At first he played in the Turkish urban backyard mi-

lieu, but soon he had more German friends than from any other group. In Turkish class in Hannover, he memorized the words of the [Turkish Republic's] founding father [Mustafa Kemal] Atatürk: "Happy is he who may call himself a Turk." But as a Kurd of Shiite-Davidic faith, his national pride remained minimal; he "never thought much of those kinds of sayings." His school career was a decisive factor in this special path. The bright, eager-to-learn boy attended extra-help classes in the afternoon, transferred to a full-day comprehensive school, and graduated from high school in good standing. A steep path, which the usually level-headed climber recounts with blazing eyes: "I proved that we can leave the underclass and make ourselves into something." [. . .]

He inquired secretly about naturalization criteria on his own and cautiously confided in a brother. When he solicited family advice on the subject one night at the kitchen table, he was met first with icy silence, then loud protest. Mahmut tabled his plans. But unlike his siblings, he still felt lost during visits to Anatolia—like an Almancı, as his relatives called him.

Before he finally handed in his naturalization application two years later while studying law in Göttingen, there were still many stages of dissociation to work through. The family disapproved of his decision to move in with his German girlfriend and was ashamed of him when he finally broke his promise of marriage to a Turkish girl that his father had arranged for him. Long talks with his fiancée made taking the step to the Göttingen town hall easier: room 1520, Residence Office, Citizenship Affairs. [. . .]

The process is just as undramatically exacting as it is crushingly laborious. Mahmut had to provide a flood of papers, from his birth certificate to his certificate from the Federal Ministry for Education and Research. Three legal processing sites assess the prerequisites, each one with more scrutiny than the previous. The Empire- and State-Citizenship Law of 1913 demands that a German-to-be must first be unrestrictedly capable of employment; second, prove an "unequivocal life change"; third, have a residence; and fourth, "be able to provide nourishment for himself and all those who depend on him." Thanks to visits to the Bureau for Foreigner Affairs and university lectures, Mahmut is in command of bureaucratic German and understands that he is subject to the general principles any applicant faces. The Federal Republic is ostensibly "not a country of immigration; it does not strive to increase the number of German citizens purposefully by way of naturalization."

Certificates, certified copies, and translations of Turkish documents are only the necessary preliminary materials; Mahmut must do much more to belong not only to the population but also to the *Volk*. His 10 years in Germany were easy to prove. Later, the district government of Braunschweig looked over his "dedication to free-willed democratic order" in accordance with the Constitutional Defense's routine inquiry. The candidate had already passed the language exams before graduating from university. The city usually waives medical health reports, but Mahmut had to go to the bureau's physician, because he has a walking handicap from a childhood palsy and an accident; the extent of an eventual restriction on his employability must be assessed. He spends three and a half hours at the Health Bureau, during which he is asked if he is a homosexual. No AIDS test, but "actually that wouldn't bother me all that much." [. . .]

His reserved demeanor in public and prudence in the formalities paid off in February 1987. After nine months, an average processing duration, the district government approved the naturalization. Braunschweig's guarantee was official but under one condition: Mahmut Erdem must have his Turkish citizenship revoked within two years. Thus began phase three of the change of allegiance: penitent journeys to the consulate and to the Domestic Bureau of the Turkish Republic. [. . .]

Ankara took another year with the exemption [from military service] and the revocation of citizenship. Mahmut was lucky once again. Thirteen months after the Turkish military released him, so did the state. One last exchange with Braunschweig followed; whoever wants to be a German has to pay an entrance fee. At least 100, at most 5,000 marks—generally three-fourths of one's gross monthly income. As a student, Mahmut was charged 62 marks. On February 28, Agent Klinnert offered his congratulations and handed over the certificate of naturalization "without flat champagne or official ceremony." [. . .]

Mahmut still has the fourth phase of the naturalization process before him—achieving inner integration. His Turkish siblings meanwhile consider him "the lost son of the family." His mother is assiduously silent about the change of allegiance with neighbors and relatives. He says he will never "assimilate through and through," because he identifies with the ideals of the multicultural society. Reverence for family, the pleasures of encounter, and hospitality, he says, are gifts that he would like to share as "a German citizen of Turkish nationality." He will continue to work on the status and role of foreigners, because, to name just one reason, the new passport does not protect him from insults on the street. As a future law-school graduate, he is specializing in foreigner law. [. . .]

Mahmut still hopes that young Turks born and raised here will receive at least the same entitlement to rights of naturalization as resettlers with German ancestry from Poland or the Soviet Union. Birthplace should be treated equally next to ancestry as grounds for recognition. At least he hopes so.

6

FOREIGNER LAW (1990)

Passed as Ausländergesetz. Translated by Tes Howell.

[. . .] Section 85. Simplified naturalization of young foreigners.

A foreigner who applies for naturalization after completing his sixteenth year and before concluding his twenty-third year may be naturalized as a general rule when he:

 1. Gives up or loses his previous nationality;

 2. Has had permanent and consistent residence in the domestic territory for eight years;

 3. Has attended school in the domestic territory for six years, at least four of which were completed in a general education facility; and

 4. Has not been convicted of a crime.

Section 86. Simplified naturalization of foreigners with long-term residence in Germany.

 (1) A foreigner who has had permanent and consistent residence in the domestic territory for 15 years and has applied for naturalization before December 31, 1995, may be naturalized when he

 1. Gives up or loses his previous nationality,

 2. Has not been convicted of a crime, and

 3. Can prove he can provide for himself and any family members entitled to aid without resorting to social or unemployment assistance; the requirement in no. 3 will be waived if the foreigner can show he is unable to do so without recourse to social or unemployment assistance for reasons beyond his control.

 (2) The foreigner's spouse and underage children can be naturalized according to par. 1 even if they have not had permanent residence in Germany for 15 years.

Section 87. Naturalization by acceptance of multiple nationalities.

 (1) Requirements section 85 no. 1 and section 86 par. 1 no. 1 will be waived if the foreigner cannot renounce his previous nationality or can only do so under particularly difficult conditions. This is to be presumed when:

 1. The law of the state of origin does not allow for the renouncement of nationality;

 2. The state of origin regularly refuses release and the foreigner has submitted an application for release to the naturalization authorities for official forwarding to his state of origin;

 3. The state of origin arbitrarily denies release from nationality or has not decided on the complete and proper release application within an appropriate time frame;

4. The request for release from nationality would mean an unreasonable hardship for members of certain groups, particularly political refugees.

(2) Requirements section 85 no. 1 and section 86 par. 1 no. 1 can be waived when the state of origin makes release from nationality dependent on military service and when the foreigner has spent the majority of his education in German schools and has grown up on federal territory according to a German way of life and is at the age where he is eligible for military service. [. . .]

7

IRINA WIESSNER

CONSERVATIVE AND MANIPULATED

First published as "Konservativ und manipuliert" in *die tageszeitung* (October 15, 1994). Translated by Tes Howell. Between reunification in 1990 and the 1999–2000 citizenship reforms, dual citizenship took on particular symbolic importance among German journalists and politicians. The following two texts exemplify the polemical entrenchment that the "double-passport" debate generated. Wießner is the federal chair of the Society for Endangered Peoples (Gesellschaft für Bedrohte Völker).

Many Turkish immigrants cannot identify with German society. The Turkish media, loyal to the state, wields great influence: A call for single citizenship only.

A large segment of the first generation and the immigrant spouses from Anatolia who later followed cannot accept the German lifestyle because of Islamic moral concepts and upbringing. A family from Anatolia, reared traditionally and in the spirit of nationalist Kemalism, convinced of the superiority of Islam and the Turkish people, does not want to accept, for example, that the daughter of German neighbors may move out of her parents' house when she is pursuing an education in the same city. A Turkish family sees it as *ayıp* (improper) when grown German children do not show the requisite respect for their parents and grandparents and do what they want instead. The family, according to many Turkish citizens, must be defended in the face of such impropriety.

This contemptuous attitude toward their German surroundings, which an extremely large portion of the Turkish ethnic group holds, arises primarily from its background and upbringing, and secondarily from its meager or nonexistent effort to get better acquainted with Germans. The Germans are not much better; ignorance and disinterest persist on both sides.

Directly related to their assessment of German society as morally inferior is the increasingly influential nationalistic, fascistic, or radically Islamic-oriented Turkish press and the powerful Islamic movement behind it, both of which warn against Westernization and Germanization.

Ankara's political influence on the Turkish minority is so strong that one ought to be wary of granting dual citizenship. Its power is evident in the Turkish media, which functions as a corrupting, anti-German influence on Turks in Germany, will not leave them alone, and in a certain way, deprives them of both native countries. [. . .]

Unfortunately, men like [Cem Özdemir] are obviously in the minority—men who are not afraid of the decision to accept a new homeland. Sometimes the attitude of German and Turkish spokespersons toward dual citizenship seems like the decision-making process of a couple considering whether to get married or not after years of living together; marriage is not actually necessary, but it does offer several advantages, security, and perhaps even a new quality of togetherness. Why should one not be able to expect a commitment to German citizenship from all migrants who envision their future here? Why should they not make a clear statement about their new country with an unequivocal citizenship commitment? No one gets upset when a European becomes a U.S. citizen. Why must we condone such indecision in Germany?

Dual citizenship, with rights on both sides, does not help overcome the rupture between cultures. Tansu Çiller, the Turkish prime minister [1993–95], called on her countrymen living abroad to transfer their savings to Turkish banks as a kind of donation to the troubled fatherland. Through this appeal, she generated pangs of guilt among many Turkish immigrants. *Hürriyet*, a newspaper with widespread circulation, also requests donations for troops in the mission against the PKK. [. . .]

Turkish voters with dual citizenship are not "neutral" voters who hold the future of the new homeland dear to their hearts. As long as they allow themselves to be manipulated so completely by the press in Turkey, they will remain "foreigners" who are just exploiting the right to vote. Through the Turkish press in Germany, Turkey will succeed in influencing German politics through pressure from Turkish voters on German parties. [. . .] With what, then, should a German party (whether Red, Green, or Black) gain the favor of Turkish voters? With reactionary women's politics? By sanctioning human-rights abuses in their old homeland? By continuing to provide military assistance for the mission against the Kurds? [. . .] Is it an illusion to expect that people, once out of their homeland, will view their former country and its government in a more critical and sophisticated light? [. . .]

Just like the native German citizen, the Turkish voter will initially have his own interests in mind before he decides on a party. But after that, the potential party's disposition toward Turkey will play a leading role. The Green Party, which advocated so vigorously for the rights of foreign migrants, will get nowhere, for its platform and stance toward Turkey reflect neither the moral concepts nor the wishes of most Turkish voters. Even the SPD has distinguished itself as too friendly toward Kurds.

However, the CDU, which steadfastly rejected dual citizenship, will surpass everyone. It stands, particularly in Bavaria, for the preservation of family values and unborn life, and its foreign policy is loyal to NATO partner Turkey when prompted; it officially denies (upon request) the existence of a Kurdish problem. Instead, the CDU talks about "fighting terrorism" and tries to resist internal calls to put pressure on Turkey, keeping its efforts as low-key as possible.

In order to keep the dependence on "foreign" votes as minimal as possible, the owners of those votes must take a side. Anyone who votes must do so only as a German citizen, regardless of national origin. [. . .]

8

FRANCO FORACI

THREE-PRONGED ARSENAL OF MALICE

First published as "Dreigliedriges Hetzarsenal" in *die tageszeitung* (October 29, 1994). Translated by Tes Howell. This article responds to Wießner's "Conservative and Manipulated," which argued against dual citizenship.

Concerning Some Leftists' Chauvinistic State of Mind

Allow me to say, Ms. Irina Wießner, that you are a racist. Leftist blows cleverly hidden under a magic cloak of university services. Part of this ideal masquerade is that you are an associate of a more or less honorable organization for the defense of human rights—the Society for Endangered Peoples. Your humanitarian mission for the disenfranchised and incapacitated of this world, especially for the Kurds, opens doors for you in the leftist scene; but your "scholarly" heart beats like that of a politicizing Turkologist—more for the arteries on the right side of the left's paralyzed body and mind.

At any rate, your minor treatise on the pages of the last *Intertaz* (October 15) reveals extreme cultural high-handedness. You represent, with no inhibition and with incisive formulations, the kind of nationalistic body of thought that I would have expected from someone of the simplistic and feather-brained ilk of a prejudice-laden Mr. [Heinrich] Lummer. Your own prejudicial Turkish treatise, presented in progressive packaging, comes to us in the form of an ostensibly serious appeal against the legal introduction of dual citizenship, a call so bleeding-heart leftist that it could make one ill. One must only be able to read between the lines.

One more thing at the outset: it would be essentially bearable to allow you to blunder on uncontradicted about avoiding unnecessary publicity, if the place and forum of your shameful remarks had not been the multicultural special feature of the *tageszeitung*. As it is, however, the feeling remains that you are probably speaking from the heart to a considerable portion of the disoriented, naive, but hopelessly ignorant German left, which considers your shocking theses potentially enlightening and absolutely knowledgeable in the search for new identities in the postcommunist era. [. . .]

Smugly wrapped up in pseudointellectual vocabulary, you repeatedly insert familiar positions and popular clichés about Turks: you maintain that many Turks here would espouse a "reactionary women's politics" if they were politically integrated. Furthermore, a considerable number would "also (continue to) stand apart from their fellow German citizens—full of suspicion and scorn." For they "cannot accept the German lifestyle because of Islamic moral concepts and upbringing." [. . .]

The upshot of your three-pronged arsenal of malice is that Turks in Germany obstinately shut themselves off from the modern age. What kind of leftist wants anything to do with unreasonable, authoritarian, religiously doctrinaire antidemocrats? First point won. Instead of the original soundtrack from the right, "Turks smell like garlic and rape our women," there is a new tune from the left à la Wießner: "Turks are machos, nationalists and fascists." Be most wary of Islamic fundamentalists. [. . .]

I dare to assume that all *tageszeitung* readers who are truly looking around their neighborhoods can come up with an array of clear counterexamples for every one of your sweeping attacks against the Turkish community. But this viewpoint does not matter; of course, you know better because of your profession.

Being an expert in Turkish regional studies does not automatically qualify you for complex political insights. From a political-science standpoint, your equation of "nationalistic Kemalism"—as you understand it—with the "superiority of Islam" is utter nonsense. By ignoring historical facts, you instrumentalize structurally incompatible elements in order to strengthen deeply rooted emotional resentments against Turks. [. . .]

It seems to me, Ms. Wießner, that you have truly taken Heinrich Lummer as a model. In his 1992 Ullstein pamphlet "Asylum," he reported about the incorrigible "Turkish charm" that is endangering our "Western fundamental values." "We cannot expect to succeed in the integration of Muslims who have given up Islam," pontificates this unrelenting opponent of the multicultural society, "and an integration of Muslims as Muslims, in turn, can only be superficial. [. . .] Foreign infiltration is threatening our country from the inside out because the German population is constantly shrinking." Another thesis reads, "The fact that a million and a half Turks have hardly integrated themselves after 20 years of being entrenched in their habits [. . .] shows how little can be expected from a 'color-blind' melting pot concept." We hear this theme more explicitly in skinhead jargon: the Turks do not want to assimilate; they're bleeding us dry. Obviously, and tomorrow they will all walk around with crooked noses, band together in banking, and rule the global economy. Déjà vu. [. . .]

Shortly before the conclusion of the third section of your tirade, you let the façade drop. Even the most ignorant person realizes by now that the Turkish example was only a vehicle for your poaching adventures. "In order to keep the dependence on 'foreign' votes as minimal as possible," you recommend that "the owners of those votes take a side. Anyone who votes must do so only as a German citizen, regardless of national origin." The multicultural world in the immigration country of Germany should coalesce with the essence of Germanness, or just be silent.

Dual citizenship is possible in Germany in certain exceptional cases. There are over 2 million dual citizens from the Elbe to Lake Constance. Most come from non-European countries, including many Turks, and are followers of the most diverse of religions. This diversity has never threatened the Federal Republic; on the contrary. Why should it be any different with a general introduction of dual citizenship? For to be a dual citizen means full membership on all levels; it means participation without the pressure of having to give up one's identity; it means a stabilizing internal bridge against cultural schizophrenia. No one will become the henchman of another nation and deal against the interests of a country in which he has built his life. Dual citizenship is an assent, not an obstacle to internal societal peace.

Allow me to say, Ms. Wießner, that you are a cunning racist.

9
SONJA MARGOLINA

ETHNICISM IN THE CLOAK OF MULTICULTURALISM

First published as "Der Ethnizismus im multikulturellen Gewand" in *die tageszeitung* (January 2, 1995). Translated by Tes Howell. Margolina (b. Moscow, 1951) has worked as a freelance journalist in Berlin since 1986.

The debate about dual citizenship demonstrates the identity problems of the left. In a modern German context, granting these civil rights would be nothing but a concession to the Turkish state.

Dual citizenship has become an *idée fixe*. I see the debate as a sham and believe that its ferocity and blindness to reality has much more to do with identity issues of the left than with discrimination against foreigners. In addition, political correctness masks insecurities and fears of immigration (not only those felt by the right).

Some 6.5 million foreigners currently live in Germany, and only 2 million of them are Turks. Some believe that their contempt for "the Germans," their antiquated women's politics, and their support for Turkey make Turks into "the foreigners" who do not want to belong and would vote conservatively if they had dual citizenship. Such a "leftist" argument against two passports is implausible. One may not refuse people political rights because of their conservatism or, for that matter, because of their outdatedness. That approach is just not democratic, and it indicates a tendency to instrumentalize foreigners for political purposes.

It is particularly false to stigmatize the Turks as an exceptionally foreign element because of their conservatism. Indeed, most immigrants/emigrants from authoritarian countries are conservative and do not condone modern German customs. Thus, in many respects, Russian Germans barely differ from Anatolian farmers: they are at a loss in this atmosphere of "individualism" and "coolness"; they miss the community spirit and extended family at home, and forbid their children, for example, to take part in sex education. Russian Germans probably also vote conservatively. One suspects, and not without reason, that the CDU wants to bring potentially like-minded voters into the country. However, this approach does not solve the historical problem of "ethnic Germans." Feelings of resentment toward the individualist West came from the preindustrial age and have no nationality; or more specifically, their national affiliation changes with time. Before World War II, Germans and their eastern neighbors cultivated these feelings; today only right-wing conservatives in Germany nurture them, whereas they are still generally disseminated in other countries—especially in Muslim states. How often have I heard Croats, Poles, or Russians complain about "the Germans"—but, of course, only when they were alone. The schizophrenic relations of emigrants and guest workers to their "second homeland" are a consequence of culture shock and inadequate integration.

[. . .] And our multiculturalists rush to play out their political-power interests against their own society. [. . .] The ideology of multiculturalism understands the preservation of ethnic identity as a basic human right. But the connection between citizenship and this identity is barely tenable. The political steps toward the elimination of an ethnically defined concept of citizenship could signify an important turning point: the rejection of a traditional German understanding of the nation as a "blood community." Dual citizenship, meanwhile, would reinscribe its legitimacy through preservation of *jus sanguinis*. It promotes loyalty to the country of origin and equates cultural identity with national belonging; the acceptance of German citizenship is seen as a betrayal of cultural roots. Turks often have reiterated this rationale to justify their refusal to accept German citizenship. The understanding that citizenship is a political agreement and actually may not have a "genetic" connection with cultural roots is all too often missing from the minorities' arguments. A concession to the ethnic at the cost of the political contributes to the notion that foreigners do not want to identify themselves "inwardly" with German culture because they are already committed to another identity. As long as the newly emerged minorities reject the idea of belonging both to a nation and to another cultural sphere, it will continue to be omitted from the dialogue, thus making the efforts of liberal elites to achieve *jus soli* superfluous.

Recently, the "right" to a collective identity and the value of difference have been popular topics of discussion. The debate includes ethnic identities in this multicultural fervor despite the fact that no one is asking what kind of abyss actually separates the so-called postmodern identity from the ethnic. In the latter case, the issue is not self-classification in a cultural milieu or a choice of relations (Gerhard Schulze), but the dissolution of the individual within a collective whole that dissociates itself from others rather than coexisting with them. Ethnicism in the cloak of multiculturalism is a meaningful step backward on the path toward archaic tribal unions and "molecular civil wars" (Hans Magnus Enzensberger). Especially after 1989, when the oppressed ethnicities gained their own states, the illusion of their "primeval innocence" was destroyed; out of the oppressed came the oppressors. [. . .]

Migrants who are willing to give up their ethnic ties in favor of social ones can be deterred from integration: they will be sufficiently armed with arguments, mottos, with the semantics of an alleged "identity of the native country." The "collective identity" discourse legitimizes a self-ghettoization among foreigners and their retreat into the "extended family" of the community, which "offers the ethnic group protection, keeps it grounded, but also limits the freedom of decision-making and the advancement of the individual" (Thankmar von Münchhausen). Because European societies are confronted with the continually growing stream of people from different cultures, the question arises whether the emerging ethnic groups should be institutionalized as minorities and consequently kept from integration. This question may be asked, but the preliminary problem of citizenship and political rights in Germany is anything but resolved. [. . .]

The German discourse on dual citizenship seems false and ideologized to me. The German and the Turkish sides argue using fetish concepts like "ancestral identity" and "cultural roots," and often shamefully misappropriate the adjective *collective*. For "collective identities" have destructive consequences everywhere. I am not against dual citizenship because of an alleged political preference for those Turks living in Germany, nor because of their manipulation at the hands of the Turkish state. I am against the equation of the cultural and the national, of the cultural and the political, against every concession of politics to ethnicity.

At the same time, I have few illusions about the curative effects of citizenship. It would be naive to hope that citizenship alone would fundamentally change the relationship of German Turks to Turkey. After all, *jus soli* does not prevent Islamists in France from increasing their influence among Algerians with French citizenship. In Islamic communities abroad, an inherent dynamic develops that the host society has great difficulty managing. It is true that racism and poverty make marginalized immigrants particularly receptive to fundamentalism, but it would be shortsighted to reduce this border-encroaching movement to racism in the host country. According to such argumentation, foreigners are still just victims of merciless Western capitalism. Sometimes the victim role is very well suited for the promotion of special interests in the power struggle. The political correctness of a perpetrator driving himself into a corner cannot be a serious answer to the challenge of immigration and the difficulties of integration.

10

JÜRGEN GOTTSCHLICH

BRAVO ALMANYA!

First printed as "Bravo Almanya!" in *die tageszeitung* (October 19, 1998). Translated by David Gramling. Gottschlich is the Istanbul correspondent for various German newspapers.

The Turkish public is reacting with enthusiasm to the Red-Green coalition's resolution on dual citizenship. "Guest-worker ideology is on its way out."

Nine hundred thousand Turks are becoming Germans, and *Bild* magazine is happy. Seldom has a headline been so widely cited in Turkey as the one from Friday's *Bild:* "Yeni Vatandaşlar Hoşgeldiniz" ("Welcome new citizens!"). "Bravo Germany" effused the tabloid *Sabah [Morning],* and the reliable *Cumhuriyet [Republic]* wrote that this development was nearly a revolution. The Germans are accepting dual citizenship, doing away with their antiquated citizenship law, and even *Bild* is all for it. Although the official reaction is reserved—the Turkish foreign ministry greeted the intentions of the new government with a moderate tone, intending to wait and see what becomes of them in concrete terms—the public's enthusiasm is widespread. From the Turkish point of view, the acceptance of dual citizenship is the decisive breakthrough.

After decades of abasement, after incessant new legal restrictions on visas and admittance for spouses and other relatives, after the shocks of the burning houses in Mölln and Solingen, this is the first big positive step for Turkish immigrants in Germany. The approximately 900,000 Turks, to whom the press here [in Istanbul] are currently referring, are those who may avail themselves of a German passport under the new regulations. There is no question that they will apply for them as well. Ismail Günidi, the Interior Ministry official in Ankara responsible for the conferral and retraction of Turkish citizenship, has already announced that many bureaucratic hurdles will be removed for those Turks who wish to assume German citizenship.

The Turkish minister responsible for citizens abroad, Rifat Serdaroğlu, was the most daring of the officials. In various interviews, he has said, "With this move, Germany has brought its citizenship law up to twenty-first-century standards." In a similar tone, the chief editor of the popular paper *Hürriyet [Freedom],* Ertuğrul Özkök, commented on the Red-Green rendezvous on

Saturday: "Finally in Germany, the ideology of the guest worker is on its way out." The twenty-first century, Özkök hopes, will bring an entirely new understanding of minorities.

The intriguing aspect is that *Hürriyet* considers the Green Party Bundestag representative Cem Özdemir as the true father of this major success. Apparently, Cem Özdemir, who has fought for so many years for the rights of the Turkish minority in Germany, has delivered at last. While *Hürriyet* in Turkey effusively praises Özdemir, the same newspaper's German edition shoots him down. In the conflict about filling the new government's commissioner of foreigner affairs position, the columnist Ertuğ Karakullukçu took great pains to make clear to his readers that the leftist Claudia Roth is preferable to the traitor Özdemir.

If current expectations are fulfilled and most Turks who are indeed entitled soon apply for a German passport, the SPD can plan on a quick million additional votes in the next elections. Of the 160,000 who can already vote, 76 percent voted SPD. In 2002, the quota could be higher.

11
REFORM OF THE STATE CITIZENSHIP LAW (1999)

Published in *Bundesgesetzblatt* 38 (1999), 1618–23. Translated by Tes Howell.

Article 1: Alteration of the Empire- and State-Citizenship Law

1. [. . .] A child born to foreign parents in domestic territory shall acquire German citizenship when one parent:

a. Has legally held permanent and consistent residence in the domestic territory for eight years and

b. Possesses a residence permit or has possessed for three years a residence permit for an unrestricted period.

2. [. . .] Where the person undertaking the obligations stipulated in article 1 states a desire to keep his foreign citizenship, German citizenship will be revoked when the statement is received by the relevant authorities. It will also be lost where no statement has been made prior to his twenty-third birthday.

3. Where the person incurring the obligation stated in paragraph 1 states a desire to keep his German citizenship, he must prove that he has given up or lost his foreign citizenship. If such proof is not provided by his twenty-third birthday, German nationality shall be lost unless the German government has already received per application the written approval of the relevant authorities to retain German citizenship. [. . .]

Article 2: Alteration of the Foreigner Law

(1) [. . .] A foreigner who has legally had permanent and consistent residence in the domestic territory for eight years is eligible for naturalization per application when he:

1. Acknowledges the liberal democratic order of the Federal Republic's Basic Law and declares that he has not pursued or supported any actions that are directed against this liberal democratic basic order, the stability or security of the federation or a state; which are intended as an illegal encroachment on the government or on constitutional institutions of the federation or a state or their members; or which endanger the external interests of the Federal Republic of Germany by application of or preparations for violence;

2. Possesses a residence permit or right of residence;

3. Can prove he can provide for himself and any family members entitled to aid without resort to social or unemployment assistance;

4. Gives up or loses his previous nationality; and

5. Has not been convicted of a crime.

The requirement in number 3 will be waived when the foreigner can show he is unable to provide without recourse to social or unemployment assistance for reasons beyond his control.

(2) The foreigner's spouse and underage children can be naturalized according to article 1 even if they have not had permanent residence in the domestic territory for eight years. [. . .]

12

JEANNETTE GODDAR

WOMEN—AN IMPEDIMENT FOR NATURALIZATION

First published as "Einbürgerungshemmnis Frau" in *die tageszeitung* (February 13–14, 1999). Translated by Tes Howell. Goddar (b. 1968) is a freelance journalist in Berlin. In this text, TIO (Treff- und Informationsort für türkische Frauen e.V.) refers to a meeting space and help line for Turkish women, operating since 1978.

Dual citizenship is said to be the great reform piece of the Red-Green coalition government. However, even if it does go into effect, despite the changeover in Hesse, fewer women will profit from citizenship reform than men because many female immigrants cannot even fulfill the prerequisites.

"We will grow old in Germany," she says. Ayşe K. is now 50. She holds an application for pension benefits in her hand: now that she is German, she finally has a right to get something back, at least a part of the money that she paid into the pension fund. She cleaned and scrubbed in a hospital for almost 20 years in Berlin-Neukölln. She has not been able to work for several years.

Not much time has elapsed since this Turkish Berliner gave up her dream of retiring in Turkey. Just two years ago, she finally decided to apply for a German passport. "I was scared," she explains in broken German, "and I never knew for sure that I wouldn't indeed go back after all." Only when it became clear that her children would never leave Germany did she accept the thought that she would stay here too. But she does not feel like a German.

For most female immigrants sitting in the rooms of the Turkish Women's Organization this morning in Berlin-Kreuzberg, the decision to apply for a German passport was purely pragmatic. "It's very useful from a bureaucratic perspective," says nurse Emine G., "and there's nothing for me in Turkey either." It was completely different for her mother. "She is already at the age where she can retire in Turkey," she says, "but she wouldn't receive any pension there as a German." Women of the first generation frequently paid into the pension funds of both countries.

"She'll receive little money in Turkey," says Aysin Yeşilay-Inan, "but she might be able to live off of it there." Aysin Yeşilay-Inan, who works in the Turkish Women's Organization as a counselor and primarily helps women fill out the countless forms, sees a dilemma in women giving up their Turkish passport when they have not yet built an existence for themselves here: "Many women have ancestral land in Turkey; it is often their only possession. In Turkish marriages, it is anything but customary to split the man's income." The women can retain ownership of the land only if they remain Turks: no Turkish passport, no Turkish inheritance. However, Yeşilay-Inan also observes that it is often easier for women to forgo the passport of their homeland. "Perhaps this is because their mind-sets are less patriotic."

A reform of the citizenship law could create at least some independence for married women who either follow their husbands or are married off to Germany without ever having seen their future life partners. This group does not only include Turkish and Arabic women who marry Turks or Arabs living here. "More and more Asian women are being brought into the country," says Thuy Nonnemann of the Berlin Vietnam House. "Many of them end up here completely helpless in catastrophic conditions—locked up, blackmailed, or abused."

They may defend themselves against these unbearable conditions only after four years—prior to that time, they receive no independent right of residence. According to Red-Green coalition plans, they could apply for German citizenship after two years of marriage. And even though perhaps only "two years of mistreatment" will be "prevented," as Hatice Pekyiğit of the Berlin help line TIO cynically remarks: two years of mistreatment is a long time. Still, all the female immigrant organizations are pushing for women to receive their own residence-permit status upon their arrival.

The frequency of cases in which women follow male immigrants to Germany has increased considerably. "Many men cannot make things work with women of the second generation," observes Pekyiğit. "So women whose behavior is more docile are flown in from Turkey. They arrive and are completely helpless because they can't speak German and don't know anyone."

The men, whom the young girls and women meet here, are "often even more conservative than their fathers in Turkey," observes the Saarbrücken psychologist Ferah Aksoy, who works mainly with young Muslim women.

"The young women hope for a great life and find to their horror that their life here is worse than in Turkey." According to Aksoy, there is no way back for most of them because of the loss of face but also because many have given up everything. A German passport in the pocket is an enormous advantage: "security always compensates somewhat for feelings of inferiority."

The significance of a new citizenship law for the majority of foreign women who have been here for some time is still unclear. Most immigrant women, working jobs typically done by women, do not believe in a sudden emancipatory effect. "Most families who came in the sixties came from traditionally conservative rural regions," explains Aksoy, "and many have hardly budged from their values." Aksoy separates the daughters of these families into roughly three groups: those who completely reflect the role modeling of their parents, those who fight for their freedom through tricks and white lies, and a small minority of self-confident immigrant women. The latter group is becoming increasingly large," says Aksoy. "This is easy to see, particularly in Berlin. But such processes take a long time."

Indeed, the self-image of the generation that comes into the world after the introduction of a new citizenship law (and receives German citizenship without active parental assistance) could change dramatically. "Today it's par for the course that parents threaten their children: if you don't behave, we'll send you back to Turkey," says Sanem Kleff of the Berlin organization Education and Science (Erziehung und Wissenschaft). "Then the story is: your grandma in Anatolia always wanted to have you with her. Young women are often enough sent back for a few years and then have serious problems when they return and still can speak only broken German."

If children automatically had a German passport, hopes Kleff, then this means of pressure would be unavailable to parents. "It is incredibly important for the socialization of the second and third generation that this sword above their head disappears."

The psychologist Aksoy observes that foreign parents are often completely overwhelmed by child rearing in a cultural area considered to be hostile, and consequently, they turn to absurd measures. But she also fears that having a German passport will not be very helpful to many young girls. "Familial pressure will remain," says Aksoy, "and when one is not raised to be independent, it is very difficult to say, 'no, I'm not going to do that right now.' "

In a study on Islamic girls and women in Giessen and Lollar, teacher Fatma Dülger found that most underage girls live with two identities: they feel simultaneously like a German and an Iranian or Turk. She also determined that the German passport gives a sense of security to the girls, of whom several already have dual citizenship. "It gives them some independence from their parents," she says. "Furthermore, there are parents who do go back to Turkey. Until now the children always had to go with them even when they were almost of age."

Dülger also considers it important that the children born here become German without having to take initiative in the process. "Up until this point, it has always been the educated who opted for a German passport and began the long bureaucratic journey. And when the parents didn't get involved, then the children were stuck."

Admittedly, though, there is also the fear that a new naturalization law, if truly passed, will bring countless disadvantages to women. For only those who do not receive welfare or unemployment benefits would be naturalized, and this is an ever-shrinking group. In the Turkish population alone, the unemployment rate is at 23.2 percent; women are overrepresented here as well as in the welfare ranks.

"Nine out of ten women who come here receive state support" says Saadet Özulusal of TIO, "or they do not apply for welfare and muddle through somehow in order not to endanger their residence-permit status." But whether someone managed to live without state assistance has never yet played a role in the application for naturalization [during 15 years of residence]. "Naturally, we welcome the new law," says Özulusal, "but we also see some problems. It seems likely that we will develop a two-class law: only those who can afford it can become a German. And it will be overwhelmingly women who will form the underclass."

The associates of ZAPO, a Berlin project oriented toward immigrants from Eastern Europe, also perceive disadvantages for their clients. "Most of these women work for unbelievably low wages or cannot find employment at all," says Hilde Hellbernd. Others slip into welfare as soon as they have children, and then do not learn the German language because they spend most of their time in the home. Consequently, they cannot find a better-paying job—and ultimately are not naturalized because of their poor German-language skills. On the journey to naturalization, women have an advantage over men in only one area: they have fewer previous convictions.

13

ROGER DE WECK

PRO: TWO PASSPORTS

First published as "Pro: Zwei Pässe" in *Die Zeit* (January 7, 1999). Translated by Tes Howell. De Weck (b. 1953, Friburg, Switzerland) became editor in chief of *Die Zeit* in 1997.

Dual Citizens — Good Citizens

Millions of people have two passports. Is this problematic? Do they have a problem? Not at all. Dual citizenship is not a danger but an opportunity. It can only be good for Europe if, for example, numerous Germans are also French and vice versa. Dual citizenship is useful, but even more useful would be triple or quadruple citizenship. Then Europe would be Europe.

Increasingly, people carry two cultures within them; they have a father and a mother tongue, a motherland and a fatherland. Or they grew up in two countries and love one just as much as the other. Or they have found a second homeland without separating from the first. It is anachronistic to want to limit these people to a single citizenship.

Citizens of two states are good citizens. They can enrich both states' commonwealth and body of thought.

The French-German Daniel Cohn-Bendit is now the German candidate of the French Greens in the European elections. That is okay, that is allowed, and almost everyone thinks that is nice. Nevertheless, dual citizenship is to remain disagreeable? If cosmopolitanism is a virtue today, then " duopolitanism" simply cannot be bad.

No German takes exception to the fact that Bernhard Vogel was first the governor of Rhineland-Palatinate and then of Thuringia. In 30 years, it will be a given for us Europeans that a good (and bilingual) politician changes locales: from Paris to Berlin, from the French cabinet to the German cabinet. Such changes will cause as little sensation as the recent move of Schleswig-Holstein's trade and commerce minister to North Rhine–Westphalia. In business, science, and culture, the leap over national borders is becoming increasingly easy, increasingly necessary. Politics will follow.

The opponents of dual citizenship have an old, incoherent image of the state. The state of the future in Europe is not the nation-state. Precisely this fact should deter the European-oriented CDU from inflating nation-state citizenship. [. . .]

Both nation and region will inspire identity as before, as the Bavarians in Germany remained the Bavarians (and in turn, within Bavaria, the Franconians are still Franconians). But national identity will—as has long been the case with regional identity—always be based on something other than citizenship. The notion of a Europe of open regions and self-contained nations is absurd. All European nations—even *étatiste* France—will one day be more culturally inspired than state-inspired nations.

Hence the uniqueness and extraordinariness of the European Union as opposed to the authoritative political system: it is neither nation nor empire, two extremely dangerous political entities. National sovereignty plays a role in the EU—nevertheless, the citizen should not be allowed to share his nationality? All or nothing: either German or French but by no means German-French. Madness.

Nothing against the French, the dual-citizenship foes will argue, but the issue here is Turks. So what? *What's the problem?* Will Germany be harmed if a young German also has a Turkish passport? Damage occurs when the young German only has a Turkish passport. He who does not have to live a divided existence will communicate and connect with others so much the better.

14

JAN ROSS

CON: ONE PASSPORT

First published as "Contra: Ein Pass" in *Die Zeit* (January 7, 1999). Translated by Tes Howell. A correspondent for *Die Zeit,* Ross has come to represent "modern conservatism" and "small government" with his 2002 book *The New Enemies of the State,* a critique of the Social Democratic administration of Gerhard Schröder.

Dual Citizens—Half Citizens

Dual citizenship has become the political mascot of enlightenment and liberalism. Whoever expresses objections to it is suspected of being a nationalist and obscurantist; or even worse, he simply does not understand where the problem lies. Is the passport not just a formality, not really that important?

One must first throw the question back to the citizenship-law reformers. They are actually the ones who overestimate the passport. They believe they hold a particularly useful instrument for foreigner integration in their hands. It is free and ideologically correct, a demonstrative act against hyper-Germanness and barroom prejudices. Unfortunately, the passport contributes very little to integration. For the issue is primarily a social problem, not a legal one, and he who pursues the legal/political path makes two mistakes. He neglects the social because he believes to have found a legal patent remedy to solve the "foreigner question." And he debases the law when he abuses it as an apparent replacement for the much more difficult task of social integration. To see the means for integration in the political status of the citizen is to misjudge the difference between state and society.

The reformers therefore overestimate the citizenship law as a remedy and an aid. At the same time, they underestimate it in its own intrinsic value, and the debate about dual citizenship demonstrates this fact. Not that dual citizenship would be inherently objectionable: the conservatives love to exaggerate the danger of divided loyalty. But a strangely dispirited and uncharitable image of one's own community manifests itself in the *routine* acceptance of dual citizenship. One cannot impute desirability to a community that could prompt its new citizens to forgo another identity for a freely chosen German one. It may also be that this currently prevailing negative self-assessment is even justified. There is not much inspiration in being a German these days, with no conception or mission, no republican humanitarian emotionalism or American sense of mission of freedom. We do not necessarily need to be like this; after all, one cannot falsify such ideals. But to be or become a country, *to which one is happily committed,* would be pleasurable and worth all efforts—politically and culturally. The treatment of citizenship as just some free gift, as something that does not cost anything and is therefore worth nothing—this attestation of low self-esteem is certainly not suited to awakening the respect of others, nor to our ambitions to cultivate the desirability of being German.

The strangest aspect of this dual-citizenship discussion is a rarely noticed contradiction voiced by its proponents. They are the ones who demand a departure from the traditional German concept of nation as a pure bloodline—the renunciation of all things ethnic and national, blood and soil *[Blut und Boden]*. They regard *ius sanguinis,* Germanness by virtue of the parents' German lineage, as a terrible anachronism. According to them, it should be replaced by the enlightened "Western" understanding of nation as a community defined by cohabitation, oriented toward the everyday, and constructed by common convictions; it should be a union of free citizens, not a fateful alliance of clan members. Constitutional patriotism instead of tribal nationalism. However, it is precisely this understanding of state that demands the conscious choice, the decision for a citizen identity.

What kind of constitutional patriots are those people who undervalue their constitutionally based citizenship so much that the process of opting for this citizenship, while having to renounce another, seems perpetually unreasonable to them? Particularly those who understand affiliation with a nation not as a natural act but rather as one of will and freedom, must be prepared to demand or make a sacrifice. The new citizens' continued dependency on the country of their familial origin is by no means excluded. One can certainly love two women. But one can be married only to one.

15

MICHAEL BRENNER

REWARDED FOR GOOD BEHAVIOR

First published as "Belohnte Bravheit: Integration vor Einbürgerung: Deutsche Judenemanzipation" in *Frankfurter Allgemeine Zeitung* (January 26, 1999). Translated by David Gramling. Brenner, professor of Jewish history at the Ludwig-Maximilian University in Munich, is author of *Jewish Culture of the Weimar Republic* (Munich: Beck, 2000).

Integration before Naturalization: The Emancipation of German Jews

"Naturalization can only come at the end of a successful integration," reads one of the core sentences of the Hessian CDU party's signature campaign. The concept of citizenship as a reward for successful proof of integration has a tradition in Germany. Whether it has proven itself valid is another story.

At the end of the eighteenth century, when liberal thinkers such as the Prussian minister of war Christian Wilhelm Dohm sought to transform German Jews from mere subjects into useful citizens, they adopted a similar approach. In order to make Jews into "happier, better people and more useful members of society" the state made them undergo an educational process and adapt to the cultural environment; only upon attaining this goal would they achieve lawful emancipation. All German states more or less followed this model during the nineteenth century. Thus, it took almost a century until the constitution of the empire no longer discriminated against Jews as second-class citizens.

A look to the West shows that this process transpired in other ways as well. In the wake of the Revolution, French Jews were emancipated overnight, so to speak—or, more precisely, over two nights, because not until a year later did the poorer and less acculturated Jews of Alsace become entitled to what their Sephardic brethren in Bordeaux had acquired immediately. Of course, two decades later Napoleon made quite conspicuous inquiries as to whether the French Jews had indeed proven themselves French, but in general the French principle was effectively the opposite of the German. France sought no prerequisites initially, and the Jews became equally enfranchised French citizens without performing preliminary tasks. In Germany, in contrast, they obtained equal rights only after they had proven themselves worthy by means of an extended process.

The question whether German anti-Semitism had a special path has not been intensively discussed since [Daniel] Goldhagen. Clearly, the answer to this question is extremely multilayered, but one thing can be said with some certainty: the debate, protracted over decades, on whether Jews enjoy equal rights or not decisively contributed to the fact that large parts of the population repeatedly questioned their Germanness even after 1870. Certainly, the "motherland of emancipation" has its own anti-Semitism and its Dreyfus Affair. But the Dreyfus Affair would not have been possible in Prussia because there were no Jewish officers there until the First World War. And whereas France and Italy featured prominent Jewish ministers, this arrangement was to remain unthinkable in Prussia and in other German states (with the single exception of Baden) until the Weimar Republic. Certainly, this de facto delay was no longer due to legal conditions but to societal consensus in the affected spheres.

Dohm and his liberal successors, who ultimately accomplished Jewish emancipation, were anything but anti-Semites. They spoke well of the Jews, who must first be taught how to become German. Their path was supposed to make Jews "happier, better people" and above all "more useful members of society." Similarly, one may not ascribe xenophobia to the supporters of the signature campaign. The "Ruttgers paper" makes clear how the Jews' usefulness for society was accentuated in those days: "Foreign fellow citizens are an enrichment to our society." But considering the not-so-joyful consequences of the German path of Jewish emancipation in the longer term, those who see "naturalization only at the end of a successful integration" must ask themselves who actually decides whether and when this integration is successful, and what effects will years of discussions and public signature campaigns have on the population?

By the time Jews finally became equally enfranchised citizens, the debate had gone on so long that, in the minds of many Germans, Jews could never be Germans. A culturally, religiously, and racially defined concept of Germanness appears to have flouted citizenship considerations. Social integration had already come up against insurmountable hurdles just at the moment of successful emancipation.

What is ultimately important for the integration of foreigners is not whether they live in Germany with one or two passports, but whether their Christian fellow citizens can imagine Muslim Germans and Black Germans in their minds. Change in citizenship law regarding ancestry criteria must thus be followed by an intensive promotion of societal acceptance of many "other" and new German citizens. The longer one discusses the tasks they must perform in order to obtain the German passport, the more barriers will be established in people's minds.

16
DIETER GRIMM
THE OTHER MAY REMAIN OTHER

First published as "Das Andere darf anders bleiben" in *Die Zeit* (February 17, 2000). Translated by David Gramling. Grimm (b. 1937) was a justice of the Federal Constitutional Court from 1987 to 1999 and subsequently became professor of public law at Berlin's Humboldt University and a member of the Global Law Faculty at New York University.

When the Constitution Was Written, No One Thought about Multiculturalism

[. . .] Uncertainty reigns supreme in legal practice. The High Administration Court in Münster decided a case concerning a female Muslim student's being excused from coeducational sports instruction on the premise of compulsory conformity, whereas the High Administration Court in Bremen adjudicated according to the preservation of identity. Clearly, overarching principles are necessary to resolve the discrepancies. Nothing is more important than examining the document upon which society has standardized the foundation of its coexistence: the constitution. One must, of course, consider that the problem of multiculturalism had not yet presented itself at the time of the enactment of the Basic Law. One cannot expect explicit answers from it, nor can one even find such relevant terms as "tolerance" and "culture."

Nonetheless, the Basic Law is a constitution that supports tolerance, even tolerance toward cultural difference. Among its most significant principles are the equality of all people—rooted in human dignity, the unrestricted development of identity, the freedom of religion and of conscience, the freedom of speech and art, the freedom to assemble and form organizations. In short, differences of opinion, plurality of religions and worldviews, and cultural diversity are legitimate according to the constitution; difference must be tolerated in principle. Each can choose his/her lifestyle. Each can also reject other lifestyles but not infringe upon their right to exist. The state must guarantee the freedom of all and may not interfere on behalf of one party over another.

The Basic Law did not establish these tenets with regard to intercultural conflicts, which no one could have foreseen in 1949, but rather in light of intracultural conflicts: of denominational conflicts that came from the various interpretations of the Christian tradition or out of political conflicts that arose from differing interpretations of the common good and—under the auspices of truth—led to civil war or repression. The Basic Law formulated its answer generally and abstractly and therefore is a valid instrument for these new conflicts. The notion that members of other cultures must conform fully and completely is unconstitutional. The freedom of religion and conscience, freedom of speech, and equality are human rights. Whoever lives here as a member of a foreign culture can lay claim to these rights and cannot simply be forced to give up his/her customs and convictions.

But that premise does not mean that the immigrant may force his/her cultural idiosyncrasies upon the native population. It also does not mean that he/she does not need to be considerate of the convictions and customs of the native population. The Basic Law is not value neutral; it is based on the value of human dignity and the consequent principles of individual self-determination and equality in freedom. For this reason, it also protects the autonomy of different social subsystems such as politics, economy, science, art, and law. After all, it is established upon a pluralistic democracy as the best form of governance reflected by these principles. After the experience of National Socialism, these principles were ascribed such a high value that they are seen as unalterable.

[. . .] The question is only whether the constitution allows or even provides for exemptions from restrictions on freedom in a conflict between a foreign culture and the German legal system. At issue is also the relation between unity and difference, equality and dispensation that demands clarification with every encounter between cultures. Here the problem of multiculturalism becomes mostly a practical one; here is where the legal arguments occur.

For example: may animals be slaughtered without anesthesia, contrary to the ban on ritual animal slaughter, if religious faith demands this act? Must a motorcycle-riding Sikh wear a helmet although his religion prescribes that he wear a turban? May a worker be fired because he performs compulsory prayers during work hours or does not show up for work on a religious holiday? Must a prisoner of Mosaic belief eat standard prison food even if it contains forbidden ingredients? May a father refuse medicinal treatment for his cancer-stricken son for religious reasons? May parents keep their daughters from continuing their education because their own culture reserves higher education for the sons? Must polygamy be allowed for a foreigner living here if it is acceptable in his culture? [. . .]

Regarding exemptions from generally applicable regulations, in and of themselves well-founded, room for tolerance is greater than usually assumed. No one should be prevented from performing religious duties just because the native population is agitated by the foreignness of the behavior or takes offense at the existence of exemptions. The obligation to wear a helmet would then most likely be resolved for the Sikhs under the freedom-of-religion principle. When a religiously ordained behavior creates disadvantages for others, but the conflicting interests can be balanced, exemptions from the generally applicable law are also possible. Prayer during working hours would then not lead to dismissal if the work flow were able to accommodate it and if compensation, through overtime perhaps, were possible.

Such exemptions are by no means new. The legal system is rather full of them in favor of certain groups: youth are not prosecuted under general criminal law. Employees who belong to the workers' council do not fall under the general limited right of cancellation. Officials are excluded from the statutory retirement insurance. Poor people do not have to pay the radio-license fee; priests do not have to serve in the military. The population's social cohesion and adherence to the laws have not suffered. One must understand that cultural difference can be a perfectly good reason for exemptions. Now and then, they are already written into the law—for example, in the case of animal slaughter. [. . .]

Clarity of legal interpretation is all the more important should a minority wish to forbid or force upon its members a behavior for the preservation of cultural identity that is in opposition to the fundamental guarantees of freedom and equality inherent to the native legal system. Society is not forced to give up its own identity in order to recognize a foreign cultural identity. In the area of equality, there are many examples of this. Forced marriage of young girls, ritual genital mutilation, exclusion from higher learning, but also dishonorable punishments or the prohibition of expression and blocked access to information, must therefore not be tolerated when they have religious or otherwise cultural roots. Not all cultural conflicts can be resolved harmoniously. In certain core areas, the only choice is between conformity and flight.

17

CHRISTIAN DEMOCRATIC UNION

WORKING PRINCIPLES FOR THE IMMIGRATION COMMISSION OF THE CDU PARTY OF GERMANY

First published as "Arbeitsgrundlage für die Zuwanderungs-Kommission der CDU Deutschlands" (November 6, 2000). Translated by Tes Howell. The Christian Democratic Union was founded in Berlin in July 1945. It is widely regarded as the center-right party on social and political issues in Germany, often working in close conjunction with the Christian Social Union of Bavaria.

[. . .] As a nation, we are responsible for our past and the construction of our future. The common ground of our cultural and historical heritage and our mutual will to freedom and unity are an expression of national identity and the basis for the convergence of people in our reunited *Volk* and state. A democratic national consciousness encourages acknowledgement of one's willingness, duties, and responsibility in the community.

However, we know that our community lives by spiritual principles that are neither self-evident nor eternally stable. A special commitment for us is to preserve, strengthen, and continue to develop the Christian-influenced fundamental values of our free democracy. This stance distinguishes us significantly from socialist, nationalist, and liberalist thinking. The foundation and orientation of our political action are a Christian understanding of people and the basic values derived from it: freedom, solidarity, and justice. [. . .]

No society can handle unrestricted immigration if it does not want to jeopardize its internal stability and identity. The Federal Republic consequently has the right to control and limit immigration—like every other country that is under comparable immigration pressure. The question is not immigration, yes or no, but rather immigration, widely unregulated as before or regulated and restricted. [. . .]

Germany must be open to qualified foreign employees, entrepreneurs, and scholars to ensure peak scientific performance, great innovative power, and economic vitality. Cosmopolitanism is a prerequisite for outstanding achievements in all areas, not just in sports.

If we want to be successful in the global competition for the "best minds," a half-hearted, indecisive gimmick or instant program like the Green Card initiative will only hurt our country; it will not be of any use to it. Whoever wants to win "the best" must receive them—and their families—with open arms and without resentment and offer them lasting, attractive employment and living prospects in the Federal Republic. [. . .]

Every state and every society must pay attention to a certain common foundation, a mutual trust and a communal spirit. The acceptance of a common canon of fundamental values is part of this foundation. A community with the most varied individual notions of living can otherwise not remain stable. Without loyalty to the underlying moral concepts of the host country and a corresponding common identity consciousness, our community can neither fulfill its duties nor remind its citizens of their responsibility for everyone's common welfare.

In addition to learning the German language, integration therefore requires a clear commitment to our system of government and constitutional law and assimilation into our social and cultural living conditions. Consequently, the values of our Christian-Western culture, those shaped by Christianity, Judaism, ancient philosophy, humanism, Roman law, and the Enlightenment, must be accepted in Germany. This does not mandate the abandonment of personal cultural and religious character but rather the approval of and assimilation into our value frameworks and rules that are meant for coexistence. [. . .]

Foreigners who want to immigrate legally and obtain permanent residence should participate in an assimilation program. This program should include German language training, but also the essentials of the Federal Republic's system of laws, the history and culture, as well as the social and professional orientation of our country. Early efforts could help to avoid separatist tendencies and the formation of parallel societies.

18

RITA SÜSSMUTH

REPORT OF THE INDEPENDENT COMMISSION ON IMMIGRATION

First published as "Bericht der Unabhängigen Kommission Zuwanderung" (July 4, 2001). Translated by Hilary Menges. In this report, the Independent Commission on Immigration presents the results of its work: "Structured Immigration—Promoting Integration." The 21-member commission was appointed on September 12, 2000, by the federal minister of the interior, Otto Schily. Süssmuth (b. 1937, Wuppertal) was president of the German Bundestag from 1988 to 1998 and chair of the Independent Commission on Immigration (2000–01).

Germany is in actuality a country of immigration. People came and have stayed; others have migrated back to their homelands or have continued their migration to other lands. Immigration has become a central public theme. Taboos have been replaced by a general recognition of this reality. Objectivity increasingly determines the public debate. [. . .]

Secure Long-Term Prosperity

The goal of an employment-oriented immigration must be to bring about long-term social prosperity, security, and freedom. Prosperity is desirable not just for its own sake but also as a precondition for Germany's capacity to live in freedom, justice, and solidarity and its capacity to fulfill its responsibilities vis-à-vis the imperative of global solidarity with poorer nations. [. . .]

World Economic Challenges

Globalization opens up economic opportunities but also places new demands on the productivity of the national economy and the people that it affects. The prosperity of the modern industrial states is based on state-of-the-art technology and knowledge. Knowledge is gaining in importance and is increasingly developed on an international basis. Simultaneously, international competition for highly qualified labor power continues to intensify, and the national organizational framework is losing importance. [. . .]

Demographic Change

With static birthrates and without further immigration, the German population is expected to sink from 82 million to 60 million by the year 2050. In this case, the number of persons capable of employment in Germany would drop from 41 million to 26 million. Individual life expectancy is rising, the number of births continues to decline, the population is generally aging. This would still be the case even if more children were born per family in the future, because today there are fewer potential parents than in earlier generations. [. . .] This predictable decrease in population will probably decrease the national economic demand. However, this decelerated growth could lead to the curtailment of business-investment activity and productivity increases. [. . .]

Access to the Job Market among Immigrants Coming to Germany for Humanitarian or Social Reasons

The commission recommends that immigrants with the intent of long-term residency, either for economic or political reasons, should be granted immediate unrestricted access to the job market. In the case of other immigrants, access to the market should be restricted to avoid a draining effect. The laws of the new market-oriented immigration system regarding access to labor should not be undermined. [. . .]

Regarding labor-market access for asylum seekers with pending applications, the current regulation granting access after a waiting period of one year should remain unchanged. In order to mitigate draining effects, the one-year waiting period stipulates that the asylum proceedings should be concluded within this time, during which an applicant is not allowed to work. [. . .]

The commission suggests that a broad package of measures be developed with creativity and determination to make Germany more attractive to qualified immigrants. This program will require combined efforts in society and politics. Failures in this regard could jeopardize the entire project of job-market-oriented immigration. [. . .]

Germany's image abroad is indelibly marked by its history, particularly the tyranny of National Socialism. Foreign media devote special attention to xenophobic assaults. Another disadvantage for us is the meager proliferation of the German language in foreign countries, exacerbated by the worldwide encroachment of the English language. [. . .]

Efforts to increase Germany's attractiveness might also motivate highly qualified Germans to either stay in or return to their country. Currently, 17,000 to 18,000 Germans work in the United States, along with more foreigners who received their natural-science degrees in Germany.

[. . .] At the close of 2000, approximately 7.3 million people with foreign citizenship were living in Germany, 64 percent of whom had been here for over 8 years; 48 percent, for at least 10 years; and 32 percent for more than 20 years. More than two-thirds of foreign children and youth living in Germany were born here. The vast majority of these people will stay for the long term.

The basic goal of avoiding multiple citizenship still stands as before. However, exceptions must be considered in various cases of hardship, and when reciprocity must be guaranteed in relation to other EU states. [. . .]

The introduction of *jus soli* prohibits the legal treatment of people as foreigners over a period of generations when they have long been an integral part of German society. The far-reaching significance of this reform should be extensively evaluated. In the social consciousness, it will henceforth become increasingly self-evident that citizenship is not inextricably tied to ethnic heritage. [. . .]

Last but not least, it is necessary to achieve as broad a consensus as possible between state authorities and residential populations to ensure legitimacy in elections. Those afforded political participation by naturalization, which includes the right to vote, are of central importance. [. . .]

The tendency to seek naturalization is not great among migrants who came to Germany before the 1973 recruitment ban. Apparently the requirements for naturalization seem unattainable to them. In recognition of far-reaching integration efforts of these people, the commission feels a more generous position on multiple citizenship is appropriate for this group of people. These immigrants, as well as German society, have neglected the acquisition of the German language, because they were expected to have a limited period of residency. During naturalization procedures, the blame for this situation should not be ascribed to these law-abiding immigrants, who have worked hard since their arrival in Germany and who have raised their children here. [. . .]

19

CENTRAL COUNCIL FOR MUSLIMS IN GERMANY

STATEMENT OF THE ISLAMIC COUNCIL ON THE REPORT OF THE IMMIGRATION COMMISSION

First published as "Stellungnahme des Islamrates zum Bericht der Zuwanderungskommission" (August 29, 2001). Translated by Hilary Menges. The Central Council for Muslims in Germany officially formed in 1994, although representatives of Islamic umbrella alliances throughout Germany had been meeting since 1986 to organize around federal legislative topics such as religious education.

The Islamic Council of the Republic of Germany welcomes the objectives described in the Immigration Commission's report about regulated immigration.

Given the backdrop of the report's reference to a new phase of integration policy, the Islamic Council expresses emphatic support for a civil society in which the foreign is understood as an opportunity for enrichment. The goal must be a culture of recognition and togetherness in equality, in which the fundamental rights and duties of the Basic Law will be accepted on the basis of difference.

Cultural differences—for example, wearing a head scarf—must be tolerated and accepted by the social majority. The disappearance of individual heritage—and identity—must not occur under integration, because this development would lead to a false equation with assimilation. It must also be expressly acknowledged that integration is not a process of removing supposed "deficiencies" among migrants. The goal is rather, a new balance between rights and duties through the clear and manifest expectation of legally guaranteed rights.

For example, the state must make an all-encompassing offer of incorporation and integration assistance to migrants and combine it with incentives in the form of increased accessibility to legal residence and work permits.

In addition, the guarantee of religious freedom is an essential prerequisite for the integration of minorities, as mentioned in the Immigration Commission's report. Instituting Islamic instruction as a proper compulsory subject at public schools is an important step toward the equalization of Muslims with the already established religious communities. In order for equal religious status to be conferred upon Islam in Germany, the recognition of Islam as a legal body of public right (in keeping with the strong conviction of the Islamic Council) is an urgent condition.

The Islamic Council emphatically demands the introduction of an antidiscrimination law in Germany, which would allow migrants to defend themselves against discrimination and its consequences. As always, people in Germany experience discrimination due to their heritage or religious convictions, whether in daily life or in the workplace. It is now necessary to translate word for word the antidiscrimination guidelines of the European Parliament, in order to bring to fruition the protection of religious minorities appropriate in a lawful democracy.

To ensure a promising and successful coexistence of the societal minority and majority, the Islamic Council advocated early on a clear and definite delimitation of the terms *integration* and *assimilation*. Gratifyingly, the report of the independent Immigration Commission took up this train of thought and currently attributes the guarantee of the existing religious beliefs of Muslims to "identity-building and identity-supporting functions." If one wants to integrate migrants as equal partners in the societal structure for the long term, integration cannot and must not mean the surrender of ancestral culture and identity. A nonbureaucratic naturalization as well as the acceptance of dual citizenship are tried and tested methods in this process.

A sustained representation of the Islamic Council's positions on integration will be further achieved through an intensified inclusion of migrants in intercultural housing projects that serve to promote integration. This program should include the establishment of home ownership as well as the participation of migrants in programs that promote economic independence through state-supported programs toward establishing one's livelihood. In this way, migrants will achieve a secure and long-term place in German society and, through their economic performance and the creation of new jobs, contribute to increased investment in the private sector.

20

PRO ASYL

COUNTERFEIT LABELS ARE BECOMING LAW

Press release first published as "Ettikettenschwindel wird Gesetz" on the PRO ASYL website (June 18, 2004). Translated by David Gramling. Members of welfare and human-rights organizations formed PRO ASYL in 1986 during the height of the asylum debate. The organization currently claims a membership of 12,000 throughout Germany. This press release presents one of several dissenting opinions that emerged in public debates in the days following the immigration compromise of June 2004.

The government and opposition are claiming, in a kind of grand-coalition harmony, that the compromise on the immigration law is of truly historical dimensions. From the perspective of PRO ASYL, the only thing with epochal significance is this vain self-celebration among politicians. At the conclusion of a multiyear political dramaturgy, they have presented a law that delivers on almost none of the promises of the past. The curtain is closing—and the central questions remain open. A swindle of labels is about to become law.

Immigration itself will hardly be possible in the future, except for an entrepreneur who can bring his first million along with him and create ten new jobs or who can promptly find employment after completing his studies. Real opportunities for immigration, which are desirable for demographic as well as economic reasons, are nowhere in sight.

PRO ASYL's view is that many one-time political declarations of intent, not only those made by the Greens but those of other Bundestag parties as well, are either absent from the bill or have been transfigured in an entirely unsatisfactory way.

Despite all of the propaganda about mutual agreement, the praxis of delay and toleration [in recognizing undocumented foreign nationals and asylum seekers] has not been dismantled. PRO ASYL's analysis of the proposed new statutes reveals that the preconditions for achieving legal residence will become even more difficult under the Foreigner Act currently in force. The new law contradicts an agreement among the Federal Assemblies of the Green Party from May 8, 2004, as well as agreements among various bodies of the SPD, Union parties, and FDP. In any case, integration will not take place for those who have been "tolerated" for several years. [. . .]

The law includes no statutes for older applications. Even the Foreigner Act passed by the Kohl administration in 1990 included this feature. In contrast to other European states, which have added right-to-remain and right-to-legalization statutes into their new foreigner laws, what is ostensibly Europe's most modern body of immigration law has missed its chance to make up for the past.

A tightening of deportation law and the introduction of sanctions in the area of integration are intensifying the repressive character of the law. The message of this law is not openness to the world but a kind of barracks mentality.

Through the introduction of so-called exit centers, the law will have an even more macabre effect: reports indicate that more people than ever are living in prisonlike conditions under the Red-Green government—or simply in prison, because there are no efforts to restrict the excessive German prison law.

In the last round of negotiations, there was a fatal intermingling of immigration issues with security dilemmas. Even though the effectiveness of the first two antiterror-law packages has not yet been assessed, the law introduces a new activist position in this regard. The legal instruments that are currently in place already cut deep into the structure of our legal state.

Despite the original resistance of the CDU, statutes for the recognition of sex-specific and nonstate persecution as grounds for asylum were included in the bill. This now-belated modernization is following up on a mandatory EU guideline. An immigration law would not have been necessary in order to achieve this step forward.

The meager result of this gigantic legislative process can be boiled down to this formula: pseudomodernization in a kind of Grand Coalition harmony. Hardly any problems will be resolved in the long term. The CDU, as announced, will continue to up the ante on security questions. German corporations will press for a neoliberal tradition of increased access for "useful" immigrants. The politically weakened SPD can call attention to this false victory, and the CDU can tout the limits [on new immigrants] that it wanted. With closed eyes, the Greens carefully catered to the coalition partners they pocketed in the last elections. For the great majority of those who have been tolerated for years and for most refugees, the law offers few options. [. . .]

21
RAINER MÜNZ
WE WOULD RATHER BE AMONG OUR OWN KIND

First published as "Wir bleiben lieber unter uns" in *Die Zeit* (June 24, 2004). Translated by David Gramling. Münz (b. 1954, Basel) is professor of population science at the Humboldt University in Berlin. In this text, "backyard preachers" refers to imams who set up makeshift mosques in urban backyards.

Despite Stoiber, Beckstein, Müller, Schily, and all the others who negotiated the Immigration Act—or better said, the Immigration Limitation Act—Germany needs immigrants. Urgently. We've known the reason for this for years. In the coming decades, the number of Germans of working age will shrink markedly, an unpleasant consequence of the low birthrate. The number of elderly will, however, steadily grow for at least 40 years. Two felicitous developments are responsible for this situation. On the one hand, the life expectancy has increased, and on the other hand, the elderly are of a generation that was not decimated in a world war.

This demographic development will most certainly affect our affluence. And it endangers our competitiveness. In the future, more and more young people with newly acquired knowledge will move into the labor market. At the same time, this shrinking number of younger people will provide for more and more old people. The result: the wiggle room for wage increases will become smaller, the retirement living standards will not be able to be maintained, Germany as a location will become unattractive, the attempt to fill the holes in the national household budget with taxes and dividends will become all the more difficult.

Two things could help us out of this predicament: a longer working life and more qualified immigrants. Of course, immigration is unpopular, and so is a higher retirement age. There is, however, no reasonable alternative to either. Even those who hope for higher birthrates through an increase in the financial subsidy for families must admit that children born next year will not be available for the labor market until 2025, and those with higher qualifications will not reach it until 2030. Far too late.

Given this insight, Germany should be in a position to generate the most modern immigration laws of Europe. In order to secure a large societal majority for this, the Red-Green federal government founded a commission under the directorship of the CDU politician Rita Süssmuth in mid-2000. Employers, unions, churches, communities, scientists, and the political parties took part.

Exactly three years ago, the Süssmuth commission suggested the following: the active selection of qualified immigrants according to the model of the classical immigration countries, the active promotion of integration through language courses and orientation for immigrants, and changes in the asylum law. The selection of highly qualified immigrants according to a point system—independent of whether they already have been offered a job—should provide Germany with a clear advantage in the international competition for economically attractive migrants. Canada and Australia have had successful experiences with this strategy for years and have thus served as a model for the commission.

This ambivalent attempt at a future-oriented immigration law has failed. The CDU rejected the plan, though its own experts, under the direction of the Saarland-based minister president Müller had made a very similar suggestion. The CSU was against it as well, and Red-Green was lacking a majority even within its own party in the Bundesrat.

The result is a compromise that does not deserve the name Immigration Act. The point system, which was actually the core of the plan, was dropped in committee. As a result, the 1973 moratorium on foreign labor recruitment has been maintained. Ambitious young people from other countries will not, for the foreseeable future, be able to settle in Germany—unless they are self-sufficient entrepreneurs with at least a million euros and ten new jobs in their suitcase. The iconoclastic idea of coaxing the best and most creative minds to Germany has thus been buried.

Nonetheless, the law provides for limited exceptions to the moratorium on recruitment: precisely for those entrepreneurs just mentioned. Second, exceptions will be made for university students, who will be granted one year after graduating to find a job. And, finally, for top-notch scientists and elite managers, an unlimited right to settle will be created. Germans, other EU citizens, and citizens of countries that have just joined the EU will continue to outrank these people in the applicant pool.

Asylum law will also be improved. Refugees who are from nonstate groups or who encounter discrimination because of their sexual orientation or the threat of genital mutilation did not have a right to asylum until now. This situation is changing. The controversial "stopgap toleration" policy will be discontinued. Asylum seekers who may not be deported to their home countries because of war or terror can receive a limited residency permit in their first year. In the second year, this situation will be standard practice.

Refugees who are recognized according to the Geneva Convention have until now only received so-called minor asylum. Now these refugees will be viewed as equal to those recognized in article 16a of the Basic Law, thus allowing them to work. Hardship commissions may also distribute a limited residency permit if an applicant is required to leave the country or may be deported.

The new feature of the law is the stipulations for internal security. The deportation of terror suspects and backyard preachers will be made easier. If deportation is not possible, the government bureaus may restrict the mobility of terror suspects and forbid them to have contact with certain other people. Security detainment for suspects who may not be deported, which the federal interior minister suggested and the CDU vehemently supported, is nowhere to be found in the new law. This kind of detainment apparently offends against the enlightened opinions of constitutional scholars and the Basic Law.

An essential demand of the commission has been fulfilled by the new law: promoting the integration of immigrants. Immigrants now have a right to language and integration courses. Until now, this right was available only to resettlers from the former Soviet Union. The estimated cost (235 million euros annually) will be covered by the federal government. Interior Minister Schily, Saarland Minister President Müller, and Bavarian Interior Minister Beckstein agreed on this stipulation at the last minute. Language and integration courses are mandatory only for immigrants who do not possess EU citizenship. If these immigrants do not take part in the course, their social assistance may be discontinued. In extreme cases, their residence permit may not be renewed.

Without a doubt, the new law offers some improvements. But it forgets about the great opportunity to open the gate for highly qualified immigrants. There will not be another change anytime soon, and an EU-wide regulation is nowhere in sight. This law does not help to shape the future.

22

ACT TO CONTROL AND RESTRICT IMMIGRATION AND TO REGULATE THE RESIDENCE AND INTEGRATION OF EU CITIZENS AND FOREIGNERS (2005)

Passed in 2005 as Zuwanderungsgesetz. Translated by Tes Howell. This law resulted from a compromise between the Social Democrats and the Christian Democrats in June 2004. As Germany's first comprehensive immigration law ever, it marks a symbolic threshold in the country's legislative and political history.

Section 1. Purpose of the Law

1) The law serves to manage and restrict the movement of foreigners into the Federal Republic of Germany. It facilitates and shapes *Zuwanderung,* or immigration, while maintaining consideration for the integration capacity and economic, labor-market interests of the Federal Republic. The law also serves to fulfill the humanitarian responsibilities of the Federal Republic. It regulates the entry, residence, employment, and integration of foreigners. Regulations in other laws remain unchanged. [. . .]

Section 19. Settlement Permits for Highly Qualified Persons

1) A settlement permit may be granted to a highly qualified person in special cases, if the Federal Institute for Labor consents. [. . .]

2) Highly qualified persons for clause 1 are:

1. Researchers with special topical knowledge,

2. Instructors in a particularly important function or research assistants,

3. Specialists and management staff with particular career experience, who receive a wage of at least double the assessment standard of state health insurance. [. . .]

Section 43. Integration Courses and Programs

1) The integration of foreigners who are living legally and permanently in the Federal Republic into economic, cultural, and societal life will be promoted.

2) Integration efforts on the part of foreigners will be supported by an offering of integration courses. Integration courses include instruction in the language, the legal order, the culture, and the history of Germany. Consequently, foreigners should become accustomed to the living conditions in federal territory to the extent that they will possess the necessary self-sufficiency to handle all aspects of everyday life without assistance from a third party. [. . .]

5

RELIGION AND DIASPORA
MUSLIMS, JEWS, AND CHRISTIANS

FREIMANN MOSQUE, 1973. Postwar Munich had a relatively large population of Muslims, many of whom had been refugees or prisoners of war. The municipal government accepted this single-minaret design after an initial objection that "though fitting for an illustration out of *A Thousand and One Nights*, it is certainly not appropriate for Munich."

THIS CHAPTER EXPLORES religious affiliation as a crucial force in migrant community building and for the cohesion of the modern nation-state. The September 11, 2001, attacks on New York City's World Trade Center, which were partially planned in Hamburg, incited an extensive debate about Islamist political organizations in German cities. September 11 also encouraged discussions among Muslims in Germany about the possibilities of a distinctly European Islam. Muslim scholar Bassam Tibi in "Between the Worlds" (2002) and social historian Hans-Ulrich Wehler in "Muslims Cannot Be Integrated" (2002) illustrate the acute tensions that inform German debates about faith and civic identity.

Some of the earliest institutional advocates for multiculturalism and the social integration of immigrants were Christian churches. In the first text in this chapter, "The Synod Speaks for Guest Workers" (1973), the Catholic Church of Germany takes a decisive position against the "rotation principle" of the guest-worker program. The Synod memo declared that, as fellow citizens and " fellow Christians," guest workers deserve stable and just employment conditions, as well as full enfranchisement in their local political communities and congregations.

Five additional texts speak to the future of Jewish communities in Germany. Recalling his childhood in Bavaria, Michael Brenner ("No Place of Honor," 2000) compares postwar Jewish identity to Islamic identity in the 1990s. An interview with author Micha Brumlik (1998) and a report on Jewish pop culture in Berlin ("The Hype over the Star of David," 1998) illustrate the symbolic role Judaism plays in the cultural imagination of 1990s Germany. Israeli president Ezer Weizman ("With a Backpack of Memories and the Staff of My Hope," 1996) and Green Party activist and member of the European Parliament Daniel Cohn-Bendit ("As a Jew—Here?" 1996) debate the meaning of Jewish life in Germany in the post-Holocaust era. These two texts are of primary significance in the context of the "fifth wave" of Russian-Jewish emigration to Germany since 1990, when hundreds of thousands of Soviet Jews accepted Germany's invitation to "return," much to the consternation of many Israeli politicians. Cohn-Bendit defends his preference to live in the Jewish diaspora in Germany, whereas President Weizman claims that Germans must eradicate every mark of racism in their society before Jews can reasonably dwell there.

The majority of these texts were written before 2001. They foreground a wide spectrum of social, educational, and civil-rights debates that are not immediately concerned with fundamentalist terrorism or a global clash of cultures. Since the labor-recruitment moratorium in 1973, religious organizations have played an emblematic role in German public discourse about cultural integration. The print media have often represented grassroot and diasporic Muslim religious organizations as a failure of, and a threat to, German civic society. Left-leaning integrationists have railed against the presence of archconservative religious leaders from Turkey and Iran, nicknamed "import imams," who conduct religious services in languages that few Germans understand. In 1980s West Germany, many Turkish supporters of the secularist principles of Mustafa Kemal, the Turkish Republic's first head of state, found themselves in the midst of radical religious organizations that were far more separatist than those they had known in Turkey. Yet Muslim community organizations have undergone major transformations in Germany since the mid-1980s. Many existing congregations offer monthly German-language worship services for third- and fourth-generation immigrants who speak German as their primary language.

In the late 1980s, the Turkish political exile Cemalettin Kaplan and his Cologne-based Muslim youth academy aroused the suspicion and consternation of German law enforcement. Kaplan quickly became a metonymic figure for pro-Iranian, theocratic movements in Germany before his death in 1995. The monolingual and semiprivate religious space of Kaplan's "caliph state" represented a new kind of cultural sovereignty in Germany, one that questioned the power of the state on several levels. Throughout the 1970s and 1980s, the federal government often monitored Muslim religious organizations' activities along with those of other domestic networks like the Red Army Faction, the Gray Wolves, and various Kurdish resistance organizations such as the PKK (Kurdistan Workers' Party).

Muslim community events in stadiums, courtyards, and mosques have generated xenophobic alarm among German politicians who view these events as indications of widespread "foreigner infiltration." One early text, "What Remains for Turks Abroad?" (1982), considers the emergence of religious political extremism in Turkish communities in Germany, citing the fact that many of the fundamentalist organizations founded in Germany would be banned as insurrectionist in Turkey. "Germany, Your Islamists" (1997) surveys the Islamic political network Milli Görüş (National Perspective), with its large-scale events and its substantial traction in Germany.

One can view head scarves, crucifixes, burkas, and other markers of religious affiliation either as mobile symbols of religious political sovereignty or merely as private aspects of one's everyday wardrobe. In Germany, they are emblematic of a political freedom that both enacts and aggravates German constitutional principles. The debate about head scarves and crucifixes became particularly relevant in the case of the Afghani-born German citizen and schoolteacher Fereshta Ludin, who was banned from wearing a head scarf while teaching in the state of Baden-Württemberg. In "The Universalist Swindle" (1998), Dilek Zaptçıoğlu contends that Ludin's religious worldview does not impair her desire and capacity to teach Goethe or Schiller any more than a Catholic's worldview affects his or her teaching style. How can religious Muslims participate in the civic culture of democratic societies? How will Soviet immigration transform Jewish Germany? Will the next decades confirm or refute the fabled "clash of civilizations" between Islamic and Judeo-Christian societies?

1

WILHELM HILPERT

THE SYNOD SPEAKS FOR GUEST WORKERS

First published as "Synode spricht für Gastarbeiter" in *Süddeutsche Zeitung* (November 24–25, 1973). Translated by David Gramling.

Synod guarantees full participation in church bodies, rejects rotation principle

The foreign employee must be respected as more than a fellow Christian and fellow citizen in church and social life. So declares the position paper "The Foreign Employee: His Position in the Church and in Society," which the common synods of the dioceses of the Federal Republic collectively compiled at Würzburg's Kilian Cathedral. The synod paper concludes that "Many German Catholics do not realize that every foreign believer is from the outset a fully enfranchised member of the pastoral congregation in which he resides. A transformation in our attitude toward the foreign fellow churches must be achieved, a transformation which priests and socially responsible lay people must always be willing to undertake." Some 3.5 million foreigners are living in the Federal Republic; among them, about 1.8 million are Catholics and 500,000 are orthodox Christians.

Foreigners will henceforth be accepted into the various bodies of the dioceses and pastoral congregations, according to an official stipulation of the synod paper. Furthermore, every diocese will have a special staff, led by a "spiritual leader in the mother language," for the spiritual guidance of foreigners.

The synods recommend that state and municipal governments relax their foreigner laws, facilitate the reunification of families, and focus the perquisites of the Labor Promotion Law toward those foreigners who come from a non-EC country. The synods have also expressed opposition to the so-called rotation principle: "Foreigners should not be sent home to their homeland after a few years just to be replaced by other foreign laborers. No one may withhold the opportunity for integration from foreign workers." Nonetheless, the willingness of individual foreign laborers to return to their homeland will be supported on a case-by-case basis. [. . .]

2

PETRA KAPPERT

WHAT REMAINS FOR TURKS ABROAD?

First published as "Was bleibt den Türken in der Fremde?" in *Frankfurter Allgemeine Zeitung* (September 25, 1982). Translated by Tes Howell. The term *Hodscha* is a German transliteration of the Turkish word *hoca*, meaning "teacher" and "spiritual leader."

The migration situation of Anatolians is partly characterized by the fact that the practice of Islam has become a defensive tactic against social discrimination. At first, government officials in Turkey showed no particular interest in the religious support of breadwinners in Germany (whose numbers now run into the hundreds of thousands). Radical sects and brotherhoods, banned and persecuted at home for their unconstitutionality and militancy, have seized the initiative and organized the construction of mosques, Islamic congregations, and extracurricular religious instruction. Organized Islam in Germany—approximately one-fifth of the Turks living here belong to religious organizations or associations—appears therefore to have become far more radical, violent, and militant than Turkey ever allowed it to be. For a long time, Turkey's official stance was that "this is Germany's problem, not ours."

The "official representatives" of the highest Turkish religious authorities, as opposed to the sect *hodschas,* or trained priests, are having a difficult time reconquering the terrain for official orthodox Islam. Competition from fundamentalist sects, partly financed by Arab oil nations, is already hard to beat. It is well known that even in religion courses (in addition to the Arabic Koran lesson), students will inevitably hear catchphrases like "Turkish children must not make friends with Germans because they are Christians, eat pork, go dancing, and do not wear head scarves," or "What is taught in (public) schools is wrong, regardless of whether the teacher is German or Turkish," or even "Teachers who are against Koran courses must be killed." Still, German authorities have little chance of intervening. Outside of Koran courses, students are not allowed to tell anyone what they have learned there, where the courses take place, or even the name of the instructor. If they disobey this order, the children will face beatings.

The courses are financially supported through parents' membership fees, ranging from 20 to 50 German marks a month, as well as through voluntary and involuntary donations. "The *hodschas* collect money for their school and other purposes. Whoever does not donate is in danger of being beaten or even killed," complains a critic of the courses in Hamburg. When confronted with the harsh words of these radical fundamentalist organizations, which incidentally try hard to convey a sense of seriousness to German authorities, this critic prefers to be silent and pay the fees.

It is estimated that more than 50 percent of Turkish schoolchildren attend Koran courses in Germany. Yet the parents are frequently not fanatical fundamentalists or absolute opponents of integration. Given the gradual loss of traditional values in their new cultural group, they are now sending children to religion courses based on the feeling that "Islam enables one to preserve a piece of the homeland," as one father put it. "Religion is one of the few supports in which one can still take pride."

3

HEINRICH BILLSTEIN

AN ISLAMIC BOOT CAMP: THE KHOMEINI FROM COLOGNE

First published as "Islamische Kaderschmiede: Der Khomeini von Köln" in *Die Zeit* (February 12, 1988). Translated by Tes Howell. The Cologne-based cleric discussed in this article, Cemalettin Kaplan, died in 1995.

A Home for Young Muslims Alarms Authorities

Neither gentleman in the truck makes an effort to disguise his presence. They observe the building from an appropriate distance, without particular caution, and note each Turkish boy and girl leaving this morning with a checkmark.

Around noon, the city officials will be there again to take out their tally sheet and note how many Turkish minors reenter this building in North Cologne.

The Cologne authorities' unusual devotion to the Turkish children at 20B Delmenhorster Street has lasted for over a year. The reason: this "boarding school for Muslim youth," where over 100 Turkish children and youths will be trained as Islamic clerics over a period of four years, does not exactly reflect German principles on the protection of minors, nor Western pedagogical concepts. Last September, the North Rhine–Westphalian regional youth-welfare department and the city of Cologne were so frightened for "the physical, spiritual, and mental welfare" of the young Muslims that they ordered immediate closure of this "monastic community." Since then, the "elite training facility employing iron discipline," as the city council classified the boarding school, has become a festering problem, now causing concern among police and legal authorities.

In their formal justification of the closure, youth-welfare officials claimed that the institution's representatives employed no trained caregivers and presented no curricular plan, despite an official request. However, what exasperated the officials most was that the children's education was modeled on Islamic-fundamentalist Iran. Law enforcement still does not know what is actually happening in this facility, which is located in a desolate industrial area. Officials do not even know the precise number of underage inhabitants.

At the same time, rumors about paramilitary training and corporal punishment stubbornly persist. Bloodthirsty videos that glorify Iran's war against Iraq are supposedly just as essential to the school's curriculum as drills in Koran proficiency. The revered Iran allegedly pays the monthly rent of 12,000 German marks for the building, which was once used as a home for asylum seekers. All this conjecture is rejected politely but resolutely by the organization's directors. The young Muslims themselves are tight-lipped on the subject. Thus, official suspicion is based on the views of the Turkish cleric Cemalettin Kaplan. His Federation of Islamic Associations and Communities established the boarding school. The Khomeini of Cologne, as his opponents call him, is viewed as the most radical of the Turkish fundamentalists who have made Cologne their European center in recent years.

The 61-year-old religious zealot wants to transform Turkey into an Islamic republic based on the Iranian model. According to Kaplan, the Turkish state, with its "repulsive democracy, has risen up like a cobra over the field of martyrs, the Islamic land of Anatole." Such declarations can be found in Kaplan's missionary periodical *Tebling* (Proclamation), which calls for an overthrow of the faithless regime in Ankara.

Due to his hateful tirades against the secular "godless Turkish Republic," the *hodscha* was sent into early retirement as a mufti (the highest religious official) of the province Adana and then expatriated to Germany. Since then, the [German] Office for the Protection of the Constitution has been on the heels of the Cologne Khomeini imitator. The North Rhine–Westphalian branch has been issuing warnings about his activities since 1985. Meanwhile, Cologne's Administrative Court forbade him to continue inciting violence from his exile location. In the court's judgment, such activity is not protected under the basic rights of freedom of religion and opinion. (By the way, this bellicose man obtained recognition as an asylum seeker long ago.) Youth-welfare officials are convinced that the *hodscha*'s ideas represent real danger for young Turks and that the minors in the home are therefore "being influenced in a manner not in accordance with the laws of the Federal Republic of Germany, and indeed to such a grievous degree that the welfare of the children and youths appears to be endangered."

The city of Cologne has been unable to enforce the closure ordered by the provincial youth-welfare office. Indeed, the city's law-enforcement personnel have a dilemma. Because the Muslim zealots are not willing to bow out voluntarily, city officials have threatened compulsory evacuation. This action would be a spectacular one for the Federal Republic, one that appears possible only by way of a massive police deployment. There are already plans for such a large-scale operation. Legally, the case is supposedly airtight.

Still the city hesitates. What to do with the young inhabitants of the home? After all, the issue is their spiritual salvation. Eike Johannis, the city-council member from Cologne-Nippes, is convinced that the children will be back in Cologne after three days if their parents do not detain them. The game would start all over again. Officials have long suspected that several minors were hidden with Turkish families or in mosques before each social-services inspection.

Consequently, law enforcement seems to fear embarrassment just as much as it fears the use of force. In the next few days, the gentlemen from the city clerk's office of the Nippes district will return to their posts in front of the house. Ultimately, they do not want to stand there empty-handed when the order for compulsory evacuation finally comes. "Otherwise all of Germany will laugh at us," predicts one of the officials.

In the coming days, at least, there will be little chance of a headline-worthy development in the pursuit of the stubborn Turks of North Cologne. After all, Carnival is here. Cologne's police officers are otherwise occupied.

4

RUDOLF WALTHER

FOULARD AND CRUCIFIX: THOUGHTS ON THE CULTURE WARS

First published as "Foulard and Kruzifix: Kulturkampfüberlegungen" in *Süddeutsche Zeitung* (August 17, 1995). Translated by David Gramling.

What behooved Bismarck to undertake a so-called cultural struggle between 1871 and 1887? His was not a struggle *for* culture, as the politically powerful Borussian professors thought, but rather a contribution to nonculture and pietistic intolerance. Certainly, Bismarck was not turning against the Catholic Church per se. This cultural struggle instead targeted the political representatives of Catholicism in the new empire; it was a preemptive campaign against the Catholic Central Party, which needed to be disciplined in the new German style. Nonetheless, the party's voting membership doubled in size during these 16 years of small-minded legalistic hick-hack. Despite its devious ingenuity, Bismarck's enterprise was a failure.

The Federal Constitutional Court's recent judgment declaring the Bavarian norm of hanging a Christian cross in every classroom unconstitutional has been decried as a modern version of the Bismarckian culture struggle and compared with the National Socialist politics of *Gleichschaltung*, or institutional consolidation. Both comparisons are absurd, because the Karlsruhe constitutional court decision does not discriminate against any minority. Instead, it ends the privileging of religion in public schools, specifically a religion that is now practiced by only a minority.

However, the menacing counterimage of a rampant Serbo-Croatian threat to public safety is masquerading about in the guise of a rhetorical question. After the judgment on August 11, 1995, the *Frankfurter Allgemeine Zeitung* aired the following thought: "What if Christian parents were to complain about Muslim girls wearing head scarves in German classrooms?" Is this position convincing at all?

In French schools, where a strict separation of church and state has prevailed since 1905, there have been repeated conflicts since the 1980s, because individual school principals have categorized head scarves as a catalyst for religious agitation. In 1989, the late-Gaullist representative Chemière barred three head-scarf-wearing girls from school. Since then, and especially since the education minister's 1994 decree, a minor war has been gathering momentum within French schools. François Bayrou prohibited the wearing of overt religious symbols. He meant head scarves among Muslim women and not the crosses around the necks of Christians or the *kippahs* of Jewish pupils. This decree violated not only the basic premise of equal treatment but also retrogressed to before the 1905 legislation separating church and state. The state interfered in the private issues of a religious minority out of domestic political motives but targeted, as Bismarck once had, the actual and imagined political ambitions of this minority.

In the case of the Karlsruhe decision, things are quite different. In schools, the cross stands for the institutionalized association of church and state. The state allows the Christian profession of faith the right to advertise with its central symbol in the neutral space of state schools. At issue here is the surviving privilege of institutions that can (but do not necessarily) violate the rights of other religions and the feeling of individual persons through a special arrangement with the state. In contrast, a girl's head scarf cannot breach the basic principle of equality among people, whether they wear a cross, a *kippah,* or nothing at all.

The common factor that makes the conflict about head scarves in France and the cross in this country comparable is simply the blindness with which the government and some journalists, in their loyalty to church and state, betray basic universalist principles of right in favor of allegedly Christian-Western convictions. Such feeble *ressentiment* does nothing more than fuel the fire among advocates for civil and holy war.

5

EZER WEIZMAN

WITH A BACKPACK OF MEMORIES AND THE STAFF OF MY HOPE

The following is an excerpt from Israeli president Ezer Weizman's speech to the German Bundestag in Bonn on January 16, 1996. First published as "Mit dem Rucksack der Erinnerungen und dem Stab meiner Hoffnung" in *Frankfurter Rundschau* (January 17, 1996). Translated by Tes Howell. Weizman (b. 1924) was the seventh president of Israel, from 1993 to 2000. His visit to Germany in 1996 catalyzed a broad debate about the future of Jewish community and identity in Germany.

[. . .] Ladies and gentlemen, this is not an easy visit for me. Only 50 years have passed since the end of that terrible war, a moment in my people's long history. It was not easy for me to visit the Sachsenhausen concentration camp. It is not easy for me to be in this country, to hear the memories and the voices that call to me from the earth. It is not easy to stand here and talk to you, my friends, in this building. Jews lived in Germany for more than a thousand years. Until the National Socialists destroyed it, this was the largest and oldest Jewish community in Europe, from the first merchants, who came here in the Romans' wake, to the scholars of the twentieth century. From Calonymus to Mendelssohn, from the ritual-murder accusations in Fulda to the horrors of the pogrom night. From stigma to the yellow star, from the anti-Semitic writings of Martin Luther to the Nuremberg Laws, from Raschi's biblical interpretation to Heinrich Heine's lyrics, Rabbenu Gershom, the light of exile, Walter Rathenau, Martin Buber, Franz Rosenzweig, Albert Einstein—these are only a few names that this country has known.

Among the millions of my people's children whom the Nazis led to their deaths were more names than we could remember today with the same measure of reverence and deep respect. Yet we do not know these names. How many unwritten books died with them? How many uncomposed symphonies remained lodged in their throats? How many scientific discoveries could not develop in their minds? Every one of them was killed here twice. Once as a child, dragged into the camps by the Nazis, and once as the adult whom he or she could not become.

National Socialism not only ripped them away from their families and people but also humanity in general. As president of the state of Israel, I can mourn for and remember them, but I cannot forgive in their name. I can only demand, ladies and gentlemen of the Bundestag and the Federal Council, that with your knowledge of the past you focus your attention on the future as well. That you recognize every impulse of racism and destroy every manifestation of neo-Nazism. That you acknowledge these elements courageously and destroy them at the root, so that they do not grow and develop branches and blossoms.

I imagine that for you as well, ladies and gentlemen, a visit from the Israeli president is not a very comfortable moment. Yet we are not meeting as private people but rather as representatives of sovereign states, and we must find a common path in order to address and accomplish the goals we set for ourselves. [. . .]

6

DANIEL COHN-BENDIT

AS A JEW—HERE?

First published as "Als Jude—hier?" in *Frankfurter Rundschau* (January 19, 1996). Translated by Tes Howell. Cohn-Bendit (b. 1945, Montauban, France) was expelled from France for revolutionary activities in 1968. In 1989, he established the Office for Multicultural Affairs in Frankfurt.

A Response to Israel's President Ezer Weizman

During a state visit this week, Israel's president Ezer Weizman expressed once again his bewilderment that Jews—50 years after the Holocaust—can still live in Germany. This statement not only offended me but also made me a little angry. My parents had to leave Germany in 1933: my father had returned already by 1949. Consequently, I feel compelled to explain why Jews live in Germany and, yes, why they can even feel comfortable here. But I will get to that later.

If Jews could not find a homeland in Germany after Auschwitz, then the same should apply to homosexuals, Sinti and Roma, and the disabled. How could even Germans, born after 1945, live in Germany with this history?

Indeed, an upbringing in Germany cannot merely consist of the cultivation of guilt. Teachers know the potential consequences for a German adolescent who learns what his or her ancestors were capable of doing to their fellow human beings. But the Germans and humankind in general will have to contemplate Auschwitz and the notion of total annihilation for some time to come.

When I was forced to leave France in 1968, I encountered a generation here that was prepared to take the collective guilt of the Germans upon itself. And, in fact, it wanted to establish a democracy that would preclude the possibility of war and Auschwitz forever. Of course, there was a naïve dimension inherent in this battle—and there still is. Germans want to be the best democrats, the best ecologists, the best pacifists, the best antinationalists, and the quintessential antiracists. It is true that this can get on one's nerves occasionally. . . .

If Weizman does not want to understand that Jews can live in a Germany where such horrible events as the murder of Turkish citizens in Solingen or Mölln occur, then he has struck a nerve in contemporary Germany. But he should kindly not forget that millions of people from Munich to Hamburg filled the streets to say no to racist terror. After *Kristallnacht,* millions of people stayed at home and acted as though they no longer knew the Jews, whose friends they had been just days before.

After the Holocaust, many issues still remain unresolved. One must ask the Germans: how could almost an entire people fall under the spell of total barbarianism? The French must explain why the French police, who picked up my grandfather, collaborated with such barbarism. Many Austrians must ask themselves why they viewed the annexation as a blessing. The list of collaboration could continue.

I have lived in Germany since 1968 because the decision to stay became a voluntary one. Ezer Weizman, as president of the state of Israel, has not only the right but also the obligation to promote Israel—a state in which devout Jews live with devout Muslims, Christians, and atheists.

Conversely, he must understand that there are many Jews who prefer to live in the diaspora. Provocatively speaking, I will go so far as to say that Israel signifies the end of Judaism and the beginning of a national Israeli consciousness. I subscribe to a different understanding of Judaism than Weizman. Having grown up in France and living in Germany, I feel comfortable as a cosmopolitan in the diaspora, but I also appreciate every multicultural society that tries to overcome one-dimensional ethnic thinking.

For this reason, I would like to return to Weizman's claim. More than 500,000 Jews lived in Germany before 1933. Germany will come to terms with itself and its history only when hundreds of thousands of Jews, together with

Muslims, Christians, and atheists, help shape the Germany of the future. Or, following Jean-Paul Sartre, when Germany is again accustomed to the fact that Jews in Germany can be employers and entrepreneurs, debtors and bankers, conservatives and Greens, ministers and independents, harlots and thieves—then being Jewish in Germany will have become normal. It is worthwhile to fight for this future.

Therefore, it makes sense to me that Jews live in Germany today and stand up for it; may this German democracy continue to improve and reform itself. I live today in Germany voluntarily and without guilt.

7

THOMAS KLEINE-BROCKHOFF

GERMANY, YOUR ISLAMISTS

First published as "Deutschland, deine Islamisten" in *Die Zeit* (June 20, 1997). Translated by David Gramling.

Crescent, Döner Kebab, Propaganda: A Visit to the Largest Rally of Muslim Fundamentalists in the Federal Republic

As though an invisible hand were showing the way, the masses stream through the gates of the Westphalian Stadium. No usher needs to interfere; everyone seems to know what to do: women left, men right. No questions, no protests. Today, at the beginning of the soccer season, the sold-out stadium is orderly, Islamically speaking. The 48-year-old Federal Republic had never seen such a sight in this enormous arena before last Saturday: nothing but women with head scarves up to the roof of the east bleachers, chaste and devout. Scarves—as far the eye can see. Were it not for the ads for "Brameier German Soccer League Bed Linens" and the challenge "Borussia—Just Do It!" one could imagine oneself back in Turkey.

But the Westphalian Stadium is quite certainly located in Dortmund, Germany. And many visitors, the younger ones at least, have a German passport or were born here as natives. A sign on the upper balcony of the women's stands confirms this fact: "We are immigrants!"

The annual rally is billed as the "Peace and Culture Festival," and many of the 40,000 guests agreeably wave the flag of the Islamic organization Milli Görüş, or National Perspective, which coordinated the event. The flag is typical: a crescent encircles the European diaspora, against a background of Islamic green. In the 1990s, missionaries have been fairly successful in the Federal Republic. For a long time Milli Görüş has covered the republic with a dense network of alliances. The organization controls around 300 of the 1,000 mosques and owns community centers that provide the devout with secular services: they can shop in their own supermarket, drop off the children at day care or the youth center, the sports club, Koran school, or a computer course; they can book pilgrimages or trips to Turkey, check out videos and books, and receive advice on income taxes or education. Milli Görüş now reaches nearly one-fifth of the 2 million German-Turks, and as much as a third of the youth, according to the Bielefeld youth researcher Wilhelm Heitmeyer.

The German majority society seems to have intentionally ignored this development, as it has ignored many events in the adjacent but strange immigrant world. But the Office for the Protection of the Constitution has been watching in recent years and has described Milli Görüş in its most recent report as "Islamic extremist," because it strives for the "displacement of the secular system of government in Turkey" and the establishment of an "Islamic theocracy."

It is hard to overlook the fact that for Milli Görüş, the old Turkish homeland continues to exist as a conceptual anchor in this Westphalian stadium as a conceptual anchor alongside the new German one. Political stars from Turkey occupy the seats of honor on the sidelines, among them three cabinet ministers and the mayor of Istanbul. It is no coincidence that they all belong to the party of the fundamentalist leader Necmettin Erbakan, a major supporter of Milli Görüş. A band dressed in old Ottoman military costumes first plays folk songs but later—repeatedly— plays the national anthem. And a chorus, numbering into the 10,000s, sings along: "my beloved fatherland Turkey." Does this sound like a religious event?

Why young native Germans go into a stadium in order to sing the Islamic hymns of their parents' home country cannot be investigated by a male reporter, at least not in the women's stands. Friendly yet determined security guards thwart every attempt—and cite the Koran in the process. The rebuttal that men and women are separated in the Federal Republic only in changing rooms, public bathrooms, and saunas is rejected confidently by the gentlemen: squatters' rights apply in the Westphalian Stadium, and this afternoon those rights belong to Milli Görüş. And so it goes when Islamists know and use not only the Koran but German law as well.

So, back to the opposite stands, where the young Sedat sits among the masses and waves the Turkish flag. At 22 years old, he has come directly from Borsigplatz, a Dortmunder. And therefore a real Borussian. Normally, he is in the stadium "for unity's sake," but today he is here "because of national sentiments" and "for religious reasons, of course." For him, it is always somehow an emotional matter, a great and real one. The Germans, he says, would not understand; they automatically call it fundamentalism, "but," he quips, "to be Borussian, that is also fundamentalism."

Years ago, Sedat's parents took him to Milli Görüş, first to the mosque, then to the courses. So that he won't lose his connection to Turkey, they reasoned at the time. So he doesn't run through the city someday with the other bellowing and drunken Borussia soccer fans. He still became a Borussia fan but does not bellow or drink. "I'm still a Muslim."

The idea that the organization teaches the youth can be seen in the halls of the Westphalian Stadium. Through the corridors under the stands, the legions roll past the vendors. Enormous architectural drawings for new mosques in Bremen and Rendsburg are plastered on concrete pillars. Next to that one can pick up the *Milli Gazete,* the semiofficial newspaper of Milli Görüş and the Turkish Welfare Party, which rails sometimes against America, sometimes against Israel, but always against secularism. A few meters farther is the Koran on CD-ROM, and then an entire selection of videos for youth.

The videotapes are covered in naïve drawings, as though the stories were fairy tales. The vendor says innocently, "all of this is for children under six, no blood or violence." On the table in front of him is a video entitled *Küçük Mücahid,* facilely translated as *"Little Mujaheddin."* The cover image shows a boy adoring a bearded religious fighter, complete with ammunition belt and machine gun. This is the Taliban's ideology, packaged for children.

Many of the videos follow a template, as the sociologist [Wilhelm] Heitmeyer's research group discovered after analyzing these films: a boy, an immigrant child, lives in a Western city, a sinful cesspool of criminality, drugs, and demoralization; the boy goes astray, but Muslims, selfless and helpful, reach out; they offer orientation, warmth, and identity through Milli Görüş.

Slowly, step by step, Milli Görüş's ideological pull encourages religious involvement. Heitmeyer's group reports that the process climaxes with the summer camps, from which many youths return completely changed. Many a girl has gone with flowing hair and returned in a head scarf.

Those who might like to speak about the head scarf this afternoon in the Westphalian Stadium, of course with women, must resort to craftiness and catch them on the way back from the restroom. Four girls from Lübeck, hardly of age, agreed to talk. Of course, they are wearing head scarves, and they are wearing the latest Islamist chic fashions: platform shoes, tight clothes (ankle length), satin shirts (with a high neckline). One need only give the signal and they all start talking: they complain about the hypocrisy of a society that proudly touts the Basic Law while discriminating against those who wear head scarves.

One of the girls describes her search for an apprenticeship. Repeatedly she was told "If you take off the head scarf, you can start today." But she does not want to do so. Last week, she went to apply at a Lübeck hospital, where she was told, "Your head scarf scares the patients." "Why?" she asked. "Do the nuns here scare the patients less?" The young woman received neither an answer nor the job.

Milli Görüş takes advantage of this situation: first, the organization hammers into the girls' heads that a good Muslim woman is one who wears the head scarf. Whoever criticizes this article of faith contributes to the negative image of Islam. In the end, Milli Görüş represents itself as a defense against the pressure to assimilate. The young women consequently feel they are agents of emancipation. Unfortunately, the conversation with the girls from Lübeck barely lasts five minutes, for a few attentive guards once again feel they have to defend the women's freedom. [. . .]

8

MEIKE WÖHLERT

THE HYPE OVER THE STAR OF DAVID

First published as "Der Hype um den Davidstern" in *Zitty* (July 1998). Translated by Hilary Menges.

Anything that qualifies as Jewish is the latest fashion. But things have not yet returned to normal—quite the opposite.

A few weeks ago, something changed at the post office. The Jewish Congregation of Berlin began to send out its newsletters not enclosed in envelopes but unwrapped. Since then, many members—especially elderly ones—have canceled their subscriptions. They don't want their neighbors to know they are Jews.

Upside-down world? Recently, Jewishness is all the rage: Jewish restaurants, shops, clubs, and cultural establishments have been cropping up all over Berlin, from the *Scheunenviertel* district to the Spandauer suburbs. Bagels must be included on the menus of the trendy cafés; tours through "Jewish Berlin" enjoy long-running success and are even offered in English. [. . .]

In June, throngs of visitors attend the Jewish Streetfest on Ryke Street; in October, curious minds will not be able to find a spot in the packed Hebrew courses at the Jewish adult-education center. The term *Jewish living* sticks to the city like döner and meatballs, gleefully complemented by the terms *new blood* or *rebirth*.

So, everything's great with the Jews? "Whatever is now happening in Berlin has absolutely nothing to do with Jews themselves," says Julius Schoeps, director of the Potsdamer Moses Mendelssohn Center for Jewish-European Studies. "It is a result of the fact that non-Jewish society has not yet come to terms with its history. It is the opposite of normalcy—it's folklore."

Schoeps is not alone in his views. Many Jews regard this overwhelming interest dubiously, because the Germans are celebrating a form of Judaism that no longer exists. Its roots were extirpated here, and as a result, the tiny, inchoate seedling is now being excessively watered, preserved, and engaged. The hype says more about the burdens of the Nazi past than about the Jewish present. The journalist Henryk M. Broder, who lives in Berlin and Jerusalem, articulates the main issue: "The fewer real Jews there are in existence, the more enthusiasm there is for Jewish culture."

Before the war, there were 160,000 Jews in Berlin; in 1945, only 5,000 remained. Until reunification, the number in West Berlin was not more than 6,000; in the East, it was just over 200. Since then, the figure has doubled to approximately 12,000—mainly due to emigrants from the former Soviet Union.

Yet the Holocaust memorial and the Jewish Museum are central civic and political topics that foster public discussion. When the head of the Jewish adult-education center was fired and then reinstated amid internal struggles, however, the topic took a more prominent place in Berlin's newspapers than in Senate decisions. In London, Paris, Amsterdam, or New York, no one would have been interested. In contrast to these cities, tried-and-true Jewish life in Berlin is only a trickling stream. To exculpate our conscience, we eat, write, and play violin at its banks.

Andrew Roth, coauthor of the English travel guide *Jewish Life in Berlin,* believes that "many people eat in Jewish restaurants to show that they are the 'other' Germans—those who at the time hid a Jew in their cellar back then." [. . .]

Hartmut Bomhoff views the enthusiasm for the façade of Judaism with particular skepticism: "It is easier to go eat in the Tabuna than to discuss the 1940s with the grandparents." And when people "run to klezmer concerts and name their children Sarah and David, Jews have nothing to do with it." Bomhoff, who was previously active in Jewish-Christian dialogues, has since retreated: "For me, the more that is appropriated from Jewishness, the bigger the chasm grows."

Professor Schoeps goes one step further. He views the current trend as "markedly dubious," because he sees anti-Semitism and fascination with Jewishness as two sides of the same coin. Although everything Jewish "is figured positively for the moment, that can quickly turn into the opposite. The exaggerated declaration of belief in Judaism corresponds to exaggerated rejection."

Gabriel Heimler, an artist and fellow Meshulash member, goes so far as to call the recasting of Judaism through socially acceptable clichés as "cultural Shoah." Henryk M. Broder's judgment does not come across so harshly: "Klezmer is as Jewish as lederhosen are German. That is okay; people need their symbols." Nevertheless, he does find the hype to be "somewhat ill-mannered." [. . .]

Broder meets many converts "who say to me, I should eat kosher and not go to the cafés on Saturday. I find it in part very funny when these people tell me what correct Jewishness is. I know what correct Jewishness is. I always have to wake my father up when he dreams of the KZ [concentration camp]." Conversion fever is running rampant in Berlin, too. Yehuda Tiechtel, a New York rabbi, has been living here for two years, and it never ceases to surprise him: "I have been in many lands and on many continents but I have never been approached by so many people who want to convert." Tiechtel says the reasons offered are quite vague for the most part, but Rabbi Tiechtel has little time for the converts: he has his hands full with the existing Jews.

Berlin has a particular meaning for Tiechtel: "Starting in this city, Hitler and the Nazis set out to destroy Judaism. And now we are bringing Jewish knowledge and self-awareness back here. It is a great revenge against Hitler!"

He says this with delight, with true enthusiasm. When people on the street react and stare at him because of his traditional black suit, he bears this attention with composure: "To live in Berlin is very different from living in New York or Israel." But he is still very open-minded: "When people react to my clothing, I explain to them what the hat and the bands are for. It is a good thing when people show interest." [. . .]

Friday evening. A man in a green uniform stands in front of the synagogue on Ryke Street. Another one blocks the entrance, holding the type of metal detector one sees at airports. Pat downs and purse searches are under way. Why? The man stares without understanding: "because there is a synagogue here," he says, shaking his head.

"Normalcy? The entrance to the Community Center in the Fasanen Street looks like the Stammheim trials! That does not exist in any other country," says Professor Schoeps. Taunting, threatening letters are daily occurrences for him and for Andreas Nachama, the head of the Jewish Congregation of Berlin. The letters represent the largest share of Berlin's approximately 100 annual punishable anti-Semitic offenses—along with destruction of property, disturbing the peace, desecration of cemeteries, and other crimes. The state police, not the "normal" criminal police, are officially responsible for handling these offenses. Precinct director Peter-Michael Haeberer explains why: "The state is not endangered when the head of the Jewish Congregation receives an abusive letter. The danger arises in the existence of a body of thought. One might think that after 50 years, it would gradually stop. But it does not stop."

Like many other members of Meshulash, Hartmut Bomhoff found the "German Manifesto" in his mailbox on May 8, 1995. That day was the 50-year anniversary of the end of the war. The manifesto declared "If you have not emigrated by May 9, you'll be in for it." He stayed and had his number removed from the phone book. [. . .]

Nicola Galliner, head of the Jewish adult-education center, does not always identify herself to strangers as a Jew. "When I want to have my peace and quiet, I'd rather not say anything. As soon as people know, they treat me differently." Or as Michael Blumenthal, the future director of the Jewish Museum, said in *Newsweek:* "During every visit to Germany, I arrive as an American and leave as a Jew." The phenomenon of being treated differently: it is an ambivalent combination of rejection, inhibition, enraptured wonderment and compulsory explanations. [. . .]

So what should young Germans do, if not ask questions when their interest is not satisfied by biting into a bagel? They can't get to know Jewish life in street signs; their grandparents took care of that. And in school they learn much about deceased Jews but very little about the living. In such a knowledge vacuum, stereotypes can spread unchecked.

In November 1998, the Meshulash group planned an exhibition entitled *Jewish Life in Berlin—Traditions and Visions.* Part of the project description read, "We invite artists to present their imagination to us: deft and futuristic, without false pathos or folkloristic touch."

9
DILEK ZAPTÇIOĞLU
THE UNIVERSALIST SWINDLE

First published as "Der universalistische Schwindel" in *die tageszeitung* (July 18, 1998). Translated by Tes Howell. Zaptçıoğlu was editor in chief of the magazine *Bizim Almanca* (Our German), and is a correspondent for the Istanbul-based newspaper *Cumhuriyet* (The Republic), as well as the German newspapers *Die Zeit* and *die tageszeitung.*

The head-scarf debate: The Muslim Fereshta Ludin is prohibited from becoming a teacher in Baden-Württemberg. For migrants in Germany, this is a fatal sign.

The discussion about the head scarf is not new. Nine years ago, France was already discussing the head scarves of young female students in Creil. The judgment in favor of the girls divided the SOS Racism movement and cost it the support of the socialists, who traditionally adhere to rigid secularism.

At that point, Germany seemed like a minor paradise for believers of every orientation. Here no one said anything when girls came to class with head scarves; upon request, they were released from physical education or swim class—situations that would make the French shake their heads. But, of course, the French did not understand that church taxes are automatically deducted from every salary in Germany and that one of the largest parties calls itself Christian Democratic.

Appearances in Germany were always deceiving: these head-scarf-wearing girls, having finished with their tolerant schools and training, were confronted with the bitter truth while on the job search (if not earlier). They had little chance as a salesperson or secretary. The human-resources staff always found some reason not to hire a young woman with a head scarf: some simply said that the girls could not work wearing such a getup.

Things were different in manufacturing: there, almost all female employees of the Muslim faith wear a head scarf, and even the cleaning ladies' heads are usually covered. The employers not only accept this practice; they explicitly welcome it for hygienic reasons.

There is, of course, a difference between the Muslim woman who cleans the classrooms and the one who stands at the board talking about Goethe and

Schiller. What signifies hygiene and religious freedom for one person is a possible sign of religious fanaticism and professional unsuitability for another, even if the employee is in no way a religious fanatic. [. . .]

In German schools, students learn about Western culture and civilization, which are historically based on Christianity. By definition, this diverges from Islam. No instruction is free of the values and norms that this part of the world has created for itself, which it declared to be universally valid, and against which there has been worldwide resistance. Therefore, a teacher with a cross around her neck is a daily phenomenon in German schools; she fits into the overall picture, whereas a teacher with a head scarf sticks out, just because she is Muslim.

School is not neutral in its worldview, and the values and norms that it imparts have universal pretenses—but they are not impartial. If Fereshta Ludin were a Muslim who felt her culture and civilization were superior to others, she would have to reject working with such lesson plans outright. She would try to teach the children about her own worldview. Given that she cannot do so in German public schools, she would go to a private school or perhaps try to establish a private Islamic school, where filling classrooms would be no problem.

But these are not her intentions at all. Fereshta Ludin is merely insisting on wearing the head scarf in the classroom. Actually, this statement is incorrect, as there is no public place where a devout Muslim may "take off" the scarf. Whether the scarf is a Muslim item or not is of little interest. If she herself feels this practice to be religious, then it is. She wants to wear the head scarf and to teach the children the same things her non-Muslim colleagues do. That she does not see this desire as a contradiction of her Islamic faith should make every secularist extremely happy, for it shows that Fereshta Ludin restricts her faith to the private sphere of the conscience and does not want it to be understood as politics.

In the French head-scarf debate, the issue was clearly the traditionally rigid perceptions of secularism and the question whether this perception should now be moderated and modernized. The debate revolved around the fact that every kind of religious or worldview-oriented symbol was forbidden in French schools—for students as well as teachers. In Germany, one is admittedly a bit more lax with such symbols, and there are schools, teachers, and even political leaders who refuse to apply constitutional court decisions to crosses in the classroom.

In short, at issue is distrust of the other, buried deep in the nation's soul. It is a distrust of every "foreigner," especially when he has become so similar to "us." When he has assimilated himself and conformed, he can be all the more dangerous and could weaken and betray us from within. So, beyond the apparently value-neutral discussions about symbols in the school, the head scarf has an important, perhaps unique, discussion-worthy aspect: how do

Germans envision their future with (Muslim) migrants, when they make them an assimilation offer that they themselves refuse to honor? [. . .]

10

MICHA BRUMLIK, ANGELIKA OHLAND, AND RAINER JUNG
JEWS IN GERMANY: A DELICATE RELATIONSHIP

First printed as "Juden in Deutschland: Eine heikle Beziehung" in *Deutsches Allgemeines Sonntagsblatt*, (September 18, 1998). Translated by David Gramling. Brumlik (b. 1947) has taught pedagogy and education at the universities of Heidelberg and Frankfurt since 1981.

There are many shared rituals among Jews and non-Jews—as well as deep divides. What's missing is normalcy.

The Jewish Congregation and the Berlin Gorki-Theater were bitterly divided over Fassbinder's *Garbage, the City and Death.* Yet, according to Micha Brumlik, a Frankfurt-based educator, journalist, and member of the Green Party, this extreme hostility arose from other sources. If it were up to him, the exchanges between Jews and non-Jews would be much less complicated.

AO/RJ: Mr. Brumlik, in 1985, you and other Frankfurt Jews prevented the staging of Rainer Werner Fassbinder's *Garbage, the City and Death,* claiming it was anti-Semitic. Now, the same production is to be staged by Berlin's Gorki-Theater, and you want the Jewish community to accept it. What led you to change your mind?

Brumlik: The Jewish community has changed significantly. In 1985, it had a sort of "coming out." The Fassbinder scandal proved how effective it can be. We have become more self-confident—despite the fact, of course, that anti-Semitism still exists. [. . .]

AO/RJ: Then may Fassbinder call a rich Jew a "rich Jew"?

Brumlik: Of course. After all, that is not a taboo, and it wasn't one back in 1985 either. In Frankfurt, it was no secret that Jewish housing speculators did treat their renters poorly. The local Frankfurt press documented it daily. [. . .]

AO/RJ: Mr. Nachama, chairman of the Jewish Congregation of Berlin, sees the Fassbinder drama squarely in the tradition of Josef Goebbels. How has he come to such an extreme position?

Brumlik: Recently, the Jewish Congregation of Berlin has been treated in a disparaging way by Berlin's municipal government. Think about the manner in which the Senate carried out the dismissal of the director of the Jewish Museum; the state had no right to treat the Jewish community like a dumb school boy. In Berlin, just like in Frankfurt 13 years ago, the underlying tensions are more important. The Fassbinder piece is only a trigger. [. . .]

AO/RJ: But in symbolic and moral spheres, the Jewish community has definite influence. For example, regarding the Holocaust memorial: would it be at all possible to reconsider the project, as long as Mr. Bubis [chair of the Central Council of Jews in Germany] wants the memorial?

Brumlik: Someone like Michael Naumann, the SPD's deputy for cultural affairs, could order up some Jewish professors and journalists from the United States to argue against the memorial. The influence the Jewish community enjoys is power derived from the mercy of the rulers. And during times of conflict, it can be just as easily withdrawn. [. . .]

AO/RJ: What would you consider normal relations between Jews and non-Jews?

Brumlik: Under "normal," I would understand everyday relationships in which all young people could treat each other impartially and without inhibition, independent of whether they have Jewish or non-Jewish parents. This yearning for normalcy is completely justifiable and legitimate. When politics or other societal powers aim to enforce this normalcy, it becomes problematic. In 1985, when we first demonstrated against the Fassbinder piece, the Frankfurt director Ruehle argued that the production depicted Jews and non-Jews as finally being able to look at each other freely. For me, that smacked of an attempt to enforce reconciliation. A parallel situation arose when Helmut Kohl and Ronald Reagan visited a military cemetery with SS graves and the former Bergen-Belsen concentration camp—on the same day. That simply doesn't fly.

AO/RJ: But this tension exists within every young German who has grown up with *The Diary of Anne Frank* and *Schindler's List.* They identify themselves with the Jewish victims, resulting in a strong philo-Semitism—and isn't this based on clichés, just as anti-Semitism is?

Brumlik: Maybe. Nevertheless, the comparison between philo- and anti-Semitism is still wrong. Why should I object if today's young people are scrupulously and arduously examining and debating Jewish and German history? If they happen to side with Jewishness, I would not tell them they are merely compulsive philo-Semites. Individual motives are the decisive factor. I thought it was terrible when former Nazis, after the war, became passionate supporters of Israel's powerful military state. One who comes to mind is Hanns-Martin Schleyer, the murdered president of the employer's union. [. . .]

AO/RJ: And where do you see German society in 1998? Are we tending toward liability, or responsibility? How about the notion that "The 15 percent who won't accept liability for their parents' guilt are the true danger."

Brumlik: Those who accept responsibility outnumber those who don't. But the 15 to 20 percent who represent right-wing extremism and right-populist positions—they are a danger. These people do not accept one bit of liability. And I suspect that this position indeed reaches into the political center.

AO/RJ: The banks that refuse to pay out money to Jewish accounts have not accepted any responsibility either. Nazis haven't been involved for a long time, but their children and grandchildren are now in positions of power.

Brumlik: This type of behavior is scandalous. But I didn't expect anything else. The heads of the banks represent the interests of the employer. It would be overconfident to expect a particular civic consciousness from them.

AO/RJ: You yourself belong to the first postwar generation of Jews in Germany. What has struck you?

Brumlik: The feeling of foreignness in the family home and the desire to leave Germany. Otherwise, I grew up relatively normal, in regard to school and the like. In the 1950s, when I was in kindergarten and school, Jewish establishments were not as intensely guarded as they are today. Young Jews in today's Germany must feel like they're in an electronic ghetto.

AO/RJ: Can one feel both Jewish and German?

Brumlik: I prefer to speak of Jews in Germany, but, of course, every Jew must define this relationship personally. However, I feel myself to be neither a Jewish German nor a German Jew. Even now. But at the moment (and I hope it comes soon) when German citizenship rights are changed and one no longer has to belong to an ethnically German people in order to be German, I will say, I am German. But such normalcy has yet to come.

11

MICHAEL BRENNER

NO PLACE OF HONOR

First published as "Nur keinen Ehrenplatz" in *Süddeutsche Zeitung* (December 2–3, 2000). Translated by Tes Howell. Michael Brenner is a professor of Jewish history and culture at the University of Munich. This text refers to the "guiding culture" debates of 2000, which will be discussed in chapter 7 in more detail.

On the Jewish Minority's Role in the Temple of the Guiding Culture

My earliest encounter with the meaning of German *Leitkultur,* or guiding culture, in the context of the Christian Western world reaches back 30 years to my first day of school. I was introduced to the wonderful German custom of emptying a schoolbag filled with candy. The question that occupied me on this day was: chocolate or bonbons? But our young teacher in that provincial Bavarian town embarrassed me with a completely different question. Right in the first hour she presented us with the clearly formulated either/or status: "Who is Catholic, and who is Protestant?" Neither one seemed familiar to me, and consequently I could not decide between the given options. When I returned home, I learned that there were other options besides the ones given. I would soon learn more about this in intensive Jewish religious instruction.

For the next 13 years, I remained the only Jewish pupil in my class, although I was supposed to notice that I wasn't; the other one naturally hung on the cross before all our eyes, as in every good Bavarian school. In my high school years, other exotic deviations from the Catholic-Protestant majority joined my class: a Muslim whose family came from Iran, a New Apostolic, and—certainly the most exotic of us all—a student behind whose name the initials *O.B.* ["without avowal"] popped up in the annual report, which did not mean that his father was the mayor but rather that he had no professed faith. Because my own religious instruction took place one afternoon a week in the Jewish community center, we played a kind of multicultural soccer during my class's religious lesson. [. . .]

Synagogue Yes, Mosque No
Until now, not much has changed in Bavaria despite clear constitutional directives. In the liberal city-state of Bremen, guiding culture is grounded in the state constitution as a guiding religion. Article 32 states, "Public schools are community schools with generally Christian-based religious instruction of nonspecific faith in biblical history." This clause was once legitimately considered a particularly progressive summary of Catholic and Protestant religious instruction. However, wouldn't one need to adjust such a passage to fit the considerably altered reality, in order to ensure appropriate instruction for other religious communities?

For a long time, Jews were the only non-Christian minority in Germany. That situation has changed. For one thing, Jews live in a more or less pluralistic society—ethnically and religiously. They are no longer the only minority but rather a small minority among others. They are, and this leads us to the other side of the coin, anything but a typical minority. After the Holocaust, a Jewish presence in Germany was and is still crucial to the survival of German democracy. Success or failure of democracy in Germany was measured abroad largely by whether a Jewish community, however small it might be, could feel at home here. The departure of Jews from Germany would have unforeseeable consequences—not for the Jews but for Germany.

It would be mistaken to view the treatment of the Jewish minority in Germany today as representative of the interaction with other religious and ethnic minorities. Fortunately, anti-Semitism is still widely considered a social taboo. However, opinions and ordinances against other religious minorities and foreigners are, on the contrary, socially acceptable. There was a time when politicians could express wonderful sentiments about their Jewish fellow citizens and in the same breath warn about the danger of foreign infiltration in Germany.

Since Heinz Galinski and Ignatz Bubis took over the consistory, this situation has changed, and the pointed words of Paul Spiegel recently have made this line even clearer. Spiegel's prediction was correct: one cannot measure the policy toward Jews by the Sunday speeches on November 9, nor by the Week of Solidarity, but by the social openness toward minorities and foreigners, "the others." Just to name two examples: it is easy to imagine a synagogue in the cityscape, but a mosque? Luckily, one can now become well informed about Jewish culture at German universities, but where can one gain sound knowledge about Turkish culture and history?

The question—how does the Jewish minority define itself in the present debate?—simply has no answer. It could make things easy for itself and take the side of established society, resume the pre-1933 tradition in the context of German-Jewish symbiosis, and place itself in the illustrious company of the Einsteins and Rathenaus, Freuds and Zweigs. As a concession, the idea of a Christian Western world would be expanded into a Jewish-Christian Western world. The Jews would then receive a place of honor, so to speak, in the not-so-roomy temple of German guiding culture. Spiegel made it clear that he is choosing the more uncomfortable path and will oppose this kind of position. According to the core of his legitimate protest against the guiding culture's prescriptions, the Jews have lived better in a pluralistic society than in a monolithically defined one.

Both empires in Central and Southeastern Europe (the Hapsburg and Ottoman, respectively), which perished in World War I, accommodated not only large but also thriving and relatively free Jewish communities. This was possible in part because they could not and did not want to be defined by a guiding culture. Under completely different premises, such circumstances also hold for the United States, which offers the modern version of a multiracial empire, in that it allows countless immigrants to realize their own cultures. For the representatives of the European nation-state model, this multiculturalism was significantly more difficult, which is why their politics wavered between assimilation and exclusion. However, even in both France and Great Britain, there has long been a multicultural and multireligious milieu because of their colonial past and the more strongly pronounced secular elements in their societies. This model is a dream for some in Germany and a nightmare for others. In any case, it is indisputable that Germany is only in the early stages compared to other Western societies.

We should be grateful to the initiators of the guiding-culture debate. They have made us aware of what some had not previously seen so clearly: that German society is still strongly influenced by Christianity, thus making the discussion about a guiding culture one about a guiding religion as well. One may support and defend this state of affairs. But one can also call it into question and assert that in a modern twenty-first-century society, Christian religions must be strong enough to give up their symbolic dominance in the public sphere, as is already the case in most Western countries.

The Jewish community has a particular task ahead of it because of its special history and legal status: it is indeed one of the smallest minorities but also the most visible in terms of its symbolic power. As such, it can advocate for other minorities and for an open society. The fact that Jewish spokespeople have recently been doing so more often has caused some irritation among established politicians. This is good.

The option is either a backward society, shaped by fears of foreign infiltration, or an open society, which earnestly questions the relevance of many guiding values—whether they be guiding cultures or religions. For a long time, the Jews, as the only minority, have been assigned the task of making their respective societies a little more colorful and flexible. This position has brought them recognition and admiration from the one, mistrust and hatred from the other. Today they are—thankfully—no longer the only ones in this role.

12

JAN ROSS

ERNST, THE MOSLEMS ARE HERE!

First published as "Ernst, die Moslems sind da!" in *Die Zeit* (December 19, 2001). Translated by David Gramling. Ernst Jünger (1895–1998), the subject of the first section of this essay, was a major literary figure of the 1920s "reactionary modernism" movement, whose texts reflect on his experiences as a soldier in World War I.

The question of the year: How are we doing with Islam? Are we tolerant enough? Or are we, on the contrary, too lax? Everywhere in Germany there is a new desire for clarity and, when necessary, conflict.

"Ernst, the Moslems are here," called Frau Jünger from downstairs, when the messengers from the University of Bilbao arrived unannounced at the poet's house in Wilflingen with news of the conferral of an honorary doctorate. A Muslim professor had made the arrangements for the award, and the bearers of the message were a group of religious comrades. The scene took place in 1989. Ernst Jünger came down, expressed his delight, and professed his sympathy with Islam. First off, the prophet Mohammed had been a warrior, which pleased the old soldier. Because of the pilgrimage to Mecca, Islam is a religion of travel, and Jünger is a passionate traveler as well. Finally, the 94-year-old soldier looked over to his Liselotte: having four wives, as the Koran allows, would also not be that bad. In any case, there was no reason to decline the offered title, and Ernst Jünger did indeed travel to Spain to accept the tribute with a respectful speech about Islam.

The man relating this story belongs to the small Muslim delegation. He narrates it with a Badish accent. Abu Bakr Rieger comes from the Black Forest and converted to Islam during law school. For a few years, he settled in Weimar as a lawyer (out of love for Goethe, he says) and was particularly happy to lead Muslim friends and visitors through the sacred sites of German national literature. Since then, he has sat in a Potsdam office and published the *Islamische Zeitung*, which has a circulation of 10,000 copies monthly. He is also the vice-chair of the Islamic Council—the second-largest Muslim umbrella organization in the Federal Republic (after the larger Central Council of Muslims)—which is regarded with suspicion by the German authorities because its dominant member organization is the Turkish-Islamic Milli Görüş organization. For Rieger, however, no mere theocratic dreams can account for the imminence of unrest and the current realities of Islam. Rather, a resistance to the economization of society generates this potential—for example, by way of the Koran's prohibition on interest accrual. Limitless capitalism dissolves the bonds of place and space in human life; Rieger rediscovered himself in Mecca, in the Kaaba center of the world. One might almost say that he became Muslim out of homesickness.

So much is going on in Germany! September 11, 2001, and the war in Afghanistan abruptly thrust Germany's Islamic world into view. Curiosity was awoken; concern as well. Otto Schily banned Metin Kaplan's Caliph State, a rather bizarre marginal group. The Bavarian interior minister Günther Beckstein is demanding the same for Milli Görüş, which, considering its 27,000 members and intimate link with Turkish domestic politics, would definitely be quite a different exercise of power. Are we tolerant enough, or are we too trusting and lax? A ruling will be handed down in Karlsruhe in mid-January on the constitutional appeal by a Muslim butcher, who was not allowed to practice ritual slaughter by authorities and courts. Politicians, school authorities, and lawyers are at odds about whether female Muslim teachers ought to be allowed to wear a head scarf in the classroom. Reflection on Islamic religious instruction has become pressing—and precisely at the moment when the role of Christianity in state-sponsored education is no longer a self-evident proposition, as the emerging conflict around Brandenburg's church-estranged life-skills curriculum demonstrates.

The discourse about foreignness, with which the majority society sees itself confronted, fluctuates peculiarly between fear of conflict and desire for self-assertion. For God's sake, a clash of civilizations must not take place, and when Italy's minister president Berlusconi spoke in Berlin on the supremacy of the West over Islam, hands flew into the air in appalled defiance. However, whether or not there was also a kind of politically incorrect self-praise in this gesture is still unclear. It is, after all, the leftists and liberals—tending on the one hand toward multiculturalism but just as bound to Enlightenment and emancipation on the other hand—who find themselves in a strange contradiction when faced with veiled Muslim women. Should one be foreigner friendly or critical of fundamentalism? Should one defend difference or fight the dark Middle Ages? Conversely, conservatives look with fascination upon Islam's loyalty to tradition and sense of family, which generates unsettling competition for indigenous Christianity and the customs of the land.

In the Mosques, the Old People Are Praying

We must do away with a certain well-meaning "interreligious fudging," says the Protestant bishop of Berlin-Brandenburg, Wolfgang Huber. A little more care should be exercised in the recently ubiquitous chatter about the "three Abrahamic religions"—Judaism, Christianity, and Islam—or in the precipitous expansion of the Jewish-Christian dialogue into the Jewish-Christian-Muslim trialogue. Huber has had enough of this "escape into the foreign," of the ostensibly progressive self-disgust that seeks to teach school-children everything about Ramadan and the Garden Hut Festival, while no longer speaking of Advent and Christmas. Berlusconi's supremacist grandiloquence is nonetheless offensive to the bishop, and the words *guiding culture* hardly pass over his lips, because "Reflection on the self need not be accompanied by a claim to supremacy." But one senses a fresh desire for clarity and differentiation, as well as a desire for conflict when it is necessary. Even the Hamburg bishop Maria Jepsen, of all people, the incarnation of the Protestant will for peace and advancement, recently decried the persecution of Christians in the Muslim world: "In many Islamic countries, Christians are seen as second-class citizens, and we must say with more clarity than ever before that when you and your Moslems call for respect and equal treatment, you must also make an effort to end the persecution in your countries."

It is not easy to say what influence strict or even fanatical Islam exerts among Muslim immigrants in the Federal Republic. One often hears that in the "third generation" of young foreigners born here, integration is failing because they are retreating into a cultural ghetto. "Fundamentalism" and the satellite dish on the roof, bringing native-language television programs into the home, play into this claim. Head scarves are on the rise: in general, they are mostly worn by girls whose mothers did not wear them. This new religious fervor that has seized the whole Islamic world since the late 1970s did not pass into the domestic diaspora quietly. The Turkish community in Germany is much more of a "quiet little people" than are the Pakistanis and Bangladeshis in England or the North Africans in France. Ultimately, though, there is still the impression that young Muslims in this country are not much more interested in religion than other youth are and that it is the old people who are assembling in the mosques, just as in the churches. The fundamental trend is not Islamization but secularization. And as for the ghetto, the "parallel society" that everyone is warning of is not so simple.

For example, the Continuing Education and Meeting Center for Muslim Women in Cologne may look like a parallel-society institution at first glance, an exclave and separate world. Men are not permitted here, at least not in the classes. Ayten Kılıçarslan, the current teacher, describes it as a free space for unobserved and unhindered coexistence, where clients and visitors can be "women in chadors or women in short-sleeved dresses." But clearly the basic disposition of the center does not come across as neutral or worldly but pious. And why should it not? Here, tradition and emancipation do not stand in opposition to one another, contrary to general expectations. In this Cologne education center, Muslim girls and women can obtain their elementary or trade-school certificates. If they have not achieved this objective yet, that might have to do with their distrustful fathers', husbands', brothers', or uncles' plans to sabotage their attendance at German public schools. Resistance to the sex-segregated and Islam-oriented world of the education center is low. Does this milieu signify a capitulation to the religious dictates of the pasha ethos? Girls and women do learn something; they can be trained for a career, win independence and self-awareness.

Ayten Kılıçarslan would prefer not to label herself as an "Islamic feminist." For her, the term suggests agitation and polemics. But many of her colleagues have fewer problems with the concept of feminism, and they all believe in advocating for the interests of their gender. The women of the center value independence from any of the male-run mosque communities, and they are quite conscious of the patriarchal material often preached in these mosques. Ayten Kılıçarslan argues that this patriarchal bent is not a necessary or even a plausible consequence of her beliefs; she considers it a mistaken social and cultural development. "We have less of a problem with Islam than with Muslim men." That statement sounds a little too grand to be true. No religion can be so cleanly separated from its historic and societal concretizations—certainly not a religion like Islam, which, according to its entire self-concept, pursues not only a faith doctrine and pious praxis but a way of life as well.

Of course, these questions may not be left to the internal dynamics of Islamic communities. It goes without saying that legal offenses and anticonstitutional propaganda cannot be tolerated. No tradition or conviction releases citizens from the duty to obey laws. But what about that gray area, where we quietly suspect that someone's acceptance of an open society's rules of play is only lip service, that internal speech differs from external speech, that something spoken in Turkish differs from that which is spoken in German? For those of us who do not understand Turkish, doesn't this suspicion sneak in? In the head-scarf debate, such righteous ruminations play a major role. One is not allowed to dislike the head scarf of a Muslim teacher in a German school merely for being a cultural irritation, an offensive impression. There are certainly no sufficient grounds to forbid such sentiments, although often enough, they are the real motive for the desire to prohibit. But behind the head scarf, is there not perhaps something else hiding, an image of women that we reject fundamentally and that is ultimately contrary to the Basic Law and geared toward an Islamic theocracy?

This year, the former Federal Constitutional Court judge Ernst-Wolfgang Böckenförde, one of the greatest teachers of constitutional law, rigorously decried the prohibition on head scarves. The German constitution is not secular; the neutrality of the state's worldview in no way compels teachers to assume religious neutrality in their civil service.

Until there is proof of an unreasonable disturbance of the peace in schools, a teacher should be able to assert his or her freedom of faith. Böckenförde, however, had more in mind than just constitutional dogmatism. Already during the dispute about the Dismissal of Radicals during the 1970s, he confronted the menace of thought control. He perceived a climate of suspicion in which a kind of constitutional-conformist worldview was demanded of the citizen as the only correct disposition. This approach doesn't work, not among believers nor among leftists.

When it comes to latent inner reservations about the stipulations of the Basic Law, Böckenförde makes an informative comparison with his own Catholic Church. Until the beginning of the 1960s, the Catholic doctrine of tolerance contradicted the Basic Law in principle; the church maintained that one must acknowledge nonbelievers and people with different beliefs only out of pragmatic considerations, for the sake of peace and equal rights. Under ideal relations, only the true religion, Catholicism, has a right to existence. This position stands in stark contradiction to the Basic Law's concept of the freedom of belief and conscience, and no devout Catholic would have been able to become a civil servant if this doctrine were imputed to him personally. Of course, this interpretation of the Basic Law did not prevail. But the Catholic Church revised its opinion and, at the Second Vatican Council of 1965, recognized religious freedom. Doctrinal opinion followed the realities of life. Only in this way do religions become compatible with modernity, not through antifundamentalist schoolmasterism. According to Böckenförde, one can and must hope for the same from Islam, because "freedom is contagious."

13

HANS-ULRICH WEHLER

MUSLIMS CANNOT BE INTEGRATED

First printed as "Muslime sind nicht integrierbar" in *die tageszeitung* (September 10, 2002). Translated by David Gramling. Wehler (b. 1931), a prominent social historian and public intellectual in Germany, is a professor of history at the University of Bielefeld. This is a follow-up interview regarding Wehler's speech at the 2002 *Deutscher Historikertag*, or German Historians' Day.

taz [die tageszeitung]: Mr. Wehler, you celebrated your seventieth birthday on the 11th of September of last year. How was it when you found out about the terrorist attacks in the United States?

Hans-Ulrich Wehler: I was in an isolated village on Crete where we had neither radio nor television. That evening my wife and I had a nice dinner. Not until the next day did we find out by telephone about the attacks. After this, we found a television in a hotel to watch. At first, I did not want to believe it.

taz: Now, a year later, German historians are meeting for a major conference in their field—and at the last moment, a panel discussion about September 11 was added. How could it be that your colleagues almost ignored this topic?

Wehler: That is the provinciality of the German historians' guild. They can easily come up with 10 experts on the Bavarian War of Succession. But when they look for just one good historian who can say something about the Near East—then it gets really difficult. In America, one would just get on the telephone with any good university's history department and drum up a few people from Berkeley, Harvard, or Stanford.

taz: What particular contributions can historians make to the debate concerning September 11?

Wehler: They can put the whole discussion into historical perspective. Islam is the only world religion that is still overtly and quickly expanding. Soon it will have overtaken Christianity. It is a militant monotheism that cannot deny its origins in a world of bellicose nomadic Arab tribes.

taz: Do you mean to say that we are indeed engaged in a "clash of cultures," as the American political scientist Samuel Huntington believes?

Wehler: I don't understand the perspective of the *multikulti* dogooders who have tossed Huntington's book into the netherworld. I doubt that the critics actually read the 550 pages. It is a quite modest analysis about how new lines of conflict arose at the end of the Cold War. You can't just summarily dismiss that with a wave of your left hand—certainly not after September 11.

taz: Doesn't the Federal Republic, with its 2.4 million Turkish immigrants, prove that a peaceful coexistence can work?

Wehler: This example shows precisely that it does not work. The Federal Republic doesn't have a foreigner problem; it has a Turk problem. This Muslim diaspora is fundamentally incapable of integration. Since its founding, the Federal Republic has coped superbly with its now 10 percent immigrant population. But as one would expect of a complex society, there is a limit.

taz: And how do you address this issue?

Wehler: One must impose strict controls. All immigration countries have put on the emergency brakes after a phase of uncontrolled immigration; the Americans and the Australians even utilized expressly racist criteria. The American immigration law of 1922–23, which was in effect for forty years, includes the artificial concept of the "Caucasian," denoting the "blond whites," who could immigrate in higher quotas.

taz: Are you making a proposal for such criteria here?

Wehler: One should not accept explosive materials into the country voluntarily. I have two brilliant Turkish students here. But one must carefully distinguish between personal experiences and the necessity for strict controls.

taz: Academic elites integrate without difficulty. Is the ability to integrate more a question of social status than of religion?

Wehler: In the Federal Republic, one can hardly speak of a Turkish elite, except for the famous tourism entrepreneur Vural Öger and a few others. Turks grow up in a religion that establishes certain barriers to integration. The fundamentalist current has a shot at a majority—both here and in Turkey.

taz: Can one stop this trend by strengthening Western-oriented forces through the prospect of European Union membership?

Wehler: This argument borders on political idiocy. Europe is shaped by the Christian tradition, by Jewish-Roman-Greek antiquity, the Renaissance, the Enlightenment, and scientific revolution. That all applies to the new member states in Eastern Europe as well. But it does not apply to Turkey. One cannot just ignore this cultural border in an act of willful self-destruction. Furthermore, accepting Turkey would give Europeans such notorious neighbors as Syria and Iraq.

taz: The U.S. government obviously wants to solve the Iraq problem with a war. If you see such a great danger in this kind of "clash of cultures," would you advocate such an attack?

Wehler: I have nothing against threats as a tool. But clearly a preventive war is being organized right now. I do not know of any preventive war in recent history that met its stated goal.

taz: Which parallels are you thinking of?

Wehler: In a moment of sobriety, the German grand admiral Tirpitz labeled World War I a German preventive war. The intention was to defuse the danger of an impending two-front war by humiliating Serbia and telling Russia to get lost. That failed fantastically.

taz: Does that mean that you compare the U.S. policy on Iraq to the German war politics of summer 1914?

Wehler: The concrete constellation is different, but the formal structure is the same. The idea is to defuse a situation by anticipating it—"prevenire," as Friedrich the Great said. This senile calculus attempts to solve political problems with one grand military strike. The Americans should read Clausewitz: war is only a means to achieve political goals. And there are no more political goals in the Near East that can justify another Gulf War.

taz: Many Americans compare Saddam Hussein with Adolf Hitler . . .

Wehler: . . . And say, "What if there had been a preventive war against Hitler?" Clearly no one planned for that—the mood in the United States would have had to be appropriate for declaring war. In European countries, which had just fought World War I, there was a deep longing for peace. And Roosevelt himself needed two years after the outbreak of the war to bring the United States in on the side of the Allies. Heaven knows whether that would have happened without the Japanese attack on Pearl Harbor.

taz: Europeans think the same today. But were these considerations correct in hindsight?

Wehler: Given the horizon of the time, they were completely correct. From the perspective of May 1945, just about anything would have been justified in order to stop such crimes against humanity. But that was asking far too much from the parties involved between 1933 and 1939. Today, however, the players are by no means overburdened. All arguments to the contrary are clearly mistaken.

taz: The federal chancellor sees this issue similarly and speaks of a "German way." Does this threaten to become another special path for the Germans?

Wehler: I find the formulation atrocious. My generation fought for decades against the "special path." The long path westward ended when the Germans finally felt comfortable in the West. For Schröder, it is just about the shabby exploitation of an election situation, not a real political possibility. Everyone knows there is only a European way.

taz: But this European way is not the American way?

Wehler: For the Europeans, there is no axis of evil. They have learned from their bloody history that pragmatic humility is a virtue. One can go into conflicts head-on, or one can quell them laterally. But one will never reach an eternal state of peace-loving happiness. We should defend this skeptical tradition.

14

FEDERAL CONSTITUTIONAL COURT

DECISION REGARDING ANIMAL SLAUGHTER AS A RELIGIOUS PRACTICE

This decision, docket number 1BvR 2284/95 from January 18, 2002, was published on the court's website www.bundesverfassungsgericht.de. Translated by Hilary Menges.

This complaint regarding the infringement of the constitution involves the granting of special authorization for religious slaughter—that is, the killing of warm-blooded animals without prior anesthetization.

At the beginning of the twentieth century, the slaughter of animals for religious purposes in keeping with Jewish rituals was largely permitted. The appropriate regulation thereof recognized predominant exceptions to the primary ban on religious slaughter without anesthetization. After National Socialism came to power in Germany, more and more states moved to ban religious slaughter. Eventually the imperative to anesthetize warm-blooded animals prior to butchering was implemented throughout Germany according to the law of April 21, 1933. According to the findings of the Federal Constitutional Court, the law's goal was to insult and violate the religious feeling and customs of the Jewish portion of society. Exceptions to the ban on religious slaughter were granted only in the case of emergency killings.

After the end of World War II, religious slaughter was for the most part tacitly tolerated, though state law did not expressly reauthorize it (for example, butchering in accordance with Islamic Sharia). Nationwide regulations regarding religiously motivated, unanesthetized slaughter were first established with the enactment of the Slaughter Law, as part of the Animal Protection Law. Since the implementation of the first Law to Amend the Animal Protection Law of August 12, 1986, the Animal Protection Law's article 1 fundamentally bans the slaughter of warm-blooded animals without anesthetization. However, article 2.2 allows the possibility of granting special exceptions on religious grounds. [. . .]

The plaintiff is a Turkish citizen and, according to his statement (which is not disputed in these proceedings), a strict Sunni Muslim. He has lived in the Federal Republic of Germany for 20 years and operates a butcher shop in Hessen, which he took over from his father in 1990. In order to provide for his Muslim customers, he was specially authorized to perform ritualistic religious slaughters without anesthetization until September 1995 (in accordance with article 2.2 of the Animal Protection Law). The butchering was carried out on his premises under veterinary supervision. In the period following, the plaintiff undertook additional applications for the granting of such authorizations. Since the June 15, 1995, decision of the Federal Constitutional Court, the requests have remained unsuccessful. [. . .]

It is alleged that the plaintiff's freedom to choose and pursue a career has been violated. Even though he is a Turkish citizen, he claims to have unlimited and unrestricted residency [in Germany]. In view of the duration of his residence in the Federal Republic of Germany, as well as his de facto German roots and his professional activities as a butcher, he claims protection under article 2.1 of the Basic Law. In addition, he claims fundamental rights protection under article 12.1 of the Basic Law.

The job of a Muslim butcher is an independent occupation, which requires certain qualifications that a normal butcher does not need to have. This occupation involves the quick and clean execution of the slaughter itself, so that the animal does not suffer unnecessarily. The job is, however, characterized much more by its religious elements, including the invocation of Allah.

The ban on religious slaughter thus affects the plaintiff as a manifest ban on his profession and thereby objectively restricts his job choices. If the decisions in question were able to persist and he were perpetually denied special authorizations, he would have to search for a new occupation. Constitutional law could only justify such a far-reaching intervention if it served to defend against demonstrable or severe danger to the good of the community. This, however, is not the case.

The Central Council of Muslims in Germany emphasizes the important meaning of animal welfare in Islam and explains that unanesthetized religious slaughter is stipulated as a mandatory component of Muslim religious practice. All significant Islamic groups in Germany share this opinion. According to a report from the Al-Azhar University of Cairo, the consumption of animal flesh not slaughtered in religious rituals is valid only in emergency situations. Such a situation, however, does not exist for Muslims in Germany. The principle of equal treatment with Jewish believers demands the authorization of religious slaughter for Muslims as well (in accordance with the Animal Protection Law). [. . .]

The court decisions in question violate the fundamental rights of the plaintiff as defined in article 2.1 in conjunction with articles 4.1 and 4.2 of the Basic Law. The authorities and the civil court have misjudged the necessity and possibility of a constitutional interpretation of article 4 of the Animal Protection Law. Therefore, applying the special-exceptions rule regarding bans on religious slaughter, they arrived at a disproportionate restriction of said fundamental right.

This decision may not be appealed.

Justices: Jaeger, Hömig, Bryde

15

BASSAM TIBI

BETWEEN THE WORLDS

First published as "Zwischen den Welten" in Berliner Tagesspiegel (May 11, 2002). Translated by David Gramling. Tibi (b. 1944, Damascus), chair of international relations at the University of Göttingen, is a German political scientist of Syrian descent.

Multicultural pathos is not enough: Whoever wants to integrate Muslims into the German community of values must offer them an identity.

Most observers tend not to interpret the newest anti-Jewish excesses of the Beurs in France as a combined effect of traditional anti-Semitism coupled with Prime Minister Ariel Sharon's new radical approach to the Palestinian autonomous regions. Instead, these observers express the opinion that the heinous deeds of Islamic Arab immigrant children from North Africa result from integration failures. Speaking as a migrant myself, I am also of the opinion that, in the case of Germany, the integration of Muslim immigrants has not been successful.

I understand immigration as steered migration. Current immigration, however, proceeds willy-nilly and without rules. [. . .] But what does integration mean, and why must it necessarily be considered a failure in Germany so far? Germany's politicians have apparently not learned any lessons from the tragic events of September 11.

Terror as a Problem of Diaspora

The terror attacks of September 11 proved in a concrete way that security issues are closely connected to immigration, given that the attacks were organized in the German Islamic diaspora. Consequently, Western countries (primarily the United States but also European states) have taken necessary steps. The British interior minister for labor, David Blunkett, voiced the opinion that Islamic migrants must accept the values of British democracy as a precondition for their integration. Islamists within the British Muslim diaspora attacked Blunkett and associated him with "right-wing extremism." But this recrimination seems to more fittingly describe his Islamist opponents, who dismiss "democracy as faithlessness" in their London community newspaper. Since September 11, it has become clear that language acquisition alone is no indicator of successful integration. The organizer of the New York terror plots, the Egyptian Islamist Mohammed Atta, came from Hamburg and spoke fluent German. These factors did not stop him from destroying the World Trade Center towers—in a certain sense the secular cathedrals of the Western world—and declaring war on Western civilization. This event demonstrates that integration belongs among the central instruments of nonmilitary struggle against terrorism.

Certainly, integration may not be decreed by law, but it also cannot be achieved merely through participation in language courses, as German immigration law prescribes. Until recently, Islamic fundamentalists had created a zone of détente within the European Muslim diaspora. Now, only the integration of Muslim migrants offers an effective means to counter religious extremism. Integration, in contrast to assimilation, does not mean changing one's own cultural identity. Instead, it offers migrants a kind of enrichment, for in the receiving country they take on a civic identity that dissolves the feeling of foreignness in favor of membership in a communal civil entity.

In a democratic society, integration means fitting oneself into a political-civil societal formation and developing a feeling of belonging to it. In the democratically designed Federal Republic, immigration for Muslim migrants means acquiring the identity of a German citizen. Whoever rejects this prospect is advocating the establishment of a parallel society and thus ignores the dangers of Balkanization.

A passport does not contribute to integration if no identity is connected to it. In contrast to the U.S. passports of Syrians living in the United States, my German passport affords me no identity. Charles Maier, an academic of German-Jewish descent who teaches at Harvard, spoke of a "citizenship of the heart" at an event entitled "Reimagined Communities and Identities: Being German." Could integration in Germany be modeled after that in the United States? It has consistently been my experience in the United States that the country offers an additional identity to people from my Islamic civilization that Germany does not provide. Here I am only a "Syrian with a German passport."

In Western Europe, there is a population of 15 million Muslims from the Mediterranean region, Asia, and Africa. Among this Muslim diaspora, there are about 3.5 million Muslims living in Germany (about 2.5 million Turks and Kurds, about half a million Arabs, and half a million from other parts of Islamic civilization). I believe that only a small portion is integrated. I myself, for example, demonstrate that naturalization does not mean integration.

Bundestag representative Cem Özdemir is one of the few integrated Muslims in Germany. At the Harvard event mentioned above, he came as a German citizen and spoke in the name of Germany. The German university does not offer me this kind of membership in a common entity. But in what form should the integration of Muslims living in Germany proceed?

"Being German" was supposed to have been redefined after 1945; it was supposed to mean nothing more than belonging to a common democratic entity, in the sense of a community of values that could include migrants as well. Since then, German democrats have been speaking of the Westernization of German political culture. "Westernness" can be found on paper in Germany, for example in the first 19 articles of the Basic Law, but it is not constitutive of the political culture of this country. We can only reach the goal of integration if both sides, Germans and migrants, exhibit a willingness to do so. Only when Germans and Muslims are willing to integrate—which until now has not been the case—can there be peaceful coexistence. However, this precondition places a demand on Muslims in Germany to harmonize Islamic values with those of Western Europe. [. . .]

Mosaic or Common Values?

Multicultural communitarianism means that different cultural communities can exist next to one another, like pieces in a mosaic, without sharing common values. Against the backdrop of the September 11 tragedy, it has become clear that the *multikulti*-communitarianism and the "free space" that it promotes lead to parallel societies and consequent security risks. To clarify the urgency of this insight, we must revisit what happened on September 11. Was the attack purely a criminal act perpetrated by a group that is connected to Bin Laden through a global network? Or was it more than that? What does it have to do with immigration and integration? One thing is clear, particularly here in Germany: we cannot merely return to business as usual and push the terror attacks out of our minds. They were far more than a criminal act; they marked an epochal turn. Not only is it necessary to better understand the world of Islam, but also to attempt to integrate Muslims living in the West. Thus, we must Westernize the Islam practiced in Germany through the integration of its supporters, just as this country has been Westernized since 1945. [. . .]

Because of their recent past, Germans are not in a position to promote integration based on their own identity. This inability is marketed as the "German virtue" of identitylessness. A society with a damaged identity is incapable of integration as long is it does not come to terms with its past. Migrants cannot share guilt for Nazi crimes with Germans, but they can share the responsibility for ensuring that nothing similar ever happens again. [. . .]

On September 11 in New York and Washington, an attack on Western civilization took place that was organized in a diasporic culture. This act of terror was the militarized form of a value conflict. In the long term, the response must be a politics of integration through which Muslims, as European citizens with European values, abhor the perpetrators of September 11 like all Western citizens do. September 11, as well as the coexistence of Germans and 10 million foreigners from all over the world, offers this country a historic chance to return to normalcy, to establish a democratic civic identity that binds Germans and foreigners into a common entity. [. . .]

16

FEDERAL CONSTITUTIONAL COURT

DECISION REGARDING THE WEARING OF HEAD SCARVES AMONG SCHOOLTEACHERS

This decision, docket number 2BvF 1436/02 from September 24, 2003, was published on the court's website www.bundesverfassungsgericht.de. Translated by Tes Howell. The plaintiff in this case is Fereshta Ludin, whose headmaster forbade her to wear a head scarf while teaching. Despite the Federal Constitutional Court's decision in her favor, a lower court later upheld the school district's right to ban Ms. Ludin from employment, and she retracted her claim in fall 2005.

The plaintiff desires a teaching position in the province of Baden-Württemberg. In her constitutional grievance, she appeals the decision handed down by the Administrative Court of the Greater School District of Stuttgart, which reviewed and rejected her employment status in elementary and middle schools on the basis of her declared intention to wear a head scarf. [. . .]

The plaintiff, born in Kabul, Afghanistan, in 1972, has lived continuously in the Federal Republic of Germany since 1987 and obtained German citizenship in 1995. She is of the Muslim faith. After passing her first state examination and completing her internship, she completed her second state examination for teaching positions in elementary and secondary schools with a concentration on middle-school German, English, civics, and economics.

The greater Stuttgart school district rejected the plaintiff's application for a teaching position in elementary and middle schools in the province of Baden-Württemberg on the basis of insufficient personal appropriateness. The reason provided for the rejection was that the plaintiff was not prepared to abstain from wearing a head scarf. It was further alleged that the head scarf is an expression of cultural segregation and thus not only a religious but also a political symbol. It is further alleged that the objective effect inherent in the head scarf, cultural disintegration, could not be reconciled with the imperative of state neutrality. In her appeal, the plaintiff claims that wearing a head scarf is not only an aspect of her personality but also an expression of her religious convictions. According to the prescriptions of Islam, wearing a head scarf is part and parcel of her Islamic identity. The decision barring her employment appears to conflict with the basic right of religious freedom according to article 4, clauses 1 and 2 of the Basic Law. Despite the responsibility of the state to remain neutral in questions of belief, it may not, according to the fulfillment of the education contract of article 7, clause 1, of the Basic Law, fail to consider religious worldview, and it must facilitate a balance between these conflicting interests. It has been suggested that the head scarf is not a religious symbol in the sense that a crucifix is religious. Moreover, as the plaintiff is a beneficiary of basic rights, her entitlement to an individually and religiously motivated action is at issue.

[According to the greater Stuttgart school district,] even if the plaintiff is not doing missionary work for her religious convictions, by wearing a head scarf while teaching, she effectively expresses her affiliation to Islam, and her students are not able to excuse themselves voluntarily. Therefore, she appears to be forcing students to negotiate with this profession of faith. Young people, whose personalities are not yet completely formed, are apparently open to influences of all kinds. From this perspective, only the objective effect of the head scarf ought to be considered. Particularly for female students of the Muslim faith, a severe normative pressure may ensue that would obstruct the school's pedagogical duty to achieve the integration of Muslim pupils. [. . .]

[According to the Federal Ministry of the Interior,] the case of the crucifix is similar to the Muslim head scarf in that, in the context of universal compulsory schooling, as opposed to fleeting encounters in daily life, one cannot escape constant confrontation with this religious symbol either. That the plaintiff is a beneficiary of basic rights does not alter the fact that the symbol she wears will inevitably be attributed to the state. However, it is important to consider that in wearing this religious symbol, she is exercising basic rights. [. . .]

In judging whether a particular article of clothing or other external sign deploys religious content or expressions of worldview, the effect of the medium of expression is to be considered equally alongside its possible meanings. The head scarf, as opposed to the Christian cross, is not in itself a religious symbol. [. . .] Head scarves worn by Muslim women are understood as a code for vastly different statements and values. [. . .]

[Research shows] that in consideration of this diversity of motivations, the meaning of the head scarf may not be reduced to a sign of the societal repression of women. Rather, the head scarf can be a voluntary means for young Muslim women to lead a self-determined life without breaking with their culture of origin. In this regard, it has not sufficiently been proven that the plaintiff, simply by wearing a head scarf, would hinder the fostering of an image of women among her Muslim students that is consonant with the worldviews of the Basic Law or its manifestation in their own lives. [. . .]

As long as no legal circumstance exists in which it can be clearly demonstrated that it is the professional duty of elementary- and middle-school teachers to abstain from displaying items that affirm their religious membership in the school or in class, the assumption of the plaintiff's insufficient appropriateness is not commensurable with article 33, clause 2 in conjunction with article 4, clauses 1 and 2, and article 33, clause 3, of the Basic Law. The decisions that led to this constitutional grievance thereby offend against the legal rights of the plaintiff, as they have been represented in these proceedings. The judgment of the Federal Administrative Court is hereby annulled, and the matter will be sent back to said court. [. . .]

This decision was reached with five yeas and three nays.

Assenting Justices: Hassemer, Sommer, Boss, Osterloh, Lübbe-Wolff

Dissenting Justices: Mellinghoff, Jentsch, Di Fabio

17

ARNFRID SCHENK

ALLAH ON THE BLACKBOARD

First published as "Allah an der Tafel" in *Die Zeit* (June 9, 2004). Translated by David Gramling.

The 700,000 Muslim students in Germany will soon receive religious instruction. In-school trials, however, are slow in coming.

It almost sounds familiar. "Pilgrims, pilgrims, you must travel, . . ." sing twelve elementary-school students, sitting around their teacher in a half circle. The melody is redolent of children's birthday parties: "Little ring, little ring, you must travel." But what kind of texts are the children chanting along to this melody? Their teacher, Ömer Aslangeçiner, laughs. Anyone who teaches Islamic religion in German has to improvise once in a while. And this revised children's song does quite well in teaching these first-graders at the Albert Schweitzer School in Lehrte near Hannover one of the five duties of every Muslim—the haj, the pilgrimage to Mecca.

For the past few months, Islamic religious instruction has been offered in the German language at eight elementary schools in Lower Saxony. This in-school trial will run until 2007. If the Ministry of Culture and the Muslims are satisfied with it, statewide implementation will be considered.

Two hours per week, Aslangeciner explains the world of Islam to his group at the Albert Schweitzer School. Most of the children were born in Germany. Their parents come generally from Turkey but also from Bosnia or Albania. Almost all of them speak German well. The teacher tells them about the prophet Muhammad, describes why Muslims fast in the month of Ramadan, and he takes them to the mosque once and explains the imam's duties, shows them where he sits and how one can find the direction toward Mecca.

In many mosques, children tend to learn to segregate themselves

The Ministry of Culture selected eight teachers and insisted that they not be strangers to the parents and school administration. Ömer Aslangeçiner has been living in Lehrte for 30 years and has taught remedial courses in heritage languages for many years. "It was very important for us to know the teachers," says Beate Fogber, the principal of the Albert Schweitzer School, "so that there would be no mistrust. We wanted to be sure that Islamist thinking would not be promoted."

Lower Saxony is joining North Rhine–Westphalia and Bavaria in closing this gap in the German school system. Some 700,000 students of the Muslim faith live in Germany. So far, they have not been able to take part in regular religious instruction under state supervision in the German language. Muslim organizations say there has been a lack of political will. State agencies say this inaction has to do with disunity among Muslims, and they demand a unified partner with whom they can negotiate.

According to the Basic Law, all organizations of faith have the right to state-sponsored religious instruction. However, the precondition is that the religious community in question must be officially recognized. Muslim groups are expected to be organized, just as Christian churches are.

Thus, religious education continues to be delegated to mosque organizations—with unpleasant consequences. It is estimated that there are 2,300 mosques in Germany. Three-fourths of them offer Koran classes, according to the Center for Turkish Studies in Essen. Approximately 70,000 Muslim youth attend these courses regularly. There is nothing about Koran classes per se that is objectionable. There, young Muslims learn faith practice, such as the ritual washing before prayer. What is problematic is the fare that is offered at many mosques in addition to the Koran classes: archconservative, somewhat radical ideas against Western ways of life are praised, and students are commanded not to enter into friendships with Christians. The instructional goal: segregation instead of integration.

In addition, the *hocas* [religious teachers] come to Germany only for a few years, hardly speak German, and do not know the children's world. So they are not in a position to promote dialogue, even if they wanted to do so.

The Marburg Islam researcher Ursula Spuler-Stegemann does not believe that regular Islamic instruction would have the effect of dissolving Koran courses. But it can offer a reasonable alternative to the questionable teachings propagated in many mosques. In order for the 40,000 students of Muslim faith in Lower Saxony to have access to enlightened religious instruction, the Ministry of Culture had to bring a large number of Muslim groups to the table: the Central Council of Muslims, which despite its name, represents only a small number of Muslims; the Turkish-Islamic Union of the Foundation for Religion (Ditip), and a newly founded organization called the Schura of Lower Saxony. Almost 90 percent of [Germany's] Muslims were represented in this way. A representative from Milli Görüş was at the table as well. [. . .]

A similar in-school trial is up and running in Bavaria, but only in one elementary school. North Rhine–Westphalia is much further along. The highest number of Muslims in Germany live here. Some 260,000 are in school. Since the 2000–01 school year, the state has been offering pupils religious studies in the German language. This year, the model project has expanded to 90 schools. Some 3,700 pupils are taking part. The curriculum was developed by the State Institute for Education in Soest, in collaboration with Muslim experts from Ankara to Cairo. This curriculum not only explores the basic questions of Islam but also issues of everyday life in Germany. The instruction is not devotionally oriented; it does not educate toward faith but instead informs students about it. Thus, it comes under the conditional title "Islamic instruction in German." [. . .]

4,500 Teachers Have to Be Trained

The case of Berlin demonstrates that some things can go awry in the attempt to establish Islamic religious instruction. Since the 2001–02 school year, the Islamic Federation of Berlin has been organizing Islam classes. After several legal proceedings, it was recognized as a religious community and thus gained exclusive rights to provide religious instruction in Berlin, without the School Department having any say in the matter. This recognition was a precipitous decision, because the federation does not represent the majority of Berlin's Muslims by a long shot, and it is commonly regarded as closely related to Milli Görüş, despite its claims to the contrary. Teachers and principals still complain, however, that more and more Muslim parents want to prevent their children from participating in class trips, coeducational sports, and sex-education classes. Many students no longer exchange gifts at Christmas parties. Many principals fear a furtive Islamization is afoot. [. . .]

If the various states do indeed attempt to implement Islam classes in the next few years, there is yet another problem. Where will the teachers come from? Religious education as a normal subject in the German language requires academically trained teachers. The jurist Martin Heckel, who has dealt with this topic extensively, estimates that 4,500 teachers will be needed. Thus far in Germany there has been no training, save for a few guest professorships. Just a short while ago, the University of Münster established a Center for Religious Studies, which will offer a teacher-training course for Islamic religious instruction starting in the upcoming winter semester. Training has also begun in Lower Saxony. There is a new continuing-education course for Islam teachers at the University of Osnabrück. These programs are being developed in collaboration with the universities of Cairo, Vienna, Tehran, and Ankara. Peter Graf, a professor of intercultural pedagogy, is directing the program. He has high hopes for a "religious-ethnic education for Muslims in the West." Existing concepts of religious instruction cannot simply be imported toward this end. They must be appropriate for the European context. Thus, religious education will become a site of dialogue.

Taking a look at Ömer Aslangeçiner's class, one has the feeling that this exchange between the religions is actually functioning quite well. Right after the Haj and Ramadan on the curriculum come Christmas, Easter, and Pentecost.

18

ZAFER ŞENOCAK

BETWEEN THE SEX PISTOLS AND THE KORAN

First printed as "Zwischen den Sex Pistols und dem Koran" in *Die Welt* (July 20, 2005). Translated by Lucy Powell.

After each terrorist attack carried out by young Muslims, we experience the same ritual. The media gropes around in the dark, excitedly trying to pin down the motives of the perpetrators and asking questions about their potential danger to the various European countries where Muslims live. Religious leaders are hastily summoned together to emphasize the importance and necessity of a dialogue between the religions as if they were there to prevent a religious war. At panel discussions of this kind, the emphasis is always on communicating how peaceful the message of the religions is. Muslim functionaries and clerics try their best to allay the worries and fears of non-Muslims. These are the stopgap measures of a nonexistent Islamic public domain, like digging graves after a terrorist attack. These brutal attacks have nothing to do with Islam and cannot be condoned in any way, they intone in unison. Clear words that have no meaning.

Because the things that have to happen are not happening. Muslims have to ask themselves why the killers come from within their own ranks. Where does the hate come from, a hate which stretches so far that it allows people not only to destroy other's lives but also their own? What is needed is not so much a dialogue between religions as between Muslims. But where will this happen? And who will lead it?

Islam has always been a community-based religion rather than a belief of the individual. Membership in the community of believers is existential for practicing Muslims. It is where Muslims receive support and familial warmth. The community is particularly attractive for all those with doubts and despairs about a modernity centered around individualism. Muslims are intensely exposed to group dynamics that starkly restrict the freedom of individuals and their development potential.

In contrast to Christianity, which, to a great extent, has a psychotherapeutic function for the individual believer, Islam makes demands on society and social life. These demands are not, however, the result of extensive thought but of memorization and emulation of a passed-down tradition. This focus has created an ideology starved of creative energy, which is predestined to break out in violence and to set latent aggression in motion. There is such a deep rift for many

Muslims between what they believe they are entitled to and what they actually experience that they find themselves in a permanent schizophrenic state.

Twenty years ago, I was working on a translation of the lyrical works of Yunus Emre, a thirteenth-century Anatolian mystic. How did I, a budding poet born in Turkey, raised in Germany, and writing in German, arrive at translating the poems of an Islamic mystic from the Middle Ages? Admittedly, the writings had aesthetic appeal. They are not only full of poetic power, they testify that Islamic literature does have individual voices, ones that describe the loneliness and doubts of lone wolves—a far cry from dogmatic convictions and group mechanics. Yunus Emre's view of the other is very different from the view one finds in religiously motivated texts by Muslim scholars. The borders between belief and nonbelief and between the religions are porous; the perception of others is not clouded by personal rhetoric; much more, it is an alienated view of one's own person.

> My love reaches out beyond my heart
> I know a way deeper inside
> Unbelieving is the one who strays from belief
> What an unbelief further inside still
> Don't say I'm in me I'm not
> There is an I further inside me . . .
> Belief and Law do not affect me
> Which direction do I take further inside?

The translation of these poems was a linguistic challenge, absolutely fascinating from a literary point of view. But they had almost no relevance to the reality of my German life and thinking. Or did they? All around me, the no-future generation was running riot. Everyone who still saw a sense in political involvement found themselves in the arms of the 68 generation, which was hungry to establish itself. Yunus Emre anchored me in another time and world. It was as if someone from my childhood was guiding me through the translation, a childhood in which Islamic culture, as lived and conceived, played a huge role.

How should one understand the general and yet amorphous term *Islamic culture?* A religion that determines the believer's way of life down to the last detail, the ultimate meaning machine focusing solely on technical functions, ensuring that believers remain fully functional through constant observation. That at least was the claim. Reality, however, provoked people to disobey the strict rules, to question the Muslim way of life. Was there in this world of prayers and regulations such a thing as a room for the senses, a form of existence for the mind? If there were such a place, then it could be found in texts of the sort left behind by Yunus Emre, the Anatolian dervish. These texts did not stonewall my surroundings and the time in which I was living and which was so far away from that in which they were written. Far more they transferred smoothly into the world of others which had long become my own. Had I not been working on Emre's oeuvre, there would have been a solid barrier between my inner world and the one in which I lived, and I would have fallen victim to the irreconcilable contradictions between the Sex Pistols and the Koran. My parents' house on the one side, school and free time on the other; Turkish origins versus a life centered around Germany. For my creative work, indeed for my entire existence, I depended on the permeability of these borders.

Every border separates and joins at the same time. It can be a fence but also a crossing. We have long lived in a world in which pain arises not from what separates but from what joins. The aesthetic agenda of the present is to find a language to describe the pain felt today by the many people who are exposed to the most diverse cultural influences. Our perception of the world is selective, but we mentally reconstruct it to a whole. But what happens when this ordering system fails? When the individual fragments can no longer be accommodated into a personally structured form? When the hard break lines become festering interfaces, the pain unbearable, the wounds incurable? The collision of contradictory worlds necessitates a translating power whose aim is not the leveling of differences but the transfer of different interpretations.

Every translation is an interpretation, shedding light on a term from different perspectives. When the luminosity wanes, much is left in the dark. And darkness breeds fear and aggression. It is understandable that after each terrorist attack carried out by young Muslims, the loud appeal for a liberal tolerant Islam is weirdly accompanied by a call for more state intervention and control. But in view of the vast philosophical and psychological dimensions of the conflict, these well-meaning objections seem to be the caricature-like gestures of a general helplessness. Is the God of the holy books really as nonviolent as we are repeatedly told these days? Is there not a raging, punishing God who demands accountability in all three monotheistic religions, who is at least as powerful as the merciful, forgiving one? Is there not a tendency in the culture of modernity, that traces back at least as far as the Renaissance, to place man in God's position, in good as in evil? And what is the tense relationship between this hubris and the relativization of power and truth, which likewise has become a cornerstone of an open, pluralistic society?

Questions that are mostly left by the wayside because we have prematurely opted to agree on the so-called common denominators such as love for one's neighbor and esteem for human life. But there's no longer any such thing as common denominators in the form of easy-to-eat chunks, just as there are no longer cultures that could be described as closed circles.

Orient and Occident, Islam and Christianity, tradition and modernity meet at best in museums or anachronistic events. What shapes people today, what makes them behave as they do, how they behave is a mishmash, an amalgamation of the huge collection of exploded fragments of cultural entities that are not clearly geographically locatable. The Taliban are not only situated in the mountains of Afghanistan but also in the minds of people living in London, New York, and the rest.

People today are suffering from a state of exhaustion provoked by diversity. This fatigue makes the call to unity dangerously attractive and a rigid modernity, which demands differentiation and individualization, ineffective. Halfheartedly formulated cosmopolitan ideals are no more likely to tackle the male rituals of religious fanatics than the newly strengthened nationalist voices.

So, a return to order? But which one? Back to which time? No, we, the enlightened, cannot return. We could attempt to understand ourselves better. Ask ourselves the questions we put to others. Start an inner dialogue before we turn our words on other people.

PROMOTING DIVERSITY
INSTITUTIONS OF MULTICULTURALISM

A TELEVISION STUDIO IN COLOGNE, 1970s. At the center is Aysim Alpman, host of *Ihre Heimat—Unsere Heimat (Your Homeland—Our Homeland)*, the WDR television station's first program to address foreigners living in Germany in their native languages. With coiffed hair and casual couture, the broadcasters pose before a backdrop of Istanbul's Blue Mosque. The staging suggests that television allows viewers to be simultaneously "here" and "there."

AMONG THE PRINCIPAL early catalysts for immigration reform in the 1970s were the Deutsche Städtetag, or the German Council of Municipalities, and the German Caritas Alliance. These groups funded and analyzed statistical research about immigrants' living conditions, legal disenfranchisement, and socioeconomic inequities. Publications by the Städtetag, like the 1973 pamphlet opening this chapter, were among the first institutional attempts to advocate for guest workers as "fellow citizens" who had chosen Germany as their new homeland. Even before the 1973 moratorium on recruitment, the Städtetag took a strong research-supported stance refuting widespread notions of disproportionately high criminality among immigrants.

In 1978, the chancellor's cabinet called for a new, permanent post in the federal government that would be responsible for promoting social integration among foreigners. Housed under the Ministry of Health and Social Order, this new office, with a staff of two, was dubbed the Office of the Federal Commissioner for the Promotion of Integration among Foreign Workers and Their Family Members. Its first appointee was Heinz Kühn, former minister president of the province of North Rhine–Westphalia.

Kühn published this chapter's second text in 1979. Known widely as the Kühn Memorandum, the paper alerted the government to the urgent need to offer willing immigrants "unconditional and permanent integration" into West German society. It opposed all coercive and financial incentives designed to persuade labor migrants to leave Germany, thus preempting the "willingness-to-return" policies of the Kohl administration.

The Ecumenical Planning Committee theses of 1980, another early text in this chapter, exemplify a new stage in an emerging multicultural doctrine. The committee believed that Germans bore the responsibility for adapting to the nation's immigrants, because guest workers had engaged in decades of unacknowledged integration already. Activist clerics and lay people alike envisioned the possibility of multiethnic collaboration and dialogue in an era of perceived mistrust.

This principle of intercultural dialogue came to the fore in a most concrete way in a 1982 leaflet—"With Each Other, Not against Each Other"—circulated by the Berlin Senate's commissioner of foreigner affairs, Barbara John. Commissioner John distributed two versions of this leaflet—one to

Berlin's immigrant residents and one to nonmigrant residents—addressing the misunderstandings between the two groups.

Heinz Kühn's successor, Liselotte Funcke, sought to bring to the foreground the humanistic principles of art as a counterweight to the labor-market concepts that had dominated immigration policy in previous eras. In 1986, her office organized the exhibition *The Other Country—Foreign Artists in the Federal Republic*. Showcasing transnational artists became a standard corrective measure for the disenfranchisement that had characterized labor migration thus far. Such endeavors generated collaboration between the federal commissioner's office and other institutions, including the European Council, the Federal Office for Political Education, Deutsche Welle Radio, and UNESCO.

Funcke's successor, Cornelia Schmalz-Jacobsen, enjoyed more financial support from the various ministries and received more frequent invitations to participate in the shaping of policy at the cabinet level, although the consultancy role of her office did not become law until 1997. Upon her appointment, the office's name changed to the slightly less cumbersome Office of the Commissioner for the Needs of Foreigners. Schmalz-Jacobsen's piece in this chapter, "Where Are the Turkish Teachers and Doctors?" (2001) emphasizes that colorful multicultural celebrations should not obscure the persistent inequity in employment and professional opportunity between migrants and nonmigrants.

In 1994, Deniz Göktürk published "The Naked and the Turks," an essay on Radio Multikulti at Sender Freies Berlin. Founded in 1994, Radio Multikulti quickly became one of the foremost purveyors of world music and multicultural entertainment, though statistics showed that immigrant listeners tended to prefer Berlin's Turkish music station FM Metropol. Göktürk's essay contrasts the lively, hybrid social world in 1990s Berlin with the earnest purposefulness of SFB's institutional programming.

Another major exemplar in this "cultural turn" in immigrant advocacy was the Workshop of Cultures, founded in 1993 in Berlin's Neukölln district. In an effort to popularize the idea of multicultural collaboration throughout and beyond the city of Berlin, the workshop began staging a yearly Carnival of Cultures in the city's predominantly Turkish district of Kreuzberg. Competing with other carnival cities, Rotterdam and London among them, the Workshop of Cultures sought to display Berlin as a global hub of multiculturalism. Critics of the event noted the relative lack of Turkish participants, as compared to the predominance of Germans wearing exotic costumes and dancing to ethnic beats. The event's organizers defended their project, stressing that the carnival did not aim to provide a radical platform but rather to inspire a celebratory occasion for citizens of diverse political positions.

The transethnic activist network Kanak Attak emerged in the late 1990s as one of the most iconoclastic expressions of resistance to institutional multiculturalism. Known for its stylized appropriation of consumer icons, Kanak Attak, whose manifesto appears in this chapter, agitated for an end to the socialist left's celebratory staging of undifferentiated ethnic essences. "Against Between," a manifesto by American German-studies scholar Leslie A. Adelson (2000), articulates a similar critique of binary readings of immigrant literature and calls for a new public debate about migrant subjectivity in German literature.

The House of World Cultures, founded in 1998 in the desolate east end of West Berlin's Tiergarten Park, was another major addition to the German multiculturalist landscape. Texts by Günther Coenen and Johannes Odenthal, both former presidents of the organization, chronicle the birth and development of the house, which seeks to bring world cultures to the Berlin stage.

We conclude this chapter with a look back and a look forward. The first of two closing texts is a retrospective tribute to the work of Barbara John, Berlin's commissioner of foreigner affairs since the early 1980s. The final text is a compilation of public responses to a pending plan to establish a German Museum of Migration.

1

THE GERMAN COUNCIL OF MUNICIPALITIES
SUGGESTIONS FOR SUPPORTING FOREIGN EMPLOYEES

First published as *Hinweise zur Hilfe für ausländische Arbeitnehmer* (Cologne: Deutscher Städtetag, 1973), 1–5. Translated by David Gramling.

The increasing number of foreign workers in the Federal Republic generates a host of new problems and tasks for municipalities, especially in metropolitan areas. The German Council of Municipalities has therefore compiled some references for foreign employees in cooperation with experts from its member cities as well as from agencies, organizations, and alliances active in the field. This compilation is organized according to the practical needs and legal foundations of concern to immigrants. Questions of integrating foreign workers (through housing and reuniting family members), assistance for children and youth, school, health, as well as counseling and information are at the center of the document's design. We have intentionally refrained from macroeconomic or demographic-political questions. Instead, the point of departure for our considerations is the fact that foreign employees in the Federal Republic must be seen in the long run as fellow citizens. In many circumstances, they must be understood as people who view the Federal Republic as their chosen homeland. On this basis, they may claim certain rights and responsibilities during their residence. [. . .]

Nonetheless, foreign employees were and continue to be underprepared for their residence in Germany and often come with false, overly optimistic expectations. Several added factors burden relations between them and Germans: unsatisfactory situations in the homeland leading to their departure; separation from family, friends, and neighbors; the often very palpable isolation in their new residence and workplaces; frustration with the realities of their new situation; the need to overcome enormous cultural and civilizational differences; the great difficulty of making themselves understood; the pressure for assimilation in the absence of regular opportunities to release pent-up aggression through conversations or in other legitimate ways; strained living conditions; and much more. These complicating factors often lead to nearly unbearable internal tensions among them, not infrequently resulting in sickness, accidents and depression. [. . .]

There should be no question that if foreign employees are to live in our country, their rights as at least temporary citizens must be guaranteed. It is therefore appropriate that, in their particularly difficult situation, they should receive special assistance. Economic, social, and humanitarian factors demand a quick integration of foreign employees into society and the working world of the Federal Republic, to the extent that it is necessary for a limited residence. Dissociating them from the German population is damaging for both parties. [. . .]

Widespread prejudices, such as the statistically debunked claim that foreign employees evince a higher rate of criminality, must be countered through consciousness-raising activities. The mass media are of paramount importance in this regard and must deliver substantive and responsible coverage. Because public political discourse and the current political situation form a feeding ground on which prejudices can be either nourished or uprooted, the media are the best basis for a mutual understanding among different nationalities. They are also the best defense against prejudice and discrimination in the interest of educating toward tolerance, political openness, and critical thinking, even among children and youth.

2

HEINZ KÜHN

THE PRESENT AND FUTURE INTEGRATION OF FOREIGN WORKERS AND THEIR FAMILIES IN THE FEDERAL REPUBLIC OF GERMANY

Published in English translation (Bonn: Memorandum of the Federal Government Commissioner, 1979). Kühn (b. Cologne, 1912, d. 1992) was appointed in 1978 to the newly created post of "Federal Commissioner for the Promotion of Integration among Foreign Workers and Their Family Members," known in common parlance as the "foreigner commissioner" or the "commissioner of foreigner affairs."

The alarming situation concerning the future prospects for 1 million foreign children and adolescents in the Federal Republic calls for large-scale efforts in order to prevent major harm to individuals and society. Current problems, and others that will most certainly arise in the near future if rapid and radical change is not undertaken, are a challenge that must be addressed now; otherwise the problems threaten to become insurmountable and will present disastrous consequences.

The measures taken thus far have obviously been inappropriately determined by the priority attached to labor market considerations. Less attention has been given to the equally important social and socio-political needs.

Therefore, the friction-generating problems of foreign workers and their families require a new and corrective approach that would take far greater account of socio-political conditions and needs. It must be recognized that an irreversible development has taken place and that social responsibility for foreign workers and their children, most of whom were recruited some years ago and have now been living in this country for a considerable time, cannot be simply recalibrated according to the labor-market situation. The apparently large number of migrants who are willing to stay in the Federal Republic (comprised particularly of members of the second and third generations) must be offered unconditional and permanent integration.

The vague notions of a "temporary" integration are incoherent and unrealistic, and the current situation is clear and intractable proof of its inadequacy. The strategy of encouraging foreign workers to return to their home countries should not be overemphasized; this option can be reasonably successful only if it focuses on those who are seriously interested in returning. But this also requires that the foreign workers concerned be fully informed about alternative possibilities.

On the basis of this analysis, the proposals put forward in this memorandum envisage a consistent integration policy with the following priorities:

1. Recognition of *de facto* immigration (while maintaining the ban on further recruitment);
2. A considerable increase in integration measures, in particular for children and adolescents, i.e. at the preschool, elementary school, and vocational training stage;
3. Abolition of all segregating measures, e.g. "nationality classes" in schools and similar concepts;
4. Acknowledging the right of young foreigners to unrestricted access to jobs and training opportunities;
5. Developing opportunities for young foreigners born and raised in the Federal Republic to opt for naturalization;
6. A general review of legislation regarding foreigners and naturalization procedures, in order to improve their legal situation and take greater account of the legitimate special interests of foreign workers and their families;
7. Improving their political rights by granting them the right to vote in local government elections after a certain period of residence;
8. Improving qualified social counseling. [. . .]

The capacity of preschools to support parents in the education of their children is particularly important for foreign families, especially in terms of integration. Parents themselves are faced with considerable difficulties that, without appropriate assistance, make them unable to prepare their children for life in the Federal Republic. [. . .]

Pilot projects have shown that an organized union for foreign staff would contribute to greater motivation among parents, as well as to improved scholastic achievement, and would not create any major initial difficulties. It would facilitate psychological access to foreign, and in particular to Turkish, families. Moreover, foreign teachers would have a special understanding for the language difficulties and the family background of the children.

The situation for foreign children and adolescents at school is characterized by insufficient school attendance, an extremely low rate of success in upper-primary education, and a remarkable underrepresentation of foreign children in secondary schools. It has been estimated that 25% or more of foreign pupils do not or only irregularly comply with their obligation to go to school. [. . .]

3

ECUMENICAL PLANNING COMMITTEE FOR FOREIGNER DAY

IN THE FEDERAL REPUBLIC WE LIVE IN A MULTICULTURAL SOCIETY: THESES FROM SEPTEMBER 24, 1980, DAY OF THE FOREIGN FELLOW CITIZEN

First published as "Wir leben in der Bundesrepublik in einer multikulturellen Gesellschaft: Thesen vom 24 September 1980 (Tag des ausländischen Mitbürgers)" in *Deutschland—Einheit in kultureller Vielfalt,* Jürgen Micksch, ed. (Frankfurt am Main: Otto Lembeck, 1991), 171–79. Translated by Tes Howell. The Foreigner Day Planning Committee included representatives from the Foreigner Bureau of the Protestant Church in Germany, the German Greek-Orthodox Church, and the German Episcopal Conference.

Different cultures, same rights: Toward a common future

Even today, small cultural and linguistic minorities are still living in Germany, such as the Danes, Frisians, and the Sorbs. [. . .] At least 30 nationalities and linguistic communities have their own church congregations with hundreds of pastors from different countries throughout the world. Through the recruitment of foreign employees and the subsequent arrival or establishment of their families here, the coexistence of different cultures has taken on a new quality and role, particularly in the industrial centers. Within the confines of the European Community, citizens of other member states (Italians and soon also Greeks, Spanish, and Portuguese) have a right to live here without having to become German nationals. Furthermore, the significant cultural influence of the United States is inestimable.

A mutual integration is necessary for future coexistence

Foreigner policy can no longer be merely a one-sided integration or assimilation policy. Mutual integration is necessary. Foreign fellow citizens have performed remarkable acts of adaptation. Now it is the task of Germans themselves to adjust to these new circumstances and conditions of multicultural collaboration.

In this coexistence of cultures, the majority should respect the claims of the minority

Foreign fellow citizens frequently form their own organizations and orient themselves increasingly on the basis of their own self-representations. Because they have few possibilities to voice opinions and participate collaboratively in society, they use their own interests as a foundation for new groups.

They should be encouraged toward this end. There will often be tensions between the objectives of such self-representation and the interests of German organizations. To a certain extent, foreigners who have had the experience of not being accepted as fellow human beings tend to mistrust even positive offers of integration into this society. Foreigner organizations contribute actively to societal life and make it possible for foreigners to collaborate in its design. Foreign and German institutions should be supported and financially assisted in comparable ways. In cultural centers, it is of primary concern that space be made available to facilitate the preservation of cultural traditions. In such centers, multicultural collaboration could be cultivated and supported in a particularly successful way.

Mutual isolation and ghettos do not promote a common future
Even if there are understandable reasons for mutual isolation, the coexistence of immigrants and natives, for which many have worked so diligently, will not improve through segregation, nationally oriented preschool programs, boarding schools, or residential ghettos. Discussion and contact are necessary and should be encouraged on all levels. [. . .]

The best places for learning about intercultural living and tolerance are kindergarten and school
Kindergartens and schools are the places where experiences of different cultural traditions collide openly and directly. Here, one has the opportunity to learn different languages as mediators of culture. Intercultural instruction is a chance to acknowledge others and to be personally enriched as a result. Instruction in the native language should be integrated into educational instruction. Immigrants' life experiences from their homelands and in the Federal Republic should be an integral part of school programs. The native language of immigrant children should be recognized as a first foreign language. [. . .]

Cultural programming should communicate differences but also commonalities among the respective cultural traditions
Community-based cultural and leisure programming should concentrate more heavily on providing different groups with opportunities for self-representation and promotion of important aspects of their respective homelands, in addition to interaction with natives. [. . .]

Owing to the nationality-transcending character of faith, congregations have a special duty in the promotion of a multicultural society
Congregations must not be content with accepting foreign parishes merely as "extensions of themselves." Christian convictions should be reason enough to work together in all congregational spheres and to stimulate an

understanding of cultural traditions that will resonate beyond the congregations. Parishes are in a good position to facilitate this collaboration through their worship offerings, common celebrations, kindergartens, discussion groups, work circles, free-time and educational opportunities, and other events. Again and again, the belief in Christ overcomes barriers between people.

New programs and communication structures in the media are necessary for a multicultural society
The media play a crucial role in arousing and communicating understanding for other cultures. [. . .] Foreigner programs should attest to the actual situation in the countries of origin, not an "illusory world." Cultural programming from these countries should be presented more frequently and translated for German-speaking contexts, in order to render unfamiliar behavior comprehensible.

The coexistence among different cultures in a multicultural society is a new chance for the future of the Federal Republic
[. . .] Coexistence with people from other cultures is a chance for an expansion of one's own horizon. If it succeeds in leading to creative communication with other cultures, it will be an important contribution toward the realization of the common culture of a European Community and to the promotion of social harmony.

As a prerequisite for such coexistence, we must grant equal political rights to ethnic and cultural minorities. The right to vote is part and parcel of this commitment.

4

BARBARA JOHN

WITH EACH OTHER, NOT AGAINST EACH OTHER

First published as a pamphlet titled "Miteinander—nicht gegeneinander" by the commissioner of foreigner affairs of the Berlin Senate (November 1982). Translated by David Gramling. The "Living Together in Berlin" campaign was one of the first government-sponsored advertising efforts to promote multiculturalism, depicting foreigners working in harmony alongside Germans on posters throughout West Berlin's bus and subway system. Commissioner of Foreigner Affairs Barbara John is the subject of another article in this chapter, "The Woman from Kreuzberg."

Dear fellow citizens,

Those of you who live in districts like Kreuzberg, Schöneberg, Tiergarten, Neukölln, Wedding, Charlottenburg, or Spandau—districts where particularly high numbers of foreigners are living—may feel somewhat overwhelmed or disadvantaged.

Feelings of this kind are entirely understandable. Sometimes they arise out of the dynamic of a fleeting encounter, while at other times they are based in negative experiences. It is, however, a mistake to remember only the bad experiences and to see the good ones as merely a matter of course. Each of you can think of a number of positive encounters. Why do we constantly fail to acknowledge the kindnesses we encounter? We should be talking more about these issues in public arenas.

If mutual understanding is not successful right off the bat, it is because we know too little about each other. Many of you come across Turkish citizens on a daily basis and have been doing so for years—on the way to work, on the street, when shopping, at home. I know from conversations with you that many behaviors of the Turkish population still remain foreign to you. This is often the case simply because we do not see or discover anything familiar in these ostensibly unusual images.

Given the limited scope of this pamphlet, I will not be able to bring you closer to the Turkish culture. By way of a few examples, I would like to encourage you, however, to be more open when coming in contact with others. I know that it is precisely at such moments when great effort is necessary from both sides. But it is worth the trouble.

Turkish citizens are simultaneously receiving a similar pamphlet. In it, I have explained why it bothers the German population when a familiar neighborhood becomes an almost foreign milieu within a short period of time.

In the past few months, I have experienced great hospitality in Turkish families and have been consistently astounded by the openness of our conversations. My eyes have been opened time and again; I had seen things in a much different light before. I continue to discover how easy it is to build bridges when both sides wish to do so.

The fact that there are people who have explicitly xenophobic intentions is shameful for us and painful for foreigners. We would all do well to take the time to bring stories of successful attempts at neighborliness into the public eye and to encourage one another by example. [. . .]

In order to continue this dialogue about our successful stories of living together, it would be helpful if you would tell me about your experiences.

With best wishes from your Commissioner of Foreigner Affairs,
Barbara John

5

BERLIN COMMISSIONER OF FOREIGNER AFFAIRS
WHAT IS GERMAN?

First published in 1991 as "Was ist Deutsch?" as part of the Berlin Senate foreigner commissioner's Living Together in Berlin poster campaign. Translated by David Gramling. These posters, often 2 meters by 3 meters in size, were common sights along Berlin subway walls, at bus shelters, and on beer coasters in the mid- and late 1990s.

What Is German?

Fir trees? Travel dreams? Cool intellect? Cold heart? Pensiveness? Xenophobia? Openness? Shock? Baseball bat? Schinkenhäger liquor? Inferiority complexes? Minority protections? Craving recognition? Development aid? Love thy neighbor? Sideswipe? Starvation diet? Pub crawl? Rostock? Solingen? Forgetfulness? Perfectionism? Know-it-all? Airlift? Roasted chicken? Helpfulness? The news? Stolen cars? Steel helmet? Social welfare? Economic Miracle? Wheel of fortune? *Berlinale?* Milk-distribution center? Love for animals? Humanity? Sentimentality? Excitability? Autonomy? Volkswagen? Kitchen collectives? Germany for the Germans? Vanity? Love of children? Cowbells? Instant soup? Martial-arts groups? First World War? Second World War? The Wall? Applause from the audience? Democracy? Equal rights, but only for me? Equal responsibilities, but only for you? Laziness? Cleaning up? Anorexia nervosa? Soccer is our life? Poets and thinkers? Judges and executioners? Hospitality? Closing the borders? Making oneself look worse than one is? Always feeling guilty? Boozing up for courage? Undermining the intellect? Family ties? Gang warfare? Workaholism? Tax evasion? Withholding love? Muscle power? Inventiveness? Wannabe? Heil Hitler? Looking for scapegoats? Uncertainty? Having visions? Constant frustration? Moralistic sermonizers? Magnanimous toward one's own mistakes? Never seeing other people's merits? Taking cautious pleasure in the foreign? Watering the neighbor's plants once in a while? Knowing hunger from when times were rough? Changing the channel during bad news reports? Pulling out the checkbook? Fire bombs? Love for the homeland? Cattiness? Kindergartens? Honesty? Getting rid of self-doubt with Schnapps? Feeling a little better afterward? Conscientious about responsibilities? Me? No pain, no gain? Traveling abroad? A summer house in Spain? Cars from Japan? Bellies? Intoxication? Warmheartedness? Beauty? Tolerance? DIN-standard? Nonconformity? In peak form? Feeling at home? Feeling foreign? Finding foreign cultures stimulating? Pracowici? Szwaby? Szkopy? Mangiakrauti? Crucco? Patates Alman? Getting worked up about anything different? Blind in the right eye? Making excuses by saying that the French and the Italians and the English and the Dutch and the Americans or everyone else are no better? White wedding? Always seeing black? Going along with every fashion? Loving the law on mandatory business hours? Technical Inspection Agency Control? Spring rolls? Stick-in-the-mud? Carefree? Go-getter? Sticking to your guns? Foreigners and Germans together? Ossis against Wessis? Wessis against Ossis? Federal Constitutional Court? BKA? Free Body Culture? MTV? Community assistance? Envy? Class? Nivea? Closing time? Striving for something higher? Sticking to one's prejudices? Grabbing? Don't want to hear it? Others first? Sticking it to others? Lothar Matthäus? Anthony Yeboah? Roy Black? Roberto Blanco? Being idle instead of doing something? Counting beans? Tormenting children? Turning on the tube? Squeaky wheels? Going wild at your local hangout? Making a clean sweep? Sitting with others at a table? Planning on a happy future? Fear of the future? Digging a grave for others? Marching with torches? Beer mugs? Detachedness? Humor? Being in a good mood? Having a better education? Never having enough? Closing off? Giving the bird? Brass music? Feeling great? Acting up? Bureaucracy? Environmental degradation? Data protection? Wanting everything? Controlling everything? The fatherland is the kingdom of heaven? We don't need anyone? We do fine on our own? A stick of butter? Garden gnome? Keeping with your own? Going beyond yourself? An emigration country? An immigration country? Sauerkraut? Political sullenness? Disturbing the peace? Squeaky-clean man? Millers always want to wander? Turning against your neighbor? Panic stories? A matter of honor? Uniforms? If you don't want to be my brother, then I'll bust in your skull? Settling your accounts? Dig in? Not asking questions? Being a role model? Being there for someone? Riding the train without a ticket? Skipping work? Thumping the law books? Putting in some effort? Not letting up? German shepherds? Being critical? Being self-critical? Lottery tickets? More appearance than reality? Federal Railway? Road rage? A little coffee? A little beer? Gretchen? Having principles? Having a constitution? Phoning the constitutional court? We are the best? Striking below the belt? Outgrowing yourself? Alertness? Dedication? Tasks? Living beyond one's means? Living Together in Berlin. The Commissioner for Foreigner Affairs of the Berlin Senate, Senate Administration for Social Issues, 65 Potsdamer Street, 10785 Berlin.

6

DENIZ GÖKTÜRK

THE NAKED AND THE TURKS

First published as "Muselmanisch depressiv: Die Nackten und die Türken im Berliner Tiergarten" in *die tageszeitung* (September 3, 1994). Translated by Tes Howell. This article was inspired by a planning meeting at the Haus der Kulturen der Welt regarding programming at Radio Multikulti.

BERLIN, SUMMER OF 1994. Extended families are grilling in the Tiergarten in temperatures over 30 degrees Celsius. Oblivious to the perennial debate on whether open flames in public parks are permitted and ecologically responsible, everyone is having a good time here: the smoke is climbing, the meat sizzling, the tea steeping, the children playing—people are sitting and talking. The hastily assembled (and barely noticed) wire bins with handwritten signs "Ashes only/Yalnız Kül" even lend a hint of multilingual legitimacy to the hustle and bustle. Territorial borders are invisible here in this nationally prescribed multicultural blend of togetherness. The nudists keep a respect-ful distance from the Turks and vice versa. Only the sociologists, stalking around with their cameras, occasionally pop into the scene. Is it a coinci-dence that the Berlin Turks have chosen the Tiergarten for their gatherings?

Green is, after all, the color of the fundamentalists—and "for the country," symbolically speaking, means something like "closer to God." Rumor has it, by the way, that extra grills are included in the Tiergarten renovation plan. [. . .]

Meanwhile, nearby in the House of World Cultures—in the center (if not the epicenter) of this "Legalize Grilling Party"—a perspiring group of ex-perts is discussing what can be done to help foreigners acculturate and in-crease their presence in the media. Some report that the newly established Radio Multikulti, which took over broadcasting for foreign citizens at Sender Freies Berlin, or Radio Free Berlin, will embrace anything but Anglo-American pop. Can world music satisfy the techno-Turks? The experts begin to trust and open up to each other: foreigners are people, too. They should not always appear in the media as a problem but as people who are normal like anyone else. Indeed, more and more TV programs are set in Turkey or have Turks playing roles in a German setting, often as cheerful snack-stand operators. After all, television is supposed to mirror reality.

Media representatives at the meeting, themselves spirited advocates for disadvantaged foreigners, do not ask whether any of these foreigners actually want this cultural programming. For the most part, those on the inside al-ready know what those on the outside need, without having to ask them. Sev-eral point out that the fiction of homogeneous cultural identity and unam-biguous group affiliation is quite outdated these days. Unexpectedly, I see myself attacked from the politically correct corner: "You and Aras Ören—you don't have the same experiences on the street as normal guest workers. You aren't really Turks anymore." It is common knowledge that origin, milieu, and education shape the habitus of every person. The German radio editor, incidentally, does not have the same experiences as the German construction worker. But how has it come to pass that I represent the same experiences as the (absent) writer Aras Ören, from whom a generation and a gender sepa-rate me? And according to which characteristics might the "normal" guest worker be distinguished? Does he resemble his television stereotype? Does he have to speak broken German and go to a mosque? Does his wife wear a head scarf? Does he buy all his supplies at the Aldi supermarket? Are his chil-dren allowed to attend college? Is there such a thing as properly and im-properly alienated Turks?

For the most part, disadvantaged Germans and their tastes are just as for-eign to German intellectuals as the foreigners are. It is much preferable to hound the contemptible German from a safe distance. Unpleasant people and situations confront us in the city all the time, and it is sometimes diffi-cult enough to tolerate one another. As a result, we move in our own circles, with our own preferences and manners, which, in and of itself, is not really objectionable. Cultural programming is also made primarily for the like-minded, although the media like to present themselves as the educators of the people. Still, we should grant others the differentiated individuality that we claim for ourselves. Instead of seeking out chimerical masses on the street, we could first try to cooperate with our own colleagues of different backgrounds, with whom a relevant dialogue would be easy to begin.

The condescendingly didactic imperative of foreigner-specific cultural activities is still prevalent; indeed, it has become doctrine. A rhetoric of consternation flourishes on both sides. Foreign youths avail themselves of this fashionable parlance and commit themselves to self-pity "between the cultures." Some youths even declare "My best friend is a foreigner," instead of standing up for their own personal history, their own characteristics and strengths. What other choice does one have with all this communally encouraged togetherness afoot: Weeks of the Foreign Citizen, intercultural writing workshops, ikebana, and painting-against-racism events? Even graffiti and hip-hop, once expressions of American subculture, have become instrumentalized as workshop topics. Meanwhile, Catholics are demanding Islamic religious instruction in German schools. Instead of dismantling barriers, all these efforts appear to be establishing borders and arming reactionaries with traditional national symbols.

Recently, young German Turkish women have started donning the crescent and star. Processes of cultural encounter and integration do not submit to cultural political prescription, certainly not to control from above. Despite all this activity, there is little cause for depression: while the experts are still discussing inside, the food outside has already been eaten.

7

RAINER BRAUN

GOOD RECEPTION: RADIO MULTIKULTI BERLIN

First published as "Gut angekommen" in *Frankfurter Rundschau* (September 24, 1996). Translated by David Gramling.

With a growing audience and a great deal of attention from media colleagues at home and abroad, there are not many radio stations in this republic for whom reputation and positive resonance among listeners has been as unanimous as with Sender Freies Berlin 4. Baptized on the Spree two years ago, Radio Multikulti has since become one of the prominent players in the bellicose market of Berlin radio.

The latest media analyses in June of this year showed Radio Multikulti with only a 0.7 percent market share, but that is only counting the German-speaking listeners. This group makes up merely a small minority of its three-year marketing plan. "Sixty percent of our listeners did not learn German as their first language," reports station chief Friedrich Voss, who is clearly "very happy" with the balance sheet after two years.

Indeed, the station's approximately 40 employees (12 full-time) have achieved astounding results. The public has accepted Radio Multikulti—with its dual character as a target broadcaster in 18 languages and as a round-the-clock German-language station. Among Berliners with Turkish passports, this specialty station is ranked fifth out of two dozen channels in the capital. Its distinct musical character should not be underestimated in this regard: unlike most radio stations, its disc jockeys do not play the expected mélange of Anglo-American rock and pop in whatever permutation. Instead, they clearly favor world-music selections from Europe, Africa, Latin America, and the Caribbean.

These innovations in the radio sector have won the staff the CIVIS prize as well as recognition from UNESCO as "Germany's Contribution to the World Decade for Cultural Development." The model character of this Berlin radio station has found no parallels throughout Europe or the ARD.

Original plans to expand the promising project throughout the federal territory have been put on hold until 2001, partially for financial reasons. This is the case because, even in Berlin, such a program owes its 3 million–mark budget to a 2 million–mark contribution from the Media Institute of Berlin-Brandenburg and another 500,000 marks from the Federal Ministry for Labor and Social Affairs. Radio Multikulti also functions in cooperation with the House of World Cultures, where its Container-Domicile is housed, as well as with the Goethe-Instituts, the ARD Institutes, BBC World, and Radio France International.

Looking to next year, Friedrich Voss has planned the introduction of a Portuguese program, an expansion of service promotions and of the world-music offerings. His plan is to "hold course on the current budget" in the hope that Radio Multikulti might soon broadcast on the old FRB 2 frequency 98.2. Because reception on the current frequency is too weak, the potential listenership of around 500,000 in the inner-city districts of Kreuzberg, Schöneberg, and Mitte has not been exhausted. [. . .] The budget for 1997 has been secured, and thereafter, it should become self-sustaining. New pledges for funding have surfaced, and now it is just a matter of the hows and what nexts. . . .

8

WORKSHOP OF CULTURES

WHY A CARNIVAL OF CULTURES IN BERLIN?

First published as "Warum ein Karneval der Kulturen in Berlin?" in 1998 on the Karneval der Kulturen website: www.karneval-berlin.de. Translated by Tes Howell. Since 1993, the Berlin/Neukölln Workshop of Cultures has sponsored an annual carnival to promote the new world capital of Berlin as a "workshop of integration."

The project Carnival of Cultures developed against the backdrop of Berlin's growing internationality, a consequence of the intensified immigration of people from all over the world. Today, the cosmopolitan city of Berlin is marked by ethnic and cultural heterogeneity. This process is taking place at a time when Berlin must struggle with the all-too-familiar consequences of German unification and redefine its role as the capital. A variety of social, economic, and cultural conflicts are emerging, noticeably beleaguering the atmosphere of the city.

Berlin has become a focal point of international interest, as well as a symbol for the path toward a unified Europe. Signs of emerging nationalism and racism are being precisely and fastidiously noted on the seismograph, as are clear efforts to promote a society built on acceptance and tolerance.

Given this situation, there are voices that seek an easing of circumstances through the "assimilation" of all that is foreign. Yet this position just does not add up; the native population does not take the burgeoning creative force of immigrant groups into consideration, nor does it succeed in understanding new cultural influences.

As the city with the highest number of foreigners in Germany (about 440,000), Berlin plays the role of a "workshop of integration." Fears of foreign infiltration can be alleviated only by a cultural praxis of diversity, by integration—and precisely not assimilation—and peaceful coexistence, established through mutual respect and tolerance. Berlin must understand its internationality as an opportunity and actively shape its role as a mediator between differing mentalities.

The Workshop of Cultures, the sponsoring organization for the Carnival of Cultures that was established in 1993 in Berlin's Neukölln district, is a place of dialogue and encounter between people of different nationalities, cultures, and religions. The workshop sees itself as a center of reciprocal cultural transfer; it wants to promote the artistic potential of immigrants living in Berlin and make them visible, audible, and accessible.

This objective gave rise to the idea for the Carnival of Cultures. There were repeated attempts to organize a carnival in Berlin, which were unsuccessful because they sought to import existing carnival traditions from Germany or abroad and did not want to fully consider the available potential in Berlin. The carnival is well suited to be a traditional model for creating a framework of integration and action for different cultural initiatives, thereby reconstituting the "carnivalesque" elements inherent to all cultures and expressing them in an energetic procession.

The carnival is not a one-dimensional event but rather an aesthetic spectacle that encourages the participants to engage in cultural performances in the various areas of creative design. In doing so, it is based on cultural practices that all cultures engage in. The costuming and masking of the participants, the setting of special rhythms and choreographies, the gloriously colorful processions in groups on the street: these are traditional customs that one finds even in cultures without a specific carnival tradition.

Carnival is a breaking-out from restrictive conditions. Carnival symbolizes pride and the joy of self-production and self-representation within the social and cultural context of a group. Carnival promotes and stimulates popular art and cultures, and increasingly those of its participants, at the highest levels. [. . .]

The Berlin Carnival of Cultures joins the tradition of more recent carnival cultures in Europe, but it is unique on a global scale because of the diversity of participating nationalities and subcultures. The professed goal is to make the carnival a festival for all Berliners—for the people living here who come from 184 nations and for native Germans as well. Even in the first year of the Berlin carnival, there were more active participants than at the tenth Rotterdam Carnival.

The Carnival of Cultures in Berlin is open to all; it can be supported by people of any cultural character as an integral part of an urban, pluralistic culture to which they feel they belong. It can be used as a platform to express consciously one's own cultural identity. Immigrant groups see the carnival as an opportunity to display a presence, to make themselves unable to be ignored and to allow Berlin to experience its multiculturality with more depth and consciousness. [. . .]

9

ANONYMOUS

WE ARE STILL OUR OWN BEST FOREIGNERS

First published as "Unsere besten Ausländer sind immer noch wir selbst" in the *Frankfurter Allgemeine Zeitung* (June 2, 1998). Translated by Tes Howell.

This weekend, in the Berlin district of Kreuzberg, where, at least on the back streets, the prophet Mohammed finds more believers than the Christian Savior, the third annual Carnival of Cultures took place. As a street procession and performance, the event gives the people of this city an opportunity to show each other the treasures of their music, their temperament, and their approach to life. Koreans displayed how to make whiplike headwear appendages twirl by spinning one's head rhythmically. Mexicans displayed how one can wear Mexican hats while singing. Belly dancers belly danced.

As the belly dancers and other ensembles marched by, one could discern the nationalizing, vitalizing effect of a multicultural ethos in a metropolitan city heavily populated by immigrants. Yet the best and the majority of the belly dancers were secondary-school teachers from Swabia, and the Brazilian street samba bands were also roughly 99 percent German—far more representatives, that is, than the nation can claim in Kreuzberg on a day without a multicultural festival. Other attractions included healers and venerably coutured fakirs with turbans, accompanied by the drumming of Far Eastern martial-arts clubs.

One thing was proven this weekend: we are still our own best foreigners, by far. The processing ensembles and happily swaying spectators proved it. Berlin's Istanbul, the former postal district SO 36—where every second building has a döner kebab stand and every third a mosque, where the twisted dagger causes havoc every day (according to the assertions of a large Hamburg paper)—became German again for a few hours on this day of cultures. Germanness ruled in its most German form—namely, in the one that avows multiculturalism. However, those whose culture and heritage are not part of the Carnival of Cultures, the city's Turks, were rarely seen on this Sunday, in the audience and in the festival procession. Perplexed bearded men and veiled women watched from shaded windows. They must have felt how small their world is—the island of Kreuzberg in the great sea of multiculturalism, where the Germans get along so nicely.

10
KANAK ATTAK
MANIFESTO

Printed in English on the organization's website, www.kanak.attak.de, in November 1998. Translation modified by David Gramling. This document is the mission statement for Kanak Attak, a transethnic activist network that formed in the mid-1990s. Several contributors to this volume, including Feridun Zaimoğlu and Mark Terkessidis, rank among its membership.

Kanak Attak is a community of different people from diverse backgrounds who share a commitment to eradicate racism from German society. Kanak Attak is not interested in questions about your passport or heritage. In fact, it challenges such questions in the first place. Kanak Attak challenges the conservative and liberal orthodoxy that good "race relations" are simply a matter of tighter immigration control. Our common position consists of an attack against the "Kanakization" of specific groups of people through racist ascriptions, denying people their social, legal, and political rights. Kanak Attak is therefore antinationalist and antiracist, rejecting every single form of identity politics supported by ethnic absolutist thinking.

Simply put, we reject everyone and everything that exploits, dominates, and humiliates people. The field of Kanak Attak's interventions includes critiques of the political and economic circumstances that allow racism to fester, the culture industries that perpetuate the commodification of racism, as well as confrontations with everyday racism, discrimination, and violence in Germany. We support the fundamental human rights of all people yet at the same time are critical of notions of "equality" that mean the subordination of difference under one hegemonic culture. We seek to challenge this dominance of a hegemonic culture that ignores racial inequality—whether it is understood as "global postmodernism" or a dull Teutonism.

The End of Dialogue Culture

Although Kanak Attak is a predominantly migrant movement, it should not be seen as the "cool voice" of the ghetto. That's how they would like it, the commercial vultures of the culture industries, which are searching for "authentic" and "exotic" human experiences to sell to those living in the gray mainstream of everyday German society. Here the figure of the young, angry migrant fits perfectly—the person who endorses the "out of the ghetto" mythology that assures complacent liberals that German society is meritocratic after all. That notion in turn is used with great commercial success by the German music and film industries to falsify a "German Dream."

Kanak Attak also distances itself from a definition of the "political" that naively suggests that all that is needed is "dialogue" and the "peaceful cohabitation" between Kanaks and the majority of this society via the Day of the Foreign Fellow Citizen and displays of folk culture and humanistic campaigns. When the weather is good and the conscience is bad, liberal Germans decorate their cars with stickers with messages such as "Foreigners, never leave us alone with the Germans!" Kanak Attak is not a friend of such multiculturalism. There are not many supporters of this concept left, a concept that never got beyond the status of local policy experiments before mainstream talk turned to the failure of the multicultural society. Thus, it was inevitable that demands for integration and assimilation would resurface. In this atmosphere, it was not German society that was examined but the migrants themselves! We were told that migrants lack tolerance. Those who do not want to "adapt" (read "assimilate") to the open society have no business in enlightened Germany. Yet tolerance is being claimed from a dominant position that does not have to examine its own complicity with subordination; existing relations of domination are being suppressed. This logic suggests that to talk openly about racism and to challenge ethnocentrism and nationalism will only cause more trouble and violence. It was capable of generating prejudice among the majority of Germans. Yet the only racists are the extremists, or so we are told.

We reject all of this. Racism has to be challenged in all its forms—from individual discrimination to violent attacks. [. . .]

Against Contemporary Certainties

Racism articulates itself at present mainly in a culturalist form. Just as in other European countries, Islam serves as a space of projection for different kinds of racisms. This is why we think we have to fight against all barriers to the recognition of Islam as an equal religious community. For us, Islam is no homogenous ideology. One must distinguish everyday religious practice from organized political Islam. Nevertheless, present-day anti-Islamism is one of the key parts of the neoracist consensus within German society. German politicians invoke false and pseudofeminist positions to defend spurious "universal" rights. This bias can be seen in the discourse about head scarves. At this point, even reactionary politicians display sympathy for oppressed women, as long as they can pin the blame on Islam.

Another racist form of argumentation that we have to attack is the idea that the "mixture of people" must somehow be regulated and controlled. This nonsense has spread too far. It hits people through the Foreigner Act in the same way that a bar bouncer regulates the "right mixture" of people inside. Well-intentioned people often point out the so-called pressure brought about by uncontrolled immigration. But migration is not the problem. The problem is those who can only think and live in ways that promote bland homogeneity. Even the tolerant and enlightened are looking for a new club if necessary, or a new part of town. Others hope for help from the Nazi parties or take the law into their own hands.

We demand not only the extension of civil rights and other privileges to all groups but question the ostensibly self-evident regulation of "inside" and "outside" and the absurdly dehumanizing living conditions that racism promotes. *Punktum e basta.*

Represent! Represent!

Kanak Attak offers a platform for Kanaks from different social areas who are sick of the facile hopping between cultures that postmodernists recommend. Kanak Attak wants to disrupt the ascription of ethnic identities and roles, the "we" and "them." And because Kanak Attak is based on attitude and not on heritage, origin, roots, or papers, nonmigrants and Germans of the second and even third generations are part of it too. But a word of caution here as well! The existing hierarchy of social life and the subject positions it imposes cannot be merely overlooked. Not all constructions are the same. So our project is caught up in the whirlwind of contradictions concerning the relation between representation, difference and the ascription of ethnic identities.

Nevertheless, we are working toward a new attitude for migrants of all generations—one that we want to bring to the stage, independently and without compromise. Whoever believes that we celebrate a potpourri of ghetto hip-hop and other clichés will be surprised. We sample, change, and adapt different political and cultural movements that operate from oppositional positions. We go back to a mixture of theory, politics, and cultural practice. This song is ours.

Now's the time! Kanak Attak!

11

JOHANNES ODENTHAL

HEIMAT ART: NEW URBAN CULTURES

First published as "Heimat Kunst—neue urbane Kulturen" in the *Heimat Kunst* brochure (Berlin: Haus
der Kulturen der Welt, 1999). Translated by Tes Howell. Odenthal is the director of the Program on
Music, Dance, and Theater in Berlin's House of World Cultures and project director of *Heimat* Art.

Krisda Duangphung of Fulda has just become the new "Mister Germany."
Bavarian composer Sandeep Baghwati is one of Germany's contemporary
music innovators. Since 1996, Ismael Ivo has been managing the dance theater at the Deutsches Nationaltheater in Weimar. Rui Horta and Amanda
Miller, representing Germany, won national prizes at the choreographers'
competition in Paris-Bagnolet. The new pop star Tarkan is one of the most
internationally popular singers from Germany. And the rappers Sabrina
Setlur and Aziza A. are defining the German hip-hop scene.

How do we imagine the German cultural landscape of the twenty-first century? Will the discourses on asylum, minorities, and integration dominate, or
will German society develop the potential for an open cultural migration?
The cultural scene in Germany will have to redefine itself amid xenophobia,
monocultural national identities (which are now experiencing a renaissance
in Eastern Europe), and the migration societies of modern metropolises in
Western Europe. However, the debate about intercultural dialogue accomplished far more in the 1970s and 1980s than it does today. With German reunification and the new national self-preoccupation, the Federal Republic
has reverted to a pre-1970s consciousness.

The project *Heimat* Art is responding to these questions and this societal
situation. Events taking place in 10 cities this spring and summer demonstrate the cultural diversity in Germany. *Heimat* Art is dedicated to the thesis
that the development of new artistic languages in Germany must be radically
intercultural, finding its impulses in the encounter, the collision, or the rup-
tures between different cultures. The question is not only "who are 'the new
Germans,'" but also "how can Germany represent itself artistically in the
coming decades?" The concept and self-image of national fine arts and cultural policy are gradually being transformed by the consequences of migration and globalization through a dynamic of open dialogue. Cultural identity
is no longer static, nor is it the consensus of a majority society pursuing integration; it is rather the exchange between equally legitimate individual and
collaborative concepts that merge and dissociate. Culture no longer attributes this concept of cultural diversity to ethnic groups. Cultural identity is a
dynamic resignification process of art and society, an experimental field in
motion. [. . .]

If we follow Vilém Flusser, the great migration theorist, a polemical dialogue arises between the natives and the "homeless" that leads to po-

groms, a change of homeland, or the liberation of natives from ties to their homeland. Homeland is a kind of unconscious entanglement in habits; migration means suffering the loss of homeland but also the immersion in an extremely constructive situation that, according to Flusser, is always the prerequisite for survival in migration. *Heimat* Art is a project of artist-migrants who take responsibility for the sometimes painful, sometimes exceedingly seductive search for a new open identity, beyond national bond, that surrenders to the existential experiment of a dialogue beyond the well-trodden path.

12

GÜNTHER COENEN

THE FIRST YEARS OF THE HOUSE OF WORLD CULTURES

First published as "Die ersten Jahre des Hauses der Kulturen der Welt" in *Zehn Jahre Haus der Kulturen der Welt* (Berlin: Haus der Kulturen der Welt, 1999), 7–9. Translated by David Gramling. Coenen was the first general secretary of the House of World Cultures from 1989 to 1992, before becoming the director of the Goethe-Institut in Athens.

[. . .] The Congress Hall had been a mixed-use building for years, and its image as an event venue had been all but lost. The hall was thought of as cold in atmosphere, technologically underequipped, and unable to be renovated, because it was protected under historical-preservation statutes. Bus 69 occasionally drove by the hall, often without any passengers, and usually the bus failed to drive all the way up to the main entrance and drove right by instead. Work began at the House of World Cultures on January 3, 1989, though the planning stages for its founding had begun in September of the previous year. The new team assembled in the open, empty space. Offices, tables, chairs, typewriters, and telephones were not yet available. It was cold and gray outside, and the long-established Congress Hall administrative staff had barricaded itself in the only available office space. Counting on the premature demise of this new experiment, the previous tenants were ready to do their part to precipitate its downfall as soon as possible. These conditions and other factors turned the initial challenge into a matter of insistent assertion. A fantastically engaged, young, creative, and highly intelligent team accepted and rose to this challenge, as did an unexpectedly engaged and numerous audience.

Looking back, it should be noted that among the conceptual underpinnings of the house was the fact that a new consciousness of the meaning of cultural differentiation had been achieved during the 1980s. Bonn and Berlin reacted to the founding of the House of World Cultures in a politically appropriate way, given the postmodern challenges of the regionalization of cultural identities, and the house thus found worldwide recognition. Audience reactions showed that more and more people were crossing the horizon of their own culture and wished to be stimulated by other traditions. Artistic engagement, emotionality, and sensuality had been generally pushed out of Western art to make room for the minimalist and conceptual turns, but these former essentials could be rediscovered through foreign art. In the early days, many critics feared that the work of the House of World Cultures might devolve into a kind of "cuddling" up to foreign cultures and would adhere to the various concepts and programs of the multicultural society. Very quickly, the staff of the house recognized that intentions were not a sufficient justification for programming. There could not be a Third World Bonus if we were to fulfill our commitment to fostering respect for foreign production. Those who came to the house had to measure up just as well as domestic artists. [. . .]

Already back in 1987, the Indian prime minister Rajiv Gandhi and federal chancellor Helmut Kohl had agreed that in the fall of 1990, the federal government would sponsor and plan a Festival of India. Delayed by the confusions of reunification, the festival was ultimately planned for 1991–92, and the house became involved in this effort. Considering its financial and physical dimensions, this festival was the most wide-ranging cultural-exchange program that the federal government had ever engaged in. [. . .] By the end of the festival, in which 350,000 people participated, the House of World Cultures had made a name for itself both in Berlin and throughout the republic, boldly claiming a new network of partners engaged in foreign cultural and political topics.

The 1990 business report of the House of World Cultures delivered an unequivocal assessment. "The tasks of the institution will increase in importance in the foreign and domestic realm, in Berlin as well as in the rest of the republic. Its engagement with foreign mentalities and foreign cultures will increasingly be a factor in the internal and external peace of this republic." It seems that the realities of this claim have not changed; neither has the necessity of maintaining and strengthening this institution.

13

LESLIE A. ADELSON

AGAINST BETWEEN: A MANIFESTO

Published in English in *Unpacking Europe*, Salah Hassan and Iftikhar Dadi, eds. (Rotterdam: NAi, 2001), 244–55. Adelson, professor of German studies at Cornell University, delivered this manifesto at Berlin's House of World Cultures in 2000.

[. . .] In May 2000, the president of Germany [Johannes Rau] gave a landmark speech in Berlin's House of World Cultures, calling for a radical reorganization of thought in all arenas of social and political life.[1] This call was issued in response to the changing face of the German nation, even before the summer's furious debates about renewed right-wing extremism. President Rau most likely did not have literature in mind when he said this, but emergent literatures certainly are one important site of cultural reorientation. More than a mere repository of treasured or controversial works of art, a nation's culture is also an activity, a creative engagement with a rapidly changing present. It actively seeks to negotiate changing values and attitudes toward a changing world.[2] This labor of culture is currently being undertaken, in ways that have yet to be grasped, by authors usually presumed to be outside German culture, even if they have somehow managed to reside on German territory or acquire German citizenship. "Between two worlds" is the place customarily reserved for these authors and their texts on the cultural map of our time, but the trope of "betweenness" often functions literally like a reservation designed to contain, restrain, and impede new knowledge, not enable it. This then is my manifesto *against between*.[3]

The notion that Turks in Germany are suspended on a bridge "between two worlds" carries with it a number of misperceptions that thwart understanding, even as they claim to promote it.

1. The "dialogue of cultures" that Johannes Rau and other public figures call for may be useful, even necessary, in the sociopolitical realm, but it fails completely, oddly enough, in the imaginative realm of social production that is often taken to represent culture. Whoever mines literary texts of the 1990s and beyond for evidence of mutually exclusive collective identities in communicative dialogue with one another is not reading this literature for its most significant innovations. This is especially true for literature written in German by authors whose cultural imagination has been profoundly influenced by many years of living, working, studying, and dreaming in the Federal Republic of Germany.

2. Despite wide recognition that political science and literary interpretation rely on different terms, media, and analytical procedures, the growing

1. Johannes Rau, "Berliner Rede/Ohne Angst und Träumereien: Gemeinsam in Deutschland leben," *Haus der Kulturen der Welt* (Berlin), May 12, 2000, n.p. See www.bundespraesident.de/reden/rau/de/00_0512.htm. The German verb *umdenken* connotes something conceptually akin to shifting gears or changing direction: *"Wir müssen in allen Bereichen des gesellschaftlichen Lebens und des politischen und staatlichen Handelns umdenken."*

2. See Agnes Heller's concept of the "present-present age" as elaborated in *A Theory of History* (London: Routledge and Kegan Paul, 1982), 44. Leslie A. Adelson discusses the concept in *Making Bodies, Making History: Feminism and German Identity* (Lincoln: University of Nebraska Press, 1993), 24.

3. This manifesto was written as a pointed intervention in a particular field of political and scholarly rhetoric in Germany at a particular historical juncture in the development of contemporary German studies on an international scale. The trope of "betweenness" may well be useful in other contexts, but such contexts are not the author's present concern.

and diverse field of Turco-German literature may well be the only sector in literary studies today in which an entrenched sociological positivism continues to hold sway. This positivist approach presumes that literature reflects empirical truths about migrants' lives and that authors' biographies explain their texts so well that reading the texts themselves is virtually superfluous. This saves readers and critics a good deal of time. Meanwhile, the literary elephant in the room goes unremarked.

3. The sociological thrust of this positivism is an epistemological holdover from the late 1970s and 1980s, when an emergent "guest-worker" literature focused on the economic exploitation of and xenophobic disdain for the underprivileged. These tropes still circulate in the reception of migrants' literature today, especially when it is written by someone presumed to represent the culture of Turkey. Aras Ören and Güney Dal are best known for their literary reflections on the "guest-worker" experience, for example, and they both continue to write in Turkish despite their long-time residence in Germany. But few people know that Ören explicitly conceived several of his novels from the 1980s as being *auf der Suche nach der gegenwärtigen Zeit* ("in search of the present")—that is, as a pseudo-Proustian series of literary reflections on the modernist legacy for an as-yet-uncharted but shared Turco-German present. Even fewer people know that the narrator of Güney Dal's tale of an industrial strike and a mutant migrant in the mid-1970s characterized foreign laborers as *ein[en] Teil lebendiger Erinnerung*, a piece of "living memory" of Germans' own class history.[4] If the sociological tensions of this earlier period cannot be reduced to an absolute cultural divide between things German and things Turkish, they are even less useful for assessing the significance of a literature that has grown only more diverse since the two postwar German states were united in 1990 and Cold War divisions began to yield to the new Europe.

4. The imaginary bridge "between two worlds" is designed to keep discrete worlds apart as much as it pretends to bring them together. Migrants are at best imagined as suspended on this bridge in perpetuity; critics do not seem to have enough imagination to picture them actually crossing the bridge and landing anywhere new. This has to do, in turn, with the national contours that are ascribed to these ostensible "worlds" linked by a bridge of dubious stability. In this model, the Federal Republic of Germany may change and the Republic of Turkey may change (though this is usually dismissed in Germany as unlikely), but what is not allowed to change is the no-

---

4. See Leslie A. Adelson, "Coordinates of Orientation: An Introduction," in Zafer Şenocak, *Atlas of a Tropical Germany*, trans. and ed. Leslie A. Adelson (Lincoln: University of Nebraska Press, 2000), xxiv; see also Zafer Şenocak and Bülent Tulay, "Germany—Home for Turks?" in *Atlas of a Tropical Germany*, 1–9. For the German original of this second essay ("Deutschland—Heimat für Türken?"), see Zafer Şenocak, *Atlas des tropischen Deutschland: Essays* (Berlin: Babel, 1992), 9–19.

tion that Turks and Germans are separated by an absolute cultural divide. Where does this leave Turco-German writers in Germany? It is absurd to assume today that they always and necessarily and only represent the national culture of Turkey. The Turkish diaspora and its lines of affiliation cannot be traced or contained by the borders of the Turkish republic, certainly not by these alone. Beyond the Cold War, German culture is already forever changed, and Turco-German literature is part and parcel of this cultural transformation.

5. Zafer Şenocak has called for "something like a negative hermeneutic" that could perhaps heal "the wounds of communication" inflicted by a public obsession, right and left, with Self and Other.[5] Such a negative hermeneutic, again in Şenocak's words, "critically interrogates what is presumed to be understood."[6] In this sense we do not need more understanding of different cultures if understanding only fixes them *as* utterly different cultures. Instead of reifying different cultures as fundamentally foreign, we need to understand culture itself differently.[7] Cultural contact today is not an "intercultural encounter" that takes place between German culture and something outside it but something happening *within* German culture between the German past and the German present. Turco-German literature has been making forays into this unfamiliar territory for some time now, but the imaginative complexity of this cultural endeavor has gone largely unrecognized to date.

6. In this context, the spatial configuration of cultural labor also needs to be understood in a radically different way. Creative writing and critical thought certainly take reference to concrete places in the world, where people and nations have loved, lost, struggled, and died. These places haunt human imagination, but the imagined spaces of cultural labor cannot be mapped or measured with surveyors' tools. The discursive model that repeatedly situates Turks and other migrants "between two worlds" relies too schematically and too rigidly on territorial concepts of "home" *[Heimat]*. Even the notion that language becomes a "home" for those in exile or diaspora presupposes that a territorial home is the place of authenticity, from which language as home can only distinguish itself in sorrow or celebration. Searching for traces of "home" in contemporary cultural production is

5. For English-language commentary on this idea, see the following texts in *Atlas of a Tropical Germany:* Adelson, "Coordinates of Orientation," xxix; Şenocak, "The Poet and the Deserters: Salman Rushdie Between the Fronts," 42; "Which Myth Writes Me?" 82; and "Beyond the Language of the Land," 68. The phrase *"so etwas wie eine negative Hermeneutik"* appears in Şenocak, "Der Dichter und die Deserteure," in *War Hitler Araber? IrreFührungen an den Rand Europas* (Berlin: Babel, 1994), 28; "Wunden der Verständigung" appears in Şenocak, "Jenseits der Landessprache," *Sirene* 9.15/16 (1996): 173.

6. Şenocak, "Which Myth Writes Me?" 82.

7. See Adelson, "Coordinates of Orientation," xxxv.

therefore a misguided venture. Creative thought is not bounded by geographical or political borders. The Turco-German literary texts that demand the most of their readers do not reflect *Orte des Denkens* ["sites of thought"] in any predictably national or even ethnic sense. Instead they are *Orte des Umdenkens* ["sites of reorientation"]—that is to say, imaginative sites where cultural orientation is being radically rethought.

7. In a series of aphorisms called "Beyond the Language of the Land," Zafer Şenocak writes, "I am not in between, for I have lost my sense of direction."[8] Here, the military language of embattled camps—familiar to readers of Samuel Huntington's *Clash of Civilizations*—alternates with the disorienting language of lyrical reflection: "Songs and salvos alternate."[9] This disorientation that arises when familiar categories are left behind becomes the very ground on which critical readers reorient themselves anew. Lest I be misunderstood, this is not a celebration of violent circumstances that deprive people of the homes, lives, and relations that matter most to them. A postmodern embrace of "nomadic" fantasies is not what I propose. What I do have in mind is an epistemological reorientation to which migrants' literature contributes at a crucial juncture in an uncharted German present. It is surely no coincidence that two of the most complex writers in this field, Zafer Şenocak and Yoko Tawada, cite the great wordsmith Paul Celan (1920–70) as one of their literary muses. For the Japanese-born Tawada, the "between" of Celan's German-language poetry does not mark a border *[Grenze]* between two distinct worlds but a threshold *[Schwelle]*, a site where consciousness of something new flashes into view. She describes a poem by Celan as *Zwischenraum*, "a *transitional* space." This is not the bridge "between two worlds" on which Turks are so often thought to be suspended. For, as Tawada elaborates, "Der Zwischenraum ist kein geschlossenes Zimmer, sondern er ist der Raum unter einem Tor. / Ich fing an, Celans Gedichte wie Tore zu betrachten und nicht etwa wie Häuser, in denen die Bedeutung wie ein Besitz aufbewahrt wird." For Tawada reading Celan, the word is a site of opening, a threshold that beckons.[10] Turco-German literature too is a threshold that beckons, not a tired bridge "between two worlds." Entering this threshold

8. For the German, see Zafer Şenocak, "Jenseits der Landessprache," *Sirene* 9.15/16 (1996): 172. (The essay also appears in *Zungenentfernung*, an essay collection published in 2001.) For the English translation, see Şenocak, *Atlas of a Tropical Germany*, 67.

9. Samuel P. Huntington, *The Clash of Civilizations and the Remaking of World Order* (New York: Simon and Schuster, 1996). For the German, see Şenocak, "Jenseits der Landessprache," 171; the English appears on p. 66 of *Atlas of a Tropical Germany*.

10. Yoko Tawada, "Das Tor des Übersetzers oder Celan liest Japanisch," *Talisman* (Tübingen: Konkursbuch, 1996), 129–30. Unless otherwise indicated, all English translations are my own. Here, I propose, "The space of transition is not a closed room but rather the space under a gate./I began to regard Celan's poems as gates and not, say, as houses in which meaning is stored like possessions."

space is an imaginative challenge that has yet to be widely met, and much
critical work remains to be done. [. . .]

14

JULIA NAUMANN

MULTIKULTI—OR WHAT?

First published as "Multikulti—oder was?" in *die tageszeitung* (June 9, 2000). Translated by Tes Howell.

A carnival does not create equal-opportunity living in a multicultural city

Organizer Anett Szabó expresses it succinctly: "When the Kurd is dancing,
the Korean is not." Approximately 184 nationalities exist in the capital. The
largest group is the Turks; the smallest are comprised of single persons from
Antigua, Bahrain, and Brunei. There are hardly any points of contact.

This disengaged coexistence breaks down once a year, or rather it is supposed to. But the Carnival of Cultures does not transform Berlin into a city
of peaceful cooperation. The event may provide for convergences and confrontations, but it has no political platform, which is the most important vehicle for advocating equal rights for different ethnic groups.

According to advertisements, the carnival, which will take place this weekend for the fifth time, is supposed to connect people from the "whole world
in a unique festival." One hundred thirteen groups from 70 countries will file
through Kreuzberg on Pentecost Sunday. In gloriously colorful costumes,
they will show the crowd their decorated floats and dance to exotic beats.
What began as a small procession in 1996 with "just" 50,000 spectators has
become the city's "*multikulti* mega-event."

Has the carnival really influenced how people live together? Isn't it actually the case that a *multikulti* show is being staged, even though "*multikulti*" is
more about paying lip service to diversity than a political and social reality?
Aren't the Turkish vegetable merchant, the Polish maid, and the Vietnamese
cigarette vendor just being presented like dancing bears?

Szabó dismisses that as "completely absurd." "When we were accused of
throwing foreigners into costumes and exhibiting them," recounts Szabó, "I
went to the participants." They just had a good laugh. According to them, the
carnival will not radically change integration politics, but it does provide "an
impetus for thought." "I believe in sustainability," says the 35-year-old Szabó.
The participants (4,200 this year) prepare all year for this special day. Very
few groups recruit people from just one country of origin; most do so from
many different countries. Consequently, a group with Polish and German
participants, for example, will perform Brazilian dances. Around half of the
dancers are German. [. . .]

Many of the participants live in binational marriages. The majority have been in Germany for some time and have secure residence status. "Architects, cooks, students, and secretaries are there, and all age groups are represented," lists Szabó. However, only a few socially marginalized groups, such as war refugees living in government residence halls, are represented. Moreover, the Vietnamese (over 8,000 of whom are living in Berlin) are not there this year. But an increasing number of Turkish groups, which had been skeptical of the carnival in its first years, are now making up the difference. At first, few Turks stood on the roadside and cheered for the floats, though the procession went through Kreuzberg. "There is no carnival in Turkey," explains Turgay Ayadini, a paralegal and musician who organizes one of four stages at the street festival, the Salon Oriental. The women with scantily covered breasts would have scared away many Turks, he says. It was reportedly difficult to get Turkish musicians to come, because they wanted a high honorarium. Meanwhile, the Turks have become more tolerant, observes Ayadini. The four-day street festival is now well attended by Turks. "That is indeed a success!" Süleyman Balcı also sees it this way. He is a social worker and organizes a float on which Turkish and Arab youth, whom he calls "intolerant," take part. The carnival, he suggests, is an effective learning experience for the youth.

In this respect, the Carnival of Cultures does perhaps truly have a *multikulti* effect, if one understands *multikulti* as cooperation among different cultures and not just in an ethnic sense. For the Green Party mayor of Kreuzberg, Franz Schulz, the carnival promotes "coexistence and cultural diversity." However, Schulz does not want to circulate among the people. "I will watch the procession from a privileged view at city hall. The parade will pass by us." There are parallels here with the carnival in Rio, where the processions are seen as the domain of the poor, and the rich sit on multilevel platforms and watch the spectacle: no encounters occur between the two.

15

CORNELIA SCHMALZ-JACOBSEN

WHERE ARE THE TURKISH TEACHERS AND DOCTORS?

First published as "Wo sind die türkischen Lehrer und Ärzte?" in *Die Zeit* (May 26, 2001). Translated by David Gramling. Schmalz-Jacobsen, a member of the Free Democratic Party, served on the Süssmuth Commission on Immigration and was the federal commissioner of foreigner affairs from 1991 to 1998.

The 40 years of immigration history in Germany are full of contradictions. Asylum seekers and refugees have been generously accepted in great numbers, millions of late resettlers with considerable family relocation needs have found a new home, and foreigners with lengthy legal residence in federal territory have approximately the same rights as Germans.

The result, nonetheless, is a contrary and agitated immigration country with frustrated immigrants, signaling a lack of normalcy and openness to the fact of migration. Efforts toward integration on both sides have been formidable, but the symptoms of segregation, even in the second and third generations, may not be overlooked.

The idea that integration is a mandatory task of the state has not yet been made official policy. Migrants are the blind spots in most school textbooks, and not just there. They hardly come up. Thirty percent of children and youth in our elementary-school classes come from a migration background, and this figure is higher in thickly settled regions. But it appears that no one has taken notice of this—neither in teacher education nor in higher education.

The number of foreign dropouts is twice that of German youth. Only recently has there been some consensus that language competency is the ticket to academic and professional success. But a federal study about language acquisition among migrants according to objective criteria is still lacking. Scientifically rigorous data on the non-German domestic population is also astoundingly meager, despite the 7.3 million foreigners and the 2.5 million resettlers who have come to us in the past ten years.

Even before the recent revision of the citizenship law [in 1999], there were 100,000 foreigners in Germany who could have become naturalized without difficulty but did not do so. The severely limited parameters for dual citizenship cannot be the sole reason for this notoriously low rate of naturalization.

Why the hesitation? The question cannot be posed to the immigrants only. We should pose it to ourselves too, the society doing the accepting. An interesting anecdote: in one Berlin district, government officials solicited and encouraged 18-year-old foreigners to pursue naturalization—with great success, because the young people felt "wanted." Subsequently, greater Berlin has become the place in Germany with the most naturalization applications.

Until Chancellor Schröder's hotly debated Green Card initiative in March 2000, foreigners were described as a threat in most areas of political debate— in all the parties. They were seen as a majority element from which society needed protection. Media, especially electronic media, are playing a significant role in the paradigm shift that politics and economics are now demanding. In the satellite age, most programs can be viewed throughout Europe, and the immigration population also takes in programming from their countries of origin. The days of "guest-worker shows" are gone for good. State radio has reduced them bit by bit. They were switched over to less attractive time slots or have been discontinued altogether. Only Sender Freies Berlin's Radio Multikulti and [Cologne's] WDR, with its all-day Funkhaus Europa, offer interesting alternatives.

Otherwise: silence. A purposeful strategy to respond to the diversity of the listeners and its expectations—not to mention its market potential—is nowhere in sight. Immigrants pay radio and television taxes, yet they are not represented anywhere in the corresponding institutions, with the exception of West German Radio. The current troupe of television entertainers and commentators does not reflect our immigration society. More must be done to contribute to integration and to raise acceptance.

Recently, an American asked me, "Where are all your Turkish teachers and doctors?" He was surprised by the "colorful" scene on the streets of our big cities and the simultaneous absence of immigrants in many aspects of daily life. His question is justified. Indeed, where are they in the offices of public agencies, in the police force, in the social-services bureaus, as teachers in kindergartens, on editorial boards, at banks, and at the post office? [. . .]

16

ECKHARD MICHELS

GERMAN AS A WORLD LANGUAGE

First published as "Weltsprache Deutsch" in *Die Zeit* (August 9, 2001). Translated by David Gramling.

With a *festschrift*, a major exhibition in Berlin, and—not to forget—a special postage stamp, one of the great German cultural institutions is about to celebrate its birthday. Fifty years ago, in Munich, on August 9, 1951, the "Goethe-Institut Inc., for the Continuing Education of Foreign German Teachers" was founded. However, the date is a little bit fudged. The prehistory of this highly praised establishment reaches back much further.

Back in the 1930s, Franz Thierfelder called the first Goethe-Institut into being. Thierfelder, born in Deutschbora in Saxony in 1896, a doctor of German philology and economics and an accomplished journalist to boot, had been the general secretary of the Deutsche Akademie, or German Academy, in Munich since 1928. The first Goethe-Institut was then founded in 1932 as a department of this academy. In contrast to the 75-year-old German Academic Exchange Service (DAAD), it seems appropriate to reduce the Goethe-Institut's history to the past 50 years. In 1945, the Americans summarily dissolved the German Academy, as well as the Institut—perhaps a bit rashly but not entirely without reason. [. . .]

The "Academy for the Scientific Investigation and Promotion of Germanness, a.k.a. the German Academy," as the official title read, was established in 1923 by professors at the University of Munich, primarily by the ecclesiastical historian Georg Pfeilschifter, the geopolitical scientist Karl Haushofer, and the historian Hermann Oncken. It was first located on Odeonplatz, then, after 1932, in the Maximilianeum. The goal was to reinvigorate Germans' cultural self-awareness after losing the world war. At the same time, the academy was supposed to promote German culture in the international arena.

No Classes for the Untermensch

This dual task formed the basis for the character of this haughtily named organization. Its "research department" billed itself as a society of scholars seeking to make Germans more familiar with their cultural heritage. Meanwhile, its "practical department," in contrast, did cultural work abroad. In order to secure the necessary clout for the new establishment, a 100-person senate was designed based on the 40 "immortals" of the Paris-based Academie Française, including distinguished, politically conservative, and exclusively male representatives of culture, science, economics, politics, and the military. At its official founding on May 5, 1925, the academy's lofty goal was to become the central organization of nongovernmental foreign cultural politics. This vision was quickly shattered, however, and language promotion remained the only cultural-political arena of its work that was not already being undertaken by other organizations such as the German Foreign Institute, which possessed far greater connections at the Reich's ministries than did the new academy. Thierfelder was the first to recognize the opportunity to give the organization a definitive profile based on continuing-education courses for foreign German teachers by establishing a special institute and language schools abroad. In 1931, the academy began to receive subsidies from the Bureau of the Exterior. [. . .]

[In November of 1941], Hitler raised the organization per "Führer's decree" to the level of a Body of Public Right. The academy was thus officially delegated the task of safeguarding the German language domestically, overseeing orthographic streamlining, and advising other agencies on the composition of official texts. More important still, the academy would continue to promote the German language abroad. [. . .]

After November 1941, the academy was swimming in money. In 1939, the Bureau of the Exterior had thrown 80,000 reichsmarks into the academy's approximately 550,000-mark annual budget. The rest was raised through business donations. In 1944, however, the budget amounted to 9 million reichsmarks; now more than 85 percent of the money came from the state. The German Academy's budget was almost 20 times that of the revered Prussian Academy of Sciences, the greatest among the traditional German scientific academies.

The financial problems were over, but now there was a lack of qualified staff, because the army had been drafting the lecturers since the end of 1941. Against its will, the academy appointed more and more women for language instruction abroad in order to reach the goal that Siebert had announced in a speech at the time of the "Führer's decree:" "We intend to help the German language assume its proper place as a world language. Whoever wishes to take a place at great Germany's table must afford the German language at least as much significance in negotiations of a diplomatic, scientific, cultural, and societal nature as he affords his own."

At the outbreak of the war, the German Academy administered more than 46 language schools with perhaps 70 teachers in 15 mostly European countries. Approximately 8,000 students had signed up. The institute's interests were particularly geared to the Balkans, a region the Reich had sought to economically permeate since the end of the 1920s. Four years later, thanks to financial bequests from the Reich's budget, the German Academy consisted of 105 lectorships—primarily in the Balkans and occupied France. These were supported by hundreds of locally recruited teaching assistants, who operated 170 smaller branches of the academy in the occupied, allied, or neutral states.

In 1942, when the Third Reich found itself at the zenith of its military power, language courses posted their all-time-high enrollments, with approximately 64,000 students. However, the academy was only allowed to promote the German language among those subjected peoples who, according to contemporary racial categories, were found to be worthy of taking part in the culture of the "master humans." Thus, there was no institute in occupied Poland, the invaded regions of the Soviet Union or in the "Protectorate of Bohemia and Moravia." [. . .]

The Goethe-Institut of the German Academy continued its training courses for foreign Germanists in Munich until summer 1944. In addition, it published teaching materials for German instruction, fulfilling one of the special directives of the regime. It published a language primer for *Volk*-Germans in the army and foreign-language volunteers in the Waffen-SS that focused primarily on military vocabulary. As the author declared to his academy colleagues, an appendix would include "the Germany Song, the Horst Wessel Song, the Flag Song, the duties of the German soldier, and the strong and irregular verbs." In addition, the primer for the Waffen-SS would be supplemented by two language lessons on the topics "family" and "honor." [. . .]

In December of 1945, the Americans demanded the dissolution of the academy, despite futile attempts by Thierfelder, who had been made commissarial general secretary. This move, however, did not prevent the directors of the newly refounded Goethe-Institut, in the 1950s, from associating themselves with the work of their predecessors. The old institute had, from a purely "disciplinary" point of view, done pioneering work in the new field of "German as a foreign language." Thus, the old academy's assessment criteria from 1935 were reimplemented verbatim for new courses at home and abroad after 1953. In this initial phase, teachers resorted to the instructional text *Spoken German*, published by the academy in 1939. However, some minor corrections were necessary for the new edition, so that language stu-

dents would not come to know Munich as the "capital of the movement."
[. . .]

Encouraged by new cultural initiatives at the Bureau of the Exterior, the
organization reopened in March 1951 in Bonn. Its directors sought to establish as close ties as possible with the work of the German Academy. The
dream of "German as a world language," which Thierfelder had suggested
in his 1938 book of the same name, was certainly dispelled. However, new
venues for German came into view in the young states of the Near and
Middle East, which were gaining emancipation from their French and British
colonial masters. German should, as the story goes, at least claim a spot
among the first five languages of the world.

Continuity with the German Academy was also important for a completely
different reason. The institut could be interpreted more or less as the right-
ful heir of the old academy. This was a condition for accessing the predecessor organization's reserve savings of some 140,000 German marks, which
after 1945, had been administered by the Bavarian state. [. . .]

The Business with Goethe

From this perspective, it appeared only appropriate to include minor or un-
compromised members of the old academy from the outset. Consequently,
three more of the eight signatories of the August 9, 1951, founders' declaration, in addition to Thierfelder, had been active in the predecessor organizations. These former academy members included Fehn Kurt Magnus, who
would remain chairperson of the Goethe-Institut until his death in 1962. In
his particular role as a director of the Reich's radio company until 1933, Magnus had been a senator of the German Academy but was deposed amid the
growing conservatism of the academy's directorship during the Nazi regime
because of his democratic past. Dora Schultz, the one woman among the
founders, had worked for the academy as a German teacher since the 1930s.
[. . .]

The Bureau of the Exterior, from which Thierfelder and Magnus sought
subsidies, made it clear from the outset that financial support would be possible only if the Institut established some distance from the academy, at least
in name. They consequently decided to revert to the former subdepartment
Goethe-Institut—a label everyone could live with.

Goethe, Johann Wolfgang, by the way, had not served as the namesake for
the predecessor institutes only because of his fame as a German poet. Even
then, in 1932, financial considerations played a role. Thierfelder, always cog-
nizant of the empty coffers of the German Academy, made a deal with the
Frankfurt Goethe Society: the new department within the academy would
permanently bear the name of the poet, if on its behalf the society would donate a third of the proceeds it collected during the 1932 Goethe Year in
Bavaria. Thierfelder was hoping for 4,000 reichsmarks, and the endeavor was

successful. And thus, the poet from Frankfurt became the worldwide patron saint of German teachers—in good times and in bad.

17
CENTRAL WELFARE OFFICE FOR JEWS IN GERMANY
RECOMMENDATIONS FOR IMMIGRANTS

First published in a bilingual Russian-German pamphlet as "Empfehlungen für Zuwanderer" (Berlin: Central Welfare Office for Jews in Germany, 2001). Translated by David Gramling.

With your decision to leave the former Soviet Union and choose Germany as your immigration country, you find yourself in a new living situation that may appear foreign to you. In order to facilitate integration, here are a few suggestions.

The entrance permit with which you came into Germany represents an invitation neither from German authorities nor from the Jewish Congregation. It only means an authorization of your application to enter Germany. Responsibility for the decision to emigrate is still in your hands.

Naturally, life in a new country is often riddled with doubts. You feel sadness about what you have lost and a longing for your homeland. At the same time, all your hopes are tied to a new life in the West. There is professional help for this kind of crisis; most feel abandoned and alone and seek out social connections with their countrymen and -women.

However, the key to integration lies in learning the German language. Successfully graduating from a German course facilitates your adjustment in a still-foreign world. Your knowledge of German can be broadened by reading books, newspapers, and magazines, as well as through television and radio.

The most intensive opportunity for learning may be found in the practical application of language knowledge in daily communication. In addition, there are many free or inexpensive options for leisure and education: public libraries, courses at junior colleges, lectures, and readings at cultural centers. You should take advantage of these opportunities in order to be able to communicate in the foreign language as soon as possible. Older immigrants should also take absolutely every opportunity to learn the German language.

It is becoming increasingly difficult to find a place to work. Imagination, initiative, and reorienting oneself to performing services of a different skill set often lead to the desired success. Be aware of employment postings in newspaper inserts, on television, and on the radio.

Be careful in filling out your applications.

Employment is an important precondition for an eventual naturalization.

The housing market in the Federal Republic of Germany is overburdened, and patience is required for locating an affordable apartment. Waiting periods of one to two years are not uncommon. It is recommended that you take the initiative and do not wait for a referral from the Social and Housing Bureaus.

Consumer goods in Germany are not scarce, because the market—the demand side, that is—determines the supply. You can think over your potential purchases without worry, because most items are widely available.

You should also be aware of available donations and secondhand stores for clothing, furniture, and electric items.

Be careful when entering into contracts! In particular, you should think very carefully when obtaining credit, buying goods on layaway, and when signing insurance contracts. You are responsible for your written agreements. Your local consumer consultant offers advice on contract agreements and can give you advice on the real worth of various goods.

However, personal liability insurance is recommended.

Take advantage of the cultural events at the Jewish Community Center. The congregations are available to you for private events (bar and bat mitzvahs, birthdays, and weddings).

You may develop your Jewish life through volunteer work such as working on the congregation newspaper, working on the development and restructuring of youth and senior centers, visiting the sick, working in Jewish charity organizations, and/or forming artistic and musical interest groups.

You can also enrich Jewish life in Germany and strengthen your own Jewish identity by active participation in worship services and in cultural events in the congregation.

Because this brochure cannot answer all of your important questions, we recommend that you turn with confidence to the congregation responsible for your place of residence.

18

WOLFGANG MACKIEWICZ

GERMAN IS NECESSARY

Published in *Deutschland* (March 2001), a publication of the Societäts-Verlag and the Press and Information Office of the German federal government. Mackiewicz authored this text as president of the European Language Council.

Language and integration: how important is it for immigrants to learn German?

The Federal Republic of Germany is characterized by regional variety—a variety mirrored in its wide range of customs, behavior patterns, and dialects. We therefore possess several identities and affinities: regional ones, national ones, and, increasingly, European ones. The notion that a language is the expression of one particular culture thus requires further qualification. Language is principally a means of communication and is capable of being dreadfully abused—as demonstrated by our own history or by a glance at the contemporary gutter press.

It is, of course, true that language is the key to understanding the culture, the way of life, and the hopes and dreams of those who live in a particular country, and for that reason, it is important that those coming here from elsewhere already speak German or else soon learn it. [. . .]

When one reflects on certain developments taking place in Germany and in other European countries, it is apparent that we are in the midst of an ir-reversible—and positive—evolution toward an increasingly multicultural so-ciety. First of all, European integration is clearly progressing apace. The po-litical will is there, and we can expect that mobility within the EU—including the present candidate countries in Central and Eastern Europe—will in-crease considerably over the next decade. This means that even more atten-tion must be paid to language acquisition, for lack of language skills contin-ues to be one of the greatest barriers to mobility.

The introduction of the Green Card for certain professions here provides further food for thought. If the Federal Republic has to rely on specialists from other parts of the world to maintain its economic position, it is our duty to in-tegrate these people: after all, they are coming here at our invitation and for a limited time only. This can only mean that we must increase both the op-portunities for and the attraction of learning the German language. We must show much more tolerance toward those who do not have a complete mastery of the language, and we must get used to the fact that communication in the workplace—and in the public sphere—will initially take place in English. I am not arguing that English should become our lingua franca but simply that it be used as a necessary first step on the road to universal multilingualism.

There also remains the question of the educational needs of the children of recent immigrants to this country. Even the most ardent advocate of lin-guistic and cultural variety should not overlook the fact that the social inte-gration of immigrants of the second generation depends on their mastering the German language. Adopting the language of their new home is not equivalent to abandoning their cultural origins. And multiculturalism does not mean cultivating one's own native language at all costs. We can be sure that in the future, mastery of multiple languages will be a decisive economic factor, both for individuals and for our society as a whole.

19
SAFTER ÇINAR
BERLIN AFTER PISA

First published in the series "Berlin nach Pisa" in *die tageszeitung* (April 9, 2002). Translated by David Gramling. In summer 2000, the Organization for Economic Collaboration and Development con-

ducted a comparative study of education systems called the Program for International Student Assessment (PISA). Approximately 180,000 15-year-old pupils from 32 participating countries were
tested for reading literacy, mathematical literacy, scientific literacy, and crosscurricular competencies.
In all four areas, German pupils scored far below average. The integration of children from underprivileged and less-educated families into the school system was particularly weak. Children from migrant families in Germany scored lower than in any other European country. Çınar, 56, is a spokesperson for the Turkish Union in Berlin-Brandenburg.

Equal opportunity cannot be the last word in the German education system.
Much to the contrary, children from poor and immigrant families experience extreme hardship. In Berlin, they primarily attend kindergartens and elementary schools in the inner city. There, the main complaint among teachers is that the students lack German skills and other linguistic capacities, and
that they show low social competence due to a correspondingly insufficient
level of pedagogy. The consequence: many German parents, along with those
from the non-German middle class, avoid those schools; social segregation
in these districts persists, and the conditions at institutions of learning are becoming increasingly severe. What to do with these kindergartens and schools
in the inner cities? How can they offer all children equal chances? [. . .]

The PISA results should not be surprising. The school system in the Federal Republic is based on social selection to a greater extent than in any
other industrialized country. This state of affairs is widely acknowledged and
widely supported as well. And since the 1980s, it has primarily affected children from migration backgrounds.

This disparity has been visible for a long time now. In recent years, children and youth with dark hair and skin color have been the ones who attend
the vocational and special schools in the city. This is less a result of their ethnic heritage than of their social heritage, for most of these children are from
working-class families.

The countries with the best results in the PISA study are either tried-and-
true immigration countries, like Canada, or states with a similar migration
percentage to ours, like Sweden, that nonetheless deal with their minorities
in a very different way—in the kindergarten as well as in schools. The federal
German education system, however, offers children of migration backgrounds no equal opportunities. It has failed in its integration efforts.

It is certainly true that problematic factors arise from the immigrants
themselves: concentrated residential districts, spouses moving from the
homeland, and media habits. But one's choice of residence, spouse, and television programs is a free one, according to the Basic Law; and putting these
basic rights in question is counterproductive. [. . .]

Throughout the educational system, the fact must be accepted that the
promotion of the mother language and culture is not a liability but a relief
measure for children, because it relies on the competences that they already
have and alleviates parents' fears of alienation, thus promoting integration. [. . .]

Of course, migrants must make efforts to develop linguistic and social competence, particularly for their children's sake. But the political sphere must establish the necessary framework. It has missed this opportunity, even in the new Immigration Act. [. . .]

20

MECHTHILD KÜPPER

THE WOMAN FROM KREUZBERG

First published as "Die Kreuzbergerin" in the *Frankfurter Allgemeine Zeitung* (May 25, 2003). Translated by Tes Howell.

Barbara John is the longest-serving commissioner of foreigner affairs in Germany. Now she has to go.

German foreigner policy appears to be women's work, at least considering the evidence in the public sphere. Politicians occupy the private side with legal moves and regulations. Early in her tenure as the foreigner liaison in Berlin, it sufficed, says Barbara John (CDU), just to say "yes" all the time when the then-senator Heinrich Lummer (CDU) said "no"—for example, when discussing Turkish guest workers' desire to bring their families to Germany. Her first "yes" was the most decisive. She pushed through an "open office" to deal with public inquiries, a bureau in which officials would talk with foreigners instead of about them. She did not want to sit somewhere in the administration and develop policy.

Profound insights about how immigrants feel and what they need—homeland—originated in John's large dingy office on Potsdamer Street. A trust developed, even a warmth, between the newly arrived and the long established. All could learn from Barbara John not to fear those foreigners who, contrary to their own plans, settled here permanently.

She calls this approach "being rooted in reality." The tall woman with the blond shock of hair and the emphatically inconspicuous clothes directs her department with grinding pragmatism. She also shows heartfelt devotion and commands the language of calm conviction and clarity. Since September 11, she has warned against "Islamophobia." Responding to accusations that she is naïvely engaging with fundamentalists, she says, "I do not negotiate with terrorists; I am talking about practical problems." Berlin journalists call John after every catastrophe in the world, for she knows how they can tap into the immigrants' opinions. She has built an infrastructure in Berlin of projects, self-help groups, and organizations that facilitate interaction between the majority society and its minorities. On October 3, 2001, the first Day of German Unity after the terrorist attacks in America, she invited people to a Day of Open Mosques. When a Palestinian father brought his children armed with fake explosives to the demonstration, she visited a Palestinian organization the following Sunday. Whoever was interested in the sentiments and opinions of Iraqi exiles during the Iraq war went to Barbara John for names of organizations where they could be found. According to John, the lengthy coexistence of foreigners and Germans has "created commonalities" that go far beyond shopping at the Turkish vegetable stand. Barbara John has transformed a sentence by Odo Marquard into her practical axiom: "Matters of principle are powerful, sometimes violent; life is fragile."

Her self-restraint on practical questions over the years has given the Catholic John a quiet self-assurance that is stunning: she argues that no religion has held out against secularism in Western culture. Why should Islam be able to do it?

Berliners have benefited from John's view that they are always more willing to integrate and become better than they normally are. She referred to Moses Mendelssohn, to Friedrich II, and to the long tradition of foreigners in Prussia; she did not talk about conflicts between majority and minority, nor did she use the language of alarmism. Everyone was expected, she would say coolly upon such occasions, not to bash in the heads of others—and with such statements, she struck the civil-social tone that characterizes her. Her successor, who comes from the "antiracism" school of thought, will face difficulties.

Barbara John is the exception to the rule that politicians in Berlin are unloved. She does not see herself as a politician in the narrow sense but rather as an administration employee. For years she has been the longest-serving German foreigner liaison. She was appointed in 1981 by Richard von Weizsäcker and "discovered" the department, which today has 28 employees; she continued on under his successors Eberhard Diepgen (CDU), Walter Momper (SPD), then again Diepgen and finally Klaus Wowereit (SPD). At the end of her term, she was rejected by a PDS senator when she offered to continue working as an unsalaried official. Senator Klaus Böger (SPD) reacted quickly. He allowed John to establish an office in his administration, and now she is back to where her career began: she coordinates efforts throughout Berlin to teach German to all children as early and as well as possible. Before she became the commissioner of foreigner affairs, John was a teacher of German as a Foreign Language; she even wrote a textbook. She will be able to do this again, now that the essential role of mastering the language has been proven irrefutable.

John credits her concentration on the secularist elements of coexistence for her popularity beyond the circle of her "clients." No one needs to feel overwhelmed or threatened by demands for "best practices," as they are now called, or for the self-evident minimum standards of civilization. When the devastating test scores of the first graders' language tests were presented, she did not speak of the tragic results. She said, "We don't have to perform miracles." Only the children can learn the language; we can only try to help them.

One rarely heard the voice of Barbara John in the often ideologically driven discussions about whether Germany was or was not an immigration country, or in the debates about the Red-Green coalition's planned immigration law. She continued to work and was her own—highly professional—spokeswoman. She accessed EU funds, attended academic conferences (to which she is often invited for her expertise) and participated in seminars to hear whether the academy had finally found a formula for conveying the most important element in a migration policy: that immigration is also an advantage for the recipient society. Meanwhile, she is an honorary professor at Humboldt University.

One could interpret Barbara John's career in two different ways: One could complain that a woman with so much experience in domestic policies still does not play a larger role. But one could also learn from her example that someone so unpretentious, persistent, straightlaced, trail-blazing, and self-reflexive must prevail—in the long term. For now, as she is sent into retirement from her post as commissioner of foreigner affairs, Barbara John has "won." There is a new discussion, "rooted in reality," about how Germany can better reconcile its own interests with those of its immigrants.

According to John, we are "an immigration country with a job market and educational system that are hostile to immigrants." The unskilled workers that Germany admits must have access to the overregulated job market. Earlier, she says, we understood ourselves as a "nonimmigration country with immigrants." In between these two poles are the 20 years of her service—and her tenacious patience. Length of service can indeed be a political virtue.

Barbara John grew up in Kreuzberg, on Manteuffel Street. The area was always poverty-stricken but now sometimes epitomizes the brighter side of a multicultural city. Whoever sees her climb out of her little car, her back seat full of banana crates for the move from one office to another, begins to understand: she belongs to a disappearing type of West Berliner, who built a democratic community with the famous postwar virtues of persistence and modesty. Barbara John has never fit in with the subsidy champions. But even they have learned to respect her.

21
VOICES IN SUPPORT OF THE MIGRATION MUSEUM

Published on the website of the proposed Migration Museum—www.migrationsmuseum.de—in 2003. Translated by David Gramling.

CEM ÖZDEMIR
First Bundestag member of Turkish descent, German member of the European Parliament

When I visited the Immigration Museum on Ellis Island near Manhattan a few years ago, I tried to imagine how it would be to walk through a comparable museum in Germany with my parents. A museum with modern museum pedagogy, in which school classes with students of different backgrounds would crowd and jostle through. But a museum that would not be limited to documenting the living conditions in a so-called guest-worker settlement at the beginning of the 1960s, one that also would show Germans the extent to which our common land has changed for the benefit of all and will continue to change, despite all of the problems that are undeniably present.

DUARTE BRANCO
Chair of the Association of Portuguese Businesses in Germany

The problematic of migration has existed in Germany for a long time, and nonetheless, ordinary citizens have hardly any means to engage with this topic in a manageable and contemplative way. Even communication about this societal phenomenon with children and adolescents has been rather difficult thus far—and usually, from a pedagogical perspective, it has been too theoretically laden and influenced by value judgments that are either dismissive or uncritically affirmative. For these reasons, it is an exceptionally welcome development that there is now a solution—a solution that demonstrates that migration can be apprehended not merely as a threat but as an enrichment. A migration museum can accomplish this task. Communicating an open attitude to the teenage generation appears very important. Germany, as a member of the European Union and an active agent in the age of globalization, cannot forgo the opportunity to prepare its next generation for today's world of international exchange. [. . .]

HEIKE MARÍA MARTÍNEZ FIGUEIRIDO
Federal Association of Spanish Social and Cultural Organizations

Finally, the history of the "guest worker" in the Federal Republic will soon become visible. Consequently, a piece of the "hidden" history of the postwar period of the Federal Republic will come to light and assert its meaning for that context. This is an important step on the path to a common future. Admitting to migrants that their history is a part of the history of the Federal Republic communicates a bit of recognition—beyond mere museum exhibitioning. Recognition of their contribution must be one of the most important political goals for nearly all autonomous organizations, for it also means that they finally belong, that they have finally arrived after 50 years.

AN IMMIGRATION COUNTRY?

THE LIMITS OF CULTURE

***KÜLTÜR* IN BERLIN-SCHÖNEBERG, 1986.** Kemal Kurt's snapshot captures a German woman beholding an urban culture that is no longer just her own. The Turkish spelling of *culture* both appropriates and undermines the dominance of a German *Kultur* to which immigrants are expected to assimilate. The poster advertises a *Begegnungsfest*—one of the many street festivals and open-air events designed to facilitate encounters between different cultures.

THIS CHAPTER CONSIDERS how immigration has reshaped the basic idea of Germany as a nation-state since 1961. The texts included here pose and reformulate inquiries about Germany's self-concept on the global stage: Is Germany an immigration country or an ethno-national community? As Theo Sommer points out, West Germans in 1985 were only slightly less than unanimous in their opposition to further immigration. Because individual states, not the federal government, were responsible for granting and regulating residency for foreign nationals, many West German cities considered imposing "one-in one-out" quotas for Turks and other guest-worker residents.

Immigration had, however, become a feature of the West German self-concept by the late 1970s, appearing prominently on party platforms and candidate agendas for the first time. The current chapter opens with a 1985 editorial in which center-left journalist Theo Sommer cautions against a relaxed-border policy between Germany and Turkey. Sommer's gradualist position is cautious in its expectations about the fragile balance of xenophobia and tolerance undergirding West German society. Political theorist Dieter Oberndörfer's 1987 essay "The Open Republic" poses this immigration question in terms of the founding concepts of the West German state. His question, whether West Germany is a constitutional republic or a nation-state, presaged the German guiding-culture debates of the early 2000s. Daniel Cohn-Bendit and Thomas Schmidt's 1991 piece, "When the West Becomes Irresistible," takes a different tack than Sommer's and Oberndörfer's articles do—framing their analysis in terms of transnational migration trends and global wealth distribution. For Cohn-Bendit and Schmid, Germany is subject to the global distribution of labor in late capitalism; national policies must heed, rather than dictate, migration phenomena.

Heiner Geissler's essay "Germany: An Immigration Country?" also from 1991, evokes a visionary multiculturalism that rejects national identity in favor of constitutional patriotism. Klaus Bade, in contrast, calls attention to social issues in post-Wall Germany that pose new challenges to Geissler's constitutional vision. A dialogue between Claus Leggewie and Daniel Cohn-Bendit, "Multiculture: Just a Motto for Church Congresses?" confronts the practical task of disseminating multicultural concepts in everyday life. As two veteran political activists on the center left, Cohn-Bendit and Leggewie agree that the multicultural message has been a failure and that much more political work lies ahead before Germany can think of itself as an open and diverse society.

The 1995 *Spiegel* article "Return to Charlottengrad" surveys Berlin's burgeoning Russian immigrant communities, suggesting that the new capital has become as much an eastern city as a western one. Since the fall of the Soviet Bloc, commercial and cultural traffic with Poland, Moscow, and the Czech Republic has been booming, and Berlin has developed into a major tourist destination for Russian consumers. "Charlottengrad" is a nickname for the affluent West Berlin neighborhood Charlottenburg, a name revived from the years just after the Russian Revolution, when tens of thousands of Russian intellectuals sought refuge in Berlin. This article tracks the westward migration of a generation of middle-class Soviet Jews and *Spätaussiedler*, or "late resettlers," who set off for Berlin in the early 1990s.

Günther Beckstein, Bavarian minister of the interior since 1993, was a member of the triumvirate of negotiators during the Immigration Act compromise of June 2004, along with Otto Schily and Peter Müller. His 1999 article "An Approach to the Guiding Culture" claims that multiculturalism prevents citizens from engaging with each other in substantive ways and promotes a general predilection toward mutual disregard. Beckstein insists that Germany take a more active role in the integration of its foreigners by compelling them to adopt the German language and the basic political values of their host country. This idea found its most controversial articulation when Bundestag member Friedrich Merz—borrowing a phrase from Islamic scholar Bassam Tibi—advocated a "freedom-based German guiding culture," or *Leitkultur* for short. According to Merz, the Basic Law espouses certain values to which immigrants must assent, including gender equity and a willingness to speak German.

Merz's concept of *Leitkultur* rapidly became the *bête noire* of millennial integration politics, earning the distinction of "most disliked neologism of 2000" from the PONS dictionary company. The final texts in this chapter debate the concept from various perspectives. Gustav Seibt chronicles German legislators' failed attempts to posit a unifying culture in the decades after National Socialism. For Seibt, even 50 years after the Third Reich, the idea of guiding values remains dangerous and impracticable. For Mark Terkessidis, in "German Guiding Culture: The Game of Origins," Merz's concept entirely disregards the socioeconomic and educational circumstances of Germany's immigrants. For Moshe Zimmermann, the proponents of guiding culture exhibit a forgetfulness about Germans' uses and abuses of "culture" in the Third Reich. Despite the short shelf-life of the guiding-culture idea in legislative politics, its central tenets of linguistic and political acculturation were absorbed into the 2005 Immigration Act. The chapter closes with speculative glances into the future of this new and belated immigration country.

1

THEO SOMMER

BREACH OF CONTRACT OR BREACH OF THE DAM?

First published as "Vertragsbruch oder aber Dammbruch?" in *Die Zeit* (July 19, 1985). Translated by Tes Howell. On July 9, 1985, West German Chancellor Helmut Kohl paid a state visit to Ankara at the invitation of the Turkish prime minister, Turgut Özal, to discuss "greater mobility" for Turkish workers in West Germany. Sommer wrote this editorial during his tenure as editor in chief of *Die Zeit*.

Bonn and the Menacing Flood of Turkish Immigrants

Fear of foreign infiltration, of a country losing its national identity? These fears have always existed, and not just in the minds of German *Blut und Boden* visionaries. "Why," lamented Benjamin Franklin in 1751, "should we endure these country bumpkins swarming into our settlements from the Rhineland, converging in a cluster, introducing their language and customs while excluding ours? Why should Pennsylvania, established by the English, become a colony of strangers who will soon become so numerous that they will Germanize us instead of us Anglicizing them?"

Franklin—philosopher, statesman, composer of streetwise aphorisms and discoverer of the lightning rod—was not a racist nor a barbarian but a man of the Enlightenment. An instinct (immutably ingrained in humans) is revealed in his lamentation: people prefer to be around their own kind, and whenever they allow friends into their inner circle, the newcomers had better conform to the language, the culture, and the value system of that group. The fears that Franklin felt about the Rhineland farmers were repeated in each subsequent immigration wave: first the Irish, Italians, and Eastern Europeans and more recently, the Hispanics and Pacific Islanders, Spanish-speaking immigrants, and Asians of various descent. These are the same fears that we West Germans are experiencing when we think about the 4.3 million foreigners who live in the Federal Republic and West Berlin—especially the 1.4 million Turks.

Every survey yields similar results: 80 percent of German citizens find that there are too many foreigners in this country, and 85 percent want restrictions on further immigration. Germans do not enjoy such consensus on any other topic. This unity spans the party spectrum, from CSU followers to the Greens. People are simply troubled by the idea that we are taking in a greater share of foreigners than we can cope with psychologically and economically.

Helmut Schmidt, as chancellor, was the first to warn us "that we cannot handle a further wave of foreigners into our country. It is counterproductive to accept people here who can obtain a higher standard of living through unemployment benefits and social welfare than if they were to work 45 hours a week in their own country." Heinz Kühn, former SPD minister president in North Rhine–Westphalia, declared even more emphatically, "whenever the number of foreigners surpasses the 10 percent threshold, any given people becomes rebellious."

For now, we are quite a bit below the Kühnian rebellion threshold: for-eigners comprise 7.1 percent of the resident population, and recent statistics demonstrate a downward trend. The threshold has been reached in 19 large German cities, and in some, it has been significantly superseded: 24 percent in Frankfurt, 18 percent in Stuttgart, 17 percent in Munich, 12.5 percent in Berlin. The prospect of a new stream of Turks pouring into the Federal Re-public after December 1, 1986, weighs heavily on the German government and people. At that point, the tolerance level, the rebellion threshold, would be surpassed.

The Association Agreement, an agreement the European Community ne-gotiated with Ankara in 1964, allows for the possibility of a new Turkish in-vasion. It stipulates that after December 1, 1986, Turks will receive the same labor mobility in EC territory that all citizens of full member states already enjoy. No one knows how many will actually take advantage of this policy. Meanwhile, the official number of those willing to migrate is 1.2 million, al-though this figure is difficult to verify. One thing is certain, though: there are officially 3.5 million unemployed in Turkey, along with millions of under-employed individuals in Anatolian villages. Many of those people will want to try their luck beyond their borders. And their dream destination will be, as before, Germany: 90 percent of all Turks who leave their homeland come to us.

It is no wonder then that the government is frantically trying to prevent a breach in the dam. Minister of the Interior Zimmermann, Foreign Secretary Genscher, and last week Chancellor Kohl all had just one goal in their dis-cussions in Ankara: to persuade the Turks not to make use of their labor-mobility rights. The government's spokesman, Ost, bluntly explained, "An increased number of workers from Turkey in Germany is not tolerable from a labor-market perspective, not to mention social and integration factors." There it was again: Helmut Schmidt's old refrain.

But what can we do? The federal government is hiding behind legal ar-guments. According to the government, the Ankara Agreement merely stip-ulates an obligation to "be guided" by the notion of freedom of movement. The freedom of movement applies only to workers, not their family mem-bers, and before the Memorandum of Understanding can become operative, there must first be a joint resolution in the EC Association Council. This pro-cess is undignified legal mumbo jumbo.

There is only one remedy, of which many will disapprove but to which there is no alternative: business according to good Levantine practices. That is, Ankara ought to completely forgo the right of labor mobility or establish a long transition period until it takes effect; in return, Bonn ought to in-crease its aid to Turkey, and not just for military spending but in areas that would directly benefit the country's economic development.

Such a plan must be possible. Of course, our productivity is not unlimited, and if West German industry avoids investing in Turkey, then the Federal Republic cannot change much with loan guarantees. For this reason, the government must make it crystal clear in the coming negotiations (scheduled for the fall) that if there is no alternative, Bonn would favor a breach of contract over a breach in the dam.

Crystal clear—exactly. No one in 1964 could have foreseen the current situation. Bonn is therefore completely justified in taking recourse to two principles that underlie all transactions between individuals and between states. The first one can be found in *clausula rebus sic stantibus*—the unspoken assumption behind all contracts, that things remain as they are. The second one is in the formula *ultra posse nemo obligatur:* no one is obligated to do more than he can achieve. We are not obliged to risk our livelihood for anyone.

The only issue is this: our productivity. Not the substance of our people, which a 7 percent proportion of foreigners does not yet jeopardize; there cannot yet be talk of "ethnomorphosis" or a "change of national allegiance." Nor is there a danger that permanent ghettos will form in our big cities—the history of all immigrations teaches us that ghettos dissolve as soon as the process of differentiation and social advancement begins among the immigrants; class ultimately becomes more important than race. Of equally little importance is the concern that undigestible groups could burden our collective body. For the process scholars call "acculturation," cultural conformity, is above all a question of time: a matter of two or three generations. The Turks might show themselves to be more resistant to the influences of their new environment than other peoples; conformity, assimilation, and integration might be slower for them, but in the end acculturation will occur. Turks in Germany first become German Turks and then finally Turkish Germans. They are already beginning to walk in the footsteps of the Szymanskis and the Cartellieris.

Is Germany therefore a melting pot? The concept of a melting pot comes from America, but today Americans hesitate to use it; the ethnic groups are too large and no longer allow themselves to be "melted" so easily. The alternative is the multicultural society, a patchwork carpet, which some in this country envision as a model for the Federal Republic: no longer integration through absorption but rather integration through the coexistence of co-equal groups in a people of peoples.

The Amish (the descendants of those rustic Rhinelanders who once angered Benjamin Franklin) have found their place in America. One may doubt that this multicultural example can be realized within the modest dimensions of our small country. One thing is certain: if the dam that has held back the Anatolian poor breaks in a year and a half, the flood of millions will wash away the beginnings of both models—integration in a melting pot and coexistence within the patchwork mosaic—without a trace.

2

DIETER OBERNDÖRFER

THE OPEN REPUBLIC

First published as "Die offene Republik" in *Die Zeit* (November 13, 1987). Translated by David Gramling. Oberndörfer, director of the Seminar for Political Science at the University of Freiburg, was born in 1929.

[. . .] The collapse of 1945 ended the dream of political unity among all people of German linguistic and ethnic heritage. This unity was realized only during seven years, from 1938 to 1945, and even then not completely. The remaining shell of Germany was divided up. In the free sector, the new republic was not effectively accomplished—understandable for the situation of that time. The Federal Republic was founded as a republic for "Germans." The Basic Law of the new republic relied on a folkish-national substratum.

According to its own self-concept, the new republic was merely a provisional political reorganization under which "Germans" could live in peace. The Basic Law allowed this "new order" only "for a transitional period." The reunification "of the German people"—a politically explosive postulate in view of Austria, the South Tyrolians, and German minorities outside of the state territory of 1937—became a constitutional mandate: "The whole German people is called upon to achieve Germany's unity and liberty in free self-definition." [. . .]

The tension established in the Basic Law between cosmopolitical norms and the folkish tradition of the nation-state has thus far not been resolved. Its political explosiveness for the legitimacy of the Federal Republic's political order was hardly recognized or was merely pushed out of its consciousness. Ethnic nationalism has remained alive to this day in the political culture of the Federal Republic. Its approach to immigration and the right of asylum demonstrates this fact very clearly. The work of several million guest workers singularly catalyzed the expansion of the German economy after internal migration ceased with the building of the Wall, and despite structural unemployment, the productivity of the German economy is still dependent on the effect of that work. In many areas, a need for additional skilled foreign-labor power is even increasing. The Federal Republic thus became a country of immigration long ago.

Still, the official version stands: "The Federal Republic is not an immigration country." As many guest workers ought to go back to their homelands as possible. Their label has been suggestive since the beginning. One expects of guests that they show gratitude and say goodbye politely after a certain period of time. Thus far, there has been no politically influential lobby for facilitating the naturalization process for foreigners or, as in the United States, for the possibility of acquiring citizenship through immigration quotas or service in the armed forces. Surely, the basic reason for this state of affairs, next to political fears about employment, is the fear of a threat to one's own ethnic-cultural substance. [. . .]

Leaving nationalism behind first demands a radical rejection of the premises of its ideological justification and full engagement in a republican constitutional praxis. The scratch test for a new republican constitutional praxis must take the form of a liberal policy on naturalization and asylum.

It was not the conceptual bases of National Socialism that gave form to racialist delusion but rather ethnic nationalism. The revolutionary power of this nationalism ensured German loyalty for the National Socialist dictatorship until the end.

The (millions of) senseless human casualties amid the collective delusion of nationalism (in both European world wars) would only make sense if they led to insight into the humanity of all peoples and overcame, not simply through theoretical but also practiced humaneness, the nationalism that separates human beings into peoples. [. . .] Republics orient their politics to the future, to the goal of the political unity of all people, through which the latent or constant state of global civil war is overcome. Only on the long path toward this goal do republics gain their historic worth and legitimacy. [. . .]

3

DANIEL COHN-BENDIT AND THOMAS SCHMID

WHEN THE WEST BECOMES IRRESISTIBLE

First published as "Wenn der Westen unwiderstehlich wird" in *Die Zeit* (November 22, 1991). Translated by Tes Howell. Cohn-Bendit (b. 1945, Montauban, France) was expelled from France for revolutionary activities in 1968. In 1989, he established the Office for Multicultural Affairs in Frankfurt under the newly elected Red-Green coalition municipal government. He is currently cochairman of the faction of the Greens/Free European Alliance of the European Parliament. With Schmidt, he published *Heimat Babylon: The Challenge of the Multicultural Society* (Hamburg: Hoffmann and Campe, 1993).

The multicultural society must be recognized as reality

There are some successes that become problematic when they materialize. At present, this is the situation in the Western world. During the decades of bloc confrontation, the problem had its roots in the superiority, attractiveness, and irresistibility of the West's social and economic model, which has consistently promoted freedom, open borders, and the dream of prosperity. One day an emergency occurred: the alternative, socialism, abandoned the race, leaving the philosophy of the West to beam brighter than ever before. But the victory may not last as long, nor be as sweet, as anticipated.

Worldwide, people are seeking to collect on the Western promise of happiness—hence the West's precarious situation. It is clear that it has not been able to make good on its promise. Because people have only one life at their disposal, they are no longer willing to wait for the arrival of this prosperity. In places where the wealth does not want to go, more and more people are willing to go to it: they migrate to those wealthy countries in the West. This mobility (voluntary or imposed), which has been growing since the beginning of the modern age, will continue to increase in the future.

It would be a fatal mistake to overinterpret this fact ideologically in one direction or another: the multicultural society should neither become a surrogate vision for the disoriented Left, nor should its undeniable problems be used to create horror scenarios about a society robbed of its identity. Modern societies do not allow themselves to be transformed back into closed ones. If things go well, Western societies will be able to deal in a reasonably civil manner with the new turmoil arising from the end of bloc confrontation and the triumphal march of Western civilization.

It is irresponsible to nurture the illusion that the problem of migration movements could be curbed by protectionist measures. One cannot fight a system of closed borders for decades just to return to it when things get serious. One cannot push for an open-borders Europe and suddenly seek to shield Western Europe from the rest of the world. And above all, one may not use popular discontent over an unsettling reality as an opportunity to propagate simplistic conceptions of the world—conceptions with which one could indeed win elections but certainly not solve problems. Modern societies are constantly formed and re-formed through condemnations—they disintegrate and destroy traditions, they tend toward imbalance, and they make it difficult for the individual to construct a clearly outlined identity. Consequently, they promote the ephemeral urge to find simple solutions and scapegoats. It is no longer an option to represent migration (an unavoidable consequence of the modern age) as a cause of all evil and as something that could be stopped with decisive national measures.

It would be no less irresponsible to distort the multicultural society into a modern Garden of Eden of harmonious multiplicity and—in an act of reverse xenophobia—to seek to expel the beloved German along with the foreigner. A kind of indignation about xenophobia, which proposes a policy of unrestricted open borders as an antidote, contains something hypocritical and dangerous. For, if history teaches anything, it is this: dealing civilly with the foreigner is not innate to any society. Much evidence suggests that reservation toward the foreign is germane to the anthropological constants of this type of contact. And the modern age, with its increasing mobility, has made this problem more ubiquitous than ever. [. . .]

States and nations like to act as though they were sovereign. Regardless of the fact that unrestricted nation-state sovereignty is undesirable (consider, for example, the federated Europe of the future), it has been an illusion for a long time. Current and future migration movements have such deep-seated motivations that no state, regardless of the measures taken, will be in a position to halt them. A country as rich as Germany has no other choice than to accept the fact that it is already and will remain an immigration country. Now the issue is how to deal with this reality. And on this point it is important to take an aggressive stance in the development of an immigration policy. [. . .]

We therefore propose an open discussion on changing the present system. Because the Federal Republic of Germany has been unable to see itself as an immigration country thus far, there is no alternative to asylum for the many who want to come to Germany for warrantable reasons. In the long run, the exaggerated use of this exceptionalist loophole will lead to a situation in which the basic institution of asylum will be weakened and decried *ad absurdum*. We argue for a restricted use of asylum procedures; it should be applied sparingly in obvious cases of political, religious, race, and/or gender-based persecution, thereby affirming its actual meaning. We would consequently gain some ground on the problem of immigration without the hysteria and demagogy that is currently raging. [. . .]

4

HEINER GEISSLER

GERMANY: AN IMMIGRATION COUNTRY?

First published as "Deutschland—ein Einwanderungsland?" in *Einwanderbares Deutschland: Oder Vertreibung aus dem Wohlstands-Paradies?* Daniel Cohn-Bendit, Liselotte Funcke, and Heiner Geissler, eds. (Frankfurt am Main: Horizonte, 1991), 9–23. Translated by Tes Howell. Geissler (b. 1930) was a member of the Bundestag and chair of the CDU/CSU faction from 1991 to 1998.

[. . .] What consequences will the single European market bring? German businesses will be forced in significantly greater measure than before to establish production and distribution sites within the EU and Germany. Whoever wants to be economically successful in the "EU abroad" must know the language and culture, the lifestyle and mentality of these countries. Not only managers and engineers but also skilled workers and employees will have to think and work European. Increasing numbers of educated and motivated young people will recognize professional opportunities in France, Italy, Spain, Great Britain, Greece, Portugal, Poland, and Hungary as a stimulus, chance, and challenge, and they will want to use these opportunities and excel in them. There are already 1.4 million foreigners from the EU states living with us. [. . .]

In a Europe characterized by manifest freedom of movement, one can be born and grow up in Germany, study in Great Britain, work later in Germany or France, and spend one's "active old age" in Italy. In Germany, the neighbor will be Belgian; the work colleague, Turkish; the daughter-in-law, Danish; and the union comrade, Spanish or Hungarian. A Europeanization, and even an internationalization, of our lives is already taking place today. An abundance of European products—food and drink, literature, music and art (as we have had for centuries), science and research, fashion, design—will become a mass experience of everyday life. These are the characteristics of an already existing and growing multicultural society. [. . .]

The vast majority of foreigners in the Federal Republic were either born here or have lived here for over 10 years. And despite this fact we have the lowest naturalization quota of all comparable European countries. Only around 14,000 foreigners are naturalized annually, but in 1988 alone, for example, 73,000 children of foreign parents were born in our country. Barbara John, the commissioner of foreigner affairs of the Berlin Senate, pointed out in 1989 that someday we will have to speak about twenty-fifth-generation foreigners if the policy on naturalization remains the same.

I know that some in our country find it unbearable to live with people who come from another culture, have another native language and a philosophy of life different from the Germans'. For my part, it is intolerable that millions of fellow citizens have fewer rights in our country. Stuttgart's mayor Rommel compares our society with the old Sparta, its Spartans and Helots, a three-class society composed of citizens with greater and lesser rights.

Constitutional Patriotism as a Concept for the Future

The laws that regulate who is or may be German are questionable and contradictory enough. An ethnic German from Kazakhstan, who has only trace amounts of German blood in his veins and whose ancestors left Germany at the time of Catherine the Great, passes for a German here. I state emphatically: I have no objections to this. But the second-generation Iranian living in Germany, who works as a senior physician at a hospital in Rüsselsheim and speaks Hessian like Heinz Schenk has the greatest difficulties getting a German passport. [. . .] The economic prosperity of the Federal Republic and its strong position in Europe and the world are not the result of German national character. It is rather the combined effects of a constitution guaranteeing unhindered development of personhood and the welfare-state concept of a social market economy that have produced a symbiosis superior to that in all other political systems. [. . .]

5

KLAUS BADE

GERMANY AND IMMIGRATION

First printed as "Deutschland und die Einwanderung" in *Das Manifest der 60: Deutschland und die Einwanderung* (Munich: C. H. Beck, 1994), 13–15. Translated by Tes Howell. A migration historian, Bade is the director of the Institute for Migration Research and Intercultural Studies at the University of Osnabrück and chair of the Federal Council on Migration.

[. . .] Global migration and refugee movements are individual and societal answers to political, economic, and ecological crisis situations. In the face of this challenge, even a country with Germany's economic strength can affect very little on its own. Pan-European solutions are needed. As Europe's most-sought-after immigration destination, a particular responsibility for the development and implementation of appropriate concepts is ascribed to Germany. Yet, as a precondition for this, Germany must overcome the problems within its own borders and not delegate them to Europe. The more unresolved national problems are tabled into Europe's future, the more difficult the road to that future will be. [. . .]

The unified Germany of the 1990s is confronting a new integration situation that is unfolding with more complexity and less clarity than its predecessor, which involved only the integration of refugees and the persecuted during the mid-1950s and the subsequent path of the "guest-worker question" in the West. The new integration situation comprises various groups of foreign as well as indigenous "foreigners." In Germany, since the late 1970s, there has been a paradoxical immigration situation without an immigration country and without an immigration agreement. De jure foreigners and de facto immigrants are living here as indigenous foreigners, the majority of whom are from third-generation families from the previous "guest-worker population." [. . .]

Along with these issues, there are German-German integration questions and experiences of alienation as well. The identity problems of many settlers from the former GDR have still not been overcome. In the East, the one-sided reformation by the West gives many people the feeling of having become foreign in their own country. This inner alienation has further exacerbated encounters with immigrant foreigners, encounters with which East Germany has had little experience anyway. Given the ambiguity of the new integration situation, many people perceive immigration as a threat, thus providing a new, dangerous theme to right-radical agitators. Social anxieties and helplessness have given rise to xenophobic scapegoat theories. [. . .]

Comprehensive legal and political answers to the challenges presented by migration and its effects are still lacking. It took more than a decade to make it to the lowest common denominator of all official government statements, the transpartisan lie that "The Federal Republic is not an immigration country." This claim stifled one of the most important and, if neglected, most dangerous areas of societal formation. [. . .]

Any new taboo or political nonrecognition, every defensive repression or neglect of these politically explosive topics, each new flight from the responsibility to negotiate because of fear of registered voters would be tantamount to reckless self-endangerment. Migration and its effects will accompany Germany and Europe far into the future: from internal immigration in the European market and its margins to continental and intercontinental immigration pressures on the East-West and South-North axis. [. . .]

6
DANIEL COHN-BENDIT AND CLAUS LEGGEWIE
MULTICULTURE: JUST A MOTTO FOR CHURCH CONGRESSES?

First published as "Multikultur—nur ein Kirchentagsmotto?" in *die tageszeitung* (January 8, 1994). Translated by David Gramling. Leggewie (b. 1950) is professor of political science at the University of Gießen and director of the Center for Media and Interactivity.

[. . .] *taz[die tageszeitung]:* You yourselves have said that the concept of the multicultural society gives rise to conservative emotions. There must be a particularly German reason for this phenomenon.

CL [Claus Leggewie]: I trace that back to the particular situation in which we found ourselves around 1989. First, can we really empirically claim that Germans have especially great difficulty accepting their condition, their metamorphosis? One cannot make this claim about the 1960s and 1970s. I believe that, based on its actions, Germany was a foreigner-friendly country in those days. [. . .] In 1982, a rightist conservative turn was proclaimed in foreigner and asylum politics. In contentious situations such as 1989, Germany quite easily tends to develop an almost laughable nationalism that is not actually germane to its culturally and regionally differentiated structure. [. . .]

DCB [Daniel Cohn-Bendit]: Now, for the first time in the history of the Federal Republic, we are experiencing a real societal conflict about immigration—for the past three or four years. Not only must the laws be held responsible for this inexcusable procrastination but the Left as well. Have not leftist sociologists completely ignored the immigration problem? Neither the student movement nor other representatives of the Left have really taken heed of the topic. The student movement knew about the living conditions of migrant farmers on the Mekong plains a whole lot better than they knew about the living conditions of Anatolian peasants working at the Opel factory in Rüsselsheim. [. . .]

taz: The established parties on the left of the spectrum (Green, AL, PDS) have a single focus: making an immigration law that determines rules for residency and can be marketed as a cure-all for racism. [. . .] Can Islam be won over to secular forms of multiculturalism?

DCB: Islam, what is Islam anyway? Ten years ago, during the Olympic Games in Sarajevo, no "Muslim problem" crossed any journalist's mind, because Muslims were naturally embedded in former Yugoslavian everyday life. "The" Islam did not exist, just as "the" Catholicism or "the" Christianity did not exist. It is true that, under the conditions of a multicultural society with religious freedom, we clearly must oppose a fundamentalistically inflected political Islam. [. . .] Yet the simple equation that Christianity means modern, enlightened spirit and Islam means backward, authoritarian ideals does not add up.

CL: Aside from the Algerian and Iranian examples, there is nothing particular to Islam that would preclude peaceful coexistence with secular cultures and religions. Unfortunately, most of the standard interpreters of the Koran, the mullahs, see it differently. The reason I make an appeal for Islam in the West is that Islam needs an intellectual basis in order to construct an alternative to this extreme rightist xenophobic Islamism. Apparently, this basis can only be found in the West—the effect of a strange, world-historical development. [. . .]

taz: In a multicultural society, democracy and human rights are inalienable. A look at Germany and the rest of the world does not exactly hold out hope for this ideal.

DCB: Whoever says the cards are stacked against us has a strong argument. Nothing is certain. But I fear the traditional form of leftist politics that always cowers in a defeatist position. The question is, to what extent can we get the idea of multicultural societies across, so that they are perceived as normal? We will need to supplement universal human rights with a formulation of the universal forms of negotiation within developing multicultural societies. At the end of this process, there will have to be a U.N. convention where the necessary framework for immigration will be articulated. If we do not understand this issue as a political project—much less as a moral one, as it has been understood thus far—it will not allow us progress. [. . .]

7

RETURN TO CHARLOTTENGRAD

First published as "Rückkehr nach Charlottengrad" in *Der Spiegel* (August 28, 1995). Translated by David Gramling.

The party begins after midnight. The tiny, nameless, unlicensed bar is filling up quickly. Almost all of the young regulars greet Vassja the bartender with a short *"Privyet."* The guests speak Russian, Czech, Polish, or French. German is found only on the menu board.

Silver tinsel hangs from the buckling paneled ceiling of the street-level space in a prewar East Berlin building. Someone has stuck barbed wire into the wall around a pink-colored poster of a Russian model. A worn-out sofa set and a pair of chrome chairs appear to have come from the salvage pile, fitting for the squatter milieu.

Vassja Linezki, 26, raised in a Moscow academic family, came to the German capital in 1990 with a backpack full of books. He was one of the first Russian squatters in Berlin. Since then, two dilapidated tenements have come into Russian hands. These youth from Kiev, Saint Petersburg, and Odessa earn their money through occasional work as bicycle messengers.

On Sundays, Russian reigns supreme in the thermal baths at Berlin's Europa-Center near the Memorial Church. Aging regulars sit sweating on marble benches in the Roman-Russian steam baths. Golden armbands, formidable earrings, and necklaces with Orthodox crosses shimmer in the steam. Tattoos from prison terms ornament many of the men's legs—on the left leg a call girl, on the right the Statue of Liberty. [. . .]

The Russians are here indeed. No other European metropolis has attracted so many Russian immigrants since the collapse of the East Bloc as the German capital has. And no other immigration group dazzles as brightly as the emigrant scene from the Commonwealth of Independent States. Strange birds and honest artisans, ambitious artists, clever intellectuals, shrewd businesspeople, and big-time profiteers are pushing their way toward Berlin.

Approximately 70,000 to 100,000 former Soviet citizens are currently living in the city, much more than in Paris or London. No one knows the exact figures. The official statistics are missing about 10,000 "Russian Germans" from Kazakhstan or Siberia; they are counted as Germans and therefore not as immigrants. Furthermore, the number of those who came to East Berlin by marriage during the GDR era is also not known. And no government agency dares to guess how many people have come illegally to Germany or how many sought asylum in vain and are now living underground here. [. . .]

The Jewish Congregation, two-thirds of whose 10,000 members are from the Commonwealth of Independent States, organizes social and cultural events. On the Berlin Radio Multikulti station, a Moscow journalist moderates a daily 20-minute program in his mother language. Lately the Spree Channel has been regularly offering Russian television programming on the cable network.

German Berlin, mesmerized by the illustrious metropolis of the 1920s, clearly longs for a renaissance of the *Russkij Berlin* of the Weimar Republic. At that time, more than 300,000 Russians contributed to Berlin's role as the cultural center of Europe. [. . .] Between 1918 and 1924, 2,200 books were produced by 86 Russian publishers in Berlin, more than in Petrograd or Moscow.

The last actress from this era still living is Vera Lourié. This elderly lady rents the four large rooms of her prewar Wilmersdorf apartment to Russian students. She herself lives surrounded by old photos in the living room. She has been putting her memoirs down on paper for years; now she is looking for a publisher for her life story, which begins in Saint Petersburg in 1901.

After her flight to the Spree in 1921, the young Lourié came in contact with all the greats. She celebrated at raging atelier parties with painters Iwan Puni and El Lissitzky and philosophized with authors like Boris Pasternak, Ilja Ehrenburg, and Viktor Shklovsky. Lourié's close friend, the eccentric author Andrej Bely, identified the mood in 1924 in "Charlottengrad," the area around the Kurfürstendamm, in this two-line formulation: "Night! Tauentzien! Cocaine! This is Berlin!"

Russians like Bely were amazed by the stoicism of the Berliners. Setting off in a broad swath through the city, the author contemplated how he could best provoke the German passersby. Headstands or absurd conversation snippets—all for naught. "Nothing surprises the Berliners," he noted. "The sobriety of everyday Berlin overcomes all of the craziness."

Just as in the 1920s, the Berliners take in the new neighbors from far-off Russia with relatively little difficulty and, with a mix of resignation and laissez-faire, watch as their city becomes increasingly Eastern.

The Russians arriving are not the poorest of the poor. They are people from the middle classes who still have some energy left and just want to live a better life in the West, learn more effectively, and earn more money. [. . .] *Business* has been the magic word for Russians since the days when the Wall was falling and duty-free commerce with the Soviet troops stationed in the GDR promised lucrative gains. Doctors closed their practices, scientists moved over to the booming import-export sector. And the saleswoman at an electronics shop remembers that "making a quick buck among the middlemen" became a kind of national sport for young people. She herself left her job as a dental hygienist and worked the flea-market stalls outside the barracks in Brandenburg's Wünsdorf for 15 marks per hour.

Those who are not attracted here by business prospects come with a lust for adventure. Money is clearly the last thing on Vassja's mind. Pure curiosity beams from his green eyes. As a Moscow philosophy student, he had wanted to get away for a long time, out of his "stuffy cage," to get to know Western Europe. But where would he go?

When Russian television reported on the squatter houses on East Berlin's Mainzer Street in 1990, the travel destination became clear. "Free apartments, music, and people who might understand us," is how Vassja and three friends imagined the new life in the West—and, with tourist visas in their back pockets, that's how it went.

Among all of the various reasons for leaving their homeland, Jewish ancestry unites most of the Russian migrants. Whereas 60 years ago being identified as a Jew in Germany meant a death sentence, these days such a notation in one's passport promises a more stable, or at least a more pleasant, life than was the case in the fragmented, openly anti-Semitic Soviet Union. [. . .]

Many Jews are becoming acquainted with Judaism only after immigrating. For the well-off, the Hanukkah party at the chic Hotel InterContinental Berlin is the society high point in December. Regular attendance at one of the five synagogues remains the exception.

Most are like Vassja, who had no connection to the Jewish religion in

Moscow. "I went to a Soviet school and naturally took part in the Pioneers," he says. He heard about the legal provisions for quota refugees only after he came to Berlin and happily laid claim to them.

[. . .] Up to 1990, the number of Russians in Berlin remained relatively low. In West Berlin after the war, almost all traces of the first Russian emigration had been eradicated. The Allies strictly controlled further entry; as late as 1975, only 174 former Soviet citizens were reported. [. . .]

More than 26,000 Russian guests booked hotel rooms in Berlin last year, most of them for an extended week of shopping. Particularly popular is the traditional Shopping Center of the West (Kaufhaus des Westens): "The Russians came promptly on the first day of the clearance sale with their translators and bought us out with cash," recounts a saleswoman from the furs department.

Boutiques and jewelers around the Kurfürstendamm have long since adjusted to the new clientele and hired Russian-speaking personnel. Even at the Friedrich Street Mercedes-Benz dealership, it is a Russian selling the cars. Ninety percent of the customers come from Moscow or Kiev; money is no object. Payment in full.

A young Russian in shorts and a Lacoste shirt nods to the woman accompanying him as he decides on a Diesel C 220 model. The price is 62,000 marks. The young woman pulls a pack full of large bills out of her shoulder bag and disappears into the backroom to make the exchange. A bit later, a man from Almaty in Kazakhstan purchases an S-Class Mercedes for more than 200,000 marks.

It is not just the Berliners but also the Russian migrants who settled in Berlin that are bothered by these climbers with a penchant for grandiosity. They fear that they are giving resident Russians a bad name and note with concern that as time goes on, more and more criminal business owners show up among the nouveau riche.

Almost every shop owner and restauranteur of Russian heritage has already had a visit from the Mafia toughs. Even in Vassja's squatter bar, two footmen have already stopped by. Those guys quickly got the picture that nothing is there for them.

The neighborhood toughs push their demands with extreme brutality. Since 1991, the police have tallied 11 homicides, more than any other foreign minority in Berlin.

For Raschel Dimant from Riga, age 51, 1994 was a sad year. "Many relatives and acquaintances of mine lost their lives," weeps this woman, who has secured the title Madame Dimant in the merchant scene at the fleamarket on the 17th of June Boulevard.

Concerns began to arise when her brother-in-law, Berlin's most prominent Russian icon merchant and antiquarian, was shot in his Ku'damm gallery by an armed robber. Madame Dimant also knew Berlin's last victim, a 27-year-old salesman murdered in March. The murderer shot this White Russian with 10 bullets.

On the day of the burial at the Russian Orthodox cemetery, various luxury limousines parked on Tegel's Wittestrasse. The mourners, clad in black, made their way through a sea of white flowers, as singers accompanied the ceremony.

For Bishop Feofan, head of the Russian Orthodox Church in Germany, such funerals are not an unfamiliar spectacle. Burials of members of the 2,000-member Berlin parish resemble those in "Italian Mafia films," says the holy man. Feodan refrains from critiquing the life choices of the victims: according to him, all are God's children in death.

Nonbelievers are less calm about these things. Without being asked, Vassja apologizes for the fact "that these kinds of people are abusing German hospitality."

Vassja, who does not regard the lack of warm water in his building "as a mark of indignity," is looking for a job to escape his existence as a sporadic landscaper for the Social Bureau. Soon he will take up his philosophy studies again, which he had broken off in Moscow. "But before that, I have to establish a legal company for the bar," he resolves.

Vassja has indeed arrived in Germany.

8

GÜNTHER BECKSTEIN

AN APPROACH TO THE GUIDING CULTURE

First published as "Annäherung an die Leitkultur" in *ifa:Zeitschrift für KulturAustausch* (March 1999). Translated by David Gramling. Beckstein (b. 1943, Hersbruck) has served as Bavarian interior minister since 1993. He was one of the primary negotiators in the Immigration Law compromise of June 2004.

Our foreign fellow citizens have made formidable contributions to the economic and cultural development of Germany. Therefore, I want to state clearly that I consider foreigners to be an enrichment. A constructive coexistence expands the horizon on both sides, promotes understanding for other cultures and ways of living, and ultimately contributes to more tolerance. Germany has impressively proven in the past decades that it is a foreigner-friendly country. We must not, however, overlook the fact that the Federal Republic has taken first place in Europe with its approximately 9 percent foreigner population. [. . .]

In many urban residential areas, the foreigner population has become disproportionately high in recent times. An article in the Berlin *Morgenpost* made me quite pensive: German residents of the Berlin district of Moabit are complaining of increasing tensions with the Turkish-Arab majority population as well as about their children being terrorized, and even speak of an outright displacement pressure. The interests of the indigenous population are constantly negated, says the declaration, which was also underwritten by integrated foreigners in Germany.

In schools as well, the problem is clear in a somewhat dramatic form. In many trade-school classes, the foreigner rate is near 80 percent, and the pupils have very little command of German. At a workshop in Munich, the Berlin commissioner of foreigner affairs reported on two schools in Berlin that, in the wake of ghetto formation, had not one student who speaks German as his or her mother language.

These specific problems strengthen my conviction that we must hand down a clear rejection of multicultural ideologies. With the concept "multicultural," a link is usually made to the notion that different foreign cultures have equal rights alongside German culture and that, endowed with the dictum of protection and support, they will be recognized as a piece of our national culture. This approach amounts to the formation of an official "state of many peoples," which neglects the concerns of the German majority population in an unacceptable way. The consequence would ultimately be to relinquish the nation as a community of laws and common destiny, a loss of identity and the feeling of belonging together, a vague "living next to" rather than the necessary "living with," and the development of segregated parallel societies. Thus, I can only agree with former federal chancellor Helmut Schmidt, who labeled it as regressive to establish a so-called multicultural society in Germany.

A crucial precondition for a burgeoning and peaceful coexistence is that we achieve real integration of our foreign fellow citizens. Real integration demands, first of all, major accomplishments from individuals. The acquisition of the German language is a first crucial step. In addition, foreign fellow citizens must devote themselves to our state and its societal and constitutional order and value system with no ifs, ands, or buts. Respecting our political, social, and cultural conditions is essential. [. . .]

All those willing to integrate are called to comprehensively use the integration offerings at the federal, provincial, municipal, and nonprofit levels and those of numerous social institutions. It must be our common goal to develop these offerings even more on all levels and to shape them as attractively as possible. To this end, the integration paper presented by the CDU/CSU faction in the German Bundestag includes an abundance of important solutions. It is my opinion that the following aspects should be strongly kept in mind.

The educational level of foreign youth needs constant improvement. This is the best way to counteract disproportional unemployment.

Learning more and better German is the nuts and bolts of integration. We must therefore constantly increase foreigners' willingness to make extensive use of the numerous offerings available.

We must exhaust all measures to counteract ghetto formation, which is counterproductive to integration. Approaches include, for example, subsidized housing allocations.

Ultimately, the goal is to not exceed a certain percentage of foreigners in educational instruction. This ideal in no way derives from xenophobic or furtive motives. We must be concerned that in an elementary-school class with more than 60 percent foreign children, the guiding image of integration is simply no longer present.

Real integration is, incidentally, only possible if the number of people to integrate is limited. No society can accept other cultures limitlessly. The integrative power of our people must not be overtaxed. The key concept for Germany's integration contribution is to be found in the field of psychology and is called *Zustimmung*, or agreement. Only when German society has the feeling that it is not overwhelmed or even endangered can integration politics really be successful. Where acceptance and integrative capacity wane, social volatility and xenophobia arise.

We are coming up against the limits of our acceptance capacity. Curbing integration through effective national, as well as European, measures is thus the imperative of the hour. The creation of an immigration law with a quota regulation is the wrong way. An additional quota would further increase the already high number of people who are immigrating as asylum seekers and refugees to join their families or on other lawful grounds. Extending migration would not only massively exacerbate the problem of unemployment among unskilled workers but would also lead to broad shortages in the social-welfare system.

Only a cautious, compassionate, and responsibility-conscious procedure, which takes the interests of the indigenous population just as seriously as those of foreigners willing to integrate, can guarantee the peaceful coexistence of people of different cultural spheres in our country in the long run. I will continue to speak for such a politics, informed by mutual tolerance and respect, with great insistence.

9

ANDREA BÖHM

HARMONY OF CULTURES?

First published as "Harmonie der Kulturen?" in *Die Zeit* (March 9, 2000). Translated by David Gramling. Böhm (b. 1961) is a U.S.-based correspondent for various German newspapers.

An immigration country needs conflict: the second part of the debate on the limits of tolerance

The concept of tolerance is like a Christmas tree decorated with too much tinsel. It must be undecorated. The more appeals or alliances for tolerance that appear in our midst these days, the greater the demand for intimacy and familiarity with the foreign will be. However, tolerance comes from enduring something, not from liking something.

That idea sounds fatalistic, but it actually creates the first precondition for pragmatism. For if one frees the concept of tolerance from the harmony imperative, space is created for conflict. In turn, conflict, according to the social philosopher Michael Walzer, is the precondition for tolerance as everyday praxis and not just as individual virtue. Without identifying conflict and acting upon it, no immigration society can come to understand how much difference it is willing and able to endure. In this abstract sense, it sounds like a harmless bit of uninspiring discourse and ethical exercise, a little political group therapy. Only the concrete questions lead to the sensitive spots—for example, to the discussion on "foreigners" and criminality.

For some time now, the Hannover-based criminologist Christian Pfeiffer has been presenting the results of his institute's youth-violence study at conferences and panel discussions. According to the study, the increase in violent crimes is actually lower than the political statistics on criminality suggest; second, it is primarily attributable to young male migrants and resettlers. Pfeiffer names three factors as reasons: poor educational instruction, social disadvantages in the family, and an imported "macho culture," primarily among Turkish immigrants, which expresses itself in the intrafamily violence of fathers against wives and children—and continues on from there. "Daughters," says Pfeiffer, "run the risk of assuming the mother's victim role, while the sons become perpetrators outside the four walls of the home." According to him, what plays out in many such Turkish families is "not tolerable." This situation is a powder keg, not because the validity of the study is dubious. Some critics say Pfeiffer is feeding munitions to the Right. But what would be the alternative? To avoid a long-overdue conflict? Pfeiffer is appealing to the "Turkish community" in Germany to deal critically with the problem. In doing so, he is risking impertinence.

Leftists have been acting like social workers in their dealings with foreigners
Such appeals to a minority "community" always entail arbitrariness, given the defining power of the majority. For example, the software designer or the law student have absolutely nothing in common with the 14-year-old repeat offender—other than their parents' country of origin. Yet violent youth offenders, and not law students, shape the image of Turkish migrants in our society.

For minorities, it is always a tightrope act to discuss their own grievances. This was observable in the United States in the early 1990s among African-Americans who engaged in an excruciating discussion of black youth violence in the cities. The primarily white media followed the process benevolently. They in no way felt compelled to ask, however, whether it is tolerable that every Afro-American between the age of 13 and 45 must live under general suspicion of being dangerous, because of the media's fixation on young black gang members.

The key principle for constructive conflict is that both parties be on an even playing field. Of greatest importance is official affirmation—that is, citizenship. Hardly any country of immigration has refused this option so adamantly as Germany has. Now, the new citizenship law will gradually correct this grievance. An open critical dialogue about violent tendencies among migrant youth remains, however, as long as their belonging in this society is in question. In the meantime, 14-year-old "Mehmet," who was born in Munich and acquired a mile-long rap sheet there, should not be deported—unless one seeks to make an ethnic problem out of a social and political one. So no one ought to be surprised when the stereotype of the combative foreigner leads to daily reports of assaulted foreigners. This type of ethnicization of conflicts is providing a disguised legitimation for hunting down the "other," even at the highest political levels, among residents of the new federal states, who never learned how to interact with foreigners. At a recent group discussion about tolerance, a Brandenburg state attorney offered an articulation of the concept: "One may find the other abominable, but one is not permitted to beat him up." Above all, one must perceive him as an acting subject.

Excluded from this new era of conflict will be one German institution that appears very sympathetic at first glance: the social service agencies. For decades, left-liberal pedagogues and social workers exercised sovereignty over the discussion on foreigners. The ethnologist Werner Schiffauer called this state of affairs "gentle assimilation." While conservatives uncompromisingly demanded adaptation, left liberals attended to foreigners through care and support mechanisms. The Commissioner of Foreigner Affairs office is a typical result of this way of thinking—interceding on behalf of an aphasic minority that is stuck on the political sidelines.

These government agencies will no longer have a right to existence if independent lobbying groups from among the "supported" people themselves come to the fore. All the more reason that mediators are helpful. They could, for instance, attend to a problem that has been smoldering between some Muslim congregations and *Der Spiegel* for some time now. The former reacted in disgust to a reprinted painting of the prophet Mohammed in a cover story on the topic of morals, because there is a ban on images in Islam. Since then, protests have been raining down upon the editorial staff. A capacity for conflict would be well exercised in this case. There are mutual allegations of intolerance: Muslims perceive a lack of respect for their religious rules, *Der Spiegel* perceives a threat to pluralism from the religious proscriptions of individual groups. Furthermore, there is clearly a need for compromise on a few ground rules, the abuse of which will not be tolerated: for example, the habit among some Turkish-language media of publishing the telephone numbers and addresses of their least-favored journalists.

Muslim believers are no longer looking only for niches in Germany where they can rest unmolested. They are now struggling for a stake in societal power and political influence. In principle, the state's tolerance limit is clear: the constitution comes before religion and the social order linked to it. Behind this principle lie countless ambiguous cases of conflict. The latest example involves the Islamic Federation of Berlin. The organization is under the control of Islamic fundamentalists and is under surveillance by the Federal Office for the Protection of the Constitution. Nonetheless, it has succeeded in presenting itself as "integrated" enough that the courts recognize its status as a religious community and grant it the right to shape Islamic religious instruction at Berlin schools. Some Germans as well as Turks applaud this recognition as a long-overdue step toward the integration of Muslim pupils, whereas others are angered by all the starry-eyed good faith. Whoever believes that these conflicts are battled along ethnic lines is mistaken. It is primarily secular immigrants who are first affected by the politicization of Islam and engage in the conflict about the limits of tolerance.

For many, the desire for a multicultural society has been a thing of the past since they read Samuel Huntington's *Clash of Civilizations* a few years ago. But behind the laborious normalcy of an immigration society, there is no way back. In the instance of the Islamic Federation, two scenarios for the future may be played out. Either the organization will soon become a fundamentalist catchall for the losers of an ethnic underclass—a kind of Nation of Islam in Germany—or the CDU will discover that Muslims with a good education, entrepreneurial spirit, patriarchal family ideals, and the deep religiosity one encounters among Islamists signal an attractive voting group.

10

JOHANNES RAU

WITHOUT FEAR AND WITHOUT ILLUSIONS: LIVING TOGETHER IN GERMANY

Translation courtesy of the German Embassy in Australia: www.germanembassy.org.au. Rau (1931–2006) was federal president of Germany from 1999 to 2004. He delivered this speech on May 12, 2000, at the House of World Cultures in Berlin.

Ladies and Gentlemen,

Thirty percent of all children in German schools come from immigrant or recently naturalized families. At some schools the proportion is 60 percent or more. In 1997 and 1998, more people from other countries left Germany than arrived. Almost 50 percent of all asylum seekers within the European Union apply for asylum in Germany. Of those that seek asylum here in Germany, around 4 percent are granted asylum. Turks alone have established more than 50,000 companies in Germany and created 200,000 jobs. The German economy will in the future not have enough qualified personnel.

These are six widely differing statements on reality in Germany—and yet they are all part of a broader picture. Immigration, refugee contingents, limitations on establishment of residence, immigrants, integration, Green Cards, asylum, deportation, repatriation—these key words have for years repeatedly returned to mold political discussion. Many individual problems and many detailed issues also form the stuff of private conversations—and also often lead to wordless confrontation. More than 7 million foreigners live in Germany. They have in the past years changed our society. But we do not give enough consideration to what this means for life in our country. And we do not act in line with this changed reality.

How we live with one another is one of the most important topics of all when we think about the future of our society. We must come to grips with this topic, because it concerns everyone in our country, even if some people have not yet noticed, because in some respects, it goes to the very heart of our constitutional order and our constitutional reality, because waiting does not solve problems but aggravates them, and lastly because it comes down to whether we can join forces to provide a good future for everyone.

Everybody knows that immigration gives rise to strong emotions in many people—good emotions as well as less admirable ones. Precisely for this reason we must talk as openly as possible about it—and as calmly and realistically as possible. Often there is too much that remains unspoken. Often we lead illusionary debates rather than tackling the broader and more fundamental topic of harmonious coexistence.

We must overcome uncertainty and fear, which can lead to xenophobia, hatred, and violence. We must overcome a blind xenophilia, which denies that there are problems or conflicts when people of differing origins live together. [. . .]

We do not need any artificial debates on whether Germany is an immigration country or an in-migration country. We must not continue to pluck isolated issues from the discussion: today Islamic religion classes in schools, tomorrow Green Cards, then work permits for seasonal workers, or the treatment of refugees from civil wars. [. . .]

It is not difficult to act in a xenophile manner in well-off areas. It is harder in places that are being changed more and more, where a "local" can no longer read the shop signs, where families from all over the world live together in the same building, where the odors of various cuisines mingle in the corridors, where foreign music is played loudly, where we encounter totally different styles of living and religious customs. Life together becomes difficult when long-established Germans no longer feel at home, when they feel like foreigners in their own country. It is one thing to enjoy multicultural radio programs in air-conditioned cars. It is another to sit on the underground or the bus and be surrounded by people whose language one cannot understand.

I can understand parents who are concerned about the educational future of their children in schools with a high percentage of foreign pupils. I have come across it myself. I can also understand that people are worried by the above-average crime rates among young foreigners and ethnic German immigrants from Eastern Europe. I can understand how girls and young women are not the only ones afraid of being harassed or intimidated by gangs of young foreigners. Anyone who does not take such fears and concerns seriously is talking past their audience, making them ask "what do they know?" Where fears and concerns are justified, an attempt must be made to find a remedy. We must explain and be able to explain why there is no alternative, at least no better one.

For example, people get worked up about asylum seekers who sit around all day in the center of town, thus creating the impression that they are happy to do nothing and be supported by the taxpayers. Far too few of them know that asylum seekers are legally prohibited from working during their first three months here and that employment offices thereafter continue to turn them away. People who know this may wonder what the point of such a rule is. But they won't accuse asylum seekers of not wanting to work.

I am deeply committed to a worldwide dialogue between cultures and religions. This is an important topic. I have, however, never viewed it as a substitute for tackling the everyday problems that arise from the coexistence of different cultures in our own country. We cannot simply talk about harmonious coexistence in the abstract; we have to look at it in a practical context.

Xenophobia is present in our society; foreigners sometimes meet with hostility. There is violence, even murder. But more dangerous still than individual acts of violence is the social climate that shrouds xenophobia in hidden or even open sympathy. There is an aggressive intolerance of foreigners, which is encouraged when the majority does not speak out against it. Anyone who does not speak out abets. We are all called upon. Politicians, policemen, the judiciary, and teachers all have a special responsibility to counteract hostile tendencies. To do this requires civil courage and support. [. . .]

When right-wing extremists proudly speak of "national liberated zones," the alarm is sounded for the rule of law and democracy, and all true patriots are given a reason to hang their heads in shame. There are reasons and explanations for racism and racist violence, but nothing can justify them. Anyone who uses violence must be punished—the quicker, the better. [. . .]

It is encouraging that the number of students of Turkish descent at our universities has doubled during the last 10 years. However, the number of foreign pupils at middle schools is three times greater than that of their German peers, and the reverse is the case at high schools. Forty percent of non-German youths with a graduation certificate from a middle school do not find an apprenticeship. We need education concepts that acknowledge that pupils from German families with a Western Christian background are no longer the normal case everywhere. This must be given greater attention in basic training and continuing education for teachers.

I would like to say a few words of encouragement to you all. Take part in our society—in your own districts and in schools, in trade unions or in sport clubs. Only if as many as possible play an active role in society can we make full use of the riches that can become available to us when people from different cultures live together. [. . .] I would like to see a diverse and vibrant Germany—peaceful and cosmopolitan. Working toward this is worth every effort. What matters is not the origins of the individual but, rather, that we create a prosperous future together.

11

HANS-HERBERT HOLZUMER

FALSE DREAMS OF A BRILLIANT NEW BEGINNING

First published as "Der falsche Traum vom glanzvollen Neustart" in *Süddeutsche Zeitung* (June 10, 2000). Translated by David Gramling.

Jewish immigrants from the Commonwealth of Independent States can make it to Germany with relative ease. But they do not find any work.

The professor had nothing but the highest opinion of Germany. During his three-month guest professorship, the Lithuanian became acquainted with a place that interested him greatly. The working conditions at the German university were superb, and he enjoyed the collegial climate. Then, back at home in Vilnius, he heard that he could return to this beautiful, hospitable country as a "quota refugee." One could even say he was courted at the German consulate. He followed this renewed invitation. But this time it was quite different.

Germany reared its bureaucratic head: the egalitarian treatment he had previously enjoyed as a professor and scientist was nowhere in sight. Instead, his path followed the "Procedural Stipulation of February 15, 1991, pursuant to the Law on Measures for Refugees Accepted in the Context of Humanitarian Assistance Actions," according to information provided by the Federal Ministry of the Interior. This path led him to the Zirndorf refugee camp, then into a dormitory on Schleissheimer Street in Munich, then into a humble subsidized apartment, which the city of Munich pays for.

Since the expiration of his six-month "integration-assistance" package, the professor has been a social-welfare recipient. He received a free German course and a continuing-education credit. Since then, he has been prohibited from taking part in government-sponsored career-development initiatives, in accordance with the Social Welfare Law Code (SGB III). His academic qualifications from the Soviet Union have no value here. Nor can he find a job adequate for his education level. In contrast to "late resettlers" from the former Soviet Union, he is not entitled to a German passport. He kept his previous identification papers, despite the fact that he can no longer return to his home country. The moratorium on recruitment continues to prevent foreign workers from taking away German jobs. The loopholes that the new Recruitment Moratorium Exception Statute is supposed to open will not be of any use to him, because he is not an IT expert with a six-figure earning potential. Maybe he should just find something to clean.

The professor's fate is anything but unusual. Many Jews from the former Soviet republics have come to Germany, especially those from states that are Muslim dominated in the post-Soviet era. "Lifelong discrimination, the impression that everyone is leaving, above-average educational qualifications, and the expectation of a good, fresh start in Germany, are among their most common motivations," summarizes Charlotte Knobloch, president of the Israeli Cultural Community of Munich and Upper Bavaria and vice president of the Central Council of Jews in Germany. "Most emigrant Jews had good careers in the Soviet Union and were relatively privileged." Therefore, their shock is all the greater. According to Knobloch, "Upon their arrival in Germany, the internationally renowned surgeon and the celebrated actress become social-welfare recipients, occupants of mass housing projects."

Romantic Expectations

The questionable aspect of these cases is the fact that the immigrants are not refugees in the classical sense, refugees for whom a certain amount of hardship is expected upon starting anew in Germany. These so-called quota refugees were often out and out recruited. A realistic image of the country has not been provided at Germany's embassies and consulates. Consequently, most immigrants cannot reasonably imagine their future situation after immigration. Their expectations of life in Germany have been romanticized, says Charlottte Knobloch.

How can this be the case? The quota policy was based on talks between the former chair of the Central Council of Jews in Germany, Heinz Galinski, and the former federal chancellor Helmut Kohl, which led to an accord on January 9, 1991. According to the Interior Ministry, the contents are "not available to third parties." Unofficially, it is said that the quota consists of an annual 80,000 people over a period of 20 years. Since then, German consular officials in Eastern Europe have been trying to fill this quota. How many have followed the call and how many are still to come is not documented in statistics, because immigrants are not counted according to religion. Since

1989, in Munich alone, more than 3,000 new congregation members have been registered, says Charlotte Knobloch. [. . .]

Strengthening the Congregations

"The answer is clear for the federal government: strengthening our Jewish congregations benefits a reunified Germany," declares the Interior Ministry. Career prospects, however, are almost entirely absent for these emigrants. The director of the Munich Labor Office, Erwin Blume, is attempting to develop an initiative to refer qualified, Russian-speaking job seekers to export-oriented firms. "We must not see this group as a problem group," he says, "but as a potential for productivity." But in the face of a bureaucracy and political sphere whose highest credo is "Germany is not an immigration country," it is doubtful that he will have much success. [. . .]

12

FRIEDRICH MERZ

IMMIGRATION AND IDENTITY: ON THE FREEDOM-BASED GERMAN GUIDING CULTURE

First published as "Friedrich Merz zum Thema: Einwanderung und Identität—Zur Diskussion um die 'freiheitliche deutsche Leitkultur' " in *die tageszeitung* (October 25, 2000). Translated by David Gramling. Merz (b. 1955, Brilon) is a member of the German Bundestag and was chair of that body's Christian Democratic Union faction from 2000 to 2002. Though his proposal of a "German guiding culture" catalyzed fierce debate about cultural pluralism and constitutional patriotism, the concept of a "guiding culture" *(Leitkultur)* was first popularized by the Syrian-born Göttingen professor Bassam Tibi (see chapter 5 in this volume) in 1996.

[. . .] Immigration and integration can be successful in the long run only if they find broad support among the population. This will necessitate a capacity for integration on both sides. The host country must be tolerant and open; immigrants who want to live with us on a long-term basis must, for their part, be ready to respect the rules of coexistence in Germany.

I have described these rules as the "liberal German guiding culture." The formulation set off knee-jerk indignation as well as broad approval. Particularly thought provoking is the comment that my critique was correct and understandable because there was no longer a generally accepted definition of what we understand our culture to be (possibly because of the long-neglected debate about standards and a basic sphere of social agreement). It is alleged that human relations are now regulated only by laws, not by a common value-oriented social consensus.

If this indication is correct, then we should argue not over concepts but rather over content.

Only when we have created clarity for ourselves can a concept for immigration and integration truly succeed.

The constitutional tradition of our Basic Law is essential to our country's culture of civil liberties. It is shaped by the absolute respect for human dignity, a person's inalienable personal rights, and by the civil rights, liberties, and the right to protection from the state, as well as civic duties.

The Basic Law is thus the most important expression of our system of values and therefore a part of German cultural identity that enables the inner coherence of our society.

German culture was shaped decisively after World War II by the European idea. As a country in the middle of Europe, Germany and the Germans have identified themselves with European integration, with a Europe of peace and freedom, based on democracy and a social market economy.

Integral to our system of freedoms is the position of the woman in our society, which was achieved only after decades of struggle. She must also be accepted by those who, primarily for religious reasons, have a much different expectation. We cannot and must not tolerate the development of parallel societies. Cultural coexistence and mutual enrichment through cultural experiences from other countries come up against their own limits, where basic consensus toward freedom, human dignity, and equality is no longer observed.

Coexistence with foreigners thus has its consequences. People of different origins can shape their future together only on the foundation of commonly accepted values. Furthermore, a successful immigration and integration policy must insist that the German language be understood and spoken. This requirement is not national linguistic chauvinism but rather a basic precondition for peaceful coexistence in our country; it is also our cultural foundation even if the Basic Law does not touch on this issue.

Whether it is the identity of our country, the constitutional patriotism, or even the liberal guiding culture that has shaped us, the immigration and integration of foreigners, which we want to and must promote, need to be oriented toward commonly held, valid standards. Whoever avoids a discussion about it or, at best, answers with hackneyed phrases, merely prepares the ground for political radicalism, which until this point has thankfully been limited to minorities on the left and the right.

13

GUSTAV SEIBT

NO GREATER COUNTRY

First published as "Kein schöner Land" in *Die Zeit* (November 2, 2000). Translated by Tes Howell.

Typically German: the historically clueless advocates for a guiding culture are following a fatal tradition and ignoring the modern feeling of *Heimat*.

Germany will have to cope with a certain amount of immigration in the coming decades, so that the demographic break in the current generation of 40-year-olds will be less problematic. The CDU is no longer disputing this fact, though it is the same party that stubbornly denied the problem as long as it called the shots. The CDU—first in the form of Jörg Schönbohm and then Friedrich Merz—has developed the concept "German guiding culture" as a new answer to these circumstances. The immigrants would be wise to adapt, especially if there is no way to do without them. The content of the idea is diffuse, applying to everything from the Basic Law and command of the German language to "Western values." Less sibylline is the new general secretary, Meyer, who is already barking that foreigners should abide by German "regulations and laws"—a paradoxical request in a situation in which foreigners cannot rely on the police to do their duty and protect their lives.

However unclear the content of the concept "guiding culture" may be, its function is clear. The phrase *guiding culture* denotes an empty space: the assimilative attraction that enables immigration societies to receive foreigners and still retain their own identity. The German guiding culture would in effect have to achieve what the United States' mythological self-image as a society of free and equal pursuers of happiness or France's universalistic self-conception of the nation and human rights accomplish. The American and French self-concept is realized particularly in both nations' capacity to look appealing beyond their borders. The situation is similar for the English gentleman's ideals as well as for the autonomous traditions of small nations like Switzerland and Holland.

The Expulsion of Spirit in Favor of the Reich

That Germany does not have such an advertiser-friendly, hospitable, and independently convincing national culture at its disposal is proven by the tense, authoritarian attempt of the coalition parties to postulate one. The more they bark, the more unattractive German culture becomes. Contrary to the claims (most prominently by Martin Walser) that this lack of appeal is simply a consequence of National Socialist crimes and the subsequently necessary self-critical assessment, this weakness arose during Bismarckian nation-state formation and was already diagnosed before World War II. In the 1935 first edition of Helmuth Plessner's famous book, *Die verspätete Nation [The Belated Nation]*, which described the Bismarck empire as a pure invention of power, he spoke of a "great power without a conception of the state," without a persuasive concept, which both France and England have embedded into the foundation of their nations. [. . .]

The sinister, exclusionary origin of the German nation-state instantly created a venomous atmosphere in the first decade after the establishment of the Reich: in the anti-Roman cultural battle that egregiously infringed on the law, in the anti-Polish policy for West Prussia, and in the Berlin anti-Semitist debate of 1878. In that nasty dispute, the imperious phrase *guiding culture* would have fit perfectly, since that debate was an equally artificial uproar over the supposed unwillingness of a small minority to conform.

Whoever uses the phrase *guiding culture* today must have forgotten much of the German history he pretends to love. For in place of a humanitarian element typical of national ideas in Western nations, a cultural darkness arose in Germans, one that the phrase *guiding culture* references with hideous precision. This missionary consciousness celebrated its most wanton excesses in the journalistic military deployment of hundreds of German professors during World War I; one can read about this "intellectual mobilization" in Kurt Flasch's recently published account. Here it becomes clear what a guiding culture can look like in Germany: Protestant, militaristic, idealistic (therefore uncompromising), apolitical, authoritarian, faintly religious, and historically philosophical. The dichotomies are familiar: culture versus civilization, spirit versus intellect, and music versus politics. What generations of enthusiastic foreigners had once seen as typically German—the subtle, the sentimental, the slightly anachronistic, the meditative, as well as the provincially endearing, the profundity of German existence—all the romantic *valeurs* of German culture (not the least of all its humor) had long been trampled underfoot by the homogeneous ideals of a society that wanted to know no parties, only Germans. Without this background, the National Socialists would not have been able to wage their war against modern art, the churches, and the Jews. [. . .]

14

MARK TERKESSIDIS

GERMAN GUIDING CULTURE: THE GAME OF ORIGINS

First published as "Deutsche Leitkultur: Das Spiel mit der Herkunft" in *Tagesspiegel* (November 4, 2000). Translated by David Gramling. Terkessidis (b. 1966) is a psychologist and freelance journalist.

Germans are racking their brains about what their guiding culture is. Skating rinks and McDonald's, Bach and Roberto Blanco, the Reeperbahn and Cardinal Ratzinger? Hülya B., a Muslim woman, knows.

Hülya B. is a trained educator and is unemployed. This is due primarily to the fact that her religious denomination is not Christian. Even her career counselor prophesied this situation, because more than two-thirds of all kindergartens in the Federal Republic are managed by church entities. For Muslim women, this means: not a chance. Of course, Hülya B. applied at state kindergartens, but the competition there is very intense. And she was informed in a roundabout way often enough on the telephone that most native parents have problems with a Turkish woman with Islamic beliefs taking care of their children. At the moment, the young woman is doing various temporary jobs. Hülya B. knows quite well what "German guiding culture" means.

Though commentators from the *Frankfurter Allgemeine* newspaper dismiss the concept as "drivel" and simultaneously a "dishonorable discussion" in the *Bild* newspaper's opinion section, *guiding culture* is anything but flowery words for most migrants. To be sure, in Germany, there is far more of something resembling a dominant culture than in other comparable European immigration societies. In the current debate, the opponents and defenders of guiding culture at least agree on one thing: that German society became culturally distinct long ago. The conflict has to do only with how it is evaluated. By and large, the liberal public finds diversity normal and wonders why the bellicose rapper mien of Turkish teenagers or the head scarves of young Muslim women are any worse than the rest of the population's private cookouts.

In the Union [CDU], by contrast, many fear the loss of values, standards, or rules of play in the face of cultural difference. According to assertions from Meyer to Goppel, foreigners always seem to be abusing the rules expected of guests: mistreating the constitution, or behaving disrespectfully toward German customs. Angela Merkel sees the "leftist idea" of the multicultural society as a failure. How much difference does Germany really tolerate?

Hülya B. is not too strict about her beliefs. She does not wear a head scarf. Were she to wear one, her problems would be all the more apparent. The case of Fereshta Ludin ultimately demonstrates that the head scarf means much more in this society than a private tendency. She was not allowed to become a teacher in Baden-Württemberg because the Ministry of Culture considered her head scarf a "symbol of cultural separation" that would not coalesce with notions of tolerance here. Although more crosses ornament school walls in the state of Bavaria, after a converse resolution by the Federal Constitutional Court, Ludin's symbolic devotion is not allowed in the school. And this, despite the fact that the learned young woman represents a model example of "integration."

Everyday Ostracism

Without a doubt, Fareshta Ludin can imagine something when she hears "German guiding culture." So can the Muslim organizations that no longer wish to practice their religion in backyard meetings and thus are applying for permission to build a mosque. The officials and inhabitants of most communities cannot bear the idea of seeing a minaret out the window. In contrast, the chimes of nearby Christian churches are felt to be normal, despite continuously dwindling significance and membership. The same thing occurs with religious instruction. For 40 years, Muslim believers have lived here. But whereas both domestic Christian denominations are taught in schools without question, the demand for a corresponding class for Muslims appears to many as a usurpation of German schools by fanatical Koran preachers.

Of course, it is not simply about Islam. How about Orthodox classes for students of Greek or Serbian origin? In contrast to France—though many natives do not know it—there is no secularism in Germany. State and religion are not strictly separated from each other. Here, the two Christian denominations are privileged, and thus far there have been hardly any attempts to introduce secularism, thus making denomination a private issue, or to equally enfranchise the beliefs of immigrants.

"Guiding culture"—really just pretty words? The dominance of an invisible guiding culture encompasses more than the religious sphere. For instance, Serhat Z. received no apprenticeship position. Meanwhile, he knows for sure that it has to do with his origin. After numerous failed attempts, he put the rule to the test. He called various middle-class businesses about an apprenticeship and gave his own name on some occasions and an invented native name on others. When his "foreign" name came up, the conversation was most often quickly over. Young people with migration backgrounds have a more difficult time obtaining an apprenticeship position. This has nothing to do with education level. Studies show that the decision makers in this country's various small businesses consider the cultural background of young migrants to be a problem. Above all, it is alleged that young men of Turkish ancestry would disturb the business culture—due, for instance, to their ostensibly higher irritability in matters of honor. [. . .]

In contrast to France or Great Britain, "we" in Germany means only the community of natives; this "we" sounds entirely exclusive for all people of non-German backgrounds. However, migrants often do not appear very forthcoming. For most natives, their communities [original in English] come across as closed off and bound to their homeland. The Turkish men's café or the head-scarved woman seem to belong to another world. Even today, many first-generation Greek immigrants know no more about their own cities than their workplace, the Greek church congregation, and the route to the airport. But maintaining an imaginary homeland or one's own tradition as a frame of reference is not always due to a defensive posture among migrants but to the conditions for acceptance in Germany. From the outset, access to citizenship was made almost impossible for migrants and thus created barriers to political participation. On top of everything, membership in a political migrant organization can be grounds for the denial of citizenship even today. Thus, there was nothing else for immigrants to do than to relocate to the community activities of cultural organizations. [. . .]

Head Scarf as Symbol

Also, the much-debated head scarves, evidently the signal par excellence for the traditionality of the "foreigner," are anything but traditional. Often enough, young, educated women of Turkish descent wear the head scarf. However, this head scarf has absolutely nothing to do with the traditional head scarf of the mothers, which leaves the hairline free and ties under the chin. Young women wear a so-called turban—a towel that covers both the whole hair and the shoulders. The "turban" has no special cultural meaning in Turkey and is worn by young Muslim women in all European countries today. Moreover, the Essen education researcher Yasemin Karakaşoğlu-Aydın discovered in a survey of "head-scarf students" that the women's families were often not very religiously oriented. To be sure, this head scarf is a religious symbol—but the decision to wear it is felt as a fully individual and particular expression of personality—once again not traditional but very modern values.

The separation of a German guiding culture from a foreign tradition, which has not been traditional for a long time, proves to be primarily strategic. The desire to maintain the separation, which the Union is now arguing for, portends a static future. In contrast, we should concern ourselves with the further dissolution of the currently existing guiding culture. We need a political framework that will put migrants' societal participation on stable ground.

To overcome the strict separation between "we" and "they," it will be necessary for both natives and migrants to identify the sites of each other's entanglements—that fragile world in between where identities appear dependent on each other in unpleasant, unsettling ways.

15

MOSHE ZIMMERMANN

THE WORD GAMES ARE OVER:
MORE IMMIGRATION, LESS GUIDING CULTURE

First published as "Das Wortspiel ist aus: Mehr Einwanderung, weniger Leitkultur" in *Süddeutsche Zeitung* (November 18, 2000). Translated by Tes Howell. Zimmermann (b. 1943, Jerusalem) is the director of the Richard-Koebner-Center for German History at the Hebrew University of Jerusalem. Paul Spiegel is president of the Central Council of Jews in Germany.

For the historian George Mosse, there was no doubt: since the rise of the Third Reich, German culture, the heir to the Enlightenment, was not to be found on German soil but abroad in exile with the *Jekkes,* the German Jews. It was the German-Jewish educated classes, he once wrote, who rescued the positive in German culture after the dictatorship, the Holocaust, and the collapse; he wrote this around the time that Helmut Kohl heralded his cultural turn in Germany. Is this what Paul Spiegel meant when he announced that he wanted to use the term *German culture* as a replacement for *German guiding culture?*

If so, then Paul Spiegel's attack is coming from the right corner: he speaks, among other things, in the name of murdered and emigrated bearers of German culture, and reacts accordingly to associations that call forth the term *guiding culture,* associations that conjure up names like Spengler, Moeller van den Bruck, or Rosenberg. And when a CDU politician described Spiegel's complaints as "exaggerated reproaches," a further association could hardly be avoided: namely, the accusation against the "exaggerated Jewish intellectualism." There the debate could begin, and the attribute *indecent*, a word one German politician used to describe Spiegel's speech, could have been the breaking point.

The Culture of the Constitution

Yet one must not take up Spiegel's alternative concept without further consideration. This phrase has caused too much harm in the past. The confrontation of culture and civilization, the application of the concept in the Third Reich, or the ghettoization of the German Jews in the "Jewish cultural alliance" delegitimized the use of this word for the modern context. Spiegel's compromise, therefore, does not help the Germans. Perhaps one should choose a word combination with "constitution" instead of "culture?" To preach the old "Germanization" in this era of the "erosion of the national culture" (Hermann Bausinger) or to plead for the "homogeneity of the German people" (Edmund Stoiber)—there's no future in this!

As an outsider and observer of the German scene, one should hardly be surprised. Again and again, a provocative term incites a furor throughout Germany: in the recent past alone, it was "moral weapon," "intellectual arson," and "derailment," terms that have stirred emotions. And now we have landed at "guiding culture." If one follows the intensive debate about orthography reform, one can sum it all up as "typically German." However, the debate over words and language must not hide the issues themselves: xenophobia, understanding of the meaning of democracy, and civic and human rights. The approximately 100 murdered victims of racism in Germany within 10 years must call forth alarm similar to the conspicuous alarm over the death toll in the current Middle East intifada. It is about the many people who understand "guiding culture" as looking down on the cultures of the "others," even if the politicians do not mean it that way. The problem does not begin with skinheads, whom Spiegel fears as the country's potential future leaders. It begins in the heads of the completely normal people who view the dark-skinned or those with accents as a potential danger. The test is the "everyday test": How does a salesperson in a department store treat a foreign-looking customer?

If the foundation consists of ethnocentrism and racism, then achievement of the next steps is merely a question of the specific socioeconomic conditions. Soon it will become quite natural to look the other way, not just due to cowardice but to consent as well. In Germany, there is currently no "Fourth Reich" in the making, but it is still a country in which racism has not lost its cultural breeding ground. However, the realization that not only the "foreigners" are endangered but also democracy altogether—and therefore all of us—this realization has not become common knowledge.

German historians, along with other intellectuals, are in the midst of a vigorous debate on the question of continuity before and after 1945. One discovers, with great dismay, the personal continuity and asks whether the presentation of the separation between personal entanglement in the system before 1945 does not rest upon a deception, whether the whole of society could truly free itself from the "original sin." As long as this question cannot be clearly answered, one must exercise the greatest caution, and indeed not only among intellectuals.

One can only escape this constellation when one dispenses with unnecessary word games and again addresses the questions of immigration. The mission should be compensating for the loss of German culture during the emigration in the 1930s with a new immigration of today, instead of provoking a national German guiding culture. For this immigration will not only enrich the pension fund but also German culture.

16
ULRICH K. PREUSS
MULTIKULTI IS ONLY AN ILLUSION

First published as "Multikulti ist nur eine Illusion" in *Die Zeit* (May 31, 2001). Translated by David Gramling. Preuss (b. 1940, Hannover) has been the president of the Berlin Central Administration of the German Federal Bank since 2002.

Germany is becoming a country of immigration. The Basic Law does not lead the way.

Now that the CDU and CSU have shifted their course, Germany is on its way toward officially becoming an immigration country. The politics of migration will from this moment on be a permanent element of German domestic politics. However, the actual challenge of this development is the following: We must transform the already existing and, to a certain extent, merely physical presence of foreigners into a self-evident status of belonging in our society. That is the core of the integration problem currently making its way into the foreground of discussion.

I am consciously speaking of foreigners but am not referring to the increasingly outmoded governmental and human-rights concept of the foreign. This concept still derives from the golden-age ideal of a homogenous polity. In those days, those who belonged to other states switched sovereign territories only in small numbers, and mostly only temporarily. In this era, the foreign was that which belonged to another state. Far into the twentieth century, it was the preeminent doctrine that one's state bound him to an exclusive and existential relationship. Foreignness in a guest country was, to a certain extent, the opposite of belonging to one's home state. This approach we may term the "state-rights" model of the foreign.

In our time of open statehood characterized by border-crossing mobility and mass migration of labor power, this exclusive and existential quality of citizenship is increasingly the mere formal-legal assignment of the individual to a common essence. Such citizenship reveals little about the identity of a person. Thus we see in the foreigner not much more than the holder of a foreigner's passport, which he, as a "German Turk," "German Russian," or "German Palestinian" often doesn't even possess anymore. Rather, he is a representative of an ethnic minority living here. In other words, the concept of the foreigner has transformed from a state legal category to a sociocultural one.

Meanwhile, the fact that many ethnic minorities live in Germany has clear consequences. The ideal of a homogenous society, which was overcome long ago, is once and for all defunct. It may not and cannot serve as a normative standard any longer. More precisely, if we officially define ourselves as a country of immigration and accept foreigners as fellow citizens, we must make room for a new normality together. This approach can succeed only if we negotiate consciously in the role of the foreigner, who, together with many others, will form a new societal reality.

Until now, the normalization of the foreigner succeeded by means of his naturalization. He thus gave up his previous citizenship and obtained the new one, after a few challenging conditions. Many liberals and leftists believe it is possible to tackle the problem of immigration and integration in this manner today as well.

But just as many conservatives have bid farewell to their illusions, leftists and liberals must also now give up that old beloved idea that naturalization—in other words, the acceptance of the immigrant into the legal community of citizens—is the solution to all integration problems. There is an eternal debate about whether foreigners should be naturalized at the end of a long and successful integration, or even at the conclusion of an assimilation process. Others maintain that the acquisition of citizenship must take place at the outset, because it is the precondition for any integration. Leftists and liberals have always fought for the second model.

Their position belongs to the honorable tradition of the universalist ideals of the French Revolution, which promises to see every naturalized person not as belonging to a foreign people but rather as a new citizen, one who does not differ from the autochthonous people in his humanity and has a consequent right to be regarded as equal. The republic unequivocally required the newcomer to adjust to the secular and human-rights-oriented political culture of France. All particular characteristics—such as origin, religion, skin color, language, customs, and traditions—by which the abstract human in the concrete individual may be recognized needed to be held separate from the public sphere and were banned to the private sphere.

This civil-rights universalism has its price, however, because precisely origin, religion, ethnicity, skin color, and language are for many people, especially outside this country, sources of self-awareness, self-respect, identity, and also pride. Those belonging to minorities in particular seek to affirm their insistence on their ethnic-cultural particularity and demonstratively avow their origin. Demanding assimilation to customs, traditions, and normative standards of the majority population would detract from their own. Nonetheless, they would not cease to be different from the majority, whether because of language, skin color, or name. Their insistence on particularity, they say, ought to communicate to the majority society that they wish to preserve their identity in an environment that is foreign and often hostile. This stance leads, particularly among young immigrants, to ethnic isolationism and sometimes even to an unconditional and aggressive identification with an abstract ethnic subject. The sad consequence: the liberatory impulse, which lies in the discovery of one's own ethnic particularity, is thus once again destroyed.

An immigration politics that relies on human-rights-oriented universalist principles is ambivalent. For whoever grants entry to immigrants, but simultaneously demands the public neutralization of their origin and culture, expects them to deny their own identity. It is common knowledge that this contradiction was the core of the French conception of immigration for decades. Still today, representatives of a rigid secularist republicanism hold fast to this idea.

In Germany, such a model has no such chances. Here, the traditionally strong territorial, religious, cultural, and political particularism has allowed for a high degree of openness toward cultural diversity, especially on the regional and local levels. At its core is the freedom of religion and conscience guaranteed by the Basic Law. Its classic theme, which is also highly pertinent these days, is the tension between the basic law of equality of responsibility for all citizens and the individual's privilege to abstain on religious grounds (consider, for example, the head-scarf question or the issue of nonparticipation in physical education). The courts have found these cases "friendly to basic rights"—that is, in favor of the "dissenters." With the one exception of compulsory taxation, a person may be freed from performing responsibilities to the state—from military duty, inoculation, school and social duties, and allegiance requirements—if he may credibly claim that these duties cause him to violate binding principles of his religion and conscience.

For a long time in our country we have coped with such conflicts without repercussions for the democratic sense of equality—especially with those (with the exception of the military objectors) that concerned members of small religious communities. The constitutional core of these conflicts was expressed each time as follows: How much freedom from duty can the egalitarian constitutional state afford? It could be only as magnanimous as the concerned community was small and as the meaning of the exception to the norms of the majority community was marginal. Now, however, Germany wants to define itself as a country of immigration, and immigrants are tossing out new questions in great numbers. Thus, it is no longer simply about the recognition of a marginal lifestyle's eccentricity and stubbornness by excusing its practitioners from communal duties. Of course, such an exception always means something that is often forgotten in the debates: namely, being shut out from the majority community. The task of an immigration society consists much more in the recognition of the cultural specificity of immigrant minorities and in making them coconstitutive bearers of the society.

For such a common entity, the concept of individual freedom from duty, which was always considered in terms of an exception, is inappropriate. Granted, this old concept may work tolerably well for the liberation of a Muslim girl from coed physical education, maybe even for the freedom from battle in exceptional cases. The concept may, for a limited time, deal even with general facts of life, like businesses' hours of operation, norms of dress, dietary regulations in state institutions, holiday regulations, or building codes for non-Christian religious buildings. But one thing is certain: these exceptionist regulations do not serve the integration of immigrants in German society. Neither are they intended for an immigration society. Here a concept oriented toward individual exceptions not only comes up against its own internal limits but also galvanizes and reifies the immigrant's role as outsider.

The fact that we must understand ourselves as a country of immigration means that we may not consider immigrants as incomplete Germans who live on the margins of society, for a certain amount of time, usually in the first generation. Exactly this fact calls for a policy of formal equality and of strict cultural neutrality toward all individuals and their cultural conditions. We should therefore take another path: the path of the Canadian philosopher Charles Taylor and his "politics of recognition," which prizes the intrinsic value of cultural differences and protects their claims to an identity—an identity that is also marked by group membership. This policy demands neither a guarantee of group-level rights (as in the citizens'-rights minority-protection model) nor a cultural relativist avowal of multicultural society. [. . .]

It is difficult to find a steady path between the Scylla of an immigration concept based on cultural assimilation and the Charybdis of a multicultural society of nationalities. Without a doubt, the Basic Law will remain the basis of this new immigration society, but this realization doesn't help us much. For the interpretation of the basic laws changes constantly, and the constitution does not prescribe a certain integration policy. The idea of declaring the "German guiding culture" as a standard for integration will necessarily fail, because no united national culture exists in a pluralistic society. Under no circumstances can it become a binding canon without simultaneously conflicting with the central principles of the Basic Law.

The Basic Law is indeed open to an immigration society, but it is not a sufficient guide toward it. Now the political task is to find a new form for this society, a form in which immigrants are assumed and accepted as equally enfranchised constituents of a self-renewing republic. The situation is entirely comparable with the entry of Germans from the former GDR. Therefore, it is a case of creating a new normality. If this effort is successful, it will be the path between a bloodless universalism and an autistic multiculturalism.

17

JÜRGEN HABERMAS AND JACQUES DERRIDA

AFTER THE WAR: THE REBIRTH OF EUROPE

First published as "Nach dem Krieg: Die Wiedergeburt Europas" in *Frankfurter Allgemeine Zeitung* (May 31, 2003). Reprinted as "February 15, or What Binds Europeans Together: A Plea for a Common Foreign Policy, Beginning in the Core of Europe," in *Constellations* (vol. 10, November 3, 2003). Translated by Max Pensky.

The Treacheries of a European Identity

[. . .] It is easy to find unity without commitment. The image of a peaceful, cooperative Europe, open toward other cultures and capable of dialogue, floats like a mirage before us all. We welcome the Europe that found exemplary solutions for two problems during the second half of the twentieth century. The EU already offers itself as a form of "governance beyond the nation-state," which could set a precedent in the postnational constellation. And for decades, European social-welfare systems served as a model. Certainly, they have now been thrown on the defensive at the level of the nation-state. Yet future political efforts at the domestication of global capitalism must not fall below the standards of social justice that they established. If Europe has solved two problems of this magnitude, why shouldn't it issue a further challenge: to defend and promote a cosmopolitan order on the basis of international law against competing visions?

Such a Europe-wide discourse, of course, would have to match up with existing dispositions, which are waiting, so to speak, for the stimulation of a process of self-understanding. Two facts would seem to contradict this bold assumption. Haven't the most significant historical achievements of Europe forfeited their identity-forming power precisely through the fact of their worldwide success? And what could hold together a region characterized more than any other by the ongoing rivalries between self-conscious nations?

Insofar as Christianity and capitalism, natural science and technology, Roman law and the Code Napoleon, the bourgeois-urban forms of life, democracy and human rights, and the secularization of state and society have spread across other continents, their legacies no longer constitute a *proprium*. The Western form of spirit, rooted in the Judeo-Christian tradition, certainly has its characteristic features. But the nations of Europe also share this mental habitus, characterized by individualism, rationalism, and activism, with the United States, Canada, and Australia. The "West" encompasses more than just Europe. Moreover, Europe is composed of nation-states that delimit one another polemically. National consciousness, formed by national language, national literatures, and national histories, has long operated as an explosive force.

However, in response to the destructive power of this nationalism, values and habits have also developed which have given contemporary Europe, in its incomparably rich cultural diversity, its own face. This is how Europe at large presents itself to non-Europeans. A culture which for centuries has been beset more than any other by conflicts between town and country, sacred and secular authorities, by the competition between faith and knowledge, the struggle between states and antagonistic classes, has had to painfully learn how differences can be communicated, contradictions institutionalized, and tensions stabilized. The acknowledgment of differences—the reciprocal acknowledgment of the other in his otherness—can also become a feature of a common identity.

The pacification of class conflicts within the welfare state and the self-limitation of state sovereignty within the framework of the EU are only the most recent examples of this. In the third quarter of the twentieth century, Europe on this side of the Iron Curtain experienced its "golden age," as Eric Hobsbawm has called it. Since then, features of a common political mentality have taken shape, so that others often recognize us as Europeans rather than as Germans or French—and that happens not just in Hong Kong but even in Tel Aviv. And isn't it true? In European societies, secularization is relatively far advanced. Citizens here regard transgressions of the border between politics and religion with suspicion. Europeans have a relatively large amount of trust in the organizational and steering capacities of the state, while remaining skeptical toward the achievements of markets. They possess a keen sense of the "dialectic of enlightenment"; they have no naively optimistic expectations about technological progress. They maintain a preference for the welfare state's guarantees of social security and for regulation on the basis of solidarity. The threshold of tolerance for the use of force against persons lies relatively low. The desire for a multilateral and legally regulated international order is connected with the hope for an effective global domestic policy, within the framework of a reformed United Nations.

The fortunate historical constellation in which West Europeans developed this kind of mentality in the shadow of the Cold War has changed since 1989–90. But February 15 shows that the mentality has survived the context from which it sprang. This also explains why "old Europe" sees itself challenged by the blunt hegemonic politics of its ally. And why so many in Europe who welcome the fall of Saddam as an act of liberation also reject the illegality of the unilateral, preemptive and deceptively justified invasion. But how stable is this mentality? Does it have its roots in deeper historical experiences and traditions?

Today we know that many political traditions that command their authority through the illusions of "naturalness" have in fact been "invented." By contrast, a European identity born in the daylight of the public sphere would have something constructed about it from the very beginning. But only what is constructed through an arbitrary choice carries the stigma of randomness. The political-ethical will that drives the hermeneutics of processes of self-understanding is not arbitrary. Distinguishing between the legacy we appropriate and the one we want to refuse demands just as much circumspection as the decision over the interpretation through which we appropriate it for ourselves. Historical experiences are only *candidates* for self-conscious appropriation; without such a self-conscious act they cannot attain the power to shape our identity. [. . .]

18
CEM ÖZDEMIR
MEHMET AND EDELTRAUD TOO

First published in English on www.opendemocracy.net (May 30, 2005).

I have asked myself for quite a while now how our society would have reacted had a catastrophe comparable to September 11, 2001, taken place in our country—perpetrated by people from a similar background. What would then happen to the already deplorable state of relations between immigrants of Muslim background and the majority population? It seems doubtful that the recent naturalization legislation, which became law on January 1, 2000, would still find a majority in both houses of the German legislature. Indeed, had the same legislation not been passed three years ago, I doubt if it would have become law in today's post–September 11 world.

In my view, this belief is not connected only to Islamic realities. It has more to do with the general nature of contact with those cultures in Germany that are experienced as "foreign." For example, relations with representatives of Jewish communities—who are automatically and collectively held responsible for the politics of Israeli prime minister Ariel Sharon, regardless of details of their work or the nature of their associations with Israel—allow us to predict what would happen in this country if another minority group suddenly found itself the center of negative national attention.

When it comes to anti-Semitism, one must take into consideration the consequences of modern German history and the subsequent "civil safe-guard system"—de-Nazification, education policy and the "watchdog role" of the U.S. media—which have resulted in a large measure of self-control among those whose opinions lean toward the anti-Semitic. However, politicians who claim they are being thanked for finally speaking "what everybody is thinking" illustrate just how thin this protective coating against anti-Semitism actually is.

A certain hierarchy of cultures, peoples, and religions appears impossible to eradicate. If I consider the very different reactions to a social phenomenon—like, for example, youth violence—I begin to lose faith in the ultimate realization of the basic principle of equality or the prohibition of violence, both stated in the German constitution. In the recent case of the juvenile repeat offender "Mehmet from Bavaria," everybody was outraged by the amount of sheer aggression shown by one young Turkish person (who was raised—and, therefore, learned his delinquency—here). His deportation to Turkey seemed to become the most pressing domestic political issue in Germany.

Meanwhile, young German people (read: children of native German parents), after setting fire to a facility for asylum seekers or torturing and beating to death an equally German youth because of his or her clothing, are considered the unfortunate ones—exceptional cases who, with patience and a lot of understanding, can be rehabilitated. Even the most passionate advocates of law and order will mutate into sympathetic sociologists of youth with compassionate hearts for the social environments of these unfortunate creatures. We can say with certainty that it does not matter to the victims which country the parents of their aggressors came from. Yet our politicians and media continue to obsess over the issue and, in so doing, further sensationalize the immigration issue.

Certainly, the aggressive media coverage of cases like Mehmet's is not representative of collective public opinion in Germany. My personal experiences alone attest to this fact—experiences, it should be noted, that many other individuals of non-German heritage, representing all sectors of society, can undoubtedly relate to.

However, in the United States, a headline like one that appeared in a major German news magazine not very long ago is simply unimaginable. The headline was used for an article describing a membership drive for the Green Party that I helped organize, in which 42 German citizens of Turkish and Kurdish origin had registered as Greens. It proclaimed, "Özdemir brought his 42 Turks." Almost 2.5 million people in Germany with Turkish passports know full well the connotation here of the intentionally chosen word *Turks*. The author of the piece was indifferent to the fact that these were naturalized citizens—German citizens. In this context, the term *Turks* carries the same implications as the now outdated terms *coloreds* and *Negroes* would have in

America. To stay with this example: not only in the United States would this journalist have had difficulty finding a newspaper likely to print something as insensitive about, say, an African American Congressman. [. . .]

Not until Germany recognizes that immigration issues affect everybody—native and nonnative Germans alike—will we have established a protective roof for every member of our society. What we have to acknowledge and, more importantly, accept is the fact that these issues do not only affect Mehmet, Giovanni, and Olga. They affect those with names like Hans, Eberhardt, and Edeltraud, too.

19

FRANZ MÜNTEFERING, CLAUDIA ROTH, AND ANGELA MERKEL

HOW SHOULD THE IMMIGRATION OF JEWS FROM THE COUNTRIES OF THE FORMER SOVIET UNION BE REGULATED IN THE FUTURE?

First published as "Wie sollte in Zukunft die Zuwanderung von Juden aus den Ländern der ehemaligen Sowjetunion geregelt werden?" in *Jüdische Allgemeine* (June 23, 2005). Translated by David Gramling.

The leaders of the parties represented in the Bundestag answer this question

FRANZ MÜNTEFERING
Leader of the Social Democratic Party

According to the rules currently in effect, people of Jewish faith or those who have at least one Jewish parent may immigrate to Germany without further preconditions. It is precisely the Eastern European immigrants who have ensured that Jewish congregations will prosper once again in Germany. But there are hurdles to overcome: insufficient language knowledge and meager prospects on the job market make integration into our society difficult. Of course, no new regulation may be accepted without consulting with the Central Council of Jews. We will continue to advocate for the further successful immigration of people of the Jewish faith.

CLAUDIA ROTH
Green Party Leader

Since 1991, more than 170,000 Jewish emigrants from the Soviet Union have come to Germany as immigrants. For us, it is an inestimable signal of faith that Jewish men and women are moving into a country that attempted to annihilate all of European Jewry 60 years ago. This movement has led to a flowering of Jewish congregations in Germany. The great enrichment that this development has provided—not only to our country but also to the Jewish congregations in our country—can be sensed when one visits synagogues in Germany. Immigration, however, also represents a challenge to those congregations. A great number of immigrants neither seek nor find their way to the Jewish congregations. This state of affairs is awkward for the congregations. But the door to Germany is also open to secular Jewish men and women. Any discussion of the regulation of Jewish immigration from Eastern Europe must be pursued in common with the representation of Jewish congregations. For us, it is clear that Jewish immigration will continue to enrich our country. It shall not be restricted.

ANGELA MERKEL
Leader of the Christian Democratic Union

I am very pleased that in recent years, many lively Jewish congregations in our country have been formed. In this regard, the immigration of Jews from Eastern Europe must be kept under consideration. These immigrants are welcome, because we intend to strengthen Jewish life in Germany, and the current legal principles for immigration have generally stood the test. It is, however, important that the people coming to Germany actually become integrated in the Jewish congregations. To ensure this, there must be a constant dialogue between the political sphere and the Jewish community in Germany.

8

LIVING IN TWO WORLDS?

DOMESTIC SPACE, FAMILY, AND COMMUNITY

SATELLITE DISHES IN BERLIN-KREUZBERG, 2005. Every night more than a million television sets in Germany tune in via satellite to a wide range of free Turkish-, Arabic-, and Asian-language channels. They allow migrants to view 24-hour programming in their native languages but cause anxiety among German media experts about the ostensible failure of national integration.

THE TEXTS IN THIS CHAPTER attempt to offer an impressionistic engagement with the "lifeworld" of migration: living rooms, bedrooms, schools, apartment complexes, rental units, deportation holding facilities, nursing homes, and makeshift encampments. A federal statute regulating accommodations for guest workers opens this chapter, followed by a 1974 interview with New German Cinema director Rainer Werner Fassbinder, in which he addresses the dilemma of representing migrant workers in his films. A 1977 article in *Der Spiegel* on "guest-worker children"—or children of recruited laborers—interviewed teenagers about their employment, their educational experiences, and the daily presence of discrimination in their lives. Two years later, the Berlin-based physician Albrecht Spieß began documenting a health anomaly among youth of transnational backgrounds: a disproportionately high number of "guest-worker children" presented psychosomatic stress symptoms such as ulcers, which are highly uncommon in patients of that age.

Another group of texts in this chapter illustrates the strained relations between German and immigrant neighbors in housing complexes and rental properties. A 1979 class-action complaint letter from the German residents of a housing complex claims that Turkish neighbors are noisy, unruly, and excessively social. Another text, a mock classified advertisement penned anonymously from the perspective of a Turkish father looking for a new apartment, sardonically recasts this stereotype of the Turkish family home. It also calls attention to the ubiquity of housing discrimination, which prevents working-class Turkish families from living outside of designated immigrant neighborhoods.

Dilek Zaptçıoğlu's 1993 piece shares the title of this chapter, "Living in Two Worlds." Her essay rebuffs the long-held fable that immigrants in Germany live in an indeterminate and troubled space "between two worlds." Cautious and passionate, Zaptçıoğlu's article attests to the affective "bilocationality" of the second generation of German Turkish youth, their experiences visiting Turkey during and after a childhood in Germany, and their sense of investment and belonging in multiple, overlapping homelands.

A second article from 1993, "At Most Half a Homeland," serves as a generational counterpoint to Zaptçıoğlu's piece, surveying the experiences of retired guest workers who, despite perennial intentions to return to their former homelands, now share their later years with other retired labor migrants in Germany. The article investigates the options for hospice, nursing homes, assisted living, and health insurance for elder immigrants, as well as the long-term health effects of decades of dangerous, repetitive physical labor in German workplaces.

A 1994 article, "Saying 'I Do' for the Certificate," explores the logistical intricacies of marriages of convenience. Refugees and lesbian and gay immigrants are particularly affected by the spousal residency statutes of German immigration law. Traditionally, German law has barred immigrants in same-gender relationships from obtaining citizenship through civil marriage as their heterosexual counterparts could. This article documents the phenomenon of "double marriages of convenience," in which two binational same-gender couples exchange partners for the purpose of civil marriage and citizenship.

A 1994 conversation between Deniz Göktürk and Wulf Eichstädt addresses the multiculturalist notion of "living together in Berlin," the idealized coexistence of migrants and nonmigrants in urban space. Under what conditions can one say that these urban residents are "living together *(Miteinanderleben)*" rather than "living next to each other *(Nebeneinanderleben)*" in the private and public spheres of the city? A 1995 article on Berlin's main deportation facility, the Krupp Street Prison, sketches out the daily life of inmates awaiting unspecified deportation dates. Because these inmates are not protected under criminal law statutes on compulsory detainment, they do not enjoy the access to health care, education, or rehabilitation measures that traditional prisoners do.

A topic often sidestepped in the political debate on immigration is the international traffic in women as wives, domestic servants, or indentured sex workers. We include a promotional essay by a German entrepreneur in the international sex trade. "The Thai wife" advertises an internet-bride service in terms of cultural encounter and enrichment, invoking the stereotypes of both the cool, rational European and the wild, passionate Asian. We decided to include this text as an example of the cooptation of multicultural discourse for even the most exploitative ends.

Klaus Hartung's article on the sprawling Kreuzberg Center apartment complex in Berlin's East Kreuzberg district chronicles one businessman's efforts to reinvigorate the insolvent, neglected structure. Since the mid-1970s, Kreuzberg has served as the quintessential urban dystopia for anti-immigration advocates throughout Germany, and the Kreuzberg Center apartment complex has been one of its defining architectural landmarks. In the 1990s, entrepreneur Peter Ackermann sought to convert the building into an economically viable mix of residential and mercantile venues by constructing playgrounds, limiting the amount of döner kebab stands, and aggressively prosecuting drug offenses in the center's corridors and stairways.

A 2001 article, "Colorful and Speechless," surveys multilingual kindergartens in Hamburg's Ottensen and Veddel districts, where in one typical kindergarten class the children speak 18 different languages. At issue in this article is the lack of funding and state support for multilingual pedagogy, as well as a dearth of qualified applicants for these low-wage teaching posts. Although the 2005 Immigration Act calls for every immigrant to learn German as a condition of citizenship, researchers are nearly unanimous in demonstrating that generation after generation of transnational youth lack access to linguistically appropriate primary education, whether bilingual or monolingual.

Frankfurt-based cultural anthropologist Regina Römhild's 2002 essay "When *Heimat* Goes Global" highlights the "transnationalization" of immigrant cultural spheres. Römhild's essay follows one of Frankfurt am Main's Uzbek teenagers, Katja, whose "normal" life depends on a network of affiliations between migrants of various backgrounds. In the most concrete ways, locality and community are multiple for Katja; she continually filters her everyday life through a prism of global connections.

"The Campsite Is Growing" reports on a Roma tent city along a German highway, whose inhabitants have left their official residences to evade the Federal Border Patrol. After the Serbo-Croatian war, the German state began sending asylum applicants back to Belgrade and other Eastern European cities. Roma teenager Demail had completed tenth grade when his parents discovered that they had to abandon their Essen apartment for a nomadic existence if they were to remain in Germany. As the interview concludes, Demail sketches out the floor plan of his former apartment on the ground of his family's tent.

The texts in this chapter focus on the private, domestic sphere in its most diverse forms: the transnational *oikos* as it is lived and practiced within the German nation-state. The chapter concludes with texts concerning two aspects of domestic life: an essay on undocumented house cleaners from Poland and a manifesto on the rights of Turkish women in response to a series of high-profile "honor killings" in Berlin.

1

THE FEDERAL MINISTRY FOR LABOR AND SOCIAL ORDER

GUIDELINES FOR HOUSING ACCOMMODATIONS FOR FOREIGN EMPLOYEES IN THE FEDERAL REPUBLIC OF GERMANY

First published as "Richtlinien für die Unterkünfte ausländischer Arbeitnehmer in der Bundesrepublik Deutschland" by the Federal Ministry for Labor and Social Order (April 1, 1971). Translated by David Gramling.

Unless otherwise stipulated by local statutes, the following guidelines are to be followed:

I. Construction design
1. The height of bedrooms and living rooms must be at least 2.30 meters. In attic spaces, the lowest clearance must be two-thirds of the floor space of each given room.
2. The floors must have a heated surface.
3. Walls and ceilings must be insulated.
4. Outer doors must be thick and must be lockable. When bedrooms and living rooms lead directly to the outside, a double door or windscreen must be installed.
5. The window panels must be at least one-tenth of the overall floor space. Windows must be thick and able to be opened. If direct ventilation is not available, sufficient ventilation systems must be installed. [. . .]

II. Living spaces
1. Accommodations must be established such that 8 square meters are provided for each person. [. . .]

III. Sleeping quarters, living quarters, infirmary spaces
1. Separate sleeping quarters must be provided for men and women.
2. In cases in which employees work different shifts, workers from different shifts must be provided with different sleeping quarters.
3. Each resident must have his/her own bed. Two beds may be installed above one another at most.
4. No room may have more than four beds.
5. Each room must have a sign in German and in the official mother language on which the legal capacity of the space is noted.
6. Provisions for each bed include a mattress, a pillow, a sufficient number of wool blankets and sheets.
7. Each new worker must receive clean sheets. [. . .]

2

RAINER WERNER FASSBINDER AND HANS GÜNTHER PFLAUM

AT SOME POINT FILMS HAVE TO STOP BEING FILMS

Published in *The Anarchy of the Imagination: Interviews, Essays, Notes,* Michael Töteberg and Leo A. Lensing, eds. (Baltimore: Johns Hopkins University Press, 1991), pp. 11–15. Translated by Krishna Winston. This 1974 interview concerns Fassbinder's film *Angst essen Seele auf* (*Ali: Fear Eats the Soul*), one of the first German films to address guest-worker issues.

HGP: Herr Fassbinder, in this film you've told a provocatively simple, simplified story. Is there a didactic program implied in your reduction of the conflicts to such a level?

RWF: It seems to me that the simpler a story is, the truer it is. The common denominator for many stories is a story as simple as this. If we'd made the character of Ali more complicated, the audience would have had a harder time dealing with the story. If the character had been more complex, the childlike quality of the relationship between Ali and Emmi would have suffered—whereas now the story's as naïve as the two people it's about. Though of course the relationships are much more complex, I realize that. But it's my opinion that each viewer has to flesh them out with his own reality. And he has an opportunity to do that when a story's very simple. I think people have to find their own opportunities for change—of course, you can go strictly by ideology, but for the larger audience, I don't think that makes much sense.

HGP: Couldn't the very simplicity of this film give the audience an excuse to dissociate themselves from the story, saying, "In reality nothing's that simple?"

RWF: They have an excuse, or actually they're forced, to dissociate themselves from the story, not at the expense of the film but rather in favor of their own reality—to me that's the crucial thing. At some point, films have to stop being films, being stories, and have to begin to come alive, so that people will ask themselves: What about me and my life? I think this film forces people—because the love between the two comes across as so clean and pure—to examine their own relationships with darker-skinned and also older people. To me that's very important. You can't make it simple enough.

HGP: On the other hand this simplicity can be incredibly provoking: for instance, when Ali's sitting in Emmi's apartment, and you see the big lonely, empty apartment and a little, lonely woman, and he's describing his room, where six of them are crammed in like sardines—the question just spontaneously occurs to you: Why doesn't Ali simply move in with Emmi?

RWF: Yes, that's what we discovered with the television series *Eight Hours Are Not a Day:* the simpler the stories, the more the viewers could do with them. The intellectuals and leftists charged that all that wasn't true anymore, but they were wrong; it was still true for the viewer, because he had a chance to translate everything into something that related to himself and his own reality. And if art, or whatever you want to call it, seizes the opportunity to get discussion going among people, it's achieved its maximum effect, I think.

HGP: To what extent does *Fear Eats the Soul* incorporate your experiences with other films? I'm thinking primarily of the films of Douglas Sirk, of course.

RWF: Yes, actually ever since I saw his films and tried to write about them, Sirk's been in everything I've done. Not Sirk himself, but what I've learned from his work. Sirk told me what the studio bosses in Hollywood told him: a film has to go over in Garmisch-Partenkirchen, in Okinawa, and in Chicago—just try to think what the common denominator might be for people in all those places. To Sirk something still mattered that most people in Hollywood don't care about anymore: making sure his work was in tune with himself, with his own personality—that is, not just produced "for the public," like those films here in Germany that none of us likes: those sex and entertainment films that the producers think the public likes, but they don't like themselves. That's the difference between a production for the masses by Sirk and one by Vohrer. Sirk hasn't done much that he's ashamed of, and I'm impressed by that.

HGP: The dramatic structure of the story of *Fear Eats the Soul* reminds me of Sirk: in the first half of the film the couple has to contend with problems that come from the outside and tend to have a stabilizing effect on their relationship. Not until this pressure from the outside lessens do your protagonists (and the film itself) confront the internal conflicts, the problems the two of them are bound to have with each other.

RWF: Yes, but that's not Sirk, that's life. In the case of minorities, outsiders, etc., it really is true that as long as they feel pressure from outside they don't get around to their own problems, because they're completely taken up with shielding themselves and assuring themselves of a kind of solidarity. As I was writing, it was hard for me to get away from that; I wondered how to work it so people wouldn't be putting so much pressure on the two of them anymore.

HGP: What's the function of the final sequence, when Ali collapses from a stomach ulcer, and the doctor at the hospital mentions that that's a common diagnosis for guest workers. Don't you have an entirely different reality forcing its way into the picture at that point?

RWF: It's true to life. I heard about it from a doctor at a clinic. She described this scene to me in detail, and I could picture it perfectly. Here you have this absolutely authentic bit of guest-worker reality breaking in, and people have to deal with that, too. Of course, the ending's meant to take this private story, which I'm crazy about and also happen to think is very important, and give it a thrust into reality, including in the mind of the moviegoer. [. . .]

3

NASTY RASCALS, LITTLE PIGS, THROW THEM OUT!

First published as " 'Gemeine Lumpen, Sauigels—rauswerfen' " in *Der Spiegel* (December 26, 1977). Translated by David Gramling.

More than a million foreign children are living in the Federal Republic. Some 45,000 of them reach working age each year but find neither an apprenticeship nor a job. They are illiterate in two languages; they speak German just as poorly as they speak their mother language. Two-thirds fail out of vocational school, make their way into the social underworld, and become day laborers. Experts are warning about the "social powder keg of tomorrow."

Sedat Manönü, an 18-year-old Turk, never wants to wait tables at a pizzeria again. Sweating away 12 hours a day for 500 marks a month, he says, "No one even sees me there; I'm not an animal, you know." Sedat, who graduated from vocational school and speaks German well, ran to the Hannover Labor Bureau week after week, but he did not receive an apprenticeship. Now he has "had enough of it," and takes piecemeal jobs here and there. He'd like to smack the friendly, smiling, and regretfully dismissive labor-bureau worker.

Francesco Pucci, now 17, came from Palermo to Mainz as a small child. His father and mother went to work every day, while Francesco skipped school and played on the streets with the Italian neighbors' kids. He stole bikes, lifted a camera from a parked car here and there, busted into vending machines. During his vocational training, he scuffled with the foreman, picked pockets, and then landed in juvenile court. Today, Francesco is unemployed and hangs around at the Mainz train station. He "will soon end up in jail"—or so fears his case manager, Sebastiano Cornelio. "It can't be helped," elaborates Cornelio. "This kind of life story is pretty typical."

All of the female students in the ninth grade at Munich's Albert Schweitzer Vocational School found apprenticeships this year, except the Spanish student Concepción Origuel. She is a 16-year-old who wants to become a physician's assistant. She applied for positions at about a dozen medical practices, went to each "with big hopes," and was "soundly rebuffed" each time. The position had already been filled. "Maybe that is natural," she says resignedly, "since usually the Germans take them." But she finds it "so dumb" that the doctors "always want to know first where I am from and what my parents do. We're not lepers or anything."

But they are treated that way—the adolescent children of foreign employees—pushed into the societal underworld, without sufficient schooling, without the least prospect of a career. They are dealt with like "disposable goods," says a representative of the Federal Youth Curatorium. They are a new disenfranchised generation who are guaranteed neither residence nor employment in the host country of the Federal Republic, a country that precipitously assigns them a spot on the bottom rung of the social ladder. As the *Frankfurter Allgemeine Zeitung* conjectures, "the difficult climb of the first generation" is followed by "the descent of the second to even lower depths."

More than a million foreign children under 21 live in the Federal Republic. For about a half of them, the Bosporus and the Peloponnesus are their foreign homelands, whereas cities like Duisburg, Stuttgart, and Munich are their familiar hometowns. About 110,000 guest-worker children are born in Germany each year. In metropolitan areas like Frankfurt and Offenbach, every second baby has a Spanish, Italian, or Turkish father.

Another 1.2 million young foreigners live back in the homeland, separated from their parents, and are waiting for entry into the Federal Republic. Many are already living illegally in the country, unbeknownst to the government. They are "foreigners who are neither foreigners nor Germans," as one Augsburg educator summarizes the situation. [. . .]

Anyone who followed their parents to Germany after December 31, 1976, [. . .] should not even attempt to obtain a work visa or an apprenticeship; both are inaccessible to them. These youth must come to terms with the fact that when they become 18, they will be unemployed foreigners and will be deported to their homeland. It is a state-sponsored idleness that drives many into the market halls and harbor dockyards, places where they can be hired illegally for low wages. [. . .]

In criminal statistics, guest-worker children "do not yet play a large role," claims a Munich police commissioner. "They behave no worse than the others; most of their crimes are petty theft in department stores, fights here and there, purse snatching." Young Greeks work Stuttgart's Leonhardplatz as hustlers; young Turks deal drugs in Berlin. Turks and Greeks also support Munich's militant rock group the Black Spiders. [. . .]

If Germans and foreigners "are not put on an even playing field soon," says Teoman Atalay, the chair of the Foreigner Advisory Board in Hannover, "violence and yet more violence will ensue, even worse than among Holland's Moroccans."

4

JUSTIN WESTHOFF

TURKISH CHILDREN WITH STOMACH ULCERS

First published as "Türkenkinder mit Magengeschwür" in *Der Tagesspiegel* (October 10, 1979). Translated by Tes Howell.

The hygienic situation of foreign fellow citizens in Berlin is considerably worse than that of the German population. Under the auspices of the Berlin Working Group on Structural Research in Health Care (BASIG), scholars from various disciplines presented this problem to the press—just in time for the Berlin Senate conference on foreigner integration in Berlin, scheduled for October 24 and 25. Using the example of Turkish women and children, BASIG spokesman Wilhelm Schraeder pointed out that the general state of health is closely related to the social situation. Foreigners are susceptible to risks beyond social discrimination; for example, language barriers make filing claims for medical benefits difficult. Moreover, there is the fear of losing one's job and—as a direct consequence of that—deportation. According to Schraeder, permanent harm from inadequate medical attention to foreigners will lead to high financial costs for society. [. . .]

Foreign children, according to Angela Zink from the Federal Public Health Department's Institute for Social Medicine and Epidemiology, are more frequently and more seriously ill than their German peers, and they are considerably more likely to become victims of accidents. Particularly more frequent are illnesses, infectious and parasitic diseases, as well as ailments of the intestinal tract, a physical response to their social situation. The Kreuzberg pediatrician Dr. Albrecht Spieß added that in his practice, five-year-olds were coming in with stomach ulcers, a phenomenon hardly conceivable among German children. Ms. Zink cited insufficiently furnished and often overcrowded apartments, the children's compulsion to reorient themselves to new nutritional habits, and the low rate of vaccination among foreign children as causes for their susceptibility.

According to Spieß, even when such illnesses are caught early, the mothers cannot devote sufficient attention to the children. They often lose their jobs because they have taken all of the legally allowed five sick days to care for their children.

5

"TOILET DECREE" FOR FOREIGNERS

First published as " 'Toilettenerlass' für Ausländer" in *Der Tagesspiegel* (October 10, 1979). Translated by Tes Howell.

STUTTGART. Whoever did not know it before can read about it now: "Sit (don't stand) on the toilet seat!" And so begins a pamphlet published by the Baden-Württemberg Ministry of Social Services, which was recently sent to local governments to be hung in bathrooms of dormitories for asylum seekers and the homeless.

Tip number 2 of this guide—which is published only in German and yet covers every detail for the predominantly non-German-speaking target audience—reads, "After purging the bowels, clean the anus carefully with at least two pieces of toilet paper, folded together, until the anus is completely clean. Use the left hand for this and as much new toilet paper as is necessary for proper cleanliness. Throw the used paper into the toilet bowl so that it is flushed with the excrement."

After the tip on how to flush the toilet come precise instructions for washing one's hands: "Allow the water flowing from the faucet to run over both hands, then put the soap in the palm of your hand and rub your palms together several times until foam develops. Now rub your hands together vigorously; then wash the lather from your hands with a lot of water." The "Recommendation for a hygienic cleaning after defecation" decrees in closing, "Dry your hands with a paper towel from the paper towel dispenser."

A spokesman for the Ministry of Social Services explained that German-language proficiency is necessary to comply with the guidelines. The spokesman addresses the question—whether a foreigner, who has never used a restroom, can even read and understand this tutorial—by adding that the ministry subsequently recommended that local health authorities translate the pamphlet into foreign languages. According to him, the lavatory regulations were sent to the authorities because of different prevailing hygiene practices—for example, of Muslims. Authorities in Hamburg had put out a similar "lavatory decree" a few years ago.

6

LETTER FROM RENTERS TO THEIR HOUSING DEVELOPMENT, "NEW HOMELAND"

First published as "Brief von Mietern an ihre Wohnungsbaugesellschaft 'Neue Heimat'" in *Der Tagesspiegel* (October 10, 1979). Translated by Tes Howell.

Dear Ms. _____ ,

"Turks Get Out" can already be seen written on the sides of buildings and construction trailers. This is clearly the opinion of the Charlottenburg population. The hatred of foreigners grows daily. So, what kind of apartment politics is the "New Homeland" (NH) playing in order to transform the redevelopment area of Klausen Place into a "Little Istanbul"? We do not want to become a second Kreutzberg *[sic]*. The foreigner-friendly employees of the NH should live with foreigners for a while and not just celebrate festivals with them. Then they would no longer sign rental contracts with them. IT IS OUTRAGEOUS to rent the apartments in a complex primarily to foreigners and to place Germans as a minority in the same house, just to document that Germans are also receiving apartments. In our case, five Germans equal two families, compared to approximately 22 foreigners equaling five families, and it must be noted that these facts are concealed when the foreigners sign the rental contract. If it must be this way, then Turks should be in one building and Germans in another. Habits and religious differences do not allow for the two to live together.

We, both German families, demand that the families [name omitted] and [name omitted] be moved and the apartments consequently vacated and rented to Germans—(but not to antisocial people such as those at 23 Seeling Street or welfare recipients). Tolerating the actions of foreigners for eight and a half months is enough. Furthermore, the rest should abide by the conditions of the rental contract and house rules. Despite several letters and meetings with the NH, not much has changed.

Statement on the Actions of the Foreigners

1. There are certainly more people living there than the number designated in the contract.
2. Loud music by [name omitted].
3. Noise from the children during quiet hours in the complex and courtyard. (In front, automobile noise; in the back, children's noise.) Soiling of the stairs and courtyard, as well as damage to the garden and the (almost daily) placing of rocks in the complex and courtyard doors to hold them open.
4. Odor in the stairwell because tenants leave apartment doors open while preparing food.
5. Constant visits by strangers during the day as well as in the evening (there is evidently a group of 35 people who go in and out from time to time).

Even tenant Mr. [name omitted] (a Turk) has stated that "it is like a hotel here" (though he does not dare complain).

It is outrageous that we have to tolerate families [name omitted]/[name omitted], who have already been evicted from several apartments and have been declared intolerable tenants.

Also, the family [name omitted] often receives visitors, sometimes up to 20 people, who bring chairs with them. They also bring with them considerable noise pollution so that we cannot sleep in our little room, because the visitors remain there late into the night. Slamming doors and running down the stairs is no rarity. In addition, the amount of garbage is larger because of increased food and drink consumption; as a result, the trash containers are always full. Products are emptied out of large cardboard boxes, which are then left next to the trash bins.

We ask for swift action in regard to our grievances.

7

MUSTAFA TEKINEZ

ARE WE NOT ALL HUMAN BEINGS?

First published as "Sind wir nicht alle Menschen?" in *Deutsches Heim, Glück allein: Wie Türken Deutsche sehen,* Dursun Akçam, ed. (Bornheim-Merten: Lamuv, 1982), 206–14. Translated by Tes Howell.

In a society, in which time is strictly organized and nerves are strained, any disruption of people's private lives is a difficult pill to swallow. No one likes people who occupy an apartment with their entire clan, who destroy the peace and quiet of their neighbors with noise, songs, and visits by friends and acquaintances. Cultural customs and conventions cannot be used here as a shield. People who run around streets and locales with pistols and knives, blocking the path for others and bothering women and young girls, are not welcome anywhere in the world. In short, these persistent, frequent misbehaviors have become a cause of misgivings in German society.

Admittedly, this fact is not enough to excuse the Germans' extreme self-centeredness, their asocial character, their rejection of foreigners (especially of Turks), or their invidious, at times hostile, behavior. Interpersonal relations cannot legitimate refusing to rent an apartment just because the potential renter is Turkish or not accepting someone as a neighbor, not allowing the person a voice in the public sphere, or endeavoring to isolate the individual everywhere.

Germans act strangely with one another, too, a phenomenon one rarely finds in other countries. There is no mutual love; at the center of all their relationships stand self-centeredness and mistrust. There are hundreds of thousands of examples. During a train trip, for example, a woman in a six-person compartment set down her bag on one seat and her coat on another so that no one would sit around her. And she did so despite the fact that the trains do not belong to her father, and everyone who has paid money has a right to a seat. When the number of men and women in a compartment reaches three, it is considered full. They sit with a sour expression, holding a newspaper, magazine, or a book. If someone opens the door and inquires after open seats, he or she is considered an intruder. They do not even look up from their reading. They hem and haw, trying to prevent the newcomer from entering. Even if the person spends hours standing in front of the compartment, no one will offer a seat. If this person has a brown skin color, is a Turk, they openly lie: "No seats here," say the Germans, who cannot lie. [. . .]

This self-centeredness and mistrust have shaped the faces of many German citizens, resulting in strained nerves and a stiff, frozen facial expression. They do not look at other people with friendly faces and laughing eyes. Only when they see their dogs does a slight smile come over their lips. But when human figures appear, this expression disappears. [. . .] I have never seen a German laughing and joking around. People who sit next to or across from each other in the same compartment do not talk to each other, do not converse. Eight, ten hours pass silently and voicelessly as though everyone were constantly ill-tempered.

8

DILEK ZAPTÇIOĞLU
LIVING IN TWO WORLDS

First published as "Leben in zwei Welten" in *Der Weltspiegel* (June 20, 1993). Translated by Tes Howell.

The "German Turks" are no homogeneous group. Social change has begun.

The first German I ever met taught a preparatory class at the German School in Istanbul. My adventure with the German language began in 1970, when I, along with other children, went through the great gates of the *Alman Lisesi* above the Genoese Galata Tower in Istanbul's Beyoğlu, the old Pera district. There were just a handful of us, and we were certainly privileged, for the German School was a private institute and charged stiff tuition fees. [. . .]

The German School was, and still is today, a multicultural educational institution. In addition to Turkish students, there were children from Greek and Armenian minority groups, students of Levantine Italian heritage, Turkish Jews, the progeny of White Russians (who had fled prior to the October Revolution), and, of course, Germans.

The latter were the children of our school's teachers, of German diplomats and consulate officials, of German businesspeople residing in Turkey, and of private individuals. They always sat together in the classroom and associated almost exclusively with each other. After school, they almost never accompanied us on our *Kafeterya* or *Sinema* visits, and because some of their parents were also their teachers, we could never persuade them to cut class when the weather was beautiful and take a trip to one of the islands near Istanbul. Our teachers never invited us to their houses. We knew only that they lived in the chic parts of Istanbul, Bebek, and Etiler and preferred to live as a "colony" among themselves. They had butcher shops where they could buy pork cutlets and pork/beef sausage and bakeries that baked those delicious German rolls and *Berliners*. Whatever consumer goods that they could not buy in Istanbul at that time (nowadays, one can find anything in Istanbul), they flew over from Germany via the consulate. We had no access to the German Ghetto.

Why am I relating all this here? After all, I was asked for an article about Turks in Germany, about their culture, customs, practices, and views. What does the German School in Istanbul have to do with the Ford worker Ahmet or the Kreuzberg produce vendor Yusuf? Or is the difference between the German colony in Istanbul and the Turkish colony in Kreuzberg not so great as it seems at first glance?

After the murders in Mölln and Solingen, the German media rediscovered the Turks. Now, while there is talk of new beginnings in the relationship with the Turkish minority, people want to know who the Turks are. Do the Turks even want to assimilate? The discussion centers on the Turks' "nonexistent will to integrate," on their "culture that has nothing to do with ours," as a *Der Spiegel* editor wrote after Solingen.

What is the Turkish culture? Is there even a "national culture"? What is, for example, the "German culture"? Clichés yield many extremes: pork knuckle versus roast lamb, church versus mosque, yodeling versus belly dancing. It becomes more dangerous when the clichés reveal their character as prejudicial: diligence versus laziness, human rights versus torture, order versus chaos, freedom versus head scarf.

Let's pause for a moment and ask ourselves whether the Germans possess a unified culture. Doesn't this notion remind us of forced *Gleichschaltung*, or social streamlining, and other phrases from National Socialism? Or of state socialism before its collapse? Isn't every liberal society "multicultural" in the sense that its individuals have completely different ways of living depending on social status, culture, and experience? Are we not condemning totalitarian regimes for this reason—because they require certain behaviors and ways of thinking, which they characterize as "national," "religious" or "socialist" culture, and do not tolerate any deviation?

The Turks have established a society in Germany and in Turkey that is every bit as heterogeneous as German, French, or British society. A Turkish doctor who works at the University Clinic in Cologne certainly has much more in common with his German colleagues than with the Turkish factory worker who came from the small village in Anatolia and only finished elementary school. In light of this fact, it is necessary to move once again away from the useless notion of "culture" to social-classification practices.

The majority of Turkish "guest workers" came to Germany from smaller hamlets in Anatolia. For these people, the recruitment contract with Turkey (dated October 30, 1961) meant the opportunity to move into a higher social class. They left their families behind and did not necessarily want to live here but rather to work and earn money. As Max Frisch rightly said, "One had called for workers, but human beings came." However, not even those who arrived realized this truth in the beginning.

When I visited Germany in the 1970s, several Turkish families lived in one apartment. They spent hardly any money and tried to save as much as possible in order to return home quickly. Their stay "abroad" was supposed to be limited to five or six years. For this reason, no one felt a need to establish a home, to increase one's German skills, let alone to ask about one's rights. The threefold motto was, "Don't stand out as objectionable; don't talk back to the German boss; don't annoy the foreigner police."

The image of the Turkish man, walking through the streets with a lowered head and furtively glancing around like a thief, epitomized the foreignness of the wandering worker.

Yes, the first generation did not feel comfortable here. Everything was strange: the kitchen, the smells, the surroundings, the language, the social etiquette. It was difficult for people to develop connections to a country in which they had no memories or personal history. Furthermore, they had come into one of the most advanced industrial nations in the world, due to precapitalist circumstances. Considering this journey into the tunnel of time, the first generation of Turks did well here despite everything, a fact that indicated their capacity to adapt.

Temporary residence abroad evolved into immigration on its own. The half-packed suitcases were unpacked in the 1980s. The negative experiences of returning to the homeland played an important role in this shift. To date, around 1.5 million Turks have returned to their homeland, following the introduced return incentives that the conservative-liberal coalition government paid in the 1980s. Turkish "Deutschländer" tried to establish new lives there with their savings. They soon noticed that not everything was as wonderful as they had imagined. They were foreign in Germany but also foreigners in Turkey.

The "employee societies," partially financed by government loans, went bankrupt and took the painstakingly saved capital of the returning immigrants with them. The children were subjected to special government measures like "integration courses" after failed attempts at entry into Turkish schools. New schools were opened for the children of returnees, and teachers from the Federal Republic were imported. After enduring assimilation pressure in the Federal Republic, the young people were now forced to integrate in Turkey.

In Istanbul, I met many of these young people who joined forces through "returnee organizations." They complained about the authoritarian educational system in Turkey, about the unusually harsh political conditions, about the strict moral rules and the social controls, under which they felt stifled.

Many were desperate about their situation and definitely wanted to return to Germany. But there were some who were the first harbingers of a new future: young people, whose perspective was influenced by a higher education, who did not feel like the ubiquitously invoked "lost generation" or like a "time bomb" on which society was sitting; they felt as though they were between two worlds, or rather living in two worlds. They were aware of the richness that their particular way of life had afforded them, and they felt at home in both countries and did not want to forsake either. The world was a small globe that people had separated into different states and upon which they had drawn senseless borders. Yes, the "Deutschländer" were different and wanted to be accepted in their differentness.

The number of these young people grew with time. Today, 1.8 million people of Turkish origin live in Germany, and 480,000 of them are under 15 years old. Over two-thirds of the Turks have been here at least 10 years and will remain. The immigration process shows no signs of abating. The third generation is growing up; it is undoubtedly more influenced by this country than by the homeland of its grandparents. Though this generation receives certain "Turkish values" from their parents, they will, however, be increasingly shaped by the customs here until their children will be distinguished from their German peers only by their appearance. Conformity to this society will certainly make their lives easier but will also remove the richness that life offers the wanderer between worlds.

The "German Turks," as they are known by some today, are not a homogeneous group. Even if they consist mainly of workers, and their children often occupy a position "at the very bottom" of German society because opportunities are not equal, there is also notable social change within the Turkish minority. Professor Faruk Şen, director of the Center for Turkish Studies in Essen, has noted for years that a Turkish middle class is slowly emerging in Germany.

Some 610,000 Turkish employees have a total annual income of 22.5 billion marks and pay 5 billion of that into the pension fund. Compare that with the mere 20 million marks that Turkish retirees receive in annual income. Many retired Germans are financed with the rest of this money. The buying power of the Turks is estimated at 50 billion marks. [. . .]

These days I speak with many Turks, other foreigners, and those who were made into foreigners. They are united in their rage. But they do not vilify "the Germans," for they know that there is no such thing. I, too, am inclined to sink into pessimism in light of the idleness of government authorities, the voicelessness of the intellectuals, and the general xenophobic atmosphere. The deep and never completely eradicated roots of racism in Germany and its manifestations—formidably violent and merciless in comparison to other countries—frighten me. Currently showing its ugly face again, this certainly does not benefit the country of Goethe and Schiller, Brecht and Benjamin. But I am not in favor of ascribing certain traits to certain "peoples" as unalterable.

Like many other foreigners who are closely connected to Germany through their biography, I wish that there would be a quick end to the resurgent barbarity in this country and that the great injustice that has befallen minorities for decades and has degraded them to objects of justice and administration be eliminated as quickly as possible. I would not like to regret that I walked through the gate of the German School in Istanbul over twenty years ago. The call "Germany to the Germans" would lead this country to a new catastrophe, be it only through the loss of the richness that living between worlds brings to everyone.

9

TANJA STIDINGER

AT MOST HALF A HOMELAND

First published as "Höchstens eine halbe Heimat" in *die tageszeitung* (May 15, 1993). Translated by Hilary Menges.

*Turkish senior citizens in Berlin: Sickness, isolation and financial woes
determine their daily lives. Few places for socialization and refuge exist for them.
Children and grandchildren are often the only ray of hope.*

BERLIN. When Zekeriya Eldemgil laughs, a row of golden teeth twinkles. At
least this afternoon he is amusing himself splendidly. Every Wednesday the
58-year-old retiree spends hours in the meeting room of the employment-
welfare center. Here, in the middle of Kreuzberg, he meets with his retired
compatriots, drinks tea, plays Tavla, gossips, and converses. "For me, this here
is an alternative diversion, otherwise there is nothing else for me to do. What
else should I do with myself?" he explains hesitantly. Zekeriya Eldemgil came
from Istanbul to Germany 28 years ago, and, like so many other Turks in his
generation, paid for the construction and preservation of Germany's economic miracle with his health.

He did piecemeal work for years and "never missed a day." Now he has a
serious metal allergy as a result of his factory labor. Three years ago, he went
into early retirement. Since then he, his wife, and his almost full-grown son
have lived on 724 marks of retirement income and 500 marks of social welfare per month. "How should this work? The rent still needs to be paid." No,
he says, slowly shaking his head, this is not how he envisioned old age.

Over 10,000 Turkish senior citizens and pensioners spend their remaining years of life in Berlin. Sickness, isolation, financial worries, and family
conflicts often determine their daily lives. Even if the condition is similar to
that of older Germans, a decisive component is added to the plight of first-
generation immigrants. "The German society has dismissed them for
decades. They consider themselves unwanted persons. They have always concentrated on their work, often above and beyond their own capacities. That's
why so many are physically and psychically ill," says Mustafa Çakmakoğlu
meditatively. The seniors are continually coming and going at the office
hours of the chair of the Turkish Community.

According to Çakmakoğlu, they almost always have language difficulties.
Because of the long-perpetuated illusion of returning home, only a few
thought it was necessary to learn the German language. "Besides, there was
no time for it, given the drudgery of work," he says curtly. At bureaus and at
the institution of social security (officially responsible for senior citizens),
they are helpless and insecure without interpreters. These problems are also
familiar to Erdoğan Özdinçer. The 57-year-old works for the foreigner information center DGB. "Many elderly come with questions and concerns; they
feel useless. And we thought, okay, we'll set up an association to solve their
problems."

Since then, the Association of Turkish Retirees has gained a membership
of over 100 members. Besides physical exercise, excursions, and meetings,
the program also offers social advising and assistance in cases of illness. "Se-

niors need contacts, too. They feel as if they have slogged away here and then are suddenly shoved into the corner and left alone," says Özdinçer.

This initiative of one's own seems to be long overdue. For people seeking help, there are not enough places of refuge. Initiatives and associations that specialize in seniors, such as the labor-welfare group, are overrun. Questions about care, housing, and sustenance for foreign employees are becoming more urgent. Increasingly, they are not remigrating back to their homelands, as the German state initially planned. Most spend the last years of their lives in a land that remains ever-foreign to them.

"Homeland," the Turkish Community's interpreter translates for Ali Ergin, "is not this here. At most a half." Ali Ergin, the 68-year-old from Ankara, came to Berlin in 1964 and worked in construction. He made a modest fortune for himself and spends half of the year in Turkey.

For most Turkish seniors, oscillation between here and there is the only possible way to live in their homeland without losing their German residency status. The threat of forfeiture lurks if one leaves the country for over six months. The physically ill prefer to remain in the Federal Republic full-time precisely because of its better medical care. Others agitatedly return to Berlin, only to find that they cannot find their way in either country.

Ergin's only ray of light was his children and grandchildren, "but I am losing them. They have no respect for me and live a different life than I do." The generational conflict bears heavily on this age group in particular. Erdogan Özdinçer summarizes: "They vacillate between pride for their children and lack of understanding for their way of life. After all, they didn't just work for their own benefit."

For 42-year-old Ayshe, who did tailoring piecework for over 20 years and retired early, her children are also her future: "I live only for them." She is also certain that they are the ones who will care for her and her husband in old age.

The Senate members responsible for foreigner representation are looking ahead, albeit timidly. Barbara John (CDU) reckons that in the future, more and more Turkish seniors will have to be placed in retirement homes and hospice. In a pilot study, she is offering Turkish women the option to receive advanced training in the area of elder care. "It is essential to prepare nursing staff who will know the language and culture of those in need of care, so they are not driven further into isolation."

This isolation is for the most part more intensive for retired Turkish women than for men. More and more elderly women visit the meeting and information center for Turkish women (TIO) in Kreuzberg. "While the men go to cafés and meet people there, the women stay at home and are responsible for the family and the household," reports Helga Göbel, a TIO worker.

Mustafa Çakmakoğlu tells of a Turkish saying that is applicable to the situation of the elderly. "One speaks of 'life between two mosques.' Our seniors belong neither to one nor the other fully. They have worked and given their all for both lands, Germany and Turkey. And now nobody knows where they should go."

10

ELKE ECKERT

SAYING "I DO" FOR THE CERTIFICATE

First published as "Das Jawort für den Schein" in *die tageszeitung* (November 22, 1994). Translated by Hilary Menges.

Immigration through the civil registry office: Foreigners marry Germans in order to stay here. The marriage certificate is bought. The more vigilant the authorities, the more imaginative the couples.

The wedding was without pomp. After the vows, the pair looked each other in the eyes shyly. The two made no more than a kissing motion. The groom threw a bashful glance at the small circle of friends, which another young man returned in kind. The registrar noticed nothing. The director of *Green Card* would have been gratified.

In the United States, marriages between strangers for the purpose of obtaining residence and work permits for the foreign partner are an alternative to immigration quotas and the yearly green-card lottery. This abuse of the law has also become a tradition in Germany in the face of insufficient immigration rights and practically dismantled asylum rights. It is a German-German history as well: the Kreuzberg freak who married a Leipzig woman seeking to emigrate had little to fear regarding criminal legal action.

If, in contrast, a German takes a Kurd or Palestinian as a husband, the Foreigner Bureau is on the scene without delay. The vigilance of civil servants inspires the fantastical imagination of the prospective spouses. In the case of the ex-Yugoslavian citizen mentioned at the beginning of the article, her German helpers found an especially original marriage variation. The husband of Milica will never "properly" marry: he is homosexual. Everything has been cleared with his boyfriend. The work of convincing Milica's boyfriend proves much harder. The young man was raised conservative, and he has been with Milica for two years. But Milica, who fled to Berlin on account of the war in April 1992, wanted to marry the gay man and not her boyfriend: "Peter is my boyfriend now, but how do I know whether or not that might change sometime?"

The two talked about marrying, but it would have been a marriage of convenience. The marriage of convenience with the homosexual friend rescues Milica from the extremely encumbering status as a refugee with a limited visa. Now she can travel and work everywhere: "If I had married Peter, I would have felt under pressure. I was afraid that if we argued I would be reproached or even be susceptible to coercion."

Doris Preiffer-Pandey from the IAF (Community Interest Group of Women Married to Foreigners) in Frankfurt suggests that fictitious marriages can also be "proper" marriages: "The separation of property, withholding household costs and alimony claims only come into question at the time of divorce; during the marriage, this is not possible." State educational loans and social security are cut off as soon as one of the partners starts earning an income. Should a partner become unable to work as a result of illness or accident, the other must "take responsibility for him just as in a real marriage."

Not even the IAF can estimate what percentage of binational marriages are actually marriages of convenience. But estimates of 50 percent to 70 percent were certainly too high and, according to Pfeiffer-Pandey, came "from people who have something against binational marriages anyway." However, at the IAF, it is well known that young men, "particularly those from North African countries like Morocco and Algeria," attempt to marry into Germany. Even in the Berlin IAF office, manager Lima Eurvello deplores the trickery of many African citizens: "Some come to Germany already having obtained the official certification of their unmarried status. They know exactly what they need in order to marry here."

For its part, the IAF advises against fictitious marriages altogether, because they bring about too many complications. Nevertheless, Pfeiffer-Pandey expresses understanding for foreigners who attempt to gain a residency permit this way: "For the inhabitants of non-European countries, with the exception of the United States, Canada, and Switzerland, it is impossible to immigrate legally. All borders are hermetically sealed." Therefore, for the past 20 years, the IAF has promoted "at least some kind of immigration quota."

Michael was introduced by a friend to a woman from Thailand, who asked him outright if he would marry her. Her offer sounded tempting to this welfare recipient: the young woman intended to pay him 8,000 marks. Her relatives had saved money for years in order to send her to Germany. Once here, she was to marry and earn money to support her family from afar. IAF associate Pfeiffer-Pandey estimates that the price tag for such fictitious marriages averages between 5,000 and 10,000 marks.

Michael acquiesced to the bargain, and the wedding took place. He suspects, though, that the Foreigner Bureau is hot on the trail of the German-Thai couple: "At the wedding at the registry office, we barely made an effort to appear 'real.' I came in jeans and a bomber jacket, and she wasn't exactly in a bridal gown." The Foreigner Bureau would have been justified in wondering, because the two officially announced a so-called separation year just a few weeks after the marriage. They want to get divorced in one year. Shortly after the marriage, the Thai woman met another man who would marry her for love and not money.

Neza, a friend of Milica's, met her future husband, Sven, in a Kreuzberg bar. Just like her friend, the Bosnian Serb fears being sent back to her bombed-out homeland, where she no longer can envision a life or job for herself. She immediately accepted the man's offer to marry her and consequently supply her with a work and residency permit, because Sven was willing to do this favor without financial compensation. He comes from Kreuzberg's autonomous scene, where marriage is usually not an issue. But marriage with a foreigner flatters the ego. According to Sven, "One is well-received in the scene when one does it." This political correctness [original in English] among independents shows solidarity on the one hand and undermines foreigner and asylum policy on the other.

The Foreigner Bureau has not remained passive in cases of suspected fictitious marriages. In addition to home visits during the night or day and questioning of neighbors, parents, or employers, the couple will be summoned to the bureau and interviewed separately there. Once a fictitious marriage has been identified, the residency permit for the foreigner partner becomes invalid, because it is contingent upon the continuance of the union through the first four years of marriage. During this time, a "marital cohabitation" in the Federal Republic must continue to exist, in keeping with the Foreigner Act.

The Regional Council in Leipzig is taking new steps to prevent abuse of the law. Karin Pergold, manager of the Leipzig-based IAF office, has noticed in her consultations that many binational couples mention that the foreign partner only received a year-long residence permit. But the foreigner law reads that "according to regulation, a three-year residence permit" can be granted. In the summer, an internal memo from the district office in Leipzig to the civil registrars was leaked to IAF. The signatories of the circulated letter requested in cases of marriage with a foreigner "that the Foreigner Bureau be broadly informed" of all the details. The possible indicators of fictitious marriage were listed in a checklist. Next to asylum seekers, the suspicion is focused on men and women from developing and third-world countries. Further "indicators" include illegal residence in the Federal Republic, difficulties in linguistic communication between the "fiancés," or an "unusual difference in age."

The circulated letter continues, "If, as a result of your inquiries, you reach the conclusion that a fictitious marriage is intended, you shall orally decline the notice of intended marriage and the performance of the wedding ceremony." A written notification should be sent "only upon the fiancés' demand." Another circulated letter recommends a further, more inconspicuous variation to the district office of registrars: in the case of suspected fictitious marriage, the written memorandum of intended marriage shall be provisionally acknowledged as received, but after a week, the couple will be orally informed of the rejection of their notice. Only if the couple insists does it become necessary that a written and legally instructive rejection follow. It is not known if a similar practice exists in other federal states.

Berlin-based attorney Petra Schlagenhauf has had her own experiences with the fictitious marriage investigations of the Foreigner Bureau. One couple "from the alternative scene" suspected of fictitious marriage was invited to the bureau for questioning. The young couple had married shortly prior to imminent deportation. Petra Schlagenhauf says, "The civil servant attempted to judge the two based on his own ideas about typical marriage. There were questions such as 'What is your husband's hobby?' or 'What TV magazine does your wife read?' "

At the end of the procedure, even the civil servant no longer felt comfortable in his own skin. In answer to the question "What stove does your wife cook on?" the young man answered irritably that he is actually the one who cooks. The couple courageously passed the difficult test; they had married for love.

11

WULF EICHSTÄDT AND DENIZ GÖKTÜRK

ALL QUIET ON THE KREUZBERG FRONT

First published as "In Kreuzberg nichts Neues" in *die tageszeitung* (November 1, 1994). Translated by Tes Howell. Göktürk discusses architecture and city planning with Eichstädt, a contributor to the International Building Exhibition, who consulted on city restoration projects in Berlin's East Kreuzberg neighborhood.

DG: The current *Intertaz* newspaper theme is "the leftists and the foreigners." Districts like Hamburg-Altona or Berlin-Kreuzberg are emerging as zones of contact. How did it happen that many foreigners, artists, social dropouts, and members of the leftist-alternative scene settled in these former working-class districts?

WE: In Berlin, the influx of foreigners began in the late 1960s, later than in other West German cities. Berlin-Kreuzberg was a special case, for this district had lost its workforce after the construction of two large satellite towns. The skilled worker who could afford it and the average working class family moved to Buckow-Rudow or the Märkisches Viertel, a new housing development in the northwest of West Berlin. In the days of the 1967 student revolts, I often spent evenings in Kreuzberg bars and heard the workers comment on the "student squabbles." At that time a classic worker population still lived there, and there wasn't a single foreigner. A vacuum then resulted from so many residents moving away to the satellite towns, and the Turkish population quickly filled it. In the early 1970s, we traveled with great enthusiasm through Kreuzberg to enjoy the food and hospitality in the new Greek and Turkish bars, which we had experienced on our international trips.

The mood soon changed, though, and the population became a displaced mass during a powerful redevelopment process that peaked in 1973–74. Familiar examples are the areas around the Wassertorplatz, the Böcklerpark, and Naunyn Street, where housing organizations evacuated the dwellings and pushed Turkish families into other demolition areas so that the people could not reside anywhere permanently. This cynical association between the city and its people outraged ever-widening spheres. Another policy existed behind the redevelopment machinery that was implemented far more aggressively in Wedding—namely, that of targeting the Turks for removal. This policy was problematic, however, because no one knew where to send them.

DG: How do the different scenes in Kreuzberg interact?

WE: We at the IBA city restoration project have strongly supported the squatters because they handle the houses with care and have been tolerant toward the foreigner population. Of course, this tolerance stems from a social romanticism and a young, middle-class ethic, but originally it was based on the premise that these young people would not compete with foreigners in the labor market. For example, a grocery vendor from Wrangel Street found that a Turkish store had taken away his customers and, with them, his livelihood. It is often said of the Turkish youth that they are brighter, more disciplined, and efficient than the German underdogs from broken families. This notion laid the foundation for hatred. Gradually, a population evolved that was capable of living together. At the time, I kept a close eye on Cuvry Street. This is a mazelike, spacious ensemble with factory buildings in the courtyard that house the alternative scene. The homes facing the front are almost exclusively occupied by Turks. The advantages, which could be gained for the Turkish population, were dependent on the squatters' having first brought the demolition machinery to a halt. The one is not imaginable without the other, even if they were to draw lines of demarcation in the houses and courtyards again. But there are no essential conflicts.

DG: People eat döner kebabs or buy vegetables in a Turkish store, but they aren't living "together."

WE: That's completely right—hardly any interaction. But there is a phenomenon here that I believe is very important. The Turks have allowed a political vacuum to develop because they had no right to vote and no political presence. Approximately one-third of the city's population has not been represented in political decisions. Because of this vacuum, the initiatives and later the Green Party's Alternative List were able to gain so much influence.

DG: Was that influence positive or negative?

WE: In terms of developing the character and specific integration makeup of Kreuzberg, it was certainly positive. But if one wants to judge the development of Kreuzberg overall, then I see things quite ambivalently today. But I think there was no other reasonable way. I would not like to lose this Kreuzberg, but it has not generated anything positive for many years. In the mid-1980s, when it became clear that our society was rich enough to paint buildings bright colors and build new facilities, we saw that we had failed. After the first great successes were achieved on the construction site, we debated intensively about how to promote social stabilization (for example, assistance for better education and jobs). But the willingness of politicians to support that project on a larger scale was practically nonexistent, and this reluctance laid a foundation for the current social conditions, which are, of course, very troubling.

A good example of this isolated coexistence is our relationship to Islam. No one associated with the German initiatives understood this phenomenon, myself included. Turkish friends who helped with our work in Kreuzberg were secularized Turks from academic families in Istanbul, who distance themselves from Anatolian devoutness. Aside from a long debate about the question of whether a mosque should be built at the Görlitzer train station square (although it was unclear who should pay for it), there was never an intelligent, thoughtful discussion in which religious experts explained or asked anything. For me, that is a clear sign that intercultural interest is fundamentally low.

DG: Where did the dialogue break down?

WE: Social coexistence consisted of dissociations that enabled the perception of the other as inferior. Many questions were left unanswered. I personally have often felt the absence of an articulation of Turkish interests by Turks themselves. Along with young Turkish intellectuals, we have spoken as representatives for the Turks, but it never resulted in legitimized political representation. No one is paying any attention to the high unemployment rate among Turkish youth. There is also no sympathy among Germans from varying social backgrounds. The new bourgeoisie of Kreuzberg is simply not interested in the underdogs. [. . .]

12

KONRAD SCHULLER

LAST DAYS ON GERMAN SOIL

First published as "Die letzten Tage auf deutschem Boden" in *Frankfurter Allgemeine Zeitung* (September 23, 1995). Translated by David Gramling.

SEPTEMBER 22, 4:10 P.M. Because of the risk of suicide, they had to take the belt away from the prisoner. He comes in with empty belt loops, presses the palm of his hand against the glass barrier in greeting, and asks that his name not be used. He doesn't have much time. The walk through the first gate, the second gate, the passport check, and the staircase to the cells has cost us 10 of the 30 minutes allotted for our visit.

This is Berlin's Krupp Street Prison. Of the 2,459 people sent back to their homelands from German deportation centers in the year 1994, most of them spent their last days in Germany here: rejected asylum seekers, felons at the end of their sentences, the mean and the mild, the sick and the healthy, youth and adults. The drug dealer sits here next to the desperate refugee, who is here not because of a crime he might have committed but because he must leave the country. This type of custody does not count as punishment. It is only supposed to ensure that the deportation candidate is on hand when the hour comes.

Boredom nags at the unnamed prisoner. Twenty-three hours in front of the communal television, one hour in the yard, day after day, month after month. Uncertainty eats away at one's sanity; it makes one's nerves vibrate. The conditions here over those months make a classical prison seem like an amusement park. Deportation custody is not supposed to accomplish reintegration into society, and consequently such efforts are neither required nor provided. In contrast to the penitentiary in Moabit right around the corner, activities, training, weekend visits, and furloughs are impossible here. Unlike criminal custody, deportation custody is only presumed to last a few days, and consequently the overcrowded residence halls and other conditions are thought to be tolerable, as the man without a belt tells us. The fact that health care is nonexistent here and medical treatment is geared toward the singular goal of ensuring that deportees are capable of transportation arises from the belief that patients' chronic illnesses are the responsibility of their home country. Thus, instead of therapy, painkillers are prescribed; instead of an expensive cast for a polio patient, only an ointment. Those infected with HIV have to eat the same institutional meals as everyone else, despite their special nutritional needs.

Our time is almost up. Only now does the man behind the glass come to the point. Activist organizations such as the Berlin Initiative against Deportation Custody have claimed over and over that the Krupp Street facility is a bastion of arbitrariness, humiliation, and even violence. A list of incidents supports this claim. One concerned a prisoner who was allegedly struck in the groin area by staff because he requested too many bathroom breaks. [. . .]

Considering these conditions and the recent provisional decision of the administrative court of Greifswald, that deportation custody requires a legal foundation, the grand coalition [CDU/SPD] in power in Berlin proposed a law that would address some of the needs of deportees. "Normal living without the freedom" was the formula with which SPD representative Barthels articulated the plan. The proposal does indeed provide for some improvements; prisoners shall be allowed to work during their custody; each shall be given his own room after six months of custody. Families will be able to stay together, and prisoners will be able to receive guests after a "certain period of time." [. . .]

13

HÜSEYIN A.

APARTMENT WANTED

First published as "Mietgesuche" in *Mittelhessische Anzeigenzeitung,* a classified-advertising newspaper in Hesse (June 16, 1996). Translated by David Gramling.

Young Turkish family with four-year-old daughter seeks a three- or four-room apartment with kitchen and bath in Gießen for 1,200 German marks, utilities included. Telephone: 0641/394685. Warning: our advertisement sounds harmless, but just like other foreign families, we aren't entirely unproblematic. We have just one daughter now, but soon we will multiply like locusts. In a few years, we will have several loud, dirty children with bad manners who will raise hell in the building. These little urchins will run around screaming all day, and you won't understand a word they are saying. If your house has a well-tended, orderly yard with beautiful flowers, plants, and trees, you will no longer recognize it after a few short minutes. Our children will promptly and completely destroy it, and we will hang our laundry out there instead. The only time the laundry will not be there is when we invite our countless relatives and acquaintances to grill with us. By the way, we slaughter our lambs in the bathtub on principle. If we move in, the entryway will smell like garlic and exotic spices. Deafening Turkish Jada music will waft from our open windows all day. At least once a week, the woman of the house will be beaten to the point that she needs hospitalization. For this reason, we will be a well-known address for the local police. A squad car will often appear and shine its searchlight in front of your house, because we will often be involved in shady dealings that threaten internal order. Knifings are normal for us. Although we are a three-person family, we will have at least twenty people in our apartment, because we are constantly having visitors. If you are one of those people who still vacations in Turkey, even though it seems that Turkish automatons are falling from the sky like dead birds, then perhaps we still have a chance to rent an apartment in your building, for apparently you will never learn your lesson. Does this sound crazy to you? We look forward to your telephone call.

14

HAJO SCHUMACHER

MORE FOREIGN THAN THE TURKS

First published as "Fremder als die Türken" in *Der Spiegel* (April 14, 1997). Translated by Tes Howell.

Multikulti is the magic word that describes the dream of peaceful coexistence. The reality, evident in the first multicultural residential project, is a long way off.

Okay, "that the Poles are strange" is something Mr. Paffrath already knew, but that "they are even stranger when they own their own apartment" was new to him; "so reserved—just strange somehow." Conciliatory, Paffrath raises his hand to his mouth and mutters, "I didn't want to say anything."

Having brought down his garbage, the early retiree now takes a walk around the block. In front of the Turkish produce store he stops to sort apples in the display: "They should all be in a row."

Paffrath knows a lot about other nationalities. At Easter, he was in London; last fall, in the Madeira sun. He sees himself as a "citizen of European culture." Do the Poles actually belong to this culture too? Mr. Paffrath thinks about this a bit. It doesn't matter anyway.

Paffrath is a guinea pig. And, as such, his tolerance is tested on a daily basis. For he is surrounded by more culture than he would like: Poles, Russian Germans, Turks, Brazilians, non-Rhenish Germans, Cambodians. Result: "You can forget about *multikulti.*"

For a year and a half, Paffrath, 55, has lived with his wife and son in Germany's first multicultural residential project in Volkhoven-Weiler, which, depending on the wind, gets polluted air from the Ford factory, Bayer Leverkusen, or Kölner City.

One hundred families purchased apartments in the rectangular building that shields a manicured courtyard from the outside world. Following the wishes of a pastor, a real-estate firm, and a dozen other like-minded citizens, the project was supposed to prove that what has failed in the nation can succeed on this small residential block.

For example, Corina Läpple, 28, from number 14, was born for such multicultural projects. She found it exciting and positive that Kim, 5, and Tom, 2, will grow up with children from all over the world. And she and her husband, the IT technician Markus, 33, were curious to get to know the children's parents.

Down in the courtyard, Mrs. Läpple hoped the multicultural life with all its great diversity would blossom in the summer: aromas of exotic food, the laughter of happy and appreciative people, children of all skin colors playing together.

Unfortunately, the German monoculture has so far been stronger. When her son toddled across the freshly seeded lawn, he was promptly "yelled at." In the pond that collects rainwater, the children are not allowed to wade because of insurance issues. And to be on the safe side, the owners of the ground-floor apartments have enclosed their towel-sized gardens with an anti-international protective hedge.

A few particularly sensitive residents even had fast-growing decorative woods planted to shield them from view. However the turbo-reforestation was against house regulations. Now meter-high walls of wooden lattice separate the lots.

"So far it hasn't been all that warm-hearted," comments Mrs. Läpple calmly. She received no replies—not even negative ones—to her invitation for brunch and Advent coffee. Only the Ouy family from Cambodia thanked her for the offer.

The Ouys, who fled torture and hunger in their homeland 20 years ago, had expected more togetherness from the project. "That will come still— maybe," hopes Mrs. Ouy politely. "At any rate, we have learned to make do everywhere we go."

And thus the residential block on Fühlinger Weg reflects the German norm regarding coexistence, tolerance, patience, and respect. Recently, the community quarreled hopelessly about the common spaces—conceived by the project's planning committee as a multicultural nucleus.

Partyers stand in opposition to those seeking peace and quiet. Mr. Paffrath, who lives across from the common room, likens parties in the isolated room to "[them] dancing in my bed." Meanwhile, a German gymnastics group is now practicing there. The community newspaper, whose goal is to promote cohesion, never made it to print. Many dismissed it as outright "silly."

The tanning salon Flamingo-Sun on the first floor is, as the neighbors joke, the most multicultural because stiff-necked neighbors can at least attain a "foreign" complexion there.

Mrs. Läpple complains that "one should really be ashamed" of some of her fellow residents. At a recent meeting, a German man complained loudly enough for all to hear about "the damn foreigners." At that point, Mrs. Läpple was looking forward to some "hopefully audible resistance."

However, the victims hung their heads and acted as though they had not heard. Afterward, someone explained to her that it makes little sense to have such discussions, because they only evoke further injury. Experience teaches that it is bad enough to be foreign in Germany; it is worse to be rebellious.

Perhaps, Mrs. Läpple supposes, it would have helped if the Society for Multicultural Living, established by the Ratingen-based real-estate firm Interboden, had let prospective buyers know from the beginning what they were planning to do. Many buyers did not learn of the firm's intention until they had signed the contract.

To avoid scaring away those people who had little interest in other cultures, the clever brokers kept several lists of new residents: this group received a list with overwhelmingly familiar German names, whereas the Läpples saw one with foreign names.

However, despite the low cost of approximately 3,500 marks per square meter, it was not only the natives who declined the offer. Many potential

Turkish buyers, fearing right-wing extremists who could be attracted by the label *multicultural,* said "no thanks."

Yet the building contractors assured them that there was no reason for panic. Following the 1993 attack on a Turkish residence in Solingen, they had begun to build particularly secure window frames and shutters that made break-ins almost impossible.

But the Islamic candidates remained skeptical. What should they think of planners who had, in the blueprints, aligned the toilets directly facing Mecca? And so, instead of the projected two-thirds, only 38 of 104 apartments went to foreigners, with a higher percentage of Germans in the project than in the surrounding concrete jungle of the Cologne suburb Chorweiler.

Meanwhile, real-estate agent Reiner Götzen, 45, is quite happy "that we do not have such enormous diversity. Otherwise, we would overload the project."

So that the foreign vitality does not bubble over, Götzen has implemented "strict German house regulations" because "the Southerner doesn't really get going until night time."

Islam expert Werner Wanzura, 54, provides mental support for the project. The pastor of the St. Cosmas and Damian congregation [. . .] has already learned something. "The Poles," explains this emissary of Pope Karol Wojtyla, "are more foreign to us than the Turks."

Various strategies were planned to improve the situation in the beginning. However, neither the promised social worker nor the announced day-care center materialized. And there is no café, which was to be a communal meeting place. The swift end to the flower shop probably scared away interested tenants.

The team behind the project showed real engagement just once. In the summer of last year, Wanzura and the Catholic educational organization put on a symposium. For two days, scholars competed in Wanzura's congregational hall over who had the most innovative idea to present.

Herbert Schnoor, former interior minister of North Rhine–Westphalia, ruminated over "the multicultural society—threat or chance?" Professor Stefan Gaitanides of Frankfurt presented on the "systemic conditions for a multicultural agreement within our democratic structure in the context of international conflicts." Professor Erich Schneider-Wessling of the Munich Academy of Fine Arts countered imaginatively with "integrative residential possibilities for people from different cultures—architectural design in cultural colors."

Mrs. Läpple was in the audience there, too. Unfortunately, she "understood nothing, to be honest." Except this: "There was no way it was about us."

15

K. BERGER

THE THAI WIFE: MEDICINE FOR GERMAN MEN DAMAGED BY WOMEN'S LIBBERS?

Published as "Die Thaifrau—Medizin für emanzengeschädigte deutsche Männer?" in 2000 at http://guide.thaifrau.de. Translated by David Gramling.

In this age of globalization, many Europeans who are disgusted by the increasing masculinization of the female in private and professional life and deeply repulsed by women's lib in this country are naturally looking beyond the borders of their own homeland. Thanks to the ways that men are open to the world and able to adjust to the customs of foreign cultures, more and more appear to be succeeding in freeing themselves from the constraints of worn-out conventions and prejudices and are searching and finding happiness in far-off lands in tropical regions.

It is also a dream among many men to conquer a woman from a land where woman can still be woman and man can still be man—not a "little guy." He can take her back to his chillier homeland and live with her for the long term.

Many have had frequent opportunities to make first contact. On vacations in tropical countries like Thailand, many encounters with the beauties of the land have taken place. In the vast majority of cases, this first encounter turned out to be a meeting between a man and a female representative of the more commercial sort.

However, men discovered to their amazement that a Thai lady, even if she is working in this particular industry, is usually endowed with much natural charm and deals with her customers in a friendlier and more cheerful way than her German counterparts do. Thus, many tolerance-oriented Europeans eventually toy with the idea of leading this lady, in whose pleasant company he has never for even a second felt like the usual john or tourist, back onto the path of virtue and considers staying with her beyond the period of the vacation.

It is no longer uncommon today for a cosmopolitan, self-confident German man to return from a vacation with an exotic woman and to become the envy of his colleagues at home. A wild Asiatic thoroughbred female can easily turn the heads of even the coolest European. This fact does not sit well with many German ladies; indeed, they may be threatened by the prospect of falling short in men's assessment of the feminine characteristics they seek. If we rely on experiential accounts, the Thai lady generally brings an acquired tendency to please the man and perceives a harmonious life together as her highest purpose. Her childlike, naive femininity and traditional sense of family could also doubtlessly awaken the desire among many men never to allow this tryst with the creature of their dreams to end.

In the moments after they have survived some hot adventure and the cool European intellect calls again, intelligent men will of course ask the question whether they could maintain their right path in the future when sharing it with a lady of the "profession," whether they will ever be able to drive the bar life out of the lady after they have succeeded in getting the lady out of the bar.

Those who do not feel up to such truly difficult tasks should not immediately become discouraged and throw in the towel but should pursue other paths that might also lead to the goal they long for. Of course, these strategies are not as fast and comfortable as the commercial contact venues, but on this more time-consuming path in search of happiness, the end result could prove significantly better.

If the opportunity should arise, one should at least make an attempt to learn 100 to 200 words in the foreign language, with a focus on the essential elements of daily life—for example, shopping, eating, drinking, sleeping, driving, man-woman relationships, and similar topics—so that nothing can stand in the way of interesting journeys of discovery outside the tourist centers. One can find smaller locations with little markets and festivals and other interesting places that are not constantly overrun with streams of tourists. In this way, with a humble knowledge of the language, one can make contact with the "normal population" and thus also automatically make contact with feminine comeliness. He who can diplomatically broach the topic of his interest in a female Thai partner on such occasions will often be surprised how quickly he will find these desired contacts.

Another alternative that could spare one elaborate traveling and effort would be a partner-placement agency, in which case one must make sure not to be ripped off by a zealous sales-oriented enterprise. Often, the marketing for such agencies uses actresses and models who are not even available but are only tempting decoys. At the same time, one can find partner-placement agencies nowadays that provide services for no fees and operate the placement agency simply in order to offer an alternative to the more commercial venues and big businesses and to assist those searching for prospective partners in their search for happiness, without much in the way of expenditure. (See examples on the Internet at http://www.thaifrau.de.)

In any case, after successful contact is established, it is the job of the one seeking a partner to make a choice and ascertain whether he intends to live together. The greatest possible number of commonalities is usually recognized to be one of the most important preconditions for realizing a harmonious partnership. With two people who come from completely different cultures and emotional worlds, no one can count on the immediate fulfillment of these preconditions. But if both partners demonstrate goodwill to accommodate each other as much as possible in this area, a very happy relationship can result. Different cultural backgrounds and interests can coalesce into a grand, functional unity. A commonly spoken and understood language is unquestionably crucial as soon as possible—so, German when the place of residence is Germany.

It could be an unpleasant surprise to the woman who has taken a great leap into our country if she suddenly finds out that her ostensible big man is making ends meet in his German homeland with resources that are relatively as meager as hers had been before. Most women become acquainted with their new environment rather quickly and soon learn to treasure and use its amenities. For some individuals, integration will of course be more difficult. It should be taken as axiomatic that the higher the level of education, the less arduous the adjustment. Problems can be expressed, explained, and solved.

Those with more simple natures do not have it so easy in this regard. They quickly pine for their former life, the home climate they are used to, their parents' house, and cheerful conversation with their own kind. Their German protector and teacher will need to take some initiative to avoid the quick withering away of his wife and must not break off connections to her homeland too severely in the initial period. In this case, it would be very helpful if it were possible for her to watch the television channel Thai TV Global Network, which is broadcast throughout Europe 24 hours a day and presents a constant and comfortable connection to her homeland and an interesting source of information.

He should exercise caution when choosing his circle of acquaintances. Some men have learned the hard way that the cheerful small Thai community in whose company his wife feels so at home is an organization of swindlers whose main vocation consists in quickly gambling away the income of their husbands. Only by immediately putting on the emergency brake—by cutting off the funds, that is—can this problem be resolved, no matter how difficult this might be. A horrible end is better than an endless horror and is the only solution in such cases. No one should believe, however, that gambling is a purely Thai problem. Germans are also significantly affected by this behavior as well.

Another problem concerns the pronounced sense of family of the Thai lady. It is not categorically a positive characteristic but rather one that could have disastrous effects for the German husband if not monitored and managed with precision. A disproportionate transfer of shared household funds to Thailand could also mean quick financial ruin for the German partner. Many Thai families are in no sense demure in expressing their desires and making demands on the daughter living in the supposedly affluent paradise, and they are uncommonly imaginative when it comes to inventing new reasons for bringing about yet another lucrative funds transfer. At the very latest, after the brother's third severe motorcycle accident or the costly burial of a grandmother that had already been financed four years earlier, a red light should go off for even the dumbest *Farang*, or foreigner, and the emergency brake should be pulled. It is also not absolutely necessary for the wife's brothers in Thailand to have a cell phone on their belts as a status symbol when it becomes clear that, since their sister's wedding in Germany, they can no longer take care of their own living costs despite available employment opportunities.

Those who consider such examples to be simply bad jokes could soon find themselves in the embarrassing position of experiencing these things live in their own intimate family circle. Men are well advised to avoid such incidents and to behave like one who never lets go of the wheel and always remains vigilant. In this way, they can be relatively certain that such unpleasant events will not arise. But in no case should one generalize from these kinds of events. That would also do injustice to the many Thai women who have adjusted very well to German conditions in happy and exemplary marriages. And men should never be discouraged from looking around among the always-fascinating beauties of Thailand for an appropriate partner.

It is said that every man is the forger of his own happiness, and taking on a vivacious Thai lady, and thus a little Sabai and Sanuk from the Thai way of life, could guarantee a meaningful dash of spice to the daily life of many a dispassionate European man.

16

KLAUS HARTUNG

ENTERPRISE KREUZBERG

First published as "Unternehmen Kreuzberg" in *Die Zeit* (August 2, 2001). Translated by David Gramling. In 2003, the Kreuzberg Museum documented local housing initiatives in the exhibition *History in the Making: Berlin at Kottbusser Gate*. Hartung (b. 1940) is a frequent commentator on Berlin economic and urban development.

Kreuzberg Center used to be a symbol of misery and the ghetto. Now it is becoming livable. Civic sensibility and business ideas, not subsidies or politicization, have helped improve conditions. Here, the citizen is making his own reforms. On the forefront: a finance attorney.

A staircase. A symbol. A simple, filigree steel construction. But who notices it? Hardly anyone who comes around "the Kotti," the Kottbus Gate—the symbolic site of civil war, ghetto, and decline in Kreuzberg—takes note of it. And whoever turns down Adelbert Street to drive through the cement mass of the New Kreuzberg Center (NKZ), would not see this staircase, only that old image of a social powder keg. He also will not see the three new maple trees, which suggest some kind of small piazza. The giant cliff of exposed concrete in the stony sea of Berlin, the concrete of a thousand social-welfare residents and Turkish hustle and bustle, has clearly established itself as a symbol. It signals failed integration, ghettoization of Turks, drug scenes. The Kreuzberg Christian Democrats were thinking of this place when they demanded that "Germany come to recognize itself again."

For the CDU godfather, Klaus Landowsky, it was Berlin's "center of criminality." According to him, "no one can get a handle on it." His suggestion in March 1998: demolish it. The NKZ was also a symbol in Turkey; the "Gallery" constructed over Adelbert Street was known as the "Galata Köprüsü," or Galata Bridge. Kurds ruled this massive bridge with their gambling salons and pool halls. The dual-purpose concrete ramps that led up to it were like fortress entrances, pasted over with layers of political posters promoting the Marxist-Leninist struggle.

"Nothing against Kurds, but no one liked to go up there. It just was not pleasant," said Hakan Kir, who now has his elegant Allianz agency in the Gallery. The cement steps have been torn out. The new ornamental steel staircase suggests a gentle disavowal of the cement fort of social problems. According to the architect Claudia Grünberg, who now works here, people noticed that "something has changed here." In 2000, city-planning senator Peter Strieder hastened to inaugurate the bridge and to announce the allocation of 7 million marks in investment capital by the "neighborhood management," to be used for building and environmental renovation.

For the new business director, Peter Ackermann, what began with the new staircase is nothing less than a "model case of integration." It is the official end of the NKZ and beginning of the Kreuzberg Center—"Kreuzberg Merkezi." That is the new name. So reads the new illuminated sign on the cement bridge over Adelbert Street, painted bordeaux and violet. The logo: a yellow sunbeam and a green point.

Utopia and Social Misery

A model case for integration? When Peter Ackermann speaks of this effort, it is a businessman speaking, not a social worker or politician. Ackermann's motto has always been "Then I'll do it myself." When he took over the Kotti situation in 1999, it was clear to him that "it's not an object that one administrates. It must be shaped." But before speaking of a model case, one must know that Ackermann's story has a prehistory. Social utopias don't just fall from the sky. On the contrary, the misery began with social utopia. When the NKZ was introduced in 1970, talk of a new world was churning. A neglected Kreuzberg would receive a showpiece, a European center of the East, a mezzanine of Kreuzberg businesses, reading rooms, a swimming pool, ateliers, department stores, terrace cafés, a cinema for drinking and smoking, a greenbelt. "Mercantile, cultural, and residential areas will form a comfortable unity with artists, street singers, hand-organ players, and bookstore shoppers." [. . .]

From the outset, the project was perceived as an impertinence. The giant cement half-shell at Kotti was only thinkable because the city's freeway and the demolition of Luisenstadt were part of the plan. For the first time, the Kreuzberg "neighborhood" rebelled and organized against it. A faction of the Berlin left housed the Organization of the Proletarian Avant-Garde and mobilized the district. A core developed that later would become the successful squatter movement. This provoked yet another political consequence: the strategies of the "mindful urban renewal." The IBA, the International Architectural Exhibit, opened at the beginning of the 1980s. There, expertise was developed for the "critical reconstruction" of the contemporary city. Berlin stood to gain much from the NKZ: a regenerative city plan, including the rescue of the Luisenstadt, a new identity of alternative neighborhood self-determination, and a paradoxical touristic allure in a new arena of Turks and the autonomous left. But the NKZ offered no such benefits.

Already during construction, technical costs were cut. No showpiece, no mezzanine with singers, only negative social selection instead. People with residence permits and urgent-appeal status moved in, mostly Turks with many children. The Social Welfare Bureau paid most of the rents. Apartments were passed on from renter to renter. It was similar with the businesses. The bazaar ruled supreme: entrepreneurial partnerships with hidden bosses, hot money and businesses with offshoot businesses. Within a bakery, one could also set up a prostitution business. The punks came, along with the winos and junkies. The place had degenerated into a "toilet" and a trash can for syringes, according to one bank sales clerk. [. . .]

With Ackermann doing it on his own, things are going quickly. Step by step. A new name, a new logo. One hundred fifty new trash cans with logos, new stairways. He secured financing for a playground next to the Mevlana Mosque. The children of the district also have a place. After three months of struggle, a pedestrian overpass is now being built to connect both wings of the building at an even level. Ackermann is pushing rigorously for a new aesthetic: display windows will no longer be pasted shut with posters. Neon signs, even if they are expensive, are being eliminated if they do not fit in. Barbed wire and fencing were immediately taken down. "No one will be driven away, no one shut out. Junkies belong to our society too." He did not want a security guard. The reason: the more the building becomes a fortress, the more negative the image is. The shop merchants and residents won out on the issue of security guards. Ackermann did not have a social utopia in mind but rather normality: "the normal neighborhood average of unemployed people, normal mix of businesses." Integration for him means above all the integration of the NKZ into Kreuzberg. The means for him is business. The high business quota (40 percent, with 80 businesses) was used as an operating standard. The monoculture of 16 *kebap* kiosks was discontinued; their contracts were not extended. Whoever wants the space must offer something new.

At Ackermann's suggestion, Turkish soups are sold on the corner of the plaza. It says so in the contract. "The man makes a roaring business!" It's too bad if he comes up with something else. Ackermann is in charge. When a contract is breached, the word is "hit the road!" A Vietnamese woman is operating a cook shop called Thay Hung. Ackermann is promoting it, because he wants to bring female entrepreneurs into this men's culture. "Ethnic meeting spots" like pool halls or karate schools were discontinued. He needs 20 to 30 percent vacancy in order to remodel. Horst Wiesner, head tenant and chair of the Renters' Advisory Board, dreams of normal establishments like Nordsee, McDonald's or even a fancy Italian restaurant in the gallery. Grünberg, the architect, wants three street cafés at the head of the plaza. "Of course, that also means that the drug scene be pushed out." The sound of what's to come. In any case, the gallery is free of youths loitering around. "The whole picture has become brighter," says the shoemaker Ibrahim Contur. A contract painter with ABM-Services is working his way through the stairways and mezzanines. The architect Grünberg is trying to turn the "backside into the frontside." The architecture has many dark corners, "dirty triangles" as Ms. Grünberg calls them. The pool hall has disappeared. In June, the homeless theater group Ratten 7 took the stage, who, together with the Ant King Peoples' Stage, is performing the Wild West show "The Song of Death." Now, at the former eyesore where the stairs and the gallery converge, a small café, the Neighborhood Café at the Kotti, greets visitors with colorful umbrellas. [. . .]

17

SUSANNE GASCHKE

COLORFUL AND SPEECHLESS

First published as "Sprachlos bunt" in *Die Zeit* (May 17, 2001). Translated by David Gramling.

Many immigrant children's German is worse than ever. If the parents do not help out, kindergartens and schools are powerless.

The bilingual kindergarten in Hamburg's Ottensen district is considered to be a model of successful foreigner integration, or "integration of migrant women and men" *[MigrantInnenimmigration]*, as one would tend to say here. Thirty-six children, who come from Turkish and German families in more or less equal proportion, are bilingually educated in the kindergarten's day care. The organization's space, which came into being in 1989 as the result of a parents' initiative, is bright and friendly. For recess, the three- to nine-year-olds go to a lushly landscaped adventure playground right outside. Food is prepared fresh daily, Turkish and German.

The director of the kindergarten is sure of a few things. First, she is certain that Turkish children in bilingual education learn German more successfully than their peers, who are only addressed in German in their kindergartens. Second, the linguistic results are so high among their pupils primarily because the classroom emphasizes respect for the culture of origin. Last, the project acts as a model for intercultural work.

Why is the coexistence of Germans and foreigners not always and everywhere so harmonious, enriching, and colorful as on this sunny May morning in Ottensen? Why, first of all, is language competency among immigrant
children in Germany recently becoming not better but consistently worse, as
the observations of pedagogical practitioners suggest?

No Multikulti *Idylls*

The answer is rather simple. Most foreign children do not grow up in idyllic
multiculturally oriented middle-class milieus but rather in problem neighborhoods in which even the residential German population has difficulty ut-
tering a grammatically correct sentence. Because the parents of many foreign children tend to rely on ghetto education, any hope of German-Turkish
peer group learning [original in English] is in vain from the outset. The few
kindergartens in Berlin's Wedding district, in Hamburg's Wilhelmsburg or in
Essen's Stoppenberg, have nice parent organizations with high ratios of academics, who themselves choose organizations on the basis of whether they
"suit" their children. A large portion of foreign parents do not seek an education for their children based on enlightened "neutral worldviews." Instead,
especially with daughters, they scrupulously monitor adherence to religious
codes of behavior, which often is tantamount to a virtual segregation from
societal contact generally considered normal.

Under these conditions, learning German is anything but easy. At the same
time, however, command of the German language is the basic precondition
for any chance of success in German society. For the 1.7 million foreign children (42 percent Turks), emphatic tolerance rhetoric is of precious little use.
They deserve a sober reexamination of the conditions of their education.
What structural barriers hinder them in language acquisition? What can the
educational system do to counteract the separatist tendency of their families?

These questions are difficult to answer, because precise knowledge about
the language competency of foreign children in Germany is largely lacking.
Their dubious class participation (especially in the higher grades of grammar
school and special schools) and dropout rate yield unequivocal conclusions
about linguistic and social disenfranchisement. However, a systematic
standard-language assessment tool does not exist. The official sector first ap-
praises language competency during the enrollment assessment—too late to
effectively prepare children with deficiencies. And the process, moreover, is
not satisfactory. School doctors cannot judge Turkish knowledge among beginning pupils; if they conclude that the children cannot speak German well,
their best option is to postpone enrollment or to make a referral to a
speech-therapy elementary school. A grotesquely failed intervention with
scant support resources: the children are not, after all, developmentally disabled. [. . .]

Kindergarten classrooms are apparently not in a position to counterbalance the inauspicious situation in the home and cannot ensure that their charges will learn German during the three years of kindergarten. One must, however, keep in mind the working conditions of these highly focused establishments: 129 children with 18 different first languages attend this day care for 2- to 11-year-olds in Hamburg's Veddel district. Two of the 12 women teachers are Turks, which means that they can be counted on to understand the Turkish children. However, a sense of uncertainty inhabits most conversations. So far, the kindergarten has only been able to mobilize extra help hours for language assistance through speech-therapy pedagogy services. "Despite this," says the teacher, "when they get to the school, the children can make themselves understood to a certain extent in German."

There is no reason to doubt this estimation. Only, from the point of view of future opportunities, the "to a certain extent" is not good enough. And a significant although not statistically established number of non-German children have never even attended a kindergarten. For this reason, the elementary and middle school next door to the Veddel kindergarten offers five classes just for those who do not speak any German. There is also a remedial class for older students who can neither read nor write. The old debate about separate versus "integrated" classes is becoming increasingly superfluous. In the classes in question, German pupils make up only 10 percent, because both the Germans and the socially mobile migrants are leaving the problem districts in droves. To deal with these consequences by extending the established feeder areas of the school, a proposal currently under discussion, is questionable. According to current pedagogical opinion, at least grammar-school children should live within walking distance of school. Besides, busing [original in English] ghetto children to the suburbs would create added social conflicts.

It would be excessively unfair to blame the coming language catastrophe only on the kindergartens. Indeed, it is somewhat difficult for some teachers to correct children at all, which is essential for second-language acquisition. However, only a few of the educators are trained in communicating German as a foreign language. In practice the particular school of thought one employs is irrelevant. Without the voluntary cooperation of the parental home, the instruction does not work. "For this reason, courses for mothers are the fulcrum and linchpin," says Andreas Pochert, author of the Berlin language-status study: "The children must keep in mind: It is important to learn German; my mother knows what is at stake and is working hard on it herself." Experts do not think highly of the idea of mandatory kindergarten or whole-day school for foreigner children. However, they are unanimous in that a daylong option is necessary.

Education politics is stuck between a rock and a hard place. If it is serious about language advancement, it is faced with a giant investment in language teachers, such as classes for parents and extra-help sessions for a clientele that cannot express its appreciation by voting. Moreover, it must communicate to German citizens that these investments will serve social peace. It needs to develop a rhetoric that makes clear to Turkish parents that forgoing mandatory measures in no way condones inaction on their part.

This means that state institutions must play a different role than they have so far. Clearly, revision of some of the integration "truths" from the early *multikulti* milieu will be necessary. For example, it is more than questionable whether the perennially demanded "instruction in the mother tongue" really serves integration. The standard argument is that mastery of the first language is allegedly essential for the acquisition of the second language. But must we not first of all delegate this responsibility to the parental home, despite the complications? It goes without saying that our education system also has duties to German culture, including raising children of any ancestry in such a way that all opportunities in life will be open to them. That principle means in part that their parents not marry them away against their will. That, as women, they also be allowed to engage in a career. That they be able to deal with open society. And learn German: read it, write it, speak it.

18

REGINA RÖMHILD

WHEN *HEIMAT* GOES GLOBAL

First published as "Wenn die Heimat global wird" in *Die Zeit* (March 14, 2002). Translated by David Gramling. Römhild is assistant professor at the Institute of Cultural Anthropology and European Ethnology at the University of Frankfurt am Main. She is director of the research project Transit Migration.

Immigrants changed our society long ago. We just haven't realized it yet.

Katja is 16 years old. She lives in the Gallus district in Frankfurt/Main and attends school there. She came to Germany as the daughter of Russian-German emigrants from Uzbekistan. Many of her friends are "also Russians," as she says. The "Russian" network of kinship connections stretches into other Frankfurt districts and the surrounding region, a network of cafés and discotheques that Katja frequents. In her own district and school class, she has more contact with "Turks" and "Yugoslavs" than anyone else. One friend is from Armenia. This distinction is important for Katja because her friend could be mistaken for a Turk based on name and appearance. Katja apparently no longer wants anything do with Turks—though only a few sentences earlier, she talked of the Turkish boys in her clique.

Katja's world illustrates what cultural anthropologists call the "transnationalization" of our society. In worlds like hers, cultural influences flow in from the most varied regions in the world. They combine into novel forms of coexistence under specific local conditions. What results is a completely normal German everyday life. Although this life has been lived a thousand times, it still remains largely invisible, even in the current debate on immigration. For Katja's everyday life contradicts the prevailing notions of integration, of coexistence in an immigration society. This integration imperative envisages that immigrants have integrated into a given German cultural landscape. To move within a migrant network like Katja, to spend time in "ethnic" clubs and organizations—in other words, those not frequented by Germans—is seen as the absence of a will to integrate, if not outright malicious refusal. In contrast, integration is seen as successful when migrants commit themselves to their German homeland.

A notion of homeland that abandons diverse, globalized relationships is a fiction. The reality in cities such as Frankfurt, Offenbach, Munich, or Stuttgart is that a third of the population does not have a German passport and speaks another language. Most of the youth with whom Katja socializes at school and in her free time come from migrant families like hers. Some were born here; others immigrated as children with their parents. Katja prefers to spend her free time at the "Yugoslavian" cafés and "Russian" clubs. She feels comfortable in the Gallus district, even though she preferred life in Höchst, where she used to live: in Höchst there were more Russian meeting spots; there was more happening. Both city districts are former workers' quarters, and many migrants still live there. Katja's experiences and her immigrant family background are considered normal here. That the Germans are by birth the majority in the Federal Republic attracts little attention in this area. From this perspective, Katja's classmate Anika appears to be an exception: she was born as a German in Germany. When the two fight, Anika is sometimes called "potato."

In the relationships youths have with one another, classification according to nationality plays a considerable role; after all, they want to distinguish themselves somehow. Still, they meet up again on the level of comparable experiences: the countries of origin are different, but they have the migrant story in common, with which they all must deal in their own way.

Katja was in Uzbekistan this year. She enjoyed seeing her grandfather again. But she can no longer take much pleasure in village life there. She cherishes the spaces of freedom that are available to her in metropolitan Frankfurt. Katja found the situation of youths in Uzbekistan depressing. She rules out returning there, at least for now. She has other plans: after secondary-school level I, she would like to apprentice as a doctor's receptionist. Katja envisions her future here, in a Germany that she shares with many others who have had similar world experiences.

Instead of acknowledging these new spheres of experience, officials still define integration as "cultural and social harmonization of immigrants with native Germans and as an assimilation of their circumstances." So reads the language of a recently published study on the status of integration in Frankfurt/Main. The Gallus district, in which Katja lives, looks good in this analysis: here, immigrants are already largely "integrated into the everyday social spheres of long-established German inhabitants of the district." Yet if Katja is "integrated," then it is primarily within the microcosm of the immigration society, as is typical for our cities. In this context, the cultural-studies scholar Mark Terkessidis speaks of "self-integration," referring to the efforts of migrants who must find their own place in this society and be creative in constructing their worlds. These strategies of self-integration imply not only an analysis of the long-established Germans' habits; at issue is also communication between immigrants of different nationalities.

Native Germans on one side, non-German immigrants on the other: does this perspective sufficiently represent the reality in which we live? Katja came to Germany as an emigrant child; she and her parents are legally Germans, with German citizenship, with a German passport. Katja, however, counts herself among the "Russians" in Germany; she sees herself as a migrant like many others. Many of her classmates were born here but are still seen as "Turks" or "Yugoslavs"—an image of the foreign that partially coincides with their own self-image, even if many of these classmates' families made use of the new citizenship law and are now Germans according to their passports. In this way, the boundaries are blurred and the ostensibly clear-cut categories interpenetrate. On the side of the Germans, there are many people with migration experience: emigrants, repatriated foreigners, mobile Germans who spend considerable time abroad on business or for pleasure. On the side of the "immigrants," there are, however, many family members who have already lived here for two or three generations. They are an inherent part of our society, and they actively help shape it as pupils, students, employees, entrepreneurs, politicians, and artists.

In contrast, the number of Germans who have settled down in families continues to decrease. The integration ideal is still based on this shrinking majority. In the future, fewer and fewer people will live their entire lives where they were born, and even the most settled people will recognize that the world around them changes unceasingly, that the world comes to them at home even if they themselves do not move. The salsa scene or the esoteric networks in the cities are examples of the development of new cultural marketplaces, in which Germans, together with non- or semi-Germans, actively participate in the globalization of their lives.

We have been living in a globalized society for a long time already, not only in the economic but also in the cultural sense. Migration is one cause of this. With it, people, things, and ideas become mobile. Meeting and dealing with foreigners has become an everyday experience. However, this everyday experience has still not found its way sufficiently into the theories that we have about them nor the notions that we derive from them. Migration, so it is still believed, changes only the migrants' lives and biography, not those of the society concerned. According to migration researcher Ludger Pries, nation-states such as Germany understand themselves as "receptacles" that must hold people and cultures together. Movements between the individual receptacles are understood as a disruption of the entire system. The desired equilibrium is achieved again only when the moving part is well adapted to— or "integrated" in—the new place.

Still, the history of "guest workers" in Germany shows that people develop their own migration projects that are only conditionally manageable by nation-states. The migrant laborers of the first generation who remained here did not tear down the bridges to their old homeland but rather maintained the familial, social, and economic relationships. International migration always creates new connections between countries and cultures and makes the imaginary receptacles of nation-states permeable. Thus, through their own "transnational" networks, the "guest workers" launched modernization developments in the European periphery. In the process, they spurred on a transnational Europeanization "from below."

In the nation-state logic, a life with two—or even more—homelands is seen as problematic; this phenomenon produces within the individual a tension that must be resolved. Migrant children, above all, are seen as "living between the worlds," suffering from an identity crisis, because they have lost their cultural roots and no longer know where they belong. Whole branches of social work, of foreigner and later intercultural pedagogy, have endeavored to help people out of this quasi-pathologic condition and to help them achieve a new cultural rootedness in Germany. As though questions of identity could be answered with an either-or decision.

An ethnographic study by Sven Sauters bears the programmatic title "We Are Frankfurt Turks." In it, youths from the second immigrant generation describe their position in a cultural sphere, for which the language of integration has no name. These German-Turkish youths are developing an independent way of "being Turkish" that does not refer to the rural homeland of their parents. In fact, Frankfurt/Main is the place from which they enact distance from their homeland. Frankfurt is the place that demands this separation from them—and enables it in the first place. For being a Frankfurt Turk is a collective project, experienced and lived as part of youth culture.

One finds identification with the city in all German migration centers: in Berlin as well as in Stuttgart, Munich, or Offenbach. For Frankfurt, statistics prove this phenomenon: according to the above-mentioned integration study, two-thirds of the surveyed youths see themselves as Frankfurters; almost half feel—partly simultaneously—connected to their parents' country of origin, but not even one-fifth identify themselves as German. Could one therefore assume, as the study concludes, that "the majority of those surveyed feel connected to the German host society?" Is the city the smallest common denominator that enables integration into German life—if not on a national level, then at least on the local one? The Frankfurt Turks contradict this notion: it is not the German Frankfurt to which they are referring, not the city as a part of the national republic, but rather the potentially cosmopolitan metropolis, which offers the social and cultural framework for their particular life plans.

Migration produces cultural pluralization, not the unified culture of the global village. When the global comes into contact with the local, the cultures distinguish themselves further; they duplicate each other in ever-new combinations. Ayse Caglar and Levent Soysal show a glimpse of this in their studies on German-Turkish youth culture in Berlin. The German audience recognizes and appreciates German-Turkish hip-hop and rap as the musical avant-garde. German-Turkish hip-hoppers, in turn, make a conscious connection with the African-American youth culture, which they use for their linguistic and musical self-stylings. Bands such as White Nigger Force, by name alone, express the fans' feeling that they are the "blacks of Germany." Kreuzberg and Brooklyn have become symbols for cultural kinship in the global sphere.

The second generation of immigrants in particular articulates itself aggressively and, in the process, adopts a political position: their spokespeople are musicians, filmmakers, and writers such as Feridun Zaimoğlu, who has made the jargon of German Turks, "kanaki speak," socially acceptable, or the political-action group Kanak Attak. The language and culture of the "ghetto kids" [original in English] have indeed become part of the commercialized German multiculture. But there are other, less spectacular forms of such cultural globalization: cafés and clubs emerging in the expensive downtown areas have established themselves in the mainstream yet still serve/cater to almost exclusively Turkish patrons, especially from the middle class. Here, one can listen to Turkish pop as it is played in Istanbul or Ankara, and the interior design is urban and fashionable. The décor here is neither ghetto nor arabesque folklore. Understood as modern and European, urban Turkey is the inspiration for this scene. The German public knows little of such places, because German multiculture has other institutions, such as the proverbial "Greek restaurant" with souvlaki, sirtaki, and shepherds' rugs on the wall—where hardly a Greek can be found.

The cultural practice of the immigration society does not abide by the ethnic sorting pattern of established multiculture, nor does it allow itself to be forced into an intercultural assimilation dialogue. It is more difficult than ever to squeeze cultures within boundaries and specifications. They migrate and change with the people.

19

ANDREAS ROSENFELDER

THE CAMPSITE IS GROWING

First published as "Der Zeltplatz wächst" in *Frankfurter Allgemeine Zeitung* (November 11, 2002). Translated by Tes Howell. The Residence Obligation Law mentioned in this text is a law requiring asylum seekers to remain in the district where they first applied for asylum.

Since Heinrich Himmler's 1938 Gypsy Decree, many German Sinti and Roma whose ancestors immigrated primarily from Hungary in the late nineteenth and early twentieth centuries have lived without citizenship or state recognition. Until 1979, the West German government did not acknowledge Sinti and Roma as victims of National Socialist genocide, and in 1983, Chancellor Helmut Schmidt released a joint statement with Opposition Leader Helmut Kohl to that effect. In the same year, the Central Council for Sinti and Roma in Germany was founded in Heidelberg.

Pity the camper: The caravan of Roma is looking for a permanent resting spot.
A look into the encyclopedia teaches us that the cultural history of nomads is rooted in the desert. Those who come from nowhere have good reason to wander around. But the images of camping, wandering clans do not reveal where the desert begins and where it ends. For, on the one hand, we know from documentaries that even the deadest desert landscapes are alive. On the other hand, U.N. conventions on desert abatement expose the creeping devastation of the earth. The origin of all nomads has long served as a dusty existential metaphor for a global society that sends even its elite troops into the desert. Still, whereas the idea of nomads surfaces increasingly in the folklore of activists, management consultants, and museum curators, Europe's most flexible inhabitants are disappearing unnoticed into the desolate peripheries. At issue are the gypsies, whose designation as Sinti and Roma appears to have been stripped of the unpleasant associations wrapped up in the term *gypsy*. And does not their caravan of several hundred Roma, who for seven months have lived in tents in German parks and swimming-pool grounds to protest their deportation to postwar Yugoslavia, reflect their nomadic fate?

Since their arrival in Europe, a mythical desert wind has accompanied the gypsies, whose name refers back to the Indian caste of the untouchables. From the beginning, foreign papers decided that their fate would be to wander. In fifteenth-century town chronicles, mysterious foreigners surfaced with forged documents from Emperor Sigismund, Pope Martin V, and King Friedrich III, which identify the bearers as Egyptian nobles whose wanderings represented God's punishment as predicted in the Bible: "For I intend," according to the prophet Ezekiel, "to make Egypt into a desert in the middle of desolate lands and leave their cities in ruins amid wasted cities for 40 years, and I intend to scatter the Egyptians among the peoples and chase them away into the lands." The legend's 40 years have passed, but the scenario continues. Yet the protection letters that brought the gypsies a provisionally peaceful tolerance have now become interstate deportation notices. Dzoni Sichelschmidt, a young man from Kosovo and speaker for the Roma caravan, keeps entire stacks of paper in his briefcase: signatures from Council of Europe members, protest letters to federal ministers, reports from the U.N. High Commissioner for Refugees, but above all, the copy of an agreement written in Cyrillic. The nine-page accord, signed on October 10, 1996, is between the Federal Republic of Yugoslavia and the Federal Republic of Germany on the repatriation of civil-war refugees, the longest-standing legal basis for last April's deportations. Sichelschmidt himself belongs to those Roma who fled to Germany in the early 1990s before the war. The governing parties during the war had found useful cannon fodder in these gypsies, who had previously enjoyed privileges for their partisan fighting under Tito.

Today, Yugoslavian civil-war refugees are the last Roma in Western Europe. Other Eastern European refugees, who fueled a blazing antigypsy backlash in the West after the Wall fell, have been repatriated to their hardly more hospitable countries of origin in the past decade. In the ruins of Yugoslavia, whose infrastructure is barely capable of handling the million refugees already there, the Roma can expect an insufferable life in poverty, under bridges and in trash dumps. For their red passports are from an era lost to the war and are nothing more than worthless paper. Sichelschmidt guesses that the Roma, presumed to be political experts, will be expected to represent the Western ideal of a multiethnic Kosovo and bring Serbia into Europe.

No gypsy believes in a multicultural Balkan, even if many families sit waiting every Wednesday on their packed suitcases. On Wednesdays, the Yugoslavian airline JAT flies to Belgrade, and on Wednesdays, some receive unannounced visitors at their doors. The Foreigners' Registration Office handles between 70 and 80 deportations a month, which adds up to thousands annually. With around 40,000 Roma in Germany, the repatriation should last a biblical 40 years.

As a means of travel, caravans held significance even before the Roma demonstrations. But now, at the head of the protest march for permanent residency in downtown Düsseldorf, which passes by the "longest bar in the world," the omnipresent caravan marches for the rights of refugees and migrants.

Leftist organizations support the Roma because of their mottos: "No God, No State, No Fatherland!" One suspects that such political romanticism originates from the same misunderstanding of homelessness as does the "Three Gypsies," sung by Nikolaus Lenau, except that the poet used more beautiful language. Meanwhile, from the loudspeakers blares Goran Bregovic's high-tempo brass music from Emir Kusturica's films, which can also be heard as background music for insurance advertisements.

Gypsy culture has long since become mass culture; no museum party manages without Macedonian funeral songs. And even the style-conscious outfit of the younger Roma—gelled back hair, upturned white collars, fitted jackets, and high-heeled leather shoes—fits into every bold fall collection. And still, there is a difference between the hip-hop dances of 15-year-old Roma girls and the folk dancing of hyper Slavic students. For the teenagers in their sparkling tennis shoes and fur-stuffed jean jackets, the Balkans are not a source of style inspiration but rather a nightmare.

Dear Ramadani, a student in the eighth grade at an Essen secondary school, and his family of eight have already received a deportation notice and now see the demonstration as their last hope: so far, Roma families have only been picked up for repatriation in their apartments or at visits to the authorities. Dear plays on the B youth team of Borussia Mönchengladbach; the soccer organization might be able to hold on to the promising new kicker. Maybe the name Ramadani will roll off the tongues of sport reporters in the future. But as a Roma, the young man from Kosovo will not show up in any player statistics. Inconspicuousness is perhaps the most striking characteristic of Roma in Germany, who often arrived here in the 1960s as guest workers.

Above all, quick adaptation separates the Roma, predominantly from Southeast Europe, from the mobile-home existence of the German-speaking Sinti, who travel through villages as rug dealers or carnies and have shielded their customs from the outside world since their experiences under National Socialism. Roma, on the other hand, strive for success under a cloak of invisibility. That the bald-headed Yul Brynner was not only one of the brothers Karamazov but also the honorary president of the International Roma Union is known only to insiders, as is the case with singer Marianne Rosenberg, designer John Galliano, and pop star Michelle, who all come from gypsy families.

Still, while remaining in one place demands neutralizing differences, the emergency maneuver of exodus, triggered at various key points in Roma history, unleashes the whole exotic aspect of nomadism. The adoption of these foreign images is the last means of attracting attention for the Roma, who have lived in Germany for over 10 years on three-month residence extensions. In a way, the archaic parade, having already passed before the Marine School in Bremerhaven, the Brandenburg Gate in Berlin, and the Documenta in Kassel Station, freezing during these winter days under a strict application of the Residence Obligation Law, reflects the provisional nature of a vagabond existence.

These nomads have no windows, just plastic holes with painted mullions that lend the tents the appearance of domesticity in this urban no man's land outside of Neuss. Emergency housing made of plywood and tarps replaces the Roma's ramshackle huts that flourished on the tattered outskirts of the Balkans. This silt-filled campsite has nothing in common with this age of trekking adventures and microfiber tents. The children catch bronchial illnesses, and according to doctors, the bacteria teem in puddles surrounding the few water sources. Nevertheless, the demonstrators will not complain because the possibility of a pestilence affecting the city would incite the authorities to break up the camp.

The Roma camp, which must move every few weeks within the city, is currently next to the autobahn. Until the night cold gets the upper hand, the family of Ardem Elmacti, known as a blonde gypsy, sits together on camping chairs. Like most Roma, the 32-year-old salesman from Belgrade, who fled to Germany as a young man and was condemned to do nothing during his best years because he lacked a work permit, has been here for over 10 years under a long-term residence provision—subject to job availability. Inside the tent, his 12-year-old son, Emran, watches television; he was born in Germany.

"What should we do?" asks the sandy-blond father. "Sacrifice a child? We are not Kurds, and we have no lobby. But we have heart." His firstborn son, Demail, 16 years old and class rep at his Essen secondary school for two years, accepts the situation with casual sarcasm: "We're on a sightseeing tour!" When the caravan began, Demail was ending the tenth grade just before the jump into *Gymnasium*—and upon hearing his fluent speech, one immediately notices the *Gymnasium* graduate in the boy with the chic wool cap. Here in Germany, he is hoping for a "completely normal life," but he envisions only hate in Yugoslavia: "We'd be crushed there." Along with his sister Esma, almost the same age, Demail acts out for fun the 82 square meters of *Heimat* that now lie abandoned in their Essen apartment: "Space heater! Balcony! Bathtub! DVD player!" However, the sound of these magic words transforms the autobahn wall, where a string of pale neon lights lines the horizon, into a shifting sand dune on the edge of an endless desert.

20

STEFAN WILLEKE

OUR PEARL JULIA

First printed as "Unsere Perle Julia" in *Die Zeit* (January 15, 2004). Translated by David Gramling.

She came from Poland, studied economics, and dreamed of true love. Now she irons our shirts. We pay her under the table—and we think that's just fine.

[. . .] Since the newspapers began writing about the police searches seeking to uncover illegal cleaning ladies, that old sense of discomfort we believed forgotten is once again present. Just a few minutes separate her from the bus stop and house number 38. She absolutely must keep her job, she says, and so she wants to be called Julia in print. Julia is 29 years old and grew up in a small town on the Polish coast. [. . .]

Julia's life takes place between number 38 and number 64 on a street with red and white single-family houses. Ironing, folding, more ironing. Eight hours a day, sometimes ten. Julia works without a work permit and is thus committing a crime. She does so voluntarily in Hamburg: vacuuming, mopping, vacuuming. She wanted it to be this way.

And we intended it to be this way too. We Germans. We middle-class people; we architects, lawyers, teachers, locksmiths, journalists, engineers. Our work contracts are in order, and yet we employ cleaning ladies, gardeners, and child-care personnel without work contracts, hoping that they will bring order into our everyday lives. The foreign help is named Julia, Svetlana, or Ben. They are from Poland, Kazakhstan, or Ghana. We do not pay taxes for them, nor health insurance, nor retirement insurance, and when the helpers are lying sick in bed, we do not pay them their illegal salary anymore. We have grown used to this arrangement, because it has always been thus. We are not criminals, we are simply having our shirts laid out, and we pay good money for it. It's only the state that is trying to cast doubt on our self-image. With the help of a new law that the cabinet will decide upon in mid-February, the government will try harder to combat illegal labor. "Working illegally is no mere peccadillo; it is tangible economic criminality that causes severe damage to the common good." So declared the Federal Ministry of Finance recently on its Internet home page.

But we click on past; we do not want to know this, not in such precise terms. The new staff unit Finance Control for Illegal Labor will send out 5,000 agents from labor bureaus and customs administrations into the land. Paragraph 11 of the new bill warns us—and our household help—of fines between 1,500 and 150,000 euros. But we do not read such texts. We do not feel addressed by them, because when people talk about illegal labor, we think of columns of mortified day laborers who snuck into Germany illegally through a sluice. In contrast, Julia smiles happily while she turns the knob on the steam iron to "wool." Her smile gives us a good conscience. [. . .]

Professor Friedrich Schneider from Linz estimated that the magnitude of the rapidly growing shadow economy in Germany in 2002 is very high: around 350 billion euros. Generated from illegal labor alone. Nine million people are working illegally, at least once in a while. [. . .]

We also do not want to know much about the minijobs the government created, which are advantageous from a taxation point of view, as a way to legalize illegal labor in the domestic sphere. Around 3 million domestic laborers in total are employed among us, and only around 2 percent of them are officially declared. [. . .]

Our unions do not want to put up any barriers to a low-salary sector, because they fear that soon our employers will only pay low wages. Should we really be concerned about this prospect? We have had our minimum-wage sector for a long time. We call it Julia, and when we are gushing about this sector to our neighbors, we say "our Julia."

21

THE TURKISH FEDERATION OF BERLIN

TEN-POINT PLAN OF THE TURKISH FEDERATION OF BERLIN FOR COMBATING INTOLERANCE TOWARD WOMEN

First published on the website of the Türkischer Bund Berlin on February 25, 2005. Translated by David Gramling.

The Turkish Federation of Berlin is concerned about the crimes committed against women in the past few months. TBB wishes to summon all societal forces to develop common strategies to preclude such events in the future. For the TBB, the main question is what values in the Basic Law are applicable here, not just values that are "German," "Turkish," or "Islamic." TBB cautions against racist tendencies in this context. We propose the following theses for discussion:

1. Zero tolerance toward violence against women
2. No tolerance for repressive attitudes advanced for religious or traditional reasons
3. Careful monitoring of values and ideas that discriminate against women
4. A public and active avowal from Turkish and Islamic organizations on the right of self-definition for women
5. Promotion of the Turkish and intra-Islamic discussion process vis-à-vis equal rights for women
6. Strict prosecution for forced marriage, a new enlightenment in the Turkish and Islamic community
7. New intercultural opportunities at educational institutions and the promotion of intercultural competence among teaching staff
8. Establishment of a chair for Islamic theology at one of the Berlin universities, and introduction of an Islamic studies track in Berlin schools
9. Implementation of mandatory participation in swimming, sports, biology, and sexual education among schoolchildren
10. Factual representation of Islamic values in public.

The TBB is ready to put all of its efforts into taking part in a factual discussion and the development of solutions.

WRITING BACK
LITERATURE AND MULTILINGUALISM

CELEBRATING TRANSNATIONAL WRITERS, 2005. Author Feridun Zaimoğlu, nick-named Germany's Malcolm X, receives the 15,000-euro Adelbert von Chamisso Prize, created to honor immigrants writing in German. Famous for his pseudo-ethnographies of migrant youth, Zaimoğlu (third from right) appears stoically resigned about the institutional domestication of his rebellious presence on the German literary scene. Linguist Harald Weinrich (far right) founded the prize in 1985.

OUR NINTH CHAPTER FOCUSES on the phenomenon that Leslie A. Adelson (see chapter 6) refers to as the "literary elephant in the room": transnational literature beyond autobiography and ethnic categorization. Rather than presenting a representative selection of immigrant fiction in Germany, the texts in this chapter shore up the interpenetrating fields of German and transnational literature: publishing and recruitment practices, awards and competitions, ironic appropriations and resignifications, trends and movements. The collection ranges from poetic critiques of Orientalism (Zafer Şenocak) to analyses of "migrant-literature" niche marketing (Klaus Pokatzky), celebratory invocations of the multilingual spirit (Harald Weinrich), and mordant repudiations of multicultural ideology (Maxim Biller). These writings do not intend to offer an aerial view of immigrant literary production; they offer a set of case studies from the industries and discourses that constitute transnational literature.

"Akif Pirinçci: I Am a Token Turk" (1982) is an early critique of the publishing industry's pursuit of representative Turks in the West German literary scene of the early 1980s. The search for and promotion of authentic voices from the second immigrant generation often ended in embarrassment. Such was the case when a token author such as Akif Pirinçci unabashedly admitted to exploiting his heralded position as a young and marketable immigrant author. In stark contrast, the linguist and literary critic Harald Weinrich, founder of the German as a Foreign Language program at the University of Munich, writes in the Goethean tradition of honoring the connections between national literature and world literature. For him, transnational authors represent an unsurpassable and enriching contribution to the canon of German literature.

These first two texts view the advent of immigrant literary production in two vastly different lights. Pokatzky ironically presents the business of publishing immigrant writers as a shortsighted marketing scheme. He suggests that the culture industry invites migrant writers to confirm the political imagination not of a mass readership but of a network of critics and publishers predisposed to valorize literary memoirs from the social margins. Weinrich, however, exemplifies an Enlightenment faith in the progressive capacity of transnational literature to enliven German culture and broaden the hermeneutic circle of the nation.

A third position emerged in a 1986 Chamisso Prize acceptance speech by the German-Turkish poet and novelist Aras Ören. Ören suggested that immigration is the quintessential face of all Europe and that immigrant writers possess unique power to investigate the conditions for literary subjectivity in global capitalism. Ören envisioned a special position for multilingual, multinational writers in the "consciousness industry" of his time; they have an opportunity to catalyze a fundamental redefinition of categories such as "European" or "German."

In 1991, when Emine Sevgi Özdamar won the prestigious Ingeborg Bachmann Prize for literature, her work seemed to signal that literature by migrants was departing from the multicultural niche reserved for them. In stylized, deceptively simple, and "broken" German, Özdamar's winning submission, an excerpt from her debut novel *Life Is a Caravanserai Has Two Doors, I Came in One, I Went out the Other,* charmed jurors and appalled critics throughout Germany and Austria. Jens Jessen's review of the Bachmann Prize proceedings, reprinted in this chapter, attributes Özdamar's success to the irreversible devolvement of literary aesthetics in Germany. Jessen emphasizes that, though Turkish high culture has produced works of literary genius, Özdamar's coming-of-age story is an underdeveloped derivative of Turkish folklore. Opposing Weinrich's claim that migration literature is world literature, Jessen contends that multilingually inflected writing is a patently immature, folkloristic simulacrum of national belles lettres. Özdamar's 1992 retrospective essay, "Black Eye and His Donkey," issues a humorous rebuttal to her critics, reflecting on her own practice of depicting guest-worker history.

In a caustic pursuit of multicultural euphemisms, Maxim Biller's 1991 essay "The Turkicized Germans" sketches a Huxleyan vision of West German labor migration and the discourses arising to represent it. Satire became a major mode of articulation for transnational writers in 1990s Germany, notably for Feridun Zaimoğlu, Wladimer Kaminer, and Osman Engin.

Zafer Şenocak's 1994 prose poem, "The Bastardized Language," places labor-migration history in the broader context of Orientalism and imperialism. In the interventional tone of Frantz Fanon and Aimé Césaire, Şenocak inquires into the asymmetrical relationship between canonical German literature and "migrant literature." How, he queries, can transnational writers in Germany be so fully aware of Goethe, Kafka, and Nietzsche, when German writers know so little about canonical Turkish writers like Nazım Hikmet?

Feridun Zaimoğlu's 1995 mock ethnography, *Kanaki Speak: 24 Discords on the Margins of Society,* was a watershed moment in transnational literature in Germany, because it both satirized and appropriated the "authentic migrant voices" of sociological multiculturalism. Since the book's publication, Zaimoğlu has played a major role in reframing migration literature in Germany as a creative and critical endeavor beyond the conceit of authentic testimonial. Şinasi Dikmen (b. 1945, Samsun, Turkey) is another of Germany's preeminent satirical voices on the traditionally earnest issues of ethnic identity, cultural categorization, and migrant experiences. Together with Muhsin Omurca, he cofounded the Knobi-Bonbon-Kabarett in 1985.

Günter Grass's speech "In Praise of Yaşar Kemal" is an example of one canonical German writer's engagement with questions of international human rights and Turkish literature. Grass delivered this speech at the Frankfurt Paulskirche in 1997, calling attention to Yaşar Kemal's Kurdish heritage and the oppressive measures the Turkish government adopted to squelch Kurdish self-determination. Abbas Maroufi, an Iranian author and journalist in German exile, appeals to Günter Grass as the symbolic standard-bearer of German literary humanism. In his open letter to Grass, Maroufi describes his family's experience of asylum in Germany and the difficulties of working as an author in exile. He appeals to the broader literary establishment to engage in the everyday political and legislative affairs of immigration.

Two texts in this chapter critique the notion of the immigrant author as a bridge between cultures. German-Japanese author and poet Yoko Tawada's short poetic essay, "I Did Not Want to Build Bridges," investigates the role language plays in the articulation of multiple identities. A profile of German-Turkish novelist Güney Dal chronicles his development from a writer of "proletarian guest-worker literature" in the 1970s to a writer of German historical fiction with his 1999 novel *Teatime at Ringside*. We conclude this collection of texts with one ironic narrative and one anti-ironic narrative. The Moscow-born author and spoken-word performer Wladimir Kaminer continues the 1990s tradition of migration satire in his essay "Why I Still Haven't Applied for Naturalization." Kaminer comically dramatizes the apoplexy of describing his entire past and future to a local immigration officer named Herr Kugler. In an earnest, almost ethnographic counterpoint to Kaminer's urban satire, Asfa-Wossen Asserate's 2003 essay "In Praise of Squareness" admires rural German culture for its spirited steadfastness and unvarnished manners. These two concluding texts, one by a Russian émigré and one by an Ethiopian prince, exemplify the variability of migrant literature in the twenty-first century.

1

KLAUS POKATZKY

AKIF PIRINÇI: I AM A TOKEN TURK

First published as "Akif Pirinçi: Ich bin ein Pressetürke" in *Die Zeit* (May 28, 1982). Translated by Tes Howell. After his ascent to stardom as an immigrant author in the field of migration literature in the early 1980s, Pirinçi (b. 1959, Istanbul) continued writing novels such as *Felidae* (1989) and *Francis* (1993). According to his publishing house, Goldmann, these later novels were translated into 17 languages and sold more than 2 million copies.

On Akif Pirinçi and the German Literary Industry

Let's be honest. We journalists have waited a long time for this: a 22-year-old Turk, resident of the Federal Republic for 13 years (his father is a truck driver, his mother a factory worker), writes a novel about his lost love, the German law student Christa. The book is a bestseller; the film adaptation is imminent. We celebrate this success and report on it gladly.

"Rhenish girl inspired young Turkish writer," lauds the *Express* in Cologne, with undertones of hometown pride. The *Trade Gazette* of the reputable German Book Trade Association advertised the book as a "modern love story, somewhere between Salinger and Bukowski." And the reviewer at the high-circulation subculture magazine *Sounds* was beside herself with praise: "All the old writers," be they Handke, Walser or Grass, will have to "grow pale with veneration" for this "great outsider novel, which deserves to go down in history with Goethe's *Werther.*"

Of course, one could argue that such praise is not to be taken seriously, because the *Trade Gazette* is more of an extended advertisement for large book publishers than an independent critical literary journal, and the *Sounds* reviewer had obviously never read one line by Goethe or Grass. Still, curiosity was piqued, and the book is being read. It has achieved a circulation of 24,000—first out of interest for the exotic author, then out of a feeling that oscillates between derision and irritation.

In the casual, often-affected tone of the disco crowd, Akif Pirinçi relates his short-lived but intimate relationship with the "lovely, sweet, beautiful Christa," which finally "ends in an emotional ice age." What the Goldmann publishing house calls "a piece of literature from contemporary Germany that surprises and whisks one away with its originality" is nothing more and nothing less than a nice little piece of entertainment—good to read before going to sleep, in the bathtub, or on the subway. In places, it is particularly funny, lively, and dynamic, but then again, it is also written with the stiff, humorless, doltish undertone of young male chauvinists. And it is very often simply clumsy and awkward; one sees all too clearly that the Goldmann readers are less interested in furthering a young author's work than in marketing him effectively to the press.

After sending his manuscript to 70 publishers—Goldmann among them—over a three-month period, Akif Pirinçci received only rejections at first, some politely packaged and others not. His mother then loaned him 3,000 marks, with which he printed 500 copies at a university copy center. His 25-year-old sister, a graphic artist, designed the cover of *Tears Always Mean the End*. The author himself distributed fliers and hung up posters advertising the book.

Sales began sluggishly; then he saw a literature program on television about "love in our times." The next day he called the moderator, Reinhard Hoffmeister, complained about the "top-heavy crap" on the show, and asked why he had not been invited on. He sent Hoffmeister his first novel, and on the next ZDF "Litera-Tour" Akif Pirinçci was allowed to promote himself for six minutes, evincing a big mouth and a cool wit.

The next day, the Goldmann Press calls from Munich: "We really like your book; we want to buy it." "But you haven't even read it," responds Akif Pirinçci. "That doesn't matter; we like it all the same." The author acquiesces and receives his contract three days later, guaranteeing him a circulation of 20,000 copies, as well as 60 pfennig per copy. Meanwhile, Pirinçci is already working on the sequel, *The Gates of Insanity*. He has sold a screenplay version of his first work to Studio Hamburg for about 20,000 marks, and is anticipating playing the lead role in the film.

He recounts this tale with a Rhenish accent over Chinese food in Andernach, the next-largest town near Weißenturm, where he is living with his parents again. "I am the token Turk," he explains over his chicken soup, "but whether they see me as a Turk or a German doesn't really matter to me; my culture consists of those things that I do. And what the people around me are doing just doesn't interest me." As a result, he "cannot stand" the question often put to him: "As a Turk, what do you think about this?" After all, his philosophy is "All cultures are alike. I don't care about culture. The only important things in this world are fucking and money and nothing else."

Whoever hopes to learn about the thoughts and feelings of the second foreigner generation will be disappointed: he writes as little as possible on Turks and their problems. "Because that is nothing new," he explains over his spring roll, "and everybody knows it."

When he came to the Federal Republic, he was nine; he taught himself German through "intensive TV and film watching." Films were/are for him "the greatest." So, with the money that he earns from his first book, after buying a Porsche, he would like to produce a "super science fiction" film, preferably in Hollywood, the "emblem of American cinema."

He had few friends in school; while the others were interested in mopeds, he sat at home and wrote scripts for radio plays and made-for-TV movies (32 altogether). The *Bayerischer Rundfunk* produced one of his short TV movies; he was 14 at the time. When he was 16 years old, he won first prize in a *Hessischer Rundfunk* contest with a science fiction radio play. He dropped out of

Gymnasium, then left secondary school altogether, then finally and half-heartedly attended vocational school. He worked with a film company in Cologne and at the opera "as a handyman" and subsequently studied in Vienna for two years at the Film and Television Academy. [. . .]

The image of the poor, lonely Akif and a series of almost identical gushing reviews that his friend, advisor, and manager, Rolf Degen, an academic journalist, was able to place in local papers and cultural journals have proven effective. Two thousand fans have written to him, although he has responded to no one ("I'm not a doctor"); a women's commune in Nuremberg sent him 10 marks to get drunk and invited him to visit (he pocketed the money and is not even thinking of visiting); and a school class outside of Hamburg invited him in vain: "I'm not going there. What am I supposed to talk about with them?" [. . .]

"One seldom sees such escapism as with Akif," says a representative of the Goldmann publishing house, "but he has gotten very far with it nonetheless." However, some are now overcome by a "guilty conscience" when they think about their author and see how he "has been systematically worn down" by too grand an accommodation from the publisher ("the contract with him is the most ridiculous we have ever put together") and by a completely uncritical public response.

2

HARALD WEINRICH

THE ADELBERT VON CHAMISSO PRIZE

First published as "Der Adelbert-von-Chamisso Preis" in *Chamissos Enkel: Literatur von Ausländern in Deutschland,* Heinz Friedrich, ed. (Munich: Deutscher Taschenbuch Verlag, 1986), 15–19. Translated by Tes Howell. The first Chamisso promotional prize to honor authors of non-German descent went to Aras Ören (b. 1939, Istanbul). Subsequent winners include Franco Biondi (1987), Zafer Şenocak (1988), Zehra Çırak (1989), Gyorgy Dalos (1995), Yoko Tawada (1996), Güney Dal (1997), SAID (2002), and Asfa-Wossen Asserate (2004).

Among the various German literary awards, the Adelbert von Chamisso Prize is given to nonnative German authors for their important contributions to German literature. It bears the name of a man who was born in France as Louis Charles Adélaïde Chamisso de Boncourt and who later, as an emigrant, became a German poet under the name Adelbert von Chamisso. Heinrich Heine declared his esteem for this author, saying "His heart is so young and vibrant; the man is not separated from the poet in him, his word is his heart, and this heart is great and beautiful and young and vibrant." We ask ourselves today whether Adelbert von Chamisso would have been this poet if fate had not placed him between two countries as it did, between two languages and—one could almost say—between two cultures. Would he have written even one line as a Frenchman, living comfortably on his estate in Champagne? I doubt it. But, tossed about by fate, he was thrown not only into a foreign world but also into a foreign literature, thus becoming part of the commonwealth of world literature by those who are cast into the world and often in opposition to it.

The creation of the Adelbert von Chamisso Prize is a signal that literature from the outside is welcome among us Germans and that we can appreciate it as an enrichment of our own literature and as a concrete piece of world literature. And even if we sometimes are not sure how to address these half-foreigner, half-native authors who often do not have a German passport but do have a German pen, we are momentarily absolved of our linguistic confusion when we name them "Chamisso's grandchildren."

What does it mean to have a German pen? The Foundation of the Adelbert von Chamisso Prize has deliberated at length whether it means nothing other than writing in the German language, as Rafik Schami does, for example. However, reflecting on how foreign writers write and publish in Germany proves that a "German pen" is at work when the texts are composed in the native language but discuss the life of foreigners in Germany. In other words, they are inspired by Germany and have their actual reading public in the German linguistic sphere. This is particularly true for Aras Ören. Accordingly, the statutes of the Adelbert von Chamisso Prize stipulate that the award be given for literary works that have been written in German by authors whose native language is not German or those which have been translated into German in the immediate context of their construction. [. . .]

We are very grateful to the Robert Bosch Foundation for its cultural engagement and for its successful contribution not only to a peaceful but also to a friendly coexistence of natives and foreigners in a country in which some foreigners do indeed experience injustice but a country in which Adelbert von Chamisso could become a German poet—a country in which a writer of Israeli origin, now living in Denmark, can introduce an Arabic author in the German language, and a country in which a Turkish writer living in the Federal Republic can introduce another Turkish writer living in West Berlin in German as well.

3

ARAS ÖREN

CHAMISSO PRIZE ACCEPTANCE SPEECH (1986)

First published as "Dankrede zur Preisverleihung" in *Chamissos Enkel: Literatur von Ausländern in Deutschland,* Heinz Friedrich, ed. (Munich: Deutscher Taschenbuch Verlag, 1986), 20–24. Translated by Tes Howell. Aras Ören (b. 1939, Istanbul) has lived in Berlin since 1969. In 1973, he became editor and director of the Turkish program at Sender Freies Berlin. In this acceptance speech, Ören accounts for himself as a German author and sketches out a preliminary vision for a new European identity. Ören writes his fiction and poetry primarily in Turkish.

[. . .] We often complain today that we as individuals are left alone in the middle of a turbulently developing world of communication technologies but are unable to communicate ourselves, often experiencing an almost complete speechlessness. It looks as though we have come up against the limits of language, to a point that we can neither go forward nor return to the past.

However, something becomes immediately apparent when one apprehends the following dual development: the paradox of rapidly expanding communication technology, on the one hand, and the relegation of the individual to a lack of communication, on the other. It is not my intention to tackle this contradiction here, but as a writer, as one who deals with the written word, I do want to direct your attention to one thing: among changing technological and social conditions, it must be our task to consider the role of art, inasmuch as it reflects humans, objects, and reality, and to change it and to redefine its function. Otherwise, we will end up in a situation in which we must content ourselves with being mere pencil pushers for the reproduction of the most varied of iconographies. In view of this new role that literature must adopt, I belong neither to those who scorn mass media nor to those who see them as a competitor that will edge out the book over time. Although for advocates of so-called *Kommunikationsfreiheit,* or freedom of communication, the issue is nothing more than the total (or as complete as possible) engagement of minds, fantasies, and consciousnesses; it would be absurd to fight against this development like one of Don Quixote's companions.

For me, the writer's task is to draw consequences from everything, to establish the "consciousness industry," as Enzensberger says, as the focus of public attention, and to watch for, develop, and cultivate new territory, thereby redefining the role of literature. And in the process, the creative spirit gains in importance. Simultaneously, this spirit avows tolerance and openness to others. Here, the issue is not only permanence but also an act of fundamental self-renewal. Almost all areas of art should anticipate some difficulty with this process.

The venture is not simple. I'm certain of that. However, I think that we can only build on this foundation in the future. Perhaps we will need additional infusions of energy. I am convinced that an important incentive can come from us, foreigners in German literature, and we stand by this task. If we can accomplish it and we are recognized in the process, then the words of Adelbert von Chamisso, in whose name this award was established and given to me (and I feel very honored to receive it), will have validity for me. Chamisso said, and I agree with these words, "I almost believe I am a German poet."

Every artist is under the influence of his contemporary historical and social conditions. That is completely natural. An important part of my experience was determined by the great migration movements from Turkey to Germany, from farm countries at the periphery to the center of Europe, from underdeveloped regions to industrial nations; it was shaped by an immigration in which I participated from the very beginning and whose witness I became. The conditions under which it took place, the many individual fates that are bound to it, have left a lasting impression on me. To remain untouched by this experience is unthinkable when you are one of those involved. To stand in the middle of it and still not take part would indicate insensitivity and indifference. This indifference certainly exists. With me, however, this was not the case because I didn't want it that way. During at least one phase of my literary creation I concentrated on this point with great persistence. This era of my literary activity is closely connected with the various immigration waves. Both ran parallel to and reflected one another.

The awareness of immigration and my literary consciousness are in constant interaction and are mutually dependent. This relationship is quite clear to me. Our awareness, shaped by immigration, disunity, the loss of our old identity, and the search for a new one are not merely characteristics of those affected by immigration—passively or actively. They are simultaneously determining factors of the new consciousness, the new identity, which Europe and all highly industrialized nations have been searching for in the past two decades of this century.

In other words, Europe is the reflection of my face, and I am the reflection of the face of Europe. My speechlessness is also Europe's. I see the phenomenon from this perspective. In my opinion, this is important, and this position distinguishes me from some Turkish colleagues and many German culture brokers who work in this field. This mutual impact signifies an expansion of my creative energies and allows them to become an integral part of the creative European zeitgeist. My search for the new language contributes to this phenomenon/movement in that it can overcome the speechlessness on the borders of language. My search for new ways of communication shows contemporaries a way out of this speechlessness. While they accompany me into the future as admonishers, my presence gives them the possibility to reconsider the repressed past. Recognition and confirmation of our literature and art can also mean the recognition and confirmation of one's own consciousness and newly created values. Only under these conditions can propositions like "The Federal Republic of Germany is a nation of culture," or "The Federal Republic of Germany is connected to the cultural community of European nations"—propositions continually reinterpreted and converted into praxis by various governments according to their political position and philosophy—be scrutinized for their substance and be compelled to provide proof of their tolerance. Only then can they be taken at their word, which was probably the original intention. To put it in the briefest of terms, our new social and cultural sphere and our literature, a product of this community, will certainly contribute to the development of a new European identity. [. . .]

We represent the tradition of today as well as the cultural heritage of to-morrow. It is my wish that the written word become a bridge of communication above and beyond all borders, connecting fantasy with fantasy, thought with thought, language with language, and individual with individual.

4

MAXIM BILLER

THE TURKICIZED GERMANS

First published as "Die getürkten Deutschen" in *Die Tempojahre* (Munich: Deutscher Taschenbuch Verlag, 1991), 247–49. Translated by Tes Howell. Biller (b. 1960, Prague) released his first prose works in 1990 while working as a journalist and satirist at the magazine *Tempo*. The following satire was among a collection of polemical essays published as *The Tempo Years* in 1991. Biller uses the German verb *türken* in his essay's title, playing on the ambiguity between two meanings: the "tricked Germans" and the "Turkicized Germans." *Lindenstrasse* is a long-running popular soap opera in Germany, which has been on the air since 1985 (see chapter 10).

We will force the subhumans to enjoy their multicultural fortune; we will bend these four and a half million foreigners into shape. Indeed, one day they will understand that one does not grab at women, that one neither laughs nor talks on the subway, that only a heathen does not have coffee and cake on Sunday, and that Khomeini, Ceaușescu, and Idi Amin were all big-time criminals. Hitler, however, was a historical mistake.

It's a given, of course, that we will continue to entrust the blacks and Turks with hauling away our garbage and living in our slums. Certainly, that is somewhat unfair, but, as a result, we can continue to shop for exotic products in their exotic shops and lead civilized discussions with them in pidgin German about their primeval homeland (out of respect for their folkloristic marginal culture)—communication of a high caliber, similar to that of guest-worker programs on ZDF.

We will teach our inferiors how to speak Hessian, to cook Swabian, and to laugh Low German. We will satisfy their youth with German heavy-metal culture, elate the elderly with German economic chauvinism, and bribe them with that placebo of emancipation: "voting rights for foreigners." They should become Germans—of a certain category, let's say, second class with an expiration date monitored by immigration. And, naturally, we won't give them German citizenship anyway. We must have order. And obviously we will label the whole thing as the charmingly enigmatic *multicultural society*. And for precisely this reason, we will not tell the blacks and Turks (one must not frighten them unnecessarily) which devil's advocate—from the *taz* to *faz*, from Daniel Cohn-Bendit to Manfred Rommel—is behind the words of the thoroughly debated multicultural society. This is a man whom we call, not without pride, the Auschwitz-pacifist Geißler. It is no coincidence that he was the one who succeeded in addressing the increasingly urgent foreigner question for our reunified, strengthened *Volk*—hidden, of course, behind a pseudoliberal mask of racial tolerance and economic magnanimity.

Hence, fellow German citizens, there is no need to panic: Heiner Geißler is not advocating for the (ha ha) multicultural society, because he really wishes for a cosmopolitization and slow dissolution of our republic. No, the Auschwitz-pacifist Geißler simply realized, with a visionary pragmatic awareness, that blacks and Turks are already here and that one can hardly throw them out now, and second, that they—quotation!—as "surplus consumers" beautifully complement the socioeconomic equilibrium of our affluent society. The fact that in his book *Zugluft*, or *Draft*, he simultaneously advocates something that has been around for a long time—the coexistence of Germans and non-Germans—will at best occur to some bogus, smart-alecky, Tamil-speaking asylum seekers and nit-picking Jewish Talmudists.

We Germans, in contrast, know that in this way, he has found a particularly clever, diplomatic method for the segregation and—watch out, no euphemism!—gentle enslavement of our foreign fellow citizens and so wants to accompany us along a promising path: the creation of a society of grandly tolerant German leaders and nameless Helots, who may work off their national and cultural frustration as minor characters on *Lindenstrasse*.

The principle is clear: The Black Turks, Islamic gypsies, and Yugoslavian Jews must never find out that the multicultural society is just a trick, a new catchword for our long-standing "We single out the foreign" game. If they do, then they might not play along. And if that happens, then God help us. Then Germany will soon be a racial hotbed of vice worse than New York and Singapore, Tel Aviv and Paris all together. Then there will no longer be a single real German.

Would that really be such a catastrophe?

5

JENS JESSEN

THE TEMPTING CALL OF VANITY

First published as "Lockruf der Eitelkeit" in *Frankfurter Allgemeine Zeitung* (July 2, 1991). Translated by Tes Howell.

Klagenfurt is on its way out: On the fifteenth Ingeborg Bachmann competition
The Ingeborg Bachmann Prize is still alive and kicking. This literature competition still takes place in Klagenfurt, and television covers it live over a period of five days—mercilessly, as though it were a tennis tournament. The authors and publishers, critics and voyeurs still stream into the studios of Austrian Radio to stare at writers reading their work and the judges adjudicating them. They still all end up every evening at the restaurants in something that once would have been called "cliques." The prattle is thunderous.

Throughout the city, the event is advertised on banners as a "week of encounters." It is clear that in Klagenfurt, sociability is everything and that literature takes a back seat.

Tedium is slowly rearing its head, though I know patience is the mark of my people. How did the imbalance between display and the dignity of the prize, between the competition's formidable organizational machinery, the pathetic texts, the helpless efforts of the jurors become as glaring as it was this year? Klagenfurt has seen its day. Much time has passed since authors such as Jurek Becker, Horst Bienek, or Brigitte Kronauer competed there for an award, since authors such as Ulrich Plenzdorf, Sten Nadolny, or Gert Hofmann received one. The last award winners were Angela Krauss and Birgit Vanderbeke. What have they written? What became of them? No one will ever ask about them again. The fact that Wolfgang Hilbig, a real writer, won the Ingeborg Bachmann Prize in the meantime must have been one last upward surge from the competition's agony.

Klagenfurt cannot even muster enough energy for scandals. No author runs from the gathering crying; no one cuts his forehead with a razor. Only a handful of Austrian authors from Graz are still protesting, for they see that Ingeborg Bachmann's reputation is in jeopardy. But it is more likely that they are actually finding that their own reputations are not being sufficiently appreciated. Even among the jurors, the once-legendary battles of giants have disappeared—like the ones between Joachim Kaiser and Marcel Reich-Ranicki, which were always reminiscent of old horror films like *King Kong versus Godzilla.*

From the last egg of Godzilla's spawn slipped a small, cute dragon named Sigrid Löffler *(Profil)* who was never very good at breathing fire. Sigrid Löffler loves "authenticity," and the worst she can say about a text is that it is "artificial" and "contrived," "invented and fabricated." But what, for heaven's sake, should literature be if not invented and fabricated? It becomes clear that this dragon is merely venomous and can no longer light fires. For the other jurors also loved the category of the authentic, and indeed not at all in the precise sense of Adorno, in which the authentic could have literary meaning if necessary, but instead seriously and naively as authentication through the persona of the author. To cite the words of Stefan Richter (Reclam Leipzig), referring to the Italian Francesco Micieli's sugarcoated children's story of sorrow and misfortune, "This is a story of wasted emotion."

The misjudgments did, however, stay within narrow borders. The jury—in general restrained, kind, and slightly confused—kept itself in check. Only the gracefully lyrical text of the Berlin author Sabine Küchler, whom Sigrid Löffler accused of lying, remained undefended. (Volker Hage: "I feel excluded from the story.") This kind of commentary was not the unsettling part. The reasons were unsettling. Volker Hage's peculiar argument resurfaced in various forms among many jurors; even Karl Corino (Hessian Radio), a juror who emphatically insists on philological accuracy, suddenly spoke of the "excluded reader." What is that supposed to mean? It was not these hermetic texts themselves that attracted such judgment.

Other jurors preferred to operate with the less-charged concept of "light fiction" (especially favored by *Der Spiegel*'s Hellmuth Karasek) or with principles unexpectedly salvaged from nineteenth-century psychological realist novels. The incomplete representation of reality and inner life was criticized, as though we had not known for some time that every text can freely construct its own world and figures. Still, it would be wrong to presume, for this reason, that the jurors subscribed to Lenin's theory of reflection. Every critic there had already proved how intelligently he could review texts if he could read and judge them silently at his desk, as is appropriate in dealing with literature. It is the fatal dictate of speech, of spontaneity, the quick-witted ideals of talk shows that make anyone who adheres to them seem stupid. It is no surprise; it is no frightening metamorphosis. These are the laws of television.

However, the jurors have consciously engaged with them. One must marvel that so few have wanted to distance themselves from the lure of the Ingeborg Bachmann Prize and its flattered vanity. For the alarming lapse in textual quality, which the jury lamented, is causally linked to the jury itself. By no means does this dilemma suggest that contemporary German-speaking literature is similarly deficient. For how could one suggest to an author that he go to Klagenfurt? Even if he were to be praised by the jury, one would have to advise him to plug both ears. How many texts were praised for solidly fulfilling their aesthetic plan, however misguided it may have been? As though the embroidered silk pillow of the housewife were art just because she indeed sought to embroider a pillow. To his credit, the Swiss Germanist Peter von Matt came close to acknowledging these failures several times.

Patience—I know the mark of my people. What grows slowly gets reproduced powerfully. In the middle of a discussion, panic suddenly overcame juror Karl Corino; he was quite worried about the future of the Ingeborg Bachmann Prize. The slowly mounting tedium had suddenly reached the jury itself. Perhaps it was for this reason that the jury members decided to stage the apparent end of the competition with the conferral of awards. The jury could have chosen scandal and awarded the first prize to Urs Alleman's etude "Baby Fucker," a virtuoso piece that was, however, treated like obscene sensationalism. This would have led to the walkout of the morally conflicted Italian juror Roberto Cazzola (*Einaudi*), thereby incapacitating the jury.

It would have been a departure with fire and brimstone. Instead, the jury chose flight into incredibility and nominated the helpless text of a German-writing Turkish woman, which plays on folkloristic elements from the fairy-tale tradition of her homeland, and which the jurors good-naturedly viewed as surrealism. For this reason, among all the others, the Ingeborg Bachmann Prize is as good as dead. Only out of the deference befitting an obituary shall we say the author's name: Emine Sevgi Özdamar. Against the backdrop of contemporary Turkish prose, which is in no way naïve or folkloristic, the choice is absurd, indeed insulting. None of the other prizewinners were able to salvage the willfully squandered credibility: neither Urs Allemann (Prize of the Kärnten State) nor Marcel Boyer (Ernst Willner Prize) nor Peter Wawerzineck (Bertelsmann Stipend) nor Hubert Konrad Frank (Kärntner Industry Stipend). The jury has met its mark. Klagenfurt is done for good.

6

EMINE SEVGI ÖZDAMAR

BLACK EYE AND HIS DONKEY

First printed as "Schwarzauge und sein Esel" in *Die Zeit* (February 25, 1992). Translated by David Herricks and Frank Krause. In the wake of the Bachmann Prize controversy (see Jessen's "The Tempting Call of Vanity" above), the German newspaper *Die Zeit* asked Özdamar to describe her experiences as a migrant writer in Germany. The following text somewhat sidesteps this topical question, opting instead to narrate her engagement with the theatrical process of staging experiential narratives about migration. *Karagöz*, or black eye, is a Turkish theatrical genre of shadow puppetry that usually serves as a vehicle for social critique and political satire.

My first play was *Karagöz in Alamania,* written in 1982. It means *"Black Eye in Germany."* I wrote it because I had discovered the letter of a Turkish guest worker. I never knew the man personally. He had gone back to Turkey for good, to his home village.

Guest worker is a term I love. When I encounter it, I always picture two people; one is just sitting there as a guest, and the other is working.

The letter was written on a typewriter. The other thing that struck me about it was that at no point did he say anything bad about Germany. He said, "A worker has no home. Wherever there is work is home for him." He wrote about his wife, who could not stand the life either in Turkey or in Germany. She was always moving from the one country to the other, and on every occasion she was pregnant.

Once, while in Germany, his wife had told him that back home in their village in Turkey, she and his uncle had eaten cherries together from the same tree. Leaving his wife on her own in Germany, he had made the 3,000-kilometer journey to Turkey, merely in order to ask his relatives which of the two had first been standing under the cherry tree. Was it his wife or his uncle? Who had first gone to the tree, and who had gone to join the other already eating cherries?

He questioned relatives and neighbors in the village. The whole affair grew out of all proportion.

While in Germany, he was politicized by Turkish students who were Maoists. Once he was with them outside a factory, handing out leaflets against the Turkish fascists. When the fascists arrived on the scene, the Maoist students disappeared, and he was left standing there alone. The Turkish fascists punched him in the face, leaving one side of it paralyzed.

I could not understand the Turkish he wrote in his letter very well.

I wanted to write a play about him and then invite him back to Germany for the premiere. I wanted to show him that his life was a novel, just as he himself had claimed that it was in his letter. So I made the journey from Germany to Turkey by train.

In Austria, some Yugoslavs joined the train. Construction workers. Some of them had deliberately smashed their fingers with hammers to get a sick note from the doctor and were now on their way home to their wives in Yugoslavia, their hands wrapped in bandages.

Greeks, Turks, and Yugoslavs were sitting together in the same train, their common language German. In Yugoslavia, a few Turkish fathers, old men, also got on the train. They had journeyed there from Turkey with empty coffins in order to take back home the bodies of their sons and daughters, killed in accidents on the roads of Yugoslavia as they made their way back from Germany. Standing in the corridor, the fathers smoked cigarettes and talked in hushed voices about the journey and about their dead children. One of them said, "This journey has robbed us of our five souls."

The Yugoslav men sang songs of love and longing about the wives they were returning to, translating them for us in their broken German. The resulting conversation was almost an oratorio, and the mistakes we made in the German language were us. All we had were our mistakes.

In my play *Karagöz in Alamania,* the figure of Karagöz is a Turkish peasant. He sets off for Germany with his talking donkey, leaving his wife behind in the village. Before they reach Germany, Karagöz and the donkey experience many things along the way. The donkey turns into an intellectual, quoting Marx and Socrates, drinking wine and smoking Camel cigarettes. Karagöz's wife is constantly on the move between Turkey and Germany, unable to stand the life in either country. The donkey gets into a conversation with Karagöz's car—an Opel Caravan—about the impending war. The car gets angry, calling for its owner, Karagöz. Karagöz beats the donkey, who, suffering a heart attack, leaves in the company of a figure who is the exact likeness of Karagöz in his youth. Karagöz no longer recognizes his former self. He journeys on again in his Opel Caravan. His journey is endless.

I directed *Karagöz in Alamania* in 1986 at the Frankfurt Playhouse. Because in their various stories and scenes in the play my characters claim to be stars, I looked for actors, professional and amateur, who were stars. For example, I found an elderly Turkish worker, Nihat, who had previously owned a kebab salon and had a good face, like a mafia type. I also found a marvelous Greek opera singer, as well as German, Turkish, and Spanish stars of the stage and screen, all good actors with wonderful faces. In addition, we had a real donkey, a sheep, and three hens. A black lamb took the place of the sheep during rehearsals on stage.

At the start of rehearsals, an almost sacred atmosphere reigned on stage. What we are doing is something special! For the first time, a play about Turks. Hushed voices, loving glances. Slow movements. The animals, too, were friends with one another. Donkey, sheep, and lamb lay down to sleep alongside each other in the same stall. The actress looking after them said, "How they love one another, the animals!"

It lasted for a week. After one week, the normal difficulties of rehearsal work began.

A short while after, the actors got cross with one another; the animals started in their turn. The donkey kicked the sheep or bared his teeth at it; the sheep bit the donkey; between the two of them, the lamb uttered a loud baaaaa. We separated the animals from each other in the stall so that they would not go on fighting during the night. The Turkish star wanted to show the German star, who was acting the part of the Turk, how to play a guest worker. The German said to him, "You caraway-chewing Turk, learn to speak English properly before you try to teach me anything." In response, the Turkish star called him an "SS man" in English.

Once, the German actress looking after the animals brought the sheep and the lamb to rehearsals and shouted, "Who has been spitting on the sheep's head backstage?" The Spanish actor responded, "You with your German love of animals, when the world is full of human beings starving to death."

The German actress slapped the Spanish actor across the face, saying, "You vain Spaniard, you."

One of the German stars greeted me every morning with the words "Good morning, Mrs. Khomeini."

Only Nihat, the former kebab-salon owner, ran to and fro among the actors, shouting, "What's going on here? What's going on here?"

One morning, another Turkish star placed a letter to me on the director's table. In it, he wrote that if I persisted in loving the gay German actor more than him, he would shortly make his feelings public in a Turkish newspaper.

I invited him for a meal, cooking Turkish food for him. He ate it, criticizing me because it was not salted enough, and so on. But he ate it with relish and drank sweet Turkish coffee. Then he told me the story of his father, who had died at the age of 36 because he felt that he was the constant target of insults. When the German star found out that I had cooked for the Turk, he wanted to make a date with me. Having arranged to meet me at 11 o'clock at night in a restaurant, he turned up two hours late. He laughed, saying, "Oh, you've been waiting for me."

One day, an actress who was playing a Turkish woman appeared at rehearsals wearing a head scarf. I asked her why. A German actor had told her that she ought to thus demonstrate her commitment to being Turkish. On one occasion, the donkey hit the Turkish star in the back of his neck. He had been holding the donkey's head fairly tightly under his arm, as if to show that the animal was a friend that he was joking with. The German stage designer threw himself onto the donkey to make it release its hold on the star's neck. We then took him to the hospital, where he received a rabies vaccination. One of the Turkish stars said, "A Turkish donkey would never do a thing like that." (The donkey was from Frankfurt.) A German star replied, "I get on very well with the donkey. He'd never do anything like that to me." But then the donkey kicked him, too. He came to me and said, "I'm going to have a word with the donkey."

During rehearsals, the father, mother, and grandmother of the Greek opera singer all died, as did the 100-year-old aunt of one of the German stars. We thus reached the premiere with several deaths in the cast, not to mention those wounded by the donkey.

I wanted to invite the worker whose letter had prompted me to write the play to the premiere. But he, too, had died—of a heart attack, at age 41, in his home village, sitting on a chair outside his shop.

The theater manager was a nice man who loved his work. When one of the actresses had to speak the lines "Me stay behind / My husband stay Germany / Fuck German woman." He said: "Please don't speak that word; otherwise, the Germans will all think that Turkish poetry consists of such expressions."

As a result, when it came to the dress rehearsal, the actress spoke the lines "My husband stay Germany / Fuck German woman."

Before the premiere, the theater, out of love for the play and without asking my permission in advance, had leaflets distributed among the audience, in which it attempted to explain the work. "In the course of the play, you will occasionally wonder, Where are we now? Are we in Turkey, or are we in Germany?. . . It may well be that you will have problems ordering the scenes in your mind. They are not logically structured as in the plays we are familiar with. . . . "

That was six years ago. I still meet with actors who were involved, or they ring me up. Then they talk about the others:

—She's got a child now, did you know?
—I met him in Berlin.
—Just now, she's singing at La Scala in Milan.

—Have you heard anything of him?

—Winter is on the way. I wonder whether she'll put on her long coat again?

They pursue one another like lovers.

7

ZAFER ŞENOCAK

THE BASTARDIZED LANGUAGE

Published as "Die bastardierte Sprache" in *War Hitler Araber? Irreführungen an den Rand Europas: Essays* (Berlin: Babel, 1994), 29–33. Translated by Tom Cheesman. Şenocak (b. 1961, Ankara) is a poet, novelist, and theorist of migration. He is a regular contributor to *Die Zeit* and *die tageszeitung* and has been an artist-in-residence in the United States at Dartmouth College, Oberlin College, and the University of California, Berkeley. His essay collection *Atlas of a Tropical Germany* has been published in translation by Leslie A. Adelson.

> *Good evening. Good evening. How far is it to you?*
> *It's far, very far. And it's far to me.*
> —INGEBORG BACHMANN, "UNDINE WALKS"

Five hundred years ago, the white man crossed over the borders of his world and encountered the Other, whom he perceived as his shadow.

Whereas he wrote, the Other only seemed to speak, sing, and dance; whereas he hid his body, the Other seemed to bare his.

He controlled his urges. He wrote poems and catechisms. The white man thought that the Other had no cares and lived in an innocent paradise created by sinners for sinners. The white man decided to destroy this paradise by fire, in order to preserve it in his memory. In order to dream of this paradise by night in wooden ships rocked back and forth by the waves. The white man hated his dream. He could not bear shadows. He was suspicious. He hated the Other; he felt that the Other reminded him of his missed opportunities.

The Other survived. He was a cross-breed: half shadow, half body; half dream, half reality. He began to write. He wrote as though he were speaking. He set off along the road, a long road. He encountered the white man in his world. He settled in the world of the white man. He lost his innocence.

The borders blurred. There were parts of the world where the borders always were blurred. There was the Mediterranean, a sea that bound shadow and body, man and woman together. A sea of their common blood. The white man discovered the Other in himself. He became aggressive, against himself, against the Other in himself. He wanted to tear him out of himself, wanted to spit him out. He founded the United White Empire. But in the United White Empire, there were too many stains, spots of many colors. The many-colored stains angered him. The white man washed them out. But the Empire did not come up completely white. The languages had touched, had gotten mixed up. There were suddenly Turks in Europe, there were Indians, there were Africans, Arabs. There were too many spots that were not completely white.

Some spots stood out against the white backdrop, grew darker, closed together into tumors. Tumors that would have to be cut out, sooner or later. The white peace was over for good. Guilt and innocence mingled and made new laws.

The white man ran out of stories to tell. He repeated his stories. He heard the Other speak out of himself, in his language: Turks who had grown up in Germany began to write. They even wrote poems. It was as if Celan and Kafka were still writing. Another from Bombay spoke up in English. It was not easy for him to make himself understood. The white man occupied him as he had once occupied India. But the man from Bombay was no longer in India; he had gone among the white men in London and was describing London. As always, the Mediterranean united everyone. It was a great sea of forgetting; the treasures of the seabed were utterly limitless. The seafarers' grandchildren lifted the shipwrecks and laid out their finds in the white man's language. The white man was annoyed. He did not want any new white men. He tolerated white only on his shirt.

Is only one white language allowed? Is there a world language? Is such a world language audible or legible, or is it too much for ears to bear? When the black whites not only sing and dance but write, what happens then? Do they become white? The Turk of German tongue knows the German, but is there a German of Turkish tongue who knows the Turk? Is there the German, the Turk? Can languages embrace cultures, can cultures embrace peoples, can peoples embrace a person?

The Turkish writer knows Goethe, Schiller, Hölderlin, Benn, Trakl, Eich, Celan, Bachmann, Kafka, Camus. And the German writer? Does he know Cansever, Uyar, Süreya? Has he ever heard the name Ibnül Emin? Does he know who Ahmet Rasim was, or Fuzuli or Nedim? The German has an idea but knows nothing; the Turk knows but has no idea. Which of the two is the ignoramus, which is the one in the dark? The German's dark ideas frighten him. But then he thinks of Prince Eugene, "Terror to the Turks," and leans back, calm again.

What the Turk knows does him little good. "Coming at a gallop from distant Asia, it stretches into the Mediterranean like a mare's head! That is our country!" So Nazım Hikmet once described Turkey. All that the European remembers of this gallop is hooves thundering on European soil, numberless wars, and devastations. In Europe's memory, the Turk is a barbarian, a blood enemy, stigmatized; there is a fixed image of him. But for 150 years, this country has been stretching intellectually, too, between modernity and tradition, between Orient and Occident. Doing the splits like this has prepared the Turkish writer of German tongue for a split identity. But it also brought on aching stiffness. His tongue is numb in many places. Language ought to bring his tongue back to life, get it moving again. How many numb places does his language have? No one knows. In the language, the taboos, stereotypes passed down by tradition, are like traps. If one locates them, they turn out to be knots that must be cut through. Afterward pain spreads. A bloodless dull pain on the border to pleasure. The tongue moves.

Words appear, spotless words. Are there such words? Has not the white man said everything? He has read the Bible, the Talmud, the Koran. He did not write any of these books but forged them all and turned all languages into silence.

And now the black whites are coming, the shadows from memory, the murdered from their hell, spitting green bile. Who will be able to bear their bile? Who will enjoy drinking it? Is it not better, the white man wonders, to rely on one's household drug cabinet, to take medicines with familiar labels? Instead of risking unknown new medicines? But the old medicines no longer cure; at best, they delay death.

No one knows what the new language will taste like. The bastardized language no one can be immune to. So, better get rid of what's in the bottles straight away. But wait, there is something that once made the white man so strong: curiosity, this inexhaustible curiosity. Maybe he will try it. The alchemists of the new language who are creating new, unspoken, fictive realities between German and Turkish, between the Koran and the Bible, between Byzantium and Asia, are hoping. Hoping for a willingness to bring their unlabeled bottles to the white man as he lies on his deathbed. They are concerned for his well-being. For if he dies, they will not have many more stories to tell either. His death will be their one theme, when they are lying beside his corpse in a damp cellar, exhausted from interrogations, from the torture inflicted on them by their last readers, the conviction hunters among the blacks. Hidden under their habits, the conviction hunters dream of the tabooed tongue, of the language in knots, of the one and only indivisible taboo. They have made a pact with the white man's corpse. They want to reinstall their unhinged language where it used to hang. They cite their prophet, taking his words into their mouths like stones. Nothing moves any more. He who makes images has departed from the way; who makes new images has fallen into an abyss, lost beyond redemption. There he meets Dante working on the last version of his inferno. He meets the Marquis; Danton; the young Büchner, who gave him a second life; Rimbaud, who was always dying of tropical fever; the syphilitic Nietzsche.

They were all heralds of the blacks in white Europe. Light is not only bright, it is dark too, barely distinguishable from the first dawn glimmer. The enlighteners are not seen before noon. They sit at long tables, dining. They are civilized. A white tablecloth covers the table right down to the floor. There is no knowing what is going on under the table. Maybe Novalis is there, dreaming of Christendom and Europe. Or a Persian ambassador is formulating a sentence for a poetry-writing privy councillor from Weimar to write down later as "A country that fails to protect foreigners is soon lost." But who is a foreigner? Djem, the King of Drinkers from Persia, is a foreigner in his own country. Writers of poetry are on their guard against the truth and more at home in damp, dark cellars than at the long tables of the enlighteners at noon. Each seeks his own language as if it were a vanished island on a worn map. These islands exist, but not on maps. One has to seek them, if need be, under the sea. Now that all parts of the earth have been discovered and disenchanted, only language can still excite the explorer. It can offer a refuge from too-curious gazes; it can expose the most hidden detail to all eyes. Language is never the color in which one imagines it. The Turkish poet of German tongue dreams at night of Djem's drinking session under the cypresses. It is a drinking session on gravestones. The sakis have lost weight. They suffer from eternal wasting disease.

There are those who wish to rip out his tongue, to make sure he dirties neither the one nor the other half of himself. They speak of "identity" and "conflicts of loyalty" between two states, two peoples, two countries, two languages. They find it difficult to imagine distances. They view everything close up and see a distorted picture of themselves. They are afraid of themselves. They do not trust the ground they walk on. Yet Djem, the poet and King of Drinkers, passes the wine around, sings in their language, and the murmuring of his friends crosses the land.

8

FERIDUN ZAIMOĞLU

PREFACE TO *KANAKI SPEAK*

First published as *Kanak Sprak: 24 Miβtöne vom Rande der Gesellschaft* (Hamburg: Rotbuch, 1995), 12–19. Translated by Tom Cheesman. Zaimoğlu (b. 1964, Bolu, Turkey) emerged in the 1990s as one of Germany's most critical and polemical voices on issues of assimilation and the idea of a "dialogue of cultures." The following text is the preface to his pseudo-ethnographic collection of transnational youth testimonies, *Kanak Sprak*.

What's life like as a Kanaki in Germany? This was the question I put to myself and others. *Kanaki,* a label that now, after 30-odd years of Turkish immigration, is no longer just an insult but a name carried with defiant pride by "guest-worker-children" of the second and, above all, the third generation. [. . .]

On the street, in the supermarket, in the disco, the talk is of *taking liberties,* of the *full boat,* of *patience hanging by a silken thread.* Classrooms fall silent when the "Turkish bastards" enter. Bright children are labeled as problem cases and end up in special schools. The Germans try to make sense of the disaster. Studies are commissioned, statistics collected, migration research yields results: it's the ambivalence caused by living in two cultures, intergenerational conflict in the Turkish family, and finally, their unwillingness to integrate. The right to vote, dual citizenship, and so on, are not even mentioned in public.

This is the climate the second generation of Kanakis is born into. They, like most Germans, take not the slightest interest in Turkey except as a holiday destination. They watch the old, exhausted guest workers pack their bags. Many Turks take advantage of the government's repatriation grants to return to the homeland, hoping to use the money to live their dreams, within their own lifetimes. Their children are torn from their familiar surroundings and endure enforced assimilation in the land of their fathers and mothers. A fair number of these children commit suicide; many come down with chronic psychosomatic illnesses. In Turkish towns and villages, they are met with hostility, as "almancı," "Deutschländer"—little Germans.

Those who stay know all this; they know they cannot go back. As Germany becomes less comfortable, even threatening, Turkish parents react by demanding absolute loyalty to tradition, explicit endorsement of the guest-worker ghetto ethos. Some rediscover religion. The straitjacket of German bureaucracy strangles any possible assimilation. The path is clear toward the complete dissolution of the group—which was never a homogenous "ethnicity." But the Kanaki as a self-confident individual exists only in his passport photo anyway. He lives with the permanent feeling of inferiority, of having lost his way, gone astray. A good number end up as sick exotica in secure wards: impotence as self-inflicted mutilation, depression, schizophrenia. Those who stay out face a new form of fashionable appropriation: multiculturalism.

Here, the Kanaki features as a glittering exhibit in the great zoo of ethnicities, available for participant observation and astonished gawking. Expert "speakers for the Turks" design colorful brochures to accompany guided tours through the *multikulti* zoo, where the Kebab Preserve is positioned next to the Peruvian Music Pavilion.

Since the late 1970s, a tear-jerking, favor-currying, public-funded "guest-worker literature" has been spreading the legend of "Ali, the poor but good-hearted Turk." This "trash collectors' prose" fixes Kanakis in the victim role. The "better Germans" are "deeply affected" by these effusions, since they reek of false authenticity and "hold up a mirror" to their self-absorbed self-criticism, and they celebrate every mistake in written German as an "enrichment" of their "mother tongue." The Turk comes to epitomize "sentiment," cheap nostalgia, and fishy "exoticism." The German commissioners of foreigner affairs, former volunteers pleased to have found work by way of state-sponsored job-creation schemes, muddle along with their scraps of knowledge. But even finding a name for their clientele is problematic: "guest-worker child," "foreign fellow citizen," or simply "Turk"? The popular voice knows better: it says "Turkish bastard" or "Kanaki."

Customs and rites are ascribed to Kanakis just like dud cards get palmed off on weak players in Black Peter, a popular card game. Seen from outside, they appear only as an amorphous lumpenproletarian mass, believed to be recognizable by means of external features and "specific characteristics." Even if they could be forced to make a final decision, Kanakis seek no cultural anchoring. They have no wish to help themselves in the supermarket of identities, nor do they desire to vanish into some egalitarian herd of exiles from lost homelands. They have their own forms of subjectivity and very clear conceptions of self-determination. They make up the real Generation X, those who have been denied all possibility of individuation, of ontogenesis.

Their underground codex long since developed, they speak a jargon of their own: Kanaki speak, a kind of creole or underworld argot with secret codes and signs. Their speech is related to the freestyle sermon of the rappers; like them, they adopt a pose to express themselves. This language decides their existence: it is a wholly private performance in words.

The verbal power of the Kanakis expresses itself in a forceful, breathless, nonstop hybrid stammering, marked with random pauses and turns of phrase invented on the spot. The Kanaki's command of his mother tongue is imperfect, and his grasp of "Allemannish" is no less limited. His vocabulary is composed of "gibberish" words and phrases known to neither language. Into his improvised metaphors and parables he weaves borrowings from high Turkish and from the dialectal slang of Anatolian villages. He emphasizes and accompanies his free-form discourse with mime and gesture. The Kanaki's rich gestural language starts from a basic posture, the so-called anchor pose: arms spread wide apart, body weight grounded through the left leg, leaving the other one free to paw the ground with the toe of the shoe, to signal that at this moment, the Kanaki is keen on having a lively conversation. When, for example, the Kanaki makes a fist with his right hand, then opens it like a fan at lightning speed, he wishes to convey his disapproval or disappointment. When he strokes an index finger, damp with spittle, across one eyebrow, he wants us to recognize his competence or a successful verbal sally. And beyond particular characteristic gestures, the signal the Kanaki is sending is, Here I stand, and everything I am says, I am showing, and creating, presence.

Because the space Kanaki kids move in is the streets, they speak a continually evolving symbolic jargon, often misunderstood as the flowery language of Orientals. My poetic reconstruction had to avoid this folklore trap. Hence, the German translation uses only the form of address "brother," not *gözüm* ("my eye"), *gözümün nuru* ("light of my eye"), and many other such expressions. The Kanaki says, in literal translation, "Hate-hand happily doles out, though breaking many own bones," and means "He who is full of hatred resorts to violence without thought of the risks." The Kanaki says, "God fucks every lame kid" and means "If one wishes to get ahead in life, one must take control of one's own fate." The literary reworking had to take account of this, as also of the fact that the Kanaki cannot be equated with the scion of conventional upper-middle-class circles who cultivates four-letter words and hangs around outside supermarkets with a can of beer in his hand, hassling passersby. [. . .]

In the German translation of Kanaki speak, language alone must vouch for the entirety of existential conditions such as gesture, metaphor, and truth to the jargon. With this "poetic reconstruction," my concern was to create a self-consistent, visible, and, yes, "authentic" image in language. In contrast to the "literature of immigrants," here Kanakis speak in their own tongue. [. . .]

Here, only Kanakis speak.

9

ŞINASI DIKMEN

WHO IS A TURK?

First published as "Wer ist ein Türke?" in *Hurra, ich lebe in Deutschland* (Munich: Piper, 1995), 75–79. Translated by Tes Howell. Dikmen (b. 1948, Samsun, Turkey) came to West Germany in 1972, becoming a popular satirist and professional comedian.

Who is a Turk? How does one recognize him, and how does one know whether someone is a Turk? These questions have been on my mind since I came to Germany. In Turkey, everyone I knew and with whom I spoke Turkish was a Turk to me. When I was young—grown-up Turks were also young once—I believed that there was only one language in the world, Turkish, which is why I thought all people on this earth were Turks.

People talked of Americans, Russians, the French, but we did not have any concrete perceptions of them. Yes, an angry Russian looks like a dangerous bear, an American is the epitome of friendliness, and a German is as loyal as a sheepdog. These were all just vague guesses, but we had never actually met one. In school, I learned French without ever having seen a live Frenchman. We learned where Paris is, how high the French culture is, and even memorized French songs.

My perceptions of Turks consisted of my parents, my siblings, my relatives, my town's residents, and all the others whom I had somehow met and seen—until I came to Germany.

In Germany, first the Germans asked, then I followed: *Who is a Turk?* Many believe a Turk is someone who has a black mustache and a Turkish passport. But there are many Turks in Europe who do not have a Turkish passport, and among them even some who have no mustache.

So, who is a Turk then? Ask a Turkish consulate official. You will certainly get the following answer: "Only the members of the consulate are Turks; the others living in Germany are just guest workers, not Turks." Now we know that not all Turkish guest workers are Turks.

Am I a Turk? Or not? If I am not a Turk, then what am I? And if I am indeed a Turk, what does that make the consulate official? I have more in common with a Greek guest worker than with this official. But this Greek cannot speak Turkish; even if he could, he would not do so in front of the other Greeks. Am I perhaps a Turkicized Turk?

When someone in Germany drives a Ford Granada, he is driving a "Turkmobile." What was the name of the Turk who designed and produced this car? What was the name of the Turk who invented the plastic shopping bag: Ali Osman or Mehmet Ali?

I was born in Turkey and raised Turkish. My parents are Turks, just like my siblings and relatives. I attended a Turkish school, came to Germany as a Turkish guest worker, and registered with the Immigration Office as a Turk. My health insurance, pension, and auto insurance all categorize me under the nationality "Turk," and I speak Turkish at home with my children (as much as possible); I love Turkish, hate Turkish, eat Turkish, sh— Turkish, and I really believed that I was Turkish—until the following incident occurred.

A few years ago, I boarded a train in Hannover to participate in a reading in Hameln. It was a good reading. The audience was nice; we had an interesting dialogue, discussing the situation of Turks, the Germans, God, and the world. After the reading, we went to a Greek restaurant where the food was practically Turkish. The next day, a lady drove me to the train station in Hannover.

I entered a compartment in which an older couple sat. I asked them politely whether there were any seats free and they answered politely, yes, please; I sat down, opened *Die Zeit*, and did what one does in Germany in such a situation—namely be quiet, be quiet, be quiet, never ask anything as long as you yourself have not been addressed. Between the lines, I thought about Elisabeth, at whose house I had spent the night and with whom I had had breakfast; I thought about her two children. Elisabeth was raising her children bilingually, Turkish-German, and despite this the children went to *Gymnasium* and were very successful. Whether Elisabeth was separated from her Turkish husband or already divorced from him, I don't remember anymore. She was a good hostess, like a Turk. She even put food for the trip in my bag. I had never experienced that. No, no, she had adopted something from the Turks. I had had many German hosts, but she was somehow different.

Was Elisabeth a Turk? I don't think so. We spoke German, although she could speak Turkish well. Was she a German? No, not that either. She was an excellent hostess and a good person.

I ate the food she had prepared for me, read on in *Die Zeit*, asked questions of no one, and was not asked anything myself. The couple chatted from

Füssen to Fulda. In Fulda, a real Turk walked into the compartment, asked the couple simply, "Free?" Before he had finished speaking, the woman barked, "No, nothing free!" The Turk, small, short, with a hand-knit vest—green, I would say Turkish green, a glaring green—plastic shopping bags in each hand, left after this curt answer. I looked at him, he looked at me as if to counter, "But there are still three seats left." I had not really comprehended what was happening; it all happened so fast. The train was full, as far as I could tell. The Turk stood right in front of our door, as if to spite us. I asked the woman, "There are still three seats left here. Why did you tell the man there weren't any?"

As always when Germans assess each other, the woman answered, in a voice that, though polite, exacted distance from the interlocutor, that she would not like to sit in a compartment with someone like that. I probed further: "What do you mean, someone like that?"

"With a Turk."

"How do you know that he is a Turk?"

"Anyone can see that right away," she answered. I should just look—that dark look and arrogance.

I responded, "The man asked politely though."

"That's what you think! But I know that Turkish glare." No, I could not possibly demand from the woman that she ruin her trip with the presence of a Turk. By no means did she want to sit with a Turk.

I didn't let up: "But you are traveling with a Turk."

"No," she said, "this is my husband."

"No, really, you are traveling with a Turk: you are traveling with me!"

At first, she didn't know what she should say. She looked at her husband and asked for help, but he didn't say a word; he studied his feet and acted as though he had heard nothing. The woman interpreted my statement as humility: one should not humiliate oneself like that just for fun.

"I'm not humiliating myself when I tell you what I am."

"Do you really think that he," she pointed to the Turk, "appreciates your humility?"

"Whether he appreciates it does not interest me; but I am a Turk, and you are, unfortunately, traveling with a Turk."

"But you can't be a Turk."

"Why not?"

"Just because."

"I'm a Turk; should I show you my passport?"

"You don't need to do that because you are not a Turk."

"Why are you so certain?"

"First of all, yes, hmm, first of all, I don't know, but, hmm, there is no way you are a Turk."

"Why not?"

"Because, hmm, because, how should I say it, hmm, because you are read-ing *Die Zeit*."

I don't know how many readers of *Die Zeit* there are in Germany—maybe one, two, three, four, five hundred thousand or a million. There are 60 mil-lion alleged Germans living in Germany. Because not all read *Die Zeit*, I guess that the Germans who do not read *Zeit* are not Germans but Turks instead.

10

BAHMAN NIRUMAND

CRAFTY GERMANS

First published as "Schlitzohrige Deutsche" in *Der Spiegel* (May 5, 1997). Translated by Tes Howell. Nirumand (b. 1936, Tehran) studied German philology and Near Eastern studies in Germany, after which he accepted a professorship at the University of Tehran. After the Iranian revolution, he fled to exile in France and Germany. He has translated Mahmud Doulatabadi's *The Old Earth* and *The Journey* into German.

WINTER, 1952. Arrival in Stuttgart. Mrs. K. was waiting for me at the main train station. The streets were nearly empty; there were many ruins and half-destroyed houses. It was wet, windy, and cold, a real German November evening in a war-torn city. I had not pictured Germany like this.

After walking for about 10 minutes, we entered a house with a bombed-out second story. There were only two apartments. In one of these apart-ments lived the K. family. I immediately found the living room pleasantly warm, small, and modestly furnished. Wooden chairs, a few photos and art prints on the walls.

Mrs. K. pointed to her stomach to ask me if I was hungry. I nodded my head unmistakably. Mrs. K. went into the kitchen and came back a few min-utes later with a steaming bowl. A horrible, vomit-inducing odor filled the room. She had prepared cauliflower soup for me. I took a piece of bread— no, it was a Swabian pretzel, which tasted good. I could not eat the soup. The meal was over; we could not talk to each other. [. . .]

If someone who knows only the Federal Republic of the 1950s were to visit Germany today, he would barely recognize this country and its inhabitants. The Germans no longer take everything so seriously; they laugh more, have more fun. Perhaps the 7 million foreigners have, as some believe, truly ruined the Germans. The proverbial virtues of the Germans such as reliability, pre-cision, industriousness, and honesty are noticeably more scarce: the Ger-mans in general have become craftier. When I bring my car into the shop today, I cannot be certain, as I was in the past, that the mechanics will actu-ally fix everything. With the truth, the Germans are not as pedantic as well. I determine that we have thus become closer in our behavior.

Yes, we have become closer. We, once foreigners, constantly run around with a date book too. We have also learned to plan our day more precisely, not to sit at a strangers' table in a restaurant, and to show up punctually when we are invited somewhere.

We have learned to deal with our culture and ourselves critically, to expose every assertion—yes, even our feelings and emotions—to gnawing doubt. This transformation is particularly obvious when we meet our countrymen or visit our home countries.

But our common 40-year history has produced important changes. I believe that the political development of Germany into a democratic modern society would not be possible in this form without the active participation of foreigners. One will certainly remember how great the political engagement of non-Germans was in this period, in which the Federal Republic completed the change from an authoritarian and hierarchically structured society into a democratic one. I am referring to the 1960s. [. . .]

The society in question emerged from the ruins of postwar Germany, from the longing for a better, more humane world. It is a society that radically rejects the crimes of National Socialism, racism, and hyper-Germanness and has opened itself up to foreign influences with joy and curiosity. But it is also a society that rejects any kind of fundamentalism—be it Christian, Islamic, or Jewish—as well as national and ethnic small-mindedness. We have built this society together since the early 1960s. With this "we," I mean Germans and foreigners. [. . .]

Naturally, I do not want to deny the necessity of existing foreign organizations, but if migrants in Germany organize themselves politically and want to shape the future of this country together, then they must accept this intercultural reality. There must be no division between Germans and non-Germans in their political views.

It is completely devious when migrants alone look after the fortune of non-Germans and constantly demand tolerance and charity from the Germans. What migrants request of Germans, they must practice themselves. They cannot demand liberalism, just to be able to preach nationalist, racist, and fundamentalist positions themselves. If they want to have equality, they must feel responsible for the future of this society.

In a city like Frankfurt am Main, 40 percent of the youth under 18 are of non-German ancestry. These are our children, whose future must be important to us. It is not enough for us to advocate only for the preservation of native-language instruction in the schools, for the right of asylum or the support of foreign organizations. [. . .]

The times are forever gone in which two societies, those of the migrants and natives, existed side by side: the one impotent and helpless, the other friendly and charitable. The open democratic society that we have built together is not dependent on the majority's tolerance of the minority. The quality needed here is a readiness to deal with conflicts permanently and to solve them together. [. . .]

The sky over Germany has become bleak: unemployment and poverty grow on a daily basis, the youth suffer from a lack of prospects, intellectuals have withdrawn into their niches, parties and unions compete for more clever pragmatism—no trace of utopia. If there is a way out of this crisis, then it will certainly not lead back to the times of early capitalism. More appropriate is further development of the modern democratic society. There is no division of Germans and non-Germans on this path. We must continue to travel it together.

11
GÜNTER GRASS
IN PRAISE OF YAŞAR KEMAL

Published as "Laudatio bei der Verleihung des Friedenspreises des Deutschen Buchhandels an den türkischen Schriftsteller Yaşar Kemal" (November 19, 1997), when Kemal was awarded the German Book Trade Association's Peace Prize. English translation printed in *Boston Review* (December, 1998). Grass (b. 1927, Danzig, Germany), famous for his poignant social critique, is the author of *The Tin Drum, Cat and Mouse,* and *Too Far Afield.* He was awarded the Nobel Prize in 1999. Yaşar Kemal (b. 1923, Adana, Turkey) is one of Turkey's foremost writers, known for his epic novels about the plight of the rural population of Southeastern Anatolia, such as *Mehmed, My Hawk, Iron Earth, Copper Sky,* and *The Legend of the Thousand Bulls.* His books have been translated into many languages.

Dear Yaşar Kemal,

You must have had your reasons for proposing me as a speaker for this occasion. I was glad to respond to your wishes and yield to the temptation to glide inland from the Mediterranean, over the flat muddy fields along the coast, then over the lands of Çukurova with its cover of blackberry bushes, wild vines, and reeds, then farther inland over the swamps, and then once again over rich farmland, myrrh-fragrant hills, plateaus, including Dikenlidüzü with its five villages, where one can already see the snow-covered peaks of the Taurus.

Yaşar Kemal is one of those writers who are content with the patch of earth allotted by birth. As in the case of Faulkner, Akhmatova, or even Joyce, all the events described circle around the site of an early injury. These writers evoke landscapes—they can also be urban landscapes—containing people who, however lost they may be in their marginal existences, fix their gaze upon the center of the world and take up residence there.

I, too, am well-acquainted with that kind of obsession. That clinging to long-lost provinces. For wherever else my sentences may have led, each of them had its roots between the flats of the Vistula and the hills of Kashubia, in the city of Danzig and its suburb Langfuhr, and in the strands along the Baltic Sea. There lie my American southern states, there I lost my Dublin, there extends my Kirghiz Steppe, and there, too, lies my Çukurova.

In this manner, in other words not so much directly as thrice removed, we, dear Yaşar Kemal, are related. Not only because you as a Kurd belong to Turkey just as I, a Kashubian on my mother's side, am, despite all the burdensome memories, nonetheless committed to Germany, but surely also because of our tendency to capture our losses in words. This obsession drives us to write against the age and to tell those stories that have not been elevated to the status of affairs of state because they deal with people who never sat on high, who did not dominate but rather were themselves dominated.

Besides, though geographically distant from each other, in certain other respects our countries are quite close, since each is burdened by lasting guilt and since in both societies the majority continues to subject its minorities to callous treatment. When this waning century was still in its infancy, hundreds of thousands of Armenians faced systematic genocide in Turkey; the German crimes, committed innumerable times against Jews and gypsies, can be designated, by way of a warning sign, with a place name: Auschwitz. We were incapable of coming to terms ourselves; our countries launched wars that kept our neighbors in constant dread. We Germans were repeatedly beaten, finally divided, and then for 40 years we faced each other, armed, and as if incorrigible; to this day the Kurdish people in Turkey is subject to the state's arbitrary use of power and military actions, and the victims are mostly women and children. Racial delirium and lack of tolerance, concealed under arrogance, wars, and the consequences of war, mark the history of our countries.

Wasn't it a high-ranking German politician who not long ago warned of the German people's becoming "interracialized"? And isn't the latent hatred of foreigners, hedged in by bureaucratese, surfacing in the deportation policies of the current German interior minister, whose harshness is echoed by bands of radical right-wing thugs? Over 4,000 refugees—from Turkey, Algeria, Nigeria—are locked up in detention centers. In newfangled German, they are known as *Schublinge* ("shovees"). We are all passive witnesses of a renewed barbarity, which this time around comes equipped with democratic safety clauses.

It is up to us to give thanks to Yaşar Kemal, and one way of doing that is to overcome the coercive policies of exclusion and deportation, to live among our Turkish neighbors without whipped-up fears, and what's more, to demand policies that would finally grant civic rights to the millions of Turks and Kurds in our country.

For decades in Berlin, or more recently in Lübeck, wherever I have lived and written, Turks were part of the street scene. Turkish children were—and are—fellow students of my children and grandchildren. And I was always certain that these daily encounters with another way of life must be fruitful, for no culture can nourish itself for long off its own resources. When in the seventeenth and eighteenth century large numbers of French refugees—the Huguenots persecuted by the absolutist state who emigrated largely to Brandenburg—arrived in Berlin, these emigrants breathed life into the economy, trade, and, not least, German literature; how shabbily the nineteenth century would have come down to us were it not for the novels of Theodor Fontane. Today one can already say the same of the enriching influence of the more than 6 million foreigners, even though in contrast to the Huguenots, who were granted civic rights in an edict, they are hampered by policies that remain exclusionary and biased against foreigners; it is not simply on walls that one encounters the slogan "Foreigners Out."

Yet the Peace Prize being awarded today by the German Book Trade Association can perhaps provide a stimulus, no, several stimuli. That would certainly be in the spirit of the prizewinner Yaşar Kemal, whose critique is not directed exclusively at the internal conditions of his country. In an article published only a couple of years ago in *Der Spiegel*, he complained about the persecution of Kurds in his country and at the same time reminded the Western democracies of their complicity. He wrote:

> On the threshold of the twentieth century one cannot deprive any people, any ethnic group, of its human rights. No state has the power to do so. After all, it was the power of the people that chased the Americans out of Vietnam, the Soviets out of Afghanistan, and brought about the miracle of South Africa. The Turkish Republic ought not, through its pursuit of this war, to enter the twenty-first century as a country laden down with curses. The conscience of humanity will help the peoples of Turkey to end this inhuman war. And in particular it is the peoples of the countries that sell weapons to the Turkish state who must help to bring this about.

Ladies and gentlemen, that appeal is also aimed at a German audience. Anybody here at this gathering in the Paulskirche who represents the interests of the Kohl-Kinkel government will know that for years the Federal Republic of Germany has condoned the supply of weapons to the Turkish Republic, which is waging a war of annihilation against its own people. After 1990, when a propitious moment opened up the possibility of German unity, supplies of tanks and armored vehicles were taken from the stockpile of the former People's Army of the German Democratic Republic and delivered to that war-torn country. We have become and continue to be accomplices. We condoned this quick, dirty business. I am ashamed of my country, which has degenerated into a purely economic entity whose government permits trade that carries death in its wake and, moreover, denies to persecuted Kurds the right of asylum.

A Peace Prize is being awarded. If this distinction honoring a writer of merit truly deserves its name, if the location of this ceremony, the Paulskirche, is to be more than a mere backdrop, if literature, such as the kind I am praising, can still provide an impetus, then I urge and exhort all of the authors, publishers, and booksellers gathered here, everybody who is conscious of his political responsibility, to respond to Yaşar Kemal's appeal, to take it further and thereby ensure that human rights are respected in his country, so that armed conflict ceases to rage and, even in the most out-of-the-way villages, peace finally reigns.

12

YOKO TAWADA

I DID NOT WANT TO BUILD BRIDGES

First published as "Ich wollte keine Brücke schlagen" in *Aber die Mandarinen müssen heute abend noch geraubt werden* (Tübingen: Konkursbuch Verlag Claudia Gehrke, 1997), 65–72. Translated by David Gramling. Tawada (b. 1960, Tokyo) studied Russian literature in Japan before emigrating to Germany in 1982, where she continued her research in German literature in Hamburg. She received the Adelbert von Chamisso Prize in 1996.

The expression *eine Brücke schlagen*, "to strike a bridge," frightens me. The shore on which I am standing suddenly becomes a hand, which holds a cudgel over the other shore. In this way, it is forced into a bond. This bond reminds me of a hyphen: German-French. The first and second world cannot be metamorphosed into a third with a magic wand. When I talk to myself, one letter accidentally steps into the place of another: a bridge or a blidge? Through the tongue's weakness, the word sounds differently than it appears. What does a word look like anyway? It is like a gap under a bridge. Under the bridge, the river is moving in its slumber. There I meet people and ask them: Shall we sit on the shore and strike a gap in the dictionary? Should we open up a gap like we open a book? Or should we build our own way swimming?

The pictures we paint from that same gap are various. One swims in the water, another builds a boat, a third sits on the shore and waits for rain. Whose gaze can take the shape of an arc? Bridges made of arched gazes may reach the other shore.

The fingers of the water touch everything that comes near: summer air, cigarette butts, fish, and the soil on the shore. The soil has no fear of the water. In this silence, no element is dissolved by the touch. The water will find us. And the wind's language? The light's sounds? They will find us as well.

13

ABBAS MAROUFI

I WILL LEAVE THIS COUNTRY: A LETTER TO GÜNTER GRASS

First published as "Ich werde dieses Land verlassen" in *Die Zeit* (October 1, 1998). Translated by Susanne Baghestani and Tes Howell. Maroufi (b. 1957, Tehran) authored the novel *Symphony of the Dead*, which was published in 1989 in Farsi. His work on the *Gardoon* journal led to his exile in Germany in 1996.

On the Absurd Life of an Iranian Writer in Exile
My dear writer friend,

I have received a letter in which I am advised to begin looking for a job and to start working finally, or else they will cut off our welfare income. I paid no attention to this letter, and the welfare payments have subsequently stopped coming.

Yesterday, I discussed this matter with a representative of the Düren city council, and he told me that according to the federal German law, all are equal and that I must find a job. But what can I do besides write? After all, there is no art or publication center where someone like me could find employment. Therefore, I am forced to give up writing, stop working on my journal, and start driving a taxi or working in a pizza place. And this esteemed representative then says, "Yes, well, there's really no shame in working; after all, you have to do something. We are in Germany; you can't just walk around doing nothing and receive welfare: everyone has to work. . . . " And I cried the whole way home and had to laugh, resoundingly, about my absurd fate. I had probably lost my mind. My God, I'm crazy. In my homeland, one was sentenced to whipping and imprisonment because of the offense of writing, and here the sentence is suddenly reversed.

One of my friends thought it was nothing. "You must draft a letter and apply for work at various places. They will write under your application that they do not need anyone; put a stamp on it, and that will be it. That's how we have done things for years. They have 4 million unemployed and don't know what to do with them. This is all just a formality; don't worry about it."

Another friend said that if you get a doctor to attest that you cannot work, then they will leave you alone.

But I can work. I work, I resist. I write six hours every day; eight hours a day, I fight in the editor's office of my journal for freedom of speech, for the writers of my *Heimat*, for my convictions. I publish a bilingual journal (in Persian and German), which I think is very useful for the relationship between the two nations. Critical literature, freedom of speech, struggle against censorship.

I play a role in the fictional literature of my country, am present in the history of the oppositional press in Iran. I have been writing for 22 years; I have taught, been beaten, interrogated, have suffered great pain, have been sentenced, have cried, and have been finally exiled.

I was familiar with defenselessness; now I am starting to understand asylum. The terms swirl about in my head: *asylum, defenselessness*. Defenselessness means that you can write down your thoughts but cannot publish them. Defenselessness means that you show resistance and must suddenly realize that there is no longer anyone standing next to you. Defenselessness means all kinds of interrogations, living in constant fear of death. But you are present, are there, you exist. You do not fear your interrogator; he fears you.

In contrast, asylum means that you write and publish in complete freedom—but never forget that you are only an asylum seeker, you poor little guy! Writing is not employment; you must work: deliver pizzas or drive a taxi. Asylum means life in a rundown neighborhood. Asylum means unemployed neighbors who sic their dogs on your guests, which rip their clothing, and afterward call the police outraged. Asylum means neighbors who dump garbage from the stairwell into your mailbox. Asylum means that the neighbor makes faces at the greeting of your daughter and turns her back on her. [. . .]

Dear Mr. Grass, why did you invite me here? Why did you not allow me to rot away under whippings and torture in my country's bloodthirsty prisons? Was I a doctor in Iran only to work as an engineer here? I was invited as an oppositional writer to your country and have requested asylum. Do you remember the days when you yourself distributed fliers for me? Did the German government want to announce to the people of this earth that it represents human rights? Thugs in Tehran have a good saying: "He who invites guests must also think about supervision."

Why didn't anyone give me a residence permit back then, when I was receiving valid invitations from other countries, so that I could have gotten a visa and disappeared into some other corner? [. . .] If Iran's regime could tolerate the thoughts of others, I would never be here. There were always 10 employees working on the editorial staff of my journal, and hundreds of writers came in and out there. Go and ask German journalists. Many of them have seen the editorial office of *Gardoon* in Tehran. We worked, never intending to become inhabitants of Europe. [. . .]

We had only 24 hours to leave Iran, Mr. Grass. You know war and exile, have seen the teeth of totalitarianism, are familiar with the concept of flight, but were you unconquerable?

I used the money of the Helman-Hamett Award and the profits from my books for the journal, called for the release of my employees, and sent faxes. I withheld the award money from my children, didn't even buy them a pair of shoes. I put up resistance. I did not defend myself before the courts but rather attacked the proponents of book burnings and exposed them. [. . .]

We know Günter Grass and Heinrich Böll and Nietzsche well, we have made them our own, but do you know anyone in Iran besides Zarathustra? Perhaps Hafis? Should I send you my novels so you can see that I represent one color out of many? Nietzsche belongs to me, as do Camus and Paz. But how many colors are you missing? You have not yet been successful establishing writing as a trade. Otherwise, I would not be a foreigner in your country, nor would I be despised. [. . .]

And you, dark-haired exile, watch out, for this is not your homeland. Your share is small, your work insignificant. And my hair is very dark, Mr. Grass, raven black. And these are the words of a dark-haired, foreign human being who has written, taught, and fought for freedom of speech for years and who has been banished, escaping the fate of slaughter, into the morass of humiliation. What is left for me to say, Mr. Grass, except that if I return to Iran one day together with the exiles of my country, I will invite you to come to the land of fortresses and castles and attacks and pillaging, to the land of loving mothers who fixed their eyes on the doorways, grieved for their children, and died in anguish. [. . .]

14

HENRYK M. BRODER

NOVELIST GÜNEY DAL: I AM NOT A BRIDGE

First published as "Romanautor Güney Dal: 'Ich bin keine Brücke' " in *Der Tagesspiegel* (May 19, 2000). Translated by David Gramling. Dal (b. 1944, Çanakkale, Turkey) has lived in Germany since 1972.

A Turkish Monarchist Who Reads Wittgenstein and Boxing Magazines

Life is clamoring at the door; one sensation chases the next. But Güney Dal remains calm. He is sitting in his Wilmersdorf apartment, listening to classical music on Radio Berlin and reading a small book: "*The Wonderful Dog*—a German-Polish picaresque novel" from 1733. "A lovely story, very old and very current," beams Dal. "A human changes into a dog. In politics, wolves change into humans. Or is it the other way around?" It is not that Güney Dal is indifferent to what is happening outside: he watches the daily show in the evening and sometimes even the news programs. It is simply that what is in the newspaper everyday is not important enough for him to put down his book for it, particularly when he is reading in order to recover from writing. He worked on his last novel for over three years; it was his sixth, and when it was completed, he felt like a painter who had exhausted all of his colors. "On some days, the words are gone. I say, Come here. And they do not come."

Güney Dal has lived in Berlin for 28 years already and has had a German passport since 1992. When he is asked whether he is a German Turk or a Turkish German, he chooses a third option, which lies somewhere in between: "I am a Turkish author." But not an "exile author," because "I do not have to live here. I could return to Turkey if I wanted to." He makes this trip twice a year, in order to see friends and relatives, but he does not want to "really live" in Turkey. "Turks have no interest in my literature." In the beginning, he admits, this "displeased" him. When he goes shopping in Kreuzberg, people tap him on the shoulder in the supermarket. "They know who I am but not what I do. Most of them read *Hürriyet* and appear content."

Words in Order to Exist

Güney Dal did not turn his back on Turkey just to land in Kreuzberg and read *Hürriyet*. The son of a customs agent, he was born in Çanakkale in the

Dardanelles in 1944, 30 kilometers away from Troy. He studied Romance languages and literatures in Istanbul after graduating from high school. He worked as a voice-over speaker on the side and dubbed lines like "I'll get the horses" in U.S. westerns. After military service, he would have become a bookseller were it not for the 1971 military putsch. Although he was not deported as an opponent of the government, he nonetheless left Turkey for Berlin, where his wife, Sunku, was already working as a solderer for Siemens.

Dal learned German at the Free University [Berlin], during which time he found a position as a warehouse worker at Schering. From 1974 to 1978, he produced SFB features; in 1979, his first novel appeared, entitled *Wenn Ali die Glocken läuten hört*, or *When Ali Hears the Bells Ring*, which was about Turkish workers on strike at Ford in Cologne—proletarian prose. "A horrible title," says Dal today, "but a good book." By the early 1980s, Dal had long since given up his job at Schering and had become one of the editors of the German-Turkish newspaper *Anadil (Mother Language)*. He "produced words, in order to exist," as he says. Every four or five years, a novel came out, as well as two short stories and an anthology of "stories from the history of Turkey."

In 1999, the novel *Teestunden am Ring*, or *Teatime at Ringside*, appeared, published by Piper and set in Berlin in the 1920s with a Turk as the main figure. Sabri Mahir, painter and philosopher, opens the Studio for Boxing and Body Cultivation on the Kurfürstendamm, where boxing takes place according to the rules of New Objectivity. No one knows how New Objectivity works in the ring, and, for this reason, Berlin's leading figures of the era meet there. Marlene Dietrich, Friedrich Hollaender and Carl Zuckmayer, Egon Erwin Kisch and Bert Brecht. He organizes a fight between Max Schmeling and Franz Diener and becomes friends with Alfred Flechtheim, the editor of the newspaper *Der Querschnitt*, who, for his part, knows many bankers, revue girls, and race-car drivers.

The story is fictitious, but truth is at its core. There was actually a Turkish boxer named Sabri Mahir. Güney Dal stumbled upon the name in a *Tagesspiegel* article. "That was 1976 or 1977, and then I carried the story around with me for 10 years until I said to myself: I am Sabri Mahir."

In the Berlin address directory from 1928, he discovered a "Sabri Mahir Bey, Boxing Manager, Bayreuther Street," who operated a studio on Tauentzien Street. Dal worked his way through issues of *Boxing World, Boxing Week, Boxing Sport Revue,* and the *Boxing Yearbook.* He read the memoirs of Vicky Baum, Max Schmeling, and Fritz Kortner; texts by Heinrich Mann, Ernst Toller, Erich Weinert, and Franz Blei; the "At-Home-Calendar" and poems by the "boxer poet" Arthur Cravan. After two years, he knew it all: where Marlene Dietrich bought her suits, who sat at which table in the Romanisches Café, and where one could obtain the best éclairs in Berlin.

Dal did his research as if he intended to direct a documentary film. In the end, he had written a novel in which "10 percent [is] authentic" and the other 90 percent reads as if it were. A society novel in which society hums in the background like an orchestra and a boxer plays the solos in the ring. Sabri Mahir is the pseudonym behind which Güney Dal can be found, a Turk in Berlin who left his homeland because he wanted to live as an individual. "Tribalism drives me nuts. I do not wish to be questioned about what the Gray Wolves are doing. I write novels, and I do not know what is happening when communists take over power in Turkey."

The Regiment of Women

Güney Dal does not belong to the Writers' Collective nor the PEN Center; he underwrites no protest resolutions and does not take part in any literary chumminess. The only author he is friends with, and speaks with almost daily on the telephone, is named Sten Nadolny. Dal also does not wish to be a "bridge between Turkey and Germany" or a "demonstrative Turk" like the Green politician Cem Özdemir, who "is always so frightfully critical and never does anything off-color." According to Dal, he should "stay in a closed room for a while and read; he knows way too little."

Güney Dal has become accustomed to the fact that his books are spoken highly of yet sell poorly. He could not live on his writing, like most authors. "I write novels, and I express myself through my novels. That is all." His wife is the "speaker of the organization." At home with the Dals, Turkish is "emphatically" spoken, although both daughters speak German better. The elder daughter, Ceren, 26, is an actor and has a role on *Linden Street;* the younger daughter, Burcu, 18, also intends to become an actor after graduation. The mother, Sunku, and the two daughters sympathize with the Greens, whereas the father, Güney, feels "conservative" and thinks that "a monarchy would be good."

A completely normal Berlin family, then: bilingual, multicultural, defined by women, and politically differentiated—only the head of household stays at home most days rather than sitting in the pub. Güney Dal puts away the picaresque novel from 1733 and reaches out for the next book, *Lectures on the Basic Principles of Mathematics,* by Ludwig Wittgenstein. Wittgenstein wrote the renowned *Tractatus logico philosophicus,* which begins with the sentence "The world is everything which is the case." According to Güney Dal, one could write an entire book about this one sentence. But he still needs a while to recover from *Teatime at Ringside.* "It is terrible, what I do. But I am content."

15

WLADIMIR KAMINER

WHY I STILL HAVEN'T APPLIED FOR NATURALIZATION

First published as "Warum ich immer noch keinen Antrag auf Einbürgerung gestellt habe" in *Russendisko* (Munich: Goldmann, 2000), 189–92. Translated by David Gramling. Kaminer (b.1967) studied dramaturgy at the Moscow Theater Institute. He has been living in Berlin since 1990 and has a weekly radio program on SFB4's Radio Multikulti. This text is the last essay in his critically acclaimed collection *Russendisko*.

Every night, outside our place on Schönhauser Avenue at the corner of Born-holmer Street, there were new, always bigger ditches. They were dug by the Vietnamese who had chosen this corner as their spot for the cigarette trade. At least that's what I surmised after seeing them out there over and over at the crack of dawn with shovels: two men and a very nice woman, who have been playing a quite enterprising role on this corner for years. "Why are the Vietnamese digging? Are they trying to make more storage space for their goods?" I wondered while walking to the District Bureau to see Herr Kugler, in yet another attempt to apply for German naturalization (already the third time). Annoying. The first time, everything went like clockwork; I had all of the photocopies with me, my financial circumstances were all cleared up, all of my residency dates and locations since birth were listed, the 500 German mark charge had been accepted, and all of our children, wives, and parents were accounted for. I talked with Herr Kugler for two hours about the mean-ing of life in the FRG, but then it turned out that I had failed at one simple task: preparing a handwritten résumé. It was supposed to be unconven-tional, brief, and honest. I took a pad of paper and pen and went into the hall. After about an hour, I had written five whole pages, but hadn't even made it to kindergarten yet. "It just isn't so easy—a handwritten résumé," I said to myself and started over. In the end, I had three drafts, all of which were interesting reading, but none of them made it as far as my first mar-riage. Dissatisfied with myself, I went home. Once there, I tried to figure out the difference between a novel and a handwritten, unconventional résumé.

Next time, I was unsuccessful because of a different problem. In a medium-sized box, I was supposed to declare the grounds for my "entry into Germany." I wracked my brains on this question. But not a single reason oc-curred to me. I came to Germany in 1990 for absolutely no reason at all. That evening, I asked my wife, who always knows the reason for things, "Why did we come to Germany back then, anyway?" She said we came to Germany for fun—to see how it was. But we wouldn't get by with those kinds of formula-tions. The clerk would think we were just applying for naturalization for fun, and not because of . . . "Why are we applying for naturalization, anyway?" I wanted to ask my wife, but she had already left for the driving school, where she would make a series of drivers' education teachers crazy and strike ter-ror into a few women lingering on the street. My wife has a very unconven-tional driving style. But that is a different story.

Then, cautiously, I gave "curiosity" as my reason for our entry into Ger-many, which appeared to sound more prudent than "fun." Then I copied off my résumé by hand from the computer screen. I put everything in a folder and went back to Herr Kugler the next day. It was very early and still dark, but I wanted to be the first one there, because the clerk at the Civil Registry

Office cannot take care of more than one foreigner a day. Then I saw the Vietnamese: they were digging again! I came a little closer. Two men were standing with frustrated expressions in the middle of a big hole. The woman was standing next to them, cursing at them in Vietnamese. The men defended themselves, languidly. I looked into the ditch. There was only water in there. All at once, it became clear to me what was going on: the Vietnamese had forgotten where they had buried their cigarettes and were searching for them everywhere, in vain.

Suddenly a wind rose up and my papers fell out of the folder and landed in the ditch. The carefully handwritten résumé, all of the reasons for my entry into Germany, the big questionnaire with my financial circumstances—everything just flew off into the wet ditch. Apparently, I'll never get naturalized. But what for, anyway?

16

ASFA-WOSSEN ASSERATE

IN PRAISE OF SQUARENESS

First published as "Lob des Spiessers" in *Manieren* (Frankfurt am Main: Eichborn, 2003), 127–30. Translated by David Gramling. Asserate (b. 1948, Addis Ababa, Ethiopia) is a prince of the imperial house of Ethiopia. After the Ethiopian revolution in 1974, he settled in Germany, where he studied law and history. He received the Adelbert von Chamisso Prize in 2004.

It will perhaps be surprising to find praise for squareness in a book about manners. Such books usually intend to teach their readers about everything that should be avoided in order not to seem petit bourgeois, provincial, square. Such is an accusation that truly stings. No one wants to be a square. Moral and aesthetic categories mix together in this accusation in a very complex way. The square is the snoop, the informer, the dissembler, the sycophant, the narrow-minded, the merciless advocate of group morals, the propagator of weak chatter and suspicion—crouching, furtive, pseudo, and unsavory. Surely, each and every well-intentioned person would prefer to elevate himself above the square, as long as this self-elevation did not then smack dangerously of squareness.

It is not just the lowly squareness that is met with disgust; certain forms of small-town lifestyle are also branded as "square," which, I am strongly convinced, do not deserve this stigma. When I came to Germany, such small-towners were the real Germans for me, just as I had imagined them in Africa. They had an immutable form—I learned later that intellectuals and the elegant set laugh about this—and it was important for them to keep to this form. They loved traditions. They celebrated family parties and Christmas in the traditional way. They knew that it is a fundamental necessity for a dignified person to have manners. Unfortunately, they just had the wrong ones, as I later found out from ridiculers of the provincial lifestyle. What was so preposterous about going to church on Sunday in a *tracht* [native dress]? *Trachts* are quite cute, after all. No, they were apparently not cute, because they were not real *trachts* but unfortunate mixed forms with loden and little flower accents, ornaments and buckhorn buttons, but also with creases and zippers and unclassical patterns that the textile industry had conjured up.

However, I still have the strong conviction that such apparel, though unsuccessful to my mind, is more honorable than the unisex free-time clothing that the masses have used to make themselves comfortable for a long time now. This "making oneself comfortable" is the true mortal enemy of manners. These days, the virtue of "honesty" has soared to quite a high status. It is more honest, one might think, for a townie to make himself comfortable in his pig stall and wallow in it: everyone has a pig stall after all. These small-towners in their awkward tracht uniforms, whom I regarded as the real Germans upon my arrival, and perhaps indeed are, did not want to wallow. They had inherited forms to which they were attempting, though with a certain aesthetic blindness, to remain true. [. . .]

Once I had the particular pleasure of staying with an industrial worker and a farmer. The son of the house sat with me at the table, while the parents stood around us, presented the food to us, and watched us eat. Here, I saw the remains of an ancient culture related to our Oriental culture: Odysseus would have been served no differently at Phäak. I am deeply grateful that I was able to have this kind of an experience in the modern West, although I know that it would be senseless to try to relive this hospitality with a middle-class social climber. Of course, the meal began with the blessing "Guten Appetit," a Gaullism that once had counted as highly elegant and had replaced the religiously inflected "blessings on the meal." Meanwhile, these days there are so many truly vulgar people who know that it is square to say "Guten Appetit" and look on triumphantly and scornfully when this blessing emerges in their presence, because they see it as the quintessence of their rise into higher spheres to know that one ought to think twice before adopting this curious "Guten Appetit" as a means to discriminate oneself from false elegance. This couple, while serving their guests, had the vague sense that mealtime is more than the silence of responding to nature's needs; they saw the ritual, the ceremonial religiosity of the meal, and, in the spirit of manners, were superior to many who believe themselves better versed in them.

A TURKISH GERMANY

FILM, MUSIC, AND EVERYDAY LIFE

HEAD-ON, 2003. Fatih Akın's prize-winning film follows Cahit (Birol Ünel), who is shown here, beer in hand, on the day of his sham wedding to Sibel, a young German Turkish woman. A rebel in a tuxedo, he is not to be assimilated into either German or Turkish society. "The melting pot," Adorno wrote, "was introduced by unbridled industrial capitalism. The thought of being cast into it conjures up martyrdom, not democracy."

THE WIDESPREAD CONSUMPTION of kebab and falafel is probably the most ubiquitous sign of the "Orientalization" of Germany. "The Coup of the Billions," an extract from Eberhard Seidel-Pielen's 1996 book, subjects the fashionable and inexpensive lunchtime favorite döner kebab to consumer analysis. For Seidel-Pielen, the kebab is an invincible cultural and culinary force, capable of uprooting Germany's most widespread everyday habits. Yet despite the internationalization of German cuisine, the apolitical "selective incorporation" typical of such culinary multiculturalism holds little sway in larger debates, such as those on citizenship law or media representation.

In the late 1970s and early 1980s, the culture of "foreigners" or "guest workers" gained some modest visibility in the context of social services, where integration was a high strategic priority. Foreigners, their food, and their folklore were conspicuously displayed at organized festivals, as Antonovic describes in "More Than Schnapps and Folklore" (1982). The paternalist and ethnographic structure of these initiatives tended to preclude serious investment and exchange between the beholder and the beheld. The "bonus for Turks in art and literature," as Tayfun Erdem called the phenomenon in his memorable 1989 polemic, signaled indifference, not genuine engagement.

Until the 1990s, radio and television stations broadcast daily half-hour programs for migrants. Writers like Aras Ören and Yüksel Pazarkaya, who had come to Germany in 1969 and 1958, respectively, worked as editors for these programs at Sender Freies Berlin and Westdeutscher Rundfunk. In 1995, Berlin launched the new station SFB 4–Radio Multikulti, integrating these various foreign-language programs into one multilingual channel that emphasized diversity and world music, targeting both minority and mainstream audiences. Meanwhile, satellite television diversified media programming extensively in the 1990s; Turks in Germany could choose among multiple television channels from Turkey and were therefore less dependent on programs produced in Germany.

However, the 1990s also saw the increasing presence of figures from migrant backgrounds speaking out in the German media. Rooted in a pejorative term for foreigners, *Kanak Kultur,* or Kanak culture, became the lingua franca of a transethnic cultural politics common to Italian-German, Serbian-

German, and other immigrant youth communities beyond the Turkish-German milieu. The circulation of transnational hip-hop through cultures of solidarity, as well as the slowly increasing representation of immigrants in German television and other media, contributed to the emergence of so-called Kanak chic in the late 1990s. The politics of Kanak Attak and its symbolic reinscription of racist tropes derived political tactics from the "Verlan" linguistic movement of suburban Paris, as well as the Black Power and Queer Nation movements. This chapter presents a case study in the practices and rhetorics of transnational pop culture.

Dietmar Lamparter's 1992 article "Discrimination of the Noble Kind" analyzes the belated emergence of corporate advertising strategies to attract immigrant consumers. German service-industry firms, observes Lamparter, have only recently begun to market their products by framing them within images of the Turkish-German middle-class home. Lamparter emphasizes that this debut of the immigrant private sphere in mass marketing is quite recent, and the newly disseminated images are reshaping the demographic profile of the average immigrant consumer. No longer, claims the article, are Turks shopping at Aldi, Germany's notoriously austere discount grocery chain. Increasingly brand conscious, immigrant consumers are willing to purchase and pursue leisure culture at the same rate that their nonmigrant counterparts do.

One cluster of texts presents responses to German-Turkish films and filmmakers. "Despite the Passport, I Am Still Not a German" chronicles the travels of Tevfik Başer from Turkey to Great Britain and then to Germany, and the genesis of his feature film *Forty Square Meters of Germany.* "Everywhere Is Better Where We Are Not" (1994) places Sinan Çetin's *Berlin in Berlin,* a comedy-melodrama about reverse assimilation, in the context of other transnational films in Britain and the United States of the early 1990s. "Is Linden Street Closed Off to Turks?" (1995) reports on the representation of migrants on network television. The last text in this chapter, a review of Fatih Akın's critically acclaimed 2003 film, *Head-On,* might represent another pivotal moment in Turkish Germany's itinerary from invisibility to chic. Here, film critic Katja Nicodemus claims that transnational migrant cultures have become so normal in Germany that they no longer need to be reconstructed and disseminated through film. Yet why are some forms of migrant popular culture more easily adopted into mainstream consumption than others? Does the global embrace of American mass culture erase or alter binary cultural distinctions like those between Turkey and Germany?

1

FEHLFARBEN
MILLITÜRK

Song released on *Monarchie und Alltag* (Weltrekord, 1980). Text by Gabi Delgado Lopez. Translated by Tes Howell. Fehlfarben, a Düsseldorf-based punk, ska-parody, and disco band, composed "Millitürk" for its 1980 gold-record recording of aggressively topical songs, here blending Soviet Bloc politics with the issue of Turkish ghettoization in Berlin. The lyrics play on the German word for military, *Militär*, and the Turkish adjective *milli*, meaning "national."

Millitürk	Millitürk
Kebab dreams in the walled-in city	Kebabträume in der Mauerstadt
Turk culture behind barbed wire	Türk-Kültür hinter Stacheldraht
New Izmir in the GDR	Neu Izmir in der DDR
Atatürk the new Man	Atatürk der neue Herr
The Nation for the Soviet Union	Milliyet für die Sowjet Union
A spy at every fast-food joint	In jeder Imbißstube ein Spion
A Turkish agent in the Central Committee	Im ZK Agent aus Türkei
Germany, Germany, everything is gone	Deutschland, Deutschland alles ist vorbei
We are the Turks of tomorrow	Wir sind die Türken von morgen

2

DANJA ANTONOVIC
MORE THAN SCHNAPPS AND FOLKLORE

First published as "Mehr als Schnaps und Folklore" in *Die Zeit* (January 8, 1982). Translated by Tes Howell.

Theater, literature, music: guest-worker culture: a culture that no one wants

Officialese can boast of yet another neologism: *Ausländerkultur,* or foreigner culture. The term has spread far beyond official records. One must ask, however, what is hiding behind this concept that well-intentioned officials from German cities and municipalities have unwittingly coined? It must have been absentmindedness to confuse the culinary with culture and define *foreigner culture* as ouzo, Turkish children dancing to folk music, and the aroma of *cevapçici*—and then to present it as such.

Cultural events of this kind are usually offered in the form of so-called foreigner festivals, in which some people become the entertainment, similar to Mr. Hagenbeck's Exhibition of Peoples before the war. Usually, the others stand there just as uncomfortably as the performers and believe that they really need to understand "those nice foreign fellow citizens."

I do not want to deny such events their unifying character: it's just that I have never seen Germans dancing or singing at organized festivities where sausages with mustard represent the highest of their culinary sentiments. The foreigners were always the dancers and cooks.

Indeed, with time, the foreigners began—without official encouragement—to articulate their own interests. After all the years during which they sought to absorb and overcome the (literally) internal and external speechlessness, after this culture shock foreigners created a real cultural scene—at first timidly, then with more confidence. Theirs is a culture that emerged out of a burst of creativity, a culture that is not merely a derivative of the hosts and culture bearers here.

In the linking of traditional values from the old homeland with the new rituals of this highly industrialized land, a guest-worker culture has indeed developed that spans the emotional space from the Atlantic to the eastern Mediterranean Sea. But this culture features everyday experiences from Bremen to Berchtesgaden: a mixed culture, idiosyncratic, unique, mostly unsubsidized, often only found in the alternative scene.

Thus, several phenomena emerge: workers join theater groups, then create pieces with often explosive political messages—from the old and the new homeland. Many of them, like the Spanish "Teatro popular" in Hannover, have opted for pantomime so that their message becomes clear to as many as possible.

Publishing houses developed, printing books that reflect the daily life of those living in backstreet tenements and suffering from isolation and the consumer society. They write about this life and poeticize it, first in the native language, then gradually in German (although the grammar is often incorrect). Music groups are emerging that preserve the simplicity of folk music, despite the profitability of Bousuki and Espagna-olé sounds. Playing the single-tone melodies of their villages, they accept that their music may be dismissed as noise.

Poets, prose writers, painters, filmmakers, musicians—an entire culture industry that interests no one, that no one wants.

Despite some discussion in mainstream magazines and some television exposure, guest-worker culture is still known only to insiders who are already involved with it: either as the non-Germans concerned or as those involved in "foreigner work." Even if prominent German publishing houses release this or that relevant book by or about foreigners, most of it remains hidden from the German public.

Official recognition comes occasionally in the form of funds from various government offices. Communities (or federal states) that have pushed through measures to offer financial assistance "for the preservation of cultural identity" are very rare. In Hamburg, where over 100,000 "foreigners from recruitment countries" pay taxes, an allocation of funds was approved for the first time in 1982 by cultural authorities: 150,000 marks, which was then quickly reduced to 75,000 marks.

Foreigner organizations and centers are generally the sites where cultural heritage is cultivated and the famous "bridge to the homeland" is maintained. The government usually supports such centers, yet there are few officials from the Culture Bureau who show their financial appreciation for the cultural meaning of these places. Before the representatives of foreigner centers and associates from the Culture Bureau began to meet, foreigners had written countless letters seeking official recognition. George Defesus, the chair of the Portuguese Cultural Center, discusses this situation in the Frankfurt-based *Zeitung von Ausländern für Deutsche—WIR [Newspaper by Foreigners for Germans—WE]:* "In our center, we currently have a theater group, a chorus, and a folk-music group. There is also a youth group, which shot a film in Portugal. We receive nothing from German authorities for all these activities. And when we compare ourselves with a German shepherd club that receives 50,000 marks . . . "

Guest workers and their culture encounter very little appreciation when negotiating official channels, but the indifference from the community is even worse. This is not merely a sign of the conflict between different cultures; it is more closely connected with the internal silence of people in an industrial society, in which human interaction and dialogue no longer have high priority. It is therefore not difficult to understand that the often-cited integration hardly materializes, although a considerable number of foreign workers can effortlessly recite the daily *Guten Appetit,* and marjoram and basil have made their way into German households.

The discomfort is noticeable on both sides. At the end of a Loccum conference on guest-worker culture last October, Christel Hartmann, a drama instructor in Berlin, summed up the situation: "As long as we Germans understand ourselves as missionaries and believe that the heathen (read: Turks) do not want to think, speak, feel, or understand the Christian (read: German) way of life, as long as we understand culture as merely a structure of thought, we, the well meaning, will be incapable of communication, and we, as Germans and foreigners trying to live together, know this. The question that accompanies this conclusion is logical: why are we, the helpers and the helping, so helpless? Because there are no suggestions for a solution."

This cluelessness and helplessness have apparently befallen the whole republic and its states as well, which are presently trying to solve these problems with a flood of laws and ordinances. It is difficult to write about guest-worker culture, to solicit more understanding. It is hard to explain how this culture could only develop in this country, in collaboration between these guest workers and Germans, when the lives of these foreign workers are being regulated by law. Their lives are indeed regulated in such a way that further prohibitions would withhold basic rights.

The words of Hakkı Keskin, a Turkish lecturer in political science at the [Free] University of Berlin, gain even more importance: "Our pleading and begging are largely ignored. How are we to cultivate our culture and make ourselves heard when we lack the personnel, the infrastructure and the financial resources necessary to exert influence? How is one supposed to talk about our culture and an integration policy worthy of being taken seriously when the legal, political, and social equality is not there? We must insist on this equality." [. . .]

3

HARK BOHM, RITA WEINERT, AND WILHELM ROTH
APPEAL FOR A NARRATIVE CINEMA

This interview was first published as "Plädoyer für das Erzählkino: Gespräch mit Hark Bohm" in *epd Film* (April 1988). Translated by David Gramling. Bohm (b. 1939, Hamburg) is a film director and producer. His 1988 film *Yasemin* won the German Film Prize and was selected as a nominee for Best Foreign Picture at the Academy Awards in 1989.

[. . .] *RW/WR [Rita Weinert/Wilhelm Roth]: Yasemin* is the story of a Turkish girl in love with a German boy, but it deals primarily with the familial conflicts that ensue. Is this a popular theme?

HB [Hark Bohm]: Youth throughout the republic, from the most southern to the most northern parts, are the largest group of moviegoers, and they deal with acquaintances in their age group just like Yasemin every day, acquaintances whom they don't know quite how to categorize—the second, or actually third, generation of immigrant Turkish workers. These people are, of course, no longer Turks. When one speaks to them on the telephone, they have the same linguistic melody, the same linguistic gestures as their German counterparts. And I have witnessed that when these young people go to Turkey to visit their grandparents, they are not accepted there as Turks but only as *Deutschler.* They speak a Turkish that reminds me of the German of my American cousins and nephews, whose parents emigrated to America. These young people, living in between, are normal for my audience. I was not attempting to narrate the story of Yasemin by calling Germans' attention to their failures in dealing with the social problems of Turkish immigrants, which is the approach of many films that I know. Instead, I tried to tell the story of the lifeworld of one such *Deutschlerin.* This issue is something simultaneously familiar and foreign for young people, who go to school with these *Deutschler,* who do apprenticeships and go to university with them. I can imagine that this topic will also provoke curiosity. The first reactions to the film confirm this. I also do not perceive myself as a self-sufficient artist. I took the working copy to the Hamburg Film House and showed it to young people in order to see how they would react, what they liked, where they lost interest, and I re-edited the film according to these discussions.

RW/WR: With this film, do you intend to raise consciousness among German youth about Islamic ways of thinking and the Turkish family structures among their acquaintances?

HB: I never intend to raise consciousness. I think a well-told story needs a conflict. This was a conflict. I am a lot less moralistic than would appear at first glance. I live in Altona [Hamburg], and Uwe, who plays the younger leading male role, is my son. He has had a Turkish girlfriend for three years now, so I understand what is actually going on there. It is also certainly true that some of the conflicts that come up between my wife and me played a role— conflicts that arise when two people have internalized different value systems. This experience is how the film project came into existence. I began to research. I never thought that I ought to teach German youth a lesson about the real internal problems of Turkish families. It is merely a very powerful, archaic conflict: precisely in the moment when a daughter falls in love, her father tries to dominate her, to keep her, only to give her away to a man who has proven himself devoted to the father's own value system.

It is uncommon for 1988 that such a young woman would fall in love for the first time at age 17. It is a very tender, even chaste love story that unfolds. Girls like Yasemin just do not permit themselves the internal urges of nature. When these urges linger and fester, there is an explosion. These girls appear to be brought up in a liberal way at first glance. There are many Turkish girls who take judo because they accompany their brothers when they are kids. In this film, the father justifies this practice to the uncle on the basis that the girl will be able to protect herself and her honor.

I discussed the representation of the father intensively with many people, and I was very lucky that Şener Şen from Berlin had done stage work before and had also dealt intensively with the psychic and social situation of labor migrants. I also had a Turkish assistant and have learned Turkish myself. [. . .]

4

ANNETTE EBENFELD-LINNEWEBER

DESPITE THE PASSPORT, I AM STILL NOT A GERMAN

First published as "Mit dem Pass werde ich noch kein Deutscher" in the *Frankfurter Allgemeine Zeitung* (April 1, 1989). Translated by Tes Howell. This article surveys the work of filmmaker Tevfik Başer (b. 1951, Eskişehir, Turkey), who achieved recognition in Germany for his feature film *Forty Square Meters of Germany* (1986), which was nominated for the Federal Film Prize in 1987. Başer's other films include *Farewell to False Paradise* (1988) and *Farewell, Stranger* (1991).

One can often find the wiry figure of Tevfik Başer up on a table. Arms spread out, feet carefully placed between wineglasses, the 38-year-old Turk never needs to be asked twice to express his zest for life—today in the form of a lively little table dance, to the delight of his numerous friends, to the stunned amusement of the other restaurant guests, and for his own pleasure as well. Nothing about this presentation seems staged or exaggerated. This high-spirited childlike joy is natural, and the applause of the uninvolved observers comes across as heartfelt, before they again turn their attention to their own tables. A folkloristic idyll of Turkish provenance on Federal Republican soil?

Cut. Concentrated and engaged, the director and screenwriter Tevfik Başer talks about himself and his new film, *Farewell to False Paradise*, the words almost somersaulting over each other, underscored again and again by his hands. (The film has already achieved distinction at festivals; the German film premiere is planned for early May.) Only the bags under his eyes betray the effort it takes to answer the repetitive questions for the umpteenth time, following the premiere of Başer's second feature film at this year's Berlinale. No, he does not consider *Farewell to False Paradise* a continuation of his first feature film, *Forty Square Meters of Germany*, the film that garnered him several awards and international recognition. Even though the second begins precisely where the first ended, with the murder of a Turk in Germany by his Turkish wife. "The reasons why the woman went to prison, why she killed her husband, didn't interest me this time. I excluded that intentionally from production (in contrast to Saliha Scheinhardt's 1983 book, *Frauen, die sterben, ohne dass sie gelebt hätten*, or, *Women Who Died without Ever Having Lived*). I wanted to concentrate on the development of the wife in prison: how she learns the language, how through this act she is in a position to assume relationships with her environment, to express herself and to make contact with other women who are stuck in similar situations. The paradox of her situation fascinated me. A woman finds her freedom in prison. Why? And when, after six years, she has completed her sentence and should be released, she wants to commit suicide because she is to be deported to Turkey where the death sentence is potentially waiting for her. That is a paradox!"

Just as paradoxical and absurd is the title of the film, *Farewell to False Paradise*. In Saliha Scheinhardt's book, the story of the Turkish woman, Elif, ends on a positive note. She is allowed to remain in Germany and is not handed over to the Turkish justice system. Başer leaves the ending of his film open. The audience is not rescued by a happy end and will not necessarily leave the theater relieved. Questions, pensiveness, and a sad seriousness remain.

In all his works, the two films and the documentaries *Between God and Earth* and *Staged Heimat*, Tevfik Başer describes the situation of his compatriots in the Federal Republic with sensitivity and earnestness, illuminating their mental states in the greatest detail. "What should I do?" shrugs the film-maker, who has lived in Hamburg for eight years. "I was born in Turkey. And the fact that I have a German passport does not make me a German. I simply have a different cultural background that will not suddenly change with a new citizenship. I am not fixated on the theme of Turks in Germany. But I do see Turkish problems when I look around. After all, the Turks have been here for 30 years, not since Saturday or Sunday. Europe has always been a multicultural society whether it wants to be or not."

And the increasing xenophobia that became evident in the last elections? "Nonsense, these people always existed. They were just so elusive. Now they have a name and can be attacked." Başer, however, admits to being less confronted with the usual problems of the Turks in the Federal Republic than are his colleagues in Kreuzberg. The calculated optimism of a privileged man in an already multinational art trade?

Cut. Tevfik Başer grew up in Eskişehir, a town of 500,000 inhabitants in northwestern Turkey, between Istanbul and Ankara. His father, now retired, was a notary public; one of his brothers, a professor, directs his own pharmaceutical institute. Başer graduated from high school in 1971 but failed the entrance exam of the College for Graphic Design and was wait-listed; he decided right then to complete the mandatory two-year military service. The decision was made too early, as he quickly learned, for a spot finally opened up and he was accepted. But the opportunity had passed, and his mother cried, because there was not even enough time to hug her son good-bye.

Two years later, his mother had reason to worry again when her son informed her on the telephone that he would set out the next day indefinitely for London. A Turkish friend living in London had made the swinging metropolis appealing to him, and that was it. With no knowledge of English or considerable capital, he became a dishwasher—as could be expected. But like the Americans, who had to learn their ideals by starting out somewhere, the dishwasher did not have to stay with his dirty pots for long. The ambitious man in his midtwenties climbed the career ladder to a managerial position following short-lived stints as cook, bartender, and headwaiter. Still, after five years, the end of all future prospects could be anticipated. Even his daytime instruction in hair styling and photography did not promise a rosy future.

Nevertheless, his attempts at photography in London rekindled the neglected dream of an artistic career and supported his first hesitant thoughts in the direction of film. Meanwhile, in Turkey, people were talking about a West German subsidized training project for photographers and graphic designers. And what was closer than the homeland? After successfully completing training as a photographer and graphic designer, Başer learned the cameraman's trade at a Turkish television station. However, that job was no longer enough for the (then) 29-year-old. He wanted to learn more so he could make films independently.

But the second attempt at a college career failed in Turkey. As a result, teachers and friends from the training project arranged for a position in Hamburg, from which he was easily able to enter a visual-communications program at the College of Fine Arts. After television companies had said no to his first feature film, *Forty Square Meters of Germany,* arguing that it was "misogynistic" and "unrealistic," these same promoters were later compelled to assist with its funding alongside Studio Hamburg.

The commitment was rewarding for all those involved, as the public resonance and elite awards demonstrate.

What has changed for the author and director because of this success? "My screenplays and exposés are now being read at least. The next film is in production, and now that the award money and my deferred honoraria from directing, producing, and writing the screenplay for *Forty Square Meters* have slowly made their way to my account, I can afford a workroom in the flat where I live—for the first time. Rich? Ha, success is like a flame. I want to make good films and experiment. That is always a risk. But I wouldn't pass up success and a little money."

5

UDO LINDENBERG

COLORFUL REPUBLIC OF GERMANY

First released as "Bunte Republik Deutschland" on the album *Bunte Republik Deutschland,* Polydor (Universal), 1989. Translated by Tes Howell. Lindenberg, one of East and West Germany's most famous rock interpreters throughout the 1980s, released this multilingual anthem to race-blindness at the height of the multiculturalism debate in West Germany. The phrase "Colorful Republic of Germany" recurred in ironic form in many leftist critiques of multiculturalism throughout the early 1990s. The italicized stanzas are in Turkish in the original.

Doesn't matter if you're an Italian
Doesn't matter if you're a smooth German
or a good-looking Turk,
or Chinese, Iroquois
Greek, or Torero.
Doesn't matter if you're a Japanese sumo wrestler
or a technician for Bolero.

Doesn't matter if you're an African,
[. . . . .]
Doesn't matter if you're an Indonesian
or an Indian.
A Capuchin, Argentinean, Franciscan, or Frenchy,
or if in your cut-off wool pants,
your balls hang freely.

Colorful Republic of Germany
whole planes full of Eskimos

just like in New York City
always something going on.
We stand on the platform and greet every train,
cuz we've had enough
of those dull, mousy Germans.

Colorful Republic of Germany . . .

That tender monster
is sleeping in the dark depths
at the base of our minds

and knits an invisible chain-link
between us and others.

Colorful Republic of Germany . . .

Colorful Republic of Germany . . .

6

TAYFUN ERDEM

DOWN WITH THE TURK BONUS!

First published as "Schluss mit dem 'Türkenbonus'!" in *Pflasterstrand* (September 23, 1989). Translated by Tes Howell. Erdem is a jazz and classical musician who grew up in Turkey. His latest album is *Dreams and Dances of a Silent Butterfly* (2004). In the beginning of this essay, Erdem alludes to two artists with Turkish backgrounds who, he alleges, unduly profit from preferential treatment: filmmaker Tevfik Başer and the painter Hanefi Yeter.

I just cannot handle all this friendliness! Since the 1970s, there has been such a great amount of foreigner friendliness in the leftist-liberal art and culture scene of this republic (especially toward the products of Turkish artists) that I have become quite suspicious!

As soon as a second-class film director makes a film about the problems of the "guest worker's wife," the film *must* be praised at least with the rating "very sensitive!" As soon as a painter from Turkey, who has borrowed almost everything from his colleague Marc Chagall, and not only in his early years, has daubed some rather meager-looking "guest-worker heads" on a canvas, he *must* have "decried the misery of his countrymen in a particularly original manner!"

And as soon as an alleged novel of an alleged author from Turkey is about to appear, which turns out to be so boring we put it down after the third page, this woman *must* be discussed flatteringly in the most prominent newspapers of this country because she has done no less than "give us an inside look at the conflicted life of guest workers from their perspective!"

This absurd comedy has nothing to do with recognition as an artist but rather nonrecognition and disregard as an artist, shamelessly sold as solidarity! This posturing has nothing to do with civility but with a "you know, actually I couldn't care less about your art" attitude. This Turk bonus is actually nothing but a passive indifference and superficiality toward the culture of the others, whether out of ignorance or lazy complacency, cautious restraint or hesitation before a *real* discovery of the other culture.

This mechanism of foreigner friendliness was of course the result of a mutual agreement. There are the professional Turks, or "artists" from Turkey, who were mostly promoted not because they command their craft very well or better than others—for example, their German colleagues—but rather because they were accidentally born in Turkey and incessantly pillory this "tragic fate of their countrymen!" The men and women from the urban cultural authorities played a primary role in this tragicomedy. For one thing, they introduced an unequivocal trend into the milieu with their constant encouragement of mediocrity under the auspices of guest-worker culture. Because the directors of the municipal theaters, concert halls, exhibition halls, or film centers also had no cultural knowledge about these "foreigners," people who have actually lived in the same city for the past 20 years, they were in no position to offer an alternative to the cultural authorities.

Furthermore, the cultural authorities' decisions were particularly important in this respect because the financial basis for the existence of a free-enterprise "foreign cultural life" is either completely lacking or is laughable in size compared to the "native" cultural offerings. In this way, several good-natured but clueless officials in public cultural bureaus could afford to arbitrarily distribute hundreds of thousands of marks for "foreigners' " events, although they knew less about the music, literature, or painting of these people than about the comet discovered yesterday in the far reaches of the universe. And as long as the annual sums in the culture budget served the goals of integration (you can also read this as assimilation) of the second and third generations' growing labor potential, this meager sum of several hundred thousand marks did not bother representatives of the political powers.

In the promotion of concerts, films, novels, and/or paintings by "professional Turks," one group played and still plays a decisive role: the social workers, the good-natured angels of our era. Just as deacons and merciful nurses took care of the sick, poor and disabled for centuries, these good-natured angels succeeded in advising their "foreign citizens" in art and culture too! What brings art in such close contact with social work? If social work is necessarily to cultivate intensive links with art, then why do we usually encounter social workers at the cultural activities of Turks but not those of Americans or the Japanese and so on?

An entirely misguided "feeling of solidarity" characterizes the third prominent role in this tragicomedy: our "alternative" friends, the remainder of the 1968 rebellion. These well-educated men and women in their midthirties and upward have managed to applaud with standing ovations at the entirely naive and unbearably banal, immeasurably boring performance of a Turkish theater group that characterizes itself, true to fashion, as being "between two worlds" or "multicultural." Astounding! Where are the impudent and critical glasses they always inevitably don for a performance by a German group, be it Heiner Müller or Shakespeare? Why do they suddenly now forget the criteria of European taste, refined throughout the centuries? How should we understand this never-ending storm of applause? As an act of encouragement, of "solidarity," or rather as an attempt to cover up with the noise of applause one's own shortcoming, one's own political failure?

But now that a new phase of the "nativized foreigner's instant residency" seems to be an irreversible reality in this country, hope is surfacing, a hope that this process could perhaps usher in the possibility for change in this society. The possibility of a new, truly organic coexistence of the natives with the foreigners, in which gushing over "non-European" cultures would be superfluous anyway, because this society would be the one that changed—not Turkey, Palestine, or Nicaragua. Ultimately, then, the bored-to-death intellectuals would no longer need to search through the constantly changing cultures of non-European countries for an illusory refuge. When the goal is to enrich one's *own* life through the appropriation of foreign cultures and not just to make a gesture of solidarity toward a "foreign" artist, then we must accept that such a goal requires a higher level of knowledge and a more detailed acquaintance. Does this mean that now everyone must be a Turkey specialist? By no means! But one thing is clear: with the prevailing consumer attitude toward "exotic" cultures, the mediocrity and boredom of a "guestworker culture" could not be superseded under even the most favorable conditions, and this is precisely the result of 15 years of the most intensive promotion in this country's leftist-liberal and foreigner-friendly public sphere. Why should a saz player (saz is a kind of long-necked lute) who actually plays monotonously make an effort to play more colorfully at the next concert when he, even in this pitiful state, can collect 1,000 marks from the promotions of a cohort of benevolent, clueless cultural department heads, only because he plays this "exotic" instrument, the saz? Behind this "promotion," behind this "preferential treatment of Turks," is there the opinion that Turks are incapable of top-notch achievements in the "civilized" Western world's culture—outside of their "own," "authentic culture"?

Cultural authorities! The charity-loving humanists of our time! And our dear, alternative friends! Finally hear the clarion call of a new era: *the first wave of "foreigners" is over!* At a time when this claim seems destined to become an irreversible reality in this republic, the second phase is beginning. *Consequently, the phase of a relatively effortless and simple solidarity is also over!* Now the time for a more critical and sensible analysis of the "aliens' " culture begins, more difficult for both sides, but all the more exciting because of it! Stop this contemptible civility in the arts that will very soon destroy us all! It is high time that this "Turk bonus" finally be abandoned! Enough with the special reclassification: they are not "foreigner films" but films! They are not "guest-worker novels" but novels! There is no "guest-worker culture," just culture! Be critical—and when necessary, merciless—toward the works of artists from Turkey. For only with a discriminating attitude can the foundations for art reception be created and the criteria for art appreciation endure the test of years to come.

7

DIETMAR H. LAMPARTER

DISCRIMINATION OF THE NOBLE KIND

First published as "Die edle Art der Diskriminierung" in *Die Zeit* (October 30, 1992). Translated by David Gramling.

Advertising: So far, the eager consumer group of 1.7 million Turks in Germany has gone overlooked.

Marketing managers' hearts ought to beat a bit faster when they think of this target audience. Turks are buying chic cars, arming themselves with the newest hi-fi components, consuming copious amounts of chocolate bars, diligently paying off their building loans, and favoring the banking industry's elite institutions during financial transactions.

But all for naught. Brand names and advertising agencies are not actually thinking about the approximately 1.7 million Turkish citizens living in Germany, despite this group's pronounced consumerism. The answer is the same whether from Philips in Hamburg, Jacobs-Suchard in Bremen, Nestlé in Frankfurt/Main or Mercedes-Benz in Stuttgart: "We do indeed know that our products are well loved among foreign fellow citizens, but we have not yet advertised to this group in particular."

Zafer Ilgar, a partner at the Berlin media agency TurkMedia, believes he knows why his countrymen in Germany have been so egregiously neglected: "In many people's minds, the image of the Turkish woman with a head scarf who shops only at Turkish shops or Aldi dies hard, as does the image of her husband in the car with shredded tires who sends all of his savings home to Anatolia." Yet German-Turkish media experts know that most Turks have been in Germany for decades and that a quarter of them were in fact born here and have adapted to the German world of commodities.

Jürgen Stolte of the Hamburg advertising agency Lintas can only confirm the advertising industry's lack of interest in foreigners thus far. As chief of market research at the Federal Republic's second largest agency, he has received "practically no" inquiries about this population in the past years. Stolte sees yet another reason for the lack of attention: practically all large market-research studies are based on the German-speaking population and consequently have not raised the issue of nationality. Foreign citizens—especially when they speak German—simply get lost in the grand masses of consumers.

Yet, even if there were reliable data about Turkish, Greek, Portuguese, or Italian consumers, it is still questionable whether many firms would have designed special advertising strategies. Georg Baums, president of the Organization of Advertising Agencies (GWA) and chief of the Düsseldorf agency group Publicis-FCA, sees the target population trait of nationality as "secondary" for the great majority of all advertised products. Attitudes and mentalities such as distinct environmental consciousness or the need for luxury are good for much more these days than differentiation among target groups. Furthermore, according to the advertising executive's firm opinion, foreigners living here would be reached through German-language advertising.

And the clientele think similarly. Communication specialist Albrecht Koch of the Nestlé agency believes that "niche marketing is not very sensible for mass products. After all, everyone wants to eat chocolate." However, Turks do not find out how good Sarotti chocolate or Maggi soup tastes on TRT International (Turkish Radio and Television), their medium of choice.

For this reason, Zafer Ilgal does not intend to accept any more of this "noble kind of discrimination." In the future, his agency intends to aggressively acquire advertisements for German sweets, business chains, cars, or pharmaceuticals for the Turkish channel TRT (accessible in Germany via satellite and cable) and the widely distributed Turkish newspapers like *Hürriyet* or *Milliyet*. Transmitting the advertisements and synchronizing television or radio spots in Turkish are no problem at all.

However, because statistic-happy Germans must first be "fed with numbers," the Berlin-based Ilgal, in cooperation with the Center for Turkey Studies at the University of Essen, has compiled a representative study about the "consumption habits of the Turkish population in the Federal Republic of Germany."

The Turkish population, the largest foreign group in Germany by about 30 percent, has a low average age—around half of the 1.7 million are between 25 and 45. This group contributes powerfully to the replenishment of retirement and unemployment insurance funds and is among the most purchase-ready consumer groups as well.

More than a quarter of Turkish households plan to buy a car in the next 12 months; about half intend to acquire a new car. A similar scenario applies to hi-fi equipment, VCRs, and personal computers. Although in this regard, the Öztürk or Kasanoğlu family owns more equipment than the Meier or Schulze family, the survey reveals that Turkish families still have above-average consumer prospects.

The Turkish household, which on average is double the size of its German counterpart, turns the washing machine on almost every day and disproportionately uses name-brand detergent. The guest workers and their descendants cannot get enough of brand-name juices and Coca-Cola. Even with their various building loan balances, immigrant citizens have it over the local residents hands down.

Of course, it is not just the upper crust that makes the difference. When it comes to brand names, only the best is good enough for foreign citizens. The number of Turkish Mercedes drivers per capita is three times higher than among their German neighbors; tanks are preferably filled at the market leader, Aral; the checking account should be at the Deutsche Bank; Persil, Ariel, or Omo is used for washing; and the sneakers must be Adidas or Nike.

Ilgar explains that this dependence on market leaders and image brands is due in part to insufficient advertising from other suppliers; others, however, suspect there are social motives behind this phenomenon. "With the purchase of a Mercedes, any visit here or at home demonstrates that one has made it," say the Mercedes communications experts. And advertisers like Georg Baum are convinced that second-generation foreigners born here already "feel like Germans" and would find being addressed as members of another nationality as rather discriminating. A young Spanish woman, raised in Germany and now working at a large German auto manufacturer in the marketing department, confirms this thesis: "It would bother me to be addressed as a Spanish woman."

Yet often the arguments for abstaining from advertising sound like excuses: for years, sales opportunities have been lost.

At least in reference to his countrymen, Ilgar can counter this idea on the basis of television and reading habits. For example, the Turkish television channel TRT reaches 30 percent more Turks daily than all German channels combined. And over 60 percent of the respondents indicate that they read the Turkish tabloid newspaper *Hürriyet* as their daily newspaper.

The wall of indifference is already crumbling. At Merci GmbH in Berlin, a division of the candy group Storck, marketing manager Hans-Georg Vornfeld is researching "preconsiderations" for translating Merci ads into Turkish. Lately at Philips, there have been intentions "to think about a targeted campaign." And even at a Swabian elite auto manufacturer, serious deliberations are under way on the question whether Turkish fans have been neglected thus far.

8

CHRISTIANE PEITZ

EVERYWHERE IS BETTER WHERE WE ARE NOT

First published as "Überall ist es besser, wo wir nicht sind" in *die tageszeitung* (May 13, 1994). Translated by David Gramling. Filmmaker Sinan Çetin (b. 1953, Van, Turkey), studied fine arts at Hacettepe University in Ankara and is based in Istanbul. His feature film *Berlin in Berlin* was released in 1993. Other

Turkish films by Çetin, including the border-comedy *Propaganda* (1999), were popular hits in Germany. He also directed the recent series of Cola Turka commercials, which use a satirical reverse-ethnographic marketing strategy.

From mainstream to auteur films, more and more foreigners are speaking for themselves

LINE 1, BERLIN-KREUZBERG. Mürtüz is sitting in the subway across from a German. The native does not appear malicious, just lost in thought. So there is no cause for a scene. Mürtüz, however, creates one anyway. He taunts the German, stares at him, makes faces and threatening gestures. He is fed up with his role as foreigner, the "other," the "Turkish fellow citizen" who gets stared at like an animal in a zoo: he's had enough. Now he is gawking back and making a fool out of the German.

Many films coming into our theaters return an angry and indignant gaze similar to this one. They are speaking out against the discourse of the foreigner-to-be-integrated, saying instead, "we'll speak for ourselves." *Berlin in Berlin* by Sinan Çetin depicts Kreuzberg from a Turkish perspective. In *Bhaji on the Beach*, the Anglo-Indian Gurinder Chadha brought together nine Indian women from three generations for a trip from Birmingham to Blackpool. In *Daughters of the Heavens,* four Chinese mothers and their U.S.-born daughters tell the story of their "American way of life." And in Jan Schüttes's *Goodbye, America,* Jewish emigrants travel back after three decades to Poland in search of children born abroad.

What is particularly interesting is that films such as these have been posting financial successes lately. Stephen Frear's *My Beautiful Laundrette* arose out of the New British Cinema niche, to the applause of film critics. Ang Lee's *The Wedding Banquet* was praised not only by the critics but also achieved mainstream success. Minority cinema is able to reach a majority. *Berlin in Berlin* even beat out *Bodyguard* as the Turkish box-office hit in Istanbul, and Gurinder Chadha's feature film debut held on for 12 weeks in the British cinemas. The case is similar in England, Germany, and in the United States.

Berlin in Berlin takes place in an old prewar apartment building in Kreuzberg. A Turkish extended family lives there, including three generations of mother; father, Mürtüz; his brothers; the grandparents; the sister-in-law, Dilber; and her son, Mustafa. Thomas, a young German engineer, secretly takes photos of the beautiful Dilber, whose jealous husband becomes enraged and dies in a physical conflict. Thomas is innocent, but Dilber's brother-in-law Mürtüz sees him only as his brother's murderer. A chase on foot through the neighborhood ends accidentally in the apartment of Thomas's pursuer. It is there, and only there, that he is safe, for whoever seeks asylum cannot be turned away—so dictates the Turkish rule of hospitality. If you go out, then you're dead, says the youngest brother. Mürtüz gripes, but the father remains obstinate, and the mother lays down the law: if we kill him here, we will be eternally cursed. This is called Allah's test.

So the German is alone in a foreign land without provisions, the guest of guest workers. He does not understand the language but is avidly learning Turkish (although he puts together only a few broken pieces of conversation). He gets used to the daily routine, the power structure, and family rituals. Gradually the hosts also adjust to the unwelcome guest. On occasion, they even play music together. But for a long time, this togetherness does not lead to a reconciliation.

An upside-down world: now the foreigners are the natives, and the German adapts accordingly. This shrewd film plot turns the concept of "living together" sought by the authorities on its head. Thomas behaves just as foreigner commissioners imagine "our fellow citizens" do. He sits in the corner piously, fixes the television, plays the guitar nicely, and speaks only when spoken to. A model asylum seeker. Integration, distorted to the point of recognizability.

Mürtüz and his brother are meanwhile living between worlds: an uncomfortable space that harbors tragic conflicts and murderous spiritual anguish, but one makes do as well as possible. The father snores in front of television commercials; the mosque-shaped alarm clock goes off early in the morning with pious melodies. Dilber masturbates. The youngest brother is accompanied by his German girlfriend. Mürtüz has a rendezvous with a married lover as the grandmother prays to the East, undisturbed. Skinheads are making trouble on the street, and on holidays, all the relatives file in. Çetin's film lurches between kitsch, porn, thriller, and comedy. To a great extent, it applies a grubby B-movie aesthetic: cinematic cheap goods. But precisely therein lies its truth. Thomas's integration remains a pious fairy tale. This peddling of Turkish family is germane to the crass realities of the business, and it corresponds quite nicely to the film tastes of its protagonists as well.

Berlin in Berlin's success in Turkish cinemas may be due in part to its breaking of sexual taboos. But its strengths lie less in scandal or in forced tragedy than in its self-irony. In no way do Turks appear here as defenseless victims. They ultimately hold the positions of power. And in this respect they are as mercilessly and candidly shown as they ever could be—furtive, sympathetic, weak, coarse, comical, invidious—which means that they are thoroughly consistent with one prejudice or the next. For instance, the brothers are outspoken machos, but they cower before the grandmother. It is hardly an accident that this time the Germans are made into clichés. In the media here, foreigners generally see themselves portrayed exactly in this way.

9

KLAUS HARTUNG

LET THE BERLINERS BARBECUE IN PEACE!

First published as "Lasst die Berliner in Ruhe grillen!" in *Die Zeit* (July 29, 1994). Translated by Tes Howell.

BERLIN. Something was missing, but what was it? The kilometer-long traffic jam of people leaving the city, the mineral-water ads; the district reform plans and the daily ozone levels; [. . .] the radio warning for skin type 3 (only 36 to 54 minutes in the sun): summer in Berlin, a marriage of crisis and heat, 95 degrees in the shade. But somehow it was still not complete. Yes, of course, there he comes, the usual summer appearance of the CDU faction chair, Volker Liepelt: the annual call to arms against barbecuing in the Tiergarten. The green lung of Berlin must remain pure. Cancer and carcinoma from charcoal on the holy grass can no longer be tolerated.

As always, he calculated how many sections of charcoal-burned grass will have to be replaced again in the fall; as always, the other parties declined to participate in the campaign. A grand coalition against the grillers has not yet been organized. The use of signs, police, and intensified ecological argumentation has long since failed. Resigned, the Greens declared that one could not campaign against people experiencing comfort and leisure in their own city. The Social Democrats call it a problem of not enough garbage cans and fixed barbecuing areas. Meanwhile, the pall of smoke sweeps across the middle of Berlin, blowing through state visits and the last processions of the Russian army.

But what appears under the barbecuing vapors is nothing other than the multicultural society as it exists in practice. Turkish extended families, equipped with all the technologies; the row of women preparing salads, men tending the grill with patriarchal solemnity. The alternative regulars with their picnic hybrids, the soccer players, the bare-chested women next to the head-scarf chastity of the Turkish women. Here, everything is mixed and divided. The multicultural scene is not a community, not a utopia. Here, no one is integrated by anyone. All remain among themselves. Tolerance is the most energy-saving form of everyday life.

Berlin possesses enough large park areas that are easier to reach than this one, especially considering that Berlin's center is increasingly separated from the rest of the city by construction sites. In the Jungfernheide or Hasenheide, one sees similar mixtures of the grill society. But they cannot compare to the mass action in the Tiergarten. The hard core of the barbecuing masses in particular gathers near the Reichstag, which is designated for the new chancellery. A coincidence? Anarchistic tendencies are not implied here; the summer is too hot for that. But their visibility amid the city skyline and government buildings is certainly relevant. If there is something connecting them, then it is a kind of self-production or self-representation of the masses in the city center.

As is generally known, immediately upon taking office, [Federal President] Roman Herzog had warned that he had quite a popular touch. Nothing would keep him, he declared, from having his usual conversations with people at the sausage stand. But these days in Berlin, one tends not to be munching on a sausage when expressing an opinion. The people's food is, after all, the döner kebab. And it is difficult to express an opinion without losing half of the garlic sauce–drenched cabbage salad. However, the federal president needs only to open his window to smell the people. And indeed, one of the great tasks of the president of the Berlin Republic is to do nothing and engage in contact with the people. But that is only another way of saying he is the first federal president who lives in a metropolis. And in this respect, he would certainly have something to do. He would have to defend himself against the Bonn administrators' constantly flickering desire for "security zones." [. . .]

Where is this cheerless atmosphere in Germany today coming from? It is the provincial spirit rearing its head; it is the inability to cope with contradictions, other lifestyles, and the loss of certainty. Nothing would be more foolish than if the capital were to try to control the summer masses in the Tiergarten and to create grill-free zones staffed by security agents. Clean, green lungs are everywhere in the German province. Whoever coughs from the barbecuing fumes in the Tiergarten should consider that urban freedom does contradict ecology.

10

DANIEL BAX AND DORTHE FERBER

IS LINDEN STREET CLOSED OFF TO TURKS?

First published as "Ist die Lindenstrasse für Türken gesperrt?" in *Der Tagesspiegel* (July 13, 1995). Translated by Tes Howell. The television show *Linden Street*, set in Munich, is Germany's longest-running soap opera. Approximately 1,000 episodes have aired since 1985.

Critique of the media's portrayal of Germany's largest migrant group is increasing

This is actually cause for celebration for the republic: last week, *Lindenstrasse,* Germany's most beloved soap opera, celebrated its tenth birthday. But some did not rejoice at the anniversary; on the contrary, numerous resentful Turkish viewers complained to West German Radio. And the liberal Turkish newspaper *Milliyet* was infuriated: "Who is responsible for this lack of accountability?" In the five hundredth episode of the beloved series, the Greek *Lindenstrasse* restaurant owner, Panaiotis Sarikakis, returned from a humanitarian goods delivery in Georgia. On the way there, the truck was stopped in Turkey. Police suspected that Sarikakis's real purpose was to bring the goods to the PKK. Only with assistance from Amnesty International and the Greek embassy was the landlord's family able to free their father from a Turkish prison, where the Turkish secret police had tortured him. Sarikakis's son Vasily could scarcely contain his rage: "no animal would do such a thing, but this has all taken place in a country—in the middle of Europe—that calls itself civilized." And in the next episode, he put a sign on the steps: "No Turks allowed."

"An abhorrent scenario," declared *Milliyet,* which then asked whether the WDR, "together with the PKK," was attempting to sabotage Turkish tourism just before the vacation season. The paper called on its readers to join the protest, publishing addresses and telephone numbers of the *Lindenstrasse* editorial office. The phones were ringing off the hook at WDR; even Cornelia Schmalz-Jacobsen, the commissioner of foreigner affairs, got involved. And the Turkish embassy sent a letter of complaint to the director of WDR, Fritz Pleitgen. The station is now considering issuing an official statement to the Turkish media. By no means did they want to denigrate Turkey, the public-relations department declares apologetically. The story was written over a year ago. At that time, no one could have guessed that there would again be tension between the two Mediterranean states. Admittedly, they conceded, it is careless that the only foreigners in the series are Greek. They did not want a German character experiencing this episode in Turkey for fear that they might legitimize the racist treatment of Germans against Turks. However, despite their good intentions to make things right for everyone, they only made it worse.

A farce? Certainly. But the incident is symptomatic of a situation that has burdened German-Turkish relations for some time: the image of Turkey in the German media is increasingly the object of criticism—in Turkey as well as among migrants living in the Federal Republic. The German media's reporting is hostile toward Turkey and tends to be pro-Kurdish, according to the condensed version of the current accusation. Many Turks reacted with increasing anger to the "mistakes" made this year. The Kreuzberg Workshop of Cultures [Werkstatt der Kulturen], along with Turkish and German journalists, recently took this development as an opportunity to organize a workshop on the "image of Turkey in the German media." They planned to debate basic principles of balanced reporting using selected newspaper articles.

The first results of the debate: there can be no accepted widespread German reporting about Turkey, because the 2 million Turks living in Germany consume the latest news from sources in their home country. The Green representative Ismail Hakkı Koşan emphasized Turks' expectations, for the Turkish press equates criticism with the acknowledgment of positive developments.

The criticism, usually exclusively in Germany, strikes many readers as offensive, prompting this demand: "Criticism of Turkey, yes, by all means. But add a teaspoon of sugar for all that medicine." In any case, the reduction of Turkey to the Kurdish conflict is a distortion. Indeed, German journalists' problems already begin with word choices, which frequently express their interpretation: is it "South East Anatolia" or "Kurdistan"? Is the PKK just the "forbidden Kurdish workers' party" or a "Marxist terror organization," its members "guerillas," "rebels" or "separatists"? These questions are difficult to answer when one considers the emotions that events in Turkey evoke.

With the detailed analysis of individual articles, it became clear that reports on Turkey from serious print media generally fulfill the journalistic criterion of balance. But why the discrepancy between the real journalistic quality of the reporting and the criticism expressed about it?

One participant noted that politics have created fertile ground for the Turks' heightened sensitivity. When someone feels excluded by the general foreign policy in Germany, he sees this confirmed through a falsely written name in a German newspaper. The result of the seven-hour discussion: the content of the reporting is much less problematic than that which is not reported. Discussion leader Thomas Hartmann then made an appeal for regular background reporting that reflects all facets of the multicultural state.

That the *Lindenstrasse* creators also make use of prevalent clichés about Turkey may be thoughtless. However, the fact that Turks exist on the fringes of the media has structural reasons: there are no representatives of the largest German migrant group on the oversight committees of public broadcasting corporations or in most editorial bureaus. To remedy this situation, Berlin's Green Party is demanding a seat for foreigners, who comprise approximately 16 percent of the city, on the Radio Council. The proposal is backed by the SPD and the PDS. However, a lack of structures can be remedied only in the long term. In the meantime, the *Lindenstrasse* team hopes that upcoming episodes will ease the current turbulence. In them, the friends of Sarikakis's son Vasily will try to calm him down.

11

THOMAS JAHN

TÜRKSÜN—YOU'RE A TURK

First published as "Türksün—Du bist Türke" in *Die Zeit* (January 12, 1996). Translated by Tes Howell.

Hip-hop, house, and pop: A new feeling of solidarity is thumping in the Turkish ghettos of Munich, Cologne, and Berlin

Some 800,000 young Turks live in Germany. Surrounded by social indifference, they have now found their homeland: in their own pop music.

Young Turkish men are waiting at the door of the Bodrum and chatting up the women, trying to get them to come inside. *Damsız girilmez* is the unwritten rule that there is no admission without a female companion. Similar to German dance clubs of the past, no man can enter a German-Turkish disco alone. "That way there aren't any lone wolves around," the bouncer explains.

As on every other weekend, the club is crowded inside. Turkish pop blares from the loudspeakers, sometimes mixed with house or hip-hop. Turkish elements surface repeatedly in the music; every once in a while, one can hear an *ud* (lute) or *tambur* (saz); other times it is the *kudüm* bass drums or *darbukka* drums that shake up the rhythm from the beat box. Everyone is dancing like crazy. There are not many Germans there. But one cannot say for sure: it is difficult to match passport to person. Twenty-five hundred people are supposed to fit in this underground dance club, which is close to the Cologne Cathedral. The Bodrum is the largest Turkish disco in Europe, at least according to its operators.

At the bar, a young Turkish couple drinks Kölsch and Efes beer. They are raving about the Bodrum. "Now I'm the host when I bring along German friends," says the stylishly dressed woman. Indeed, as a German, one feels like a foreigner in the Bodrum. "Now you're in Turkey," says the man. But no one here is xenophobic, contrary to what happens outside these walls.

Turkish discos are springing up all over Germany, radio programs such as *Turkish Kisses* (through the Berlin commercial broadcaster Kiss) are being produced, and German-Turkish pop bands are quickly gaining popularity. These are signs of a change in climate: after the murderous attacks in Solingen and Mölln, for example, and the open xenophobia, the approximately 800,000 Turkish youths living in Germany are searching more intensively for their own identity. And they are finding it in their cultural roots. "The ethnic revival is hardly surprising," says Yasemin Karakaşoğlu from the Center for Turkish Studies at the University of Essen. "Young people notice that there's no place reserved for them in the German world. They run into prejudices wherever they go."

But they are also not welcomed with open arms in Turkey. There, they are unflatteringly nicknamed the *Almancı* or *Deutschländer*. The name implies that they support the Germans, that they even belong to them. This label effects a painful exclusion, for it makes them homeless. Sociologists call this an "identity gap." Not yet at home here, no longer at home there—the youth fill this emptiness in their own way, with a mixture of Turkish nostalgia and pop modernity.

"*Türksün!* You are a Turk! In Germany! Understand that; don't forget it!" reads a line of text from Cartel, one of the most well-known German-Turkish bands. With Turkish rap texts and Middle Eastern–influenced hip-hop, they aggressively address the problems of German-Turkish youths. They warn against TV and drugs, slander "snot-nosed proles," and rap about everything that is still interesting: discos, sex, cars, and xenophobia.

"Being famous is annoying. Every Turk turns to look at you," says Alper A., the 27-year-old rapper from Cartel. The Germans, however, never turn around. No one recognizes the eight men from Cartel, whom Turkish fans exalted to the pantheon of pop music. A year ago, they still belonged to three unknown hip-hop bands from Kiel, Nuremberg, and Berlin. Now they are superstars on the Bosporus: for weeks, they held the number one spot of the charts; every Turkish child can rap along with their *"Araba yok"* ["No Car"] or "Posse Attack."

So far, Cartel has sold 312,000 albums in Turkey, almost exclusively cassettes. With these records, they went platinum: a "German" group had never accomplished that before. How was such success possible? "The image of a country, from which only guest workers come, weighs heavily on the souls of the Turks," says cultural expert Karakusoğlu. "Frankly, they have waited for this occasion to assert an image of a modern and, above all, a European country." With MTV as its medium, Cartel has become known in Turkey.

"Now it's your turn, skinheads, we will get you!": a line from a Cartel song reflects the anger of many young German Turks. "For us, hip-hop is like an outlet," says Alper A. Hip-hop offers cohesion, a defense against those elements that threaten to tear the young *Deutschländer* apart: the music is both Western and Middle Eastern, the language half Turkish, half German. The hip-hoppers rummage through their parents' record collections in order to find traditional Turkish sounds that they can mix into their pieces. Barış Manço meets Run DMC. Old and new work just as well together as old and young. The "ethnic revival" is not a recollection of past values but rather a fusion of two galaxies. The result is the universe of the Kanaks.

Kanaks. This term means turning the tables. This is the point for Cartel. The band took the term by which Turks have long been abused in Germany and made a proud, aggressive trademark out of it. The model for this comes from the United States. American racists had coined the curse word *nigger;* today, however, blacks use this word themselves. Today in Germany, right-wing extremists look increasingly foolish when they yell "Kanake!" on the street.

"Certainly, one cannot compare the history of African-Americans in the U.S. with the situation of the Turks in Germany," explains 21-year-old Erci E., the youngest member of Cartel. But parallels nevertheless exist. Now the stream of news flows between the Turkish "ghettos," between Munich's Hasenbergl district, Cologne's Mülheim district, or Berlin's Kreuzberg district. And since Cartel's success in Turkey, young people there are also learning about the everyday life of the *Deutschländer* and hearing, perhaps for the first time, their language: *Kanak Sprak,* the language of the Kanaks.

Kanak Sprak is vernacular jargon that only German Turks understand. Similar to the powerfully eloquent American rappers, the Kanaks hammer out with staggering speed words and expressions that do not even exist in German or Turkish. "Our Turkish is that of a five-year-old in Turkey. Every language evolves but we don't hear any of that in Germany," says Fatih Cevikkollu, an actor and rapper in the German-Turkish group Shakkáh from Cologne. "We have developed a German system of speaking Turkish. To a Turk, that must sound like playing a VHS cassette on a Beta recorder."

"God fucks weak people": an example from Feridun Zaimoğlu, who recently published a book about (and entitled) *Kanak Sprak*. Translated, the sentence means whoever wants to move forward in this world must take his life into his own hands. The author researched for a year and a half in the "Kanak ghetto" to compile "24 discords from the margins of society." Whether one listens to Ali, the 23-year old-rapper from Da Crime Posse; Hasan, the 13-year-old drifter; or Faruk, 26 years old and unemployed, all 24 stories allow a glimpse into a world that is right in front of our eyes and yet still so far away.

"When I tell a German that instead of a skin, he's got icing like on a donut in the coffee shop," says 25-year-old unemployed Fikret, it reflects the desperation of the Germans. He continues, "The German, man, feeds on crisis, shits crisis, and infects you with this nasty virus that festers in you and rattles you until doomsday." Büjük Ibo, an 18-year-old packer, explains that young Turks receive no help from their parents: "Our good ol' dads gamble in the bars or grow a beard and go to the mosque; our mothers get fat and make 'em dinner, and where are we?"

This feeling of abandonment underlies the hip-hop family's promise to provide security: "Cartel is like a *family* that keeps getting bigger," says Ozan Sinan, the 23-year-old manager of Cartel. [. . .] According to him, Cartel will not last much longer in its current form. Only a few concerts in December and January, and then it is over. "Cartel will live on, as a group, as a new project with new Turkish crews," says Alper A.

Cartel is not popular everywhere. The patriotic poses of the band particularly bother leftist circles, for example. "They call us racists and fascists because we use the Turkish flag despite Turkey's human-rights violations; one can hardly deny those abuses," says Ali from Cartel. But why does the band use national symbols? "Because we *are* Turks," answers Ali. "Just because there are gaps in government policy doesn't mean that we should throw away the Turkish flag." Despite all this controversy, Cartel is seen as politically correct, not the least because of its attitude toward the Kurdish conflict. Two of the band's Turkish concerts took place in Kurdish cities, and Cartel is quite firm on the subject: "Kurds and Turks are brothers and sisters, and whoever wants to break them apart is a traitor; you have to explain that to your children."

12

EBERHARD SEIDEL-PIELEN

THE BILLION-MARK COUP

First published as "Der Milliardencoup" in *Aufgespießt: Wie der Döner über die Deutschen kam* (Berlin: Rotbuch, 1996), 41–44. Translated by Tes Howell. The now thoroughly German word *döner* comes from the Turkish verb *dönmek*, "to turn," connoting the rotating vertical spits at kebab stands on which cured lamb and other meats are cooked.

"Döner theft in the S-Bahn!" startled, horrified Berliners cry out in the summer of 1995. A young man attacks a passenger, violently wrests the döner kebab from him, and escapes. "Have we come so far that people will kill for a handful of döner?" concerned retirees ask themselves. "Can it be that the smell of meat and garlic sauce can rob döner junkies of all self-control?" I ask myself. And must we anticipate new forms of drug-related crimes in the future? But the retirees know their city better. They vividly remember another headline: "Döner Murder on Alexander Square!" On December 16, 1992, an unidentified individual shot the döner vendor Gamal H. four times. "Did he not want to pay protection money? Was it the Mafia? Was he a pimp? Or just a medical student?" The rumors swept through the city.

Undoubtedly, the döner kebab has changed the republic. Everywhere, we find serious people concentrating intensely with humbly bent upper bodies and animalistic wide-open eyes and jaws, as they devour these pockets of meat. Gone is the genteel bockwurst posture: the little sausage held delicately between thumbs, index and middle fingers, the ring finger and pinkie elegantly extended. The döner demands full bodily investment: two hands, flexible jaws, well-cultivated motor skills, and agile backs.

"This guy must have gone totally crazy! Aren't there any more important research topics? Once more, he is giving us Turks this slippery fatty döner and exotic belly-dancer image." During preparation for this book, I encountered blank looks at first. "You will get swift critique from the Turkish intellectuals if you write a study of the döner," warned one interlocutor. For döner consumption is like a bordello visit: hundreds of thousands do it every day, but those who perform the service are denied societal recognition. "Turkish culture is more than the döner," "not just kebab and shortened pant legs," "Turks are not just kebab vendors," and "Turkish businesspeople have more to offer than the döner." So read the headlines when Germans are supposed to be shaken up and have their alleged cultural ignorance exposed; when a Turkish cultural organization wants to make people aware of its ambitious program, or when a foreigner initiative pleads for attention to its political cause.

Our dysfunctional relationship to the number one Turkish export is easy to explain. More than cultural offensives, friendship festivals, and moral appeals, the döner has promoted intercultural encounter. This process is painful—making each person's modest yet significant role clear, questioning the rules of the game. Hans and Mustafa strike up a conversation not at night school or in the halls of high culture but rather at the döner stand, where one's plans for a first trip to Turkey originate. It holds more validity for the Eastern part of the country than for the West. If anyone taught the citizens of the former GDR that reunification concerns not only the Germans in East and West but also the 2 million immigrants from Turkey, it was these "uneducated" and simple döner vendors, the *Kebapçi*. They were the advance team. Hardly had the Wall fallen when they dared to go into the Wild East. They— not the state-subsidized, civil-servant integration specialists—have built functional bridges of understanding by the sweltering heat of the döner grill. On a daily basis, they brave their customers' repetitive, curious questions: "Mehmed, what's it really like down there?" "Heinz, do you really believe that we drive around in donkey carts? Go to Antalya. You have never experienced such a vacation as you can have there." The kebab vendors are the true, ever- present ambassadors of Turkish culture. They have accomplished more for German-Turkish relations than journalists have.

To fully appreciate the döner producer's contributions to the nutritional situation in Germany, let us look briefly to the past: "The younger immi- grants really miss their familiar, sharply seasoned dishes," reported the Berlin *Tagesspiegel* compassionately in June of 1956. The consequences were alarming: "Thus, the economics student Vecdi Demirkol has lost 14 pounds in two years and—despite his love for Berlin—gets indigestion just thinking about Berlin food." In 1956, 100 Turks were living in the city. Culinary mar- tyrdom united merchants, intellectuals, craftsmen, and students. Without protection or alternatives, they were exposed to pickled pork knuckle, pea pudding, meatballs, cabbage rolls, herring filet with potatoes, curry, and bockwurst. As of 1945, there was no Turkish restaurant nearby that could serve as a possible place of refuge, and the shops lacked so much of what Turks needed for the native menu. Zucchini? Negative. Eggplant? Unknown. *Sucuk, lokum, pita,* and *baklava?* Foreign words. Yogurt, goat cheese, olives, lamb? If one can even find these products, they are sold at astronomically high prices. At least, they are beyond the financial resources of a student. At this point, the EC market was just in the process of development and the ex- change rate of the German mark was not yet so consumer friendly as it is today. And naturally there was not a Turkish vegetable vendor on every cor- ner supplying his compatriots with the essentials. The small Turkish com- munity moved closer together out of necessity: "It is lucky that the Turks are so hospitable, that they invite each other now and then to a banquet of na- tive foods. Aram Peştemalcı, the rug dealer, even roasts a whole mutton on a skewer sometimes so that his guests will feel at home with him."

We do not know whether the student Demirkol belonged to Peştemalcı's circle of friends. However, 15 years later, it is clear his suffering would have been over. Export and import businesses, as well as vegetable markets, opened in the early 1970s, when 40,000 Turks were living in Berlin. Several resolute vendors started up their grills in Berlin-Kreuzberg and Schöneberg, offering sliced veal and lamb in flat bread for 2 to 3 marks per portion. They had no idea that they were laying the foundation for an industry that would experience fantastic revenue increases each year. Twenty-five years later, this is an industry that is ready to conquer the European, yes even the Turkish, market.

The approximately 720 million kebab sandwiches consumed each year prove that Germany is into the döner. According to statistics, every citizen eats a kilogram of döner annually. A dense network of an estimated 10,000 döner vending sites makes the Germans the leading "Orientalists" of the Western Hemisphere. There is one döner stand for every 8,000 inhabitants—a formidable ratio. In Hoyerswerda, that cozy town in Saxony, where right-wing extremists declared the city "foreigner-free" after the first postwar pogrom in 1991, the ratio is even higher. Here, 15 döner skewers turn for 60,000 citizens every day. [. . .]

As for the döner industry's success in serious numbers: around 200 tons of döner are consumed daily in Germany: 25 tons in Berlin, 35 tons in the five new federal states, 140 tons in western Germany. Two hundred tons a day, which yield approximately 72,000 tons or 72 million kilograms per year. That translates into 720 million döner kebab sandwiches a year being passed across the counter. With a consumer price of about 5 marks, the döner industry makes around 3.6 billion marks annually.

This trend may be comforting for multiculturalists, antimonopolists, and anti-American activists: in the Federal Republic, the industry makes more from döner sandwiches than the gastrogiants with their entire product menu, compared with the 3,600 million marks in döner revenue annually:

1. McDonald's Germany: sales 2,600 million marks, 570 franchises
2. Mitropa AG/DS GmbH: 529 million marks, 597 franchises
3. Mövenpick Gesellschaften Deutschland: 359 million marks, 45 franchises
4. Nordsee Deutsche Hochseefischerei GmbH: 356 million marks, 292 franchises
5. Burger King GmbH: 340 million marks, 94 franchises
6. Wienerwald GmbH: 233 million marks, 170 franchises

Still more telling than a nationwide assessment is the success of McMahmud over the hamburger giant McDonald's in Berlin and the new states: 920 million döner marks here compared to a shabby 350 million McDonald's marks. [. . .]

This success is neither sensational nor an accident of history. The Berliner Turks are just continuing a tradition. In the seventeenth century, the Huguenots brought the sausage to the Spree via Frankfurt. After 1945, the

Americans provided their tomato ketchup and curry—necessary help for the development of the Berlin currywurst. And now the döner has made its way here as well. [. . .]

13

GUNNAR LÜTZOW

OKAY, WE ARE KANAKS

First published in English in the *Berliner Morgenpost International* (March 28, 1999). Translation modified by David Gramling.

[. . .] It is Friday evening in Hip-Hop Land, and normalcy prevails. Young people are celebrating the conclusion of the international East Meets West Hip-Hop Festival on the Insel der Jugend ("Youth Island") in Berlin's Treptow district. There is no trace of the aggressiveness that is often experienced at hip-hop concerts in Berlin. The sweet smell of cannabis can be noticed only occasionally, and even the graffiti artists are sticking to their canvasses. And though many of the kids are wearing the proper sneakers, MTV is nowhere to be seen.

The Berlin band Islamic Force, which has meanwhile broken up, used to call itself Ka.Nak, which can mean both the reappropriated pejorative *Kanake* or "flowing blood" in Turkish. On its current album, the Berlin rap trio Die 3. Generation sings: "You're afraid to go to the disco, 'cuz someone might pull a gun on you and say, 'Auf Wiedersehen, Kanake!' "

Ethem Bozkurt is 22 and grew up in the Neukölln district. He explains how the band Kanaks With Brains got its name. "The expression *Kanak* is normally used as an insult against us. When a German sees someone with dark hair, the first thing he says is "Kanake." What we did was to change something negative into something positive: Okay, we're Kanaks. We're proud of it. Now listen to what we have to say."

The group was founded in 1992; raps in German, Turkish and English; and enjoys success in Turkey and a cult status among the kids in Kreuzberg. Though the band does not sell many records in Germany, it has not given up hope. Says Özgür Bozkurt, "A couple of years ago, with all those antiforeigner activities going on, many foreigners embraced their own form of nationalism. But you can't respond to nationalism with nationalism. You have to deal with this problem differently, on the basis of international understanding, particularly when you've been living here for 20 or 30 years. You have to deal with it in a considerate way—with 'brains,' as it were."

For Ethem and Özgür Bozkurt, this task requires making it clear in no uncertain terms that they are not letting the wrong people make demands on them. "We once had a show at a festival against racism in Mühlheim, and there were a lot of Turkish kids from the area there. They clearly identified with me," says Ethem. "But then they gave the Gray Wolves salute. I had to interrupt the show to say, Hey, kids—take your hands down." The Gray Wolves is a chauvinist Turkish organization active in Germany that has participated in numerous violent activities.

For Özgür Bozkurt, the question of dual identities does not even exist: "Whether I'm a German, a Turk, or a Chinese is of no importance to me whatsoever. We are entering the twenty-first century, and this question is truly medieval."

The rapper Aziza A. ("Mighty Sister") is no longer interested in categories either. "I believe that I and many other Turks are a lot further along on the German-Turkish thing. For me, it is no longer a question how much of me is Turkish. We live here in Berlin, and I'm a Berliner: it's that simple!" However, the 27-year-old "Oriental hip-hop pioneer's" experiences with some of her fellow Berliners are not exactly pleasant. "I had a job in a record store in Gropiusstadt, and I sometimes heard the customers say things like 'Something like that should not be allowed to work here.' And once I had an early-morning interview with the magazine *Fritz,* and the guy, whose name I have forgotten, asked me why I don't do belly dancing instead of rap. Unfortunately, I only woke up after that. But I'll get that guy."

On her debut album, *Es ist Zeit ("It's About Time"),* the self-confident young woman takes issue with the traditional idea of how young women should behave. Regarding her familial relations, she also does not fit into any of the usual clichés: "My parents laid the foundations of my upbringing, and they give me a lot of support—but the media prefer scandals. On television, you only hear about the kids of foreigners when they become radical and when families react in radical ways. No one wants to see the other side, because it's not interesting enough. There is an incredible diversity, but only the extremes are shown. And that makes me sick."

And so it is better not to ask Aziza A. (whose second CD will be appearing in the fall) about being a role model for other young women in the male-dominated scene or even about a message for other young Berlin women of Turkish origin: "I don't have a message; I just make my kind of music. I am not an 'ambassador,' and I'm not a politician—though I do have my own opinion. It would be stupid if I only made my music for certain people, because that again would be a kind of dissociation. My music is for everyone."

14

STEPHAN LEY

THE *DEUTSCHLÄNDER* HARDLY READ ANYTHING GERMAN

First published as "Die 'Deutschländer' lesen kaum Deutsches" in *Die Welt* (October 29, 1999). Translated by Tes Howell.

Turks in the Federal Republic stay informed primarily through media from their homeland

For days, the German media have been reporting on the battle of yeas and nays on the Red-Green government coalition. Flipping open Germany's Turkish press summary, Press Bureau Chief Renko Thiemann, who is also Information Bureau chief, discovers what Turkish newspapers are thinking about all this activity. Once a week, at the federal government's request, the University of Essen's Center for Turkish Studies (ZfT) generates a press summary of six daily newspapers. How are these papers representing and commenting on German domestic and foreign politics, the pension issue, the citizenship- and employment-rights debates, as well as the debate on EU entry for the land on the Bosporus?

Around 2.2 million Turks live in Germany and inform themselves via homeland sources, which, although broadly unnoticed in the public eye, have established a parallel media landscape. Press wholesalers in areas with high numbers of Turkish residents sell about as many Turkish papers as German multiregional daily newspapers. Throughout the country, over 210,000 of these papers are delivered daily. On sale are mass-distribution papers like the nationalist *Hürriyet (Freedom)*, the right-leaning *Sabah (Morning)*, the extremist national *Türkiye*, the social-democratic *Milliyet (Nation)*, which is geared mostly toward academics, the Islamist newspapers *Milli Gazete (National Newspaper)* and *Zaman (Time)*, and also the leftist *Evrensel (Universal)* and the Kurdish *Özgür Politika (Free Politics)*. The intellectual weekly *Cumhuriyet (The Republic)* plays no major role in Germany. Beyond these publications, there are two sports newspapers, two weeklies, a business paper, and six tabloids. Besides these "homeland exports," there are also newspapers and magazines in Germany fully manufactured by Turkish suppliers.

Cable and satellite make it possible to access radio and TV stations from Turkey. Germany also has Turkish-language radio and television stations. Four of these are exclusively for the European market. TRT-INT, for instance, is owned by the Turkish state and is thus politically dependent on the current government but always broadcasts in the spirit of Kemal Atatürk. The commercial stations concentrate on pure entertainment, while channel 7 of the Refah Party —now *Fazilet* (Virtue)—delivers Islamist propaganda that negatively represents Turks living in Germany and particularly distorts Germans.

Certainly, the greater share of the news in the Turkish media has to do with the Turkish homeland. As a result, Turks living in Germany find themselves in a media isolation. The ZfT recently determined that 60 percent do not feel sufficiently informed about Germany. The less knowledge about Germany they have, the more dominant the use of heritage-language media becomes. "Media diversity often cannot protect against media ghettoization," suggests Reyhan Güntürk of ZfT.

This situation persists despite the fact that Turkish newspapers distributed here in Germany have so-called Europe Page inserts. These pages deal exclusively with German and European themes. This practice is an improvement from the 1960s, when fully assembled newspapers were simply sent from Turkey to Frankfurt-area printers and distributed in virtually unaltered form.

The predominance of tabloids in the Turkish media landscape may account for the bright colors of Turkish multiregional newspapers in Germany. Television plays an important role in this domain, and newspapers must market themselves with expensive advertising specials and aggressive headlines. For this reason, the gray areas are not dealt with very well. In the context of a reading public that can access the English *Financial Times* and the French *Le Monde* in German newspapers' press summaries, but cannot access Turkish news there, Turkish papers can publish and polemicize free of restrictions. Friend and foe are clearly delineated.

At the beginning of the year, federal Green Party representatives criticized the growing tensions between Cem Özdemir and *Hürriyet*. After complaining about Turkish press coverage in a Bundestag speech, he was put under police protection. According to him, these newspapers' role in hindering integration was no longer tolerable. Because the papers do not present all the details, German-Turkish dysphoria results. The press often gladly operates with stereotypes of the sort that Cem Özdemir sees as dangerous for Germans' and Turks' coexistence. "It causes people, in part, to feel they are in an enemy land."

Andreas Goldberg, managing director of the Center for Turkish Studies, has sensed some efforts to represent news as objectively as possible, but the classification of events is often extortive and polemical. Headlines like "This German is our enemy" and "Let's teach the television commentators a lesson" are not difficult to find. Those who do not subscribe to the thought prohibition on Kurdish themes in Turkey, those who allegedly slight Turkish honor, must be prepared to appear on the front page along with their photo, address, telephone number, and fax number. Although there are approximately 190 Turkish journalists working throughout Germany, the Istanbul bureau columnists still set the editorial tone.

Ertuğ Karakullukçu, chief commentator at *Hürriyet*, has gained a dubious reputation—not only for mercilessly stomping German news events into the floor or praising them to the heavens but for the fact that his reckless commentaries often pillory individual journalists. For example, he has attacked Wolfgang Koydl, Turkey correspondent for the *Süddeutsche Zeitung*, for comparing the Kurdish problem with the Kosovo conflict, and Delik Güngör, a journalist at the *Berliner Zeitung*, whom he accused of inciting negative sentiments against *Hürriyet* for mishandling the Cem Özdemir situation.

The danger lies in drawing generalizations from specific events. For instance, a report on the arson attack on Turkish families was titled with the blanket declaration "Germans burn Turks." The case was similar in 1997 after an apartment burning in Krefeld. Suspicion landed quickly on German radical rightists. However, it turned out that the fire had been the tragic end of a family drama: the Turkish father had set the fire himself.

15

MARK TERKESSIDIS

MIGRANTS' STRUGGLE FOR REPRESENTATION

First published as "Vertretung, Darstellung, Vorstellung: Der Kampf der MigrantInnen um Repräsentation" on the Web site of the European Institute for Progressive Cultural Policies, www.eipcp.net (November 2000). Translated by Tes Howell. Terkessidis (b. 1966) is a freelance journalist for *Die Zeit, die tageszeitung, Spex,* and WDR.

The greatest problem in migrants' struggles has always been the "invention" of a political subject, the representation of a "we." In Great Britain in the 1970s, minorities organized around the collective term *black.* The goal in that context was a far-reaching resistance coalition confronting racism. However, in the past decade, mobilization under this banner became increasingly difficult. First of all, social and ethnic differences within this identity construction became evident. Second, the emerging global mass culture absorbed "black" cultural resistance methods into its reservoir of strategies. In France's migrant protests of the early 1980s, a similar collective concept was applied: *beur.* Here, too, the representative expression oriented itself around the majority's racist attitude toward a certain group of immigrants: *Beur* was a word play on the attribute *arabe.*

In the mid-1980s, the protests in France became noticeably quieter. [. . .] Cultural resistance among migrants in France eventually became a national variant of global mass culture: one need only consider the success of musicians such as Rachid Taha or French hip-hop.

In Germany, there has been practically no political organization among migrants to improve their situation here. Because the Federal Republic is relatively strict in limiting naturalization, migrants have been left with either the political horizon of the "native country" or that of nonpolitical "cultural" organizations. The creation of a political "we" in migrants' struggles has not been successful: the community structures continue to remain segregated. The starting points for the protest in Great Britain and France—racism and a lack of equality—were defused in Germany from the start, for most migrants today still assume that as "foreigners" they will be treated differently. What remains is at best a moral appeal to humanity. [. . .]

On the level of public images, a "racist" exoticism dominates, though the large immigrant groups continue to be underrepresented. Indeed, despite the differences in all three countries, there is a similar, dual process at work: the political articulation of migrants has decreased (or was nipped in the bud), and the cultural practices of "foreigners" have meanwhile occupied a prominent space in the public sphere of immigration countries. Apparently, immigrants' struggles for appropriate political representation have led to strengthened visibility in the cultural field (or were anticipated there). This visibility may indeed cause interesting effects, but it does not alter the unjust balance of power.

In the meantime, this visibility among migrants is contributing to a situation in which a new national "we" can be represented in immigration countries—a "we" that is no longer understood as primarily nationalistic but rather as open, tolerant and "mixed," equipped for global competition. The entrance of migrants into the cultural sphere demands a proper measure of self-exoticizing of the participants. (They must project an image as authentic voices of difference—be it of "their" culture, the "life between the cultures," the "hybridity," the "ghetto," etc.). [. . .]

In the face of this dual process, it is reasonable to take a closer look at the concept of representation. In recent years, this expression has become a central category in the theoretical discussion. In cultural studies, foreign and self-representations of migrants are subjected to analysis or are ascribed a subversive potential. Representation has at least two, actually three, different elements. First, the concept signifies nothing more than that something is replaced by something else taking its place. The first element of representation is then substitution. The political meaning of representation as substitution continued to grow in the modern age. With the introduction of absolutism, the ruler himself began to represent the whole people. At the end of the eighteenth century, the people finally began to represent themselves—through elected representatives in parliament.

This type of substitution prompted the second element of representation: embodiment. In the second half of the nineteenth century, a process of state-sponsored cultural homogenization followed the introduction of popular rule. The cultural standardization of the population was supposed to offer the guarantee of a stable consensus. This required an all-encompassing embodiment of the people into a uniform literary language, traditions, buildings, flags, coins, and so on. In this way, communities were to be created that had not previously existed in such a form. Benedict Anderson coined the term *imagined community* for this phenomenon.

In this circumlocution lies the third element of representation, combining substitution and embodiment: the perception, or, to appropriate the psychoanalyst Jacques Lacan's terminology, the imaginary. Lacan clarified the concept with the "mirror stage" of the small child—with that jubilating moment in which the child recognizes himself in the mirror. In this moment, the child welds together his heterogeneous "fragmented body" with an "I" (in the Freudian sense) through the imaginary perception of his own unity. The members of the *Volk* must always be induced to perceive themselves as a unity. This collective self-perception succeeds through the production of an imaginary excess: this event requires a mirror.

This mirror emerges on the level of embodiment. On the internal and positive level, the "invention" of traditions creates a reflective ground for the perception of unity. On the external and negative level, it produces the "others" of European history: the "wild ones," the slaves, the colonized, the inhabitants of the third world, and also the migrants. These others served as a mirror in which the subjects of the West could find their reflection. Because "they" were wild, savage, fanatic, secretive, and intolerant, "we" always appeared to be civilized, peace loving, industrious, democratic, open, and tolerant. In relation to the non-Western "other," representation functioned primarily as a technique for wielding power.

This idea that the others serve as a mirror to the Western imaginary also exerts influence on the self-perception of the other. The "objective gaze" of the white man, which Frantz Fanon so vividly described in *Black Skin, White Masks,* is always an element of one's own perception. In this respect, the politics of migrants, as with every other antiracist politics, was always an extremely difficult struggle for representation, in which substitution and embodiment mixed in the field of the imaginary in a highly complicated manner. The opponent of the antiracist struggles is not simply on the outside; the opponent is involved in the construction of one's own identity. Recourse to ethnic community, or tradition, played an immense role in migrants' struggles, and with good reason: the value of one's own background increases, a background that is always viewed as inferior by the majority and the "objective gaze" in one's self. This tradition is just as much an invention as the perceptions that the "objective gaze" produces. And often enough, this tradition remains strongly dependent on this "gaze." [. . .]

16

ZAFER ŞENOCAK AND MARTIN GREVE
COMING TO LIFE

First published as "Aufbruch ins Leben" in *Zitty* (March 30, 2000). Translated by Tes Howell. Greve is the author of a 2003 book on music among Turkish immigrants in Germany.

[. . .] It is necessary to depart from two preconceptions: first, there is the notion of bilateral cultural exchange, whereby the cultures of different states— Germany and Turkey, for example—meet as though they were at an international match, carefully separated from one another, in order to gauge or marvel at each other from a distance. Both cultural teams have long since found themselves in a permanent internal dysfunction. Moreover, countless additional players who can no longer be attributed to a national team are running around on the playing field: the migrants and their descendants. How would one define "German culture" today? The still-prevalent right to define culture exclusively as an expression of national identity has been over-hauled by reality.

In Germany, there are not even any clichés about Turkish high culture. In this country, Anatolian folk dances, playing the saz, and the döner kebab all ubiquitously symbolize an absolute "Turkishness." This situation indicates that on the state level, German-Turkish cultural exchange is essentially a one-way street to Turkey. Turkish cultural institutions are virtually absent in the German public sphere.

Second, the idealization of culture as a means for international under-standing and integration of minorities is common. Since the 1970s, when it became clear that the recruited guest workers were not just staying overnight, any kind of German-Turkish cultural encounter was absorbed through social integration. *Culture* stood as a key term for foreignness as well as for overcoming it. Cultural encounter and exchange became concepts fraught with unreasonable expectations; but artistic work, in contrast, was downgraded to a triviality, and the artists themselves became the bearers of prescribed political messages. Even today, the cultural promotion of so-called foreigners has amounted to nothing more than patronizing assistance with a social objective. The quality of artistic work comes second. The aes-thetic questions, concepts, and problems of non-German artists living here have difficulty penetrating the feuilletons. In the public sphere, one still finds the illusion of an unrealistic cultural homogeneity.

Today, German-Turkish culture is part of the cultural life in Germany and therefore falls into the scope of German politics. Cultural policy makers are essential, not the foreign minister or commissioner of foreigner affairs. Ex-amining the available potential and connecting with existing structures of cultural life is less a problem of money or new and costly institutions than a problem of coordinating the increasing supranational, transcultural inter-actions. There must be an informed liaison between artistic production and German cultural institutions and their political administration. The political structure of the Federal Republic necessitates decentralization as well as the national coordination of these regional liaisons. The establishment of such a network should thus be carried out under the overall leadership of Culture Minister Michael Naumann.

Currently, North Rhine–Westphalia is setting up the first German-Turkish culture coordination office in Duisburg. Berlin also urgently needs such an institution, a kind of agency for cultural administration that contributes to the legibility of the new cultural landscape of Germany. With their focus on German-Turkish culture, such liaisons can surely function as pilot projects and allow for future gradual expansion to the whole spectrum of the new German international cultural mélange.

17

OLIVER HÜTTMANN

COUNTRY CODE TR

First published as "Kennzeichen TR" in *Die Woche* (November 17, 2000). Translated by David Gramling.

Young German Turks are taking music, film, television, theater, and literature by storm. After Leitkultur, will Leitkültür be next?

Ertan Ongun is in his midtwenties. He smokes weed, does snuff, shoots up, hawks the junk in his crib, goes out high, and holds up the gambling salons on the other side of the street. He steals cars, extorts money, and whoever hassles him will get hassled back, because "I am the Kanake you Germans always warned about."

This figure sounds like one of the horror scenarios from Friedrich Merz, who has been galloping through the land like the bellwether of German culture as if a dark, garlic-stinking stranger with a crooked dagger were breathing down his neck. But the CDU-faction chief does not even need to look around for this dark fantasy; this guy is for real. He lives in Kiel, Schleswig-Holstein, is now clean, and three years ago, he told his life story to author Feridun Zaimoğlu, who recounted it in his book *Scum (Abschaum)*. Of course, the good citizens are clamoring that he is reinforcing the cliché of the "criminal foreigner." Now the book *Kanak Sprak* [see chapter 9] is becoming a film, directed by Lars Becker. And Zaimoğlu is almost amused that "the golden geese of integration will ponder whether this film is fresh meat for xenophobes."

A bizarre climate is at large in Germany these days. Merz finds it necessary to drum up a "discussion about immigration and integration," while Hamburg's social democratic Bureau for Foreigners is plastering the city with the slogan "Naturalization—now!" as if the terms for building loan contracts were running out. "Politicians have long ignored the simple fact that we have been living in an immigration society for a long time. In fact, they have rejected it," says Zaimoğlu. "But even without them, something is happening." In the multicultural underbrush, many clearings have developed where more and more model examples of German-Turkish careers have emerged.

Recently, the lifestyle press has been celebrating the "Kanak chic" of boutiques, galleries, bars, or discos, like the Berlin SO36, where youth of both cultures embrace each other amid Oriental beats and Western beer. Last summer, the singer Tarkan climbed the German Hit Parade, and German viewers sent the German-Turkish group Sürpriz to the "Grand Prix." The RTL weather girl, Nazan Üngör, appears on the screen as if a matter of course. The 30-year-old ex-model Erol Sander is a star among the TV Turk-men. Two pilot films based on the crime show *Sinan Toprak—Der Unbestech-liche* (The Incorruptible) achieved such high ratings that the commissar will soon be going to series.

Of course, trendy noise-making and commercial calculation is at work here. For example, various studies' findings that young German Turks are "market-conscious, acquisitive, dedicated viewers" have astonished private channels. Nevertheless, a paradigm shift is beginning to take place. Tayfun Bademsoy, director of the Berlin casting agency Foreign Faces [original in English], claims that industry has finally caught on that daily life in *Almanya* can only be represented coherently when Turkish fellow citizens are pre-sented free from exotic stylization.

Directors like Yüksel Yavuz *(April Children)* or Kutluğ Ataman *(Lola and Billy the Kid)* deal somewhat autobiographically with the socialization and sit-uation of Germans of Turkish ancestry, from the parents' loyalty to tradition to Western milieus and modernity. They are not only rendering the victim cinema films of the 1980s like Hark Bohm's *Yasemin* obsolete but the token Turk as well. "He used to be capable only of playing ferocious knife mug-gers," says Fatih Akın, who released the critically acclaimed milieu drama *Short Sharp Shock*. Now he has gone a step further. His film *In July*, with Chris-tiane Paul and Moritz Bleibtreu, only peripherally refers to a Turkish back-ground. Next year, Hakan Orbeyi will appear on screen as the fat, shy, provin-cial Sumo Bruno, in which his ancestry is not emphasized, while Birol Ünel played the role of the ur-German *leitfigur* Siegfried.

The old ways of seeing under Country Code D are no longer in effect. Ac-cording to Zaimoğlu, "the third generation in particular has no more inter-est in thinking about the stingy concepts of integration and assimilation, in busying themselves with luxury definitions like culture, identity, and home-land, because people have gotten beyond the Turkish folklorists and the Turk Information Service." Luk Piyes also approaches the embarrassing linguistic hairsplitting ("German of Turkish descent," "German from Turkey") with a clear self-concept: "I am a Cologne boy. One who has his friends and his roots there." The actor, nominated as 1995's Face of the Year, plays Ertan Ongun in *Kanak Attack* and is the "German Brad Pitt," according to *Bravo*.

Erol Sander does not want anything to do with the folklore clamor either. Raised in Bavaria, he was sent to an international religious school, where he served as an altar boy. "If I were in Turkey," he says, "I would feel like I were from the Middle Ages." Still, he played the typical Turk in order to break into television. Industrious, professional, innovative, sexy: in this country, that's how one becomes fit not only for salons but also for society. "The first guest workers were a migrant underclass," declares Zaimoğlu. "For them—I know from my father—it went like this: when you are outside, you have to behave inconspicuously. So you walk around with downcast eyes."

The guardians of popular diversity are not exactly happy about this emancipation. The hype has already been denounced as a bourgeois media trick to obscure quotidian racism and social problems. Or the climbers get pigeonholed as well-behaved quota foreigners willing to be bought out for their conformity. Amidst all this, Zaimoğlu works it aggressively as a gifted and merciless self-marketer and states dryly, "German Turks are no homogenous Community" [original in English].

Furthermore, given current developments, it appears that they are more foreign to one another than ever before. The winners are just as little representative of all Turks raised in Germany as the loser Ertan Ongun. And even if down-home Germans like vacationing in Turkey and choose döner kebab as their favorite fast food, the Turkish milieu is still no more comprehensible to them.

"Our life is Kanake, our sweat is Kanake, our gold chains are Kanake. Our whole style is Kanake," chants Ongun in *Kanak Attack*. "The phenomenon of being conspicuous, of becoming conspicuous, can certainly have a daunting effect, and, in misguided cases, can lead to the reproduction of an Anatolian masculinity type," says Zaimoğlu. "Ertan Ongun is a kind of mix of villain from the projects and Neger-Kalle. When he takes a look at himself, he is German White Trash [original in English], never having passed eighth grade and unable to make ends meet with the available resources, because his parents have been in this country only for a few decades. He is at the bottom of the social hierarchy, along with many Germans themselves. This has therefore nothing to do with the image of the criminal foreigner. Media and politicians have hammered this image into people's heads over decades by way of fantasy and resentment."

After 40 years, Turkish migrants have come to the same threshold that the African-American population of the United States crossed long ago. They are beloved in show business and sports but disparagingly tolerated in daily life. "But if they can play soccer well, they will be encouraged anyway and will say 'I love America,' " says Luk Piyes, who works on a project for drug addicts of all cultures. "I, too, would like to be proud of this country where I was born and where I live. But compare the German with the French national team. How many 'foreigners' are put in the game over there?"

He sees *Kanak Attack* primarily as a film that one should "see with cola and popcorn and laugh." Of course, reality is much more blatant than the film.

18
KATJA NICODEMUS
GETTING REAL

First published as "Ankunft in der Wirklichkeit" in *Die Zeit* (February 2, 2004). Translated by David Gramling. This text profiles Fatih Akın (b. 1973), who directed *Weed* (1996), *Short Sharp Shock* (1998),

In July (2000), *Solino* (2002), and *Crossing the Bridge* (2005), a musical portrait of Istanbul. His 2003 feature film, *Head-On*, won prizes at the Berlinale Film Festival and the European Film Prize.

Fatih Akın, the son of Turkish parents, born in Hamburg, transformed the Berlinale into a German cinema triumph at the last second. His film *Head-On* narrates a love story with a kind of unruliness and directness that seemed to strike like a fist into the festival and its far too many self-compromising films. God knows the festival was not lacking in couples who lose themselves in relationship excesses and self-obsession as Akın's figures do. But *Head-On,* this crude, pining film that often loses itself in melodramatic flourishes, must have affected the jury just like an honest corner bar in the middle of an emotionless sea of images.

Akın's film is the first German winner of the Golden Bear since Reinhard Hauff's *Stammheim* 18 years ago, and the Turkish ancestry of the director lends a meaning to this jury decision that reaches beyond the film itself. With the grand gesture of an international award, the jury referenced a migration cinema that has been representing Germany as an immigration country for at least 20 years, despite its unwillingness to become one. It is a cinema that has been moving intentionally between the worlds and has achieved, in *Head-On,* a wonderfully free perspective on its own community.

Indeed, the great strength of the Berlinale winners lies in their earnest impertinence, calling out all forms of political correctness. This includes the way Akın represents the German-Turkish milieu of Hamburg-Altona. "I want to fuck," says his heroine, the young Sibel, right at the beginning, "and not just one guy—lots." Because her own Turkish family, with its traditional moral convictions, stands in the way of her plan, she enters into a marriage of convenience. Her fake husband, who is also from Turkey, is a drunken, coked-out burnout named Cahit and lives in a studio apartment strewn with beer bottles. With unabashed lust, Birol Ünel acts far beyond the cliché of the industrious greengrocer next door. "Why don't you just fuck your wives?" he says to the men of Sibel's family while they play cards, in order to undermine their faux-pious distinction between bordello visits and domestic acts of procreation. This late-punk outlaw does not even speak Turkish anymore. Later, when looking for Sibel in Istanbul, he easily makes friends with a taxi driver who grew up in Munich.

Scorsese Needed a Lot Longer

Gone are the days when films like Tevfik Başer's *Forty Square Meters of Germany* told the tale of isolation in a strange land and, in an impulse of enlightenment, put forth the so-called guest worker as a victim of an economically oriented foreigner politics who couldn't care less about integration. It's different now that the spotlight of the Berlinale triumph and the sound bite of the "Turkish renewal of German cinema" is promptly making the rounds in the international press. *Head-On* marks not the beginning but rather the continuation of a film movement that made its way into film-studies programs in the middle of the 1990s. Unnoticed by a broader public, the material of this generation of German-Turkish directors can no longer be reduced to the integration problems of their parents. The balancing act between familial constraint and urban socialization has been retained but has moved into the background. With a wild sense of conviction, the young directors stormed the aesthetic media of the cinema and breathed new life into the most varied genres, nourishing the narratives with their own world of experiences.

"Scorsese and the other Italian-Americans needed 70 years to begin making their films. The French Algerians needed 30 years for their *cinéma beur*. We are faster. We're starting now," announced Akın in 1998 as his film debut, *Short Sharp Shock*, came into the cinemas. Even back then, he set his story in the context of a brotherly friendship between a Turk, a Serb, and a Greek in his own backyard of Hamburg-Altona. Between red-light bars, Turkish sofas, and Serbian weddings, the living image of a city district developed, along with its minor gangsters, hookers, and neighborhood big guns.

Almost at the same time as Akın's directing debut, his colleague Thomas Arslan began his trilogy of Berlin films, which look into the life rhythms of their heroes with a wonderful coolness. In *Siblings,* for example, the camera complicitly follows the brothers Erol and Ahmed on their paths through Berlin's Kreuzberg neighborhood. It is precisely through the conscious concentration on the perspective of the kids that the paths through the neighborhood come to be expressed in a "cruising" sense for life, which can no longer be defined as German, Turkish, or German-Turkish. This communal walking through the city quite naturally ensures the development of a friendship and the symbolic appropriation of a terrain.

Both Arslan and Akın and their colleague Yüksel Yavuz narrate from a perspective that is metacultural and ultimately reaches over and beyond the sociological world. In contrast to the *Banlieu* films of the Maghrebian migrant children, for example, which quickly made their way out of the Paris slum suburbs of Sarcelles and Romainville and into the heart of the French cinema, their work is not an engaged expression of sociopolitical efforts. It is a cinema that is unconcerned with juvenile delinquency, social hot topics, cultural isolation, or ghettoization and that lacks a certain mediated feel. For years, the German film industry has been leering jealously at the impressive, angry, melancholic films coming out of the French suburbs. One should not forget, however, that the *Banlieu* cinema arose in a marginal sphere that the directors quickly forced into the role of a societal pathology with a certain automatism. German-Turkish cinema arose, at least topographically, from the center of the cities. Therefore, it could claim a normality from the beginning that the French-Arab suburban teenagers cannot claim even today.

Campaign against Normality

One needs only to think of the ease with which Thomas Arslan follows a young girl through Kreuzberg in his *A Fine Day,* which is perhaps one of the most beautiful Turkish-German films. His young actor-heroine breaks up with her boyfriend, dubs a film, appears at a casting call, and does a few small errands. In this way, an easy summerlike abeyance emerges out of the movements and walks of the main actress, Serpil Turhan. Arslan's naturalistic use of light, reduced forms of expression, and story consisting of tangentially narrated situations, demand a wide-eyed attentiveness from the viewer. This is no film for *multikulti* labels, nor for hymns about the New German Cinema. But one that, with its hip T-shirts, minor cultural abjections, and a perfectly bilingual heroine, narrates from a perspective of a globalized world affected by migration movements, a world that has become so infinitely normal that one can no longer say a new word about it.

After *Head-On* appeared at the Berlinale, it became shockingly clear that this cinema is not alone in needing to defend its own normality over and over. Who would have thought that Fatih Akın would have to clarify for the hundredth time, at the press conference about his film, the unpleasant connotation of the words *guest worker* and defend himself against this label? Who would have thought that *Bild* magazine would use the Berlinale triumph as a witch hunt against Sibel Kekilli, the main figure of *Head-On*? The talk was of a "hot-blooded German film diva" or the "porn star in real life." What is scandalous is not the ostensible exposé but the greasy gestures with which this actress is being defamed in order to adopt her director as an ephemeral success—German in a no-less-greasy way. They report on his "wavy, wiry black head of hair, wonderfully olive-colored skin," and capacity, nonetheless, to speak "Hamburgerish like Hans Albers." "They are making us Germans and Turks into one country," writes the newspaper in reference to Fatih Akın.

Of course, that Germany, for which not only directors like Fatih Akın, Thomas Arslan, and actresses like Sibel Kekilli stand, does not need to be constructed by the cinema anymore. One can refuse to recognize it, just as one can ignore the Cologne Cathedral or the Siegessäule. This Germany is there, it is the only possible one, and soon it will sweep the last lovers of guiding culture out of its irrevocable future with contented disdain.

GLOBAL ALREADY?

BERLIN, POTSDAMER PLATZ, 2005. After the Wall fell, multinational corporations hired world-renowned architects to quickly fill the no-man's-land between East and West with an ultramodern urban center befitting a global city. The soaring office buildings signal the unity of high finance and postindustrial design. Though invisible here, Berlin's bustling immigrant neighborhoods are just around the corner from this hub of transnational commerce.

T HE TEXTS IN THIS EPILOGUE address the friction between global and national forces before and after German reunification. Claus Leggewie's 1990 essay "The Foreign Self" asks whether a modern democratic society can mature without undergoing a fundamental alienation from itself through immigration. Frank-Olaf Radtke's 1991 piece "In Praise of In-Difference" questions the relevance of multiculturalism in late modernity. For Radtke, the overwhelming anonymity of the modern public sphere privileges social roles and industrial functions over ethnic or cultural identities. Multiculturalism, in his view, applies communitarian concepts of identity that have been obsolete for over a century.

Of paramount importance in the 1993 petition protesting the General Agreement on Tariffs and Trade, signed by hundreds of European filmmakers and artists, is the global distribution of cultural and aesthetic labor. Although the Federal Republic of Germany joined GATT in October 1951, its free-trade principles only began to alarm artists and filmmakers in the 1990s, when their state arts funding came under fire from market-driven Hollywood. The question underlying this dilemma was whether national culture industries truly offer products of unique value in the global flow of content. Directors Wim Wenders and Volker Schlöndorff defended state-subsidized art as a crucial counterweight to the global "free market" in popular culture.

Tom Stromberg's 1999 piece "The End of Pure Culture" celebrates the convergence of business marketing, event culture, and traditional high art at the millennium. Pure art objects, he contends, have undergone a process of contamination that robs them of their role as arbiters of national culture. Whereas Stromberg optimistically heralds this marriage of marketing and curating, Michael Naumann's essay of the same year warns of the gradual impoverishment that corporate-sponsored art portends.

Ulrich Beck's "What Comes after the Volkswagen-Export Nation?" calls attention to the fact that West Germany's re-entry into the international community after the Third Reich depended upon its ability to become a legitimate export nation. In the 1950s, this new economic nationalism began to demand an influx of non-German labor to ensure steady growth. Beck points out that, in the recent decades of high globalization, this export status has become both superfluous and impracticable, and German politicians have had to reframe the national self-image in terms of an ever-changing global distribution of labor. For Beck, the ideas driving contemporary German economic and immigration policy lack the imagination necessary for this "second modernity" of globalization.

The epilogue concludes with five pieces that address the global/local nexus that has emerged in the past 10 years. Hartmut Böhme's essay "Global Cities and Terrorism" surveys the interplay between the September 11, 2001, attacks in New York and the consolidation of power in global trade capitals requiring highly concentrated immigrant labor forces. Andreas Tzortzis's 2002 report on the Hamburg Al-Qaeda cell responsible for planning the September 11 attacks examines the lingering consequences for the Hamburg neighborhood where the cell's apartment was located. Another global/local dilemma involves the highly publicized comical case of "Florida Rolf," a German retiree living out his days in Florida while collecting German social-welfare checks. The juxtaposed images of the noncitizen guest worker and the sun-bronzed retiree perplexed the German press, raising new questions about civic privilege in a transnational era.

Novelist Christoph Hein's 2004 essay "Third World Everywhere" closes this epilogue, and our collection, on an unsteady note. The effects of free-trade globalization have left the eastern territory of Germany in a state of neglect, upheaval, and susceptibility to corporate power brokering. What kind of future does the former GDR presage for Germany and Europe: a hinterland desperately in need of economic reform, or an accidental avant-garde of transnational capital?

1

CLAUS LEGGEWIE

THE FOREIGN SELF: XENOLOGICAL CONSIDERATIONS

First published as "Das fremde Selbst: Xenologische Betrachtungen" in *Multi Kulti: Spielregeln für die Vielvölkerrepublik* (Berlin: Rotbuch, 1990), 97–109. Translated by David Gramling.

[. . .] It would be stimulating and timely to reorient the problem of "discursive communication"—which tends toward the philosophy of language and pragmatics but remains far afield from actual lifeworlds—back to the social reality of multicultural societies. It is there that the truly common, mundanely different languages and regional dialects are spoken. How do "dialogues of the minds" actually function—not among European intellectuals in the Centre Pompidou (between Lyotard and Habermas, for example)— but in the actual *Tohuwabohu* around us, in a train station, in a classroom, in a government office building? Among the discourse genres, is there still, as philosophers like Manfred Frank believe, actually "a context of traditions common to one population, which, along with its habits and conventions, manage the interplay among propositions of different regimes and genres in a very motivating way"? Where are the limits of this population drawn? Is Jean-François Lyotard's critique not merely an esoteric, but actually a germane, gloss of the collapse of the "habitualities," a collapse that the age-old notion of the One World is desperately seeking to conceal?

"Speaking in different tongues," the old Babylon problem, illustrates the classic philosophers' debate on the loss of rational metaphysical purity: the question whether universal principles of communication are (or have become) obsolete and could themselves be critically described as ethnocentric maxims. Less resigned than relieved, French poststructuralists postulate multiplicity without any kind of unifying bond or basic rationale; ultimately, they allege, we have paid dearly for our "longing for the whole and the one," and the "murmur of the desire to begin the terror yet again" can still be heard at every step. "The answer is: war on the whole. . . let us activate the differences." If we did so, we would be *native speakers* [original in English] of "Babylonish" or listeners in a local jargon only comprehensible within the immediate context of communities of speech. [. . .] It is not only "neoconservative" authors or "neo-Aristotelians" who—often with very good reason—have returned to Old Europe and the Land of the Occident. Liberal and left circles have wrestled their way out of the missionary progress model of world dominance, and out of animal-moralistic self-castigation, to an enlightened (or cynical) self-assertion for Europe. Everything will depend on avoiding the consequential development of an ideology of fortification. [. . .]

The advantage of a multicultural community lies not in the sum of its ostensible substances but in diagramming its changing relations and crossings.

In this sense, only societies that are pluralistically alienated from themselves could ever truly become societies at all.

Those who draw the facile conclusion that foreigners are basically "humans like you and I" are shielding themselves from the efforts of living with difference. Whoever claims that he can see eye to eye with the foreign better than he can with his own is posturing as a congenial protector and selfless snob. Both of these positions, prominent in the European history of ideas in the form of noble cosmopolitanism and anticivic exoticism, attempt to fix the foreign or to dissolve it, to not allow it to approach or engage the self in any way. [. . .]

2

FRANK-OLAF RADTKE

IN PRAISE OF IN-DIFFERENCE: ON THE CONSTRUCTION OF THE FOREIGN IN THE DISCOURSE OF MULTICULTURALISM

First published as "Lob der Gleich-Gültigkeit: Zur Konstruktion des Fremden im Diskurs des Multi-kulturalismus" in *Das Eigene und das Fremde: Neuer Rassismus in der Alten Welt?* Uli Bielefeld, ed. (Hamburg: Junius, 1991), 90–96. Translated by Tes Howell. The German *Gleich-gültigkeit* implies both indifference and equal validity.

[. . .] Multiculturalism seeks to define plurality, and its diversity of lifestyles and forms, as a social normality. Inherent in this proposition is a structural characteristic of the modern differentiated society that had been identified long before contemporary migration and refugee movements arose. Modern societies are divided into a diversity of contradictory life spheres, in which vastly different rules, norms, and values are in effect, which the individual must be able to command all at once. However, to the extent that multiculturalism links plurality and diversity to "ethno-national background," it anthropologizes ethnicity and thus establishes a particular historical construction of community (and of foreignness) as a constant. [. . .]

When there is a simultaneous, massive presence of social members in one place (particularly in large cities), it becomes impossible to continue operating on the basis of the traditional differentiation of self/other or friend/enemy. The dichotomous distinction between inside and outside is expanded to a tri-valence. [. . .] In modern societies, one has contact with more people than one can know. One must face the possibility of encountering one another without a word of greeting on the streets and squares, in buses and elevators, without believing this behavior to be impolite or even hostile. The *greeting-less* encounter is a form of modern sociality in which the necessity of distinction has been suspended. One has learned to react to perceived differences without judgment, therefore with *apathy* and *indifference*.

Functionally differentiated societies have divided themselves into spheres in which distinct principles prevail (Hannah Arendt), and these principles affect interactions with foreigners. The schism of inside and outside recurs in modern society as the difference between "public" and "private." The functional precondition of the public sphere is indifference toward the "neutral foreigner"; the passerby is the same as oneself. Here, indifference means "being uninvolved." The passerby is any other person followed by countless others. In the public sphere of the street and the market, one carries on with business, accesses services, and satisfies the requirements of conduct; one encounters others through specific functional roles that make it possible to disregard otherwise observable characteristics. Only these functional roles (trash collector, waiter, doctor, or apartment tenant) are of any importance. Indifference here means that the actions of legitimate and functional role players have equal validity. The power of anticipating that the waiter act like a waiter and the doctor like a doctor is so great that the fact that he has characteristics of another lineage, another religion or region, or another ethnic group can generally be overlooked. Experience indicates that the danger of a potentially dysfunctional reciprocity, prompting insecurity and threat, will not arise, because the execution of functional roles is not dependent upon these characteristics.

It is a different story in the private sphere, where nonspecified relations allow the perception of all personal traits. They become downright topical when what is at issue is not functional performance but interaction with the whole person instead. Indifference has no place in the private sphere. It would inevitably be attributed to the person, perceived as coolness and insensitivity. What guards against the possibility of such an aggravation is the principle of exclusiveness, which determines admittance criteria and establishes itself as the principle of community building.

By observing that the principle of indifference implied in the aforementioned model is not practiced in the private sphere, multicultural discourse makes the demanding proposal that one pay attention to ethnic difference—emphatically and in certain ways. It claims that ethnicity should be understood as difference and should not be used as a reason for differentiation (that is, discrimination) in the social process. Not merely the functional roles but also the cultural characteristics should be recognized as equally valid and relativized. One culture or ethnicity should be like the others and thus insignificant for concrete interaction. Difference should be experienced and lived consciously, not as a threat but as a stimulus.

This proposal has its consequences. It reintroduces an instance of nonspecialization into the public and social sphere of the modern, functionally differentiated society that has already lost its objective significance. The indisputable observation that some individuals and social institutions share this approach changes nothing. They and their interpretations lag behind actual development. Society has advanced beyond the forms of communication used to describe it. Multiculturalism discourse thus reinforces traditional thinking. In the various contexts of differentiated societies, inside and outside, self and other, respectively, affect only certain subsystems, the rules of which are functionally determined. Distinction according to ethnic criteria, however, signals the construction of an almost immutable comprehensive characteristic that belongs to earlier forms of community building. Multiculturalism offers a regressive solution of the inside-outside problematic, not a progressive-modern one. [. . .]

3

AN APPEAL BY EUROPEAN AUTHORS, ACTORS, AND PRODUCERS FOR A CULTURAL EXCEPTION IN GATT NEGOTIATIONS

First published as "Aufruf der europäischen Autoren, Schauspieler und Produzenten für die kulturelle Ausnahme in den GATT Verhandlungen" in *Frankfurter Allgemeine Zeitung* (September 28, 1993). Translated by David Gramling. Signatories included Hark Bohm, Gérard Dépardieu, Volker Schlöndorff, Lina Wertmüller, Wim Wenders, and Eric Rohmer.

The final negotiations on the General Agreement on Tariffs and Trade are fast approaching. Regarding film, radio, and television, the position that large American firms have assumed and that their administrations have unreservedly supported is absolutely clear.

It is the goal of these large firms to complete the final phase in the conquest of a market that they almost entirely dominate already; they will annihilate the creative powers of Europe.

The space that would be left for European creative production would then be reduced to its most rudimentary form, and European production would see itself robbed of one of its most meaningful developments: the Europe of culture.

In an effort to counter the threat the American incursion poses to the fundamental right of multilateral and pluralistic creativity, we inventors, actors, authors, and producers support the Commission of the European Communities in its firm resolve to rigorously protect cultural production in film, radio, and television on our continent.

We take note of the efforts of Sir Leon Britten, vice president of the Commission of the European Communities, and of Pinheim, the commissioner in charge of the GATT negotiations for radio and television. Particularly noteworthy was the latter's declaration before the European Parliament on March 23, 1993, that the American position is untenable. These men share our conviction that culture is not a commodity and that the [European] Community must therefore make no concessions regarding radio and television.

We support the commission in its intentions 1) to demand the inclusion of a permanent cultural exception clause in the GATT Agreement, 2) to defend the global import of the directive "Television without Borders" without reservation, 3) to demand unequivocal exceptions to those GATT provisions that endanger the unlimited duration of the agreements on coproductions to which all member states are bound. The same applies to European funds supporting the production and distribution of works in film, radio, and television.

We demand that the commission refuse to commit to any stipulations that would consequently limit the future capacity of the Community to promote cultural development in Europe, particularly in film, radio, and television.

We expect the commission and the Council of Ministers to demonstrate the decisiveness, political courage, and fortitude necessary to counter this development; they are in a unique position to defend Europe from the cultural "dumping" that has never been so pervasive as it is today.

4

TOM STROMBERG

THE END OF PURE CULTURE

First published as "Das Ende der Reinkultur" in *Der Tagesspiegel* (July 31, 1999). Translated by David Gramling.

No reason for cultural pessimism. Business is discovering culture as a means for self-representation—and art is using business strategies.

> *Art is not a mirror for reflecting reality but a hammer with which it is shaped.*
> —KARL MARX

[. . .] No word in this century has effected such a comparably ponderous entrance, indeed a triumphal procession, as the word *culture*. Corporate culture, game culture, fight culture, team culture, alternative culture, counterculture, performance culture, city culture, event culture, television culture, discourse culture, memory culture, driving culture, fan culture, online culture, subsidy culture, struggle culture. [. . .] There are always "new cultures" coming to the fore in this culture of cultures. One, however, has completely served out its term: pure culture. Artistic events in this aseptic form are hardly to be found anymore. [. . .]

Leading entrepreneurs recognize that they can no longer place their product in the foreground of their advertisements. Instead, the goal is to insinuate oneself with the potential target group via an identification with the attitude toward life that the product seeks to convey. A mode of address is needed whose mechanisms cannot be invented from scratch. One must make use of what is currently available, and what could be closer at hand for reaching the potential customer than his "cultural identity"? "Event marketing" [original in English] is the magic phrase, whether it be an avantgarde theater troupe introducing a new brand of automobile or the choreographer who can make a shoe advertisement into a visual experience. A live happening presented by the producer for the purchaser secures consumers and a solid connection to a new audience—that is, consumer group. [. . .]

Art is opening its protected spaces and it is doing so quite literally. In the future, theaters will be open all day and will be sites of urban communication. All year long, museums will be the stage of societal life, and gallery openings will play only a small part in it. Combination tickets including all of a city's cultural institutions are likewise a matter of course, as will be Miles-and-More-Tickets for repeat art customers. [. . .]

Yet the end of pure culture is the beginning of a wonderful friendship with the other. Culture does not lose itself in the event, and the moment when the stage enfranchises the gaze and the tension becomes unbearable will be no less than fascinating. The second the impossible is suddenly occurring and the second everything is failing are moments that can only be experienced live and that elide service to anything in particular. They will thus remain irreplaceable, and such is the essence of art.

5

MICHAEL NAUMANN

AN ENDLESS SERIES OF WORLD FORMATIONS

First published as "Eine endlose Aufeinanderfolge von Weltbildungen" in the *Heimat Kunst* brochure (Berlin: Haus der Kulturen der Welt, 2000). Translated by Tes Howell. Naumann was the federal liaison for culture and media affairs in the administration of Gerhard Schröder.

As true as it probably is that products are replicated throughout the global culture, consequently exerting pressure on local markets, it is also true that these local markets simultaneously "contextualize" or "acculturate" such products. The Chinese restaurant tastes Spanish in Spain, just as it tastes Bavarian in Munich. In many other cases, local culture finds ways to situate the import within a native cultural context. Or it quickly declares the import to be its own product: to Iranians, the samovar has long passed for just as much of an autochthonous invention as tea. Cultures are adaptive and insatiable. The time when cosmopolitanism connoted the word *cappuccino* is over. [. . .]

Culture is threatened in an era of globalization, especially when its content is handled like a tradable stock. It is apparent everywhere that the culture industry is shaped by friendly and unfriendly takeovers. Cultural products must be marketable and, most important, globally marketable, which means that the business-management directives of rationalization and resource optimization apply to culture as well. In an era of worldwide exchange of equivalent values, cultural production and financial futures are subject to universal norms of standardization, profitability and banality. Brash and favorably priced is how each product must approach the expo of world cultures—generally intelligible, or, in other words, brought to the lowest common denominator. The public sets the tone, and the corporate executive benefactor directs from his office. Consequently, music producers tend to rearrange economically reliable tone sequences in new ways and throw them into the market. There is the giantism of mass art projects, the museum imperialism; there is, there is, there is. [. . .]

Who are actually the winners and losers in this process of globalization? In the sphere of culture—as opposed to economy—I can imagine a great number of winners. For the trend toward uniformity of culture will undoubtedly promote a countertendency toward niche formation. Monopolies on culture will not be able to persist: the new and uncomfortable, the uncertain and provocative, the fantastic and crazy—everything that still constitutes art—will seek and find another place of refuge. [. . .]

6
ULRICH BECK
WHAT COMES AFTER THE VOLKSWAGEN-EXPORT NATION?

First published as "Was könnte an die Stelle einer VW-Export Nation treten?" in *Was ist Glabalisierung?* (Frankfurt am Main: Shurkamp, 1997). Reprinted in Ulrich Beck, *What Is Globalization?* (Cambridge: Polity Press, 2000), 19–26. Translated by Patrick Camiller.

Overcoming the division of Germany involves much more than incorporating the GDR into the Federal Republic. As it is accompanied by the overcoming of the division of Europe, it spells the end of an epoch and the beginning of a new phase of European history.

What this shift entails, and what it presupposes, may be explained by reference to the understanding postwar West Germany had of itself and of contemporary trends. At the time, there were a number of optics that meshed together: reconstruction, internal democratization, suppression of any debate about the Nazi terror, struggle for reunification. These historical goals were far from constituting an obvious unity. Indeed, they tended to conflict with one another, permitting or even compelling different emphases and priorities. Nevertheless, they were all bound together by the project of making Germany an export nation.

The goal of mass-producing certain goods (Volkswagen, Mercedes, Siemens, and so on) and conquering world markets with "German workmanship" concentrated cultural energies and cranked up the engine of wealth. It was this "economic miracle" that laid the basis for internal democratization, for a reckoning with the organized mass murder of the Nazi period, and above all, of course, for reconstruction in both an inward and outward sense.

The Bonn Republic attempted to associate the goals of production and market conquest with a cultural-political drive to link up with Western modernity. Thus, the decisive source of legitimacy and consent was a seemingly eternal more of everything: affluent society, mass consumption, social security. Political freedom was subordinate to these.

More and more people, however, are now profoundly disturbed by the fact that the sources of affluence have begun to dry up or are bubbling forth in an extremely unequal pattern. Other goals—reconstruction, union with the GDR—have been achieved and exhausted or else become superfluous; facing us everywhere are the unexpected consequences of success. Still other goals have to be spelled out afresh according to the new world situation.

Germany's conception of itself as an export nation—the underside of German mark nationalism—no longer carries much weight. One of the key challenges is the fact that the countries of Southeast Asia, and soon also China, can now cheaply and efficiently produce the goods that previously gave German brands their lead: cars, machinery, refrigerators. Furthermore, the markets for mass-produced goods have shifted to other parts of the world (South America, Eastern Europe, China, and so on), where they can now be serviced more cheaply on the spot. The result is again that the "export-nation" model of success is running out of steam. Or else the onward march of mass-produced goods—with the motorcar as the best example—has been called into question by an awareness of their ecological consequences.

In the manner of a prayer wheel, politicians and business leaders invoke "innovation" and "the courage to take risks" as ways to survive on the world market. But this emphasis suggests a thoroughly antiquated understanding of "innovation" to continue betting on mass-produced goods and the export-nation model, as if to waddle along, with all the zest of a lame duck, behind what others can already do better and cheaper. The race to catch up on the so-called markets of the future (information technology, genetic engineering, human genetics), which is being so loudly heralded on all sides, is itself an expression of the prevailing cognitive blockages and the lack of fantasy. Innovation in world society is a relational concept. It means being forced to invent and do what others are not (or not yet) able to do. One cannot keep ahead simply by longing to match others. The whole debate over "locational factors," much of it borrowed from military strategy, is blind or even hostile to innovation.

The real question, then, is what combination of culture, politics, and economics could appear in place of the Volkswagen-exporting nation? Which innovations in marketing and culture can carry us forward into the second modernity? The world market rewards difference. So the point is to discover and develop, as a potential source of strength, things that have been condemned as, for example, regional peculiarities. [. . .]

[We must pursue] an end to the blockages involved in the image of cultural homogeneity. It is these blockages, in fact, which make the "export nation" ridiculously ill adapted for the diversity of world society in the second modernity. Just to take a banal example from the small Lower Bavarian town of Straubing, children from 24 different countries of origin can now be found in the middle school there—yet in the minds of people, parties, and government departments at the national level, the fiction still prevails that Germany can avoid becoming a multicultural society and thus maintain the *ius sanguinis* with a good conscience.

7

ARMIN NASSEHI

MINARETS IN UPPER BAVARIA

First published as "Minarette in Oberbayern" in *Die Zeit* (November 30, 2000). Translated by David Gramling.

The inventors of guiding culture, as well as its critics, are mistaken

What holds the world, the innermost German world, together is up for debate. And what other word should come to mind on this matter for Germans? Culture.

Culture—for us, it was always the stuff from which to fashion a unity or particularity that would ascribe more bad than good to our "merely civilized" neighbor nations, with their newfangled political inventions. And it was not just culture as a common form or tradition that was supposed to hold the innermost parts of the German world together. Culture was the supreme instance of a communitarian bond, which, for familiar reasons, has had to wait all too long for that Hegelian "reality of the moral idea" in the form of a single state. Culture is the superindividual aspect of the people's spirit that secures the unity of the common entity, which—and here is the inherited Hegelian construction of "the Germans"—may come into being only through the subordination of all particularities. To this extent, the culture of the people's spirit has always been a *Leitkultur,* or guiding culture. The particulars are worth nothing, and the whole is worth everything, because it is common knowledge that the true exists only as a whole—at least for the guiding culture of the people's spirit, which Hegel borrowed from Herder. This notion is precisely what is living on in the current meeting of the (people's) minds.

The debate is just as controversial as it is conventional. One side uses the field of culture to pontificate on the nation's purity and integrative power; the other side relies on the legal culture of our liberal constitution. The first thus focuses primarily on the guiding culture of German self-will and its integrative power; whereas the other cites a guiding culture of tolerance whose ample heart can cope with ethnic and religious plurality as well. [. . .]

Paradoxically, observing the world as culture creates awareness of a foundational uncertainty. The paradox of culture consists in intending to overcome contingency through emphasizing contingency—that is, through comparison, through confrontation with other possibilities, through observation of the foreign. To make this paradox invisible, culture furnishes everything we observe with a special reflective form, with a particular lofty dignity and self-justification that defers comparison by treating its own perspective as unconditional. In order to preclude us from recognizing this state of affairs, culture elicits devotion, and in opposing devotion's coercive force, one can do no better than to employ other, equally contingent devotions. The function of national culture was always to affirm the historically unprecedented reality of territorially delineated nation-states with inclusive, sovereign borders. The promise of inclusive belonging beyond all regional, ethnic, and class differences made it possible for nation-states to subjugate the other functional areas of society such as economy, law, science, education, even religion and art, to the self-description of the national culture. The patriotic movements of the eighteenth century sought a cultural self-image *sine ira et studio,* without rage or zeal. Ultimately, comparison was supposed to bring about an awareness of those among one's own deficits still awaiting (self-) enlightenment.

In the nineteenth century, amid the consolidation of modern nation-states, comparison primarily functioned as self-stabilization. This form of explicit culture suffers irremediably under a paradoxical birth defect. It embeds itself into a symbolic horizon of meaning in order to stabilize its practitioners. Yet this function is corrupted by the fact that each of one's own horizons moves in the horizon of other horizons. Only by enhancing the grandeur of one's self-description can this predicament be resolved, and Europe of the nineteenth century is full of national-cultural self-concepts that animate all functional spheres of society into a national foreclosure, contaminating societal communication almost entirely. Cosmopolitan patriotism became the exclusive state-political nationalism allowing state politics to stylize itself as a fulcrum of national guidance. How this presumption of homogeneity conceals all sorts of heterogeneity among classes, regions, interests, and ideas has been described well and often enough. But these descriptions simply confirm the historical success of this model.

The institutions and routines of nation-states are ultimately geared toward homogeneity, even if societal praxis suggests everything but homogeneity. Despite the inclusive power of political self-description, twenty-first-century nation-states are experiencing an inability to control economics or science on a national-cultural level, and even law or education (not to mention religion). In this sense, the imperative of a guiding culture was discredited long ago. [. . .]

It is, however, incomprehensible to me why critics of the CDU's helpless yet strategically clever invective are doing discourse on a nineteenth-century level. Whoever counters one insistence on identity with another indeed establishes a difference but has already lost in the process. [. . .] The unhappy Friedrich Merz had only mentioned the obscene word in passing, and already the media were typing up everything the educated citizen needs in order to confirm old Friedrich Nietzsche's claim that the clearest badge of the Germans is the fact that the question "What is German?" never dies out.

No one is interested in the reality of immigration

The discussants are only re-enacting what political and media logics prescribe for them. Politics styles itself as resolving problems and invents problems it believes itself capable of resolving. And the media are grateful when a Christian regional party stresses that no one wants to see minarets in Upper Bavarian villages. But what should one see in Upper Bavarian villages? Apparently if one stiffens up with indignation and sets off menacingly for a candlelight vigil, one falls for the joke of the debate and its system of conflicts. I read the guiding-culture debate in the following terms: political actors are stirring up the semantics by which only those fears and worries will be generated that can then be politically cured.

What I have termed the birth defect of culture can be detected in the fact that a guiding culture must be demanded at all. It is already recognized that societal reality is more multicultural than the political actors who live in the conceptual world of the nineteenth century are capable of observing. And the multicultural debate should not simply be based on ethnic culture and immigration. What modern society admits in terms of styles and forms of living, milieus, and biographical discontinuities would have caused our country to become a "multicultural" society even without immigrants. [. . .]

People love crises. They beg to be overcome, transcended, and overpowered. They offer politics the chance to style itself as decisive. To associate this crisis with a societal crisis, however, would be wrong. The reality of immigration is more stable and successful than the public debates would have us believe. And the problems of migrants, above all those of the younger generation, are anything but problems that could be resolved via culture and devotions to any kind of guiding culture. Only through the security of dependable legal entitlement and political offers of inclusion, through sanctionable rules for quotidian areas of conflict, could these problems be overcome. No one seems to be interested in the empirical reality of immigration. To have a debate about that would be exciting. It would offer a view of ourselves, of a societal reality that is as much an unspectacular success as an unspectacular failure, just like any other aspect of modern society indicates. All this has very little to do with commitments to a guiding culture— whichever kind it might be.

8

HARTMUT BÖHME

GLOBAL CITIES AND TERRORISM

First published as "Global Cities, Terrorismus" in *Lettre International* (Winter 2001). Translated by David Gramling.

Fragile Urbanity in a Networked World

[. . .] The "super-American city": this fantasy betrays the equation of society with city. Modern life is city life. Cultural regions and traditions are cut off from the functional spaces of economy and technology. In place of the local and historical, globalization takes the stage—spatially comprehensive and ahistorical, framed by networks of technology, commerce, telecommunication, and economics. Internal segmentation of cities and a hunger for surface area destroyed the historically heterogeneous and cultural heterotope. According to Robert Musil, the atomization of human activities and the subsequent dissolution of the social, the historical, and the regional lead to the dominance of the abstract over the concrete. That Musil speaks of the "super-American" indicates that this city type is certainly an American invention but reaches "beyond" America and becomes a model for modern evolution in general. Without inquiring into the particulars of European urban development, we can say that the reconstruction of bombed-out German cities, or, if you will, the refurbishment and expansion of the European city, followed Musil's model of functional compartmentalization and spatial dispersion to a great extent. The old cities, characterized by concentration, copresence, synchronicity, and a mix of people and functions, were broadly subjugated to a systemic and decontextualized model.

All of the urbanistic ideas after 1970—the postmodern city, the reaestheticization of cities, the college city, the fractal city, the career of the heterotope, the rediscovery of the regional and the historical, the valorization of city culture and urban society, the promotion of neighborhood identity, the cultural modes of reading cities as texts, the attempts to establish new forms of multifunctional, multicultural intermingling, the emphasis on difference over homogeneity, the strengthening first of the center, then of the periphery through which the city and the suburbs became the object of architectural and urbanistic reformulations, the discovery of nature in the city and urban ecology or opposing endeavors to again delimit "country" from "city" and to implement qualitative density in place of surface area expansion—all of these reforms ultimately reference the "super-American city" or what might also be called the Fordist and Keynesian city. The first two-thirds of the twentieth century can be considered an attempt to create cities without qualities for the man without qualities—that is, to build a functional enclosure for techno-economic modernity and to sociotechnically generate a corresponding human species. The last third of the century, in contrast, brought forth a hectic pluralization of urbanistic, cultural styles in order to escape functionalism. Perhaps this postmodern discursive vibrancy saw its end on September 11, 2001.

Fragmented Urban Geography

On that day, the Twin Towers of the World Trade Centers and a reported 4,000 people were pulverized in an act of terrorist violence previously unimaginable. What should be analyzed here is not the psychological trauma but the various symbolic, cultural, urban, and global political configurations. More than any other complex in downtown Manhattan, the Twin Towers represented the new economy that has spatially materialized in global cities. It is not only in the physiognomic sense that the Twin Towers gave the southern tip of Manhattan a new imprint as the ultimate triumph of functionalistic *claritas*. Along with the severely damaged World Financial Center, the Wall Street markets—which acted as the foremost emblem of the electronic economy—and the surrounding bank centers composed the central nervous system of globalization. The latter is no longer based on the classic sectors of production of goods but on the power of financial streams and economic services to steer and control. A geography is thus created that is radically distinct from the old ideal of sovereign nation-states and their associated economies. This geography is based upon a few cities, or actually certain areas within them, that represent an extremely concentrated control relay on the worldwide landscape of flows (Manuel Castells). This space of invisible, autopoietic streams of capital is managed with the assistance of gigantic information systems. For this reason, the new Manhattan downtown, as well as the new global cities, are effects of the information-technology revolution. They are essentially cybercities that are materially manifest in only a few exceedingly concentrated architectonic ensembles. The pyramidal form of world cities, composed of a center with concentric suburbs encamped around it, is no longer characteristic of globalized space. Instead economic, information-technological, and scientific infrastructures and elite groups have been implanted in the old centers, in industrial districts, or in newly constructed areas. Their architectural form frames the hardware of the centralized control power of a global network with a series of secondary and tertiary nodes.

In the case of the Twin Towers, it was not the "heart of America" that was affected but the material symbol of what Saskia Sassen has called the epoch's new triangulation: alongside the classical institutions of nation-states and the global economy, global cities have, since 1970, established themselves as self-standing control systems. Along with New York, these hubs include London and Tokyo. The Twin Towers were, iconographically speaking, the *axis mundi* of this transnational economic form, even if it originates in and is controlled by the United States.

In terms of urban geography, this new economy had severe and paradoxical effects. A few decades ago, New York was still a metropolis of industrial production and cargo handling, with corresponding social stratifications and channels of immigration, as well as ethnic and/or class-specific neighborhood development. The spatial structure was framed by the dynamic tension between center and periphery and the ethnic enclaves characteristic of a classic immigration city with its own socioeconomic networks (Robert Ezra Park). The spatial orientation pointed eastward toward Europe, where the mass of immigrants came from. Correspondingly, whites composed the great majority of the urban population. Within three decades, they became a minority: today, African-Americans, Latinos, and Asians compose about 55 percent to 60 percent combined. At the same time, with the increase in multiethnic dispersion and new demographic profiles, the downfall of New York as an industrial "production machine" and, urbanistically speaking, as a social "integration machine became final" (H. Hässermann). And thus began the rise of New York as a capital of finance and industrial services, linked with the steep increase in highly qualified economic and finance management and geared toward telecommunications and mammoth computational capacities, which recruited nationally as well as internationally.

The new New York elites in no way lived and operated in place-bound ways. Rather, they generated an extraordinary need for lower, small-segment services primarily rendered by the new immigrant population. This culturally geographically uprooted, globally active, extremely labor intensive, highly paid, consumptive, and culturally demanding management elite is in need of an unprecedented concentration of culturally, domestically, and semi-publicly specialized services geared toward lifestyle promotion. This shift has turned the Manhattan of the past decades into a space of radiating attractions, touristically and otherwise.

In the wake of these demographic and economic-industrial shifts, the politics of desegregation was brought to a close. Since then, segregation has been increasing in all global and megacities, not only in the former melting pot of New York. Taking Los Angeles as an example, Edward W. Soja has described the post-Fordist urbanization strategies that lead to the dissolution of the dual city and create new geographies. The deindustrialization of classical industrial sectors leads to 1) a newly industrialized technopolis with large surface area (which may be anywhere—in Korea or in Orange County near Los Angeles); 2) global cities that function as local control relays for a globally operating expansion of capital in cyberspace. Through it, as Soja says, "almost every corner of the world can be made into the backyard hinterland of such global cities." Global cities are indeed materially and locally present—for example, in Manhattan or Frankfurt am Main. As control cerebra, they are even dependent on local compressions.

Operatively, however, they are equally influential in a South African gold mine, a Thai textile factory, an Arab oil deposit, an Argentinean auto factory, even in a Colombian coca-growing area, a Siberian natural-gas deposit, or an Indonesian tropical-wood-processing plant. Thus, it is true that, in the new spatial ordering of the earth, the global is localized into a few points, and the local is everywhere globalized (Soja). Both of these complementary geographies enact segregation in new ways—that is, they create pure, heavily guarded, high-security, technologically defended, armed, deintegrated, fortresslike social spaces for the new elites, which are encased by a powerful cloak of totally dependent service workers. The production of segregation itself becomes the service of specialized security forms but also of urban police. These exclusion politics are reflexes of a new form of social segregation, polarization, and urban fragmentation, which have formed ethnically multiple, permanent, and desperate underclasses in the center and on the margins of cities, which no longer must be penetrated via security politics but only need to be kept satiated. [. . .]

One effect of this segregation is that the elites in Manhattan, Frankfurt, Hong Kong, Tokyo, São Paulo, and London evince more social, cultural, habitual, and economic commonalities among one another than with their countrymen a few miles away in the slums, favelas, *banlieues,* and misery districts.

In addition, globalization means a completely new segregation dynamic, which again creates a new spatial order upon the globe. Urbanistic concepts such as desegregation, assimilation, or integration and development politics have been dissolved by new inner-city, inner-societal, planetary, and ecological fragmentation of cultural-historical as well as natural-historical resources and traditions. In that the global cities had created a structural complementarity between space, race, poverty, and desperation in one sphere and a spatially concentrated control mechanism in the other, they form the model of the terrestrial, spatial order of the future. [. . .] Against this background, the recent terror attacks may be interpreted anew. The dual forms of the localization of the global and the globalization of the local have been combined here with the highest-caliber marksmanship. It is an uncanny inversion of space by which the periphery and the center coincided, and this is the catastrophe—the catastrophe of the spatial ordering of a globalization that corresponds not only to the new economy but also to the global power politics of the United States.

We will remember what the urbanists demanded for the sociocultural spatial order of large cities: cities need immigration, which today has mostly taken on the form of multicultural migration. They need promising strategies for economic and social desegregation, without destroying the enclaves of the ethnic "subsidiariat" economy and the sociocultural networking of disparate, regionally self-organizing populations. That means two things are needed: on the one hand, cultural pluralization and socioeconomic multidimensionality linked to true paths of access rich with alternatives, integration, assimilation, and advancement into the macrospace of the city; necessary on the other hand is the extraordinary closeness of life and reproductive forms in the meso- and microspaces of the neighborhoods, which must in no way be allowed to be explained away and excluded as abandoned zones. The poverty economy in districts of ethnic migration and in the proletarian and subproletarian districts of the new underclasses and housing classes has, as cynical as it may sound, a basic function for the survival of cities. This distributive economy must thus be "left to its own devices." Cities everywhere need spaces of encounter and transit for economic and sociocultural intermingling, exchange, contact, mutual penetration, and diversification; this principle has been called the politics of visibility. Well-intentioned desegregation is just as counterproductive in this regard as exclusionary segregation. To allow spaces of voluntary segregation to emerge is just as essential as municipal political measures promoting opportunities for spatial and cultural integration. [. . .]

9

ANDREAS TZORTZIS

VANQUISHING THE GHOST OF MOHAMMED ATTA

First published in English on October 26, 2002, by Deutsche Welle World (www.dw-world.de).

Berlin artist Stephan Hoffstadt has taken over the Hamburg apartment shared by Mohammed Atta and two members of the Hamburg terror cell for the next three days. He hopes to normalize the image of the notorious address.

In a real-estate market as tight as Hamburg's these days, it's an absolute steal.

Three rooms, a full kitchen and bathroom, and just 20 minutes with the train to downtown Hamburg. All for a little less than 500 euros a month.

But since the previous tenants moved out, there have been no takers. The reason: those same three tenants carried out the worst terrorist attack in history a little over a year ago.

Days after the September 11 attacks, police and media descended on the apartment on Marienstrasse 54 where investigators believe Mohammed Atta, Said Bahaji, and Ramzi Binalshibh plotted the attacks that killed more than 3,000 in the United States. Camera teams beamed photos of the unassuming white façade across the world, investigators scoured the three rooms, and no one has wanted to live there since.

This weekend, Berlin artist Stephan Hoffstadt will direct a three-day exhibition in the apartment, marking the first time the public has been let into the so-called terror nest. With an exhibit titled *Marienstrasse 54 Space Clearing*, Hoffstadt hopes to normalize the image of an apartment associated with so much tragedy.

Exhibit Avoids September 11 Themes

"It would be naïve to think we could neutralize the connotation," Hoffstadt told *DW-WORLD*. "But we're convinced that we can create an effect of 'space clearing.' That people come there and say, 'Hey, it's just an empty, banal, meaningless apartment, with a kitchen and bathroom.' "

Documentary films about the Harburg district where the apartment is located, an art installation by Berlin artist Katrin Glanz, and live readings by an actor form the program of the twice-daily shows. The rooms will remain bare, aside from Glanz's installation. The walls are the same white they were when Atta and his crew moved out in March 2001.

No Longer Just Another Building

Roughly six months earlier, police came to the apartment building up on a small hill a day after the September 11 attacks. Germany's FBI, the state police, even American investigators poked around the cleaned-out apartment. They covered the white walls in graphite powder, searching for fingerprints, and then repainted everything.

Rental agent and landlord Thomas Albrecht has told reporters that though many prospective tenants have come by to take a look, none seem willing to move into the apartment, located 200 meters from the Technical University in Harburg, where most of the terror cell studied.

It's not so much the terror cell's legacy as the continuous media storm that scares prospective tenants off, Albrecht has said. Since September 11, camera teams of every nationality have set up crews across the narrow street from the house's façade. Tenants, sick of the hassle, slam their doors in the faces of curious reporters. Hoffstadt says his project will stop at least some of that.

"The media has been waiting for a long time for someone to move in and do a story," he said. "Every three days, people call up the real-estate agent and ask 'Is someone in?' After our project, this story won't be as interesting anymore. We will have taken a piece of this sensation away."

For many of the residents in the neighborhood, that sensation has already faded. Sebastian Strunck, a 21-year-old electronics student at TU Harburg, has lived in Marienstrasse 54, one floor above the apartment, for a month now.

"I don't understand why people don't move in there," he said, noting the tight real-estate market has an especially hard effect on students. "I would move there. It's not like I think Mohammed Atta's ghost haunts it or anything."

10

GERMANS OUTRAGED OVER "FLORIDA ROLF" CASE

First published in English on August 30, 2003, on Deutsche Welle World (dw-world.de).

A controversial case of a Florida-based German pensioner drawing huge welfare benefits from Germany has sparked an angry debate among politicians and led the government to review the country's welfare laws.

Sixty-four-year-old German Rolf J. lives in a comfortable Miami Beach apartment on Florida's east coast and spends much of his time strolling the beach near his home. So far so good.

But a recent report in a German paper that Rolf J. was living it up in Florida at the cost of Germany's overburdened welfare system was too much for some Germans to digest. The mass-selling *Bild* newspaper said that a Lower Saxony court had ruled German welfare officials had to continue paying the full cost of Rolf J.'s beach apartment for another six months.

Life at the beach paid for by welfare

Media reports revealed that when welfare officials tried to reduce his housing allowance to 600 euros ($655.70) monthly, down from the current 875 euros, Rolf J. hired a lawyer—paid for by welfare authorities—who convinced the court his client could not find suitable accommodation for 600 euros and could suffer depression if forced to move away from his neighborhood. A psychiatrist also testified that Rolf J.—dubbed "Florida Rolf" by the colorful *Bild* daily—might commit suicide if forced to return to Germany.

The court then ordered welfare authorities to continue paying his current full rent for another six months, in addition to the 730 euros per month in living costs and 146 euros for a cleaner on account of Rolf J.'s being classified as handicapped. Rolf J.'s total welfare benefits, it emerged, amounted to almost 1,900 euros per month.

Politicians call for end to "sweet life under palms"

The case has triggered anger in Germany, which faces painful social reforms on account of its cash-strapped welfare and health systems and spiraling unemployment. Politicians are now calling for a revamp of the country's generous welfare laws.

Bavarian premier and head of the conservative Christian Social Union (CSU) Edmund Stoiber said in an interview with *Bild* that Chancellor Schröder and his government should completely strike out paragraphs in legal social law that regulate welfare benefits for Germans living abroad. "That will finally spell the end of a sweet life under palms for Florida Rolf and others like him at the cost of the taxpayer," Stoiber said. "I'm also in favor of banks, life-insurance companies, and property offices giving unrestricted information about the personal wealth of welfare recipients," he said.

German social and health minister Ulla Schmidt said people had a right to be upset at the Rolf J. case. "Such court decisions unhinge the sense of justice in Germany," the Social Democrat told the *Leipziger Volkszeitung*. This week, the minister announced the regulations would be changed as soon as possible. "Social welfare can't be there to finance a good life for Germans in Florida," she said.

German media reports said the minister was planning that in the future only hospital patients who cannot return to Germany on health grounds and Germans in foreign imprisonment can draw welfare from Germany. In addition, Schmidt is reportedly making provisions so that those over 70 are not affected by the planned new regulations.

This week, Chancellor Schröder announced he wanted to use the headline-grabbing case of Florida Rolf as an occasion to change the existing law. The Florida Rolf case is a "really horrible" example of abusing the social system, Schröder said in a television interview.

According to *Bild*, currently 1,055 Germans in 83 countries receive welfare, which is estimated to cost a total of 5.5 million euros.

"I've done enough for Germany"

However, the present row in Germany over the misuse of the welfare system did not seem to affect the main figure in the eye of the storm.

Interviewed by *Bild*, Rolf J., who said he was once a millionaire banker but suffered a breakdown after losing his fortune and wife, remained unruffled. "I always paid my taxes, and I lost my father in the war. I've done enough for Germany," he said.

11

CHRISTOPH HEIN

THIRD WORLD EVERYWHERE

First published as "Dritte Welt überall" in *Die Zeit* (September 30, 2004). Translated by David Gramling. Hein (b. 1944) has emerged as one of the most prominent eastern German writers since the fall of the Berlin Wall. His latest novel, *Landnahme*, appeared in 2004.

East Germany as avant-garde of globalization: When capital flees, nationalism returns

Both high art and the art of war are well acquainted with the avant-garde. They both know that the avant-garde is in possession of knowledge that will eventually become common knowledge in a society—but not until two decades, or two battles, later. It is the task of the avant-garde to react quickly to new situations and crucial changes of which the general public is still unaware. For this reason, the actions of the avant-garde generally appear incomprehensible or even mad. Visionaries displace those norms that are currently considered valid—and thus give the appearance of madness.

The East German provinces are the poor regions of Germany. The province of Mecklenburg–Western Pomerania is the poorest among them. The unemployment rate in the city of Anklam is hovering at 50 percent. Politicians and journalists appear afraid when they speak about the region. They are concerned, because they continue to refer to Mecklenburg and Anklam as the "taillights" of Germany, but they already suspect that this province and this city represent the avant-garde of Germany; they are our future.

An academic debate has arisen about whether the new Monday demonstrations are justified or are simply donning disingenuous garb. What is being overlooked, however, is a newly salient difference, one that aptly describes the changes afoot in society: a new distribution of tasks and the splitting of the demonstrators.

The reason the demonstrations of 1989 [in the GDR] had such a consequential, unforeseeable effect was that they were buttressed by exit-visa applications, escape via Eastern Europe (Hungary and Prague), and by a threat that the governing administration felt to be even more dangerous: "We're staying here." This mix introduced a stimulus into a society that sought to muffle a perplexed clique by offering easements on travel restrictions. It was nothing more than the announcement that citizens would be allowed to travel abroad that swept a whole state off the globe.

Now, however, there is a new distribution of roles. One sector of society took to the streets and demonstrated. This sector said, "We are the people and we will stay—out in the streets but still in the country nonetheless." But capital took over in the other sector—that of the exit-visa applicants and the escape to Eastern Europe (and Asia). Capital also fled into the more accessible low-wage countries and tax shelters.

The first of these escape acts led to a consumer paradise, whereas the goal of the other is the production paradise. The former was and is very costly for us, and the other will be much more costly; it may cost us our democracy. The government hardly has any means to react to it. Neither the current nor the future government can react, neither the German nor any other European government—unless it is one of the low-wage countries, one of the newly conquered paradises of profit. And we are only at the beginning of this globalizing development, or more precisely that which counts as and is recognizable as globalization: the use and exploitation of differences in living standards, wages and tax laws. This process set in at the beginning of the 1990s and developed rapidly after a hesitant beginning. The state cannot control this development. The globally operating profiteer is hardly within reach of national laws; state power and national law end at the border of the country.

European legislation does not even make it to the borders of Europe; there are European states that offer loopholes to this traveling capital, in order to secure the existence and survival of their own population. These movements of capital are no longer manageable by national governments, because they can only be controlled on a limited basis. All states have to fulfill different functions, but the most important from the states' perspective is to defend themselves from external and internal enemies. Every state in the world is based on only one foundation, and if this is withdrawn from it, it will collapse like a house of cards. The existential foundation of any given state is taxation, a compulsory measure that no one has been able or permitted to revoke since the invention of the state. Globalization has brought an end to this compulsory measure. When a sufficient economic power is present, taxation has even become negotiable. Successful flight and exit-visa applications must bring any state to its senses. It cannot fend off tax relief or tax exemption, or else emigration will manifest and the state will not only have to sacrifice its taxes but also provide for the other unemployed who are left. Neither a mayor nor a chief of state, neither a local authority nor a finance minister can respond to the demand for tax exemption by enforcing tax laws, because firms would then certainly follow through on their announced emigration. This tax revenue will outwit the state as well as the municipality, and the army of the unemployed will increase—the army that the state will then have to care for. States are, however, increasingly incapable of caring for them, if the revenue is not available to do so. A state cannot allow itself to be made susceptible to coercion; it may not consent to coercion: such is the consensus of all democratic states in case of terrorist attacks. Yet when its existential basis is revoked, this state doctrine is clearly obsolete. In order to keep entrepreneurs in the country or to tempt them into the country, gifts must be distributed: real estate is offered to potential employers at no cost, and closing costs are covered by the municipality. Often, even a multiyear or ten-year tax exemption becomes the lesser evil for the state, an evil that is supposed to stave off the greater one. The social net must be adjusted to correspond to the dwindling revenues, because it is not only the air that is growing thin. An end is not in sight; China, India and Korea's mouths are watering. The African continent will be next.

In Saigon, European employers pay an hourly wage of 6.5 cents. They are paying much more than the Vietnamese bourgeoisie, who pay a maximum of 5.5 cents. *Ex oriente lux:* this light is both glowing and tempting. Globalization has blazed a path that leads to the mutual realignment of the first and third worlds. But the goal is not the desire for a more just world but rather the exploitation of the current decline of profit maximization. This development, however, has suicidal tendencies. Henry Ford's old wisdom—that it is not just products but also consumers that have to be produced if an economy and a common good are to be kept stable—has been disregarded since the beginning of this kind of globalization. In the future, Europeans, increasingly excluded from production, will no longer be those consumers who can boost the national or global economy with 6-cent-per-hour workers.

A crash is imminent. For Asia, especially for China and India, this kind of globalization represents a development stimulus that will promote both states to the forefront of the global economy. In Europe, jobs continue to emigrate, and the social network has become a silken thread that cannot absorb anything more.

The 1-euro job, against which the Union parties could have organized mass protests only a few years ago, has already been accepted by job searchers as a reasonable possibility. But globally speaking, can they, in the long run, hold out against the 6-cent jobs? Europeans will continue to defend themselves against the coming conflict. Denial among the populace is thus unsupportable. It is possible that the fall of the Moscow empire was not the epochal break; this end simply made the break possible. Perhaps the true epochal break is the division of the world into a first, second, and third one. And because the first and second ones can no longer be paid for, it is only the third world that is left for all of us. This outcome is of course hard to imagine. But the idea that one great *Kulturnation* ran into the arms of fascism and was capable of mass murder and genocide was also once unimaginable. Just as unimaginable as the nonviolent breakdown of the heavily armed Moscow empire. "Unimaginable" means very little historically and is only a testament to our limited capacity for imagination. Europe's heads of state will, like honest cashiers, show their empty pockets and then later—as dishonest electoral candidates and against their better judgment—they will speak of a silver lining in the clouds of doubt. Who will be the saviors is unclear. Certainly, it will be an angel, the Angel of Light or the fallen, beaten, disrobed angel, the Angel of Darkness. Given our previous historical experiences, the national and nationalistic parties will soon gain in power and influence.

In 1946, one year after the Second World War, Thomas Mann said that the epoch of fascism had not ended and would not end for a long time. I read this sentence as a young man and did not understand it; it appeared hysterical and devoid of any understanding of the world. After all, fascism had just been completely and finally defeated. Today, however, I fear that back then, Thomas Mann had a clear vision of the horizon—far before his time.

1955   On May 23, the North Atlantic Treaty Organization decides to end the occupation of the Federal Republic of Germany (West Germany) and declares the country "fully sovereign." West Germany becomes a member of NATO, but the former occupying troops remain stationed there. The German Democratic Republic (East Germany), occupied by the Soviet Union, joins the Warsaw Pact.

On December 20, the West German government signs the first bilateral labor-recruitment agreement with Italy for 100,000 laborers in Rome.

1956   The Treaty of Brussels establishes the European Economic Community, allowing citizens to move between member states. This initial Common Market includes West Germany, France, Italy, Belgium, the Netherlands, and Luxembourg. The Turkish Republic applies for membership in the EEC as well, but its application is denied.

1960   Some 686,000 foreign workers, mostly from Italy, live in West Germany (1.2 percent of the population).

West Germany signs bilateral recruitment agreements with Spain and Greece.

1961   On August 12–13, the Berlin Wall is built, cutting off the flow of migration from East to West Germany. (Some 3.8 million East Germans had fled East Germany for West Germany between 1949 and 1961.)

On October 30, West Germany signs a bilateral recruitment agreement with the Turkish Republic. A central recruitment office is established in Istanbul, and by the year's end, 7,000 Turkish workers have moved to Germany.

The invention of the birth-control pill (*Antibabypille*) leads to a sharp decline in the West and East German birthrate, with long-term consequences for demographics, education, social welfare, and migration.

1962   In March, conflicting information about income-tax rates leads Turkish miners in Essen and Hamburg to stage a strike. Twenty-six workers are fired and deported.

1963   West Germany signs a recruitment agreement with Morocco.

The International Committee for Information and Social Action founds a monthly newspaper, *Anadolu,* for Turks living in Germany.

Ludwig Erhard (CDU) succeeds Konrad Adenauer (also CDU), West Germany's first chancellor since 1949.

In December, the Auschwitz trial in Frankfurt am Main commences and continues until 1966. It follows previous trials in Ulm (focusing on war crimes on the Eastern front) in 1958 and the Eichmann trial in Jerusalem in 1961.

1964   West Germany signs a bilateral recruitment agreement with Portugal.

The West German and Turkish republics renew their guest-worker agreement.

The WDR radio station begins Turkish-language broadcasts under the name Köln Radyosu throughout West Germany.

On September 10, Armando Rodrigues de Sá from Portugal is welcomed as the millionth guest worker at Cologne-Deutz train station. He receives a motorcycle as a present from the West German Association of Employers.

1965   West Germany and Israel establish diplomatic relations.

West Germany signs a recruitment agreement with Tunisia.

Some 2,700 Turks live in West Berlin.

In April, the West German Bundestag passes the Foreigner Act, the first piece of legislation since the 1938 Foreigner Police Decree to regulate residency criteria for noncitizens. Guest workers who have been employed in West Germany for five years may now receive an automatic five-year renewal of their work permit, regardless of whether they are citizens of an EC country. This new regulation applies to 400,000 non-EC workers.

1966   East Germany signs the Pendlervereinbarung (Commuter Accord) with Poland, making it easy for Poles to cross the border for temporary work.

1967   The Ausserparlamentarische Opposition (Extra-Parliamentary Opposition) in West Germany stages demonstrations against the Vietnam War.

On June 2, Benno Ohnesorg, a West German student, is killed by a police officer during a demonstration in West Berlin against the shah of Iran, Mohammed Reza Pahlavi, who is visiting West Germany.

1968   West Germany signs a bilateral recruitment agreement with Yugoslavia.

1969   A total of 2 million foreigners live in West Germany. Italians are the largest group.

Willy Brandt of the SPD becomes chancellor of West Germany and seeks better ties with East Germany, Poland, and the Soviet Union.

The West German government signs an accord with South Korea, leading to the recruitment of 10,000 nurses and 8,000 miners within the next few years.

1970   About 1 million guest workers come to Germany this year alone. Immigration stays at a peak over the subsequent two years. Most foreign workers find jobs in food-service, construction, mining, automotive, steel, and metalworking industries.

1971   Erich Honecker succeeds Walter Ulbricht as leader of East Germany.

The Islamic political organization Milli Görüş (National Perspective) forms under the name Turkish Union of Germany. Its leader, Necmettin Erbakan, a professor at Istanbul's Technical University who holds a doctorate from the Technical University of Aachen, is banned from party politics in the Turkish Republic. Consequently, the Milli Görüş movement begins to gain momentum in West Germany.

1972   The West German radio station WDR holds a contest to come up with alternatives to the label *guest worker*, which many people have come to see as a euphemism. The station accepts none of the 32,000 entries and decides that *foreign employee* is the most appropriate term.

On September 5, at the Summer Olympics in Munich, Palestinian terrorists take 11 Israeli athletes hostage. All the hostages, five of the kidnappers, and one police officer are shot.

On December 21, Chancellor Willy Brandt's *Ostpolitik* (politics of rapprochement with eastern Europe) culminates in the Grundvertrag, or Basic Treaty, which recognizes the FRG and GDR as two separate states, but not separate nations, thus easing the East-West conflict of the Cold War. Brandt also signs treaties with the Soviet Union and Poland. *Ostpolitik* goes back to Egon Bahr's speech of 1963, which argued for "change through rapprochement."

1973   Some 2.6 million guest workers now reside in West Germany. A total of 14 million guest workers had come between 1955 and 1973; 11 million to 12 million returned home.

Both West and East Germany become members of the United Nations, a "global association of governments facilitating cooperation in international law and security, economic development, and social equity."

East Germany signs an accord with North Vietnam for contract laborers who will work in industrial centers, such as Chemnitz and Erfurt, for a maximum of five years.

On July 30, *Der Spiegel*'s cover headline reads, "The Turks are coming—Save yourself if you can!" Turks now account for 23 percent of all foreigners living in West Germany.

From August 24 to 30, a wildcat strike among Turkish employees at the Cologne Ford factory leads to press debates about the "politicization of foreign workers."

In October, a global oil crisis begins after Arab countries restrict deliveries and increase prices.

On November 23, West Germany halts the recruitment of guest workers. By the end of the year, 4 million foreigners live in Germany.

1974   East Germany signs an accord with Algeria for contract workers.

Brandt resigns after revelations of espionage surface about one of his aides. The new chancellor, Helmut Schmidt (SPD), continues Brandt's *Ostpolitik*.

On November 13, the West German government decrees that any family member of a guest worker arriving after November 30, 1974, will not be permitted to work.

1975   In April, the West German government announces that no foreigners may move to a neighborhood or region where the percentage of foreigners exceeds 12 percent of the entire population. This law is repealed in 1976 on constitutional grounds.

Songwriter and performer Wolf Biermann, who had immigrated from West to East Germany in 1953 at age 17, is stripped of his East German citizenship while on tour in West Germany. This punishment for his long-standing criticism of the GDR's Stalinist policies leads to protests among East German writers and intellectuals, including Christa Wolf.

The newly formed G6 convenes for a three-day summit to discuss issues of common concern. This "Group of Six" includes the heads of state of six major industrial democracies: France, Italy, Japan, the

United Kingdom, the United States, and West Germany. This international group would become the G8 upon the accession of Canada and Russia in 1991.

Poland allows 161,000 ethnic Germans to emigrate to West Germany.

1977   Romania allows 10,000 to 13,000 ethnic Germans per year to emigrate to West Germany. A decade later, in 1988, the government's payment to Romania per ethnic German emigrant would increase from some $2,600 to $5,600.

From July to October, the West German terrorist organization Red Army Faction commits a series of murders and kidnappings of prominent politicians and industrialists. Also known as the Baader-Meinhof Group, the RAF trained with Palestinian guerrilla groups and was supported by the East German secret police.

1978   West Germany's first commissioner of foreigner affairs, Heinz Kühn, argues that the country must recognize itself as an "immigration country." He writes a memorandum suggesting that the government consider adopting policies that focus on cultural and political, as well as economic, integration.

Amendments to the general administrative regulations of the Foreigner Act grant immigrants a permanent residence permit after five years.

1979   West Germany takes in 2,500 South Vietnamese "boat people"; a total of 35,000 refugees from Southeast Asia come to Germany during the next few years.

The American television series *Holocaust* airs in West Germany and attracts 20 million viewers, more than half the adult population. The world watches how the nation reacts to Hollywood's presentation of Nazi atrocities.

1980   East Germany signs further recruitment agreements with North Vietnam and an accord with Mozambique for contract workers.

The number of asylum applications in West Germany doubles in one year, from just over 50,000 in 1979 to 107,000 in 1980. Concern grows about refugees' abuse of the right to asylum for economic reasons. On June 18, the government introduces an emergency measure to restrict the number of fraudulent asylum seekers entering the country.

On September 12, a military putsch in Turkey boosts the number of asylum applications by Turkish and Kurdish political opponents of the Turkish government.

1981   The immigrant population in West Germany is 7.5 percent of the total population.

Some 135,000 Poles seek political asylum in West Germany.

West Germany restricts immigration from non-EC member states. Spousal immigration is restricted, and immigration of dependents is limited to children 16 years of age and under.

1982   On May 26, Semra Ertan sets herself on fire in the Hamburg marketplace to protest growing xenophobia.

On August 1, the Asylum Procedure Act goes into effect. It contains regulations to speed up asylum applications.

Helmut Kohl (CDU) is inaugurated as chancellor. He will become the "unification chancellor" and remain in office until 1998.

On December 18, an ordinance amending the Foreigner Act goes into effect, requiring visas for foreigners from non-EC counties for stays of longer than three months.

1983   West German unemployment reaches a postwar record of 2.3 million, leading to widespread sentiments that "too many foreign workers are stealing our jobs."

On August 30, asylum applicant Cemal Altun commits suicide by jumping out of the window of a West Berlin Administrative Court building to avoid deportation to Turkey.

On November 28, a new law for the promotion of voluntary return (Das Gesetz zur Förderung der Rückkehrbereitschaft) offers jobless guest workers 10,500 German marks to return to their countries of origin.

1985   Mikhail Gorbachev, the new general secretary of the Soviet Communist Party, introduces his political platform of perestroika and glasnost, which allows ethnic Germans to emigrate.

Civil war in Sri Lanka brings large numbers of Tamil refugees to West Germany for political asylum.

Some 31,000 Iranian political refugees, fleeing the Iran-Iraq War (1980–88), seek asylum. They follow the first wave of highly educated Iranian refugees after Ayatollah Khomeini's Islamic revolution of 1979.

The Adelbert von Chamisso Prize, a prize for authors whose first language is not German, is conferred for the first time. Aras Ören is the first recipient.

1986   East Germany signs an accord with China for contract workers.

1988   Some 4.5 million foreigners live in West Germany, accounting for 7.3 percent of the population.

The number of ethnic Germans leaving Eastern Europe to settle in West Germany continues to rise: 202,645 come in 1988.

Roughly 60,000 contract workers from North Vietnam and other communist countries such as Angola and Mozambique enter East Germany.

1989   On October 9, 70,000 protesters in the East German city of Leipzig shout, "We are the people."

On November 4, over 1 million people in East Berlin demand democracy and free elections. The GDR government resigns on November 7.

On November 9, East German border police open the Berlin Wall. Some 1 million persons per day visit West Berlin. More than 200,000 East Germans *(Übersiedler)* move to West Germany. Between 1989 and 1993, 1.4 million East Germans migrate to the West.

East Germany deports some 60 percent of its 90,000 foreign contract workers (mainly from Vietnam, Angola, and Mozambique).

Haus der Kulturen der Welt (House of World Cultures) opens in the former Congress Hall in Berlin. The new organization is dedicated to the promotion of intercultural understanding.

1990   Some 5 million foreigners live in West Germany (8 percent of the population), 192,000 in East Germany.

In February, Chancellor Kohl receives assurances from Gorbachev that the Soviet Union supports the reunification of Germany.

Some 200,000 Russian Jews ("quota refugees") are granted special asylum status.

TRT, Turkey's state-run television and radio corporation, begins daily broadcasts to Germany via cable.

The Bundestag passes a new Foreigner Act, reaffirming the principle of *ius sanguinis,* by which only those of German "blood" heritage (children born to German parents) receive automatic German citizenship. Naturalization procedures become easier, yet the legislature rejects dual citizenship.

On July 1, East German currency is permanently discontinued and the West German mark becomes the common monetary unit.

On September 12, the Zwei-plus-Vier-Vertrag (Two-plus-Four Treaty) is signed in Moscow between the GDR, the FRG, France, Russia, the United Kingdom, and the United States, affirming the reunification of the two Germanys. Germany receives full sovereignty by accepting the existing borders (that is, by giving up eastern provinces in Poland and Russia). The treaty calls for Russia to withdraw troops from the former GDR by 1994.

On October 3, the German Democratic Republic (16.3 million citizens) is dissolved into the Federal Republic of Germany. With a population of 79 million, the reunified Germany becomes the largest country in the European Community.

On November 24, neo-Nazis in the former East German city of Eberswalde murder Amadeo Antonio from Angola.

Following the overthrow and execution of Romanian leader Nicolae Ceaușescu, more than 100,000 ethnic German Romanians flee the country. The number of ethnic German immigrants from Eastern Europe rises to close to 400,000, with the greatest number coming from Poland.

After the collapse of the Soviet Union, 2 million ethnic Germans immigrate to Germany during the next years.

1991   Emine Sevgi Özdamar, a Turkish writer and actress living in Düsseldorf and Berlin, wins the Ingeborg Bachmann Prize. Controversy over the quality of "German" literature ensues.

On February 15, a resolution of the federal states' prime ministers allows acceptance of Jewish immigrants from the Soviet Union as *Kontingentflüchtlinge,* or quota refugees. The resolution also allows Jewish immigrants to keep dual citizenship. Some 170,000 Russian Jews immigrate to Germany over the next decade.

The Bundestag names Berlin the new capital of unified Germany.

On September 30, an arson attack on a home for asylum seekers in the former East German city of Hoyerswerda injures 30 people.

1992   Immigration to Germany reaches a new record with 1,219,348 new admissions. Some 440,000 asylum seekers file applications; 230,000 ethnic Germans enter from Poland, Romania, and the former Soviet Union. Another 350,000 refugees flee the war in Bosnia to find "temporary protection" in Germany.

On February 7, the Maastricht Treaty on the European Union is signed. The treaty establishes new forms of cooperation between member-state governments in defense, justice, security, agriculture, the environment, energy, and transportation.

In May, ARTE (Association relative à la télévision Européenne), a bilingual television-programming venture, is inaugurated. Funded by the French and German governments, it focuses on cultural programs of transnational interest.

In August, hundreds of right-wing youths attack a reception center for asylum seekers and a home for Vietnamese contract workers in Rostock-Lichtenhagen, while bystanders from the neighborhood watch and applaud.

On November 22, an arson attack in Mölln kills a Turkish woman, her granddaughter, and her niece.

1993   On May 29, Saime Genç (4), Hülya Genç (9), Gülüstan Öztürk (12), Hatice Genç (18), and Gürsün İnce (27) die in an arson attack at Lower Werner Street in Solingen, West Germany. They were all female members of a family that had lived in Germany for 23 years. The attack leads to pro-Turkish, antiracist demonstrations throughout the country and a public discussion about right-wing extremism in Germany. Close to 3 million Germans protest against racism in nightly candlelight vigils *(Lichterketten)* across Germany.

On June 30, an amendment to the Foreigner Act gives those who were born in Germany or have lived there for at least 15 years legal entitlement to naturalization. Otherwise, the Empire- and State-Citizenship Law of 1913 still governs the naturalization of foreigners.

On July 1, changes in the Basic Law go into effect following the "asylum compromise." The annual quota of persons who can receive recognition as ethnic Germans is set at 220,000.

Teams of the German Soccer League participate in the project "Peacefully with One Another" by wearing a badge on their uniforms that reads "My friend is a foreigner."

1994   Leyla Onur and Cem Özdemir become the first elected Bundestag representatives of Turkish descent. Onur has served in the European Parliament as a German delegate since 1989.

1995   Some 7 million noncitizens live in Germany.

Germany joins other countries in urging Turkey to exercise moderation in its military operations against the Kurds in northern Iraq.

The Treaty of Schengen (originally from 1985) goes into effect, abolishing passport and border controls at most of the EU's internal borders. "Schengen Europe" consists of Austria, Belgium, France, Germany, Greece, Italy, Luxembourg, the Netherlands, Malta, Portugal, and Spain. The latter three become main entry points for African immigrants.

After the Dayton Peace Accords in December, most Bosnian refugees are sent back. About 80,000 remain.

The World Trade Organization is created to enable, oversee, and extend free trade among the member states. Germany, along with 75 other member states, is one of the founding members. (All 25 EU member states are WTO members.)

1996   The German Bundestag passes a law to protect minorities that stipulates that nobody shall be disadvantaged on the basis of gender, sexual preference, heritage, race, language, origin, faith, religious belief, political views, or disability.

On May 15–16, the first Carnival of Cultures takes place in Berlin.

1997   On November 1, the Act to Amend Foreigner and Asylum Provisions goes into effect, facilitating the expulsion and deportation of noncitizens who have committed a crime.

Germany implements visas for children from Bosnia, Herzegovina, the Yugoslav Republic, Croatia, Macedonia, Slovenia, Turkey, and Tunisia.

1998   According to the Ministry of the Interior, 9.37 million noncitizens live in Germany. Some 2.1 million are Turks, and one out of four foreigners in Germany is from another EU state.

The Islamic Federation in Berlin brings successful legal action against the state, obtaining permission to offer Islamic religious education (in the Turkish language) in the city's public schools. Teachers of Islam are recruited from Turkey.

Interior Minister Manfred Kanther declares 1998 the Year of Security, introducing higher penalties for illegal immigration.

In February, at the Conference of German Interior Ministers it is decided to continue deporting asylum seekers to Algeria, despite widespread violence and persecution in that country. In 1997, only 2 percent of Algerian asylum requests were accepted. The state of North Rhine–Westphalia institutes an option for battered noncitizen women to receive self-standing visas.

In March, the coalition government rejects reform of the 1913 Empire- and State-Citizenship Law.

In May, Foreign Minister Klaus Kinkel declares that Germany will withdraw aid from countries that resist Germany's efforts to deport their citizens. This decision affects approximately 70,000 individuals from Ghana, Nigeria, Togo, Gambia, Sudan, Vietnam, Bangladesh, Sri Lanka, Pakistan, and India.

In July, the CDU election platform calls for reducing government-subsidized housing for foreigners and rejecting the possibility of dual citizenship. The state of Baden-Württemberg prohibits Muslim women educators from wearing head scarves in the classroom.

A general election victory for Gerhard Schröder (SPD) leads to a coalition with the Green Party.

In November, the newly appointed commissioner of foreigner affairs, Marieluise Beck (Green Party), plans to campaign for Germany's image as a "country of immigration."

1999   Close to 4 million ethnic Germans *(Aussiedler)* have immigrated to Germany since 1950, including 2 million since 1990.

In January, the CSU, under the leadership of Edmund Stoiber, begins a petition campaign against dual citizenship because of its "massive potential for violence." Observers credit this campaign for the party's win in the elections in the state of Hesse.

In February, demonstrations take place in many German cities against Turkish commandos' arrest of the Kurdish PKK party leader Abdullah Öcalan, fugitive chief of the Kurdistan Workers Party, in Kenya. Some 60,000 Kurds live in Berlin, most of them from Turkey. Many of the 7,000 Iraqis, 2,000 Iranians, and 1,300 Syrians living in Germany have Kurdish ancestry.

France and Germany's interior ministers declare that the two countries will formulate a common deportation practice, as well as common goals for immigration politics.

On May 1, the Treaty of Amsterdam goes into effect, amending the Maastricht Treaty and transferring responsibility for asylum and migration policy to the EU. The member states agree to make Europe a common "area of freedom, security and justice."

In June, the ministers of education from 29 European countries pledge in the so-called Bologna Declaration to create a common European standard for higher education and academic degrees, including the introduction of undergraduate (bachelor) and post-graduate levels by 2010. The large-scale reform gives students and teachers freedom of mobility in Europe.

2000   The new citizenship law takes effect. Children born to foreigners in Germany automatically receive German citizenship, as long as one parent has been a legal resident for at least eight years. Children can also hold the nationality of their parents but must select a single country of citizenship no later than at age 23.

The German government creates a foundation, Erinnerung, Verantwortung, Zukunft (Remembrance, Responsibility, and Future), to compensate the millions of people who were forced into labor (*Zwangsarbeiter* or *Fremdarbeiter*) under the Nazis.

Germany has 7.3 million legal resident foreigners; 2 million of them are Turkish citizens, of whom 750,000 were born in Germany. About a third of non-Germans are from other European countries.

The PISA study is published, which evaluates performance in reading and mathematics among 15-year-olds in the 32 states of the Organization for Economic Cooperation and Development. In this survey, German students finish in the lower third. The public is shocked by the results and attributes them to German-language deficiencies among immigrant youth.

In February, Chancellor Schröder announces his Green Card initiative at a computer-trade show in Hannover, creating an exception to the ban on the recruitment of foreign labor for 20,000 foreign computer specialists to fill gaps in domestic expertise. Some 17,000 people apply for a Green Card over the next four years; their residency is limited to a maximum of five years.

In July, a bombing attack in Düsseldorf injures nine immigrants from the former Soviet Union.

In August, a court finds three teenage skinheads guilty of murdering Alberto Adriano, a father of three, who had come to East Germany from Mozambique in the 1980s.

On November 9, 200,000 Germans march in Berlin to show their opposition to an upsurge in neo-Nazi, antiforeigner, and anti-Semitic violence. Banners read, "We stand for a humane and tolerant Germany, open to the world."

On November 10, the Bundestag backs a ban against the extremist right-wing NPD. The ban fails when the Federal Constitutional Court discovers that many of the party's leaders were undercover agents from the German secret services.

A Jewish high school in Berlin graduates its first class since 1938.

2001   In May, the so-called Süssmuth report on German immigration is delivered to the Bundestag. It argues for new legislation on immigration. The pros and cons of restricting immigration are debated until summer 2004.

In August, Interior Minister Otto Schily presents his draft for a comprehensive immigration law.

On September 11, Mohammed Atta, who lived in Hamburg from 1993 to 2000, crashes a plane into New York City's World Trade Center. A student of urban planning at the Technical University of Hamburg and a citizen of Egypt and Saudi Arabia, Atta was the leader of an Al-Qaeda cell in Hamburg that included several hijackers. He entered the United States in June 2000.

2002   On January 1, euro notes and coins replace the German mark as official currency. The euro is shared by 12 of the EU's 25 members.

A Reform rabbinical seminary, Abraham Geiger College, is established in Potsdam. Increasingly, German universities offer Jewish Studies departments or institutes.

The suicide of an Algerian asylum seeker who had spent eight months in the holding section of the Frankfurt Airport intensifies churches' and refugee organizations' critiques of federal government procedures. Claiming no fault, the government releases seven detainees on humanitarian grounds.

On December 18, Germany's Federal Constitutional Court nullifies Germany's new Immigration Act because of an irregularity in voting.

2003   In November, the European Justice and Home Affairs Council introduces biometrics in EU visas and residence permits. The Visa Information System takes effect to further harmonize national laws in visa processing, combat illegal immigration, and increase security within the EU.

2004   Seven of 16 German states consider the head scarf a religious symbol and forbid public-school teachers to wear it in the classroom.

Some 3.5 million Muslims (about 4 percent of the population) live in Germany.

Ten new countries (Czech Republic, Poland, Hungary, Estonia, Latvia, Lithuania, Malta, Slovakia, Slovenia, and Cyprus) join the European Union.

In February, Fatih Akın's *Gegen die Wand /Head-On* wins first prize at the Berlin Film Festival.

On May 24, the CDU, CSU, SPD, FDP, and Green Party agree on a compromise, and both houses of Parliament pass the Immigration Act.

On October 12, Germany deports Metin Kaplan (the so-called Caliph of Cologne) to Turkey after an eight-year trial. Kaplan was the leader of the forbidden Islamist group Kalifatstaat. Kaplan had called for the assassination of his political rival Ibrahim Sofu, who was shot in 1997.

Approximately 150,000 Germans leave Germany for the United States, Canada, Switzerland, Austria, and 200 other countries. This number of German emigrants is the highest in the postwar period, 18 percent more than in 2003.

On November 21, 20,000 Muslims demonstrate in Cologne against the use of violence in the name of Islam. "Terror has neither a religion nor a nationality," says Rıdvan Çakır, director of the Turkish-Islamic Religion Organization. German politicians from all parties participate. Claudia Roth, leader of the Green Party, declares, "Islam should not only be tolerated as a guest-worker religion but must be recognized as part of our own culture."

2005   On January 1, the new Immigration Act takes effect and opens the door to legal immigration, thus officially recognizing Germany as an "immigration country."

Of an overall population of 82.5 million, 7.3 million are non-German; 1.8 million are Turks; about a half million are Italians and people from former Yugoslavia.

An estimated 200,000 Jews reside in Germany, making it the third largest and the fastest growing Jewish community in a European country. About half of them are represented by the Central Council of Jews in Germany.

Since 2000, 1 million immigrants have become German citizens.

Germany has an estimated 1.4 million undocumented residents.

The Bundesamt für Migration and Flüchtlinge (Government Office for Migration and Refugees) provides free integration courses *(Integrationskurse)*, which consist of 600 hours of German-language instruction and 30 hours of "orientation." The classes are mandatory for all immigrants and permanent residents who do not speak the language.

On February 3, Germany announces record postwar unemployment of more than 5 million people. Unemployment among migrants lies between 20 and 40 percent.

One in four marriages are between Germans and members of other ethnic groups.

The birthrate sinks to a historic low of 680,000, about half of what it was during the mid-1960s; 8.5 babies were born in Germany for every 1,000 residents—the lowest number in Europe.

Nearly 18,000 foreign doctors work in Germany (12,500 from EU countries, 3,800 from Asia, 1,591 from Russia, 1,265 from Iran, 1,265 from Greece, and 820 from Africa). About 12,000 German doctors have moved abroad.

On February 7, Hatun Sürücü, a 24-year-old Turkish-German woman, is shot by her three brothers because she violated the honor of her family by "living like a German." For the German media, the crime of "honor killing" affirms the dangers of "parallel worlds" and "misguided tolerance."

In the so-called visa affair, Foreign Minister Joschka Fischer is accused of allowing lax handling of visa applications in the former Soviet Union. In 1999, the German Embassy in Kiev, Ukraine, issued more than 150,000 visas for Germany without a security check, leading to illegal immigration and human trafficking.

On May 18, a German court strips three naturalized Turkish Islamists of their German citizenship because they failed to disclose their affiliation to Milli Görüş, the largest Islamist group in Germany (with 26,500 members), known for its opposition to Western democratic principles. According to the court, citizenship is restricted to those who pledge allegiance to the German constitution.

In June, Germany places restrictions on the immigration of Jews from the former Soviet Union. Applicants must now obtain a certificate from a synagogue in Germany affirming that they will be accepted into the community. The law passes with the consent of the Central Council of Jews in Germany, which represents some 105,000 of the estimated 180,000 Jews living in Germany today.

France and the Netherlands vote against a European constitution.

Stern magazine claims that no fewer than 200,000 Russians live in Berlin.

The European Union starts negotiations with Turkey about joining the union.

In November, following the death of two teenagers chased by police, two weeks of riots by immigrant youth throughout low-income neighborhoods in 300 French cities lead to debates in Germany about whether such riots could also happen in Berlin. The commentators are cautiously optimistic, claiming that immigrants seem to be better integrated in Germany than in France.

On November 22, after very close elections, the Social Democrats and the Christian Democrats form a grand coalition and vote in Angela Merkel (CDU) as federal chancellor of Germany. She is the first female chancellor and the first chancellor from the former East Germany.

Two exhibitions present the history of immigration in Germany. *Projekt Migration* opens in Cologne, and *Zuwanderungsland Deutschland: Migrationen 1500–2000 (Immigration Country Germany: Migrations 1500–2000)* opens in Berlin. The former is organized by DOMiT, a documentation and research center for the study of migration; the Cologne Kunstverein; and other organizations. The latter is sponsored by the German Historical Museum.

On December 20, only a few German newspapers mark the fiftieth anniversary of the first guest-worker treaty with Italy.

Asylanten: Pejorative term for asylum seekers (*Asylsuchende* or *Asylbewerber*)—that is, refugees from non-European countries who seek protection from political or other persecution.

Ausländer: Foreigner, a person without a German passport. Etymologically, the word refers to someone who lives in *elende*, which is Middle High German for "misery."

Ausländerbeauftragte: Commissioner of foreigner affairs, a position established by federal and municipal governments in the late 1970s to foster the integration of labor migrants and their family members.

Aussiedler: Resettlers. The term refers to repatriated ethnic Germans who emigrated to Germany. (See also *Spätaussiedler* and *Volksdeutsche*.)

Doppelpass: Originally a one-two pass in soccer, now "double passport," a catchphrase commonly invoked in the dual-citizenship debates of the 1990s.

Duldung: Toleration. Technical term for deferment of deportation for up to one year in the case of asylum seekers and refugees.

Einbürgerung: Naturalization. Immigrants can now obtain German citizenship (*Staatsbürgerschaft*) after eight years of residency.

Einwanderungsland: Immigration country. From 1913 to 2000, German citizenship was primarily based on *ius sanguinis*, not *ius soli*—the law of blood, not the law of territory. The Immigration Act of 2005 was the first law to officially acknowledge Germany as an immigration country.

Flüchtling: Refugee. After 1945, *Flüchtling* was a term for expellees *(Heimatvertriebene)* from Eastern Europe who came to settle in Germany. Many such refugees organized themselves into the Sudetendeutsche Landsmannschaft and, with the support of the CSU, became a strong political interest group in postwar Germany. Approximately 12 million such refugees were integrated into West and East Germany between 1945 and 1950.

Gastarbeiter: Guest worker. A term for labor migrants from 1955 to 1973, this neologism replaced *Fremdarbeiter*, or foreign worker, a term that gained notoriety under National Socialism.

Green Card: Unlike its American counterpart, the German Green Card was a five-year work permit available to highly qualified workers in the computer and information-technology industries.

Grundgesetz: Basic Law, the constitution of the Federal Republic of Germany, drafted in 1949.

Heimat: Native land, homeland, or home. This untranslatable German word connotes romantic yearning for a sense of belonging and suggests pastoral landscapes and regionalism, as in *Heimatfilm.*

Heimatvertriebene: Expellees from their homeland, mainly from Eastern Europe after Germany's defeat in 1945. (See also *Flüchtling.*)

Kanake: The German *Kolonial-Lexikon* of 1920 lists "kanaka" as a word for *human* in indigenous Polynesian languages, later used by Europeans to refer to Pacific Islanders. In recent decades, the word became an ethnic slur against "southern" migrants; it was reappropriated in the 1990s by Feridun Zaimoğlu's book *Kanak Sprak* and by the activist network Kanak Attak.

Kontingentflüchtlinge: Refugees as part of a special quota who received residency permits (circumventing the strict asylum law). Vietnamese boat people, refugees from Kosovo, and, after 1990, some 200,000 Russian Jews entered the country as "quota refugees."

Leitkultur: Guiding culture. Conservative politician Friedrich Merz mobilized the term in October 2000 and triggered widespread debate in the German media. Whether the term meant "constitutional patriotism," belief in Western values, German-language skills, or "order and cleanliness" was never clarified.

Mitbürger: Fellow citizen. The term is often used in the context of *Ausländische Mitbürger,* or foreign fellow citizens, who have no legal citizenship status.

Multikulti: Diminutive term for multiculturalism. The term is used either to promote cultural diversity, as in Berlin's Radio Multikulti, or to caricature the "relativist ethos" of multiculturalism as utopian or naïve.

Parallelgesellschaft: Literally, parallel society. This term has become a catchword for the perceived collapse of multicultural society and a retreat into ghettos.

Schengen–Europa: A recent term referring to the 1985 Treaty of Schengen (a town in Luxembourg), signed by Belgium, France, Germany, Luxembourg, and the Netherlands. The agreement ends all border checkpoints and customs controls among European countries.

Spätaussiedler: Literally, late resettlers. The term refers to ethnic Germans from the "East" (Russia, Hungary, Romania) who immigrated to Germany after 1992. Today's *Spätaussiedler* need to prove German descent more thoroughly and take a test to demonstrate that they have "actively engaged in a German way of life" *(deutsche Lebensart).*

Übersiedler: Germans who moved from East Germany to West Germany.

Volk: People, folk. Connotes the ineffable essence of an organic entity determined by blood and territory.

Volksdeutsche: Ethnic Germans. Popularized under National Socialism, the term sought to denote members of the greater German Reich. This group included so-called Volga Germans (farmers who have settled in Russia along the Volga River since the eighteenth century), Baltic Germans, and Germans in colonies in Eastern Europe.

Zuwanderung: Literally, "in-migration" or "added migration." Marking a subtle linguistic difference from *Einwanderung* (immigration), legislators called the 2005 Immigration Act *Zuwanderungsgesetz,* suggesting—maybe in a last act of rhetorical resistance to the concept of U.S.-style immigration—a difference between a native core population and additions to that population. Germany, then, is a *Zuwanderungsland,* not an *Einwanderungsland.*

BIBLIOGRAPHY

Nonfiction and Scholarly Works

Adelson, Leslie A. *Making Bodies, Making History: Feminism and German Identity*. Lincoln: University of Nebraska Press, 1993.

———. *The Turkish Turn in Contemporary German Literature: Toward a New Critical Grammar of Migration*. New York: Palgrave, 2005.

Ahonen, Pertti. *After the Expulsion: West Germany and Eastern Europe, 1945–1990*. New York: Oxford University Press, 2003.

Akashe-Böhme, Farideh. *Die islamische Frau ist anders*. Gütersloh: Gütersloher Verlagshaus, 1997.

Akbulut, Nazire. *Das Türkenbild in der neueren deutschen Literatur, 1970–1990*. Berlin: Köster, 1993.

Alba, Richard, Peter Schmidt, and Martina Wasmer, eds. *Germans or Foreigners? Attitudes Toward Ethnic Minorities in Post-reunification Germany*. New York: Palgrave, 2003.

Allinger, Elke. *. . . da sind wir keine Ausländer mehr: Eingewanderte ArbeiterInnen in Berlin, 1961–1993*. Berlin: Die Geschichtswerkstatt, 1993.

Amirsedghi, Nasrin, and Thomas Bleicher, eds. *Literatur der Migration*. Mainz: Donata Kinzelbach Verlag, 1997.

Amodeo, Immacolata. *"Die Heimat heisst Babylon." Zur Literatur ausländischer Autoren in der Bundesrepublik Deutschland*. Opladen: Westdeutscher Verlag, 1996.

Anderson, Benedict. *Imagined Communities: Reflections on the Origin and Spread of Nationalism*. London/New York: Verso, 1991.

Angenendt, Steffen, ed. *Migration und Flucht: Aufgaben und Strategien für Deutschland, Europa und die Internationale Gemeinschaft*. Munich: Oldenbourg, 1997.

———, ed. *Asylum and Migration Policies in the European Union*. Berlin: Europa Union Verlag, 1999.

Ansay, Tugrul, and Volkmar Gessner. *Gastarbeiter in Gesellschaft und Recht*. Munich: Beck, 1974.

Appadurai, Arjun. *Modernity at Large: Cultural Dimensions of Globalization*. Minneapolis: University of Minnesota Press, 1996.

Ardagh, John. *Germany and the Germans*. London: Hamish Hamilton, 1987.

Arens, Hiltrud. *"Kulturelle Hybridität" in der deutschen Minoritätenliteratur der achtziger Jahre*. Tübingen: Stauffenberg, 2003.

Argun, Betigül Ercan. *Turkey in Germany: The Transnational Sphere of Deutschkei*. New York: Routledge, 2003.

Ayim, May, and Silke Mertins. *Grenzenlos und unverschämt*. Berlin: Orlanda Frauenverlag, 1997.

Bade, Klaus J., ed. *Auswanderer-Wanderarbeiter-Gastarbeiter: Bevölkerung, Arbeitsmarkt und Wanderung in Deutschland seit dem 19. Jahrhunderts.* Ostfildern: Scripta, 1984.

―――, ed. *Das Manifest der 60: Deutschland und die Einwanderung.* Munich: Beck, 1994.

―――, ed. *Deutsche im Ausland—Fremde in Deutschland. Migration in Geschichte und Gegenwart.* Munich: Beck, 1992.

―――, ed. *Ausländer, Aussiedler, Asyl: Eine Bestandsaufnahme.* Munich: Beck, 1994.

―――, ed. *Die multikulturelle Herausforderung: Menschen über Grenzen—Grenzen über Menschen.* Munich: Beck, 1996.

―――, and Myron Weiner, eds. *Migration Past, Migration Future: Germany and the United States.* Providence, R.I.: Berghahn, 1997.

―――, and Rainer Münz. *Migrationsreport 2000. Fakten—Analysen—Perspektiven.* Frankfurt am Main: Campus, 2000.

―――. *Europa in Bewegung: Migration vom späten 18. Jahrhundert bis zur Gegenwart.* Munich: Beck, 2000.

―――, and Rainer Münz. *Migrationsreport 2002.* Frankfurt am Main: Campus, 2002.

―――, Michael Bommes, and Rainer Münz. *Migrationsreport 2004.* Frankfurt am Main: Campus, 2004.

―――, ed. *Sozialhistorische Migrationsforschung.* Göttingen: Vandenhoeck & Ruprecht, 2004.

Baier, Lothar. *Die verleugnete Utopie: zeitkritische Texte.* Berlin: Aufbau Taschenbuch Verlag, 1993.

Balibar, Etienne. *We, the People of Europe? Reflections on Transnational Citizenship.* Princeton, N.J.: Princeton University Press, 2004.

Barbieri, William A. *Ethics of Citizenship: Immigration and Group Rights in Germany.* Durham, N.C.: Duke University Press, 1998.

Bassewitz, Gert von, and Kunstamt Kreuzberg. *Morgens Deutschland, Abends Türkei.* Berlin: Fröhlich und Kaufmann, 1981.

Bauböck, Rainer. *Transnational Citizenship: Membership and Rights in International Migration.* Brookfield, Vt.: E. Elgar, 1994.

Baumann, Martin. *Migration, Religion, Integration: Buddhistische Vietnamesen und Hinduistische Tamilen in Deutschland.* Marburg: Diagonal-Verlag, 2000.

Beck, Ulrich. *What Is Globalization?* Trans. Patrick Camiller. Cambridge: Polity Press, 2000.

Beck-Gernsheim, Elisabeth. *Juden, Deutsche und andere Erinnerungslandschaften: Im Dschungel der ethnischen Kategorien.* Frankfurt am Main: Suhrkamp, 1999.

Behrends, Jan C., Thomas Lindenberger, and Patrice G. Poutrus. *Fremde und Fremd-Sein in der DDR: Zu historischen Ursachen der Fremdenfeindlichkeit in Ostdeutschland.* Berlin: Metropol, 2003.

Beier-deHaan, Rosmarie, ed. *Zuwanderungsland Deutschland: Migrationen 1500–2005.* Berlin: Deutsches Historisches Museum, 2005.

Beitter, Ursula E. *Literatur und Identität: Deutsch-deutsche Befindlichkeiten und die multikulturelle Gesellschaft.* New York: P. Lang, 2000.

―――. *The New Europe at the Crossroads: Europe's Classical Heritage in the Twenty-first Century.* New York: P. Lang, 2001.

Benhabib, Seyla. *The Intellectual Challenge of Multiculturalism and Teaching the Canon.* New York: Routledge, 1996.

————. *The Claims of Culture: Equality and Diversity in the Global Era.* Princeton, N.J.: Princeton University Press, 2002.

————. *The Rights of Others: Aliens, Residents, and Citizens.* New York: Cambridge University Press, 2004.

Benz, Wolfgang. *Integration ist machbar: Ausländer in Deutschland.* Munich: Beck, 1993.

Berger, John, and Jean Mohr. *A Seventh Man: A Book of Images and Words about the Experience of Migrant Workers in Europe.* Harmondsworth, England: Penguin, 1975.

Bergmann, Sven, and Regina Römhild, eds. *Global Heimat. Ethnografische Recherchen im transnationalen Frankfurt.* Frankfurt am Main: Institut für Kulturanthropologie und Europäische Ethnologie, 2003.

Bergmann, Werner, and Rainer Erb. *Anti-Semitism in Germany: The Post-Nazi Epoch Since 1945.* New Brunswick, N.J.: Transaction Publishers, 1997.

Berman, Russell A., Azade Seyhan, and Arlene Akiko Teraoka, eds. *Minorities in German Culture. New German Critique,* no. 46 (Special Issue, Winter 1989).

Bhabha, Homi, ed. *Nation and Narration.* London/New York: Routledge, 1990.

————. *The Location of Culture.* London/New York: Routledge, 1994.

Bickle, Peter. *Heimat: A Critical Theory of the German Idea of Homeland.* Rochester, N.Y.: Camden House, 2004.

Bielefeld, Uli. *Das Eigene und das Fremde: Neuer Rassismus in der Alten Welt?* Hamburg: Junius, 1991.

Bielefeldt, Heiner, and Wilhelm Heitmeyer. *Politisierte Religion: Ursachen und Erscheinungsformen des modernen Fundamentalismus.* Frankfurt am Main: Suhrkamp, 1998.

Bierwirth, Waltraud, and Nihat Öztürk, eds. *Migration hat viele Gesichter: 50 Jahre Einwanderungsgeschichte(n).* Essen: Klartext, 2003.

Bill, Edgar. *Immigration and Homelessness in Europe.* Bristol, England: Policy Press, 2004.

Bingemer, Karl, Edeltraut Meistermann Seeger, and Edgar Neubert. *Leben als Gastarbeiter: Geglückte und missglückte Integration.* Cologne: Westdeutscher Verlag, 1970.

Bloch, Alice, and Carl Levy, eds. *Refugees, Citizenship and Social Policy in Europe.* New York: St. Martin's Press, 1999.

Bommes, Michael. *Migration und nationaler Wohlfahrtsstaat: Ein differenzierungstheoretischer Entwurf.* Opladen: Leske + Budrich, 1999.

————, and Andrew Geddes, eds. *Immigration and Welfare: Challenging the Borders of the Welfare State.* New York: Routledge, 2000.

————. *International Migration Research: Constructions, Omissions, and the Promises of Interdisciplinarity.* Burlington, Vt.: Ashgate, 2005.

Borneman, John, and Jeffrey Peck, *Sojourners: The Return of German Jews and the Question of Identity.* Lincoln: University of Nebraska Press, 1995.

Borrelli, Michele, ed. *Minderheiten in der Bundesrepublik.* Stuttgart: Metzler, 1973.

Bremer, Peter. *Ausgrenzungsprozesse und die Spaltung der Städte: Zur Lebenssituation von Migranten.* Opladen: Leske + Budrich, 2000.

Brenner, Michael. *After the Holocaust: Rebuilding Jewish Lives in Postwar Germany.* Trans. Barbara Harshav. Princeton, N.J.: Princeton University Press, 1997.

Brettell, Caroline, and James Frank Hollifield, eds. *Migration Theory: Talking Across the Disciplines.* London/New York: Routledge, 2000.

Brinker-Gabler, Gisela, and Sidonie Smith, eds. *Writing New Identities: Gender, Nation and Immigration in Contemporary Europe.* Minneapolis: University of Minnesota Press, 1997.

Broder, Henryk M. *A Jew in the New Germany.* Urbana: University of Illinois Press, 2004.

Bröskamp, Bernd. *Schwarz-weisse Zeiten: AusländerInnen in Ostdeutschland vor und nach der Wende: Erfahrungen der Vertragsarbeiter aus Mosambik: Interviews, Berichte, Analysen.* Bremen: IZA, 1993.

Brubaker, Rogers. *Citizenship and Nationhood in France and Germany.* Cambridge, Mass.: Harvard University Press, 1992.

———. *Nationalism Reframed: Nationhood and the National Question in the New Europe.* New York: Cambridge University Press, 1996.

Brumlik, Micha. *Jüdisches Leben in Deutschland seit 1945.* Frankfurt am Main: Jüdischer Verlag bei Athenäum, 1986.

———, and Hartmut M. Griese. *Der gläserne Fremde: Bilanz und Kritik der Gastarbeiterforschung und Ausländerpädagogik.* Opladen: Leske + Budrich, 1984.

Bubis, Ignatz. *Juden in Deutschland.* Berlin: Aufbau Taschenbuch Verlag, 1996.

Bukow, Wolf-Dietrich, and Roberto Llaryora. *Mitbürger aus der Fremde: Soziogenese ethnischer Minoritäten.* Opladen: Westdeutscher Verlag, 1988.

Butterwegge, Christoph, ed. *Medien und multikulturelle Gesellschaft.* Opladen: Leske + Budrich, 1999.

———, and Gudrun Hentges, eds. *Zuwanderung im Zeichen der Globalisierung: Migration-, Integrations- und Minderheitenpolitik.* Opladen: Leske + Budrich, 2003.

Caporaso, James, Thomas Risse, Maria Green Cowles, Peter J. Katzenstein, Thomas Risse-Kappen, eds. *Transforming Europe: Europeanization and Domestic Change.* Ithaca, N.Y.: Cornell University Press, 2001.

Castles, Stephen. *The Age of Migration: International Population Movements in the Modern World.* New York: Guilford Press, 2003.

Cesarani, David, and Mary Fulbrook, eds. *Citizenship, Nationality and Migration in Europe.* London/New York: Routledge, 1996.

Chakrabarty, Dipesh. *Provincializing Europe: Postcolonial Thought and Historical Difference.* Princeton, N.J.: Princeton University Press, 2000.

Chambers, Iain. *Migrancy, Culture, Identity.* London/New York: Routledge, 1994.

Chapin, Wesley D. *Germany for the Germans? The Political Effects of International Migration.* Westport, Conn.: Greenwood Press, 1997.

Cheah, Pheng, and Bruce Robbins, eds. *Cosmopolitics: Thinking and Feeling Beyond the Nation.* Minneapolis: University of Minnesota Press, 1998.

Cheesman, Tom, and Karin Yeşilada, eds. *Zafer Şenocak.* Cardiff: University of Wales Press, 2003.

Chiellino, Carmine. *Am Ufer der Fremde: Literatur und Arbeitsmigration, 1870–1990.* Stuttgart: Metzler, 1995.

———. *Fremde: A Discourse of the Foreign.* Trans. Luise von Flotow. New York: Guernica, 1995.

———, ed. *Interkulturelle Literatur in Deutschland: Ein Handbuch.* Stuttgart: Metzler, 2000.

———. *In Sprachen leben: Meine Ankunft in der deutschen Sprache.* Dresden: Thelem, 2003.

Cohn-Bendit, Daniel, Liselotte Funcke, and Heiner Geißler. *Einwanderbares Deutsch-*

land: Oder Vertreibung aus dem Wohlstands-Paradies? Frankfurt am Main: Horizonte, 1991.

Cohn-Bendit, Daniel, and Thomas Schmid. *Heimat Babylon: Das Wagnis der multikulturellen Demokratie.* Hamburg: Hoffmann und Campe, 1992.

Cornelius, Wayne A., Philip L. Martin, and James F. Hollifield, eds. *Controlling Immigration: A Global Perspective.* Stanford, Calif.: Stanford University Press, 1994.

Dauenhauer, Bernard P. *Citizenship in a Fragile World.* Lanham, Md.: Rowman & Littlefield Publishers, 1996.

Dayıoğlu-Yücel, Yasemin. *Von der Gastarbeit zur Identitätsarbeit: Integritätsverhandlungen in türkisch-deutschen Texten von Şenocak, Özdamar, Ağaoğlu und der On-line-Community vaybee!* Göttingen: Universitätsverlag, 2005.

Demir, Mustafa, and Ergün Sönmez. *Die anderen Deutschen: 40 Jahre Arbeitsmigration: Von Gastarbeitern zur nationalen Minderheit.* Berlin: Verlag für Wissenschaft und Bildung, 2001.

Derrida, Jacques. *The Other Heading: Reflections on Today's Europe.* Bloomington: Indiana University Press, 1992.

DOMiT (Dokumentationszentrum und Museum über die Migration aus der Türkei e.V.), ed. *40 Jahre Fremde Heimat—Einwanderung aus der Türkei in Köln.* Cologne: DOMiT, 2001.

Döring, Hans-Joachim. *Es geht um unsere Existenz: Die Politik der DDR gegenüber der Dritten Welt am Beispiel von Mosambik und Äthiopien.* Berlin: Links, 1999.

Dunkel, Franziska, and Gabriella Stramaglia-Faggion, eds. *Zur Geschichte der Gastarbeiter in München: "für 50 Mark einen Italiener."* Munich: Buchendorfer, 2000.

Eley, Geoff, and R. G. Suny, eds. *Becoming National: A Reader.* New York: Oxford University Press, 1996.

Elsaesser, Thomas. *Fassbinder's Germany: History, Identity, Subject.* Amsterdam: University of Amsterdam Press, 1996.

Elsner, Eva-Maria, and Lothar Elsner. *Zwischen Nationalismus und Internationalismus: Über Ausländer und Ausländerpolitik in der DDR, 1949–1990.* Rostock: Norddeutsche Hochschulschriften, 1994.

Enzensberger, Hans Magnus. *Civil Wars: From L.A. to Bosnia.* New York: New Press, 1994. (Contains "The Great Migration.")

Eryılmaz, Aytaç, and Matilde Jamin, eds. *Fremde Heimat = Yaban Sılan Olur: Eine Geschichte der Einwanderung aus der Türkei.* Ausstellungskatalog des Essener Ruhrlandmuseums. Essen: Klartext, 1998.

Even, Herbert, and Lutz Hoffmann. *Soziologie der Ausländerfeindlichkeit: Zwischen nationaler Identität und multikultureller Gesellschaft.* Weinheim: Beltz, 1984.

Fachinger, Petra. *Rewriting Germany from the Margins: "Other" German Literature of the 1980s and 1990s.* Montreal: McGill University Press, 2001.

Faist, Thomas. *Social Citizenship for Whom? Young Turks in Germany and Mexican Americans in the United States.* Aldershot/Brookfield, Vt.: Avebury, 1995.

———. *The Volume and Dynamics of International Migration and Transnational Social Spaces.* New York: Oxford University Press, 2000.

———, and Eyüp Özveren, eds. *Transnational Social Spaces: Agents, Networks, and Institutions.* Burlington, Vt.: Ashgate, 2004.

Farin, Klaus, and Eberhard Seidel-Pielen. *Skinheads.* Munich: C. H. Beck, 1993.

Fassmann, Heinz, and Rainer Münz. *European Migration in the Late Twentieth Century:*

Historical Patterns, Actual Trends, and Social Implications. Brookfield, Vt.: E. Elgar, 1994.

Fehrenbach, Heide. *Race After Hitler. Black Occupation Children in Postwar Germany and America.* Princeton, N.J.: Princeton University Press, 2005.

Fijalkowski, Jürgen. *Aggressive Nationalism, Immigration Pressure, and Asylum Policy Disputes in Contemporary Germany.* Washington, D.C.: German Historical Institute, 1993.

Finzsch, Norbert, and Dietmar Schirmer, eds. *Identity and Intolerance: Nationalism, Racism, and Xenophobia in Germany and the United States.* Cambridge: Cambridge University Press, 1998.

Fischer, Gerhard. *Debating Enzensberger: "Great Migration" and "Civil War."* Tübingen: Stauffenburg, 1996.

Fischer, Sabine, and Moray McGowan. *Denn du tanzt auf einem Seil: Positionen deutschsprachiger MigrantInnenliteratur.* Tübingen: Stauffenburg, 1997.

Franzen, K. Erik, and Hans Lemberg. *Die Vertriebenen: Hitlers letzte Opfer.* Berlin: Propyläen, 2001.

Frederking, Monika. *Schreiben gegen Vorurteile. Literatur türkischer Migranten in der Bundesrepublik Deutschland.* Berlin: Express, 1985.

Frei, Kerstin. *Wer sich maskiert, wird integriert: Der Karneval der Kulturen in Berlin.* Berlin: Schiler, 2003.

Frieben-Blum, Ellen, Klaudia Jacobs, and Brigitte Wiessmeier, eds. *Wer ist fremd? Ethnische Herkunft, Familie und Gesellschaft.* Opladen: Leske + Budrich, 2000.

Friedrichsmayer, Sara, Sara Lennox, and Susanne Zantop, eds. *The Imperialist Imagination.* Ann Arbor: University of Michigan Press, 1998.

Fritsche, Klaus. *Vietnamesische Gastarbeiter in den europäischen RGW-Ländern.* Cologne: Bundesinstitut für Ostwissenschaftliche und Internationale Studien, 1991.

Geddes, Andrew. *Immigration and European Integration: Towards Fortress Europe?* Manchester: Manchester University Press, 2000.

————, and Adrian Favell, eds. *The Politics of Belonging: Migrants and Minorities in Contemporary Europe.* Aldershot, England: Ashgate, 1999.

Geiersbach, Paul. *Bruder, muss zusammen Zwiebel und Wasser essen! Eine türkische Familie in Deutschland.* Berlin: Dietz, 1982.

————. *Ein Türkenghetto in Deutschland: Gott auch in der Fremde dienen.* Berlin: Mink-Verlag, 1989.

Gelbin, Cathy S., Kader Konuk, and Peggy Piesche, eds. *Aufbrüche: Kulturelle Produktion von Migrantinnen, Schwarzen und jüdischen Frauen in Deutschland.* Königstein/Taunus: Ulrike Helmer, 1999.

Geller, Jay Howard. *Jews in Post-Holocaust Germany.* Cambridge: Cambridge University Press, 2005.

Gilman, Sander. *On Blackness without Blacks: Essays on the Image of the Black in Germany.* Boston: Hall, 1982.

————, and Karin Remmler. *Jews in Today's German Culture.* Bloomington: Indiana University Press, 1995.

————, and Jack Zipes, eds. *The Yale Companion to Jewish Writing and Thought in German Culture, 1096–1996.* New Haven, Conn.: Yale University Press, 1997.

Göktürk, Deniz, and Barbara Wolbert, eds. *Multicultural Germany: Art, Performance, and Media. New German Critique* 92 (Special Issue, Spring/Summer 2004).

Gottschlich, Jürgen. *Die Türkei auf dem Weg nach Europa*. Berlin: Links Verlag, 2004.

Green, Simon. *The Politics of Exclusion: Institutions and Immigration Policy in Contemporary Germany*. Manchester: Manchester University Press, 2004.

Greve, Martin. *Die Musik der imaginären Türkei: Musik und Musikleben im Kontext der Migration aus der Türkei in Deutschland*. Stuttgart: Metzler, 2003.

Griese, Christiane, and Helga Marburger. *Zwischen Internationalismus und Patriotismus: Konzepte des Umgangs mit Fremden und Fremdheit in den Schulen der DDR*. Frankfurt am Main: IKO-Verlag für Interkulturelle Kommunikation, 1995.

Grimm, Reinhold, and Jost Hermand, eds. *Blacks and German Culture*. Madison: University of Wisconsin Press, 1986.

Gruber, Ruth Ellen. *Virtually Jewish: Reinventing Jewish Culture in Europe*. Berkeley: University of California Press, 2002.

Gundara, Jagdish S., and Sidney Jacobs. *Intercultural Europe: Diversity and Social Policy*. Brookfield, Vt.: Ashgate, 2000.

Habermas, Jürgen. *The Inclusion of the Other: Studies in Political Theory*. Ciaran Cronin and Pablo De Greif, eds. Cambridge, Mass.: The MIT Press, 1998.

———. *The Postnational Constellation: Political Essays*. Trans. Max Pensky. Cambridge, Mass.: The MIT Press, 2001.

Hailbronner, Kay, ed. *Immigration Admissions: The Search for Workable Policies in Germany and the United States*. Providence, R.I.: Berghahn, 1997.

Hailbronner, Kay, David Martin, and Hiroshi Motomura, eds. *Immigration Controls: The Search for Workable Policies in Germany and the United States*. Providence, R.I.: Berghahn, 1998.

Hamm, Horst. *Fremdgegangen Freigeschrieben: Einführung in die deutsche Gastarbeiterliteratur*. Würzburg: Königshausen und Neumann, 1988.

Hammar, Thomas. *European Immigration Policy: A Comparative Study*. Cambridge: Cambridge University Press, 1985.

Han, Petrus. *Soziologie der Migration*. Stuttgart: Lucius and Lucius, 2005.

Hanagan, Michael P., and Charles Tilly. *Extending Citizenship, Reconfiguring States*. Lanham, Md.: Rowman & Littlefield, 1999.

Hannerz, Ulf. *Transnational Connections: Culture, People, Places*. London/New York: Routledge, 1996.

Hansen, Georg. *Die Deutschmachung: Ethnizität und Ethnisierung im Prozess von Ein- und Ausgrenzungen*. Münster: Waxmann, 2001.

Hansen, Randall, and Patrick Weil, eds. *Towards a European Nationality: Citizenship, Immigration and Nationality Law in the EU*. New York: Palgrave, 2001.

Hassan, Salah, and Iftikhar Dadi, eds. *Unpacking Europe*. Rotterdam: NAi Publishers, 2001.

Haus der Kulturen der Welt, *Heimat Kunst*. Berlin: Haus der Kulturen der Welt, 2000.

Heckmann, Friedrich. *Die Bundesrepublik: ein Einwanderungsland?* Stuttgart: Klett-Cotta, 1981.

———. *Ethnische Minderheiten, Volk und Nation: Soziologie inter-ethnischer Beziehungen*. Stuttgart: Enke, 1992.

Hedetoft, Ulf, and Mette Hjort. *The Postnational Self: Belonging and Identity*. Minneapolis: University of Minnesota Press, 2002.

Hefner, Margarete, Manfred Scholer, and Klaus Grabicke, eds. *Der Gastarbeiter als Konsument.* Göttingen: Schwartz, 1978.

Heinemann, Karl-Heinz, and Wilfried Schubarth, eds. *Der antifaschistische Staat entlässt seine Kinder: Jugend und Rechtsextremismus in Ostdeutschland.* Cologne: Papy-Rossa, 1992.

Heinze, Hartmut. *Migrantenliteratur in der Bundesrepublik Deutschland: Bestandsaufnahme und Entwicklungstendenzen zu einer multikulturellen Literatursynthese.* Berlin: Express Edition, 1986.

Heitmeyer, Wilhelm, and Reimund Anhut, eds. *Bedrohte Stadtgesellschaft: Soziale Desintegrationsprozesse und ethnisch-kulturelle Konfliktkonstellationen.* Weinheim: Juventa, 2000.

Herbert, Ulrich. *A History of Foreign Labor in Germany, 1880–1980: Seasonal Workers, Forced Laborers, Guest Workers.* Ann Arbor: University of Michigan Press, 1990.

———. *Hitler's Foreign Workers.* Cambridge: Cambridge University Press, 1997.

———. *Geschichte der Ausländerpolitik in Deutschland: Saisonarbeiter, Zwangsarbeiter, Gastarbeiter, Flüchtlinge.* Munich: Beck, 2001.

Herminghouse, Patricia, and Magda Müller, eds. *Gender and Germanness: Cultural Productions of Nation.* Providence, R.I.: Berghahn, 1997.

Herzog, Todd, and Sander L. Gilman, eds. *A New Germany in a New Europe.* London/New York: Routledge, 2001.

Hochstadt, Steve. *Mobility and Modernity: Migration in Germany, 1820–1989.* Ann Arbor: University of Michigan Press, 1999.

Hoerder, Dirk, and Leslie Page Moch, eds. *European Migrants: Global and Local Perspectives.* Boston: Northeastern University Press, 1996.

———. *Cultures in Contact: World Migrations in the Second Millennium.* Durham, N.C.: Duke University Press, 2002.

Holert, Tom, and Mark Terkessidis, eds. *Mainstream der Minderheiten: Pop in der Kontrollgesellschaft.* Berlin/Amsterdam: Edition ID-Archiv, 1996.

Hollifield, James F. *Immigrants, Markets, and State: The Political Economy of Postwar Europe.* Cambridge, Mass.: Harvard University Press, 1992.

Hollinger, David A. *Postethnic America: Beyond Multiculturalism.* New York: Basic Books, 2000.

Horrocks, David, and Eva Kolinsky, eds. *Turkish Culture in German Society Today.* Providence, R.I.: Berghahn, 1996.

Howard, Mary, ed. *Interkulturelle Konfigurationen: Zur deutschsprachigen Erzählliteratur von Autoren nichtdeutscher Herkunft.* Munich: Iudicium, 1997.

Hunn, Karin. *"Nächstes Jahr kehren wir zurück . . .": Die Geschichte der türkischen "Gastarbeiter" in der Bundesrepublik.* Göttingen: Wallerstein, 2005.

Huntington, Samuel P. *The Clash of Civilizations and the Remaking of World Order.* New York: Simon & Schuster, 1996.

Ireland, Patrick. *Becoming Europe: Immigration, Integration, and the Welfare State.* Pittsburgh, Pa.: University of Pittsburgh Press, 2004.

Jacobmeyer, Wolfgang. *Vom Zwangsarbeiter zum heimatlosen Ausländer: Die Displaced Persons in Westdeutschland, 1945–1951.* Göttingen: Vandenhoeck & Ruprecht, 1985.

Jacobson, David. *Rights across Borders: Immigration and the Decline of Citizenship.* Baltimore: Johns Hopkins University Press, 1996.

Jahrbuch für Kulturpolitik 2002/3. Thema: Interkultur. Essen: Klartext, 2003.

Jameson, Frederic. *The Geopolitical Aesthetic: Cinema and Space in the World System.* London: British Film Institute, 1992.

————, and M. Miyoshi. *The Cultures of Globalization.* Durham, N.C.: Duke University Press, 1998.

Jankowsky, Karen Hermine, and Carla Love, eds. *Other Germanies: Questioning Identity in Women's Literature and Art.* Albany: State University of New York Press, 1997.

JanMohamed, Abdul R., and David Lloyd, eds. *The Nature and Context of Minority Discourse.* New York: Oxford University Press, 1990.

Jarausch, Konrad H., ed. *After Unity: Reconfiguring German Identities.* Providence, R.I.: Berghahn, 1997.

Joppke, Christian. *Challenge to the National State: Immigration in Western Europe and the United States.* Oxford: Oxford University Press, 1998.

Jung, Matthias, Thomas Niehr, and Karin Böke. *Ausländer und Migranten im Spiegel der Presse: Ein diskurshistorisches Wörterbuch zur Einwanderung seit 1945.* Wiesbaden: Westdeutscher Verlag, 2000.

Kaes, Anton. *From Hitler to Heimat: The Return of History as Film.* Cambridge, Mass.: Harvard University Press, 1989.

Kahn, Charlotte. *Resurgence of Jewish Life in Germany.* Westport, Conn.: Praeger, 2004.

Kastoryano, Riva. *Negotiating Identities: States and Immigrants in France and Germany.* Princeton, N.J.: Princeton University Press, 2002.

Katsoulis, Haris. *Bürger zweiter Klasse: Ausländer in der Bundesrepublik.* Frankfurt am Main/ New York: Campus, 1978.

Katzenstein, Peter J. *Policy and Politics in Germany: The Growth of a Semisovereign State.* Philadelphia: Temple University Press, 1987.

Kaya, Ayhan. *Sicher in Kreuzberg: Constructing Diasporas: Turkish Hip-Hop Youth in Berlin.* Piscataway, N.J.: Transaction Publishers, 2001.

Keim, Inken. *Gastarbeiterdeutsch: Untersuchungen zum sprachlichen Verhalten türkischer Gastarbeiter.* Tübingen: Narr, 1978.

Kessler, Mario. *Die SED und die Juden: Zwischen Repression und Toleranz: Politische Entwicklungen bis 1967.* Berlin: Akademie, 1995.

Kiesel, Doron, and Rosi Wolf-Almanasreh. *Die multikulturelle Versuchung: Ethnische Minderheiten in der deutschen Gesellschaft.* Arnoldshainer Texte, v. 71. Frankfurt am Main: Haag + Herchen, 1991.

Kiesel, Doron, Astrid Messerschmidt, and Albert Scherr, eds. *Die Erfindung der Fremdheit: Zur Kontroverse um Gleichheit und Differenz im Sozialstaat.* Frankfurt am Main: Brandes & Apsel, 1998.

Klee, Ernst. *Gastarbeiter: Analysen und Berichte.* Frankfurt am Main: Suhrkamp Verlag, 1972.

Kleff, Sanem. *BRD—DDR: Alte und neue Rassismen im Zuge der deutsch-deutschen Einigung.* Frankfurt am Main: Verlag für Interkulturelle Kommunikation, 1990.

Kleßman, Christoph, and Georg Wagner, eds. *Das gespaltene Land: Leben in Deutschland, 1945–1990: Texte und Dokumente zur Sozialgeschichte.* Munich: Beck, 1993.

Klopp, Brett. *German Multiculturalism: Immigrant Integration and the Transformation of Citizenship.* Westport, Conn.: Praeger, 2002.

Kloss, Heinz. *Deutsch in der Begegnung mit anderen Sprachen.* Tübingen: Narr, 1974.

Knecht, Michi, and Levent Soysal, eds. *Plausible Vielfalt: Wie der Karneval der Kulturen denkt, lernt und Kultur schafft.* Berlin: Panama Verlag, 2005.

Knight, Ute, and Wolfgang Kowalsky. *Deutschland nur den Deutschen? Die Ausländerfrage in Deutschland, Frankreich, und den US.* Erlangen: Straube Verlag, 1992.

Ködderitzsch, Peter, and Leo Müller. *Rechtsextremismus in der DDR.* Göttingen: Lamuv, 1990.

Kolb, Holger. *Einwanderung und Einwanderungspolitik am Beispiel der deutschen Green Card.* Osnabrück, Germany: Der Andere Verlag, 2002.

Kolinsky, Eva. *Deutsch und türkisch leben: Bild und Selbstbild der türkischen Minderheit in Deutschland.* Bern: P. Lang, 2000.

Kölnischer Kunstverein und Dokumentationszentrum und Museum über die Migration in Deutschland e.V. (DOMiT), et al., eds. *Projekt Migration.* Cologne: DuMont, 2005.

Köpp, Günther, and Hans-Dietrich von Löffelholz. *Ökonomische Auswirkungen der Zuwanderung nach Deutschland.* Berlin: Duncker & Humblot, 1998.

Körber-Stiftung, ed. *Nation und Integration von Migranten in Deutschland.* Hamburg: Körber-Stiftung, 1997.

———. *Religion—ein deutsch-türkisches Tabu? / Türk-Alman İlişkilerinde Din Tabu Mu?* Hamburg: Körber-Stiftung, 1997.

Koslowski, Rey. *Migrants and Citizens.* Ithaca, N.Y.: Cornell University Press, 2000.

Kosta, Barbara, and Helga Kraft, eds. *Writing Against Boundaries: Nationality, Ethnicity and Gender in the German-Speaking Context.* Amsterdam/New York: Rodopi, 2003.

Kramer, Jane. *Politics of Memory: Looking for Germany in the New Germany.* New York: Random House, 1996.

Krane, Ronald. *Manpower Mobility Across Cultural Boundaries: Social, Economic, and Legal Aspects: The Case of Turkey and West Germany.* Leiden, Netherlands: Brill, 1975.

———, ed. *International Migration in Europe.* New York: Praeger, 1979.

Kubat, Daniel, ed. *The Politics of Migration Policies: The First World in the 1970s.* New York: Center for Migration Studies, 1979.

Küchler, Ulla. *Fadime: Eine türkische Familie in Deutschland.* Munich: Kunstmann, 1991.

Kurthen, Hermann, ed. *Immigration, Citizenship, and the Welfare State in Germany and the United States.* Stamford, Conn.: JAI Press, 1998.

———, Werner Bergmann, and Rainer Erb, eds. *Antisemitism and Xenophobia in Germany after Unification.* New York: Oxford University Press, 1997.

Kymlicka, Will. *Multicultural Citizenship: A Liberal Theory of Minority Rights.* New York: Oxford University Press, 1996.

Lachmann, Günter, and Ayaan Hirsi Ali. *Tödliche Toleranz. Die Muslime und unsere offene Gesellschaft.* Munich: Piper, 2005.

Lajos, Karl, ed. *Die zweite und dritte Ausländergeneration.* Opladen: Westdeutscher Verlag, 1991.

Lamping, Dieter. *Über Grenzen: Eine literarische Topographie.* Göttingen: Vandenhoeck & Ruprecht, 2001.

Lang, Barbara. *Mythos Kreuzberg: Ethnographie eines Stadtteils 1961 bis 1995.* Frankfurt am Main: Campus, 1998.

Laufer, Peter. *Exodus to Berlin: The Return of the Jews to Germany.* Chicago: Ivan R. Dee, 2003.

Lavenex, Sandra. *The Europeanisation of Refugee Policies: Between Human Rights and Internal Security.* Aldershot, England: Ashgate, 2001.

Layton-Henry, Zig, ed. *The Political Rights of Migrant Workers in Western Europe*. London: Sage, 1990.

Layton-Henry, Zig, and Czarina Wilpert. *Challenging Racism in Britain and Germany*. New York: Palgrave, 2003.

Legge, Jerome S. *Jews, Turks, and Other Strangers: The Roots of Prejudice in Modern Germany*. Madison: University of Wisconsin Press, 2003.

Leggewie, Claus, ed. *Multi Kulti: Spielregeln für die Vielvölkerrepublik*. Berlin: Rotbuch, 1990.

———, and Zafer Şenocak, eds. *Deutsche Türken / Türk Almanlar*. Reinbek: Rowohlt, 1993.

Lemmen, Thomas. *Islamische Organisationen in Deutschland*. Bonn: Friedrich-Ebert-Stiftung, 2000.

Lengfeld, Holger. *Entfesselte Feindbilder: Über die Ursachen und Erscheinungsformen von Fremdenfeindlichkeit*. Berlin: Edition Sigma, 1995.

Lester, Rosemarie. *"Trivialneger": Das Bild des Schwarzen im westdeutschen Illustriertenroman*. Stuttgart: Heinz, 1982.

Leung, Maggi. *Chinese Migration in Germany: Making Home in Transnational Space*. Frankfurt am Main: IKO Verlag, 2005.

Linke, Uli. *German Bodies: Race and Representation after Hitler*. London/New York: Routledge, 1999.

Loh, Hannes, and Murat Güngör. *Fear of a Kanak Planet: Hip Hop zwischen Weltkulturen und Nazi-Rap*. St. Andrä-Wördern: Hannibal, 2002.

Lorbeer, Marie, ed. *Multikulturelles Berlin*. Berlin: Elefanten Press, 1984.

Lützeler, Paul Michael. *Europäische Identität und Multikultur: Fallstudien zur deutschsprachigen Literatur seit der Romantik*. Tübingen: Stauffenburg, 1997.

Malchow, Barbara. *Die fremden Deutschen*. Reinbek: Rowohlt, 1990.

Manfrass, Klaus. *Türken in der Bundesrepublik, Nordafrikaner in Frankreich*. Bonn: Bouvier, 1991.

Marshall, Barbara. *The New Germany and Migration in Europe*. Manchester: Manchester University Press, 2000.

Martin, Philip L. *The Unfinished Story: Turkish Labour Migration to Western Europe*. Geneva: International Labor Organization, 1991.

———. *Germany: Reluctant Land of Immigration*. Washington, D.C.: The American Institute for Contemporary German Studies, 1998.

Maturi, Giacomo. *Arbeitsplatz, Deutschland: Wie man südländische Gastarbeiter verstehen lernt*. Mainz: Krausskopf, 1964.

Mayer, Hans. *Außenseiter*. Frankfurt am Main: Suhrkamp, 1975.

Mayer, Ruth, and Mark Terkissidis, eds. *Globalkolorit: Multikulturalismus und Populärkultur*. St. Andrä-Wördern: Hannibal, 1998.

Mecheril, Paul, and Thomas Teo. *Andere Deutsche: Zur Lebenssituation von Menschen multiethnischer und multikultureller Herkunft*. Berlin: Dietz Verlag, 1994.

Mehrländer, Ursula. *Soziale Aspekte der Ausländerbeschäftigung*. Bonn: Neue Gesellschaft, 1974.

———. *Ausländerforschung 1965 bis 1980: Fragestellungen, theoretische Ansätze, empirische Ergebnisse*. Bonn: Neue Gesellschaft, 1987.

Meier-Braun, Karl-Heinz. *"Gastarbeiter" oder Einwanderer?* Berlin: Ullstein, 1980.

————, and Yüksel Pazarkaya. *Die Türken: Berichte und Informationen zum besseren Verständnis der Türken in Deutschland.* Berlin: Ullstein, 1983.

————. *Deutschland, Einwanderungsland.* Frankfurt am Main: Suhrkamp, 2002.

Micksch, Jürgen, ed. *Deutschland—Einheit in kultureller Vielfalt.* Frankfurt am Main: Otto Lembeck, 1991.

Miles, Robert, and Dietrich Thränhardt, eds. *Migration and European Integration: The Dynamics of Inclusion and Exclusion.* London: Pinter, 1995.

Milich, Klaus J., and Jeffrey Peck, eds. *Multiculturalism in Transit: A German-American Exchange.* New York: Berghahn, 1998.

Moch, Leslie Page. *Moving Europeans: Migration in Western Europe since 1650.* Bloomington: Indiana University Press, 2003.

Modood, Tariq, and Pnina Werbner, eds. *The Politics of Multiculturalism in the New Europe: Racism, Identity, and Community.* London/New York: Zed Books, 1997.

Morgenstern, Christine. *Rassismus: Konturen einer Ideologie: Einwanderung im politischen Diskurs der Bundesrepublik Deutschland.* Hamburg: Argument Verlag, 2002.

Morley, David. *Home Territories: Media, Mobility and Identity.* London/New York: Routledge, 2000.

Morley, David, and Kevin Robins. *Spaces of Identity: Global Media, Electronic Landscapes and Cultural Boundaries.* London/New York: Routledge, 1995.

Motte, Jan, and Rainer Ohliger, eds. *Geschichte und Gedächtnis in der Einwanderungsgesellschaft: Migration zwischen historischer Rekonstruktion und Erinnerungspolitik.* Essen: Klartext, 2004.

Motte, Jan, Rainer Ohliger, and Anne von Oswald, eds. *50 Jahre Bundesrepublik—50 Jahre Einwanderung: Nachkriegsgeschichte als Migrationsgeschichte.* Frankfurt am Main: Campus, 1999.

Müller, Christian Th., and Patrice Poutrus, eds. *Ankunft—Alltag—Abreise: Migration und Interkulturelle Begegnung in der DDR-Gesellschaft.* Vienna/Cologne: Böhlau, 2005.

Münz, Rainer, and Myron Weiner, eds. *Migrants, Refugees, and Foreign Policy.* Providence, R.I.: Berghahn, 1997.

————, Wolfgang Seifert, and Ralf Ulrich, eds. *Zuwanderung nach Deutschland. Strukturen, Wirkungen, Perspektiven.* Frankfurt am Main: Campus, 1997.

————, and Rainer Ohliger, eds. *Diasporas and Ethnic Migrants: Germany, Israel and Post-Soviet Successor States in Comparative Perspective.* London/Portland, Ore.: Frank Cass, 2003.

Murphy, Richard Charles. *Guestworkers in the German Reich: A Polish Community in Wilhelmian Germany.* New York: Columbia University Press, 1983.

Naficy, Hamid, ed. *Home, Exile, Homeland: Film, Media, and the Politics of Place.* London/New York: Routledge, 1999.

————. *An Accented Cinema: Exilic and Diasporic Filmmaking.* Princeton, N.J.: Princeton University Press, 2001.

Neapel—Bochum—Rimini: Arbeiten in Deutschland—Urlaub in Italien [Italienische Zuwanderung und Deutsche Italiensehnsucht im Ruhrgebiet]. Katalog zur Ausstellung des Westfälischen Industriemuseums. Essen: Klartext, 2003.

Nirumand, Bahman. *Im Namen Allahs.* Cologne: Dreisam-Verlag, 1990.

————. *Angst vor den Deutschen: Terror gegen Ausländer und der Zerfall des Rechtsstaates.* Reinbek: Rowohlt, 1992.

Ohliger, Rainer, Karen Schönwalder, and Triadafilos Triadafilopoulos, eds. *European*

Encounters: Migrants, Migration, and European Societies since 1945. Burlington, Vt.: Aldershot, 2003.

Ong, Aihwa. *Flexible Citizenship: The Cultural Logics of Transnationality.* Durham, N.C.: Duke University Press, 1999.

Ostergaard-Nielsen, Eva. *Transnational Politics: Turks and Kurds in Germany.* London: Routledge, 2003.

Otyakmaz, Berrin Özlem. *Auf allen Stühlen: Das Selbstverständnis junger türkischer Migrantinnen in Deutschland.* Cologne: ISP, 1995.

Özdemir, Cem. *Ich bin Inländer: Ein anatolischer Schwabe im Bundestag.* Munich: Deutscher Taschenbuch Verlag, 1997.

———. *Currywurst und Döner: Integration in Deutschland.* Bergisch Gladbach: G. Lübbe, 1999.

Pagenstecher, Cord. *Ausländerpolitik und Immigrantenidentität: Zur Geschichte der "Gastarbeit" in der Bundesrepublik.* Berlin: Bertz, 1994.

Pallaske, Christoph. *Migrationen aus Polen in die Bundesrepublik in den 1980er und 1990er Jahren.* Münster: Waxmann Verlag, 2002.

Palm, Dorothee. *Frauengeschichten: Musliminnen in Deutschland erzählen aus ihrem Leben.* Cologne: Teiresias, 2000.

Parekh, Bhikhu C. *Rethinking Multiculturalism: Cultural Diversity and Political Theory.* Cambridge, Mass.: Harvard University Press, 2000.

Peck, Jeffrey M. *Being Jewish in the New Germany.* Camden, N.J.: Rutgers University Press, 2006.

Picardi-Montesardo, Anna. *Die Gastarbeiter in der Literatur der Bundesrepublik Deutschland.* Berlin: Express Edition, 1985.

Pickus, Noah M., ed. *Immigration and Citizenship in the Twenty-First Century.* Lanham, Md.: Rowman & Littlefield, 1998.

Piper, Nicola. *Racism, Nationalism and Citizenship: Ethnic Minorities in Britain and Germany.* Brookfield, Vt.: Ashgate, 1998.

Preuss, Ulrich Klaus, and Ferran Requejo, eds. *European Citizenship, Multiculturalism, and the State.* Baden-Baden: Nomos, 1998.

Probul, Amrei. *Immigrantenliteratur im deutschsprachigen Raum: Ein kurzer Überblick.* Frankfurt am Main: R. G. Fischer, 1997.

Rabinbach, Anson, and Jack Zipes. *Germans and Jews since the Holocaust: The Changing Situation in West Germany.* New York: Holmes & Meier, 1986.

Rapport, Nigel, and Andrew Dawson, eds. *Migrants of Identity: Perceptions of Home in a World of Movement.* New York: Berg, 1998.

Reeg, Ulrike. *Schreiben in der Fremde: Literatur nationaler Minderheiten in der Bundesrepublik Deutschland.* Essen: Klartext, 1988.

Riemann, Wolfgang. *Über das Leben in Bitterland: Bibliographie zur türkischen Deutschland-Literatur und zur türkischen Literatur in Deutschland.* Wiesbaden: O. Harrassowitz, 1990.

Rifkin, Jeremy. *The European Dream: How Europe's Vision of the Future Is Quietly Eclipsing the American Dream.* New York: Penguin, 2004.

Rogers, Alisdair, and Jean Tillie. *Multicultural Policies and Modes of Citizenship in European Cities.* Burlington, Vt.: Ashgate, 2001.

Röhrich, Wilfried. *Vom Gastarbeiter zum Bürger: Ausländer in der Bundesrepublik Deutschland.* Berlin: Duncker & Humblot, 1982.

Römhild, Regina. *Die Macht des Ethnischen: Grenzfall Russlanddeutsche*. Frankfurt am Main: P. Lang, 1998.

Rommelsbacher, Birgit. *Anerkennung und Ausgrenzung: Deutschland als multikulturelle Gesellschaft*. Frankfurt am Main: Campus, 2002.

Rushdie, Salman. *Imaginary Homelands: Essays and Criticism, 1981–1991*. London: Granta, 1992.

Sassen, Saskia. *Globalization and Its Discontents: Essays on the New Mobility of People and Money*. New York: New Press, 1998.

———. *Guests and Aliens*. New York: New Press, 2000.

———. *Denationalization: Economy and Polity in a Global Digital Age*. Princeton, N.J.: Princeton University Press, 2003.

Sauter, Sven. *Wir sind "Frankfurter Türken": Adoleszente Ablösungsprozesse in der deutschen Einwanderungsgesellschaft*. Frankfurt am Main: Brandes & Apsel, 2000.

Schiffauer, Werner. *Die Gewalt der Ehre: Erklärungen zu einem deutsch-türkischen Sexualkonflikt*. Frankfurt am Main: Suhrkamp, 1983.

———. *Die Migranten aus Subay: Türken in Deutschland: Eine Ethnographie*. Stuttgart: Klett-Cotta, 1991.

———. *Fremde in der Stadt*. Frankfurt am Main: Suhrkamp, 1997.

———. *Die Gottesmänner: Türkische Islamisten in Deutschland: Eine Studie zur Herstellung religiöser Evidenz*. Frankfurt am Main: Suhrkamp, 2000.

Schissler, Hanna, ed. *The Miracle Years: A Cultural History of West Germany, 1949–1968*. Princeton, N.J.: Princeton University Press, 2001.

Schissler, Hanna, and Yasemin N. Soysal, eds. *The Nation, Europe, and the World: Textbooks and Curricula in Transition*. New York: Berghahn, 2005.

Schmalz-Jacobsen, Cornelia, Georg Hansen, and Rita Polm, eds. *Ethnische Minderheiten in der Bundesrepublik Deutschland: Ein Lexikon*. Munich: Beck, 1997.

Schneider, Jens. *Deutsch sein: Das Eigene, das Fremde und die Vergangenheit im Selbstbild des vereinten Deutschland*. Frankfurt am Main: Campus, 2001.

Schönwälder, Karen. *Einwanderung und ethnische Pluralität: Politische Entscheidungen und öffentliche Debatten in Grossbritannien und der Bundesrepublik von den 1950er bis zu den 1970er Jahren*. Essen: Klartext, 2001.

Schröter, Hiltrud. *Mohammeds deutsche Töchter*. Königstein: U. Helmer, 2002.

Schuck, Peter, and Rainer Münz, eds. *Paths to Inclusion: The Integration of Migrants in the United States and Germany*. New York: Berghahn, 1998.

Schwarzer, Alice. *So sehe ich das!: Über die Auswirkung von Macht und Gewalt auf Frauen und andere Menschen*. Cologne: Kiepenheuer & Witsch, 1997.

Seibert, Wolfgang. *Nach Auschwitz wird alles besser: Die Roma und Sinti in Deutschland*. Hamburg: Libertäre Assoziation, 1984.

Seidel-Pielen, Eberhard. *Unsere Türken: Annäherung an ein gespaltenes Verhältnis*. Berlin: Elefanten Press, 1995.

———. *Aufgespießt: Wie der Döner über die Deutschen kam*. Hamburg: Rotbuch, 1996.

Seifert, Wolfgang. *Geschlossene Grenzen—offene Gesellschaften? Migrations- und Integrationsprozesse in westlichen Industrienationen*. New York: Campus, 2000.

Şen, Faruk, and Andreas Goldberg. *Türken in Deutschland: Leben zwischen zwei Kulturen*. Munich: Beck, 1994.

Şen, Faruk, and Hayrettin Aydın. *Islam in Deutschland*. Munich: Beck, 2002.

Şenocak, Zafer. *Atlas of a Tropical Germany. Essays on Politics and Culture, 1990–1998*. Trans. and ed. Leslie A. Adelson. Lincoln: University of Nebraska Press, 1999.

Seufert, Gunter, and J. J. Waardenburg. *Turkish Islam and Europe = Turkischer Islam und Europa: Europe and Christianity as Reflected in Turkish Muslim Discourse and Turkish Muslim Life in the Diaspora*. Istanbul/Stuttgart: Franz-Steiner-Verlag, 1999.

Seyhan, Azade. *Writing Outside the Nation*. Princeton, N.J.: Princeton University Press, 2001.

Shafi, Monika. *Balancing Acts: Intercultural Encounters in Contemporary German and Austrian Literature*. Tübingen: Stauffenburg, 2001.

Shohat, Ella, and Robert Stam. *Unthinking Eurocentrism: Multiculturalism and the Media*. London/New York: Routledge, 1994.

Sieg, Katrin. *Ethnic Drag: Performing Race, Nation, Sexuality in West Germany*. Ann Arbor: University of Michigan Press, 2002.

Siegler, Bernd. *Auferstanden aus Ruinen: Rechtsextremismus in der DDR*. Berlin: Edition Tiamat, 1991.

Sölçün, Sargut. *Sein und Nichtsein: Zur Literatur in der multikulturellen Gesellschaft*. Bielefeld: Aisthesis, 1992.

Sollors, Werner. *The Invention of Ethnicity*. New York: Oxford University Press, 1991.

———. *Neither Black Nor White Yet Both: Thematic Explorations of Interracial Literature*. Cambridge, Mass.: Harvard University Press, 1999.

Sørensen, Jens Magleby. *The Exclusive European Citizenship: The Case for Refugees and Immigrants in the European Union*. Brookfield, Vt.: Avebury, 1996.

Soysal, Levent. "Projects of Culture: An Ethnographic Episode in the Life of Migrant Youth in Berlin." Ph.D. diss., Harvard University, 1999.

Soysal, Yasemin N. *Limits of Citizenship: Migrants and Postnational Membership in Europe*. Chicago: The University of Chicago Press, 1994.

Steinmann, Gunter, and Ralf E. Ulrich, eds. *The Economic Consequences of Immigration to Germany*. Heidelberg: Physica-Verlag, 1994.

Steyerl, Hito, and Encarnación Gutiérrez Rodríguez, eds. *Spricht die Subalterne Deutsch? Migration und postkoloniale Kritik*. Münster: Unrast Verlag, 2003.

Straube, Hanne. *Türkisches Leben in der Bundesrepublik*. Frankfurt am Main: Campus, 1987.

Taberner, Stuart, ed. *German Literature in the Age of Globalisation*. Birmingham, England: Birmingham University Press, 2004.

———, and Frank Finlay, eds. *Recasting German Identity*. Rochester, N.Y.: Camden House, 2002.

Taylor, Charles. *Multiculturalism: Examining the Politics of Recognition*. Princeton, N.J.: Princeton University Press, 1994.

Tebbutt, Susan. *Sinti and Roma: Gypsies in German-Speaking Society and Literature*. New York: Berghahn, 1998.

Teitelbaum, Michael S., and Jay Winter. *A Question of Numbers: High Migration, Low Fertility, and the Politics of National Identity*. New York: Hill & Wang, 1998.

Teraoka, Arlene. *East, West, and Others: The Third World in Postwar German Literature*. Lincoln: University of Nebraska Press, 1996.

Terkessidis, Mark. *Kulturkampf: Volk, Nation, der Westen und die Neue Rechte*. Cologne: Kiepenheuer & Witsch, 1995.

————. *Migranten*. Hamburg: Rotbuch, 2000.

————. *Die Banalität des Rassismus: Migranten zweiter Generation entwickeln eine neue Perspektive*. Bielefeld: Transcript, 2004.

Tertilt, Hermann. *Turkish Power Boys: Ethnographie einer Jugendbande*. Frankfurt am Main: Suhrkamp, 1996.

Thränhardt, Dietrich, ed. *Europe, a New Immigration Continent: Policies and Politics in Comparative Perspective*. Münster: Lit, 1992.

————. *Einwanderung und Einbürgerung in Deutschland*. Münster: Lit, 1998.

Thum, Bernd, and Thomas Keller, eds. *Interkulturelle Lebensläufe*. Tübingen: Stauffenburg Verlag, 1998.

Tichy, Roland. *Ausländer rein! Warum es kein "Ausländerproblem" gibt*. Munich: Piper, 1990.

Traverso, Enzo. *The Jews and Germany: From the "Judeo-German Symbiosis" to the Memory of Auschwitz*. Lincoln: University of Nebraska Press, 1995.

Treibel, Annette. *Migration in modernen Gesellschaften: Soziale Folgen von Einwanderung, Gastarbeit und Flucht*. Weinheim/Munich: Juventa, 1999.

Treichler, Andreas. *Wohlfahrtsstaat, Einwanderung und ethnische Minderheiten: Probleme, Entwicklungen, Perspektiven*. Wiesbaden: Westdeutscher Verlag, 2002.

Tsiakalos, Giorgios. *Ausländerfeindlichkeit*. Munich: Beck, 1983.

Vertovec, Steven, and Peach Ceri, eds. *Islam in Europe: The Politics of Religion and Community*. New York: St. Martin's Press, 1997.

Vertovec, Steven, and Robin Cohen, eds. *Conceiving Cosmopolitanism: Theory, Context, and Practice*. New York: Oxford University Press, 2002.

Veteto-Conrad, Marilya. *Finding a Voice: Identity and the Works of German-Language Turkish Writers in the Federal Republic of Germany to 1990*. New York: P. Lang, 1990.

Vink, Maarten Peter. *Limits of European Citizenship: European Interaction and Domestic Immigration Policies*. New York: Palgrave Macmillan, 2005.

Von Moltke, Johannes. *No Place Like Home: Locations of Heimat in German Cinema*. Berkeley: University of California Press, 2005.

Waldhoff, Hans-Peter, Dursun Tan, and Elçin Kürsat-Ahlers, eds. *Brücken zwischen Zivilisationen: Zur Zivilisierung ethnisch-kultureller Differenzen und Machtungleichheiten: Das Türkisch-Deutsche Beispiel*. Frankfurt am Main: IKO, 1997.

Watts, Meredith W. *Xenophobia in United Germany: Generations, Modernization and Ideology*. New York: St. Martin's Press, 1997.

Weibel, Peter, and Slavoj Žižek, eds. *Inklusion, Exklusion: Probleme des Postkolonialismus und der globalen Migration*. Vienna: Passagen, 1997.

Weicken, Helmuth. *Ausländische Arbeitskräfte in Deutschland*. Düsseldorf: Econ Verlag, 1961.

Weidacher, Alois, ed. *In Deutschland zu Hause: Politische Orientierungen griechischer, italienischer, türkischer und deutscher junger Erwachsener im Vergleich*. Opladen: Leske + Budrich, 2000.

Weidenfeld, Werner, ed. *Das europäische Einwanderungskonzept*. Gütersloh: Bertelsmann Stiftung, 1994.

Welz, Gisela. *Inszenierungen kultureller Vielfalt: Frankfurt am Main und New York City*. Berlin: Akademie, 1996.

Werner, Jan. *Die Invasion der Armen: Asylanten und illegale Einwanderer*. Mainz: Hase and Koehler, 1992.

Wicker, H.-R. *Rethinking Nationalism and Ethnicity: The Struggle for Meaning and Order in Europe.* New York: Berg, 1997.

Wiener, Antje. *"European" Citizenship Practice: Building Institutions of a Non-State.* Boulder, Colo.: Westview Press, 1998.

Wilson, Rob, and Wimal Dissanayake, eds. *Global / Local: Cultural Production and the Transnational Imaginary.* Durham, N.C.: Duke University Press, 1996.

Wlecklik, Petra. *Multikultur statt Deutschtum? Antirassismus zwischen Folklore und ethnischem Mythos.* Bonn: Protext, 1996.

Wolbert, Barbara. *Migrationsbewältigung: Orientierungen und Strategien: Biographisch-interpretative Fallstudien über die "Heirats-Migration" dreier Türkinnen.* Göttingen: Edition Herodot, 1984.

———. *Der getötete Pass: Rückkehr in die Türkei: Eine ethnologische Migrationsstudie.* Berlin: Akademie, 1995.

Zank, Wolfgang. *The German Melting-Pot: Multiculturality in Historical Perspective.* New York: St. Martin's Press, 1998.

Zaptçıoğlu, Dilek. *Die Geschichte des Islam.* Frankfurt am Main/New York: Campus, 2002.

———. *Türken und Deutsche.* Frankfurt am Main: Brandes & Apsel, 2005.

Zetterholm, Staffan, ed. *National Cultures and European Integration: Exploratory Essays on Cultural Diversity and Common Policies.* Providence: Berg, 1994.

Literary Works

Anthologies

Abate, Carmine, ed. *Zwischen Fabrik und Bahnhof.* Bremen: CON Medien- und Vertriebsgesellschaft, 1981.

Acevit, Ayşegül, and Birand Bingül, eds. *Was lebst Du? Jung, deutsch, türkisch—Geschichten aus Almanya.* Munich: Knaur, 2005.

Ackermann, Irmgard, ed. *Als Fremder in Deutschland: Berichte, Erzählungen, Gedichte von Ausländern.* Munich: Deutscher Taschenbuch Verlag, 1982.

———, ed. *In zwei Sprachen leben: Berichte, Erzählungen, Gedichte von Ausländern.* Munich: Deutscher Taschenbuch Verlag, 1983.

———, ed. *Türken deutscher Sprache: Berichte, Erzählungen, Gedichte.* Munich: Deutscher Taschenbuch Verlag, 1984.

———, ed. *Fremde Augenblicke: Mehrkulturelle Literatur in Deutschland.* Bonn: Inter Nationes, 1996.

———, and Harald Weinrich, eds. *Eine nicht nur deutsche Literatur: Zur Standortbestimmung der "Ausländerliteratur."* Munich: Piper, 1986.

Akçam, Dursun, ed. *Deutsches Heim—Glück allein: Wie Türken Deutsche sehen/Alaman Ocağı: Türkler Almanları Anlatıyor.* Trans. Helmut Oberdick. Bornheim-Merten: Lamuv, 1982.

Aparicio, G., Suleman Taufiq, and Bernd Böhm, eds. *Wir sind fremd, Wir gehen fremd: Gedichte: Anthologie "Ausländer schreiben"; Bd. 1.* Aachen: Verlag KLENKES, 1979.

Biondi, Franco, Carmine Chiellino, and Giuseppe Giambusso. *Die Tinte und das Papier: Dichtung und Prosa italienischer Autorinnen in Deutschland: Anthologie.* Bochumer Italien-Studien, 1. Aachen: Shaker, 1999.

Biondi, Franco, Jusuf Naoum, Rafik Schami, and Suleman Taufiq, eds. *Im neuen Land.* Bremen: CON Medien- und Vertriebsgesellschaft, 1980.

Blum, Eva Maria, and Amt für Multikulturelle Angelegenheiten Frankfurt am Main. *Mit Koffern voller Träume . . . : Ältere Migrantinnen und Migranten erzählen*. Frankfurt am Main: Brandes & Apsel, 2001.

Breithaupt, Susanne. *Wahlheimat Berlin: Ältere Menschen erinnern sich: Miteinander Leben in Berlin*. Berlin: Ausländerbeauftragte des Senats, 1994.

Chiellino, Carmine. *Nach dem Gestern: Aus dem Alltag italienischer Emigranten = Dopo Ieri: Dalla vita di emigranti italiani*. Südwind Zweisprachig. Bremen: CON, 1983.

Esselborn, Karl. *Über Grenzen: Berichte, Erzählungen, Gedichte von Ausländern*. Munich: Deutscher Taschenbuch Verlag, 1987.

Förderzentrum Jugend schreibt. *Täglich eine Reise von der Türkei nach Deutschland: Texte der 2. türkischen Generation in der Bundesrepublik*. Fischerhude: Verlag Atelier im Bauernhaus, 1980.

Friedrich, Heinz, ed. *Chamissos Enkel: Literatur von Ausländern in Deutschland*. Munich: Deutscher Taschenbuch Verlag, 1986.

Göktürk, Deniz, and Zafer Şenocak, eds. *Jedem Wort gehörte ein Himmel: Türkei literarisch*. Berlin: Babel, 1991.

Hamm, Horst, Wolfgang Jung, and Heidi Knott, eds. *Flucht nach Deutschland: Lebensberichte*. Freiburg im Breisgau: Dreisam-Verlag, 1988.

Hölzl, Luisa Costa, and Eleni Torossi, eds. *Freihändig auf dem Tandem: Dreissig Frauen aus elf Ländern*. Südwind-Literatur. Kiel: Neuer Malik Verlag, 1985.

Jänicke, Julika, Helmut Lotz, and Kai Precht, eds. *Taxi-Geschichten*. Munich: Deutscher Taschenbuch Verlag, 2002.

Knott, Heidi, Horst Hamm, and Wolfgang Jung, eds. *Heimat Deutschland? Lebensberichte von Aus- und Übersiedlern*. Pfaffenweiler: Centaurus-Verlagsgesellschaft, 1991.

Lappin, Elena, ed. *Jewish Voices, German Words: Growing up Jewish in Postwar Germany and Austria*. Trans. Krishna Winston. New Haven, Conn.: Yale University Press, 1994.

Ljubic, Nicol, ed. *Feuer, Lebenslust! Erzählungen deutscher Einwanderer*. Stuttgart: Klett-Cotta, 2003.

Lorenz, Günter Wolfgang, and Yüksel Pazarkaya, eds. *Aber die Fremde ist in mir: Migrationserfahrung und Deutschlandbild in der türkischen Literatur der Gegenwart*. Stuttgart: Institut für Auslandsbeziehungen, 1985.

Lottmann, Joachim, ed. *Kanaksta: Von Deutschen und anderen Ausländern*. Generation Berlin. Berlin: Quadriga, 1999.

Madjderey, Abdolreza, ed. *Ausländer schreiben deutsche Gedichte*. Munich: K. Friedrich, 1984.

Ney, Norbert, ed. *Sie haben mich zu einem Ausländer gemacht—Ich bin einer geworden: Ausländer schreiben vom Leben bei uns*. Reinbek: Rowohlt, 1984.

Oguntoye, Katharina, and May Opitz. *Farbe bekennen: Afro-deutsche Frauen auf den Spuren ihrer Geschichte*. Frankfurt am Main: Fischer, 1992.

Özkan, Hülya, and Andrea Wörle, eds. *Eine Fremde wie ich: Berichte, Erzählungen, Gedichte von Ausländerinnen*. Munich: Deutscher Taschenbuch Verlag, 1985.

Pazarkaya, Yüksel, Dragutin Trumbetas, and Viktor Augustin, eds. *Heimat in der Fremde? Drei Kurzgeschichten: Texte in zwei Sprachen*. Stuttgart: Ararat, 1979.

Robertson, Ritchie, ed. *The German-Jewish Dialogue: An Anthology of Literary Texts, 1749–1993*. New York: Oxford University Press, 1999.

Saalfeld, Lerke v., ed. *"Ich habe eine fremde Sprache gewählt": Ausländische Schriftsteller schreiben deutsch.* Gerlingen: Bleicher Verlag, 1998.

Schaffernicht, Christian, ed. *Zu Hause in der Fremde: Ein bundesdeutsches Ausländer-Lesebuch.* Fischerhude: Atelier im Bauernhaus, 1981.

Schierloh, Heimke, ed. *Das Alles für ein Stück Brot: Migrantenliteratur als Objektivierung des "Gastarbeiterdaseins."* Frankfurt am Main: P. Lang, 1984.

Schulte, Christoph, ed. *Deutschtum und Judentum: Ein Disput unter Juden in Deutschland.* Stuttgart: Reclam, 1993.

Taufiq, Suleman, ed. *Dies ist nicht die Welt, die wir suchen: Prosa, Lyrik und Fotos von Ausländern.* Essen: Klartext, 1983.

Trojanow, Ilija, ed. *Döner in Walhalla. Texte aus der anderen deutschen Literatur.* Cologne: Kiepenheuer & Witsch, 2000.

Tuschick, Jamal, ed. *Morgen Land: Neueste deutsche Literatur.* Frankfurt am Main: Fischer Taschenbuch, 2000.

Single-Author Editions

Abate, Carmine. *Den Koffer und weg! Erzählungen.* Südwind-Literatur. Kiel: Neuer Malik Verlag, 1984.

Ağaoğlu, Adalet. *Die zarte Rose meiner Sehnsucht.* Trans. Wolfgang Scharlipp. Stuttgart: Ararat, 1979.

Aktoprak, Levent. *Ein Stein der blühen kann: Gedichte.* Berlin: Express Edition, 1985.

Akyün, Hatice. *Einmal Hans mit scharfer Sosse.* Munich: Goldmann, 2005.

Alafenisch, Salim. *Die Nacht der Wünsche: Roman.* Stuttgart: Weitbrecht, 1996.

———. *Amira, Prinzessin der Wüste.* Ravensburg: Ravensburger, 2001.

Arjouni, Jakob. *Happy Birthday, Türke! Roman.* Zürich: Diogenes, 1987.

———. *Mehr Bier: Roman.* Zürich: Diogenes, 1987.

———. *Ein Mann, ein Mord: Ein Kayankaya Roman.* Zürich: Diogenes, 1991.

———. *Magic Hoffmann: Roman.* Zürich: Diogenes, 1996.

———. *Kismet: Ein Kayankaya Roman.* Zürich: Diogenes, 2001.

———. *Idioten: Fünf Märchen.* Zürich: Diogenes, 2003.

———. *Hausaufgaben: Roman.* Zürich: Diogenes, 2004.

Asserate, Asfa-Wossen. *Manieren.* Frankfurt am Main: Eichborn, 2003.

Atabay, Cyrus. *Die Worte der Ameisen: Persische Mystik in Versen und Prosa.* Hamburg: Claassen, 1971.

———, and Ulrich Erben. *Puschkiniana: Gedichte.* Düsseldorf: Eremiten-Presse, 1990.

Ateş, Seyran. *Grosse Reise ins Feuer.* Berlin: Rowohlt, 2003.

Ayata, Imran. *Hürriyet Express: Storys.* Cologne: Kiepenheuer & Witsch, 2005.

Ayşe (pseud.) and Renate Eder. *Mich hat keiner gefragt: Zur Ehe gezwungen: Eine Türkin in Deutschland erzählt.* Munich: Blanvalet, 2005.

Bahadınlı, Yusuf Ziya. *Zwischen zwei Welten: Texte in zwei Sprachen.* Berlin: Ararat, 1980.

Banciu, Carmen-Francesca. *Fenster in Flammen: Erzählungen.* Berlin: Rotbuch, 1992.

———. *Vaterflucht: Roman.* Berlin: Volk & Welt, 1998.

———. *Berlin ist mein Paris: Geschichten aus der Hauptstadt.* Berlin: Ullstein, 2002.

———, and Georg Aescht. *Ein Land voller Helden: Roman.* Berlin: Ullstein, 2000.

Baykurt, Fakir. *Die Friedenstorte: Barış çöreği.* Stuttgart: Ararat, 1980.

————. *Nachtschicht und andere Erzählungen aus Deutschland.* Zürich: Unionsverlag, 1984.

Becker, Thorsten. *Sieger nach Punkten: Roman.* Reinbek: Rowohlt, 2004.

Biller, Maxim. *Wenn ich einmal reich und tot bin: Erzählungen.* Cologne: Kiepenheuer & Witsch, 1990.

————. *Die Tempojahre.* Munich: Deutscher Taschenbuch Verlag, 1991.

————. *Land der Väter und Verräter: Erzählungen.* Cologne: Kiepenheuer & Witsch, 1994.

————. *Esra.* Cologne: Kiepenheuer & Witsch, 2004.

————. *Bernsteintage: Sechs neue Geschichten.* Cologne: Kiepenheuer & Witsch, 2004.

Biondi, Franco. *Passavantis Rückkehr: Erzählungen 1.* Fischerhude: Atelier im Bauern- haus, 1982.

————. *Die Tarantel: Erzählungen 2.* Fischerhude: Atelier im Bauernhaus, 1982.

————. *Abschied der zerschellten Jahre: Novelle.* Südwind-Literatur. Kiel: Neuer Malik Ver- lag, 1984.

————. *Die Unversöhnlichen, oder, im Labyrinth der Herkunft: Roman.* Die Grenzenlose Bibliothek. Tübingen: Heliopolis, 1991.

————. *Ode an die Fremde: Gedichte 1973–1993.* Sankt Augustin: Avlos, 1995.

————. *In deutschen Küchen: Roman.* Frankfurt am Main: Brandes & Apsel, 1997.

Böll, Heinrich. *Gruppenbild mit Dame.* Cologne: Kiepenheuer & Witsch, 1971.

Chiellino, Gino. *Mein fremder Alltag.* Kiel: Neuer Malik-Verlag, 1984.

————. *Sehnsucht Sprache: Gedichte 1983–1985.* Kiel: Neuer Malik-Verlag, 1987.

————. *Ich in Dresden: Eine Poetikdozentur.* Wortwechsel, v. 2. Dresden: Thelem, 2003.

Çileli, Serap. *Serap: "wir sind eure töchter nicht eure ehre . . ."* Michelstadt: Neuthor- Verlag 2002.

Çırak, Zehra. *Vogel auf dem Rücken eines Elefanten: Gedichte.* Cologne: Kiepenheuer & Witsch, 1991.

————. *Fremde Flügel auf eigener Schulter: Gedichte.* Cologne: Kiepenheuer & Witsch, 1994.

————. *Leibesübungen: Gedichte.* Cologne: Kiepenheuer & Witsch, 2000.

Cumart, Nevfel. *Unterwegs zu Hause: Gedichte.* Düsseldorf: Grupello, 2003.

Dal, Güney. *Wenn Ali die Glocken läuten hört.* Trans. Brigitte Schreiber-Grabitz. Berlin: Edition der 2, 1979.

————. *Europastrasse 5: Roman.* Trans. Carl Koss. Hamburg: Buntbuch, 1981.

————. *Vögel des falschen Paradieses / Yanlış Cennetin Kuşları.* Trans. Eva Warth- Karabulut. Frankfurt am Main: Dağyeli, 1985.

————. *Der enthaarte Affe: Roman.* Trans. Carl Koss. Munich: Piper, 1988.

————. *Teestunden am Ring: Roman.* Trans. Carl Koss. Munich: Piper, 1999.

Demirkan, Renan. *Schwarzer Tee mit drei Stück Zucker.* Cologne: Kiepenheuer & Witsch, 1991.

————. *Die Frau mit Bart: Eine Erzählung.* Cologne: Kiepenheuer & Witsch, 1994.

————. *Es wird Diamanten regnen vom Himmel: Roman.* Cologne: Kiepenheuer & Witsch, 1999.

————. *Der Mond, der Kühlschrank und ich: Heimkinder erzählen.* Cologne: Kiepenheuer & Witsch, 2001.

————. *Über Liebe, Götter und Rasenmähn: Geschichten und Gedichte über die Liebe.* Mu- nich: Alliteraverlag, 2003.

Dikmen, Şinasi. *Wir werden das Knoblauchkind schon schaukeln: Satiren.* Berlin: Express Edition, 1985.

———. *Der andere Türke: Satiren.* Berlin: Express Edition, 1986.

———. *Hurra, ich lebe in Deutschland.* Munich: Piper, 1995.

Dischereit, Esther. *Übungen jüdisch zu sein: Aufsätze.* Frankfurt am Main: Suhrkamp, 1998.

El Hajaj, Mustapha. *Vom Affen der ein Visum sucht.* Wuppertal: Peter Hammer Verlag, 1969.

Engin, Osman. *Deutschling: Satiren.* Berlin: Express Edition, 1985.

———. *Der Sperrmüll-Efendi.* Reinbek: Rotbuch, 1991.

———, and Til Mette. *Alles Getürkt! Neue Geschichten zum Lachen.* Rororo Tomate. Reinbek: Rowohlt, 1992.

———. *Kanaken-Gandhi: Satirischer Roman.* Berlin: Elefanten Press, 1998.

———. *Oberkanakengeil: Deutsche Geschichten.* Berlin: Espresso, 2001.

———. *Götterratte: Roman.* Munich: Deutscher Taschenbuch Verlag, 2004.

Erzeren, Ömer. *Eisbein in Alanya: Erfahrungen in der Vielfalt des deutsch-türkischen Lebens.* Hamburg: Edition Körber-Stiftung, 2004.

Filip, Ota. *Grossvater und die Kanone: Roman.* Frankfurt am Main: Fischer, 1981.

———. *Tomatendiebe in Aserbaidschan und andere Satiren.* Frankfurt am Main: Fischer, 1981.

———. *Café Slavia: Roman.* Frankfurt am Main: Fischer, 1985.

———. *Die Sehnsucht nach Procida: Roman.* Frankfurt am Main: Fischer, 1988.

———. *Doch die Märchen sprechen Deutsch: Geschichten aus Böhmen.* Munich: Langen Müller, 1996.

———. *Die stillen Toten unterm Klee: Wiedersehen mit Böhmen.* Munich: Langen Müller, 1997.

———. *Der siebente Lebenslauf: Autobiographischer Roman.* Munich: Herbig, 2001.

———. *Das andere Weihnachten: Mährische Geschichten.* Munich: Langen Müller, 2004.

Fleischmann, Lea. *Dies ist nicht mein Land: Eine Jüdin verlässt die Bundesrepublik.* Hamburg: Hoffmann and Campe, 1980.

Füruzan. *Logis im Land der Reichen: Wie eine türkische Schriftstellerin das Leben ihrer Landsleute in Deutschland sieht.* Trans. Zehra Oyan. Munich: Deutscher Taschenbuch Verlag, 1985.

Grass, Günter. *Die Blechtrommel.* Neuwied/Berlin: Luchterhand, 1959.

———. *Unkenrufe.* Göttingen: Steidl, 1992.

Grün, Max von der. *Leben im gelobten Land: Gastarbeiterporträts.* Darmstadt: Luchterhand, 1975.

Gruša, Jiří. *Der Babylonwald: Gedichte 1988.* Stuttgart: Deutsche Verlags-Anstalt, 1991.

———. *Wandersteine: Gedichte.* Stuttgart: Deutsche Verlags-Anstalt, 1994.

Honigmann, Barbara. *Soharas Reise.* Berlin: Rowohlt, 1996.

———. *Damals, dann und danach.* Munich: Hanser, 1999.

———. *Ein Kapitel aus meinem Leben.* Munich: Hanser, 2004.

Kalkan, Hülya, and Peter Hilliges. *Ich wollte nur frei sein: Meine Flucht vor der Zwangsehe.* Berlin: Ullstein, 2005.

Kamenko, Vera, and Marianne Herzog. *Unter uns war Krieg: Autobiographie einer jugoslawischen Arbeiterin.* Berlin: Rotbuch, 1978.

Kaminer, Wladimir. *Russendisko*. Munich: Goldmann, 2000.

———. *Militärmusik: Roman*. Munich: Goldmann, 2001.

———. *Schönhauser Allee*. Munich: Goldmann 2001.

———. *Mein Deutsches Dschungelbuch*. Munich: Goldmann, 2003.

———. *Ich mache mir Sorgen, Mama*. Munich: Goldmann, 2003.

Kara, Yadé. *Selam Berlin*. Zurich: Diogenes, 2003.

Karaoulis, Kostas. *Die Finsternis*. Frankfurt am Main: Brandes & Apsel, 1988.

Karasholi, Adel. *Wenn Damaskus nicht wäre: Gedichte*. Munich: A1, 1992.

———. *Also sprach Abdulla: Gedichte*. Munich: A1 Verlag, 1995.

Kelek, Necla. *Die fremde Braut: Ein Bericht aus dem Innern des türkischen Lebens in Deutschland*. Cologne: Kiepenheuer & Witsch, 2005.

Kromschröder, Gerhard. *Als ich ein Türke war*. Frankfurt am Main: Eichborn, 1983.

Kurt, Kemal. *Scheingedichte/Şiirimsi*. Berlin: Express Edition, 1986.

———. *Was ist die Mehrzahl von Heimat? Bilder eines türkisch-deutschen Doppellebens*. Reinbek: Rowohlt, 1995.

———. *Ja, sagt Molly: Roman*. Berlin: Hitit, 1998.

Moníková, Libuše. *Die Fassade: M.N.O.P.Q*. Munich: Hanser, 1987.

———. *Eine Schädigung*. Munich: Deutscher Taschenbuch Verlag, 1990.

———. *Treibeis: Roman*. Munich: Hanser, 1992.

———. *Prager Fenster: Essays*. Munich: Hanser, 1994.

———. *Der Taumel: Roman*. Munich: Hanser, 2000.

Müller, Herta. *Drückender Tango: Prosa*. Bucharest: Kriterion, 1984.

———. *Niederungen: Prosa*. Berlin: Rotbuch, 1984.

———. *Reisende auf einem Bein*. Berlin: Rotbuch, 1989.

———. *Eine warme Kartoffel ist ein warmes Bett*. Hamburg: Europäische Verlagsanstalt, 1992.

———. *Der Wächter nimmt seinen Kamm: Vom Weggehen und Ausscheren*. Reinbek: Rowohlt, 1993.

———. *Herztier: Roman*. Reinbek: Rowohlt, 1994.

———. *In der Falle. Bonner Poetik-Vorlesung*. Göttingen: Wallstein, 1996.

———. *Heute wär ich mir lieber nicht begegnet: Roman*. Reinbek: Rowohlt, 1997.

———. *Der fremde Blick, oder, das Leben ist ein Furz in der Laterne*. Göttingen: Wallstein, 1999.

———. *Der König verneigt sich und tötet*. Munich: Hanser, 2003.

Nadolny, Sten. *Selim; Oder, die Gabe der Rede: Roman*. Munich: Piper, 1990.

Naoum, Jusuf. *Der rote Hahn: Erzählungen des Fischers Sidaoui*. Darmstadt: Luchterhand, 1974.

———. *Der Scharfschütze*. Fischerhude: Atelier im Bauernhaus, 1983.

———. *Karakuş und andere orientalische Märchen*. Frankfurt am Main: Brandes & Apsel, 1986.

———. *Sand, Steine und Blumen: Gedichte aus drei Jahrzehnten*. Frankfurt am Main: Brandes & Apsel, 1991.

———. *Nura: Eine Libanesin in Deutschland: Roman*. Wuppertal: Hammer, 1996.

Oliver, José F. A. *Auf-Bruch: Lyrik*. Berlin: Das Arabische Buch, 1987.

———. *Weil ich dieses Land liebe: Lyrik*. Berlin: Das Arabische Buch, 1991.

———. *Gastling: Gedichte*. Berlin: Das Arabische Buch, 1993.

———. *Nachtrandspuren: Gedichte*. Frankfurt am Main: Suhrkamp, 2002.

————, and Peter Schlack. *Heimat und andere fossile Träume: Lyrik.* Berlin: Das Arabische Buch, 1993.

Ören, Aras. *Was will Niyazi in der Naunystrasse: Ein Poem.* Trans. Gisela Kraft. Berlin: Rotbuch, 1973.

————. *Deutschland, ein türkisches Märchen: Gedichte.* Düsseldorf: Claassen, 1978.

————. *Mitten in der Odyssee: Gedichte.* Düsseldorf: Claassen, 1980.

————. *Die Fremde ist auch ein Haus: Berlin-Poem.* Berlin: Rotbuch, 1980.

————. *Bitte nix Polizei: Kriminalerzählung.* Trans. Gisela Kraft. Düsseldorf: Claassen, 1981.

————. *Eine verspätete Abrechnung, oder Der Aufstieg der Gündoğdus: Auf der Suche nach der Gegenwart I.* Trans. Zafer Şenocak and Eva Hund. Frankfurt am Main: Dağyeli, 1988.

————. *Berlin Savignyplatz: Auf der Suche nach der Gegenwart V.* Trans. Deniz Göktürk. Berlin: Elefanten Press, 1995.

————. *Unerwarteter Besuch: Auf der Suche nach der Gegenwart VI.* Trans. Deniz Göktürk. Berlin: Elefanten Press, 1997.

————. *Granatapfelblüte: Auf der Suche nach der Gegenwart II.* Trans. Eva Hund and Zafer Şenocak. Berlin: Elefanten Press, 1998.

————. *Sehnsucht nach Hollywood: Auf der Suche nach der Gegenwart IV.* Trans. Deniz Göktürk. Berlin: Elefanten Press, 1999.

Özakin, Aysel. *Soll ich hier alt werden? Erzählungen.* Hamburg: Buntbuch, 1982.

————. *Die Leidenschaft der Anderen.* Hamburg: Buntbuch, 1984.

————. *Das Lächeln des Bewusstseins: Erzählungen.* Hamburg: Buntbuch, 1985.

————. *Du bist willkommen: Gedichte.* Hamburg: Buntbuch, 1985.

————. *Zart erhob sie sich bis sie flog: Ein Poem.* Hamburg: Galgenberg, 1986.

————. *Der fliegende Teppich: Auf der Spur meines Vaters.* Reinbek: Rowohlt, 1987.

————. *Die blaue Maske: Roman.* Frankfurt am Main: Luchterhand Literaturverlag, 1989.

————. *Glaube, Liebe, Aircondition: Eine türkische Kindheit.* Hamburg: Luchterhand, 1991.

————. *Die Vögel auf der Stirn: Roman.* Frankfurt am Main: Luchterhand, 1991.

————. *Deine Stimme gehört dir: Erzählungen.* Hamburg: Luchterhand, 1992.

————, and Jeremy Gaines. *Die Zunge der Berge: Roman.* Munich: Luchterhand Literaturverlag, 1994.

Özdamar, Emine Sevgi. *Mutterzunge.* Berlin: Rotbuch, 1990.

————. *Das Leben ist eine Karawanserei hat zwei Türen, aus einer kam ich rein, aus der anderen ging ich raus.* Cologne: Kiepenheuer & Witsch, 1992.

————. *Die Brücke vom goldenen Horn: Roman.* Cologne: Kiepenheuer & Witsch, 1998.

————. *Der Hof im Spiegel: Erzählungen.* Cologne: Kiepenheuer & Witsch, 2001.

————. *Seltsame Sterne starren zur Erde: Wedding—Pankow 1976/1977.* Cologne: Kiepenheuer & Witsch, 2003.

Özdemir, Hasan. *Zur schwarzen Nacht flüstere ich deinen Namen: Gedichte.* Berlin: Schiler, 1994.

————. *Das trockene Wasser: Gedichte.* Berlin: Das Arabische Buch, 1998.

————. *Vogeltreppe zum Tellerrand: Gedichte.* Berlin: Das Arabische Buch, 2000.

Özdoğan, Selim. *Es ist so einsam im Sattel, seit das Pferd tot ist: Roman.* Berlin: Rütten & Loening, 1995.

————. *Nirgendwo & Hormone: Roman.* Berlin: Rütten & Loening, 1996.

————. *Ein gutes Leben ist die beste Rache: Stories.* Berlin: Rütten & Loening, 1998.

————. *Mehr: Roman.* Berlin: Rütten & Loening, 1999.

————. *Im Juli: Roman.* Hamburg: Europa, 2000.

————. *Ein Spiel, das die Götter sich leisten: Roman.* Berlin: Aufbau, 2002.

————. *Trinkgeld vom Schicksal: Geschichten.* Berlin: Aufbau, 2003.

————. *Die Tochter des Schmieds: Roman.* Berlin: Aufbau, 2005.

Pak, Kwang-seoug. *Ich war ein koreanischer Gastarbeiter in Deutschland.* Frankfurt am Main: Fischer, 2001.

Pazarkaya, Yüksel. *Irrwege = Koca Sapmalar: Gedichte in zwei Sprachen.* Frankfurt am Main: Dağyeli, 1985.

————. *Rosen im Frost: Einblicke in die türkische Kultur.* Zürich: Unionsverlag, 1989.

————. *Der Babylonbus: Gedichte.* Frankfurt am Main: Dağyeli, 1989.

Pirinçci, Akif. *Tränen sind immer das Ende: Roman.* Munich: Goldmann, 1980.

————. *Felidae: Roman.* Munich: Goldmann, 1990.

————. *Der Rumpf: Roman.* Munich: Goldmann, 1992.

————. *Yin: Roman.* Munich: Goldmann, 1997.

————. *Die Damalstür: Roman.* Munich: Goldmann, 2001.

————. *Salve Roma! Roman.* Frankfurt am Main: Eichborn, 2004.

Rock, Zé do. *Fom winde ferfeelt: Ain Buch.* Berlin: Edition Diá, 1995.

————. *Ufo in der Küche: Ein Autobiografischer Seiens-Fikschen.* Leipzig: G. Kiepenheuer, 1998.

————. *Deutsch gutt, sonst Geld zurück: A Siegfriedische und Kauderdeutsche Ler- Und Textbuk.* Munich: A. Kunstmann, 2002.

SAID. *Wo ich sterbe ist meine Fremde: Gedichte.* Munich: P. Kirchheim, 1987.

————. *Dann schreie ich, bis Stille ist: Gedichte.* Tübingen: Heliopolis, 1990.

————. *Selbstbildnis für eine ferne Mutter.* Munich: P. Kirchheim, 1992.

————. *Landschaften einer fernen Mutter.* Munich: Beck, 2001.

————. *Aussenhaut, Binnenträume: Gedichte.* Munich: Beck, 2002.

Savaşçı, Fethi. *München im Frühlingsregen: Erzählungen und Gedichte.* Frankfurt am Main: Dağyeli, 1987.

Schami, Rafik. *Das letzte Wort der Wanderratte: Märchen, Fabeln und phantastische Geschichten.* Südwind-Literatur. Kiel: Neuer Malik, 1984.

————. *Der erste Ritt durchs Nadelöhr.* Kiel: Neuer Malik Verlag, 1985.

————. *Eine Hand voller Sterne: Roman.* Weinheim: Beltz & Gelberg, 1987.

————. *Sieben Doppelgänger.* Munich: Hanser, 1999.

————. *Die dunkle Seite der Liebe.* Munich: Hanser, 2004.

Scheinhardt, Saliha. *Drei Zypressen.* Berlin: Express Edition, 1984.

————. *Und die Frauen weinten Blut.* Berlin: Express Edition, 1985.

————. *Von der Erde bis zum Himmel Liebe: Eine Erzählung vom Leben und Sterben des aufrechten Bürgers C.* Reinbek: Rowohlt, 1990.

————. *Sie zerrissen die Nacht: Erzählung.* Freiburg: Herder, 1993.

————. *Die Stadt und das Mädchen: Roman.* Freiburg: Herder, 1993.

————. *Liebe, meine Gier, die mich frisst: Erzählung.* Herder Spektrum. Freiburg: Herder, 1994.

————. *Lebensstürme: Roman.* Frankfurt am Main: Brandes & Apsel, 2000.

————. *Töchter des Euphrat: Roman.* Frankfurt am Main: Brandes & Apsel, 2005.

Seligmann, Rafael. *Die jiddische Mamme: Roman.* Frankfurt am Main: Eichborn, 1990.

———. *Mit beschränkter Hoffnung: Juden, Deutsche, Israelis.* Hamburg: Hoffmann and Campe, 1991.

———. *Der Musterjude: Roman.* Hildesheim: Claassen, 1997.

———. *Der Milchmann: Roman.* Munich: Deutscher Taschenbuch Verlag, 1999.

Şenocak, Zafer. *Flammentropfen.* Frankfurt am Main: Dağyeli, 1985.

———. *Das senkrechte Meer: Gedichte.* Berlin: Babel, 1991.

———. *Fernwehanstalten: Gedichte.* Berlin: Babel, 1994.

———. *War Hitler Araber? IrreFührungen an den Rand Europas: Essays.* Berlin: Babel, 1994.

———. *Der Mann im Unterhemd.* Berlin: Babel, 1995.

———. *Die Prärie: Roman.* Hamburg: Rotbuch, 1997.

———. *Gefährliche Verwandtschaft: Roman.* Munich: Babel, 1998.

———. *Der Erottomane: Ein Findelbuch.* Munich: Babel, 1999.

———. *Zungenentfernung: Bericht aus der Quarantänestation: Essays.* Munich: Babel, 2001.

Siege, Nasrin. *Shirin.* Weinheim: Beltz & Gelberg, 1999.

Tawada, Yoko. *Wo Europa anfängt.* Tübingen: Konkursbuch, 1991.

———. *Die Kranichmaske, die bei Nacht strahlt.* Tübingen: Konkursbuch, 1993.

———. *Ein Gast.* Tübingen: Konkursbuch, 1993.

———. *Aber die Mandarinen müssen heute abend noch geraubt werden.* Tübingen: Konkursbuch, 1997.

———. *Verwandlungen: Prosa, Lyrik, Szenen und Essays.* Tübinger Poetik-Vorlesung. Tübingen: Konkursbuch, 1998.

———. *Überseezungen.* Tübingen: Konkursbuch, 2002.

———. *Das nackte Auge.* Tübingen: Konkursbuch, 2004.

Torkan. *Tufan: Brief an einen islamischen Bruder.* Hamburg: Perspol, 1983.

———. *Allnacht: Roya und Alp-Traum.* Hamburg: Perspol, 1987.

———. *La Bibla: Die Botschaft der Isa nach der Übertragung.* Hamburg: Perspol, 1995.

Torossi, Eleni. *Tanz der Tintenfische.* Kiel: Engl & Lämmel, 1986.

Wallraff, Günter. *Ganz unten.* Cologne: Kiepenheuer & Witsch, 1985.

Zaimoğlu, Feridun. *Kanak Sprak: 24 Misstöne vom Rande der Gesellschaft.* Hamburg: Rotbuch Verlag, 1995.

———. *Abschaum: Die wahre Geschichte von Ertan Ongun.* Hamburg: Rotbuch, 1997.

———. *Koppstoff: Kanaka Sprak vom Rande der Gesellschaft.* Hamburg: Rotbuch, 1998.

———. *Liebesmale, Scharlachrot: Roman.* Hamburg: Rotbuch, 2000.

———. *German Amok: Roman.* Cologne: Kiepenheuer & Witsch, 2002.

———. *Leinwand: Roman.* Hamburg: Rotbuch, 2003.

———. *Zwölf Gramm Glück: Erzählungen.* Cologne: Kiepenheuer & Witsch, 2004.

Zaptçıoğlu, Dilek. *Der Mond isst die Sterne auf.* Munich: Bertelsmann, 2001.

Literary Works Available in English

Anthologies

Ackermann, Irmgard, ed. *Foreign Viewpoints: Multicultural Literature in Germany.* Bonn: Inter Nationes, 1999.

Harnisch, Antje, Anne Marie Stokes, and Friedemann J. Weidauer, eds. *Fringe Voices:*

An Anthology of Minority Writing in the Federal Republic of Germany. New York: Berg, 1998.

Morris, Leslie, and Karen Remmler, eds. *Contemporary Jewish Writing in Germany: An Anthology.* Jewish Writing in the Contemporary World. Lincoln, NE: University of Nebraska Press, 2002.

Opitz, May, Katharina Oguntoye, and Dagmar Schultz, eds. *Showing Our Colors: Afro-German Women Speak Out.* Trans. Anne V. Adams, et al. Amherst, Mass: University of Massachusetts Press, 1992.

Single-Author Editions

Arjouni, Jakob. *Happy Birthday, Turk!* Trans. Anselm Hollo. New York: Fromm International, 1993.

———. *And Still Drink More! A Kayankaya Mystery.* Trans. Anselm Hollo. New York: Fromm International, 1994.

———. *One Death to Die: A Kayankaya Mystery.* Trans. Anselm Hollo. New York: Fromm International, 1997.

———. *Idiots: Five Fairy Tales and Other Stories.* Trans, Anthea Bell. New York: Other Press, 2005.

Baykurt, Fakir. *A Report from Kuloba and Other Stories.* Trans. Joseph S. Jacobson and Viola N. Jacobson. Holladay, Utah: Southmoor Press, 2000.

Cumart, Nevfel. *Waves of Time: Poems = Wellen der Zeit: Gedichte.* Trans. Eoin Bourke. Düsseldorf: Grupello, 1998.

Grass, Günter. *The Tin Drum.* Trans. Ralph Mannheim. New York: Vintage, 1990.

———. *The Call of the Toad.* Trans. Ralph Mannheim. New York: Harcourt, 1992.

Gruša, Jiří. *The Questionnaire, or, Prayer for a Town & a Friend.* Trans. Peter Kussi. New York: Farrar Straus & Giroux, 1982.

Moníková, Libuše. *The Façade: M.N.O.P.Q.* Trans. John E. Woods. New York: Knopf, 1991.

Müller, Herta. *The Passport.* Trans. Martin Chalmers. London: Serpent's Tail, 1989.

———. *The Land of Green Plums.* Trans. Michael Hofmann. London: Granta, 1999.

———. *The Appointment.* Trans. Michael Hulse and Philip Boehm. New York: Metropolitan Books, 2001.

Özdamar, Emine Sevgi. *Mother Tongue.* Trans. Craig Thomas. Toronto: Coach House Press, 1994.

———. *Life Is a Caravanserai: Has Two Doors, I Came in One, I Went out the Other.* Trans. Luise Von Flotow-Evans. London: Middlesex University Press, 2000.

Schami, Rafik. *A Hand Full of Stars.* Trans. Rika Lesser. New York: Dutton Children's Book, 1990.

Tawada, Yoko. *The Bridegroom Was a Dog.* New York: Kodansha America, 1998.

———. *Where Europe Begins.* Trans. Susan Bernofsky and Yumi Selden, with a preface by Wim Wenders. New York: New Directions, 2002.

FILMOGRAPHY

The following selection of films offers various perspectives on migration, mobility, dislocation, and *Heimat* (homeland/home). The focus is on Germany, although the list includes a few prominent films from other European countries to encourage comparative readings. The films are in chronological order.

1950

Schwarzwaldmädel/The Black Forest Girl (West Germany 1950, Hans Deppe, 100 min.)

1951

Grün ist die Heide/The Heath Is Green (West Germany 1951, Hans Deppe, 91 min.)

1952

Rosen blühen auf dem Heidegrab/Roses Bloom on the Grave in the Meadow (West Germany 1952, Hans H. König, 90 min., b/w)
Toxi (West Germany 1952, Robert A. Stemmle, 89 min., b/w)

1955

Ich denke oft an Piroschka/I Often Think of Piroschka (West Germany 1955, Kurt Hoffmann, 92 min.)

1958

Toxi lebt anders/Toxi Has a Different Life (West Germany 1958, Peter Schier-Grabowski, documentary, 27 min.)

1960

Kirmes/The Fair (West Germany 1960, Wolfgang Staudte, 102 min., b/w)

1961

Bis zum Ende aller Tage/Girl from Hong Kong (West Germany 1961, Franz Peter Wirth, 95 min.)

1964

Der geteilte Himmel/The Divided Heaven (East Germany 1964, Konrad Wolf, 116 min., b/w)

1965

Ruf der Wälder/Call of the Forest (Austria 1965, Franz Antel, 85 min.)

1966

Abschied von Gestern/Yesterday Girl (West Germany 1966, Alexander Kluge, 88 min., b/w)

1968

Lebenszeichen/Signs of Life (West Germany 1968, Werner Herzog, 91 min., available on DVD with English subtitles)

1969

Jagdszenen aus Niederbayern/Hunting Scenes from Bavaria (West Germany 1969, Peter Fleischmann, 88 min., b/w)

Katzelmacher (West Germany 1969, R. W. Fassbinder, 88 min., b/w, available on DVD with English subtitles)

1972

Aguirre, der Zorn Gottes/Aguirre, the Wrath of God (West Germany/Peru/Mexico 1972, Werner Herzog, 100 min., available on DVD with English subtitles)

Lass jucken, Kumpel! (West Germany 1972, Franz Marischka, 95 min.)

1973

Geh, zieh dein Dirndl aus/Love: Bavarian Style (West Germany 1973, Siggi Götz, 85 min.)

Pane e cioccolata/Bread and Chocolate (Switzerland 1973, Franco Brusati, 112 min., available on DVD with English subtitles)

1974

Alice in den Städten/Alice in the Cities (West Germany 1974, Wim Wenders, 110 min., b/w)

Angst essen Seele auf /Ali: Fears Eats the Soul (West Germany 1974, R. W. Fassbinder, 93 min., available on DVD with English subtitles)

1975

Dar Ghorbat/In der Fremde/Far from Home (West Germany 1975, Sohrab Shahid Saless, 91 min.)

1976

Otobüs/The Bus (Turkey 1976, Tunç Okan, 84 min.)

Shirins Hochzeit/Shirin's Wedding (West Germany 1976, Helma Sanders-Brahms, 120 min., b/w)

1977

Stroszek (West Germany 1977, Werner Herzog, 115 min., available on DVD with English subtitles)

1978

Aus der Ferne sehe ich dieses Land/I See This Land from Afar (West Germany 1978, Christian Ziewer, 98 min.)

Deutschland im Herbst/Germany in Autumn (West Germany 1978, Rainer Werner Fassbinder, Alexander Kluge, Edgar Reitz, Volker Schlöndorff, and others, 123 min., color and b/w, available on VHS with English subtitles)

Die Schweizermacher/The Swissmakers (Switzerland 1978, Rolf Lyssy, 107 min.)

1979

Die Blechtrommel/The Tin Drum (West Germany/France/Poland/Yugoslavia 1979, Volker Schlöndorff, 142 min., available on DVD with English subtitles)

Die Ehe der Maria Braun/The Marriage of Maria Braun (West Germany 1979, R. W. Fassbinder, 120 min., available on DVD with English subtitles)

1980

Gölge/Schatten/Shadow (West Germany 1980, Sema Poyraz, 90 min.)

Ordnung/Order (West Germany 1980, Sohrab Shahid Saless, 96 min., b/w)

Palermo oder Wolfsburg (West Germany/Switzerland 1980, Werner Schroeter, 175 min.)

Theo gegen den Rest der Welt/Theo against the Rest of the World (West Germany 1980, Peter F. Bringmann, 106 min.)

1982

Fitzcarraldo (Peru/West Germany 1982, Werner Herzog, 158 min., available on DVD with English subtitles)

Moonlighting/Schwarzarbeit (United Kingdom/West Germany 1982, Jerzy Skolimowski, 97 min.)

Die Sehnsucht der Veronika Voss/Veronika Voss (West Germany 1982, R. W. Fassbinder, 104 min., b/w, available on DVD with English subtitles)

Stadt der verlorenen Seelen/City of Lost Souls (West Germany 1982, Rosa von Praunheim, 89 min.)

Der Stand der Dinge/The State of Things (West Germany/Portugal/United States 1982, Wim Wenders, 121 min., b/w)

1983

Empfänger unbekannt/Addressee Unknown (West Germany 1983, Sohrab Shahid Saless, 86 min.)

Utopia (West Germany 1983, Sohrab Shahid Saless, 198 min.)

Zwischen Gott und Erde/Between God and Earth (West Germany 1983, Tevfik Başer, documentary)

1984

Heimat – Eine deutsche Chronik/Heimat—A Chronicle of Germany (West Germany 1984, Edgar Reitz, 924 min., 11 parts, available on DVD with English subtitles)

Die Kümmeltürkin geht (West Germany 1984, Jeanine Meerapfel, documentary, 88 min.)

Schlaf der Vernunft (West Germany 1984, Ulla Stöckl, 82 min., b/w)

1985

Die Abschiebung (West Germany 1985, Marianne Lüdcke)

My Beautiful Laundrette (United Kingdom 1985, Stephen Frears, 97 min., available on DVD in the United States)

Le Thé au harem d'Archimède/Tea in the Harem (France 1985, Mehdi Charef, 110 min.)

1986

40 Quadratmeter Deutschland/Forty Square Meters of Germany (West Germany 1986, Tevfik Başer, 80 min.)

Günter Wallraff—Ganz unten (West Germany 1986, Jörg Gförer, documentary, 100 min.)

Das kalte Paradies/Cold Paradise (Switzerland 1986, Bernard Safarik, 90 min.)

1987

Bagdad Café/Out of Rosenheim (West Germany/United States 1987, Percy Adlon, 95 min., available on DVD with English subtitles)

Drachenfutter/Dragon Chow (West Germany 1987, Jan Schütte, b/w, available on VHS with English subtitles)

Der Himmel über Berlin/Wings of Desire (West Germany/France 1987, Wim Wenders, 127 min., b/w and color, available on DVD with English subtitles)

Sammy and Rosie Get Laid (United Kingdom 1987, Stephen Frears, 101 min., available on VHS)

Sierra Leone (West Germany 1987, Uwe Schrader, 92 min.)

1988

Abschied vom falschen Paradies/Farewell to False Paradise (West Germany 1988, Tevfik Başer, 92 min.)

Looking for Langston (United Kingdom 1988, Isaac Julien, 45 min., b/w and color, available on VHS)

Polizei (Turkey 1988, Şerif Gören, 88 min., available on VHS or VCD in Turkey)

Yasemin (West Germany 1988, Hark Bohm, 70 min., available on VHS in Germany)

1990

I'm British But... (United Kingdom 1990, Gurinder Chadha, documentary, 30 min.)

Journey of Hope/Reise der Hoffnung (Switzerland/United Kingdom/Turkey 1990, Xavier Koller, 109 min., available on VHS with English subtitles)

Das serbische Mädchen/The Serbian Girl (West Germany/Yugoslavia 1990, Peter Sehr, 92 min.)

Töchter zweier Welten/Daughters of Two Worlds (Germany 1990, Serap Berrakkarasu, documentary, 60 min.)

1991

Allemagne neuf zéro/Germany Year Nine Zero (France 1991, Jean-Luc Godard, 62 min.)
Happy Birthday, Türke! (Germany 1991, Doris Dörrie, 109 min., available on VHS in Germany)
Ilona und Kurti (Austria 1991, Reinhard Schwabenitzky)
Lebewohl, Fremde! (Germany 1991, Tevfik Başer, 100 min.)
Sommer in Mezra (Germany 1991, Hussi Kutlucan, 81 min.)
Young Soul Rebels (United Kingdom 1991, Isaac Julien, 105 min., available on DVD)

1992

Herzsprung (Germany 1992, Helke Misselwitz, 87 min.)
Langer Gang/Passages (Germany 1992, Yilmaz Arslan, 79 min., available on VHS)
Mercedes Mon Amour (Germany/France/Turkey 1992, Tunç Okan, 90 min.)
Schattenboxer (Germany 1992, Jens Becker and Lars Becker, 77 min.)
Wild West (United Kingdom 1992, David Attwood, 85 min., available on VHS)
Zweite Heimat—Die Chronik einer Jugend/ Second Heimat (Germany, Edgar Reitz, 1992, 1,532 min., television series, available on DVD with English subtitles)

1993

Babylon 2 (Switzerland 1993, Samir, 91 min.)
Berlin in Berlin (Turkey 1993, Sinan Çetin, 99 min.)
Bhaji on the Beach (United Kingdom 1993, Gurinder Chadha, 101 min., available on VHS)
Dann lieber gleich ins falsche Paradies/I'd Rather Go Straight to the False Paradise! (Germany 1993, Imrad Karim, 45 min.)
Gorilla Bathes at Noon (Germany/Yugoslavia 1993, Dusan Makavejev, 83 min., available on VHS with English subtitles)
Schwarzfahrer/Fare Dodger/Black Rider (Germany 1993, Pepe Danquart, 12 min., b/w, available on DVD with English subtitles)
Warheads (France/Germany 1993, Romuald Karmakar, 179 min., documentary, available on DVD)

1994

Ekmek Parası/Geld für Brot/Money for Bread (Germany 1994, Serap Berrakkarasu, documentary, 104 min.)
Lisbon Story (Germany/Portugal 1994, Wim Wenders, 100 min.)
Mach die Musik leiser (Germany 1994, Thomas Arslau, 85 min.)
Mein Vater, der Gastarbeiter/My Father, the Guest Worker (Germany 1994, Yüksel Yavuz, documentary, 52 min.)
Voll Normaal (Germany 1994, Ralf Huettner, 91 min., available on DVD)
Weltmeister/World Champion (Germany 1994, Zoran Solomun, 71 min.)

1995

La Haine/Hate (France 1995, Mathieu Kassovitz, 96 min., available on DVD)
Mädchen am Ball/Girls on the Ball (Germany 1995, Aysun Bademsoy, documentary, 29 min.)

Das Versprechen/The Promise (Germany/France/Switzerland 1995, Margarethe von Trotta, 115 min., b/w and color, available on VHS)

1996

Getürkt!/Weed (Germany 1996, Fatih Akın, 12 min.)

Ich bin die Tochter meiner Mutter/Ben annemin kızıyım/I Am the Daughter of My Mother (Germany 1996, Seyhan Derin, documentary, 89 min.)

Salut cousin!/Hey, Cousin! (France 1996, Merzak Allouache, 98 min., available on VHS)

1997

Filmart Takes Position: Alien/Nation — The Filmreel (Austria 1997, 60 min.)

Geschwister — Kardeşler/Siblings (Germany 1997, Thomas Arslan, 82 min., available on VHS)

Ein Mädchen im Ring/Girl in the Ring (Germany 1997, Aysun Bademsoy, documentary)

Nach dem Spiel/After the Game (Germany 1997, Aysun Bademsoy, documentary, 60 min.)

1998

Alles wird gut/All Will Be Well (Germany 1998, Angelina Maccarone, 88 min.)

Aprilkinder/April Children (Germany 1998, Yüksel Yavuz, 85 min., available on VHS with English subtitles from Internationes)

Ein Engel schlägt zurück/An Angel Strikes Back (Germany 1998, Angelina Maccarone, 83 min., color)

Ich Chef, Du Turnschuh/Me Boss, You Sneaker (Germany 1998, Hussi Kutlucan, 92 min.)

Kurz und schmerzlos/Short Sharp Shock (Germany 1998, Fatih Akın, 100 min., available on DVD)

Die leere Mitte/The Empty Center (Germany 1998, Hito Steyerl, documentary, 62 min., color)

Yara/The Wound (Germany 1998, Yılmaz Arslan, 98 min.)

1999

Beautiful People (United Kingdom 1999, Jasmin Dizdar, 107 min., available on DVD)

Dealer (Germany 1999, Thomas Arslan, 74 min., color, available on VHS)

Deutsche Polizisten/German Police (Germany 1999, Aysun Bademsoy, documentary, 60 min.)

East Is East (United Kingdom 1999, Damien O'Donnell, 96 min., available on DVD)

Geboren in Absurdistan/Born in Absurdistan (Austria 1999, Houchang Allahyari, 116 min., available on DVD)

Güneşe Yolculuk/Reise zur Sonne/Journey to the Sun (Turkey/Germany/Netherlands 1999, Yeşim Ustaoğlu, available on DVD with English subtitles)

Lola und Bilidikid/Lola and Billy the Kid (Germany 1999, Kutluğ Ataman, 95 min., available on DVD with English subtitles)

Menschen auf der Treppe/People on Stairs (Germany 1999, Hatice Ayten, documentary, 34 min.)

Otomo (Germany 1999, Frieder Schlaich, 85 min., available on DVD)

Passing Drama (Germany 1999, Angela Melitopoulus, experimental documentary video, 66 min.)

Sonnenallee/Sun Alley (Germany 1999, Leander Haussmann, 101 min., available on VHS)

2000

Auslandstournee/Tour Abroad (Germany 2000, Ayşe Polat, 91 min.)

Code Inconnu/Code Unknown (France/Germany/Romania 2000, Michael Haneke, 118 min., available on DVD)

Dreckfresser/Dirt for Dinner (Germany 2000, Branwen Okpako, documentary, 73 min.)

Erkan und Stefan (Germany 2000, Michael Herbig, 87 min., available on DVD)

Freunde/Friends (Germany 2000, Martin Eigler, 100 min., available on DVD)

Im Juli/In July (Germany 2000, Fatih Akın, 99 min., available on DVD with English subtitles)

Kanak Attack (Germany 2000, Lars Becker, 86 min., available on DVD)

Lost Killers (Germany 2000, Dito Tsintsadze, 100 min.)

Die Unberührbare/No Place to Go (Germany 2000, Oskar Roehler, 110 min., b/w, available on DVD)

2001

Anam/My Mother (Germany 2001, Buket Alakuş, 86 min.)

Escape to Paradise (Switzerland 2001, Nino Jacusso, 90 min.)

Die Grenze—Granica/Border (Germany 2001, Robert Thalheim, 95 min., short documentary)

Mondscheintarif/Moonlight Tariff (Germany 2001, Ralf Huettner, 93 min.)

My Sweet Home (Germany/Greece 2001, Fillipos Tsitos, 86 min.)

Der schöne Tag/A Fine Day (Germany 2001, Thomas Arslan, 74 min.)

Trdnjava Evropa/Fortress Europe (Slovenia 2001, Zelimir Zilnik, 80 min., available on VHS)

Wie Zucker im Tee/Like Sugar in Tea (Germany 2001, Hatice Ayten, documentary, 70 min.)

Wir haben vergessen zurückzukehren/We Have Forgotten to Return (Germany 2001, Fatih Akın, documentary, 60 min.)

2002

Bend It Like Beckham (United Kingdom/Germany 2002, Gurinder Chadha, 112 min., available on DVD)

Dirty Pretty Things (United Kingdom 2002, Stephen Frears, 97 min., available on DVD)

Elefantenherz (Germany 2002, Züli Aladağ, 95 min., available on DVD)

Ghetto-Kids (Germany/France 2002, Christian Wagner, 90 min., available on DVD)

Karamuk (Germany 2002, Sülbiye Günar, 97 min.)

Madrid (Germany 2002, Daphne Charizani, 81 min.)

Occident (Romania 2002, Cristian Mungio, 105 min.)

Solino (Germany 2002, Fatih Akın, 124 min., available on DVD)

Was nicht passt, wird passend gemacht/If It Don't Fit, Use a Bigger Hammer (Germany 2002, Peter Thorwarth, 101 min., available on DVD)

Zwischen den Sternen/Among the Stars (Germany 2002, Seyhan Derin, 86 min.)

2003

Alltag/ Everyday Life (Germany 2003, Neco Çelik, 91 min.)

Angst isst Seele auf/Fear Eats the Soul (Germany 2003, Shahbaz Noshir, 13 min., available with English subtitles on the Criterion Collection DVD of *Ali: Fear Eats the Soul*)

Gegen die Wand/Head-On (Germany 2003, Fatih Akın, 121 min., available on DVD with English subtitles)

Good Bye Lenin! (Germany 2003, Wolfgang Becker, 121 min., available on DVD with English subtitles)

Kleine Freiheit/A Little Bit of Freedom (Germany 2003, Yüksel Yavuz, 100 min., available on DVD)

Lichter/Distant Lights (Germany 2003, Hans-Christian Schmid, 105 min., available on DVD)

Milchwald/This Very Moment (Germany/Poland 2003, Christoph Hochhäusler, 87 min., available on DVD)

Schussangst/Gun-Shy (Germany 2003, Dito Tsintsadze, 105 min.)

Wenn der Richtige kommt/When the Right One Comes Along (Switzerland/Germany 2003, Oliver Paulus and Stefan Hillebrand, 78 min.)

2004

Alles auf Zucker!/Go for Zucker (Germany 2004, Dani Levy, 90 min., available on DVD)

En Garde (Germany 2004, Ayşe Polat, 94 min.)

Exils (France/Japan 2004, Tony Gatlif, 104 min.)

Heimat 3 — Chronik einer Zeitenwende (Germany 2004, Edgar Reitz, 679 min., television serial, available on DVD)

Heimkehr/Homecoming (Germany/Croatia 2004, Damir Lukacevic)

Jarmark Europa (Germany 2004, Minze Tummescheit, documentary, 124 min.)

Lautlos/Silent (Germany 2004, Mennan Yapo, 94 min.)

November (Germany 2004, Hito Steyerl, 25 min.)

Status Yo! (Germany 2004, Till Hastreiter, 118 min.)

Süperseks (Germany 2004, Torsten Wacker, 95 min., available on DVD)

Yugotrip (Germany 2004, Nadya Derado, 90 min.)

2005

Eine andere Liga/ A Different League (Germany 2005, Buket Alakuş, 100 min.)

Aufstellung/Lineup (Germany 2005, Harun Farocki, 12 min.)

Brudermord (Luxembourg/Germany/France 2005, Yılmaz Arslan, 90 min.)

Crossing the Bridge—The Sounds of Istanbul (Germany/Turkey 2005, Fatih Akın, documentary, 90 min., available on DVD)

Deutschländersiedlung/Germany in Turkey: Gated Communities (Germany 2005, Aysun Bademsoy, documentary, 80 min.)

Drei gegen Troja/Three Against Troy (Germany 2005, Hussi Kutlucan, 90 min.)

Fremde Haut/Unveiled (Germany/Austria 2005, Angelina Maccarone, 97 min.)
Kebab Connection (Germany 2005, Anno Saul, 96 min., available on DVD)
One Day in Europe (Germany/Spain 2005, Hannes Stöhr, 100 min.)
Unkenrufe/The Call of the Toad (Germany/Poland 2005, Robert Glinski, 98 min.)
Was lebst Du?/ What Do You Live? (Germany 2005, Bettina Braun, documentary, 84
    min.)

INTERNET RESOURCES

AiD: Ausländer in Deutschland: www.isoplan.de
Amnesty International Deutschland: www.amnesty.de
Amt für multikulturelle Angelegenheiten, Frankfurt: www.stadt-frankfurt.de
Antirassistisch-Interkulturelles Informationszentrum Berlin: www.aric.de
Arbeiterwohlfahrt: Bundesverband: www.awo.org
Ausländer in Deutschland: Fakten gegen Vorurteile: www.loester.net
Bahnhof Köln-Deutz: Migrantengeschichten aus 40 Jahren:
    www.angekommen.com
Beauftragte der Bundesregierung für Migration, Flüchtlinge und Integration:
    www.integrationsbeauftragte.de
Der Beauftragte für Integration und Migration, Berlin: www.berlin.de
Berliner Institut für Vergleichende Sozialforschung: www.emz-berlin.de
Bundesamt für Migration und Flüchtlinge: www.bamf.de
Bundesministerium des Innern: www.bmi.bund.de
Bundeszentrale für politische Bildung: www.bpb.de
Bündnis für Demokratie und Toleranz: www.buendnis-toleranz.de
Café Babel: www.cafebabel.com
Center for International and European Law on Immigration and Asylum:
    www.migration.uni-konstanz.de
Civitas—initiativ gegen den Rechtsextremismus in den neuen Bundesländern:
    www.jugendstiftung-civitas.org
D-A-S-H: Für Vernetzung gegen Ausgrenzung: www.d-a-s-h.org
Deutsche Welle World: www.dw-world.de
Dokumentations- und Informationszentrum für Rassismusforschung:
    www.dir-info.de
Dokumentations- und Kulturzentrum Deutscher Sinti und Roma:
    www.sintiundroma.de
DOMiT: Dokumentationszentrum und Museum über die Migration in Deutsch-
    land: www.domit.de
Einbürgerung: www.einbuergerung.de
Europa: Gateway to the European Union: www.europa.eu
Europäisches Migrationszentrum: www.emz-berlin.de
European Council on Refugees and Exiles: www.ecre.org
European Institute for Progressive Cultural Policies: www.eipcp.net
Filmportal: Internetplattform für Informationen zum deutschen Film:
    www.filmportal.de
Forschungsstelle für interkulturelle Studien: www.fist.uni-koeln.de

Friedrich-Ebert-Stiftung: Online-Portal zum Thema Interkulturalität, Migration und Integration: www.fes.de
German History in Documents and Images: www.germanhistorydocs.ghi-dc.org
Germany Info: German Embassy, Washington, D.C.: www.germany.info
Goethe-Institut: Cultures on the Move: www.goethe.de
Haus der Kulturen der Welt, Berlin: www.hkw.de
Heimat in Deutschland: www.heimat-in-deutschland.de
Herbert-Quandt-Stiftung: Trialog der Kulturen: www.h-quandt-stiftung.de
History of Germany: Primary Documents: www.library.byu.edu
Ibero-Amerika in Berlin: www.latinos-in-berlin.de
Institut für Auslandsbeziehungen: www.cms.ifa.de
Institut für Migrationsforschung und Interkulturelle Studien: www.imis.uos.de
International Organization for Migration: www.iom.int
Jugend für Toleranz und Demokratie—gegen Rechtsextremismus, Fremden-feindlichkeit und Antisemitismus: www.entimon.de
Kanak Attak: www.kanak-attak.de
Karneval der Kulturen: www.karneval-berlin.de
Migration Information Source: www.migrationinformation.org
Migration News: www.migration.ucdavis.edu/mn
Migration und Bevölkerung: Netzwerk Migration in Europa: www.migration-info.de
Migrationsmuseum: www.migrationsmuseum.de
Mut gegen rechte Gewalt: Die Internet-Plattform gegen Rechtsextremismus: www.mut-gegen-rechte-gewalt.de
Netzwerk Migration in Europa: www.network-migration.org
Open Democracy: www.opendemocracy.net
PortalGlobal—Kultur in der Brotfabrik: www.portalglobal.de
PRO ASYL: www.proasyl.de
Projekt Migration: www.projektmigration.de
Qantara.de: Dialogue with the Islamic World: www.qantara.de
Rat für Migration: www.rat-fuer-migration.de
RBB: Radio Multikulti, Berlin: www.multikulti.de
Statistisches Bundesamt Deutschland: www.destatis.de
Stiftung Zentrum für Türkeistudien: www.zft-online.de
TRANSIT: www.german.berkeley.edu/transit
Transit Migration: www.transitmigration.org
Türkischer Bund in Berlin-Brandenburg: www.tbb-berlin.de
United Nations International Migration and Development: www.unmigration.org
Verband für Interkulturelle Arbeit: www.via-bund.de
Villa Global: Museen Tempelhof-Schöneberg: www.villaglobal.de
WDR Funkhaus Europa: www.wdr5.de
Werkstatt der Kulturen: www.werkstatt-der-kulturen.de
Zentralrat der Juden in Deutschland: www.zentralratdjuden.de
Zentralrat der Muslime in Deutschland: www.islam.de
Zentrum für zeithistorische Forschung Potsdam: www.zzf-pdm.de
Zuwanderungsrecht: www.zuwanderung.de

CREDITS

Introduction

Photo. Portable plenitude. Copyright © Bildarchiv Stiftung Preussischer Kulturbesitz Berlin.

1. Working Guests

Photo. The millionth guest worker. Photo: Alfred Koch; copyright © DOMiT. 1 All rights reserved, Frankfurter Allgemeine Zeitung, Inc., Frankfurt. Provided by the Frankfurter Allgemeine Archive. 2 Reprinted with the permission of the Presse- und Öffentlichkeitsarbeit/Arbeitsstab der Beauftragten der Bundesregierung für Migration, Flüchtlinge und Integration. 3 Reprinted with the permission of SPIEGEL-Verlag Rudolf Augstein GmbH & Co. Hamburg. 4 Reprinted with the permission of C. H. Beck Verlag, Munich. 5 Reprinted with the permission of Bonnier Media Deutschland GmbH, Munich. 6 Copyright Victrola Records. 7 Reprinted with the permission of Klartext Verlag GmbH, Essen. 8 All rights reserved, Frankfurter Allgemeine Zeitung, Inc., Frankfurt. Provided by the Frankfurter Allgemeine Archive. 10 Reprinted with the permission of SPIEGEL-Verlag Rudolf Augstein GmbH & Co. Hamburg. 11 Courtesy of the DOMiT—Dokumentationszentrum und Museum über die Migration in Deutschland e.V., Cologne. 12 Reprinted with the permission of Zeit-Verlag GmbH, Hamburg. 13 Reprinted with the permission of Süddeutsche Zeitung GmbH, Munich. 15 Reprinted with the permission of Zeit-Verlag GmbH, Hamburg. 16 Reprinted with the permission of Süddeutsche Zeitung GmbH, Munich. 17 Reprinted with the permission of Süddeutsche Zeitung GmbH. 18 Reprinted with the permission of the author. 19 Reprinted with the permission of Zeit-Verlag GmbH, Hamburg. 20 Reprinted with the permission of the author.

2. Our Socialist Friends

Photo. Solidarity and progress. Copyright © Neues Deutschland Archiv. 6 Reprinted with the permission of Waxmann Verlag, Munich. 8 Reprinted with the permission of Zeit-Verlag GmbH, Hamburg. 12 Reprinted with the permission of Waxmann Verlag, Munich. 13 Reprinted with the permission of Zeit-Verlag GmbH, Hamburg. 14 Reprinted with the permission of Waxmann Verlag, Munich. 15 Reprinted with the permission of SPIEGEL-Verlag Rudolf Augstein GmbH & Co. Hamburg. 16 All rights reserved, Frankfurter Allgemeine Zeitung, Inc., Frankfurt. Provided by the Frankfurter Allgemeine Archive. 17 All rights reserved, Frankfurter Allgemeine Zeitung, Inc., Frankfurt. Provided by the Frankfurter Allgemeine Archive. 18 All rights reserved, Frankfurter Allgemeine Zeitung, Inc., Frankfurt. Provided by the Frankfurter Allgemeine Archive.

3. Is the Boat Full?

Photo. Solingen. Photo: copyright © Manfred Vollmer. 1 Reprinted with the permission of SPIEGEL-Verlag Rudolf Augstein GmbH & Co. Hamburg. 3 Reprinted with the permission of Hohenrain-Verlag GmbH, Tübingen. 4 Reprinted with the permission of Zeit-Verlag GmbH, Hamburg. 5 Copyright MZee Verlag. 6 Reprinted with the permission of SPIEGEL-Verlag Rudolf Augstein GmbH & Co. Hamburg. 8 Reprinted with the permission of Süddeutsche Zeitung GmbH, Munich. 9 Copyright Aufbau Media. 10 Copyright Orlanda Verlag, Berlin and Africa World Press, Lawrenceville, NJ. 11 Reprinted with permission of Verlag Kiepenheuer & Witsch, Cologne. 12 Reprinted with the permission of Süddeutsche Zeitung GmbH, Munich. 13 Reprinted with the permission of TAZ Verlags- und Vertriebs GmbH, Berlin. 14 Reprinted with the permission of TAZ Verlags- und Vertriebs GmbH, Berlin. 15 Reprinted with the permission of Verlag Der Tagesspiegel GmbH, Berlin. 16 Copyright BMG Music. 17 Reprinted with the permission of TAZ Verlags- und Vertriebs GmbH, Berlin. 21 Reprinted with the permission of the IZ Medien GmbH, Berlin.

4. What Is a German?

Photo. Demonstrating for visa reform. Source: Waltraud Bierwirth and Nihat Öztürk, eds. *Migration hat viele Gesichter* (Essen: Klartext, 2003), 28. 5 Reprinted with the permission of Zeit-Verlag GmbH, Hamburg. 7 Reprinted with the permission of TAZ Verlags- und Vertriebs GmbH, Berlin. 8 Reprinted with the permission of TAZ Verlags- und Vertriebs GmbH, Berlin. 9 Reprinted with the permission of TAZ Verlags- und Vertriebs GmbH, Berlin. 10 Reprinted with the permission of TAZ Verlags- und Vertriebs GmbH, Berlin. 12 Reprinted with the permission of TAZ Verlags- und Vertriebs GmbH, Berlin. 13 Reprinted with the permission of Zeit-Verlag GmbH, Hamburg. 14 Reprinted with the permission of Zeit-Verlag GmbH, Hamburg. 15 All rights reserved, Frankfurter Allgemeine Zeitung, Inc., Frankfurt. Provided by the Frankfurter Allgemeine Archive. 16 Reprinted with the permission of Zeit-Verlag GmbH, Hamburg. 20 Reprinted with the permission of Pro-Asyl. 21 Reprinted with the permission of the author.

5. Religion and Diaspora

Photo. Freimann mosque. Source: Sabine Kraft, *Islamische Sakralarchitektur in Deutschland: Eine Untersuchung ausgewählter Moschee-Neubauten* (Berlin: LIT, 2002), 336. 1 Reprinted with the permission of Süddeutsche Zeitung GmbH, Munich. 2 All rights reserved, Frankfurter Allgemeine Zeitung, Inc., Frankfurt. Provided by the Frankfurter Allgemeine Archive. 3 Reprinted with the permission of Zeit-Verlag GmbH, Hamburg. 4 Reprinted with the permission of Süddeutsche Zeitung GmbH, Munich. 6 Reprinted with the permission of the author. 7 Reprinted with the permission of Zeit-Verlag GmbH, Hamburg. 8 Reprinted with the permission of Zitty Verlag GmbH, Berlin. 9 Reprinted with the permission of TAZ Verlags- und Vertriebs GmbH, Berlin. 10 Reprinted with the permission of the author. 11 Reprinted with the permission of Süddeutsche Zeitung GmbH, Munich. 12 Reprinted with the permission of Zeit-

Verlag GmbH, Hamburg. 13 Reprinted with the permission of TAZ Verlags- und Vertriebs GmbH, Berlin. 14 Reprinted with the permission of Verlag Der Tagesspiegel GmbH, Berlin. 17 Reprinted with the permission of Zeit-Verlag GmbH, Hamburg. 18 Reprinted with the permission of the author.

6. Promoting Diversity

Photo. A television studio in Cologne. Copyright © Gipa Press. 6 Reprinted with the permission of TAZ Verlags- und Vertriebs GmbH, Berlin. 7 Reprinted with the permission of the author. 9 All rights reserved, Frankfurter Allgemeine Zeitung, Inc., Frankfurt. Provided by the Frankfurter Allgemeine Archive. 11 Copyright Kulturveranstaltungen des Bundes in Berlin GmbH, Berlin. 12 Copyright Kulturveranstaltungen des Bundes in Berlin GmbH, Berlin. 13 Reprinted with the permission of TAZ Verlags- und Vertriebs GmbH, Berlin. 15 TAZ Verlags- und Vertriebs GmbH, Berlin. 16 Reprinted with the permission of the author. 19 Reprinted with the permission of TAZ Verlags- und Vertriebs GmbH, Berlin. 20 All rights reserved, Frankfurt Allgemeine Zeitung, Inc., Frankfurt. Provided by the Frankfurter Allgemeine Archive. 21 Reprinted with the permission of DOMiT—Dokumentationszentrum und Museum über die Migration in Deutschland e.V., Cologne.

7. An Immigration Country?

Photo. *Kültür* in Berlin-Schöneberg. Photo: Kemal Kurt; © DOMiT. 1 Reprinted with the permission of Zeit-Verlag GmbH, Hamburg. 2 Reprinted with the permission of Zeit-Verlag GmbH, Hamburg. 3 Reprinted with the permission of the authors. 4 Reprinted with the permission of the author. 5 Reprinted with the permission of the author. 6 Reprinted with the permission of TAZ Verlags- und Vertriebs GmbH, Berlin. 7 Reprinted with the permission of SPIEGEL-Verlag Rudolf Augstein GmbH & Co. Hamburg. 8 Reprinted with the permission of the author. 9 Reprinted with the permission of Zeit-Verlag GmbH, Hamburg. 11 Reprinted with the permission of Süddeutsche Zeitung GmbH, Munich. 12 Reprinted with the permission of TAZ Verlags- und Vertriebs GmbH, Berlin. 13 Reprinted with the permission of the author. 14 Reprinted with the permission of the author. 15 Reprinted with the permission of Süddeutsche Zeitung GmbH, Munich. 16 Reprinted with the permission of Zeit-Verlag GmbH, Hamburg. 17 Reprinted with the permission of Blackwell Publishing, Ames, IA. 18 Reprinted with the permission of the author. 19 Reprinted with the permission of the Jüdische Presse GmbH, Berlin.

8. Living in Two Worlds?

Photo. Satellite dishes in Berlin-Kreuzberg. Photo © Anton Kaes. 1 Reprinted with the permission of the Johns Hopkins University Press. 3 Reprinted with the permission of SPIEGEL-Verlag Rudolf Augstein GmbH & Co. Hamburg. 4 Reprinted with the permission of Verlag Der Tagesspiegel GmbH, Berlin. 5 Reprinted with the permission of Verlag Der Tagesspiegel GmbH, Berlin. 7 Reprinted with the permission of Lamuv Verlag, Göttingen. 8 Reprinted with the permission of SPIEGEL-Verlag Rudolf Augstein GmbH & Co. Hamburg. 9 Reprinted with the permission of TAZ Verlags- und Vertriebs GmbH, Berlin. 10 Reprinted with the permission of TAZ

Verlags- und Vertriebs GmbH, Berlin. 11 Reprinted with the permission of TAZ Verlags- und Vertriebs GmbH, Berlin. 12 All rights reserved, Frankfurter Allgemeine Zeitung, Inc., Frankfurt. Provided by the Frankfurter Allgemeine Archive. 13 Reprinted with the permission of DOMiT—Dokumentationszentrum und Museum über die Migration in Deutschland e.V., Cologne. 14 Reprinted with the permission of SPIEGEL-Verlag Rudolf Augstein GmbH & Co. Hamburg. 15 Reprinted with the permission of thaifrau.de. 16 Reprinted with the permission of Zeit-Verlag GmbH, Hamburg. 17 Reprinted with the permission of Zeit-Verlag GmbH, Hamburg. 18 Reprinted with the permission of the author. 19 All rights reserved, Frankfurter Allgemeine Zeitung, Inc., Frankfurt. Provided by the Frankfurter Allgemeine Archive. 20 Reprinted with the permission of Zeit-Verlag GmbH, Hamburg.

9. Writing Back

Photo. Celebrating transnational writers. Photo © Robert Bosch Stiftung. 1 Reprinted with the permission of Zeit-Verlag GmbH, Hamburg. 2 Reprinted with the permission of Deutscher Taschenbuch Verlag GmbH & Co., Munich. 3 Reprinted with the permission of the author. 4 Reprinted with the permission of Deutscher Taschenbuch Verlag GmbH & Co., Munich. 5 All rights reserved, Frankfurt Allgemeine Zeitung, Inc., Frankfurt. Provided by the Frankfurter Allgemeine Archive. 6 Reprinted with the permission of Verlag Kiepenheuer & Witsch, Cologne. 7 Reprinted with the permission of the author. 8 Reprinted with the permission of EVA Europäische Verlagsanstalt GmbH & Co, Hamburg. 9 Reprinted with the permission of Piper Verlag GmbH, Munich. 10 Reprinted with the permission of the author. 11 Reprinted with the permission of Steidl Verlag, Göttingen. 12 Reprinted with the permission of Konkursbuch Verlag GmbH, Tübingen. 13 Reprinted with the permission of Suhrkamp Verlag GmbH, Frankfurt am Main. 14. Reprinted with the permission of the author. 15 Reprinted with the permission of Verlagsgruppe Random House GmbH, Munich. 16 Reprinted with the permission of Eichborn AG, Frankfurt.

10. A Turkish Germany

Photo. *Head-On*, 2003. Photo: Kerstin Stelte; © WÜSTE Filmproduktion. 1 Copyright Weltrekord. 2 Reprinted with the permission of Zeit-Verlag GmbH, Hamburg. 3 Reprinted with the permission of the authors. 4 All rights reserved, Frankfurter Allgemeine Zeitung, Inc., Frankfurt. Provided by the Frankfurter Allgemeine Archive. 5 Copyright Universal Berlin. 6 Copyright *Pflasterstrand*. 7 Reprinted with the permission of Zeit-Verlag GmbH, Hamburg. 8 Reprinted with the permission of TAZ Verlags- und Vertriebs GmbH, Berlin. 9 Reprinted with the permission of Zeit-Verlag GmbH, Hamburg. 10 Reprinted with the permission of Verlag Der Tagesspiegel GmbH, Berlin. 11 Reprinted with the permission of Zeit-Verlag GmbH, Hamburg. 12 Reprinted with the permission of EVA Europäische Verlagsanstalt GmbH & Co, Hamburg. 13 Reprinted with the permission of the Berliner Morgenpost GmbH, Berlin. 14 Reprinted with the permission of the author. 15 Reprinted with the permission of the author. 16 Reprinted with the permission of Zitty Verlag GmbH, Berlin. 17 Copyright *Die Woche*. 18 Reprinted with the permission of Zeit-Verlag GmbH, Hamburg.

Epilogue: Global Already?

Photo. Berlin, Potsdamer Platz. Photo © Anton Kaes. 1 Reprinted with the permission of the author. 2 Reprinted with the permission of Hamburger Edition, Hamburg. 4 Reprinted with permission of the author. 5 Copyright Kulturveranstaltungen des Bundes in Berlin GmbH, Berlin. 6 Reprinted with the permission of Polity Press, Cambridge. 7 Reprinted with the permission of the author. 8 Reprinted with the permission of the author. 9 Reprinted with the permission of Deutsche Welle World, Bonn. 10 Reprinted with the permission of Deutsche Welle World, Bonn. 11 Reprinted with the permission of the author.

Photo. Ausgang. Photo © Bosse Küllenberg.

Despite great efforts, it has not been possible in every case to locate all rights holders. The editors and publisher apologize for any unintended errors or omissions, which they will seek to correct in future printings.

INDEX

Italicized page numbers indicate authors of selections. Bolded page numbers refer to illustrations.

WEIMAR AND NOW: GERMAN CULTURAL CRITICISM

EDWARD DIMENDBERG, MARTIN JAY, AND ANTON KAES, GENERAL EDITORS

Text: 10/12 Baskerville
Display: DIN
Compositor: Binghamton Valley Composition, LLC
Printer and binder: Maple-Vail Manufacturing Group